500 SEASONAL RECIPES

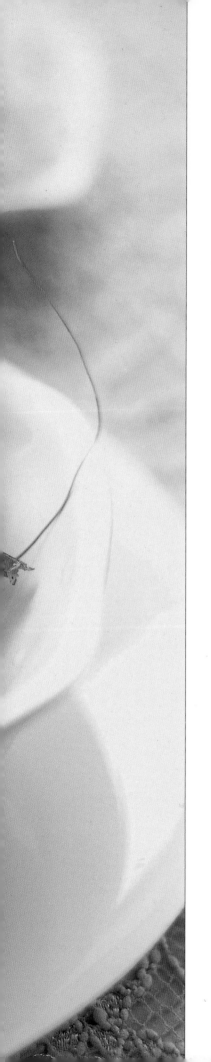

500 SEASONAL RECIPES

MAKING THE MOST OF FRESH PRODUCE THROUGH SPRING, SUMMER, AUTUMN AND WINTER:
CLASSIC AND TRADITIONAL DISHES SHOWN IN OVER 500 PHOTOGRAPHS   ANNE HILDYARD

greene&golden

This edition is published by greene&golden,
an imprint of Anness Publishing Ltd, Blaby Road, Wigston,
Leicestershire LE18 4SE; info@anness.com

www.annesspublishing.com

If you like the images in this book and would like to
investigate using them for publishing, promotions or
advertising, please visit our website www.practicalpictures.com
for more information.

NOTES

Bracketed terms are intended for American readers.
For all recipes, quantities are given in both metric and imperial
measures and, where appropriate, in standard cups and spoons.
Follow one set of measures, but not a mixture, because they
are not interchangeable.
Standard spoon and cup measures are level. 1 tsp = 5ml,
1 tbsp = 15ml, 1 cup = 250ml/8fl oz.
Australian standard tablespoons are 20ml.
Australian readers should use 3 tsp in place of 1 tbsp for
measuring small quantities.
American pints are 16fl oz/2 cups. American readers should
use 20fl oz/2.5 cups in place of 1 pint when measuring liquids.
Electric oven temperatures in this book are for conventional
ovens. When using a fan oven, the temperature will probably
need to be reduced by about 10–20°C/20–40°F. Since ovens
vary, you should check with your manufacturer's instruction
book for guidance.
The nutritional analysis given for each recipe is calculated per
portion (i.e. serving or item), unless otherwise stated. If the
recipe gives a range, such as Serves 4–6, then the nutritional
analysis will be for the smaller portion size, i.e. 6 servings.
The analysis does not include optional ingredients, such as salt
added to taste.
Medium (US large) eggs are used unless otherwise stated.

PUBLISHER'S NOTE

Although the advice and information in this book are believed
to be accurate and true at the time of going to press, neither
the authors nor the publisher can accept any legal
responsibility or liability for any errors or omissions that may
have been made nor for any inaccuracies nor for any loss,
harm or injury that comes about from following instructions or
advice in this book.

ETHICAL TRADING POLICY

At Anness Publishing we believe that business should be
conducted in an ethical and ecologically sustainable way, with
respect for the environment and a proper regard to the
replacement of the natural resources we employ.
As a publisher, we use a lot of wood pulp in high-quality paper
for printing, and that wood commonly comes from spruce
trees. We are therefore currently growing more than
750,000 trees in three Scottish forest plantations: Berrymoss
(130 hectares/320 acres), West Touxhill (125 hectares/
305 acres) and Deveron Forest (75 hectares/185 acres). The
forests we manage contain more than 3.5 times the number
of trees employed each year in making paper for our books.
Because of this ongoing ecological investment programme,
you, as our customer, can have the pleasure and reassurance
of knowing that a tree is being cultivated on your behalf
to naturally replace the materials used to make the book
you are holding.
Our forestry programme is run in accordance with the UK
Woodland Assurance Scheme (UKWAS) and will be certified
by the internationally recognized Forest Stewardship Council
(FSC). The FSC is a non-government organization dedicated to
promoting responsible management of the world's forests.
Certification ensures forests are managed in an
environmentally sustainable and socially responsible way.
For further information about this scheme, go to
www.annesspublishing.com/trees

Publisher: Joanna Lorenz
Editor: Anne Hildyard
Recipes: Pepita Aris, Catherine Atkinson, Josephine Bacon,
Jane Bamforth, Alex Barker, Ghillie Basan, Judy Bastyra,
Georgina Campbell, Jacqueline Clark, Maxine Clark, Judith H.
Dern, Matthew Drennan, Joanna Farrow, Marina Filippelli, Jenni
Fleetwood, Christine France, Yasuko Fukuoka, Brian Glover,
Nicola Graimes, Anja Hill, Deh-Ta Hsiung, Christine Ingram,
Becky Johnson, Emi Kasuko, Lucy Knox, Janet Laurence, Biddy
White Lennon, Sara Lewis, Christine McFadden, Maggie
Mayhew, Jane Milton, Janny de Moor, Sallie Morris, Suzannah
Olivier, Keith Richmond, Rena Salaman, Miguel Castro e Silva,
Ysanne Spevak, Marlena Spieler, Christopher Trotter, Linda
Tubby, Suzanne Vandyck, Sunil Vijayakar, Kate Whiteman,
Carol Wilson, Jenny White, Jeni Wright and Annette Yates
Copy Editor: Jay Thundercliffe
Proofreading Manager: Lindsay Zamponi
Production Controller: Don Campaniello

Front cover shows Chicken Wings with Blood Oranges
– for recipe, see page 207.

A CIP catalogue record for this book is available from the
British Library.

Contents

Introduction 6

Spring

Soups 8

Salsas and Snacks 14

Salads 24

Vegetable Dishes 34

Fish and Shellfish Dishes 40

Meat Dishes 48

Desserts 58

Drinks 66

Summer

Soups 68

Dips and Salsas 74

Appetizers and Snacks 76

Salads 84

Vegetable Dishes 90

Fish and Shellfish Dishes 100

Meat Dishes 108

Desserts 118

Drinks 130

Autumn

Soups 132

Relishes and Snacks 140

Salads 150

Vegetable Dishes 156

Fish and Shellfish Dishes 166

Meat Dishes 174

Desserts 182

Drinks 192

Winter

Soups 194

Relishes and Snacks 198

Salads 208

Vegetable Dishes 214

Fish Dishes 224

Meat Dishes 232

Desserts 242

Drinks 250

Index 252

Introduction

For many people, the simple fact that they spend their entire lives in an urban environment means that they are out of touch with seasonal food, particularly in today's global marketplace, where the

supermarkets stack their shelves with the same produce all year round. It wasn't so long ago that every meal people ate was prepared using seasonal ingredients, because there was no means of transporting international produce between countries. People ate as nature intended them to and their diet was dictated by what grew locally, which was therefore entirely dependent on the seasons. There is little sense or benefit in eating fruit, vegetables, meat and fish that have been flown in

from halfway around the world to fill the supermarkets all year, when you can enjoy native ingredients that have been grown, reared or caught a matter of miles from your home. There are many benefits from basing your diet on seasonal produce. Locally grown, reared and caught food will often cost less, because there isn't a premium to pay for ingredients that are scarcer; it will always be fresher and therefore tastier and more nutritious; and it will be less damaging to the environment due to the reduction in energy needed to transport and grow the produce.

Another important aspect of buying local ingredients is that you will be supporting farmers and producers in your area, meaning that you will promote the local economy. There is also an added

incentive when you buy fruit, vegetables and meat from your own country. You can either buy organic produce, which should be naturally grown or reared, or you can check that the animals are raised or caught in a humane, ethically responsible manner, and also that the money you spend on food promotes fair terms of trade for producers.

Fresh foods will vary depending on where you live in the world, but check out the fruit and vegetables that are in season in your country

and look out for them in your local supermarket. Usually, when an ingredient is in season, the store or market will have an abundance of that ingredient and will ensure that the product is clearly identified to encourage shoppers to buy it.

This comprehensive recipe book highlights the benefits and delights of cooking and eating in a more natural way, using seasonal produce whenever possible. It can be daunting at first trying to prepare meals based mainly on which foods are in season rather than cooking whatever you feel like eating, but the wealth of delicious and varied recipes in this book will soon show that it is easy to choose seasonal foods. While using local seasonal recipes is the ideal, occasionally more exotic ingredients, which grow only in tropical countries, are needed in a recipe for flavour or colour.

Spring is traditionally a time of culinary celebration after the winter months. Fresh green produce, various meats and berries begin to appear, providing opportunities to cook dishes such as Asparagus and Pea Soup, Herb-crusted Rack of Lamb with Puy Lentils, and Rhubarb and Raspberry Crumble. By the summer, the harvest from the land and sea is in progress and many fruits and vegetables are plentiful. Enjoy dishes such as Classic Gazpacho, Mackerel with Nutty Bacon Stuffing, and Strawberry Cream Shortbreads. With the advent of autumn, there is still much of the summer produce available and other delicious items are coming into season. It is a great time to try Mushroom and Bean Paté, Roast Duck with Prunes and Apple, and Old-fashioned Apple Cake. Winter is not the dull culinary season many people think it is, because some fantastic ingredients are available, enabling you to create dishes such as Seared Mixed Onion Salad, Sea Bass with Leeks, and, of course, Christmas Pudding.

The 500 tempting recipes in this book are clearly explained step by step and most show the finished dish so you can see what you are aiming to create. The recipes are divided into sections based on the seasons so that you can work through the book and buy what is available, fresh and of good quality, as the year progresses. Each season features every kind of dish, from soups and appetizers to vegetable, meat and fish dishes, and includes desserts and healthy drinks and juices. Whatever the season or the occasion, you can be sure of finding a recipe that makes the most of the delicious seasonal produce available.

Chilled Avocado Soup with Cumin

This chilled avocado soup, which is also known as green gazpacho, was invented in Spain. This mild, creamy soup is packed with the flavours of spring.

Serves 4

3 ripe avocados
1 bunch spring onions (scallions), white parts only, trimmed and roughly chopped
2 garlic cloves, chopped
juice of 1 lemon
1.5ml/¼ tsp ground cumin
1.5ml/¼ tsp paprika
450ml/¾ pint/scant 2 cups fresh chicken stock, cooled, and all fat skimmed off
300ml/½ pint/1¼ cups iced water
salt and ground black pepper
roughly chopped fresh flat leaf parsley, to serve

1 Starting half a day, or several hours, ahead to allow time for chilling, put the flesh of one avocado in a food processor or blender. Add the spring onions, garlic and lemon juice and purée until smooth.

2 Add the second avocado and purée, then the third, with the spices and seasoning. Purée until smooth.

3 Gradually add the chicken stock. Pour the soup into a metal bowl or other suitable container and chill.

4 To serve, stir in the iced water, then season to taste with plenty of salt and black pepper. Garnish with chopped parsley and serve immediately.

Cook's Tip
When avocados are plentiful and inexpensive, peel them, remove their stones (pits) and mash the flesh with lemon juice, then place in small containers in the freezer. Thaw in the refrigerator and use to make soups or dips.

Watercress Soup

Watercress and garden cress are nutritious aquatic leaf vegetables that can commonly be found growing wild in the spring. The peppery flavour of cress makes it ideal for sauces, salads and soups.

Serves 4

25g/1oz/2 tbsp unsalted butter or vegetable oil
1 large onion, chopped
1 leek, white part only, chopped
1 garlic clove, roughly chopped
2 large potatoes, peeled and cubed
1.5 litres/2½ pints/6¼ cups hot chicken or vegetable stock
1 bay leaf
1 large bunch of watercress, well rinsed, large stems removed, roughly chopped
1 large bunch of garden cress, rinsed, large stems removed, chopped (see Cook's Tip)
salt and ground black pepper
50g/2oz watercress leaves, to garnish

1 Heat the butter or oil in a large pan over medium-high heat. Stir in the onion, then sauté for 2–3 minutes. Add the leek, garlic and potatoes. Sauté for 5 minutes more, stirring until the mixture becomes fragrant.

2 Pour in the chicken or vegetable stock and add the bay leaf. Bring to the boil, reduce the heat to medium-low, cover and simmer for 20–30 minutes, until the potatoes are tender.

3 Stir in the watercress and garden cress. Simmer, uncovered, for 3 minutes and no longer, to preserve the fresh green colour and cook the cress lightly.

4 Remove the bay leaf. With a hand-held blender or in a food processor, purée the soup until smooth or until it reaches the desired consistency. Season to taste with salt and pepper.

5 Reheat if necessary, ladle into warm bowls and serve, garnished with fresh watercress leaves.

Cook's Tip
If you can't locate garden cress, use two bunches of watercress.

Chilled Avocado Soup Energy 148kcal/613kJ; Protein 1.9g; Carbohydrate 2.2g, of which sugars 1.1g; Fat 14.6g, of which saturates 3.1g; Cholesterol 0mg; Calcium 18mg; Fibre 2.9g; Sodium 6mg.
Watercress Soup Energy 598kcal/2515kJ; Protein 19.9g; Carbohydrate 76.3g, of which sugars 14.3g; Fat 25.9g, of which saturates 14.5g; Cholesterol 53mg; Calcium 602mg; Fibre 13.7g; Sodium 348mg.

Bacon and Leek Soup

Traditionally, this often made two courses or even two meals – the bacon and vegetables for one and the broth for the other.

Serves 4–6
1 piece unsmoked bacon, weighing about 1kg/2¼lb

500g/1lb 2oz/4½ cups leeks
1 large carrot, finely chopped
1 large potato, sliced
15ml/1 tbsp fine or medium oatmeal
handful of fresh parsley
salt and ground black pepper

1 Trim the bacon of excess fat, put it in a large pan and pour over enough cold water to cover. Bring to the boil, then discard the water. Add 1.5 litres/2¾ pints cold water, bring to the boil, then cover and simmer gently for 30 minutes.

2 Thickly slice the white and pale green parts of the leeks, reserving the dark green leaves. Add the sliced leek to the pan with the carrot, potato and oatmeal. Bring the soup back to the boil. Cover the pan and simmer gently for a further 30–40 minutes, until the vegetables and bacon are tender.

3 Slice the reserved dark green leeks very thinly and finely chop the parsley.

4 Lift the bacon out of the pan and either slice it and serve separately or cut it into bitesize chunks and stir these back into the soup.

5 Adjust the seasoning to taste, adding pepper, but it may not be necessary to add salt. Bring the soup to the boil. Add the sliced dark green leeks and parsley, and simmer very gently for about 5 minutes before serving.

> **Variation**
> *A chunk of beef or lamb may be used instead of the bacon, and other root vegetables may be added. Shredded cabbage is also popular.*

Asparagus and Pea Soup

This bright and tasty soup is ideal for using up bundles of fresh asparagus during the short spring harvest.

Serves 6
350g/12oz asparagus
2 leeks
1 bay leaf
1 carrot, roughly chopped
1 celery stick, chopped
few stalks of fresh parsley

1.75 litres/3 pints/7½ cups cold water
25g/1oz/2 tbsp butter
150g/5oz fresh garden peas
15ml/1 tbsp chopped fresh parsley
120ml/4fl oz/½ cup double (heavy) cream
grated rind of ½ lemon
salt and ground black pepper
shavings of Parmesan cheese, to serve

1 Cut the woody ends from the asparagus, then set the spears aside. Roughly chop the woody ends and place them in a large pan. Cut off and chop the green parts of the leeks and add to the asparagus stalks with the bay leaf, carrot, celery, parsley stalks and the cold water. Bring to the boil and simmer for about 30 minutes. Strain the stock and discard the vegetables.

2 Cut the tips off the asparagus and set aside, then cut the stems into short pieces. Chop the remainder of the leeks.

3 Melt the butter in a large pan and add the leeks. Cook for 3–4 minutes until softened. Add the asparagus stems, peas and parsley. Pour in 1.2 litres/2 pints/5 cups of the asparagus stock. Boil, reduce the heat and cook for 6–8 minutes. Season well.

4 Purée the soup in a food processor or blender. Press through a fine sieve (strainer) into the rinsed-out pan. Stir in the cream and lemon rind.

5 Bring a small pan of water to the boil and cook the asparagus tips for 2–3 minutes or until tender. Drain and refresh under cold water. Reheat the soup, but do not boil.

6 Ladle the soup into six warmed bowls and garnish with the asparagus tips. Serve with Parmesan cheese and black pepper.

Bacon and Leek Soup Energy 337kcal/1422kJ; Protein 51.4g; Carbohydrate 11.3g, of which sugars 3.3g; Fat 10g, of which saturates 3.6g; Cholesterol 33mg; Calcium 44mg; Fibre 2.7g; Sodium 1860mg.
Asparagus and Pea Soup Energy 184kcal/759kJ; Protein 4.9g; Carbohydrate 7.2g, of which sugars 4.4g; Fat 15.3g, of which saturates 9.1g; Cholesterol 36mg; Calcium 56mg; Fibre 3.9g; Sodium 39mg.

Carrot and Orange Soup

This traditional, bright and tasty soup is always popular in the spring and summer seasons. It has a wonderfully creamy consistency and vibrantly fresh citrus flavour.

Serves 4
50g/2oz/¼ cup butter
3 leeks, sliced
450g/1lb carrots, sliced

1.2 litres/2 pints/5 cups chicken
  or vegetable stock
rind and juice of 2 oranges
2.5ml/½ tsp freshly
  grated nutmeg
150ml/¼ pint/⅔ cup Greek
  (US strained plain) yogurt
salt and ground black pepper
fresh sprigs of coriander (cilantro),
  to garnish

1 Melt the butter in a large pan. Add the leeks and carrots and stir well, coating the vegetables with the butter. Cover and cook for about 10 minutes, until the vegetables are beginning to soften but not colour.

2 Pour in the stock and the orange rind and juice. Add the nutmeg and season to taste with salt and pepper. Bring to the boil, lower the heat, cover and simmer for about 40 minutes, or until the vegetables are tender.

3 Leave to cool slightly, then purée the soup in a food processor or blender until smooth.

4 Return the soup to the pan and add 30ml/2 tbsp of the yogurt, then taste the soup and adjust the seasoning, if necessary. Reheat gently.

5 Ladle the hot soup into warmed individual bowls and put a swirl of the remaining yogurt in the centre of each serving. Sprinkle the fresh sprigs of coriander over each bowl to garnish, and serve the soup immediately.

> **Cook's Tip**
> *Use a good, home-made chicken or vegetable stock if you can, for the best results.*

Spiced Red Lentil Soup

Crispy shallots and a parsley cream top this rich soup, which is light yet warming on cold spring days.

Serves 6
5ml/1 tsp cumin seeds
2.5ml/½ tsp coriander seeds
5ml/1 tsp ground turmeric
30ml/2 tbsp olive oil
1 onion, chopped
2 garlic cloves, chopped
1 smoked bacon hock

1.2 litres/2 pints/5 cups
  vegetable stock
275g/10oz/1¼ cups red lentils
400g/14oz can chopped tomatoes
15ml/1 tbsp vegetable oil
3 shallots, thinly sliced

For the parsley cream
45ml/3 tbsp chopped fresh parsley
150ml/¼ pint/⅔ cup Greek (US
  strained plain) yogurt
salt and ground black pepper

1 Heat a frying pan and add the cumin and coriander seeds. Roast them over high heat for a few seconds, shaking the pan until they smell aromatic. Transfer to a mortar and crush using a pestle. Mix in the turmeric; set aside.

2 Heat the oil in a large pan. Add the onion and garlic and cook for 4–5 minutes. Add the spice mix and stir for 2 minutes.

3 Place the bacon in the pan and pour in the stock. Bring to the boil, cover and simmer gently for 30 minutes.

4 Add the lentils and cook for 20 minutes until the lentils and bacon are tender. Stir in the tomatoes and cook for 5 minutes.

5 Remove the bacon and set it aside to cool slightly. Process the soup in a food processor or blender until almost smooth. Return the soup to the rinsed-out pan. Cut the meat from the hock, discarding skin and fat, then add to the soup and reheat.

6 Heat the vegetable oil in a frying pan and fry the shallots for 10 minutes. Remove from the pan and drain on kitchen paper.

7 For the parsley cream, stir the parsley into the yogurt and season well. Ladle the soup into bowls and add a dollop of the parsley cream to each. Pile some shallots on to each and serve.

Carrot Soup Energy 206kcal/856kJ; Protein 5g; Carbohydrate 15.8g, of which sugars 14.2g; Fat 14.4g, of which saturates 8.3g; Cholesterol 27mg; Calcium 111mg; Fibre 5.8g; Sodium 131mg.
Spiced Red Lentil Soup Energy 235kcal/991kJ; Protein 13g; Carbohydrate 28.4g, of which sugars 3.7g; Fat 8.8g, of which saturates 2.2g; Cholesterol 21mg; Calcium 66mg; Fibre 2.9g; Sodium 40mg.

Cream of Vegetable Soup

This seasonal soup is light in flavour yet satisfying enough for a lunchtime snack.

Serves 6
30ml/2 tbsp olive oil
2 large onions, finely diced
1 garlic clove, crushed
3 large floury potatoes, finely diced
3 celery sticks, finely diced
1.75 litres/3 pints/7 1/2 cups vegetable stock
2 carrots, finely diced
1 cauliflower, chopped
15ml/1 tbsp chopped fresh dill
15ml/1 tbsp lemon juice
5ml/1 tsp mustard powder
1.5ml/1/4 tsp caraway seeds
300ml/1/2 pint/1 1/4 cups single (light) cream
salt and ground black pepper
shredded spring onions (scallions), to garnish

1 Heat the oil in a large pan, add the onions and garlic and fry them for a few minutes until they soften. Add the potatoes, celery and stock and simmer for 10 minutes. Stir in the carrots and simmer for a further 10 minutes.

2 Add the cauliflower, dill, lemon juice, mustard powder and caraway seeds and stir well, then simmer for 20 minutes. Reserve some of the vegetables to add texture when serving.

3 Process the soup in a food processor or blender until smooth, return it to the pan and stir in the cream. Season, add the reserved vegetables, then serve, garnished with spring onions.

Variations
All sorts of vegetables can be used in a mixed soup, so the variations on this 'cream of vegetable' recipe are endless, depending on the season. However, the trick for success is to combine complementary flavours in balanced quantities. Parsnips and swede (rutabaga) can be added in relatively small proportions (too much will dominate). Courgettes (zucchini) and squash are good and they lighten the heavier vegetables. Add tender broccoli tops, spinach, lettuce and/or watercress about 5 minutes before the end of cooking for a fresh flavour.

Crab Soup with Coriander Relish

Prepared fresh crab is readily available in spring, of good quality and convenient – perfect for creating an exotic seafood and noodle soup in minutes.

Serves 4
45ml/3 tbsp olive oil
1 red onion, finely chopped
2 red chillies, seeded and finely chopped
1 garlic clove, finely chopped
450g/1lb fresh white crab meat
30ml/2 tbsp chopped fresh parsley
30ml/2 tbsp chopped fresh coriander (cilantro)
juice of 2 lemons
1 lemon grass stalk
1 litre/1 3/4 pints/4 cups good fish or chicken stock
15ml/1 tbsp Thai fish sauce
150g/5oz vermicelli or angel hair pasta, broken into 5–7.5cm/ 2–3in lengths
salt and ground black pepper

For the relish
50g/2oz/1 cup fresh coriander (cilantro) leaves
1 green chilli, seeded and chopped
15ml/1 tbsp sunflower oil
25ml/1 1/2 tbsp lemon juice
2.5ml/1/2 tsp ground roasted cumin seeds

1 Heat the oil in a pan and add the onion, chillies and garlic. Cook over low heat for 10 minutes until the onion is very soft.

2 Transfer the cooked onion and chillies to a bowl and stir in the crab meat, parsley, coriander and lemon juice. Set aside.

3 Bruise the lemon grass with a rolling pin or pestle. Pour the stock and fish sauce into a pan. Add the lemon grass and bring to the boil, then add the pasta. Simmer, uncovered, for about 3–4 minutes or until the pasta is just tender.

4 Meanwhile, make the relish. Using a mortar and pestle, make a coarse paste with the coriander, chilli, oil, lemon juice and cumin.

5 Remove and discard the lemon grass from the soup. Stir the chilli and crab mixture into the soup and season it well. Bring to the boil, then reduce the heat and simmer for 2 minutes.

6 Ladle the soup into four warmed bowls and put a spoonful of the relish in the centre of each. Serve immediately.

Cream of Vegetable Energy 202Kcal/840kJ; Protein 5.1g; Carbohydrate 16.5g, of which sugars 9.4g; Fat 13.2g, of which saturates 6.7g; Cholesterol 28mg; Calcium 100mg; Fibre 3.9g; Sodium 38mg.
Crab Soup Energy 425Kcal/1773kJ; Protein 26.7g; Carbohydrate 50.7g, of which sugars 1.4g; Fat 12.6g, of which saturates 1.6g; Cholesterol 81mg; Calcium 198mg; Fibre 1.3g; Sodium 632mg.

Curried Salmon Chowder

A hint of mild curry paste really enhances the flavour of this soup, without making it too spicy. Grated creamed coconut adds a luxury touch, while helping to amalgamate the flavours. Served with chunks of warm bread, this soup makes a substantial and rich appetizer.

Serves 4
50g/2oz/¼ cup butter
2 onions, roughly chopped

10ml/2 tsp mild curry paste
150ml/¼ pint/⅔ cup white wine
300ml/½ pint/1¼ cups double
 (heavy) cream
50g/2oz/½ cup creamed coconut,
 grated or 120ml/4fl oz/½ cup
 coconut cream
2 potatoes, about
 350g/12oz, cubed
450g/1lb salmon fillet, skinned
 and cut into bitesize pieces
60ml/4 tbsp chopped fresh
 flat leaf parsley
salt and ground black pepper

1 Melt the butter in a large pan, add the onions and cook for about 3–4 minutes until beginning to soften. Stir in the curry paste. Cook for 1 minute more.

2 Add 475ml/16fl oz/2 cups water, the wine, double cream and creamed coconut or coconut cream. Stir well and season with salt and pepper. Bring the mixture to the boil, stirring constantly until the creamed coconut has dissolved.

3 Add the potatoes and simmer, covered, for about 15 minutes or until they are almost tender. Do not allow them to break down into the liquid.

4 Add the fish and cook gently so as not to break it up for about 2–3 minutes until just cooked. Add the parsley and adjust the seasoning. Serve immediately.

Cook's Tip
There is a wide choice of curry pastes available. Select a concentrated paste for this recipe, rather than a 'cook-in-sauce' type of paste. If you cannot find a suitable paste, cook a little curry powder in melted butter over low heat and use instead.

Chicken and Lentil Broth

An old-fashioned spring favourite, this version is given more body by the addition of Puy lentils.

Serves 4
2 leeks, cut into 5cm/2in
 fine julienne
115g/4oz/½ cup Puy lentils

1 bay leaf
few sprigs of fresh thyme
2 skinless chicken breast fillets
900ml/1½ pints/3¾ cups good
 chicken stock
8 ready-to-eat prunes, cut
 into strips
salt and ground black pepper
fresh thyme sprigs, to garnish

1 Bring a small pan of salted water to the boil and cook the julienne of leeks for 1–2 minutes. Drain and refresh under cold running water. Drain again and set aside.

2 Pick over the lentils to check for any small stones or grit. Put into a pan with the bay leaf and thyme and cover with cold water. Bring to the boil and cook for 25–30 minutes until tender. Drain and refresh under cold water.

3 Put the chicken fillets in a pan and pour over enough stock to cover them. Bring to the boil and poach gently for about 15–20 minutes until tender. Using a draining spoon, remove the chicken from the stock and leave to cool.

4 When the chicken is cool enough to handle, cut it into strips. Return it to the stock in the pan and add the lentils and the remaining stock. Bring just to the boil and add seasoning.

5 Divide the leeks and prunes among four warmed bowls. Ladle over the hot chicken and lentil broth. Garnish each portion with a few fresh thyme sprigs and serve immediately.

Cook's Tip
Julienne is a name for foods cut into long, thin strips – usually vegetables, but also meat and fish. For perfect julienne leeks, cut them into 5cm/2in lengths. Cut each in half lengthways, then with the cut side down, slice the leek into thin strips.

Curried Salmon Energy 837kcal/3466kJ; Protein 26.3g; Carbohydrate 16.6g, of which sugars 3.6g; Fat 71.8g, of which saturates 41.2g; Cholesterol 186mg; Calcium 74mg; Fibre 0.9g; Sodium 158mg.
Chicken and Lentil Energy 210kcal/891kJ; Protein 26.3g; Carbohydrate 23.8g, of which sugars 9.8g; Fat 1.7g, of which saturates 0.3g; Cholesterol 53mg; Calcium 43mg; Fibre 5g; Sodium 52mg.

Galician Broth

This hearty soup needs long, slow cooking to give the flavours time to develop fully.

Serves 6

450g/1lb gammon (smoked or
   cured ham), in one piece,
   soaked overnight in cold water
2 bay leaves
2 onions, sliced
10ml/2 tsp paprika
675g/1½lb baking potatoes, cut
   into 2.5cm/1in chunks
225g/8oz spring greens (collards)
425g/15oz can haricot (navy) or
   cannellini beans, drained
ground black pepper

1 Drain the gammon and put it in the ceramic cooking pot with the bay leaves and onions. Pour over just enough fresh cold water to cover the gammon. Switch to high, cover and cook for 1 hour.

2 Skim off any scum, then re-cover and cook for 3 hours. Check and skim the broth once or twice if necessary.

3 Using a slotted spoon and a large fork, carefully lift the gammon out of the slow cooker and on to a board. Add the paprika and potatoes to the broth and cook for 1 hour.

4 Meanwhile, discard the skin and fat from the gammon and cut the meat into small chunks. Add it to the slow cooker and cook for 2 hours, or until the meat and potatoes are tender.

5 Remove the cores from the greens, then roll up the leaves and cut into thin shreds. Add to the slow cooker with the beans and cook for 30 minutes.

6 Remove the bay leaves from the broth, season with black pepper to taste and serve piping hot.

> **Cook's Tip**
> *Bacon knuckles can be used instead of the gammon. The bones will give the stock a delicious flavour. If there is any broth left over, you can freeze it and use it as stock for another soup.*

Sweet-and-sour Vegetable Borscht

There are many variations of this classic and colourful Eastern European soup: this one includes plentiful amounts of cabbage, tomatoes and potatoes, and it is served piping hot.

Serves 6

1 onion, chopped
1 carrot, chopped
4–6 raw or plain cooked beetroot
   (beet), 3–4 diced and 1–2
   coarsely grated
400g/14oz can tomatoes
4–6 new potatoes, cut into
   bitesize pieces
1 small white cabbage,
   thinly sliced
1 litre/1¾ pints/4 cups
   vegetable stock
45ml/3 tbsp sugar
30–45ml/2–3 tbsp white wine or
   cider (apple) vinegar
45ml/3 tbsp chopped fresh dill,
   plus extra to garnish
salt and ground black pepper
sour cream, to garnish
buttered rye bread, to serve

1 Put the onion, carrot, diced beetroot, tomatoes, potatoes and cabbage in a large pan. Pour in the stock and bring to the boil. Reduce the heat and cover the pan. Simmer the soup for about 30 minutes, or until the potatoes are tender.

2 Add the grated beetroot, sugar, wine or cider vinegar to the soup and continue to cook for 10 minutes.

3 Taste for a good sweet–sour balance and add more sugar and/or vinegar if necessary. Season to taste.

4 To serve, stir in the chopped dill and ladle the soup into bowls. Garnish each portion with sour cream and more dill. Serve with rye bread.

> **Variation**
> *To make meat borscht, place 1kg/2¼lb chopped beef in a large pan. Pour over water to cover and crumble in 1 beef stock (bouillon) cube. Bring to the boil, then reduce the heat and simmer until tender. Skim any fat from the surface, then add the vegetables and proceed as above.*

Galician Broth Energy 273kcal/1147kJ; Protein 21.4g; Carbohydrate 33.7g, of which sugars 5.3g; Fat 6.7g, of which saturates 2g; Cholesterol 17mg; Calcium 113mg; Fibre 6.7g; Sodium 974mg.
Sweet-and-sour Borscht Energy 46kcal/196kJ; Protein 1.6g; Carbohydrate 9.8g, of which sugars 6.4g; Fat 0.4g, of which saturates 0.1g; Cholesterol 0mg; Calcium 22mg; Fibre 1.9g; Sodium 29mg.

Apple and Leek Relish

Fresh and tangy, this simple relish of sliced leeks and apples with a lemon and honey dressing can be served with a range of cold meats as part of a spring buffet or for a springtime barbecue when the weather is good enough to eat outdoors. For the best result, make sure you use slim young leeks and tart, crisp apples.

Serves 4
2 slim leeks, white part only,
    washed thoroughly
2 large apples
15ml/1 tbsp chopped fresh parsley
juice of 1 lemon
15ml/1 tbsp clear honey
salt and ground black pepper,
    to taste

1 Thinly slice the leeks. Peel and core the apples, then slice the flesh thinly.

2 Place the sliced leek and apple into a large serving bowl and add the fresh parsley, lemon juice and honey. Season to taste with salt and ground black pepper.

3 Toss the ingredients thoroughly with two wooden spoons until they are well combined. Leave the bowl to stand in a cool place for about an hour before serving, to allow the flavours to blend together.

Variation
This relish could also be made with a mixture of pears and apples, if you prefer. The variation in texture between the softer pear slices and the crisp, tart apples will add extra interest to the relish.

Cook's Tip
When buying leeks, look for slim ones with firm white stems and bright green leaves. Avoid those that are discoloured in any way.

Guacamole

One of the best-loved Mexican salsas, this blend of creamy avocado, tomatoes, chillies, coriander and lime now appears on tables the world over. Ready-made guacamole usually contains mayonnaise, which helps to preserve the avocado, but this is not an ingredient in traditional recipes.

Serves 6–8
4 medium tomatoes
4 ripe avocados, preferably fuerte
juice of 1 lime
1/2 small onion
2 garlic cloves
small bunch of fresh coriander
    (cilantro), chopped
3 fresh red fresno chillies
salt
tortilla chips, to serve

1 Cut a cross in the base of each tomato. Place the tomatoes in a heatproof bowl and pour over boiling water to cover.

2 Leave the tomatoes in the water for 3 minutes, then lift them out using a slotted spoon and plunge them into a bowl of cold water. Drain. The skins will have begun to peel back from the crosses. Remove the skins completely. Cut the tomatoes in half, remove the seeds with a teaspoon, then chop the flesh roughly and set it aside.

3 Cut the avocados in half then remove the stones (pits). Scoop the flesh out of the shells and place it in a food processor or blender. Process until almost smooth, then scrape into a bowl and stir in the lime juice.

4 Chop the onion finely, then crush the garlic. Add both to the avocado and mix well. Stir in the coriander.

5 Remove the stalks from the chillies, slit them and scrape out the seeds with a small sharp knife. Chop the chillies finely and add them to the avocado mixture, with the chopped tomatoes. Mix well.

6 Check the seasoning and add salt to taste. Cover closely with clear film (plastic wrap) or a tight-fitting lid and chill for 1 hour before serving as a dip with tortilla chips. If it is well covered, guacamole will keep in the refrigerator for 2–3 days.

Apple and Leek Relish Energy 59kcal/252kJ; Protein 1.9g; Carbohydrate 12.5g, of which sugars 11.8g; Fat 0.6g, of which saturates 0.1g; Cholesterol 0mg; Calcium 27mg; Fibre 3.4g; Sodium 4mg.
Guacamole Energy 262kcal/1083kJ; Protein 3.2g; Carbohydrate 5g, of which sugars 3g; Fat 25.4g, of which saturates 5.4g; Cholesterol 0mg; Calcium 37mg; Fibre 5.5g; Sodium 15mg.

Salsa Verde

There are many versions of this classic green salsa. Try this springtime version drizzled over chargrilled squid, or with jacket potatoes served with a green spring salad.

Serves 4
2–4 fresh green chillies, halved
8 spring onions (scallions)

2 garlic cloves
50g/2oz salted capers
sprig of fresh tarragon
bunch of fresh parsley
grated rind and juice of 1 lime
juice of 1 lemon
90ml/6 tbsp olive oil
about 15ml/1 tbsp green
    Tabasco sauce
ground black pepper

1 Halve and seed the chillies and trim the spring onions. Halve the garlic cloves. Place in a food processor and pulse briefly.

2 Use your fingers to rub the excess salt off the capers. Add them, with the tarragon and parsley, to the food processor and pulse again until the ingredients are quite finely chopped.

3 Transfer the mixture to a bowl. Mix in the lime rind and juice, lemon juice and olive oil, stirring lightly so the citrus juice and oil do not emulsify.

4 Add the green Tabasco sauce, a little at a time, and ground black pepper to taste.

5 Chill the salsa in the refrigerator until ready to serve, but do not prepare it more than 8 hours in advance.

> **Cook's Tips**
> • Some salted capers are quite strong and may need rinsing in water before use. If you prefer, you can use pickled capers in the recipe instead.
> • If you prefer a little more fire in your salsa verde then simply increase the amount of green Tabasco sauce to taste.
> • Take care not to touch your eyes after chopping chillies because the oil from the chillies will cause irritation.

Grilled Spring Onions

Spring onions mark the return of better weather, and this simple dish is the perfect way to serve them.

Serves 6
3 bunches plump spring
    onions (scallions)
olive oil, for brushing

For the romesco sauce
2–3 mild dried red chillies
1 large red (bell) pepper, halved
    and seeded

2 tomatoes, halved and seeded
4–6 large garlic cloves, unpeeled
75–90ml/5–6 tbsp olive oil
25g/1oz/¼ cup hazelnuts,
    blanched
4 slices French bread, each about
    2cm/¾in thick
15ml/1 tbsp sherry vinegar
squeeze of lemon juice (optional)
chopped fresh parsley, to garnish

1 Prepare the sauce. Soak the dried chillies in hot water for about 30 minutes. Preheat the oven to 220°C/425°F/Gas 7.

2 Place the pepper, tomatoes and garlic on a baking sheet and drizzle with 15ml/1 tbsp oil. Roast, uncovered, for 35 minutes, until the pepper is blistered and blackened and the garlic is soft. Cool slightly, then peel the pepper, tomatoes and garlic.

3 Heat the remaining oil in a frying pan and fry the hazelnuts until lightly browned, then transfer to a plate. Fry the bread in the same oil until light brown on both sides, then transfer to the plate with the nuts and leave to cool. Reserve the oil.

4 Drain the chillies, discard the seeds, then place the chillies in a food processor. Add the peppers, tomatoes, garlic, hazelnuts and bread together with the reserved oil. Add the vinegar and process to a paste. Check the seasoning and set aside.

5 Trim the roots from the spring onions so that they are about 15–18cm/6–7in long. Brush with oil.

6 Heat an oiled ridged grill (broiler) pan and cook the onions for about 2 minutes on each side, turning once and brushing with oil. Serve immediately with the sauce.

Salsa Verde Energy 158kcal/652kJ; Protein 0.9g; Carbohydrate 1.1g, of which sugars 1g; Fat 16.8g, of which saturates 2.4g; Cholesterol 0mg; Calcium 35mg; Fibre 1g; Sodium 6mg.
Grilled Onions Energy 442kcal/1843kJ; Protein 8g; Carbohydrate 39.2g, of which sugars 3g; Fat 28.5g, of which saturates 3.3g; Cholesterol 0mg; Calcium 100mg; Fibre 2.5g; Sodium 121mg.

Rye Bread with Sour Cream

In this dish, sour cream is mixed with shallots, spread on slices of dark rye toast, and served with seasonal radishes and chives to counterbalance the tangy flavour of the sour cream.

200g/7oz/scant 1 cup sour cream
45ml/3 tbsp chopped fresh chives
1–2 shallots, finely chopped
salt and ground black pepper
8–10 red radishes, sliced paper
   thin, to serve

Serves 4
4 thick slices dark rye bread
15g/½oz/1 tbsp unsalted
   butter, softened

1 Toast the rye bread under a hot grill (broiler) and spread with the softened butter.

2 In a large bowl, mix the sour cream with 15ml/1 tbsp of the chopped chives. Season with salt and black pepper, then stir in the shallots.

3 Spread a thick layer of the mixture on each slice of toast. Cover with radish slices to cover the topping completely.

4 Season again with salt and ground black pepper. Sprinkle with the remaining chives before serving.

> **Variation**
> If you prefer, you can replace the sour cream with an equal quantity of quark. This soft, unripened cow's cheese is similar in flavour to sour cream but has a slightly richer texture.

> **Cook's Tip**
> Miniature versions of these snacks on small toasted bread squares make great finger food or canapés for serving at a drinks party.

Eggs Mimosa

The use of the word 'mimosa' describes the fine yellow and white grated egg which looks not unlike the flower of the same name. It can be used to finish any dish, adding a light touch.

1 garlic clove, crushed
Tabasco sauce, to taste
15ml/1 tbsp virgin olive oil
salt and ground black pepper
20 chicory (Belgian endive) leaves
   or small crisp green lettuce
   leaves, to serve
basil leaves, to garnish

Serves 20
12 hard-boiled eggs, peeled
2 ripe avocados, halved and
   stoned (pitted)

1 Reserve two hard-boiled eggs, halve the remainder and put the yolks in a mixing bowl.

2 Blend or beat the yolks with the avocados, garlic, Tabasco sauce, oil and salt and pepper. Check the seasoning. Pipe or spoon this mixture back into the halved egg whites.

3 Push the remaining egg whites through a sieve (strainer) and sprinkle over the filled eggs. Sieve the yolks on top. Arrange each half egg on a chicory leaf and place them on a serving platter. Sprinkle the basil over the egg halves before serving.

> **Variation**
> If radicchio is available, you can use these red leaves instead of the chicory leaves, if you prefer. Or try a mixture of both, alternating the colours you use when assembling the dish.

> **Cook's Tip**
> Chicory is available in the winter as well as early spring. Choose leaves that are brightly coloured and still crisp, avoiding any limp, pale specimens. Store any unwashed leaves in an airtight container in the refrigerator for up to 3 days.

Rye Bread Energy 203kcal/845kJ; Protein 4.2g; Carbohydrate 17.3g, of which sugars 5.2g; Fat 13.6g, of which saturates 8.3g; Cholesterol 38mg; Calcium 80mg; Fibre 1.8g; Sodium 190mg.
Eggs Mimosa Energy 79kcal/327kJ; Protein 4.1g; Carbohydrate 0.5g, of which sugars 0.2g; Fat 6.8g, of which saturates 1.6g; Cholesterol 114mg; Calcium 22mg; Fibre 0.6g; Sodium 43mg.

Asparagus and Egg Terrine

This terrine is a delicious and light choice. Make the hollandaise sauce well in advance and warm through gently when required.

Serves 8
150ml/¼ pint/⅔ cup milk
150ml/¼ pint/⅔ cup double (heavy) cream
40g/1½oz/3 tbsp butter
40g/1½oz/3 tbsp flour
75g/3oz herby cream cheese
675g/1½lb asparagus spears, cooked

a little oil
2 eggs, separated
15ml/1 tbsp chopped fresh chives
30ml/2 tbsp chopped fresh dill
salt and ground black pepper
dill sprigs, to garnish

For the hollandaise sauce
15ml/1 tbsp white wine vinegar
15ml/1 tbsp fresh orange juice
4 black peppercorns
1 bay leaf
2 egg yolks
115g/4oz/½ cup butter, melted and cooled slightly

1 Heat the milk and cream in a pan to just below boiling point. Melt the butter in another pan, stir in the flour and cook for 2–3 minutes. Whisk in the milk and beat until smooth. Stir in the cream cheese, season to taste and leave to cool slightly.

2 Trim the asparagus to fit the width of a 1.2 litre/2 pint/5 cup loaf tin (pan). Lightly oil the tin and then place a sheet of baking parchment in the base. Preheat the oven to 180°C/350°F/Gas 4.

3 Beat the yolks into the sauce mixture. Whisk the whites until stiff and fold in with the chives, dill and seasoning. Layer the asparagus and egg mixture in the tin, starting and finishing with the asparagus. Cover the top with foil. Place the tin in a roasting pan; half fill with hot water. Cook for 45–55 minutes until firm.

4 To make the sauce, put the vinegar, juice, peppercorns and bay leaf in a small pan and heat until reduced by half. Cool the sauce slightly, then whisk in the egg yolks and the butter over very gentle heat. Season and keep warm over a pan of hot water.

5 Allow the terrine to cool, then chill. Invert on to a serving dish, remove the parchment and garnish with the dill. Cut into slices and pour over the warmed sauce.

Hot Avocado Halves

If you make the basil oil ahead of time, or buy a ready prepared basil oil, this is an ultra-simple dish that can be ready in a flash. It makes an eye-catching first course and is an excellent appetite teaser to serve at a spring barbecue.

Serves 6
3 ready-to-eat avocados
105ml/7 tbsp balsamic vinegar

For the basil oil
40g/1½oz/1½ cups fresh basil leaves, stalks removed
200ml/7fl oz/scant 1 cup olive oil

1 To make the basil oil, place the leaves in a bowl and pour boiling water over. Leave for 30 seconds. Drain, refresh under cold water and drain again. Squeeze dry and pat with kitchen paper to remove as much moisture as possible.

2 Place the dried basil leaves in a food processor or blender with the oil and process to a purée. Put into a bowl, cover and chill overnight.

3 Line a sieve (strainer) with muslin (cheesecloth), set it over a deep bowl and pour in the basil purée. Leave undisturbed for 1 hour, or until all the oil has filtered into the bowl. Discard the solids and pour into a bottle, then chill.

4 Prepare the barbecue. Cut each avocado in half and prize out the stone (pit). Brush with a little of the oil.

5 Heat the balsamic vinegar gently in a pan, on the stove or on the barbecue. When it starts to boil, simmer for 1 minute, or until it is just beginning to turn slightly syrupy.

6 Once the flames have died down, position a grill (broiler) rack over the coals to heat. When the coals are hot, or with a light coating of ash, heat a griddle until a few drops of water sprinkled on to the surface evaporate instantly.

7 Lower the heat a little, place the avocado halves cut side down and cook for 30–60 seconds until branded with grill marks. Serve hot with the vinegar and extra oil drizzled over.

Asparagus Terrine Energy 359kcal/1483kJ; Protein 6.6g; Carbohydrate 7.1g, of which sugars 3.2g; Fat 34.1g, of which saturates 20.2g; Cholesterol 175mg; Calcium 87mg; Fibre 1.6g; Sodium 179mg.
Hot Avocado Halves Energy 222kcal/916kJ; Protein 1g; Carbohydrate 1g, of which sugars 0.3g; Fat 23.8g, of which saturates 4.1g; Cholesterol 0mg; Calcium 6mg; Fibre 1.7g; Sodium 3mg.

Tortilla Wrap with Tabbouleh

To be successful, tabbouleh needs spring onions, lemon juice, plenty of fresh herbs and lots of black pepper.

Serves 6
175g/6oz/1 cup bulgur wheat
30ml/2 tbsp chopped fresh mint
30ml/2 tbsp chopped fresh flat leaf parsley
1 bunch spring onions (scallions), sliced
1/2 cucumber, diced
50ml/2fl oz/1/4 cup extra virgin olive oil
juice of 1 large lemon
1 ripe avocado, stoned (pitted), peeled and diced
juice of 1/2 lemon
1/2 red chilli, seeded and sliced
1 garlic clove, crushed
1/2 red (bell) pepper, seeded and finely diced
salt and ground black pepper
flat leaf parsley, to garnish
4 wheat tortillas, to serve

1 To make the tabbouleh, place the bulgur wheat in a large heatproof bowl and pour over enough boiling water to cover. Leave for 30 minutes until the grains are tender but still retain a little resistance to the bite. Drain thoroughly in a sieve, then tip back into the bowl.

2 Add the mint, parsley, spring onions and cucumber to the bulgur wheat and mix thoroughly. Blend together the olive oil and lemon juice and pour over the tabbouleh, season to taste and toss well to mix. Chill for 30 minutes to allow the flavours to mingle.

3 To make the avocado mixture, place the avocado in a bowl and add the lemon juice, chilli and garlic. Season and mash with a fork to form a smooth purée. Stir in the red pepper.

4 Warm the tortillas in a dry frying pan and serve either flat, folded or rolled up with the tabbouleh and avocado mixture. Garnish with parsley, if using.

Cook's Tip
The soaking time for bulgur wheat can vary. For the best results, follow the instructions on the packet and taste the grain every now and again to check whether it is tender enough.

Potato Skewers with Mustard Dip

These potatoes are ideal for the spring barbecue and have a great flavour and a deliciously crisp skin. Try these tasty kebabs served with a thick, garlic-rich dip.

Serves 4
For the dip
4 garlic cloves, crushed
2 egg yolks
30ml/2 tbsp lemon juice
300ml/1/2 pint/1 1/4 cups extra virgin olive oil
10ml/2 tsp wholegrain mustard
salt and ground black pepper

For the skewers
1kg/2 1/4lb small new potatoes
200g/7oz shallots, halved
30ml/2 tbsp olive oil
15ml/1 tbsp sea salt

1 Prepare the barbecue for cooking the skewers before you begin. To make the dip, place the garlic, egg yolks and lemon juice in a blender or a food processor fitted with the metal blade and process for a few seconds until the mixture is thoroughly combined and smooth.

2 Keep the blender motor running and add the oil very gradually, pouring it in a thin stream, until the mixture forms a thick, glossy cream. Add the mustard and stir the ingredients together, then season with salt and black pepper. Chill until ready to use.

3 Par-boil the potatoes in their skins in boiling water for about 5 minutes. Drain well and then thread them on to metal skewers, alternating with the shallots.

4 Brush the skewers with oil and sprinkle with salt. Cook over a barbecue for 10–12 minutes, turning occasionally. Serve immediately, accompanied by the dip.

Cook's Tips
• New potatoes have the firmness necessary to stay on the skewer. Don't be tempted to use other types of small potato.
• These are just as delicious prepared under the grill (broiler): preheat the grill and continue as per step one above.

Tortilla Wrap Energy 336kcal/1408kJ; Protein 7.2g; Carbohydrate 53.9g, of which sugars 3.3g; Fat 11.4g, of which saturates 1.9g; Cholesterol 0mg; Calcium 88mg; Fibre 3.2g; Sodium 173mg.
Potato Skewers with Dip Energy 488kcal/2024kJ; Protein 4.3g; Carbohydrate 29.5g, of which sugars 4.1g; Fat 40g, of which saturates 6.1g; Cholesterol 65mg; Calcium 28mg; Fibre 2.2g; Sodium 49mg.

Fried New Potatoes with Aioli

Serve these crispy little golden new potatoes dipped into a wickedly garlicky mayonnaise – then watch them disappear in a matter of minutes. They make an ideal accompaniment to most dishes or they are equally tasty as a snack.

Serves 4
1 egg yolk
2.5ml/¹/₂ tsp Dijon mustard
300ml/¹/₂ pint/1¹/₄ cups extra
    virgin olive oil
15–30ml/1–2 tbsp lemon juice
1 garlic clove, crushed
2.5ml/¹/₂ tsp saffron strands
about 20 baby, new or
    salad potatoes
vegetable oil, enough for
    shallow frying
salt and ground black pepper

1 For the aioli, put the egg yolk in a small mixing bowl with the mustard and a pinch of salt. Mix until combined. Beat in the olive oil very slowly, drop by drop, then in a thin stream. Add the lemon juice.

2 Season the aioli with salt and ground black pepper, then add the crushed garlic and beat the mixture thoroughly until well combined.

3 Place the saffron in a small bowl and add 10ml/2 tsp of hot water. Press the saffron firmly, using the back of a teaspoon, to extract the colour and flavour, and leave it to infuse (steep) for around 5 minutes. Beat the saffron and the infused liquid into the aioli.

4 Cook the potatoes in their skins in boiling salted water for 5 minutes, then turn off the heat. Cover the pan and leave for about 15 minutes. Drain the potatoes, then dry them thoroughly in a clean dish towel.

5 Heat a 1cm/¹/₂in layer of vegetable oil in a deep pan. When the oil is very hot, add the potatoes and fry them quickly, turning them occasionally until they are crisp and golden brown all over. Drain them thoroughly on kitchen paper and serve hot with the saffron aioli.

Lacy Potato Pancakes

These pretty, lacy potato pancakes are utterly delectable served as an accompaniment to a seasonal fish dish or smoked salmon. These small pancakes make attractive and delicious canapés at a spring party or barbecue.

Serves 6
6 large potatoes
1 leek, finely sliced
1 carrot, grated (optional)
15g/¹/₂oz butter
15ml/1 tbsp vegetable oil
salt and ground black pepper

1 Peel the potatoes with a vegetable peeler or knife. Roughly grate the potato flesh into a large bowl.

2 Add the finely sliced leek and grated carrot, if using, to the potato, and mix together well until all the ingredients are thoroughly combined.

3 Heat the butter and oil in a large frying pan and when hot, add spoonfuls of the potato mixture to make pancakes, measuring about 7.5cm/3in.

4 Fry the pancakes, turning once, until golden brown on both sides. Season with salt and pepper and serve hot.

Variation
You can add various toppings to these little pancakes. Try a dollop of sour cream and a sprinkling of finely chopped red onion, or a spoonful of natural (plain) yogurt mixed with some diced and drained cucumber.

Cook's Tip
Don't be tempted to use new potatoes for this recipe. The potatoes need to be the floury variety to bind together properly. The waxy texture of new potatoes won't bind together in the same way.

Fried New Potatoes Energy 795kcal/3282kJ; Protein 2.9g; Carbohydrate 20.1g, of which sugars 1.6g; Fat 78.7g, of which saturates 10.5g; Cholesterol 50mg; Calcium 13mg; Fibre 1.3g; Sodium 16mg.
Lacy Potato Pancakes Energy 182kcal/767kJ; Protein 3.9g; Carbohydrate 33.1g, of which sugars 3.3g; Fat 4.6g, of which saturates 1.8g; Cholesterol 5mg; Calcium 20mg; Fibre 2.7g; Sodium 38mg.

Caramelized Shallot and Garlic Tarte Tatin

In this recipe, shallots are caramelized in butter, sugar and vinegar before being baked beneath a layer of Parmesan pastry. Serve with spring vegetables for the perfect seasonal feast.

Serves 4–6
300g/11oz puff pastry, thawed if frozen
50g/2oz/¼ cup butter
75g/3oz/1 cup freshly grated Parmesan cheese

For the topping
40g/1½oz/3 tbsp butter
500g/1¼lb shallots
12–16 large garlic cloves, peeled but left whole
15ml/1 tbsp golden caster (superfine) sugar
15ml/1 tbsp balsamic or sherry vinegar
45ml/3 tbsp water
5ml/1 tsp chopped fresh thyme, plus a few extra sprigs, to garnish (optional)
salt and ground black pepper

1 Roll out the pastry into a rectangle. Spread the butter over it, leaving a 2.5cm/1in border. Sprinkle the Parmesan on top. Fold the bottom third of the pastry up to cover the middle and the top third down. Seal the edges, give a quarter turn and roll out to a rectangle, then fold as before. Chill for 30 minutes.

2 For the topping, melt the butter in a 23–25cm/9–10in heavy pan that will go in the oven. Add the shallots and garlic, and cook until lightly browned. Sprinkle the sugar over the top and increase the heat a little. Cook until the sugar begins to caramelize, then turn the shallots and garlic in the buttery juices.

3 Add the vinegar, water, thyme and seasoning. Cook gently, with the pan partly covered, for 5–8 minutes, until the garlic is just tender. Leave to cool.

4 Preheat the oven to 190°C/375°F/Gas 5. Roll out the pastry to the diameter of the pan and lay it over the shallots and garlic. Prick the pastry with a sharp knife, then bake for 25–35 minutes, or until the pastry is risen and golden. Set aside to cool for 5–10 minutes, then invert the tart on to a serving platter. Sprinkle with thyme sprigs, if you like, and serve.

Grilled Goat's Cheese Toasts with Beetroot

Beetroot are considered a delicacy when they are freshly dug out of the ground in late spring and early summer. This recipe adds a new dimension to the beetroot, and the goat's cheese marries well with its earthy sweetness.

Serves 6
6 small raw beetroot (beets)
6 slices French bread
6 slices (250g/9oz) goat's cheese
30ml/2 tbsp walnut oil
salt and ground black pepper

1 Cook the beetroot in boiling salted water for 40 minutes until tender. Leave to cool slightly, then remove the skin and slice the beetroot.

2 Toast the French bread slices on both sides. Arrange the beetroot slices in a fan on the toasted bread, then place a slice of goat's cheese on top of each.

3 Place the slices on a grill (broiler) pan and grill (broil) until the cheese has melted and is golden brown and bubbling. Serve immediately, drizzled with a little walnut oil and black pepper ground on top.

Variation
If you prefer, you can use other varieties of cheese in place of the goat's cheese. Try grated mature (sharp) Cheddar for a tangy flavour. You could also use a milder flavoured cheese such as mozzarella, which is great for melting.

Cook's Tip
Always cook beetroot in their skins. If you peel them before cooking then the colour will leach out into the cooking water, taking many of the nutrients of the vegetable with it.

Shallot Tarte Tatin Energy 618kcal/2567kJ; Protein 12.8g; Carbohydrate 35.5g, of which sugars 9.6g; Fat 48.2g, of which saturates 22.8g; Cholesterol 79mg; Calcium 313mg; Fibre 3g; Sodium 605mg.
Grilled Goat's Cheese Energy 290kcal/1215kJ; Protein 13.3g; Carbohydrate 26.7g, of which sugars 5g; Fat 15.2g, of which saturates 7.9g; Cholesterol 39mg; Calcium 114mg; Fibre 1.9g; Sodium 530mg.

Pilchard and Leek Potato Cakes

This is a simple supper using a selection of basic store-cupboard ingredients, which makes it ideal for a quick and easy midweek meal. Using canned pilchards that come in tomato sauce gives a greater depth of flavour to the finished dish. It is also a great way to use the last of the spring leeks.

Serves 6
225g/8oz potatoes, diced
1 small leek, very finely chopped
5ml/1 tsp lemon juice
425g/15oz can pilchards in
    tomato sauce, boned and flaked
salt and ground black pepper

For the coating
1 egg, beaten
75g/3oz/1½ cups fresh
    white breadcrumbs
vegetable oil for frying
salad leaves, cucumber ribbons
    and lemon wedges, to garnish
mayonnaise and bread rolls,
    to serve (optional)

1 Cook the potatoes in a pan of lightly salted boiling water for about 10–15 minutes or until tender. Drain thoroughly, then mash, and set aside to cool.

2 Add the leek, lemon juice and pilchards with their tomato sauce to the cooled mashed potato. Season with salt and ground black pepper and then beat well with a wooden spoon until you have formed a smooth paste. Chill in the refrigerator for 30 minutes.

3 Place the beaten egg on a plate and the breadcrumbs on a separate plate. Divide the mixture into six pieces and shape into cakes with your hands. Dip each cake in the egg and then the breadcrumbs.

4 Heat the oil in a frying pan over medium-high heat. When hot, shallow-fry the fishcakes on each side for about 5 minutes until golden brown.

5 Drain the fishcakes on kitchen paper and place on serving plates. Garnish with salad leaves, cucumber ribbons and lemon wedges for squeezing over the cakes. Serve with mayonnaise and bread rolls, if you like.

Prawn, Egg and Avocado Mousse

A light and creamy mousse with lots of chunky texture and a great mix of flavours. Serve on the same day you make it but chill the mousse really well first.

Serves 6
a little olive oil
1 sachet gelatine
juice and rind of 1 lemon
60ml/4 tbsp mayonnaise
60ml/4 tbsp chopped fresh dill
5ml/1 tsp anchovy essence (paste)
5ml/1 tsp Worcestershire sauce
1 large avocado, ripe but just firm
4 hard-boiled eggs, peeled
    and chopped
175g/6oz/1 cup cooked prawns
    (shrimp), chopped if large
250ml/8fl oz/1 cup double
    (heavy) or whipping cream,
    lightly whipped
2 egg whites, whisked
salt and ground black pepper
dill or parsley sprigs, to garnish
warmed Granary (whole-wheat)
    bread or toast, to serve

1 Prepare six small ramekins. Lightly grease the dishes with olive oil, then wrap a baking parchment collar around the top of each and secure with tape. This ensures that you can fill the dishes as high as you like, and the extra mixture will be supported while setting and it will look really dramatic when you remove the paper. Alternatively, prepare just one small soufflé dish.

2 Dissolve the gelatine in the lemon juice with 15ml/1 tbsp hot water in a small bowl set over hot water, until clear, stirring occasionally. Allow the mixture to cool slightly, then blend in the lemon rind, mayonnaise, dill and and anchovy essence and Worcestershire sauce.

3 In a medium bowl, mash the avocado; add the eggs and prawns. Stir in the gelatine mixture and then fold in the cream, egg whites and seasoning to taste. When evenly blended, spoon into the ramekins or soufflé dish and chill for 3–4 hours. Garnish with the herbs and serve with bread or toast.

Variation
Other fish can be used in place of prawns (shrimp). Substitute the same quantity of smoked trout or salmon, or cooked crab meat.

Pilchard Potato Cakes Energy 294kcal/1229kJ; Protein 16.9g; Carbohydrate 17.1g, of which sugars 1.9g; Fat 18.1g, of which saturates 2.4g; Cholesterol 71mg; Calcium 243mg; Fibre 1.3g; Sodium 374mg.
Prawn Mousse Energy 406kcal/1677kJ; Protein 11.8g; Carbohydrate 1.7g, of which sugars 1.3g; Fat 39.3g, of which saturates 17.2g; Cholesterol 248mg; Calcium 85mg; Fibre 1.3g; Sodium 191mg.

Steamed Crab Dim Sum with Chives

These delectable Chinese-style dumplings have a wonderfully sticky texture and make a perfect snack. You can make them in advance, and steam them just before serving.

Serves 4

150g/5oz fresh white crab meat
115g/4oz/½ cup lean minced (ground) pork
30ml/2 tbsp chopped Chinese chives
15ml/1 tbsp finely chopped red (bell) pepper
30ml/2 tbsp sweet chilli sauce
30ml/2 tbsp hoisin sauce
24 fresh dumpling wrappers (available from Asian stores)
Chinese chives, to garnish
chilli oil and soy sauce, to serve

1 Place the crab meat, pork and chopped chives in a bowl. Add the red pepper, sweet chilli and hoisin sauces and mix well to combine.

2 Working with 2–3 wrappers at a time, put a small spoonful of the crab meat and pork mixture into the centre of each wrapper. Brush the edges of each wrapper with water and fold over to form a half-moon shape. Press and pleat the edges to seal, and tap the base of each dumpling to flatten.

3 Cover with a clean, damp cloth and make the remaining dumplings in the same way. Arrange the dumplings on one or more lightly oiled plates and fit inside one or more tiers of a bamboo steamer.

4 Cover the steamer and place over simmering water (making sure the water does not touch the steamer). Steam for 8–10 minutes, or until the dumplings are cooked through and become slightly translucent.

5 Make a dipping sauce by mixing equal amounts of chilli oil and soy sauce in a bowl.

6 Divide the dumplings among four plates. Garnish with Chinese chives and serve immediately with the sauce.

Chilli Crabs

These crabs are perfect for eating with fingers at a barbecue. Give guests crab crackers for the claws and have some finger bowls or hot towels to hand as it will be messy!

Serves 4

2 cooked crabs, each about 675g/1½lb
90ml/6 tbsp sunflower oil
2.5cm/1in piece fresh root ginger, peeled and chopped
2–3 garlic cloves, crushed
1–2 red chillies, seeded and pounded to a paste
175ml/6fl oz/¾ cup tomato ketchup
30ml/2 tbsp soft brown sugar
15ml/1 tbsp light soy sauce
salt
120ml/4fl oz/½ cup boiling water
hot toast and cucumber chunks, to serve

1 To prepare the crabs, twist off the large claws, then turn the crab on its back with its mouth and eyes facing away from you. Using both of your thumbs, push the body, with the small legs attached, upwards from beneath the flap, separating the body from the main shell in the process. Discard the stomach sac and grey spongy lungs known as 'dead men's fingers'.

2 Using a teaspoon, scrape the brown creamy meat from the large shell into a small bowl.

3 Twist the legs from the body. Cut the body section in half. Pick out the white meat. If liked, pick out the meat from the legs, or leave for guests to remove at the table.

4 Heat the oil in a wok and gently fry the ginger, garlic and fresh chilli paste for 1–2 minutes without browning. Stir in the ketchup, sugar and soy sauce, with salt to taste and heat gently.

5 Stir in the crab meat together with the claws and crab legs, if these were reserved. Pour in the boiling water, stir well and cook over high heat until heated through.

6 Pile the crab and crab claws mixture on serving plates with the chunks of cucumber and serve with pieces of toast.

Steamed Dim Sum Energy 146kcal/617kJ; Protein 15.3g; Carbohydrate 14.8g, of which sugars 5.2g; Fat 3.3g, of which saturates 0.7g; Cholesterol 45mg; Calcium 35mg; Fibre 0.5g; Sodium 961mg.
Chilli Crabs Energy 232kcal/971kJ; Protein 8.5g; Carbohydrate 21.8g, of which sugars 21g; Fat 12.9g, of which saturates 1.5g; Cholesterol 19mg; Calcium 28mg; Fibre 0.8g; Sodium 1347mg.

Pastry Tartlets with Seafood and Chicken Fillings

These tasty tartlets make ideal appetizers or party food and are full of the flavours of spring.

Makes 18
200g/7oz/generous 1½ cups plain (all purpose) flour
125g/4¼oz/9 tbsp butter
150ml/¼ pint/⅔ cup cold water

For the prawn (shrimp) filling
40g/1½oz/scant ¼ cup butter
20g/¾oz/scant ¼ cup plain (all-purpose) flour
475ml/16fl oz/2 cups single (light) cream
275g/10oz cooked prawns (shrimp)
salt and ground white pepper

25ml/1½ tbsp chopped fresh dill sprigs, to garnish

For the chicken and asparagus filling
65g/2½oz/5 tbsp butter
225g/8oz fresh asparagus, cut into 2cm/¾in pieces
15ml/1 tbsp cooking oil
225g/8oz skinless chicken breast fillets, cut into 2cm/¾in cubes
20g/¾oz/scant ¼ cup plain (all-purpose) flour
475ml/16fl oz/2 cups single (light) cream
salt and ground white pepper
45ml/3 tbsp chopped fresh parsley, to garnish

1 Preheat the oven to 200°C/400°F/Gas 6. Sift the flour into a large bowl. Cut the butter into small pieces, add to the flour and rub in until the mixture resembles fine breadcrumbs. Gradually add the water and mix to form a dough. On a lightly floured surface, roll out the pastry and cut circles to fit 7cm/2¾in diameter fluted tartlet tins (muffin pans). Cut a 13cm/5in square of foil to line each pastry shell and fill with a handful of dried peas or beans to help the pastry keep its shape. Chill for at least 30 minutes to rest the pastry, then bake for 10–15 minutes until crisp and golden. Remove the beans and foil for the final 5 minutes.

2 To make the prawn filling, melt the butter in a pan over medium heat and stir in the flour. Cook the roux for 3–5 minutes until pale beige. Slowly stir in the cream and cook, stirring constantly, for about 5 minutes, until thickened. Stir the prawns into the sauce and heat gently for 3–4 minutes. Season well with salt and black pepper.

3 To make the chicken and asparagus filling, melt 25g/1oz/ 2 tbsp of the butter in a frying pan over medium heat. Add the asparagus, toss to coat evenly with butter and cook, stirring, for about 4 minutes, until tender. Remove and set aside on a plate. In the same pan, heat the cooking oil over a medium heat. Add the chicken and cook for about 5 minutes, stirring, until it is no longer pink. Set aside.

4 Melt the remaining butter in a pan over a medium heat and stir in the flour. Cook the roux for 3–5 minutes until pale beige-coloured. Slowly stir in the cream and cook, stirring constantly, for about 5 minutes until the sauce has thickened. Add the asparagus and chicken and heat for 3–4 minutes. Season well.

5 Fill half the tart cases with the creamed prawns, and sprinkle with fresh dill. Fill the rest with the chicken and asparagus, and sprinkle with fresh parsley. Serve immediately.

Salmon, Sesame and Ginger Fishcakes

These light fishcakes are scented with the exotic flavours of sesame, lime and ginger. They make a tempting springtime appetizer served simply with a wedge of lime for squeezing over, but are also perfect for a light lunch or supper, served with a crunchy, refreshing salad. In this case, you may want to use the mixture to make a smaller number of larger fishcakes, which will take a few more minutes each side to cook through.

Makes 25
500g/1¼lb salmon fillet, skinned and boned
45ml/3 tbsp dried breadcrumbs
30ml/2 tbsp mayonnaise
30ml/2 tbsp sesame seeds
30ml/2 tbsp light soy sauce
finely grated zest of 2 limes
10ml/2 tsp finely grated fresh root ginger
4 spring onions (scallions), sliced
vegetable oil, for frying
salt and ground black pepper
spring onion (scallion) slivers, to garnish
lime wedges, to serve

1 Finely chop the salmon and place in a bowl. Add the breadcrumbs, mayonnaise, sesame seeds, soy sauce, lime zest, ginger and spring onions and use your fingers to mix well, distributing all the ingredients evenly.

2 With wet hands, divide the mixture into 25 portions and shape each one into a small round cake.

3 Place the cakes on a baking sheet lined with baking parchment, cover and chill for several hours or overnight.

4 When you are ready to cook the fishcakes, heat about 5cm/2in vegetable oil in a wok.

5 Working in batches, shallow fry the fishcakes over medium heat for 2–3 minutes on each side.

6 Drain the fishcakes well on kitchen paper and serve warm or at room temperature, garnished with spring onion slivers and plenty of lime wedges for squeezing over.

Tartlets Energy 274kcal/1138kJ; Protein 9g; Carbohydrate 11g, of which sugars 1.7g; Fat 21.9g, of which saturates 13.4g; Cholesterol 95mg; Calcium 83mg; Fibre 0.6g; Sodium 131mg.
Salmon Fishcakes Energy 83kcal/343kJ; Protein 4.6g; Carbohydrate 1.6g, of which sugars 0.2g; Fat 6.5g, of which saturates 0.9g; Cholesterol 11mg; Calcium 16mg; Fibre 0.2g; Sodium 117mg.

Parsley and Rocket Salad

A light dish, but full of spring greens, this salad is perfect for a lunchtime snack. Use the best Parmesan cheese – parmigiano reggiano – for a great taste experience.

Serves 6

1 garlic clove, halved
115g/4oz good white bread, cut into 1cm/½in thick slices
45ml/3 tbsp olive oil, plus extra for shallow frying
75g/3oz rocket (arugula) leaves
75g/3oz baby spinach

25g/1oz flat leaf parsley, stalks removed
45ml/3 tbsp salted capers, rinsed and dried
40g/1½oz Parmesan cheese, pared into shavings

For the dressing

25ml/1½ tbsp black olive paste
1 garlic clove, finely chopped
5ml/1 tsp Dijon mustard
75ml/5 tbsp olive oil
10ml/2 tsp balsamic vinegar
ground black pepper

1 To make the dressing, whisk the black olive paste, garlic and mustard together in a bowl. Gradually whisk in the olive oil, then the vinegar. Adjust the seasoning with black pepper – the dressing should be sufficiently salty.

2 Preheat the oven to 190°C/375°F/Gas 5. Rub the halved garlic clove over the bread and cut or tear the slices into bitesize croûtons.

3 Toss them in the oil and place on a small baking sheet. Bake for 10–15 minutes, stirring once, until golden brown. Cool on kitchen paper.

4 Place the rocket, spinach and parsley in a large salad bowl. Mix together until well combined.

5 Heat a shallow layer of olive oil in a frying pan. Add the capers and fry briefly until crisp. Scoop out straight away and drain on kitchen paper.

6 Toss the dressing and croûtons into the salad and divide it among six bowls or plates. Sprinkle the Parmesan shavings and the fried capers over the top and serve immediately.

Potato and Radish Salad

Radishes add a splash of crunch and peppery flavour to this honey-scented spring salad. Usually, potato salads are dressed in a thick sauce. This one, however, is quite light and colourful with a tasty yet delicate dressing of honey and mustard.

Serves 4–6

450g/1lb new or salad potatoes

For the dressing

45ml/3 tbsp olive oil
15ml/1 tbsp walnut or hazelnut oil (optional)
30ml/2 tbsp wine vinegar
10ml/2 tsp coarse-grain mustard
5ml/1 tsp honey
about 6–8 radishes, thinly sliced
30ml/2 tbsp chopped chives
salt and ground black pepper

1 Cook the potatoes in their skins in a large pan of boiling salted water until just tender. Drain well and leave to cool slightly. When cool enough to handle, cut the potatoes in half, but leave any small ones whole. Place in a large bowl.

2 To make the dressing, place the oils, vinegar, mustard and honey in a bowl and season to taste with salt and pepper. Whisk together until thoroughly combined.

3 Toss the dressing into the potatoes in the bowl while they are still cooling and leave to stand for 1–2 hours to allow the flavours to penetrate.

4 Finally, mix in the sliced radishes and chopped chives and chill in the refrigerator until ready to serve.

5 Just before serving, toss the salad mixture together again, as some of the dressing may have settled on the bottom, and adjust the seasoning.

> **Variation**
> Sliced celery stick, diced red onion and/or chopped walnuts would make good alternatives to the radishes if you are unable to find any.

Parsley Salad Energy 262kcal/1084kJ; Protein 9.8g; Carbohydrate 12.7g, of which sugars 3.5g; Fat 19.3g, of which saturates 3.7g; Cholesterol 7mg; Calcium 437mg; Fibre 4.5g; Sodium 565mg.
Potato and Radish Salad Energy 108kcal/451kJ; Protein 1.5g; Carbohydrate 13g, of which sugars 1.9g; Fat 5.9g, of which saturates 0.9g; Cholesterol 0mg; Calcium 8mg; Fibre 0.9g; Sodium 36mg.

Potato Salad with Egg and Lemon

The tangy flavour of this salad makes it ideal for a spring barbecue.

Serves 4
900g/2lb new potatoes
1 small onion, finely chopped
2 hard-boiled eggs, shelled

300ml/½ pint/1¼ cups mayonnaise
1 garlic clove, crushed
finely grated (shredded) rind and juice of 1 lemon
60ml/4 tbsp chopped fresh parsley, plus extra for garnishing
salt and ground black pepper

1 Scrub or scrape the potatoes. Put them in a pan, cover with cold water and add a pinch of salt. Bring to the boil, then simmer for 15 minutes, or until tender.

2 Drain the potatoes and allow to cool. Cut them into large dice, season well with salt and black pepper and combine with the chopped onion.

3 Halve the eggs and set aside the yolk. Roughly chop the whites and place in a mixing bowl. Stir in the mayonnaise. Mix the garlic, lemon rind and lemon juice in a small bowl and stir into the mayonnaise mixture, combining thoroughly.

4 Stir the mayonnaise mixture into the potatoes, coating them well, then fold in the chopped parsley. Press the egg yolk through a sieve (strainer) and sprinkle on top. Serve cold or chilled, garnished with parsley.

Avocado, Onion and Spinach Salad

The simple dressing gives a sharp tang to this sophisticated spring salad.

Serves 4
1 large red onion, cut into wedges
300g/11oz ready-made polenta, cut into 1cm/½in cubes
olive oil, for brushing

225g/8oz baby spinach leaves
1 avocado
5ml/1 tsp lemon juice

For the dressing
60ml/4 tbsp extra virgin olive oil
juice of ½ lemon
salt and ground black pepper

1 Preheat the oven to 200°C/400°F/Gas 6. Place the onion wedges and polenta cubes on a lightly oiled baking sheet and bake for 25 minutes, or until the onion is tender and the polenta is crisp and golden, turning everything frequently to prevent sticking. Leave to cool slightly.

2 Meanwhile, make the dressing. Place the olive oil and lemon juice in a screw-top jar. Add salt and pepper to taste, close the jar tightly and shake vigorously to combine.

3 Place the spinach in a serving bowl. Peel, stone (pit) and slice the avocado, then toss the slices in the lemon juice to prevent them from discolouring. Add to the spinach with the onions.

4 Pour the dressing over the salad and toss gently to combine all the ingredients. Sprinkle the polenta croûtons on top or hand them round separately.

Watercress and Pear Salad

A refreshing light salad, this dish combines peppery watercress, soft juicy pears and a tart dressing. Dunsyre Blue has a sharp flavour with a crumbly texture.

Serves 4
2 bunches watercress, thoroughly washed and trimmed
2 ripe pears
salt and ground black pepper

For the dressing
25g/1oz Dunsyre Blue cheese
30ml/2 tbsp walnut oil
15ml/1 tbsp lemon juice

1 To make the dressing, crumble the Dunsyre Blue into a bowl, then mash into the walnut oil, using a fork.

2 Whisk in the lemon juice to create a thickish mixture. Add a little more cheese to thicken it further, if necessary. Season.

3 Arrange a pile of watercress on the side of four plates.

4 Peel and slice the two pears, then place the pear slices to the side of the watercress, allowing half a pear per person.

5 Drizzle the dressing over the salad. The salad is best served immediately at room temperature. If you want to chill it for a while, take it out of the refrigerator 30 minutes before serving and only add the dressing at the last minute.

> **Cook's Tips**
> • Choose ripe Comice or similar pears that are soft and juicy.
> • If you want to get things ready in advance, peel and slice the pears, then rub with some lemon juice; this will stop them discolouring so quickly.

> **Variation**
> For a milder, tangy dressing use Dolcelatte cheese instead.

Potato Salad Energy 723kcal/3000kJ; Protein 8.4g; Carbohydrate 39.1g, of which sugars 5.1g; Fat 60.4g, of which saturates 9.6g; Cholesterol 151mg; Calcium 68mg; Fibre 3.2g; Sodium 403mg.
Avocado Salad Energy 442kcal/1838kJ; Protein 9.3g; Carbohydrate 57.4g, of which sugars 1.8g; Fat 18.8g, of which saturates 2.7g; Cholesterol 0mg; Calcium 105mg; Fibre 3.9g; Sodium 81mg.
Watercress Salad Energy 106kcal/442kJ; Protein 2.3g; Carbohydrate 7.6g, of which sugars 7.6g; Fat 7.6g, of which saturates 1.8g; Cholesterol 5mg; Calcium 81mg; Fibre 2g; Sodium 91mg.

Spinach and Roast Garlic Salad

Don't worry about the amount of garlic in this spring salad. During roasting, the garlic becomes sweet and subtle and loses its strong, pungent taste.

450g/1lb baby spinach leaves
50g/2oz/½ cup pine nuts, lightly toasted
juice of ½ lemon
salt and ground black pepper

Serves 4
12 garlic cloves, unpeeled
60ml/4 tbsp extra virgin olive oil

1 Preheat the oven to 190°C/375°F/Gas 5. Place the garlic in a small roasting pan, toss in 30ml/2 tbsp of the olive oil and roast for about 15 minutes, until the garlic cloves are slightly charred around the edges.

2 While still warm, transfer the roasted garlic to a large salad bowl. Add the spinach leaves, pine nuts and lemon juice, along with the remaining olive oil and a little salt. Toss well and add ground black pepper to taste.

3 Serve the salad immediately, inviting guests to squeeze the softened garlic purée out of the skin to eat.

> **Variation**
> You can use a mixture of young spinach leaves and other spring salad leaves, if you prefer, for this salad. Try combining the spinach leaves with a handful of watercress or rocket (arugula) leaves.

> **Cook's Tip**
> The spinach leaves need to be young and tender for this salad. Packets of baby spinach are often sold in the salad sections of supermarkets, or look out for them appearing in local grocers in the springtime.

Globe Artichoke Salad

This salad first course is a great way to make the most of artichokes. It is equally good served hot or cold.

Serves 4
4 artichokes
juice of 1 lemon

900ml/1½ pints/3¾ cups home-made vegetable stock and water mixed
2 garlic cloves, chopped
1 small bunch parsley
6 whole peppercorns
15ml/1 tbsp olive oil, plus extra for drizzling

1 To prepare the artichokes, trim the stalks of the artichokes close to the base, cut the very tips off the leaves and then divide them into quarters. Remove the inedible hairy choke (the central part), carefully scraping the hairs away from the heart at the base of the artichoke.

2 Squeeze a little of the lemon juice over the cut surfaces of the artichokes to prevent discoloration.

3 Put the artichokes into a pan and cover with the stock and water, garlic, parsley, peppercorns and olive oil. Cover with a lid and cook gently for 1 hour, or until the artichokes are tender. They are ready when the leaves come away easily when pulled.

4 Remove the artichokes with a slotted spoon. Boil the cooking liquid hard to reduce by half, then strain.

5 To serve, arrange the artichokes in small serving dishes and pour over the reduced juices. Drizzle over a little extra olive oil and lemon juice. Provide finger bowls and a bowl for the leaves.

6 To eat, pull a leaf away from the artichoke and scrape the fleshy part at the base with your teeth. Discard the remainder of the leaves and then eat the heart at the base.

> **Variation**
> If you can find tiny purple artichokes with tapered leaves, they can be cooked and eaten whole as the chokes are very tender.

Spinach and Garlic Salad Energy 234kcal/966kJ; Protein 6.1g; Carbohydrate 6g, of which sugars 3.7g; Fat 20.8g, of which saturates 2.3g; Cholesterol 0mg; Calcium 240mg; Fibre 4.6g; Sodium 23mg.
Globe Artichoke Salad Energy 59kcal/245kJ; Protein 0.7g; Carbohydrate 7.8g, of which sugars 7.3g; Fat 3.1g, of which saturates 0.5g; Cholesterol 0mg; Calcium 25mg; Fibre 2.4g; Sodium 61mg.

Grilled Spring Onions and Asparagus with Parma Ham

This is a good choice of first course for mid to late spring, when both spring onions and asparagus are at their best. The smokiness of the grilled vegetables goes well with the sweetness of the air-dried ham.

Serves 4–6
2 bunches (about 24) plump
  spring onions (scallions)
500g/1¼lb asparagus
45–60ml/3–4 tbsp olive oil
20ml/4 tsp balsamic vinegar
8–12 slices Parma or San
  Daniele ham
50g/2oz Pecorino cheese
sea salt and ground black pepper
extra virgin olive oil, to serve

1 Trim the root, outer skin and the top off the spring onions. Cut off and discard the woody ends of the asparagus. Use a vegetable peeler to peel the bottom 7.5cm/3in of the spears.

2 Preheat the grill (broiler). Toss the spring onions and asparagus in 30ml/2 tbsp of the oil. Place on two baking sheets and season.

3 Grill (broil) the asparagus for 5 minutes on each side, until just tender when tested with the tip of a sharp knife. Protect the tips with foil if they seem to char too much.

4 Grill the spring onions for about 3–4 minutes on each side, until tinged with brown. Brush the vegetables with more oil as you turn them.

5 Arrange the vegetables on individual plates. Season with pepper and drizzle over the vinegar. Lay 2–3 slices of ham on each plate and shave the Pecorino over the top.

> **Cook's Tip**
> If more convenient, the trimmed and peeled asparagus spears can be roasted at 200°C/400°F/Gas 6 for 15 minutes.

Broad Bean Salad

The Moroccan technique of marrying broad beans with preserved lemons creates a flavourful side salad.

Serves 4
2kg/4½lb broad (fava) beans
  in the pod
60–75ml/4–5 tbsp olive oil
juice of ½ lemon
2 garlic cloves, chopped
5ml/1 tsp ground cumin
10ml/2 tsp paprika
small bunch of fresh
  coriander (cilantro)
1 preserved lemon, chopped
handful of black olives, to garnish
salt and ground black pepper

1 Bring a large pan of salted water to the boil. Meanwhile, pod the broad beans. Put the shelled beans in the pan and boil for about 2 minutes.

2 Drain and refresh the beans under cold running water. Drain well. Slip off and discard the thick outer skin to reveal the smooth, bright green beans underneath.

3 Put the beans in a heavy pan and add the olive oil, lemon juice, garlic, cumin and paprika. Cook the beans gently over a low heat for about 10 minutes, then season to taste with salt and pepper and leave to cool in the pan until warm.

4 Transfer the beans to a serving bowl, and add the pan juices. Finely chop the coriander and add to the beans with the lemon. Toss, then garnish with the black olives and serve.

> **Cook's Tip**
> To make preserved lemons, scrub and quarter lemons almost through to the base, then rub the cut sides with salt. Pack tightly into a large sterilized jar. Half fill the jar with more salt, adding some bay leaves, peppercorns and cinnamon, if you like. Cover completely with lemon juice. Cover with a lid and store for 2 weeks, shaking the jar daily. Add a little olive oil to seal and use within 1–6 months, washing off the salt before use.

Grilled Spring Onions Energy 109kcal/450kJ; Protein 8g; Carbohydrate 2.9g, of which sugars 2.8g; Fat 7.3g, of which saturates 1.4g; Cholesterol 15mg; Calcium 47mg; Fibre 1.9g; Sodium 312mg.
Broad Bean Salad Energy 272kcal/1143kJ; Protein 16.6g; Carbohydrate 24.6g, of which sugars 2.9g; Fat 12.7g, of which saturates 1.8g; Cholesterol 0mg; Calcium 142mg; Fibre 13.6g; Sodium 21mg.

Grilled Halloumi and Bean Salad

Halloumi, the hard, white salty goat's milk cheese that squeaks when you bite it, grills really well and is the perfect complement to fresh spring vegetables.

Serves 4
20 baby new potatoes, total weight about 300g/11oz
200g/7oz extra-fine green beans, trimmed
675g/1½lb broad (fava) beans, shelled weight 225g/8oz
200g/7oz halloumi cheese, cut into 5mm/¼in slices
1 garlic clove, crushed to a paste with a large pinch of salt
90ml/6 tbsp olive oil
5ml/1 tsp cider vinegar or white wine vinegar
15g/½oz/½ cup fresh basil leaves, shredded
45ml/3 tbsp chopped fresh savory
2 spring onions (scallions), finely sliced
salt and ground black pepper

1 Thread five potatoes on to each of four skewers, and cook in a large pan of salted boiling water for about 7 minutes or until they are almost tender.

2 Add the green beans and cook for 3 minutes more. Add the broad beans and cook for just 2 minutes. Drain all the vegetables in a large colander.

3 Refresh the cooked broad beans under cold water. Pop each broad bean out of its skin to reveal the bright green inner bean. Place in a bowl, cover and set aside.

4 Preheat a grill (broiler) or griddle. Place the halloumi slices and the potato skewers in a wide dish. Whisk the garlic and oil together with a generous grinding of black pepper. Add to the dish and toss the halloumi and potato skewers in the mixture.

5 Cook the cheese and potato skewers under the grill or on the griddle for about 2 minutes on each side.

6 Add the vinegar to the oil and garlic remaining in the dish and whisk to mix thoroughly. Toss in the beans, herbs and spring onions, with the cooked halloumi. Serve immediately with the potato skewers.

Beetroot and Red Onion Salad

This spring salad looks especially attractive when it is made with a mixture of red and yellow beetroot.

Serves 6
500g/1¼lb small raw beetroot (beets)
75ml/5 tbsp water
60ml/4 tbsp olive oil
90g/3½ oz/scant 1 cup walnut halves
5ml/1 tsp caster (superfine) sugar, plus a little extra for the dressing
30ml/2 tbsp walnut oil
15ml/1 tbsp sherry vinegar
5ml/1 tsp soy sauce
5ml/1 tsp grated (shredded) orange rind
2.5ml/½ tsp ground roasted coriander seeds
5–10ml/1–2 tsp orange juice
1 red onion, halved and very thinly sliced
15–30ml/1–2 tbsp chopped fresh fennel
75g/3oz watercress or mizuna leaves
handful of beetroot (beet) leaves (optional)
salt and ground black pepper

1 Preheat the oven to 180°C/350°F/Gas 4. Place the beetroot in an ovenproof dish in a single layer and add the water. Cover tightly and roast for 1–1½ hours, or until they are just tender.

2 Cool, then peel the beetroot. Slice or cut them into strips and toss with 15ml/1 tbsp of the olive oil in a bowl. Set aside.

3 Heat 15ml/1 tbsp of the remaining olive oil in a small frying pan. Fry the walnuts until starting to brown. Add the sugar and cook, stirring, until starting to caramelize. Season with pepper and 2.5ml/½ tsp salt, then turn them on to a plate to cool.

4 In a bowl, whisk together the remaining olive oil, the walnut oil, sherry vinegar, soy sauce, orange rind and coriander seeds. Season with salt and pepper and add a pinch of caster sugar. Whisk in orange juice to taste.

5 Separate the onion slices and add them to the beetroot. Pour over the dressing and toss the ingredients well. Just before serving, toss with the fennel, watercress and beetroot leaves, if using. Transfer to individual plates and sprinkle with the caramelized nuts.

Grilled Halloumi Energy 393kcal/1635kJ; Protein 16.5g; Carbohydrate 20.8g, of which sugars 3.4g; Fat 27.7g, of which saturates 9.4g; Cholesterol 29mg; Calcium 263mg; Fibre 6.3g; Sodium 215mg.
Beetroot Salad Energy 238kcal/986kJ; Protein 3.8g; Carbohydrate 8g, of which sugars 7.4g; Fat 21.4g, of which saturates 2.2g; Cholesterol 0mg; Calcium 36mg; Fibre 2.3g; Sodium 116mg.

Avocado, Orange and Almond Salad

A wonderful combination of creamy avocado with oranges and tomatoes.

Serves 4

2 tomatoes, peeled
2 small avocados
60ml/4 tbsp extra virgin olive oil
30ml/2 tbsp lemon juice
15ml/1 tbsp chopped fresh parsley
2–3 oranges, peeled and sliced
    into thick rounds
small onion rings
25g/1oz/¼ cup toasted almonds
10–12 black olives
salt and ground black pepper

1 Chop the tomatoes into quarters, remove the seeds and chop the flesh roughly. Cut the avocados in half, remove the stones (pits) and carefully peel away the skin. Cut into chunks. Mix the olive oil, lemon juice and parsley. Season, then toss the avocado and tomatoes in half of the dressing.

2 Arrange the sliced oranges on a plate and sprinkle with the onion rings. Drizzle with the remaining dressing. Spoon the avocados, tomatoes, almonds and olives on top and serve.

Date, Orange and Carrot Salad

A colourful salad featuring fresh dates and orange flower water.

Serves 4

1 Little Gem (Bibb) lettuce
2 carrots, finely grated
2 oranges
115g/4oz fresh dates, pitted and
    cut into eighths, lengthways
25g/1oz/¼ cup toasted whole
    almonds, chopped
30ml/2 tbsp lemon juice
5ml/1 tsp caster (superfine) sugar
1.5ml/¼ tsp salt
15ml/1 tbsp orange flower water

1 Separate the lettuce leaves and arrange them in the bottom of a salad bowl. Place the grated carrot in a mound on top.

2 Peel and segment the oranges and arrange them around the carrot. Pile the dates on top, then sprinkle with the almonds. Mix the lemon juice, sugar, salt and orange flower water and sprinkle over the salad. Serve chilled.

Leek and Fennel Salad

This is an excellent salad for early spring, when leeks are are still available and the new season of tomatoes are just starting to begin.

Serves 6

675g/1½lb leeks
2 large fennel bulbs
120ml/4fl oz/½ cup olive oil
2 shallots, chopped
150ml/¼ pint/⅔ cup dry white
    wine or white vermouth
5ml/1 tsp fennel seeds, crushed
6 fresh thyme sprigs
2–3 bay leaves
pinch of dried red chilli flakes
350g/12oz tomatoes, peeled,
    seeded and diced
5ml/1 tsp sun-dried tomato
    paste (optional)
good pinch of sugar (optional)
75g/3oz/¾ cup small black
    olives, to garnish
salt and ground black pepper

1 Cook the leeks in boiling salted water for 4–5 minutes. Using a slotted spoon, place them in a colander to drain and cool. Then cut into 7.5cm/3in lengths. Reserve the cooking water.

2 Trim and slice the fennel. Keep the tops for a garnish. Cook the fennel in the reserved water for about 5 minutes, drain, then toss with 30ml/2 tbsp of olive oil. Season to taste.

3 On a ridged cast iron griddle, grill (broil) the vegetables until they are tinged deep brown, then place them in a large shallow dish and set aside.

4 Heat the remaining oil, the shallots, white wine or vermouth, crushed fennel seeds, thyme, bay leaves and chilli flakes in a large pan and bring to the boil over a medium heat. Lower the heat and simmer for 10 minutes.

5 Add the diced tomatoes and cook briskly until the dressing has thickened. Add the tomato paste and adjust the seasoning, adding a pinch of sugar, if you like.

6 Toss the fennel and leeks in the dressing and chill. Bring the salad back to room temperature and garnish it with fennel fronds and olives before serving. Season with plenty of ground black pepper.

Avocado Salad Energy 286kcal/1183kJ; Protein 3.5g; Carbohydrate 7.3g, of which sugars 6.4g; Fat 27.1g, of which saturates 4.4g; Cholesterol 0mg; Calcium 70mg; Fibre 4.4g; Sodium 575mg.
Date Salad Energy 138kcal/582kJ; Protein 3.6g; Carbohydrate 21.8g, of which sugars 21.4g; Fat 4.7g, of which saturates 0.4g; Cholesterol 0mg; Calcium 90mg; Fibre 3.9g; Sodium 18mg.
Leek and Fennel Salad Energy 193kcal/800kJ; Protein 2.8g; Carbohydrate 6.7g, of which sugars 5.9g; Fat 14.7g, of which saturates 2.2g; Cholesterol 0mg; Calcium 53mg; Fibre 4.6g; Sodium 297mg.

Prawn Noodle Salad with Fragrant Herbs

A light salad with all the tangy flavour of the sea. Instead of prawns, you can also use squid, scallops, mussels or crab.

Serves 4
1/2 cucumber
115g/4oz cellophane noodles, soaked in hot water until soft
1 small green (bell) pepper, seeded and cut into strips
1 tomato, cut into strips
2 shallots, finely sliced
16 cooked peeled prawns (shrimp)
salt and ground black pepper
fresh coriander (cilantro), to garnish

For the dressing
15ml/1 tbsp rice wine vinegar
30ml/2 tbsp Thai fish sauce
30ml/2 tbsp lime juice
2.5ml/1/2 tsp grated (shredded) fresh root ginger
1 lemon grass stalk, finely chopped
1 fresh red chilli, seeded and finely sliced
30ml/2 tbsp roughly chopped fresh mint
few sprigs of tarragon, roughly chopped
15ml/1 tbsp snipped fresh chives
pinch of salt

1 To make the dressing, combine all the ingredients in a small bowl and whisk well.

2 Peel the cucumber, then scoop out the seeds and cut the flesh into batons.

3 Drain the noodles, then plunge them in a pan of boiling water for 1 minute. Drain, rinse under cold running water and drain again well.

4 In a large bowl, combine the noodles with the green pepper, cucumber, tomato and shallots. Lightly season with salt and pepper, then toss with the dressing.

5 Spoon the noodles on to individual serving plates, arranging the prawns on top. Garnish with a few coriander leaves and serve immediately.

Salmon with Avocado Salad

Use only the freshest of salmon for this delicious spring salad featuring marinated salmon.

Serves 4
2 very fresh salmon tails, skinned and filleted, 250g/9oz in total
juice of 1 lemon
10cm/4in dashi-konbu seaweed, wiped with a damp cloth and cut into 4 strips
1 ripe avocado

4 shiso or basil leaves, stalks removed and cut in half lengthways
115g/4oz mixed leaves such as lamb's lettuce or frisée
45ml/3 tbsp flaked (sliced) almonds, toasted in a dry frying pan until just slightly browned

For the miso mayonnaise
90ml/6 tbsp good mayonnaise
15ml/1 tbsp miso paste
ground black pepper

1 Cut the first salmon in half crossways at the tail end where the fillet is not wider than 4cm/1½in. Next, cut the wider part in half lengthways. This means the fillet from one side is cut into three. Cut the other fillet into three pieces, in the same way.

2 Pour the lemon juice into a wide, shallow plastic container and add two of the dashi-konbu pieces. Lay the salmon fillets in the base of the container and sprinkle with the rest of the dashi-konbu. Marinate for 15 minutes, then turn and leave for another 15 minutes. The salmon will change to a pink 'cooked' colour. Remove from the marinade, wipe with kitchen paper and cut the salmon into 5mm/¼in thick slices against the grain.

3 Halve the avocado and sprinkle with a little of the remaining salmon marinade. Remove the avocado stone (pit) and skin, then carefully slice to the same thickness as the salmon.

4 Mix the miso mayonnaise ingredients in a small bowl. Spread about 5ml/1 tsp on to the back of each of the shiso or basil leaves, then mix the remainder with 15ml/1 tbsp of the remaining marinade to loosen the mayonnaise.

5 Arrange the salad leaves on four plates. Add the avocado, salmon, shiso leaves and almonds and toss lightly. Drizzle over the remaining mayonnaise and serve immediately.

Salmon Salad Energy 432kcal/1787kJ; Protein 16.2g; Carbohydrate 2.3g, of which sugars 1.4g; Fat 39.8g, of which saturates 6.2g; Cholesterol 48mg; Calcium 54mg; Fibre 2.3g; Sodium 134mg.
Prawn Noodle Salad Energy 156kcal/653kJ; Protein 7.4g; Carbohydrate 29.4g, of which sugars 5.4g; Fat 0.7g, of which saturates 0.1g; Cholesterol 49mg; Calcium 68mg; Fibre 2.1g; Sodium 417mg.

Prawn Salad

A pretty combination of pink prawns and green avocado, this salad makes a stylish light meal.

Serves 4

450g/1lb cooked peeled
   prawns (shrimp)
juice of 1 lime
3 tomatoes
1 ripe but firm avocado
30ml/2 tbsp hot chilli sauce
5ml/1 tsp sugar
150ml/¼ pint/⅔ cup
   soured cream
2 Little Gem (Bibb) lettuces,
   separated into leaves
salt and ground black pepper
fresh basil leaves and strips of
   green (bell) pepper, to garnish

1 Put the prawns in a large bowl, add the lime juice and salt and pepper. Toss lightly and leave to marinate.

2 Cut a cross in the base of each tomato. Place the tomatoes into just-boiled water for 30 seconds, then remove with a slotted spoon and plunge into cold water. Drain, then peel off the skins. Chop the flesh into 2cm cubes, discarding the seeds.

3 Halve, pit and skin the avocado and chop into 2cm chunks. Add the chopped avocado and tomato to the prawns.

4 Mix the hot chilli sauce, sugar and soured cream in a bowl. Fold into the prawn mixture. Line a bowl with lettuce leaves, then top with the prawns. Chill for at least 1 hour, then garnish with fresh basil and strips of green pepper.

Seafood Salad with Fragrant Herbs

The luscious combination of prawns, scallops and squid, makes this an ideal choice for a springtime celebration.

Serves 4–6

250ml/8fl oz/1 cup fish stock
350g/12oz squid, cut into rings
12 raw king prawns (jumbo
   shrimp), peeled, with tails intact
12 scallops
50g/2oz cellophane noodles, soaked
   in warm water for 30 minutes
½ cucumber, cut into thin batons
1 lemon grass stalk, finely chopped
2 kaffir lime leaves, finely shredded
2 shallots, thinly sliced
30ml/2 tbsp chopped spring
   onions (scallions)
30ml/2 tbsp fresh coriander
   (cilantro) leaves
12–15 mint leaves, coarsely torn
4 fresh red chillies, seeded and
   cut into slivers
juice of 1–2 limes
30ml/2 tbsp Thai fish sauce
fresh coriander (cilantro) sprigs,
   to garnish

1 Pour the fish stock into a medium pan and bring to the boil. Cook each type of seafood separately in the stock for 3–4 minutes. Remove with a slotted spoon and set aside to cool.

2 Drain the noodles. Using scissors, cut them into short lengths, about 5cm/2in long. Place them in a serving bowl and add the cucumber, lemon grass, kaffir lime leaves, shallots, spring onions, coriander, mint and chillies.

3 Pour the lime juice and fish sauce over the noodle salad. Mix well, then add the seafood. Toss lightly. Garnish with the fresh coriander sprigs and serve immediately.

Chicken and Broccoli Salad

Gorgonzola makes a tangy dressing that goes well with chicken and the classic spring vegetable: broccoli. Serve for a lunch or supper dish with ciabatta.

Serves 4

175g/6oz broccoli florets, divided
   into small sprigs
225g/8oz/2 cups dried farfalle
   pasta or other shapes
2 large cooked skinless chicken
   breast fillets

For the dressing
90g/3½oz Gorgonzola cheese
15ml/1 tbsp white wine vinegar
60ml/4 tbsp extra virgin olive oil
2.5–5ml/½–1 tsp finely chopped
   fresh sage, plus extra sage
   sprigs to garnish
salt and ground black pepper

1 Cook the broccoli florets in a large pan of salted boiling water for 3 minutes. Remove with a slotted spoon and rinse under cold running water, then spread out on kitchen paper to drain and dry.

2 Add the pasta to the broccoli cooking water, then bring back to the boil and cook according to the packet instructions. When cooked, drain the pasta, rinse under cold running water until cold, then leave to drain and dry, shaking occasionally.

3 Remove the skin from the cooked chicken breasts and cut the meat into bitesize pieces.

4 To make the dressing, put the cheese in a large bowl and mash with a fork, then whisk in the wine vinegar followed by the oil and sage and salt and pepper to taste.

5 Add the pasta, chicken and broccoli to the dressing. Toss well, then adjust the seasoning and serve, garnished with sage.

> **Variation**
> *Try adding a sprinkling of roughly chopped toasted walnuts just before serving.*

Prawn Salad Energy 221kcal/920kJ; Protein 21.8g; Carbohydrate 3.8g, of which sugars 3.5g; Fat 13.2g, of which saturates 5.9g; Cholesterol 242mg; Calcium 141mg; Fibre 1.3g; Sodium 232mg.
Seafood Salad Energy 137kcal/578kJ; Protein 20g; Carbohydrate 10.2g, of which sugars 1.2g; Fat 1.8g, of which saturates 0.4g; Cholesterol 171mg; Calcium 61mg; Fibre 0.9g; Sodium 154mg.
Chicken Salad Energy 472kcal/1977kJ; Protein 25.3g; Carbohydrate 42.5g, of which sugars 2.5g; Fat 23.5g, of which saturates 6.8g; Cholesterol 52mg; Calcium 151mg; Fibre 2.8g; Sodium 310mg.

Asparagus, Bacon and Leaf Salad

As an accompaniment, this excellent spring salad turns a plain roast chicken or simple grilled fish into an interesting meal, or makes an appetizing first course or light lunch. Sweeten the French dressing with honey for the best flavour.

Serves 4
500g/1¼lb medium asparagus
130g/4½oz thin-cut smoked back (lean) bacon
250g/9oz mixed leaf salad or frisée lettuce leaves
100ml/3½fl oz/scant ½ cup French dressing
ground black pepper

1 Trim off any tough stalk ends from the asparagus and cut the spears into three, setting the tender tips aside. Heat a 1cm/½in depth of water in a frying pan until simmering.

2 Reserve the asparagus tips and cook the remainder of the spears in the water for about 3 minutes, until almost tender. Add the tips and cook for 1 minute more. Drain and refresh under cold, running water.

3 Place the bacon in a frying pan without adding any butter or oil. Heat it gently until the fat runs, then increase the heat and fry the bacon until it is golden and crisp.

4 Drain the cooked bacon on a sheet of kitchen paper and then set it aside to cool slightly. Use kitchen scissors to snip it into bitesize pieces.

5 Place the frisée or mixed leaf salad in a bowl and add the bacon. Add the asparagus and a little black pepper to the salad. Pour the dressing over and toss the salad lightly, then serve before the leaves begin to wilt.

> **Cook's Tip**
> A wide range of different salad leaves is readily available – frisée has feathery, curly, slightly bitter-tasting leaves and is a member of the chicory family. Frisée leaves range in colour from yellow-white to yellow-green and are very pretty.

Warm Salad of Bayonne Ham

With a lightly spiced nutty dressing, this warm salad is as delicious as it is fashionable, and makes an excellent choice for some seasonal entertaining.

4 eggs, hard-boiled and quartered
50g/2oz Bayonne ham, cut into strips
juice of ½ lemon
salt and ground black pepper

Serves 4
225g/8oz new potatoes, halved if large
50g/2oz French (green) beans
115g/4oz young spinach leaves
2 spring onions (scallions), sliced

For the dressing
60ml/4 tbsp olive oil
5ml/1 tsp ground turmeric
5ml/1 tsp ground cumin
50g/2oz/⅓ cup shelled hazelnuts

1 Cook the potatoes in a pan of boiling salted water for about 10–15 minutes, or until tender, then drain well.

2 Cook the green beans in a pan of boiling water for about 2–3 minutes, then drain well.

3 Place the drained potatoes and green beans with the spinach leaves and spring onions in a large bowl. Toss with your hands until the ingredients are well combined.

4 Arrange the hard-boiled egg quarters on the salad and sprinkle the strips of ham over the top. Sprinkle with the lemon juice and season with plenty of salt and pepper.

5 To make the dressing, heat all the ingredients in a large frying pan and continue to cook, stirring frequently, until the nuts have just turned golden. Pour the hot, nutty dressing over the salad. Serve immediately.

> **Variation**
> Replace the potatoes with a 400g/14oz can mixed beans and peas. Drain and rinse the beans and peas, then drain again. Toss lightly with the green beans and spring onions (scallions).

Asparagus Salad Energy 259kcal/1068kJ; Protein 9.5g; Carbohydrate 3.6g, of which sugars 3.5g; Fat 23g, of which saturates 4.6g; Cholesterol 17mg; Calcium 53mg; Fibre 2.7g; Sodium 519mg.
Warm Salad Energy 323kcal/1341kJ; Protein 12.4g; Carbohydrate 10.9g, of which sugars 2.2g; Fat 25.8g, of which saturates 4.2g; Cholesterol 199mg; Calcium 105mg; Fibre 2.3g; Sodium 270mg.

Warm Chorizo Salad with Baby Spinach

Spanish chorizo sausage contributes an intense spiciness to this hearty warm salad. Young spinach leaves have enough flavour to compete with the chorizo and add extra colour to this delectable spring salad.

Serves 4
225g/8oz baby spinach leaves
90ml/6 tbsp extra virgin olive oil
150g/5oz chorizo sausage,
  very thinly sliced
30ml/2 tbsp sherry vinegar
salt and ground black pepper

1 Discard any tough stalks from the spinach. Pour the oil into a large frying pan and add the chorizo sausage. Cook gently for 3 minutes, until the sausage slices start to shrivel slightly and begin to colour.

2 Add the spinach leaves to the chorizo, and then remove the pan from the heat. Toss the spinach in the warm oil until it just starts to wilt.

3 Add the sherry vinegar and a little salt and pepper to the pan and stir to combine. Toss the ingredients briefly, then transfer to a salad bowl and serve immediately, while the salad is still warm.

Cook's Tip
Chorizo can be bought cooked or raw. Use the cooked version for this dish. If using the raw sausage, ensure that it is cooked for longer during step 1 above.

Variation
Watercress or rocket (arugula) could be used instead of the spinach, if you prefer. For an added dimension use a flavoured olive oil – rosemary, garlic or chilli oil would work perfectly.

Marinated Chicken Salad with Spring Onions

Hot, spicy, garlicky and a little sweet, the chicken is perfectly tempered by the mild spring leaves in this attractive salad.

Serves 4
900g/2lb skinless chicken breast
  fillet or boneless thighs
2 round (butterhead) lettuces
vegetable oil
4 spring onions (scallions), shredded

For the marinade
60ml/4 tsp gochujang chilli paste
45ml/3 tbsp mirin or rice wine
15ml/1 tbsp dark soy sauce
4 garlic cloves, crushed
25ml/5 tsp sesame oil
15ml/1 tbsp grated fresh
  root ginger
2 spring onions (scallions),
  finely chopped
10ml/2 tsp ground black pepper
15ml/1 tbsp lemonade

1 Place all the ingredients for the marinade in a large mixing bowl. Mix well until combined.

2 Cut the chosen chicken into bitesize pieces, add to the bowl and stir to coat it with the marinade. Transfer to an airtight container and marinate in the refrigerator for about 3 hours.

3 Remove the outer leaves from the heads of lettuce, keeping them whole. Rinse well, drain, and place on a serving dish.

4 Lightly coat a heavy griddle pan or frying pan with vegetable oil and place it over medium heat (the griddle can also be used over charcoal if you are cooking the chicken pieces over a barbecue). Griddle or fry the chicken for 15 minutes, or until the meat is cooked and has turned a deep brown. Increase the heat briefly to scorch the chicken and give it a smoky flavour. Serve by wrapping the chicken pieces in lettuce leaves with a few shredded spring onions.

Cook's Tip
If you are unable to obtain gochujang chilli paste from your local Asian food store, substitute a regular chilli purée.

Warm Chorizo Salad Energy 300kcal/1238kJ; Protein 5.6g; Carbohydrate 4.5g, of which sugars 1.4g; Fat 29g, of which saturates 7g; Cholesterol 18mg; Calcium 111mg; Fibre 1.4g; Sodium 364mg.
Chicken Salad Energy 279kcal/1178kJ; Protein 55g; Carbohydrate 2g, of which sugars 2g; Fat 5.7g, of which saturates 1.1g; Cholesterol 158mg; Calcium 39mg; Fibre 0.9g; Sodium 405mg.

Spring Asparagus with Egg

With a unique, delicious flavour, asparagus heralds the arrival of spring and its short season is celebrated with a range of delicious dishes such as this simple appetizer.

Serves 4

16 white or green
    asparagus spears

115g/4oz/½ cup clarified butter
4 hard-boiled eggs, finely chopped
grated rind and juice of ½ lemon
salt and ground black or
    white pepper
a handful of fresh parsley,
    chopped, to garnish

1 Trim the asparagus spears or snap them so that the tender stalk separates from the tougher base. Soak the spears in a bowl of cold water, refreshing the water a couple of times; this makes the stalks more juicy and easier to peel.

2 Bring a pan of salted water to the boil. Peel the asparagus if necessary (see Cook's Tip), and add the spears to the pan. Blanch the spears for about 5 minutes (depending on the thickness of the stalks) or until they are just tender.

3 Drain the asparagus and pat dry with kitchen paper. Arrange on individual plates or on a serving platter and keep warm.

4 Heat the clarified butter in a frying pan for about 3 minutes, until pale brown. Add the chopped hard-boiled eggs, and season with salt and pepper.

5 Cook the mixture for 45 seconds, stirring constantly, then add the lemon juice. Pour the mixture over the warm asparagus, sprinkle with the lemon rind and freshly chopped parsley and serve immediately.

> **Cook's Tip**
> *Green asparagus seldom needs peeling but white asparagus has a tougher, woodier stem, so removing the tougher skin near the base improves the texture and lets the stalks cook evenly.*

Stir-fried Spring Greens

Garlic enhances the slightly bitter flavour of spring greens, and they taste great with bacon and chillies.

Serves 6

450g/1lb spring greens (collard)

15ml/1 tbsp vegetable oil
150g/5oz smoked streaky (fatty)
    bacon, in one piece
2 garlic cloves, crushed
1.5ml/¼ tsp crushed dried chillies
salt

1 Cut off the stalks from the greens. Lay the leaves flat on top of each other and roll into a cigar shape and slice very thinly. Heat the oil in a frying pan. Cut the bacon into small cubes and sauté gently in the oil for 5 minutes, or until golden brown. Lift out with a slotted spoon and drain on kitchen paper.

2 Increase the heat, add the crushed garlic and dried chillies to the oil remaining in the pan, and stir-fry for 30 seconds. Add the spring greens and toss until just tender. Season to taste with salt, stir in the bacon cubes and serve immediately.

Florets Polonaise

Spring vegetables become something very special with this pretty egg topping.

Serves 6

500g/1¼lb mixed vegetables,
    such as cauliflower, broccoli,
    romanesco and calabrese

50g/2oz/¼ cup butter
finely grated rind of ½ lemon
1 large garlic clove, crushed
25g/1oz/½ cup fresh
    breadcrumbs, lightly baked or
    grilled (broiled) until crisp
2 eggs, hard-boiled
sea salt and ground black pepper

1 Trim the vegetables and break into florets. Place in a steamer over a pan of boiling water for 5–7 minutes, until just tender. Toss in butter or oil and transfer to a serving dish.

2 Meanwhile, combine the lemon rind, garlic, seasoning and breadcrumbs. Finely chop the eggs and mix with the remaining ingredients. Sprinkle the mixture over the vegetables and serve.

Stir-fried Greens Energy 106kcal/438kJ; Protein 5g; Carbohydrate 3.8g, of which sugars 3.7g; Fat 7.9g, of which saturates 2.2g; Cholesterol 16mg; Calcium 38mg; Fibre 1.6g; Sodium 320mg.
Florets Polonaise Energy 71kcal/297kJ; Protein 5.2g; Carbohydrate 4.7g, of which sugars 1.4g; Fat 3.6g, of which saturates 0.7g; Cholesterol 32mg; Calcium 57mg; Fibre 2.3g; Sodium 50mg.
Spring Asparagus Energy 313kcal/1289kJ; Protein 9.3g; Carbohydrate 2.2g, of which sugars 2.1g; Fat 29.8g, of which saturates 16.6g; Cholesterol 252mg; Calcium 61mg; Fibre 1.7g; Sodium 245mg.

Asparagus with Lemon Sauce

A simple egg and lemon dressing brings out the best in asparagus. Serve the asparagus as an appetizer or side dish; alternatively, enjoy it for a light supper, with bread and butter to mop up the juices.

Serves 4

675g/1½lb asparagus, tough
  ends removed, and tied in
  a bundle
15ml/1 tbsp cornflour (cornstarch)
2 egg yolks
juice of 1½ lemons
salt

1 Cook the bundle of asparagus in a tall pan of lightly salted, boiling water for 7–10 minutes.

2 Drain the asparagus well and arrange the spears in a large serving dish. Reserve about 200ml/7fl oz/scant 1 cup of the cooking liquid.

3 Blend the cornflour with the cooled, reserved cooking liquid then place in a small pan. Bring to the boil, stirring constantly, and cook over a gentle heat until the sauce thickens slightly. Remove the pan from the heat and leave to cool slightly.

4 Beat the egg yolks thoroughly with the lemon juice and gradually stir into the cooled sauce. Cook over very low heat, stirring constantly, until the sauce is fairly thick. Be careful not to overheat the sauce or it may curdle. As soon as the sauce has thickened, remove the pan from the heat and continue stirring for 1 minute. Taste and season with salt. Set aside the sauce to cool slightly.

5 Stir the cooled lemon sauce, then pour a little over the cooked asparagus. Cover the vegetables and chill in the refrigerator for at least 2 hours before serving with the rest of the sauce to accompany.

Cook's Tip
For a slightly less tangy sauce, add a little caster (superfine) sugar with the salt in step 4.

Risotto with Asparagus

Fresh farm asparagus only has a short spring season, so make the most of it in this tasty risotto.

Serves 3–4
225g/8oz fresh asparagus
750ml/1¼ pints/3 cups vegetable
  or chicken stock
65g/2½oz/5 tbsp butter
1 small onion, finely chopped
275g/10oz/1½ cups risotto rice,
  such as Arborio or Carnaroli
75g/3oz/1 cup freshly grated
  Parmesan cheese
salt and ground black pepper

1 Bring a pan of water to the boil. Cut off any woody pieces on the ends of the asparagus stalks, peel the lower portions, then cook in the water for 5 minutes. Drain the asparagus, reserving the cooking water, refresh under cold water and drain again. Cut the asparagus diagonally into 4cm/1½in pieces. Keep the tip and next-highest sections separate from the stalks.

2 Place the stock in a pan and add 450ml/¾ pint/scant 2 cups of the asparagus cooking water. Heat to simmering point, and keep it hot.

3 Melt two-thirds of the butter in a large, heavy pan or deep frying pan. Add the onion and fry until it is soft and golden.

4 Stir in all the asparagus except the top two sections. Cook for 2–3 minutes. Add the rice and cook for 1–2 minutes, mixing well to coat it with butter. Stir in a ladleful of the hot liquid. Using a wooden spoon, stir until the stock has been absorbed.

5 Gradually add the remaining stock, a little at a time, allowing the rice to absorb the liquid before adding more, and stirring all the time.

6 After 10 minutes, add the remaining asparagus sections. Continue to cook as before, for about 15 minutes, until the rice is al dente and the risotto is creamy.

7 Off the heat, stir in the remaining butter and the Parmesan. Grind in a little pepper, and taste for salt. Serve immediately.

Asparagus with Lemon Energy 96kcal/399kJ; Protein 6.4g; Carbohydrate 9.4g, of which sugars 5.8g; Fat 3.8g, of which saturates 1g; Cholesterol 101mg; Calcium 59mg; Fibre 2.9g; Sodium 8mg.
Asparagus Risotto Energy 629kcal/2616kJ; Protein 20.1g; Carbohydrate 71.9g, of which sugars 2.7g; Fat 27.9g, of which saturates 16.5g; Cholesterol 71mg; Calcium 344mg; Fibre 1.6g; Sodium 408mg.

Scrambled Eggs with Asparagus

Delightfully tender fresh asparagus and sweet peas burst with the taste of spring and make perfect partners to eggs. The secret of scrambling is to keep the heat under the pan low and serve the eggs while they are still creamy.

Serves 4
1 bunch thin asparagus
30–45ml/2–3 tbsp tiny raw
*   mangetouts (snow peas)*
8 large (US extra large) eggs
30ml/2 tbsp milk
50g/2oz/¼ cup butter
salt and ground black pepper
sweet paprika, for dusting

1 Prepare the asparagus. Using a large sharp knife, cut off and discard any hard stems. Cut the stems into short lengths, keeping the tips separate. Shell some of the fatter mangetout pods, to extract the tiny peas.

2 Place the stems into a pan of boiling water and simmer for about 4 minutes. Add the asparagus tips, and cook for another 4–6 minutes. If including some pea pod strips, cook them for about 2 minutes.

3 Break the eggs into a bowl. Add the milk, salt and black pepper and beat with a whisk until well combined.

4 Melt the butter in a large frying pan and pour in the eggs, scrambling them by pulling the cooked outsides to the middle with a wooden spoon.

5 When the eggs are almost cooked, drain the asparagus and pea pod strips, if using, and stir them gently into the eggs. Sprinkle the peas over the top, and dust lightly with a little paprika. Serve immediately.

Variation
You can replace the asparagus with mangetouts (snow peas) if you are unable to find any. String 150g/5oz mangetouts, then slice them diagonally into two or three pieces. Cook in boiling water for 2 minutes.

Cheese and Asparagus Flan

The asparagus season in spring is short, so you need to make the most of it with this delicious flan.

Serves 5–6
175g/6oz/1½ cups plain
*   (all-purpose) flour*
40g/1½oz/3 tbsp lard or white
*   cooking fat, diced*

40g/1½oz/3 tbsp butter, diced
300g/11oz asparagus spears
75g/3oz mature (sharp) Cheddar
*   cheese, grated*
3 spring onions (scallions), sliced
2 eggs
300ml/½ pint/1¼ cups double
*   (heavy) cream*
freshly grated nutmeg
salt and ground black pepper

1 To make the pastry, sift the flour and a pinch of salt into a bowl and add the lard and butter. With your fingertips, rub the fats into the flour until the mixture resembles fine breadcrumbs. Stir in 45ml/3 tbsp cold water until the mixture can be gathered together into a ball. Wrap and chill for 30 minutes.

2 Put a flat baking sheet in the oven and preheat to 200°C/400°F/Gas 6. Roll out the pastry on a lightly floured work surface and use it to line a 20cm/8in flan tin (pan).

3 Line the pastry case (pie shell) with baking parchment and add a layer of baking beans. Put the tin on to the baking sheet in the oven and cook for 10–15 minutes until set. Remove the beans and parchment, return the pastry to the oven and cook for a further 5 minutes, until light golden brown. Remove the flan and reduce the temperature to 180°C/350°F/Gas 4.

4 Meanwhile, cook the asparagus in lightly salted boiling water for 2–3 minutes until only just tender. Drain, rinse and pat dry. Cut the spears into 2.5cm/1in lengths, leaving the tips whole.

5 Sprinkle half the cheese in the base of the cooked pastry case and add the asparagus and the spring onions. Beat the eggs with the cream and season with salt, pepper and nutmeg. Pour over the asparagus and top with the remaining cheese.

6 Return the flan to the oven and cook for 30 minutes or until just set. Leave for 5 minutes before cutting and serving.

Scrambled Eggs Energy 252kcal/1045kJ; Protein 13.8g; Carbohydrate 1.3g, of which sugars 1.2g; Fat 21.7g, of which saturates 9.7g; Cholesterol 408mg; Calcium 78mg; Fibre 0.6g; Sodium 219mg.
Cheese Flan Energy 547kcal/2266kJ; Protein 10.4g; Carbohydrate 24.7g, of which sugars 2.4g; Fat 45.6g, of which saturates 26.2g; Cholesterol 165mg; Calcium 184mg; Fibre 1.8g; Sodium 167mg.

Garganelli with Spring Vegetables

Fresh, brightly coloured spring vegetables both look and taste good when served with pasta.

Serves 4

1 bunch asparagus, about 350g/12oz
4 young carrots
1 bunch spring onions (scallions)
130g/4½oz shelled fresh peas
350g/12oz/3 cups dried garganelli
60ml/4 tbsp dry white wine
90ml/6 tbsp extra virgin olive oil
a few sprigs fresh flat leaf parsley, mint and basil, leaves stripped and chopped
sea salt and ground black pepper
freshly grated Parmesan cheese or premium Italian-style vegetarian cheese, to serve

1 Trim off and discard the woody part of each asparagus stem, then cut off the tips on the diagonal. Cut the stems on the diagonal into 4cm/1½in pieces. Cut the carrots and spring onions on the diagonal into similar-sized pieces.

2 Bring a large pan of lightly salted water to the boil. Add the carrots, peas, asparagus stems and tips. Bring the water back to the boil, then reduce the heat and simmer the vegetables for about 6–8 minutes, until tender. The asparagus tips will cook quickly, so remove them from the pan with a slotted spoon as soon as they are ready.

3 Meanwhile, cook the pasta in salted boiling water for 10–12 minutes, or according to the instructions on the packet, until the garganelli are just tender.

4 Drain the asparagus, carrots and peas and return them to the pan. Add the white wine, olive oil and sea salt and black pepper to taste, then gently toss over medium to high heat until the white wine has reduced and the vegetables glisten with the olive oil.

5 Drain the garganelli and transfer it into a warmed large bowl. Add the vegetables, spring onions and fresh herbs and toss well.

6 Divide the pasta among four warmed individual plates and serve immediately, with freshly grated cheese.

Peas and Carrots with Bacon

Springtime lets you indulge in one of the season's treats: fresh peas. Sweet and tender, they are delicious eaten raw, or can be accompanied by young carrots, pearl onions, garden lettuce and salty bacon or cured ham. This dish is especially good served with roast pork or beef for a traditional Sunday meal.

Serves 4–6

8 young carrots, thinly sliced
1.6kg/3½lb fresh peas in pods or 575g/1¼lb/5 cups frozen peas
40g/1½oz/3 tbsp butter
115g/4oz rindless smoked bacon, cut into fine strips
100g/3¾oz/⅔ cup baby or small pearl onions, peeled and left whole
100ml/3½fl oz/scant ½ cup chicken stock
1 small lettuce, cut in thin strips
pinch of sugar and grated nutmeg
salt and ground black pepper
chopped fresh parsley, to garnish, optional

1 Bring a pan of salted water to the boil. Add the carrots and cook for 3 minutes. Remove with a slotted spoon and set aside.

2 Pod the peas and add them to the pan of boiling water. Cook for 2 minutes, then drain and add the peas to a bowl of iced water to stop them from cooking any further. Drain and set aside.

3 Melt 25g/1oz/2 tbsp of the butter in a large frying pan. Add the bacon and sauté for 3 minutes, then add the onions and sauté for 4 minutes. When the onions are translucent, add the carrots and sauté for 3 minutes until they are glazed.

4 Pour in the stock, cover and cook for 10–15 minutes, or until all the liquid has been absorbed. Add the lettuce and cook for 3–5 minutes until the strips have wilted.

5 Add the peas, with the remaining butter. Simmer for 2–3 minutes until the peas are just tender. Add the sugar and nutmeg, season and stir to mix. Spoon into a warmed bowl, garnish with parsley, if using, and serve.

Garganelli Energy 738kcal/3092kJ; Protein 29.5g; Carbohydrate 74g, of which sugars 5.2g; Fat 38.1g, of which saturates 10.4g; Cholesterol 38mg; Calcium 492mg; Fibre 4.3g; Sodium 416mg.
Peas and Carrots Energy 141kcal/585kJ; Protein 9.8g; Carbohydrate 15.5g, of which sugars 7.4g; Fat 4.9g, of which saturates 1.5g; Cholesterol 10mg; Calcium 49mg; Fibre 5.8g; Sodium 311mg.

Pea and Mint Omelette

Serve this deliciously light omelette with crusty bread and a green salad for a fresh lunch full of spring flavours. When they are not in season, use frozen shelled peas instead of fresh ones.

Serves 2
4 eggs
50g/2oz/¹/₂ cup fresh peas
30ml/2 tbsp chopped fresh mint
a knob (pat) of butter
salt and ground black pepper

1 Break the eggs into a large bowl and mix with a fork until just combined; do not beat. Season well with salt and pepper and set aside.

2 Bring a large pan of lightly salted water to the boil over high heat. Add the fresh peas and cook them for about 3–4 minutes until tender.

3 Drain well in a colander and add to the eggs in the bowl. Stir in the chopped fresh mint and swirl with a spoon until thoroughly combined.

4 Heat the butter in a medium frying pan until foamy. Pour in the egg mixture and cook over a medium heat for 3–4 minutes, drawing in the cooked egg from the edges from time to time, until the mixture is set underneath, but remains slightly moist on the surface of the omelette.

5 Finish off cooking the omelette under a hot grill (broiler) until set and golden. Carefully fold the omelette over, cut it in half and serve immediately.

> **Variation**
> *When young broad (fava) beans are in season, use them instead of peas. Shell the beans and cook them in boiling salted water for 3–4 minutes until just tender. Meanwhile, grill (broil) 3–4 rashers (strips) of bacon. Add the beans to the egg mixture instead of the peas and crumble the bacon over the omelette when it is almost cooked.*

Braised Lettuce and Peas

This light vegetable dish is based on the classic French method of braising peas with lettuce and spring onions in butter, and is delicious served with simply grilled fish or roast duck. A sprinkling of chopped fresh mint makes a fresh, flavoursome and pretty garnish, and gives the dish a lovely springtime taste.

Serves 4
50g/2oz/¹/₄ cup butter
4 Little Gem (Bibb) lettuces, halved lengthways
2 bunches spring onions (scallions), trimmed
400g/14oz shelled peas (about 1kg/2¹/₄lb in pods)
salt and ground black pepper

1 Melt half the butter in a wide, heavy pan over low heat. Add the lettuces and spring onions.

2 Turn the vegetables in the butter until they are well coated, then sprinkle in salt and plenty of ground black pepper. Cover the pan, and cook the vegetables very gently for 5 minutes, stirring once.

3 Add the peas to the pan and turn them in the buttery juices. Pour in 120ml/4fl oz/¹/₂ cup water, then cover and cook over low heat for a further 5 minutes.

4 Uncover the pan and increase the heat to reduce the liquid to a few tablespoons.

5 Stir in the remaining butter and adjust the seasoning. Transfer to a warmed serving dish and serve immediately.

> **Variations**
> • *If you like, you can braise about 250g/9oz baby carrots with the lettuce.*
> • *Cook 115g/4oz chopped smoked bacon or pancetta in the butter. Use one bunch of spring onions (scallions) and stir in some chopped parsley.*

Lettuce and Peas Energy 161kcal/670kJ; Protein 9.1g; Carbohydrate 15.9g, of which sugars 6.8g; Fat 7.4g, of which saturates 3.7g; Cholesterol 13mg; Calcium 73mg; Fibre 6.5g; Sodium 47mg.
Pea Omelette Energy 208kcal/865kJ; Protein 14.6g; Carbohydrate 3.3g, of which sugars 0.6g; Fat 15.7g, of which saturates 5.8g; Cholesterol 391mg; Calcium 79mg; Fibre 1.2g; Sodium 172mg.

Rice with Green Peas, Mint and Dill

This plain buttery pilaff is a a great one to serve with fried or grilled chicken and fish dishes. Dotted with fresh green peas, it is delicious served hot or at room temperature. It makes an attractive addition to a springtime buffet spread or an early barbecue.

Serves 4
15ml/1 tbsp olive oil
25g/1oz/2 tbsp butter
1 onion, finely chopped
350g/12oz/1¾ cups long
    grain rice, thoroughly rinsed
    and drained
750ml/1¼ pints/3 cups chicken
    stock or water
200g/7oz/1¾ cups fresh or
    frozen peas
1 small bunch dill,
    finely chopped
1 small bunch mint, leaves
    finely chopped
salt and ground black pepper

1 Heat the oil and butter in a heavy pan and stir in the chopped onion. Cook, stirring frequently, for about 5–6 minutes until softened.

2 Add the rice to the pan. Stir well to coat it in the butter and onion. Pour in the chicken stock or water.

3 Season with salt and black pepper and bring the stock to the boil. Reduce the heat and simmer for 10 minutes, or until almost all the liquid has been absorbed.

4 Toss the peas into the rice with half the fresh herbs. Cover the pan with a clean dish towel and a lid and leave the rice to steam with the peas for a further 10 minutes.

5 Transfer the cooked rice mixture to a serving dish, garnish with the remaining fresh herbs, and serve the pilaff hot or at room temperature.

> **Variation**
> To make a more substantial rice dish, you can add diced carrot and diced artichoke bottoms with the peas in step 4.

Aubergine and Spinach Pie

Aubergines layered with spinach, feta cheese and rice make a flavoursome and dramatic filling for a spring pie. It can be served warm or cold in elegant slices.

Serves 12
375g/13oz shortcrust pastry,
    thawed if frozen
45–60ml/3–4 tbsp olive oil
1 large aubergine (eggplant),
    sliced into rounds
1 onion, chopped
1 garlic clove, crushed
175g/6oz spinach, washed
4 eggs
75g/3oz/½ cup crumbled
    feta cheese
40g/1½oz/½ cup freshly grated
    Parmesan cheese
60ml/4 tbsp natural (plain) yogurt
90ml/6 tbsp creamy milk
225g/8oz/2 cups cooked white or
    brown long grain rice
salt and ground black pepper

1 Preheat the oven to 180°C/350°F/Gas 4. Roll out the pastry thinly and use to line a 25cm/10in flan tin (pan). Prick the base all over and bake in the oven for 10–12 minutes until the pastry is pale golden.

2 Heat 30–45ml/2–3 tbsp of the oil in a frying pan and fry the aubergine slices for 6–8 minutes on each side until golden. Lift out and drain well on kitchen paper.

3 Add the onion and garlic to the oil remaining in the pan, then fry over a gentle heat for 4–5 minutes until soft, adding a little extra oil if necessary.

4 Chop the spinach finely, by hand or in a food processor. Beat the eggs in a large mixing bowl, then add the spinach, feta, Parmesan, yogurt, milk and the onion mixture. Season well with salt and ground black pepper and stir thoroughly to mix.

5 Spread the rice in an even layer over the base of the part-baked pastry case (pie shell). Reserve a few aubergine slices for the top, and arrange the rest in an even layer over the rice.

6 Spoon the spinach and feta mixture over the aubergines and place the remaining slices on top. Bake for 30–40 minutes until lightly browned. Serve the pie while warm, or leave it to cool.

Rice with Green Peas Energy 437kcal/1819kJ; Protein 10.5g; Carbohydrate 77g, of which sugars 2.3g; Fat 9.3g, of which saturates 3.8g; Cholesterol 13mg; Calcium 57mg; Fibre 3.2g; Sodium 43mg.
Aubergine Pie Energy 257kcal/1075kJ; Protein 6.5g; Carbohydrate 23.8g, of which sugars 2.1g; Fat 15.8g, of which saturates 4.7g; Cholesterol 73mg; Calcium 99mg; Fibre 1.5g; Sodium 267mg.

Steamed Lettuce-wrapped Sole

Dover sole fillets are in season in spring, and are excellent cooked this way. Lemon sole, trout, plaice, flounder and brill can also be used in this recipe.

Serves 4
2 large sole fillets, skinned
15ml/1 tbsp sesame seeds
15ml/1 tbsp sunflower or
 groundnut (peanut) oil
10ml/2 tsp sesame oil
2.5cm/1in piece fresh root ginger,
 peeled and grated
3 garlic cloves, finely chopped
15ml/1 tbsp soy sauce or Thai
 fish sauce
juice of 1 lemon
2 spring onions (scallions),
 thinly sliced
8 large soft lettuce leaves
12 large fresh mussels, scrubbed
 and bearded

1 Cut the sole fillets in half lengthways. Season; set aside. Prepare a steamer.

2 Heat a heavy frying pan until hot. Toast the sesame seeds lightly but do not allow them to burn. Set aside in a bowl until required.

3 Heat the oils in the frying pan over medium heat. Add the ginger and garlic and cook until lightly coloured; stir in the soy sauce or fish sauce, lemon juice and spring onions. Remove from the heat; stir in the toasted sesame seeds.

4 Lay the pieces of fish on baking parchment, skinned-side up; spread each evenly with the ginger mixture. Roll up each piece, starting at the tail end. Place on a baking sheet.

5 Plunge the lettuce leaves into the boiling water you have prepared for the steamer and immediately lift them out with tongs or a slotted spoon. Lay them out flat on kitchen paper and gently pat them dry. Wrap each sole parcel in two lettuce leaves, making sure that the filling is well covered to keep it in place.

6 Arrange the fish parcels in a steamer basket, cover and steam over simmering water for 8 minutes. Add the mussels and steam for 2–4 minutes, until opened. Discard any that remain closed. Put the parcels on individual warmed plates, halve and garnish with mussels. Serve immediately.

Seafood and Spring Onion Skewers

Serve these tasty skewers with the tartare sauce dip.

Serves 4
675g/1½lb monkfish tail, filleted,
 skinned and membrane removed
1 bunch thick spring
 onions (scallions)
75ml/5 tbsp olive oil
1 garlic clove, finely chopped
15ml/1 tbsp lemon juice
5ml/1 tsp dried oregano
30ml/2 tbsp chopped fresh flat
 leaf parsley
12–18 small scallops or large
 raw prawns (shrimp)
75g/3oz/1½ cups fine fresh
 breadcrumbs
salt and ground black pepper

For the tartare sauce
2 egg yolks
300ml/½ pint/1¼ cups olive oil,
 or vegetable and olive oil mixed
15–30ml/1–2 tbsp lemon juice
5ml/1 tsp French mustard
15ml/1 tbsp chopped gherkin
15ml/1 tbsp chopped capers
30ml/2 tbsp chopped fresh flat
 leaf parsley
30ml/2 tbsp chopped fresh chives
5ml/1 tsp chopped fresh tarragon

1 First make the tartare sauce. Whisk the egg yolks and a pinch of salt. Whisk in the oil, a drop at a time at first. When about half the oil is incorporated, add it in a thin stream, whisking all the time. Stop when the mayonnaise is very thick.

2 Whisk in 15ml/1 tbsp lemon juice, then a little more oil. Stir in all the mustard, gherkin, capers, parsley, chives and tarragon. Add lemon juice and seasoning to taste.

3 Cut the monkfish into 18 pieces and cut the spring onions into 18 pieces about 5–6cm/2–2½in long. Mix the oil, garlic, lemon juice, oregano and half the parsley with seasoning. Add the seafood and spring onions, then marinate for 15 minutes.

4 Mix the breadcrumbs and remaining parsley together. Toss the seafood and spring onions in the mixture to coat. Soak nine bamboo skewers in cold water.

5 Preheat the grill (broiler). Thread the seafood and spring onions on to the skewers. Drizzle with the marinade, then cook for 5–6 minutes in total, turning once and drizzling with more marinade. Serve immediately with the tartare sauce.

Steamed Sole Energy 118kcal/492kJ; Protein 15.3g; Carbohydrate 0.9g, of which sugars 0.9g; Fat 5.9g, of which saturates 0.7g; Cholesterol 41mg; Calcium 46mg; Fibre 0.3g; Sodium 359mg.
Seafood Skewers Energy 385kcal/1598kJ; Protein 20.3g; Carbohydrate 7.8g, of which sugars 0.7g; Fat 30.5g, of which saturates 4g; Cholesterol 67mg; Calcium 43mg; Fibre 0.6g; Sodium 139mg.

Spring Crab Cakes

Unlike fishcakes, crab cakes are bound with egg and mayonnaise or tartare sauce instead of potatoes, which makes them light in texture. Spring onions add a delicious seasonal touch. If you like, they can be grilled instead of fried; brush with a little oil first.

Serves 4
450g/1lb mixed brown and white
   crab meat
30ml/2 tbsp mayonnaise or
   tartare sauce
2.5–5ml/½–1 tsp mustard powder
1 egg, lightly beaten
Tabasco sauce
45ml/3 tbsp chopped fresh parsley
4 spring onions (scallions), finely
   chopped (optional)
50–75g/2–3oz/½–¾ cup dried
   breadcrumbs, preferably
   home-made
sunflower oil, for frying
salt, ground black pepper and
   cayenne pepper
chopped spring onions (scallions),
   to garnish
red onion marmalade, to serve

1 Put the crab meat in a bowl and stir in the mayonnaise or tartare sauce, with the mustard and egg. Season with Tabasco, salt, pepper and cayenne.

2 Stir the parsley, spring onions, if using, and 50g/2oz/½ cup of the breadcrumbs into the crab meat. The mixture should be just firm enough to hold together; depending on how much brown crab meat there is, you may need to add some more breadcrumbs to get the right consistency.

3 Divide the mixture into eight portions, roll each into a ball with slightly dampened hands and then flatten each one slightly to make a thick flat disc.

4 Spread out the crab cakes on a platter and place them in the refrigerator to chill for about 30 minutes before frying.

5 Pour the sunflower oil into a shallow pan to a depth of about 5mm/¼in. Fry the crab cakes in two batches until golden brown on both sides. Drain well on kitchen paper and keep hot while you finish cooking the cakes. Serve with a spring onion garnish and red onion marmalade.

Hot Crab Soufflés

These delicious little soufflés must be served as soon as they are ready, so seat your guests at the table before taking the soufflés out of the oven.

Serves 6
50g/2oz/¼ cup butter
45ml/3 tbsp fine wholemeal
   (whole-wheat) breadcrumbs
4 spring onions (scallions),
   finely chopped
15ml/1 tbsp Malaysian or mild
   Madras curry powder
25g/1oz/2 tbsp plain
   (all-purpose) flour
105ml/7 tbsp coconut milk or milk
150ml/¼ pint/⅔ cup
   whipping cream
4 egg yolks
225g/8oz white crab meat
mild green Tabasco sauce
6 egg whites
salt and ground black pepper

1 Use some of the butter to grease six ramekins or a 1.75 litre/3 pint/7½ cup soufflé dish. Sprinkle in the fine wholemeal breadcrumbs, roll the dishes or dish around to coat the base and sides completely, then tip out the excess breadcrumbs. Preheat the oven to 200°C/400°F/Gas 6.

2 Melt the remaining butter in a pan, add the spring onions and Malaysian or mild Madras curry powder and cook over low heat for about 1 minute, until softened. Stir in the flour and cook for 1 minute more.

3 Gradually add the coconut milk or milk and cream, stirring constantly. Cook until smooth and thick. Remove the pan from the heat, stir in the egg yolks, then the crab. Season with salt, black pepper and Tabasco sauce.

4 In a grease-free bowl, beat the egg whites stiffly with a pinch of salt. Using a metal spoon, stir one-third into the crab mixture to slacken it; then gently fold in the rest. Spoon into the dishes or dish.

5 Bake the soufflé in the preheated oven until well risen and golden brown, and just firm to the touch. Individual soufflés will be ready in about 8 minutes; a large soufflé will take about 15–20 minutes. Serve immediately.

Crab Cakes Energy 285kcal/1187kJ; Protein 23.9g; Carbohydrate 10.3g, of which sugars 0.9g; Fat 16.7g, of which saturates 2.4g; Cholesterol 134mg; Calcium 178mg; Fibre 0.8g; Sodium 768mg.
Hot Crab Soufflés Energy 270kcal/1122kJ; Protein 14g; Carbohydrate 11.6g, of which sugars 2.2g; Fat 18.9g, of which saturates 12.1g; Cholesterol 181mg; Calcium 123mg; Fibre 1g; Sodium 426mg.

Soft-shell Crabs with Chilli and Salt

If fresh soft-shell crabs are unavailable, you can buy frozen ones in Asian supermarkets. Allow two small crabs per serving, or one if they are large.

Serves 4
8 small soft-shell crabs, thawed
   if frozen
50g/2oz/½ cup plain
   (all-purpose) flour
60ml/4 tbsp groundnut (peanut)
   or vegetable oil

2 large fresh red chillies, or 1 green
   and 1 red chilli, seeded and
   thinly sliced
4 spring onions (scallions) or
   a small bunch of garlic
   chives, chopped
sea salt and ground black pepper

To serve
shredded lettuce, mooli (daikon)
   and carrot
light soy sauce, for dipping

1 Pat the crabs dry all over with kitchen paper. Season the flour with a little black pepper and coat the crabs lightly with the mixture.

2 Heat the oil in a shallow pan until very hot, then put in the crabs (you may need to do this in two batches). Fry for 2–3 minutes on each side, until the crabs are golden brown but still juicy in the middle. Drain the cooked crabs well on kitchen paper and keep hot.

3 Add the sliced chillies and spring onions or garlic chives to the oil remaining in the pan and cook gently, stirring frequently, for about 2 minutes until just softened. Sprinkle over a generous pinch of salt, then spread the chilli and onion mixture on to the crabs.

4 Mix the shredded lettuce, mooli and carrot together. Arrange on plates, top each portion with two crabs and serve, with a bowl of light soy sauce for dipping.

> **Cook's Tip**
> If you can't locate any mooli (daikon), use celeriac instead.

Stuffed Spider Crab

Stuffed spider crab is the perfect dish to accompany a chilled beer on a sunny spring afternoon.

Serves 2–3
1 bay leaf
6 black peppercorns
1 onion
4 fresh parsley sprigs
500ml/17fl oz/generous 2 cups
   white wine

1 live spider crab, weighing about
   1kg/2¼lb
1 egg yolk
175ml/6fl oz/¾ cup olive oil
15ml/1 tbsp pickles, drained
   and chopped
5ml/1 tsp Worcester sauce
few drops of Tabasco sauce
5ml/1 tsp brandy
1 hard-boiled egg, chopped
sea salt

1 Fill a large pan with water, measuring the quantity as you pour it in. Add the bay leaf, peppercorns, onion, parsley, white wine and 15ml/1 tbsp sea salt for every 1 litre/1¾ pints/4 cups water. Bring to the boil, add the crab, cover tightly and cook about 40 minutes. (Allow 20 minutes per 500g/1¼lb crab.)

2 Remove the crab and leave until cool enough to handle. Break off the claws and legs. Turn the crab upside down and break off the tail flap. Insert a sturdy knife between the body and the back shell and twist it. Using your thumbs, press the body away from the shell. Remove and discard the gills.

3 Scoop out the brown meat into a bowl. Halve the body and scoop out the white meat into another bowl. Crack the claws with the back of a knife and pick out the meat. Place the back shell on a board and press down behind the eyes. When it snaps, remove and discard it, including the stomach. Add the brown meat to the first bowl. Clean the back shell and reserve.

4 Blend the egg yolk into the brown meat. Gradually add the oil, whisking constantly. When half of it has been incorporated, add it in a steady trickle, whisking until it resembles mayonnaise.

5 Add the white meat and pickles and stir in the Worcestershire sauce, Tabasco and brandy. Pile into the reserved shell and sprinkle with the egg. Serve with the legs to break at the table.

Soft-shell Crabs Energy 306kcal/1280kJ; Protein 37.6g; Carbohydrate 10g, of which sugars 0.5g; Fat 13g, of which saturates 1.5g; Cholesterol 144mg; Calcium 262mg; Fibre 0.5g; Sodium 1101mg.
Stuffed Spider Crab Energy 507kcal/2093kJ; Protein 16.4g; Carbohydrate 0.3g, of which sugars 0.2g; Fat 48.6g, of which saturates 7.3g; Cholesterol 167mg; Calcium 40mg; Fibre 0g; Sodium 290mg.

Crab Bake

Crabs are popular on coastal bar menus, especially fresh crab open sandwiches. Dry gin brings an extra dimension to this delicious dish. Serve hot with rice, or fresh crusty bread, and a leafy spring salad.

Serves 4 as an appetizer
225g/8oz cooked white crab meat
juice of ½ lemon
15ml/1 tbsp chopped fresh herbs, such as parsley, chives and fennel
20ml/4 tsp dry gin
5ml/1 tsp smooth Dijon mustard
5ml/1 tsp wholegrain Dijon mustard
60ml/4 tbsp grated hard cheese
ground black pepper

For the béchamel sauce
1 small onion
3 cloves
300ml/½ pint/1¼ cups milk
½ bay leaf
25g/1oz/2 tbsp butter
25g/1oz/¼ cup plain (all-purpose) flour

1 First make an infusion for the béchamel sauce: stud the onion with the cloves, and then put it into a small pan with the milk and bay leaf. Bring slowly to the boil, then allow to infuse (steep) for 15 minutes, and strain.

2 Preheat the oven to 180°C/350°F/Gas 4 and butter four gratin dishes. Toss the crab meat in the lemon juice. Divide it among the dishes and add a pinch of herbs to each. Sprinkle each dish with 5ml/1 tsp gin and pepper.

3 Melt the butter for the sauce in a pan, stir in the flour and cook over low heat for 1–2 minutes. Gradually add the infused milk, stirring to make a smooth sauce. Simmer for 1–2 minutes.

4 Blend the béchamel sauce with the two mustards and use to cover the crab. Sprinkle the cheese on top, and bake for about 20–25 minutes, or until hot and bubbling. Serve immediately.

Cook's Tip
The recipe can also be divided between two larger dishes to serve two as a main course.

Stir-fried Noodles in Shellfish Sauce

Classic spring vegetables such as asparagus and spring onions are given a delicious Chinese twist here. The seasonal flavours marry perfectly with the egg noodles and seafood.

Serves 6–8 as an appetizer 4 as a main course
225g/8oz Chinese egg noodles
8 spring onions (scallions), trimmed
8 asparagus spears, plus extra steamed asparagus spears, to serve (optional)
30ml/2 tbsp stir-fry oil
5cm/2in piece fresh root ginger, peeled and cut into very fine batons
3 garlic cloves, chopped
60ml/4 tbsp oyster sauce
450g/1lb cooked crab meat (all white, or two-thirds white and one-third brown)
30ml/2 tbsp rice wine vinegar
15–30ml/1–2 tbsp light soy sauce

1 Put the noodles in a large pan or wok, cover with lightly salted boiling water, place a tight-fitting lid on top and leave for 3–4 minutes, or for the time suggested on the packet. Drain and set aside.

2 Cut off the green spring onion tops and slice them thinly. Set aside. Cut the white parts into 2cm/¾in lengths and quarter them lengthways. Cut the asparagus spears on the diagonal into 2cm/¾in pieces.

3 Heat the stir-fry oil in a pan or wok until very hot, then add the ginger, garlic and white spring onion batons. Stir-fry over high heat for 1 minute.

4 Add the oyster sauce, crab meat, rice wine vinegar and soy sauce to taste. Stir-fry for about 2 minutes, until the crab and sauce are hot.

5 Add the noodles to the pan or wok and toss for about 2–3 minutes until heated through. At the last moment, toss in the spring onion tops and serve with a few extra asparagus spears, if you like.

Crab Bake Energy 224kcal/936kJ; Protein 17.4g; Carbohydrate 9.6g, of which sugars 4.5g; Fat 11.9g, of which saturates 7.4g; Cholesterol 73mg; Calcium 282mg; Fibre 0.4g; Sodium 489mg.
Noodles Energy 385kcal/1622kJ; Protein 28.5g; Carbohydrate 45.9g, of which sugars 6.4g; Fat 10.9g, of which saturates 2.2g; Cholesterol 98mg; Calcium 167mg; Fibre 2.4g; Sodium 1233mg.

White Fish Dumplings

Served on a bed of spring
vegetables, these fish
dumplings are delicious.

Serves 4
500g/1¼lb white fish fillets,
   diced, plus their bones
2 eggs, separated
5ml/1 tsp salt
2.5ml/½ tsp ground white pepper
a pinch of cayenne pepper
200ml/7fl oz/scant 1 cup double
   (heavy) cream
25ml/1½ tbsp vegetable oil
1 onion, chopped
1 small celery stick, chopped
300ml/½ pint/1¼ cups white wine
50g/2oz/¼ cup butter
30ml/2 tbsp plain (all-purpose) flour
15ml/1 tbsp chopped fresh dill
salt and ground black pepper
cooked spring vegetables, to serve

1 Place the diced fish in the bowl of a food processor and
blend until finely chopped, slowly adding the egg whites, salt,
pepper and cayenne pepper. Transfer to a bowl and place in the
freezer for 20 minutes. Beat in 100ml/3½fl oz/scant ½ cup of
the cream, then set aside in the refrigerator.

2 Heat the oil in a pan, add the onion and celery and fry for
about 5 minutes, until softened. Add the fish bones and cook
for 10 minutes. Pour in half of the wine and enough water to
just cover the bones. Bring to the boil, then simmer for about
20 minutes. Strain the stock into a clean pan. You should have
about 400ml/14fl oz/1⅔ cups. Bring back to the boil.

3 Shape the fish mixture into balls and add to the hot stock in
batches. Cook for 5 minutes, turning them during cooking.
When ready, remove with a slotted spoon and keep warm.

4 Melt the butter in a pan, stir in the flour to make a roux,
then stir in a ladleful of the stock. Bring to the boil, stirring, until
the sauce boils and thickens.

5 Stir the remaining wine and the remaining cream into the
sauce, return to the boil, then remove from the heat. Whisk in
the egg yolks and dill, then taste and add salt and pepper
according to taste. Pour the sauce over the dumplings and
serve hot, on a bed of cooked early summer vegetables.

Salmon Fishcakes

The secret of a good
fishcake is to make it with
freshly prepared fish and
potatoes, home-made
breadcrumbs and plenty of
fresh herbs, such as dill and
parsley or tarragon.

Serves 4
450g/1lb cooked salmon fillet
450g/1lb freshly cooked
   potatoes, mashed
25g/1oz/2 tbsp butter, melted or
   30ml/2 tbsp olive oil
10ml/2 tsp wholegrain mustard
15ml/1 tbsp each chopped fresh
   dill and chopped fresh parsley
   or tarragon
grated rind and juice of ½ lemon
15g/½oz/2 tbsp wholemeal
   (whole-wheat) flour
1 egg, lightly beaten
150g/5oz/2 cups dried
   breadcrumbs
60ml/4 tbsp sunflower oil
sea salt and ground black pepper
rocket (arugula) leaves and
   chives, to garnish
lemon wedges, to serve

1 Flake the cooked salmon, discarding any skin and bones.
Put it in a bowl with the mashed potato, melted butter or oil
and wholegrain mustard, and mix well.

2 Stir the herbs and the lemon rind and juice into the fish and
potato mixture. Season to taste with plenty of sea salt and
ground black pepper.

3 Divide the mixture into eight portions and shape each into a
ball, then flatten into a thick disc. Dip the fishcakes first in flour,
then in egg and finally in breadcrumbs, making sure that they
are evenly coated with crumbs.

4 Heat the oil in a frying pan until it is very hot. Fry the
fishcakes in batches until golden brown and crisp all over. As
each batch is ready, drain on kitchen paper and keep hot.
Garnish with rocket and chives and serve with lemon wedges.

> **Cook's Tip**
> *Any fresh white or hot-smoked fish is suitable. Always buy
> organically farmed fish, or sustainably caught wild fish.*

Fish Dumplings Energy 600kcal/2484kJ; Protein 27.7g; Carbohydrate 6.5g, of which sugars 2.4g; Fat 46.4g, of which saturates 24.8g; Cholesterol 248mg; Calcium 73mg; Fibre 0.5g; Sodium 205mg.
Fishcakes Energy 586kcal/2453kJ; Protein 29.8g; Carbohydrate 49.9g, of which sugars 3.2g; Fat 31g, of which saturates 7.2g; Cholesterol 117mg; Calcium 79mg; Fibre 1.3g; Sodium 266mg.

Salted Salmon with Potatoes in Dill Sauce

Salted salmon is a refreshing alternative to the more commonly known gravlax recipe. This dish is delicious with potatoes and dill.

Serves 6–8
200g/7oz/2 cups sea salt
50g/2oz/¹⁄₂ cup caster
   (superfine) sugar
1kg/2¹⁄₄lb salmon, scaled, filleted
   and boned
1 litre/1³⁄₄ pints/4 cups water
675–900g/1¹⁄₂–2lb new potatoes

For the béchamel and dill sauce
25g/1oz/2 tbsp butter
45ml/3 tbsp plain
   (all-purpose) flour
750ml/1¹⁄₄ pints/3 cups milk
120ml/4fl oz/¹⁄₂ cup double
   (heavy) cream
freshly grated nutmeg (optional)
25g/1oz/¹⁄₄ cup chopped fresh dill
salt and ground black pepper

1 Mix together 100g/4oz/1 cup of the salt and the sugar. Cover the fish fillets with the mixture and put in a plastic bag. Seal the bag and put the fish on a plate in the refrigerator overnight.

2 The next day, make a brine by mixing the remaining salt and the water in a bowl. Place the salmon in the brine and leave in the refrigerator for another night.

3 Remove the salmon from the brine and cut into 5mm/¹⁄₄in slices. If large, cut the potatoes in half then cook in boiling water for about 20 minutes until tender.

4 Meanwhile, make the béchamel sauce. Melt the butter in a pan, add the flour and cook over low heat for 1 minute, stirring to make a roux. Remove from the heat and slowly add the milk, stirring all the time, to form a smooth sauce. Return to the heat and cook, stirring, for 2–3 minutes until the sauce boils and thickens. Stir in the cream, nutmeg if using, salt and pepper to taste and heat gently.

5 Drain the potatoes and add to the sauce with the dill. Serve the salted salmon with the potatoes in béchamel and dill.

Salmon Rolls with Asparagus and Butter Sauce

The green spears of asparagus appear each year as a welcome sign of spring. The green contrasts beautifully with the pink salmon in this recipe.

Serves 4
4 thick or 8 thin asparagus spears
4 very thin slices salmon fillet,
   each weighing about 115g/4oz
juice 1 lemon
1 bunch fresh parsley, chopped
salt and ground black pepper

For the butter sauce
1 shallot, finely chopped
6 peppercorns
120ml/4fl oz/¹⁄₂ cup dry white wine
60ml/4 tbsp double (heavy) cream
200g/7oz/scant 1 cup butter, cut
   into small cubes

1 Steam the asparagus spears for 6–8 minutes, according to their size, until tender. Refresh under cold running water, drain and set aside.

2 The slices of salmon should be wide enough to roll around the asparagus. Don't worry if they have to be patched together. Place the slices on a surface, season with salt and pepper, lay one or two asparagus spears across each slice and then roll the salmon around them. Place the rolls on a rack over a pan of boiling water, sprinkle with lemon juice, and cover and steam for 3–4 minutes until tender.

3 To make the butter sauce, put the shallot, peppercorns and wine in a small pan and heat gently until the wine has reduced to a tablespoonful. Strain and return to the pan. Add the cream, bring to the boil, and then lower the heat.

4 Add the butter to the sauce in small pieces, whisking all the time until well incorporated before adding another piece. Do not allow the sauce to boil or it will separate. Season the sauce to taste, if necessary.

5 Stir the chopped parsley into the sauce, and serve immediately with the salmon rolls.

Salted Salmon Energy 407kcal/1699kJ; Protein 26.4g; Carbohydrate 22.6g, of which sugars 5.9g; Fat 24g, of which saturates 9.7g; Cholesterol 85mg; Calcium 155mg; Fibre 1g; Sodium 118mg.
Salmon Rolls Energy 694kcal/2867kJ; Protein 25.7g; Carbohydrate 2.4g, of which sugars 2.1g; Fat 62.5g, of which saturates 33.4g; Cholesterol 187mg; Calcium 55mg; Fibre 0.6g; Sodium 362mg.

Salmon with Asparagus

This spring dish is light and colourful. Asparagus makes the ideal accompaniment for salmon when it is in season. The hollandaise sauce requires concentration, but it's so good with both fresh salmon and asparagus, that it's well worth mastering.

Serves 4

bunch of 20 asparagus
    spears, trimmed

4 salmon portions, such as fillets
    or steaks, about 200g/7oz each
15ml/1 tbsp olive oil
juice of ½ lemon
25g/1oz/2 tbsp butter
salt and ground black pepper

For the hollandaise sauce
45ml/3 tbsp white wine vinegar
6 peppercorns
1 bay leaf
3 egg yolks
175g/6oz/¾ cup butter, softened

1 Peel the lower stems of the asparagus. Stand in a deep pan; cook in salted boiling water for about 1 minute, or until just beginning to become tender, then remove from the pan and cool quickly under cold running water to prevent further cooking. Drain.

2 To make the hollandaise sauce: in a small pan, boil the vinegar and 15ml/1 tbsp water with the peppercorns and bay leaf until reduced to 15ml/1 tbsp. Leave to cool. Cream the egg yolks with 15g/½oz/1 tbsp butter and a pinch of salt. Strain the vinegar into the eggs and set the bowl over a pan of boiling water. Remove from the heat.

3 Whisk in the remaining butter, no more than 10g/¼oz/1½ tsp at a time, until the sauce is shiny and has the consistency of thick cream. Season with salt and pepper.

4 Heat a ridged griddle pan or grill (broiler) until very hot. Brush the salmon with oil, sprinkle with the lemon juice and season. Cook the fish for 3–5 minutes on each side, depending on the thickness. The fish should be moist and succulent within.

5 Melt the butter in a separate large pan and gently reheat the asparagus in it for 1–2 minutes before serving with the fish and hollandaise sauce.

Farfalle with Salmon and Dill

This quick, luxurious sauce for pasta has become very fashionable, but wherever you have it, it will taste delicious. Dill is the classic herb for cooking with fish, but if you don't like its aniseed flavour, substitute parsley or a little fresh tarragon. The fresher the herbs, the better the taste, so it is always worth growing some in pots or in the garden.

Serves 4
6 spring onions (scallions), sliced
50g/2oz/¼ cup butter
90ml/6 tbsp dry white wine
    or vermouth
450ml/¾ pint/scant 2 cups
    double (heavy) cream
freshly grated nutmeg
225g/8oz smoked salmon
30ml/2 tbsp chopped fresh dill
freshly squeezed lemon juice
450g/1lb/4 cups fresh farfalle
salt and ground black pepper
fresh dill sprigs, to garnish

1 Using a sharp cook's knife, slice the spring onions finely. Melt the butter in a large pan and fry the spring onions for about 1 minute, stirring occasionally, until softened.

2 Add the wine or vermouth to the pan. Increase the heat and bring the mixture to the boil. Let it boil vigorously to reduce the liquid to about 30ml/2 tbsp.

3 Stir in the cream and add salt, pepper and nutmeg to taste. Bring to the boil, then simmer for 2–3 minutes until thickened.

4 Cut the smoked salmon into 2.5cm/1in squares and stir into the sauce, together with the dill. Add lemon juice to taste.

5 Cook the pasta in a large pan of boiling salted water for 2–3 minutes, or until it rises to the surface of the liquid. Drain well. Toss with the sauce. Spoon into serving bowls and serve immediately, garnished with sprigs of dill.

> **Cook's Tip**
> If you can't find fresh pasta, use dried, and cook in boiling water for 12 minutes or according to the instructions on the packet.

Farfalle with Salmon Energy 1162kcal/4846kJ; Protein 30g; Carbohydrate 86.5g, of which sugars 6.8g; Fat 77.4g, of which saturates 46.1g; Cholesterol 206mg; Calcium 104mg; Fibre 3.5g; Sodium 1180mg.
Salmon with Asparagus Energy 834kcal/3449kJ; Protein 46.5g; Carbohydrate 2.8g, of which sugars 2.7g; Fat 7.7g, of which saturates 31.6g; Cholesterol 358mg; Calcium 102mg; Fibre 2.1g; Sodium 401mg.

Salmon with Spicy Pesto

This is a great way to bone salmon steaks to give a solid piece of fish.

Serves 4
4 salmon steaks, each about
    225g/8oz
30ml/2 tbsp sunflower oil
finely grated rind and juice
    of 1 lime
salt and ground black pepper

lime wedges, to serve
red chilli, shredded finely

For the pesto
6 fresh mild red chillies, seeded
    and roughly chopped
2 garlic cloves
30ml/2 tbsp pumpkin or
    sunflower seeds
finely grated rind and juice of 1 lime
75ml/5 tbsp olive oil

1 Place a salmon steak flat on a board. Insert a very sharp knife close to the top of the bone. Staying close to the bone all the time, cut to the end of the steak to release one side of the steak. Repeat with the other side.

2 Place one piece of salmon skin side down and hold it firmly with one hand. Insert a small sharp knife under the skin and, working away from you, cut the flesh off in a single piece. Repeat with the remaining salmon steaks.

3 Wrap each piece of fish into a circle, with the thinner end wrapped around the fatter end. Tie with kitchen string. Place in a shallow bowl.

4 Rub the oil into the boneless fish rounds. Add the lime juice and rind to the bowl. Cover and marinate in the refrigerator for 2 hours.

5 Make the pesto. Put the chillies, garlic, pumpkin or sunflower seeds, lime rind and juice and seasoning into a food processor. Process until well mixed. With the machine running, gradually add the olive oil through the feeder tube. The pesto will slowly thicken and emulsify. Scrape it into a bowl. Preheat the grill (broiler).

6 Drain the salmon and place the rounds in a grill pan. Grill (broil) for 5 minutes on each side or until opaque. Serve with the spicy pesto and lime wedges. Garnish with chilli shreds.

Teriyaki Salmon Fillets with Ginger Strips

Bottles of teriyaki sauce – a lovely rich Japanese glaze – are available in most large supermarkets and Asian stores. Serve the salmon with sticky rice or soba noodles for a healthy, light meal.

Serves 4
4 salmon fillets, 150g/5oz each
75ml/5 tbsp teriyaki marinade
150ml/¼ pint/⅔ cup
    sunflower oil
5cm/2in piece of fresh root
    ginger, peeled and cut into
    matchsticks

1 Put the salmon in a shallow, non-metallic dish and pour over the teriyaki marinade. Cover with clear film (plastic wrap) and chill for 2 hours.

2 Meanwhile, heat the sunflower oil in a small pan and add the ginger. Fry for 1–2 minutes, stirring constantly, until golden brown and crisp. Remove with a slotted spoon and drain on kitchen paper. Set aside until ready to serve the salmon.

3 Heat a griddle pan until smoking hot. Remove the salmon from the marinade and add, skin side down, to the pan. Cook for 2–3 minutes, then turn over and cook for a further 1–2 minutes, or until cooked through.

4 Remove from the pan and divide among four serving plates. Top the salmon fillets with the crispy fried ginger.

5 Pour the marinade into the pan and cook for 1–2 minutes. Pour over the salmon and serve immediately.

Cook's Tip
In Japanese cuisine, teriyaki sauce is traditionally made by mixing and heating soy sauce, sake or mirin, and a sweetener such as sugar or honey. The sauce is reduced, then used to marinate meat which is then grilled or broiled. Sometimes ginger or garlic is added to the sauce.

Teriyaki Salmon Energy 239kcal/995kJ; Protein 24.8g; Carbohydrate 2.1g, of which sugars 1.7g; Fat 13.3g, of which saturates 2.3g; Cholesterol 58mg; Calcium 93mg; Fibre 0.3g; Sodium 323mg.
Salmon with Pesto Energy 653kcal/2719kJ; Protein 50.5g; Carbohydrate 1.4g, of which sugars 0.1g; Fat 49.6g, of which saturates 7.5g; Cholesterol 122mg; Calcium 60mg; Fibre 0.5g; Sodium 111mg.

Roasted Duckling on a Bed of Honeyed Potatoes

The rich flavour of duck combined with these sweetened potatoes glazed with honey makes an excellent treat for a dinner party or special occasion.

Serves 4

1 duckling, giblets removed

60ml/4 tbsp light soy sauce
150ml/¼ pint/⅔ cup fresh orange juice
3 large floury potatoes, cut into chunks
30ml/2 tbsp clear honey
15ml/1 tbsp sesame seeds
salt and ground black pepper

1 Preheat the oven to 200°C/400°F/Gas 6. Place the duckling in a roasting pan. Prick the skin well all over with a fork.

2 Mix the soy sauce and orange juice together and pour over the duck. Cook in the oven for 20 minutes.

3 Place the potato chunks in a bowl and stir in the honey; toss to mix well. Remove the duckling from the oven and spoon the potatoes all around and under the duckling.

4 Roast for a further 35 minutes and remove from the oven. Toss the potatoes in the juices so the underside will be cooked and turn the duck over. Place back in the oven and cook for a further 30 minutes.

5 Remove the duckling from the oven and carefully scoop off the excess fat, leaving the juices behind.

6 Sprinkle the sesame seeds over the potatoes, season with salt and pepper and turn the duckling back over, breast side up, and cook for a further 10 minutes. Remove the duckling and potatoes from the oven and keep warm, allowing the duck to stand for a few minutes.

7 Pour off the excess fat and simmer the juices on the stove for a few minutes. Serve the juices with the carved duckling and the potatoes.

Duck and Sesame Stir-fry

For a special family meal that is a guaranteed success, this is ideal. It tastes fantastic and cooks fast, so you'll be eating in no time.

Serves 4

250g/9oz boneless duck meat
15ml/1 tbsp sesame oil
15ml/1 tbsp vegetable oil

4 garlic cloves, finely sliced
2.5ml/½ tsp dried chilli flakes
15ml/1 tbsp Thai fish sauce
15ml/1 tbsp light soy sauce
120ml/4fl oz/½ cup water
1 head broccoli, cut into small florets
coriander (cilantro) and 15ml/1 tbsp toasted sesame seeds, to garnish

1 Cut all the duck meat into bitesize pieces. Heat the oils in a wok or large, heavy frying pan and stir-fry the garlic over medium heat until it is golden brown – do not let it burn, otherwise it will give the food a bitter taste.

2 Add the duck to the pan and stir-fry for a further 2 minutes, until the meat begins to brown.

3 Stir in the chilli flakes, fish sauce, soy sauce and water. Add the broccoli and continue to stir-fry for about 2 minutes, until the duck is just cooked through.

4 Serve on warmed plates, garnished with coriander and the toasted sesame seeds.

Cook's Tip
Broccoli has excited interest recently since it is claimed that eating this dark green vegetable regularly can help to reduce the risk of some cancers. Broccoli is a source of protein, calcium, iron and magnesium, as well as vitamins A and C.

Variation
Pak choi (bok choy) or Chinese flowering cabbage can be used instead of broccoli.

Roasted Duckling Energy 806kcal/3341kJ; Protein 20.8g; Carbohydrate 32.3g, of which sugars 6.4g; Fat 66.8g, of which saturates 17.9g; Cholesterol 0mg; Calcium 53mg; Fibre 2.1g; Sodium 403mg.
Duck and Sesame Stir-fry Energy 165kcal/686kJ; Protein 17.4g; Carbohydrate 2.3g, of which sugars 2g; Fat 10.6g, of which saturates 1.8g; Cholesterol 69mg; Calcium 72mg; Fibre 2.9g; Sodium 345mg.

Escalopes of Chicken with Vegetables

This is a quick and light dish – ideal for a sunny day in spring, when it is too hot to slave over the stove for hours or to eat heavy meals. Flattening the chicken breast fillets thins and tenderizes the meat and also speeds up the cooking process. The fresh tomato mayonnaise brings out the sweet flavour of the potatoes.

Serves 4
4 skinless chicken breast fillets,
 each weighing 175g/6oz

juice of 1 lime
120ml/4fl oz/½ cup olive oil
675g/1½lb mixed baby potatoes,
 carrots, fennel (sliced if large),
 asparagus and peas
sea salt and ground black pepper
fresh flat leaf parsley sprigs,
 to garnish

For the tomato mayonnaise
150ml/¼ pint/⅔ cup mayonnaise
15ml/1 tbsp sun-dried
 tomato paste

1 Lay the chicken portions between two sheets of clear film (plastic wrap) or baking parchment and beat them flat with a rolling pin. Season the chicken with salt and pepper and sprinkle with the lime juice.

2 Heat 45ml/3 tbsp of the oil in a frying pan or griddle pan and fry the chicken for 10 minutes on each side, or until cooked.

3 Meanwhile, put the potatoes and carrots in a pan with the remaining oil and season with sea salt. Cover and cook over medium heat for 10–15 minutes, stirring frequently.

4 Add the fennel to the pan of vegetables and cook for a further 5 minutes, stirring frequently. Finally, add the asparagus and peas and cook for 5 minutes more, or until all the vegetables are tender.

5 To make the sauce, mix together the mayonnaise and sun-dried tomato paste in a small bowl. Spoon the vegetables on to a warmed large serving platter or individual plates and arrange the chicken on top. Serve the tomato mayonnaise with the chicken and vegetables. Garnish with sprigs of flat leaf parsley.

Chicken with Peas

This Italian dish strongly reflects the traditions of Mediterranean cuisine, and makes the most of tasty, seasonal spring produce.

Serves 4
4 skinless chicken breast fillets
plain (all-purpose) flour, for dusting
30–45ml/2–3 tbsp olive oil
1–2 onions, chopped
¼ fennel bulb, chopped (optional)

15ml/1 tbsp chopped fresh
 parsley, plus extra to garnish
7.5ml/1½ tsp fennel seeds
75ml/5 tbsp dry Marsala
120ml/4fl oz/½ cup
 chicken stock
300g/11oz/2¼ cups petits pois
 (baby peas)
juice of 1½ lemons
2 egg yolks
salt and ground black pepper

1 Season the chicken with salt and pepper, then dust generously with flour. Shake off the excess flour; set aside.

2 Heat 15ml/1 tbsp oil in a pan, add the onions, fennel, if using, parsley and fennel seeds. Cook for 5 minutes.

3 Add the remaining oil and the chicken to the pan and cook for 2–3 minutes on each side, until lightly browned. Remove the chicken and onion mixture from the pan and set aside.

4 Deglaze the pan by pouring in the Marsala and cooking over a high heat until reduced to about 30ml/2 tbsp, then pour in the stock. Add the peas and return the chicken and onion mixture to the pan. Cook over very low heat while you prepare the egg mixture.

5 In a bowl, beat the lemon juice and egg yolks together, then gradually add about 120ml/4fl oz/½ cup of the hot liquid from the chicken and peas, stirring well to combine.

6 Return the mixture to the pan and cook over a low heat, stirring, until the mixture thickens slightly. (Do not allow the mixture to boil or the eggs will curdle and spoil the sauce.) Serve the chicken immediately, sprinkled with a little extra chopped fresh parsley.

Chicken with Peas Energy 319kcal/1338kJ; Protein 42g; Carbohydrate 9.1g, of which sugars 5.9g; Fat 10.7g, of which saturates 2.2g; Cholesterol 206mg; Calcium 67mg; Fibre 4.2g; Sodium 150mg.
Escalopes of Chicken Energy 513kcal/2143kJ; Protein 44g; Carbohydrate 18.9g, of which sugars 9g; Fat 29.6g, of which saturates 4.7g; Cholesterol 141mg; Calcium 41mg; Fibre 3.2g; Sodium 251mg.

Baked Chicken with Broad Beans

This dish is a delightful combination of baked marinated chicken with juicy rice, broad beans and sausage. It should, ideally, be prepared with free-range chicken, which is tastier and more tender. If the chicken is not free-range, reduce the cooking time by half.

Serves 6

1 free-range chicken, weighing
   about 1.8kg/4lb, cut
   into portions
2 garlic cloves, chopped
50ml/2fl oz/¼ cup white wine
sea salt

For the rice
800g/1¾lb/5⅔ cups shelled
   broad (fava) beans, thawed
   if frozen
105ml/7 tbsp olive oil
2 onions, chopped
1 sausage with little fat or salpicão
1 bay leaf
750ml/1¼ pints/3 cups
   chicken stock
250g/9oz/1¼ cups long grain rice

1 Season the chicken portions with salt and place in an ovenproof dish. Sprinkle with the garlic, pour over the wine and leave to marinate for 2 hours.

2 Preheat the oven to 160C/325F/Gas 3. Cover the dish of chicken portions and bake in the oven for about 1½ hours, until cooked through. Meanwhile, pop the beans out of their skins by squeezing gently between your finger and thumb.

3 About 55 minutes before the end of the chicken's cooking time, heat the olive oil in a pan. Add the onions and cook over a low heat, for 5 minutes, until softened. Add the sausage, bay leaf and 300ml/½ pint/1¼ cups of the stock and simmer for 30 minutes.

4 Remove the sausage and bay leaf from the pan. Discard the bay leaf, cut the sausage into small cubes and return it to the pan. Add the remaining stock and bring to the boil, then add the rice and cook for about 10 minutes.

5 Add the broad beans and cook for about 5 more minutes, until tender and still moist. Serve the chicken with the juicy rice handed round separately.

Broad Beans with Sausages

When broad beans come into season in spring, they are said to 'jump' from the field into the pot, and this dish is undoubtedly a bean-lover's dream. Nowadays, you can prepare it throughout the year, as beans don't lose much quality when they are frozen. Nevertheless, extremely tender young beans are best and will need only a little cooking, especially if you have the patience to pop them from their skins first.

Serves 4

30ml/2 tbsp olive oil
1 onion, chopped
150g/5oz black pudding
   (blood sausage)
150g/5oz chouriço sausage
50g/2oz/⅓ cup diced bacon
1 garlic clove, chopped
400g/14oz shelled broad
   (fava) beans
15ml/1 tbsp paprika
150–300ml/¼–½ pint/⅔–1¼
   cups chicken stock
chopped fresh coriander (cilantro),
   to garnish

1 Heat the olive oil. Add the onion and cook over low heat, stirring, for about 5 minutes, until the onion has softened.

2 Meanwhile, cut the black pudding and sausage into small pieces. Add them to the pan with the bacon and garlic and simmer gently, stirring occasionally, for 20 minutes.

3 Pop the beans out of their skins and add to the pan with the paprika. Stir, then add enough stock to cover and simmer until the beans are just tender. Garnish with the coriander.

> **Cook's Tip**
> Serve this as a main dish with poached eggs and crusty bread.

> **Variation**
> As a variation, cut 150g/5oz black pudding (blood sausage) in 1.5cm/⅔in slices and fry, then add to the cooked beans.

Baked Chicken Energy 823kcal/3429kJ; Protein 52.6g; Carbohydrate 50.9g, of which sugars 2.1g; Fat 45g, of which saturates 11.1g; Cholesterol 205mg; Calcium 104mg; Fibre 8.8g; Sodium 417mg.
Broad Beans Energy 286kcal/1191kJ; Protein 15.1g; Carbohydrate 16.7g, of which sugars 2.4g; Fat 18.1g, of which saturates 5.2g; Cholesterol 29mg; Calcium 103mg; Fibre 6.9g; Sodium 626mg.

Dutch Asparagus

White asparagus is a popular vegetable in many parts of Europe, particularly in Holland, where it is widely available from mid May until the end of June. You can use fresh green asparagus as a suitable substitute if the white variety is not available.

Serves 4

2kg/4½lb finest white asparagus
25ml/1½ tbsp salt
8–12 small new potatoes, peeled
4 eggs
8 slices unsmoked cooked ham
100g/3¾oz/scant ½ cup
   butter, melted
pinch of freshly grated nutmeg
chopped fresh parsley, to garnish

1 Rinse the asparagus and trim about 2cm/¾in from the base, reserving the trimmings. Using a vegetable peeler, carefully peel the spears from the tips downwards. Put the peel and trimmings in a pan and cover with a clean dish towel, leaving the sides overhanging.

2 Place the asparagus spears on the dish towel, fold in the overhang and add cold water to cover and the salt. Cover the pan and bring to the boil, then lower the heat and poach gently for 10 minutes.

3 Remove the pan from the heat and leave to stand for 15–20 minutes. Test the asparagus is tender by pricking the ends with a fork; they should be soft but not mushy.

4 Meanwhile, cook the potatoes in a pan of boiling water for 20 minutes, until tender. Drain and keep warm.

5 Hard-boil the eggs in another pan of boiling water for 10 minutes. Refresh under cold running water, shell and halve.

6 Using a slotted spoon, remove the asparagus from the pan and drain on kitchen paper. Pour the butter into a sauceboat.

7 Arrange the asparagus spears on individual plates and garnish with ham, hard-boiled egg halves and warm potatoes sprinkled with nutmeg and chopped parsley. Serve immediately with the melted butter.

Lamb Kebabs with Mint Chutney

These little round lamb kebabs owe their exotic flavour to ras el hanout, a North African spice blend. Dried rose petals can be found in Moroccan and Middle Eastern stores.

Serves 4–6

30ml/2 tbsp extra virgin olive oil
1 onion, finely chopped
2 garlic cloves, crushed
35g/1¼oz/5 tbsp pine nuts
500g/1¼lb/2½ cups minced
   (ground) lamb

10ml/2 tsp ras el hanout
10ml/2 tsp dried pink rose
   petals (optional)
salt and ground black pepper
18 short wooden or metal skewers
150ml/¼ pint/⅔ cup natural
   (plain) yogurt and 7.5ml/
   1½ tsp rose harissa, to serve

For the fresh mint chutney
40g/1½oz/1½ cups fresh mint
   leaves, finely chopped
10ml/2 tsp sugar
juice of 2 lemons
2 apples, peeled and finely grated

1 If using wooden skewers, soak them in cold water for 30 minutes. Heat the oil in a frying pan on the stove. Add the onion and garlic and fry gently for 7 minutes. Stir in the pine nuts. Fry for about 5 minutes more, or until the mixture is slightly golden, then set aside to cool.

2 Make the fresh mint chutney by mixing together all of the ingredients. Set aside.

3 Prepare the barbecue. Place the minced lamb in a large bowl and add the ras el hanout and rose petals, if using. Tip in the cooled onion mixture and add salt and pepper. Using your hands, mix well, then form into 18 balls. Drain the skewers and mould a ball on to each one. Once the flames have died down, rake a few hot coals to one side. Position a lightly oiled grill rack over the coals to heat.

4 When the coals are cool, or with a thick coating of ash, place the kebabs on the grill over the part with the most coals. If it is easier, cover the barbecue with a lid or tented heavy-duty foil so that the heat will circulate and they will cook evenly all over. Serve with the yogurt, mixed with the rose harissa, if you like.

Dutch Asparagus Energy 491kcal/2035kJ; Protein 31.4g; Carbohydrate 22.7g, of which sugars 11.1g; Fat 31g, of which saturates 15.7g; Cholesterol 273mg; Calcium 176mg; Fibre 9.3g; Sodium 835mg.
   Lamb Kebabs Energy 257kcal/1070kJ; Protein 17.2g; Carbohydrate 5.1g, of which sugars 4.5g; Fat 18.8g, of which saturates 6g; Cholesterol 64mg; Calcium 33mg; Fibre 0.6g; Sodium 59mg.

Sweet-and-sour Lamb

Enjoy this simple dish when lamb appears in the stores.

Serves 4

8 French-trimmed lamb loin chops

90ml/6 tbsp balsamic vinegar
30ml/2 tbsp caster
　　(superfine) sugar
30ml/2 tbsp olive oil
salt and ground black pepper

1 Put the lamb chops in a shallow, non-metallic dish and drizzle over the balsamic vinegar. Sprinkle with the sugar and season. Turn the chops to coat in the mixture, then cover with clear film (plastic wrap) and chill for 20 minutes.

2 Heat the olive oil in a large frying pan and add the chops, reserving the marinade. Cook for 3–4 minutes on each side. Pour the marinade into the pan and leave to bubble for about 2 minutes, or until reduced slightly. Remove from the pan and serve immediately.

Lamb with Oregano and Basil

Lamb leg steaks are chunky with a sweet flavour and go well with oregano and basil. However, you could also use finely chopped rosemary or thyme. Serve with couscous.

Serves 4

4 large or 8 small lamb leg steaks
60ml/4 tbsp garlic-infused olive oil
1 small bunch of fresh oregano,
　　roughly chopped
1 small bunch of fresh basil, torn
salt and ground black pepper

1 Put the lamb in a shallow, non-metallic dish. Mix 45ml/3 tbsp of the oil with the oregano, basil and some salt and pepper, reserving some of the herbs for garnish. Pour over the lamb and turn to coat in the marinade. Cover and chill for up to 8 hours.

2 Heat the remaining oil in a large frying pan. Remove the lamb from the marinade and fry for 5–6 minutes on each side, until slightly pink in the centre. Add the marinade and cook for 1–2 minutes until warmed through. Garnish with the reserved herbs and serve.

Lamb Casserole with Broad Beans

This dish is ideal for using the abundance of lamb in spring. It is slowly simmered on top of the stove until the chunks of stewing lamb are meltingly tender. The casserole is flavoured with a large amount of garlic, and plenty of dry sherry adds richness to the sauce. The addition of broad beans adds attractive colour.

Serves 6

45ml/3 tbsp olive oil

1.3kg–1.6kg/3–3½lb lamb fillet,
　　cut into 5cm/2in cubes
1 large onion, chopped
6 large garlic cloves, unpeeled
1 bay leaf
5ml/1 tsp paprika
120ml/4fl oz/½ cup dry sherry
115g/4oz shelled fresh or frozen
　　broad (fava) beans
30ml/2 tbsp chopped fresh parsley
salt and ground black pepper
mashed or boiled potatoes,
　　to serve (optional)

1 Heat 30ml/2 tbsp of the oil in a large flameproof casserole. Add half the lamb cubes to the pan and cook for 45 minutes until evenly browned on all sides. Transfer to a plate and set aside. Brown the rest of the meat in the same way and remove from the casserole.

2 Heat the remaining oil in the pan, add the onion and cook for about 5 minutes until softened and just beginning to turn brown. Return the browned lamb cubes to the casserole and stir in with the onion.

3 Add the garlic cloves, bay leaf, paprika and sherry to the casserole. Season with salt and ground black pepper. Bring the mixture to the boil, then reduce the heat. Cover the pan with a tight-fitting lid and simmer very gently for 1½–2 hours, until the meat is tender.

4 About 10 minutes before the end of the cooking time, stir in the broad beans. Re-cover the pan and place back in the oven until the meat and beans are tender.

5 Stir in the chopped parsley just before serving. Accompany the casserole with mashed or boiled potatoes, if you like.

Sweet-and-sour Lamb Energy 258kcal/1077kJ; Protein 19.6g; Carbohydrate 7.9g, of which sugars 7.9g; Fat 16.7g, of which saturates 6g; Cholesterol 76mg; Calcium 12mg; Fibre 0g; Sodium 87mg.
Lamb with Oregano Energy 466kcal/1938kJ; Protein 40g; Carbohydrate 0.7g, of which sugars 0.6g; Fat 33.7g, of which saturates 12g; Cholesterol 152mg; Calcium 66mg; Fibre 1.3g; Sodium 180mg
Lamb Casserole Energy 541kcal/2258kJ; Protein 50.8g; Carbohydrate 3.5g, of which sugars 1.2g; Fat 33.7g, of which saturates 13.8g; Cholesterol 190mg; Calcium 45mg; Fibre 1.6g; Sodium 221mg.

Herb-crusted Rack of Lamb with Puy Lentils

This lamb roast is quick and easy to prepare but looks impressive when served. It is the perfect choice for springtime entertaining. The delicate flavour of the lentils is the perfect complement to the rich meat.

Serves 4

2 x 6-bone racks of lamb, chined
50g/2oz/1 cup fresh white or
    wholemeal (whole-wheat)
    breadcrumbs
2 large garlic cloves, crushed
90ml/6 tbsp chopped mixed fresh
    herbs, plus sprigs to garnish
50g/2oz/¼ cup butter, melted or
    50ml/3½ tbsp olive oil
sea salt and ground black pepper
new potatoes, to serve

For the puy lentils

1 red onion, chopped
30ml/2 tbsp olive oil
400g/14oz can Puy lentils, rinsed
    and drained
400g/14oz can chopped tomatoes
30ml/2 tbsp chopped fresh flat
    leaf parsley

1 Preheat the oven to 220C/425F/Gas 7. Trim any excess fat from the lamb, and season with salt and pepper.

2 Mix together the breadcrumbs, garlic, herbs and butter or oil, and press on to the fat sides of the lamb. Place in a roasting pan and roast for 25 minutes. Cover with foil; stand for 5 minutes before carving.

3 Cook the onion in the olive oil until softened. Add the lentils and tomatoes and cook gently for 5 minutes, or until the lentils are piping hot. Stir in the parsley and season to taste.

4 Cut each rack of lamb in half and serve with the lentils and new potatoes. Garnish with herb sprigs.

> **Cook's Tips**
> Your butcher will be happy to prepare the racks of lamb for you if you are unsure of the process. Chining involves removing the backbone from the ribs.

Roast Leg of Lamb with Rosemary and Garlic

This is a classic combination of flavours, and always popular in the spring lamb season. Serve as a traditional Sunday lunch with roast potatoes and vegetables.

2 garlic cloves, finely sliced
leaves from 2 sprigs of
    fresh rosemary
30ml/2 tbsp olive oil
salt and ground black pepper

Serves 4–6

1 leg of lamb, total weight
    approximately 1.8kg/4lb

1 Preheat the oven to 190°C/375°F/Gas 5. Using a small sharp knife, make slits at 4cm/1½in intervals over the lamb, deep enough to hold a piece of garlic.

2 Push the slices of garlic and the fresh rosemary leaves into the slits in the leg of lamb.

3 Place the lamb in a large roasting pan. Drizzle the olive oil over the top of the lamb and then gently rub it all over the meat with your fingers. Season with plenty of salt and ground black pepper.

4 Place the pan in the preheated oven and roast the lamb for 25 minutes per 450g/1lb of lamb, plus another 25 minutes. The lamb should still be slightly pink in the middle.

5 Remove the lamb from the oven and leave to rest for about 15 minutes before carving.

> **Cook's Tips**
> • Leaving the lamb to rest before carving gives the meat time to relax after the cooking process and ensures a tender result.
> • In addition to roast potatoes and vegetables, you could also serve the classic accompaniment to lamb – mint sauce.

Herb-crusted Lamb Energy 639kcal/2673kJ; Protein 51.5g; Carbohydrate 28.2g, of which sugars 1.9g; Fat 36.4g, of which saturates 16.7g; Cholesterol 171mg; Calcium 89mg; Fibre 4.9g; Sodium 294mg.
Roast Lamb Energy 518kcal/2177kJ; Protein 61.3g; Carbohydrate 18.1g, of which sugars 1.5g; Fat 22.8g, of which saturates 8.2g; Cholesterol 200mg; Calcium 21mg; Fibre 1.1g; Sodium 138mg.

Veal Casserole with Broad Beans

This delicate stew, flavoured with sherry and plenty of garlic, is a spring dish made with new vegetables. For a delicious flavour be sure to add plenty of fresh parsley just before serving. Lamb can also be used and is equally good cooked in this way.

Serves 6

45ml/3 tbsp olive oil

1.3–1.6kg/3–3½lb veal, cut into 5cm/2in cubes
1 large onion, chopped
6 large garlic cloves, unpeeled
1 bay leaf
5ml/1 tsp paprika
240ml/8fl oz/1 cup fino sherry
100g/4oz/scant 1 cup shelled, skinned broad (fava) beans
60ml/4 tbsp chopped fresh flat leaf parsley
salt and ground black pepper

1 Heat about 30ml/2 tbsp olive oil in a large flameproof casserole on top of the stove. Add half the cubed veal to the hot oil and cook, stirring occasionally, for 5–6 minutes until well browned on all sides.

2 Transfer the browned meat to a plate. Add the remaining half of the meat to the pan and brown in the same way. Remove from the pan when done.

3 Add the remaining olive oil to the pan. Add the onion to the pan and cook, stirring frequently, for 5 minutes until softened. Return the browned veal to the casserole and stir well to mix with the onion.

4 Add the garlic cloves, bay leaf, paprika and sherry to the pan and mix to combine the ingredients. Season with salt and plenty of black pepper.

5 Boil until the mixture is at simmering point, then cover the pan with a tight-fitting lid and cook very gently for 30–40 minutes.

6 Add the broad beans to the casserole about 10 minutes before the end of the cooking time. Check the seasoning and stir in the chopped parsley just before serving.

Leg of Lamb with Parsley

This dish is typical of traditional Dutch cooking. At one time, the meat would have been roasted on a spit, but here it is cooked in a roasting bag. It is served with cauliflower, a popular Dutch vegetable. It is also good with crusty bread and a glass of red wine.

Serves 4

1kg/2¼lb boned leg of lamb
2 shallots, finely chopped
60ml/4 tbsp finely chopped fresh parsley
1 cauliflower, cut into florets
pinch of freshly grated nutmeg
salt

1 Put a wide, flat, ovenproof dish in the oven and preheat to 200°C/400°F/Gas 6.

2 Using a sharp knife, make diamond-shaped incisions into the fat side of the meat. Rub the inside and outside of the lamb with salt. Stuff the bone cavity with the shallots and parsley. Roll up, with the fat on the outside and tie with kitchen string.

3 Put the lamb into a roasting bag and seal loosely. Place the bag on the preheated dish and roast for 45 minutes.

4 Remove the lamb from the oven and increase the temperature to 240°C/475°F/Gas 9. Hold the bag over a bowl to collect the cooking juices and cut off one of the lower corners. Remove and discard the bag.

5 Return the lamb to the dish and roast for a further 15 minutes, until tender but still pink in the middle.

6 Put an ice cube in the cooking juices to help remove the fat, then strain into a sauceboat. Keep warm.

7 Meanwhile, cook the cauliflower in a pan of boiling water for 3–5 minutes, until tender-crisp.

8 Drain the cauliflower well, arrange around the meat and sprinkle with nutmeg. Serve immediately, handing the sauce around separately.

Veal Casserole Energy 352kcal/1473kJ; Protein 47.4g; Carbohydrate 3.6g, of which sugars 1.3g; Fat 11.6g, of which saturates 2.8g; Cholesterol 182mg; Calcium 34mg; Fibre 1.2g; Sodium 244mg.
Leg of Lamb Energy 500kcal/2088kJ; Protein 54.1g; Carbohydrate 5.3g, of which sugars 4.3g; Fat 29.3g, of which saturates 13.3g; Cholesterol 190mg; Calcium 75mg; Fibre 3.1g; Sodium 231mg.

Veal and Ham Pie

Popular for over two centuries, this classic pie is moist and delicious. The flavours of the two tender meats marry perfectly in the delicate filling.

Serves 4
450g/1lb boneless shoulder of
    veal, diced
225g/8oz lean gammon (smoked
    or cured ham), diced
15ml/1 tbsp plain
    (all-purpose) flour
large pinch each of dry mustard
    and ground black pepper
25g/1oz/2 tbsp butter

15ml/1 tbsp sunflower oil
1 onion, chopped
600ml/1 pint/2½ cups chicken
    or veal stock
2 eggs, hard-boiled and sliced
30ml/2 tbsp chopped
    fresh parsley
cabbage and mashed potato,
    to serve

For the pastry
175g/6oz/1½ cups plain
    (all-purpose) flour, plus extra
    for rolling
75g/3oz/6 tbsp butter
iced water, to mix
beaten egg, to glaze

1 Preheat the oven to 180°C/350°F/Gas 4. Mix the veal and gammon in a bowl. Season the flour with the mustard and freshly ground black pepper, then add it to the meat and toss well. Heat the butter and oil in a large, flameproof casserole until sizzling, then cook the meat mixture in batches until golden on all sides. Use a draining spoon to remove the meat from the pan.

2 Cook the onion in the fat remaining in the casserole until softened, but not coloured. Gradually stir in the chicken or veal stock, then replace the meat mixture and stir until thoroughly combined. Cover and cook in the oven for 1½ hours, or until the veal is tender.

3 To make the pastry, sift the flour into a bowl and rub in the butter until the mixture resembles fine crumbs. Mix in enough iced water to bind the mixture into clumps, then press these together with your fingertips to make a dough.

4 Spoon the veal mixture into a 1.5 litre/2½ pint/6¼ cup pie dish. Arrange the slices of hard-boiled egg on top and sprinkle with the parsley.

5 Roll out the pastry on a lightly floured work surface to about 4cm/1½in larger than the top of the pie dish. Cut a strip from around the edge of the pastry, dampen the rim of the pie dish and press the pastry strip on it. Brush the pastry rim with beaten egg and cover it with the pastry lid.

6 Press the pastry around the rim to seal in the filling and cut off any excess. Use the blunt edge of a knife to tap the outside edge of the pastry, pressing it down with your finger as you seal in the filling. Pinch the pastry between your fingers to flute the edge. Roll out any remaining pastry trimmings and cut out decorative shapes to garnish the top of the pie.

7 Brush the top of the pie with beaten egg and bake for 30–40 minutes, or until the pastry is well-risen and golden brown. Serve hot with slightly crunchy, steamed green cabbage and creamy mashed potato.

Braised Veal with Prunes

This creamy stew contains tender pieces of veal with fruity prunes. Serve with a selection of spring vegetables.

Serves 4
20 ready-to-eat prunes
100ml/3½fl oz/scant ½ cup
    brandy
2.5ml/½ tsp grated lemon rind
65g/2½oz/5 tbsp butter
600g/1lb 6oz braising veal, diced
200ml/7fl oz/scant 1 cup veal
    stock or water

30ml/2 tbsp lemon juice
1 thyme sprig
1 bay leaf
200ml/7fl oz/scant 1 cup
    whipping cream
5ml/1 tsp potato flour or
    cornflour (cornstarch)
salt and ground black pepper
chopped fresh parsley, to garnish

To serve
young peas
carrots
small new potatoes

1 Put the prunes in a bowl, add the brandy and lemon rind, cover and soak overnight.

2 Melt the butter in a pan, add the veal and cook over medium heat, stirring frequently, for about 10 minutes, until evenly browned. Season and add the stock or water, lemon juice, thyme and bay leaf. Lower the heat, cover and simmer for 1 hour, until tender.

3 Arrange the vegetables in a ring on a warm serving plate. Using a slotted spoon, transfer the veal to the centre of the plate and keep warm.

4 Bring the cooking liquid to the boil and reduce slightly, then stir in the cream. Remove and discard the thyme and bay leaf. Season the sauce with salt and pepper.

5 Mix the potato flour or cornflour with 15ml/1 tbsp cold water to a paste in a small bowl and stir into the sauce until thickened and smooth. Add the prunes with their soaking liquid and warm through.

6 Pour the sauce over the veal, sprinkle the vegetables with parsley and serve immediately.

Veal Pie Energy 621kcal/2595kJ; Protein 42.4g; Carbohydrate 39.2g, of which sugars 2.6g; Fat 33.8g, of which saturates 17.2g; Cholesterol 281mg; Calcium 128mg; Fibre 2.3g; Sodium 1007mg.
Braised Veal Energy 610kcal/2536kJ; Protein 34.4g; Carbohydrate 19.9g, of which sugars 18.7g; Fat 37.9g, of which saturates 22.4g; Cholesterol 213mg; Calcium 86mg; Fibre 3.5g; Sodium 286mg.

Tagine of Beef with Peas and Saffron

This slow-cooked tagine is a great dish to serve in the spring. It can be made with beef or lamb and is quick and easy to prepare. Saffron imparts a pungent taste and delicate colour. The peas, tomatoes and tangy lemon added towards the end of cooking enliven the rich, gingery beef mixture and the brown olives finish it off.

Serves 6
1.2kg/2½lb chuck steak or braising
    steak, trimmed and cubed
30ml/2 tbsp olive oil

1 onion, chopped
25g/1oz fresh root ginger, peeled
    and chopped
5ml/1 tsp ground ginger
pinch of cayenne pepper
pinch of saffron threads
1.2kg/2½lb shelled fresh peas
2 tomatoes, peeled, seeded
    and chopped
1 preserved lemon, chopped
a handful of brown kalamata olives
salt and ground black pepper
crusty bread or plain couscous,
    to serve

1 Put the cubed chuck or braising steak in a tagine, flameproof casserole or heavy pan with the olive oil, chopped onion, fresh and ground ginger, cayenne pepper and saffron, and season with salt and ground black pepper.

2 Pour in enough water to cover the meat completely and bring to the boil. Reduce the heat, cover the pan with a tight-fitting lid and simmer for about 1½ hours, or until the meat is very tender. Continue to cook the meat for an extra 30–45 minutes, if necessary.

3 Add the peas, tomatoes, preserved lemon and olives to the pan. Stir well and cook on a slightly higher heat, with the lid off, for about 10 minutes, or until the peas are tender and the sauce has reduced slightly.

4 Taste the sauce to check the seasoning, adding more salt or pepper if necessary. Spoon into warmed serving bowls and serve with crusty bread or plain couscous.

Spiced Beef Roll

Rolled beef is the Dutch meat of choice for special occasions, such as this spring-inspired feast. The distinctive Amsterdam onions lend a unique taste to the gravy – use normal onions if you can't find any.

Serves 4
50g/2oz/¼ cup butter
1kg/2½lb rolled beef, spiced with
    white pepper, grated nutmeg,
    ground mace and ground gloves

1 x 450g/1lb jar Amsterdam
    onions (Amsterdamse uien)
300ml/½ pint/1¼ cups red wine
15ml/1 tbsp cornflour (cornstarch)
30ml/2 tsp sugar
1.5kg/3¾lb young marrowfat
    peas, or garden peas, shelled
    weight 500g/1¼lb
100g/3¾oz sliced smoked bacon
800g/1¾lb small potatoes
2 spring onions (scallions), sliced
salt and ground black pepper
apple sauce, to serve

1 Start preparing this dish the day before you intend to serve it. Melt the butter in a flameproof casserole over medium heat until lightly browned. Add the beef and cook on all sides, including the ends, until browned. Lower the heat, add 30ml/ 2 tbsp of the juice from the onion jar, cover and simmer gently, turning the beef occasionally, for 2 hours.

2 Transfer the beef to a plate, leave to cool, then chill in the refrigerator overnight. Transfer the cooking juices to a bowl, leave to cool and chill in the refrigerator overnight.

3 The next day, skim off and discard any fat from the surface of the cooking liquid. Reserve the solidified frying fat. Remove and discard the string from the roll of beef. Cut it into 5mm/¼in thick slices, then reassemble into a roll shape and tie with string.

4 Add the wine or water to the cooking liquid, pour into a large pan and bring to the boil. Mix the cornflour with 30ml/ 2 tbsp water to a paste in a small bowl and stir into the cooking liquid. Cook, stirring constantly, for 1 minute and season to taste with salt and pepper. Add the beef to the pan and warm through over a very low heat for 20 minutes.

5 Heat half the frying fat in a frying pan. Drain the Amsterdam onions, pat them dry with kitchen paper and add them to the pan. Cook over low heat, stirring occasionally, for 10 minutes, until they are evenly browned. Sprinkle with the sugar, shake the pan well, remove from the heat and keep warm.

6 Cook the peas in boiling water for 15 minutes. Drain, garnish with onions and keep warm. Dry-fry the bacon in a frying pan until crisp. Remove from the pan and drain on kitchen paper.

7 Cook the potatoes in boiling water for 15 minutes, until tender. Drain well and pat dry with kitchen paper. Melt the remaining frying fat in a large frying pan, add the potatoes and cook, turning frequently, until browned all over.

8 To serve, remove and discard the kitchen string. Arrange the meat slices on a shallow plate. Surround them with spring onions, potatoes and peas, garnished with fried bacon. Ladle some sauce over the meat. Pour the rest in a sauceboat. Serve immediately with apple sauce as a side dish.

Tagine of Beef Energy 492kcal/2049kJ; Protein 57.9g; Carbohydrate 25.6g, of which sugars 7g; Fat 18.2g, of which saturates 6g; Cholesterol 126mg; Calcium 61mg; Fibre 10.1g; Sodium 134mg.
Spiced Beef Roll Energy 913kcal/3813kJ; Protein 74.5g; Carbohydrate 66.7g, of which sugars 19.8g; Fat 40.4g, of which saturates 18.2g; Cholesterol 185mg; Calcium 89mg; Fibre 9.5g; Sodium 650mg.

Venison Medallions with Dumplings

Venison is lean and full-flavoured. This recipe makes a spectacular dinner party dish – it gives the appearance of being difficult to make but is actually very easy.

Serves 4
600ml/1 pint/2½ cups
    venison stock
120ml/4fl oz/½ cup port
15ml/1 tbsp sunflower oil
4 X 175g/6oz medallions
    of venison

chopped parsley, to garnish
steamed baby vegetables, such as
    carrots, courgettes (zucchini)
    and turnips, cooked, to serve

For the dumplings
75g/3oz/⅔ cup self-raising (self-
    rising) flour
40g/1½oz beef suet (US chilled,
    grated shortening)
15ml/1 tbsp chopped fresh
    mixed herbs
5ml/1 tsp creamed horseradish
45–60ml/3–4 tbsp water

1 First make the dumplings: mix the flour, suet and herbs and make a well in the middle. Add the horseradish and water, then mix to make a soft but not sticky dough. Shape the dough into walnut-sized balls and chill in the refrigerator for up to 1 hour.

2 Place the venison stock in a large pan. Bring to the boil and simmer vigorously until the stock has reduced by half.

3 Add the port to the stock and continue boiling the mixture until reduced again by half, then pour the reduced stock into a large frying pan.

4 Heat the stock until it is simmering and add the dumplings. Poach them gently for 5–10 minutes, or until risen and cooked through. Use a draining spoon to remove the dumplings from the pan.

5 Smear the sunflower oil over a non-stick griddle, and heat until very hot. Add the venison medallions and cook for 2–3 minutes on each side.

6 Place the venison medallions on warm serving plates and pour the sauce over. Serve with the dumplings and the vegetables, garnished with parsley.

Venison Stew

This simple yet deeply flavoured stew makes a wonderful supper dish, incorporating rich red wine and sweet redcurrant jelly with the depth of the bacon.

Serves 4
1.3kg/3lb stewing venison
    (shoulder or topside), trimmed
    and diced
50g/2oz/¼ cup butter
225g/8oz piece of streaky (fatty)
    bacon, cut into 2cm/¾in lardons

2 large onions, chopped
1 large carrot, peeled and diced
1 large garlic clove, crushed
30ml/2 tbsp plain
    (all-purpose) flour
½ bottle red wine
beef stock
1 bay leaf
sprig of fresh thyme
200g/7oz button (white)
    mushrooms, sliced
30ml/2 tbsp redcurrant jelly
salt and ground black pepper
mashed potato and vegetables,
    to serve

1 Pat dry the venison pieces thoroughly using kitchen paper. Set to one side.

2 Melt the butter in a pan, then brown the bacon lardons over medium heat, stirring occasionally. Reduce the heat to medium and add the onions and carrot; stir in and brown lightly.

3 Add the venison to the pan along with the garlic and stir into the mixture. Sprinkle on the flour and mix well.

4 Pour in the wine and beef stock to cover, along with the herbs, mushrooms and redcurrant jelly.

5 Cover the pan and simmer over low heat until the meat is cooked, approximately 1½–2 hours. Serve immediately with creamy mashed potato and spring vegetables of your choice.

> **Cook's Tip**
> *This dish can be cooked and then left until required – a couple of days if need be. The flavours will be enhanced if it has been left for a while. Simply reheat and serve when needed.*

Venison Medallions Energy 393kcal/1651kJ; Protein 29.1g; Carbohydrate 33.4g, of which sugars 6.4g; Fat 16.3g, of which saturates 7.5g; Cholesterol 67mg; Calcium 136mg; Fibre 2.3g; Sodium 189mg.
Venison Stew Energy 727kcal/3045kJ; Protein 83.8g; Carbohydrate 17.5g, of which sugars 14.4g; Fat 31.3g, of which saturates 13.8g; Cholesterol 226mg; Calcium 70mg; Fibre 2.9g; Sodium 985mg.

Rhubarb and Ginger Wine Torte

The springtime harvest of rhubarb provides the opportunity to make this wonderful dessert. The classic combination of rhubarb and ginger is used in this luxury frozen torte to make a dish that is refreshingly tart.

Serves 8
500g/1¼lb rhubarb, trimmed
115g/4oz/generous ½ cup caster (superfine) sugar
30ml/2 tbsp water
200g/7oz/scant 1 cup cream cheese
150ml/¼ pint/⅔ cups double (heavy) cream
40g/1½oz/¼ cup preserved stem ginger, finely chopped
a few drops of pink food colouring (optional)
250ml/8fl oz/1 cup ginger wine
175g/6oz sponge fingers
fresh mint or lemon balm sprigs, dusted with icing (confectioners') sugar, to decorate

1 Chop the rhubarb roughly and put it in a pan with the sugar and water. Cover and cook very gently for 5–8 minutes until the rhubarb is just tender. Process in a food processor or blender until smooth, then leave to cool.

2 Beat the cheese in a bowl until softened. Stir in the cream, rhubarb purée and ginger, then food colouring, if you like. Line a 900g/2lb/6–8 cup loaf tin (pan) with clear film (plastic wrap).

3 Pour the mixture into a shallow freezer container and freeze until firm. Alternatively, churn in an ice cream maker.

4 Pour the ginger wine into a shallow dish. Spoon a thin layer of ice cream over the bottom of the tin. Working quickly, dip the sponge fingers in the ginger wine, then lay them lengthways over the ice cream in a single layer, trimming to fit.

5 Spread another layer of ice cream over the top. Repeat the process, adding two to three more layers and finishing with ice cream. Cover and freeze overnight.

6 Transfer to the refrigerator 30 minutes before serving, to soften the torte slightly. To serve, briefly dip in very hot water then invert on to a flat dish. Peel off the lining and decorate.

Ginger and Kiwi Sorbet

Freshly grated root ginger gives a lively, aromatic flavour to this exotic sorbet.

300ml/½ pint/1¼ cups water
5 kiwi fruit
fresh mint sprigs or chopped kiwi fruit, to decorate

Serves 6
50g/2oz fresh root ginger
115g/4oz/generous ½ cup caster (superfine) sugar

1 Peel the ginger and grate it finely. Put the sugar and water in a pan and heat gently until the sugar has dissolved. Add the ginger and cook for 1 minute, then leave to cool. Strain into a bowl and chill until very cold.

2 Peel the kiwi fruit, place the flesh in a blender and process to form a smooth purée. Add the purée to the chilled syrup and mix well.

3 Pour the kiwi mixture into a freezer container and freeze until slushy. Beat the mixture, then freeze again. Repeat this beating process one more time, then cover the container and freeze until firm.

4 Alternatively, use an ice cream maker. Freeze the mixture following the manufacturer's instructions, then transfer to a freezer container and freeze until required.

5 Remove the sorbet from the freezer 10–15 minutes before serving, to allow it to soften slightly. Spoon into glass bowls, then decorate with mint sprigs or pieces of chopped kiwi fruit and serve immediately.

Cook's Tip
Fresh ginger root is widely available and is easy to spot with its knobbly shape and pale brown skin. Look for smooth skin and firm solid flesh. Any left over can be wrapped and stored in the refrigerator for up to three weeks. Use a sharp knife for peeling.

Rhubarb Torte Energy 398kcal/1658kJ; Protein 3.9g; Carbohydrate 29.4g, of which sugars 25.2g; Fat 26.8g, of which saturates 16.2g; Cholesterol 100mg; Calcium 132mg; Fibre 1.2g; Sodium 111mg.
Ginger and Kiwi Sorbet Energy 100kcal/426kJ; Protein 0.7g; Carbohydrate 25.3g, of which sugars 25.2g; Fat 0.3g, of which saturates 0g; Cholesterol 0mg; Calcium 23mg; Fibre 1g; Sodium 3mg.

Rhubarb and Raspberry Crumble

A fruit crumble cries out to be eaten on the sofa. It sits beautifully in a bowl, stays where it should – on the spoon and in the mouth – and willingly accepts lashings of cream. The classic fruit to use is rhubarb, preferably the first of the spring when it is bright pink and tender.

Serves 4
675g/1½lb fresh forced rhubarb, cut into large chunks
a pinch of ground allspice
grated rind and juice of 1 lime
175g/6oz/scant 1 cup golden caster (superfine) sugar
225g/8oz fresh or frozen raspberries
custard or clotted cream, to serve

For the crumble
115g/4oz/1 cup plain (all-purpose) flour
pinch of salt
50g/2oz/½ cup ground almonds
115g/4oz/½ cup cold butter
115g/4oz/1 cup blanched almonds, chopped
50g/2oz/¼ cup golden caster (superfine) sugar

1 Preheat the oven to 200°C/400°F/Gas 6 and put a baking sheet inside to heat up. Put the rhubarb in a pan with the allspice, lime rind and juice and sugar. Cook over a gentle heat for 2 minutes, stirring occasionally, until the chunks of rhubarb are tender but still hold their shape.

2 Pour the rhubarb into a sieve (strainer), set over a bowl to catch the juices. Leave to cool. Reserve the juices for later.

3 To make the crumble, put the flour, pinch of salt, ground almonds and butter into a food processor and process until the mixture resembles fine breadcrumbs. Transfer into a bowl and stir in the blanched almonds and sugar.

4 Spoon the rhubarb into a large ovenproof dish, and stir in the raspberries. Sprinkle the almond mixture evenly over the surface, mounding it up a little towards the centre.

5 Place the dish on the baking sheet in the oven and bake for 35 minutes until crisp and golden on top. Cool for 5 minutes before serving with custard or clotted cream and the warmed, reserved rhubarb juices.

Rhubarb and Ginger Ice Cream

The classic combination of spring rhubarb and root ginger is brought up to date by blending it with mascarpone to make this pretty blush-pink ice cream.

Serves 4–6
5 pieces of stem ginger
450g/1lb trimmed rhubarb, sliced
115g/4oz/½ cup caster (superfine) sugar
30ml/2 tbsp water
150g/5oz/⅔ cup mascarpone
150ml/¼ pint/⅔ cup whipping cream
wafer cups, to serve (optional)

1 Using a sharp knife, roughly chop the stem ginger and set it aside. Put the rhubarb slices into a pan and add the sugar and water. Cover and simmer for 5 minutes until the rhubarb is just tender and still bright pink.

2 Transfer the mixture into a food processor or blender, process until smooth, then leave to cool. Chill if time permits.

3 BY HAND: Mix together the mascarpone, cream and ginger with the rhubarb purée.
USING AN ICE CREAM MAKER: Churn the rhubarb purée for 15–20 minutes until it is thick.

4 BY HAND: Pour the mixture into a plastic tub or similar freezerproof container and freeze for 6 hours or until firm, beating once or twice during the freezing time to break up the ice crystals.
USING AN ICE CREAM MAKER: Put the mascarpone into a bowl, soften it with a wooden spoon, then gradually beat in the cream. Add the chopped ginger, then transfer to the ice cream maker and churn until the ice cream is firm. Serve as scoops in bowls or wafer baskets.

> **Cook's Tip**
> *If the rhubarb purée is rather pale, add a few drops of pink colouring when mixing in the cream.*

Rhubarb Crumble Energy 812kcal/3403kJ; Protein 14.2g; Carbohydrate 88.1g, of which sugars 65.1g; Fat 47.4g, of which saturates 16.9g; Cholesterol 61mg; Calcium 345mg; Fibre 7.7g; Sodium 191mg.
Rhubarb Ice Cream Energy 221kcal/924kJ; Protein 3.6g; Carbohydrate 22.1g, of which sugars 22.1g; Fat 13.8g, of which saturates 8.6g; Cholesterol 37mg; Calcium 94mg; Fibre 1.1g; Sodium 10mg.

Soft Fruit and Meringue Gateau

This recipe takes five minutes to make but looks and tastes as though a lot of preparation went into it.

Serves 6
400g/14oz/3½ cups mixed small strawberries or raspberries

30ml/2 tbsp icing (confectioners') sugar
750ml/1¼ pints/3 cups vanilla ice cream
6 meringue nests (or 115g/4oz meringue)

1 Dampen a 900g/2lb loaf tin (pan) and line it with clear film (plastic wrap). If using strawberries, chop them into small pieces. Put them in a bowl and add the raspberries and icing sugar. Toss until the fruit is beginning to break up but do not let it become mushy.

2 Put the vanilla ice cream in a bowl and break it up with a fork. Crumble the meringues into the bowl and add the soft fruit mixture.

3 Fold all the ingredients together until evenly combined and lightly marbled. Pack into the prepared tin and press down gently to level. Cover and freeze overnight. To serve, invert on to a plate and peel away the clear film. Serve the gateau in fairly thick slices.

Variation
Other soft spring fruits, such as the first blackcurrants at the end of May, can be used in this dessert. Choose whatever is in season in the store. It is fun to pick your own berries if you have the facility in your area.

Cook's Tip
Use the best vanilla ice cream you can find for this dish – it will make all the difference to the final dessert. If you have the time you could make your own at home.

Raspberry Muesli Layer

As well as being a delicious, low-fat, high-fibre dessert, this can also be served for a quick, healthy breakfast to supply one of your five a day fruit and vegetables. Serve it when you want a zingy start to the day during the spring.

Serves 4
225g/8oz/1⅓ cups fresh or frozen and thawed raspberries

225g/8oz/1 cup low-fat natural (plain) yogurt
75g/3oz/¾ cup Swiss-style muesli (granola)

1 Reserve four raspberries for decorating at the end, and then spoon a few raspberries into four stemmed serving glasses or glass dishes.

2 Top the raspberries with a generous spoonful of natural yogurt in each glass.

3 Sprinkle a generous layer of the muesli over the yogurt.

4 Repeat the process until the raspberries and all the other ingredients are used up. Top each with a whole raspberry and serve immediately.

Variation
This dessert can be made with other fruits, depending on what is available. If available, strawberries, blueberries or cherries will be tasty variations.

Cook's Tip
This recipe can be made in advance and stored in the refrigerator for several hours, or overnight if you are planning on serving it for breakfast.

Fruit Gateau Energy 334kcal/1404kJ; Protein 6.1g; Carbohydrate 52.6g, of which sugars 51.2g; Fat 10.9g, of which saturates 7.7g; Cholesterol 31mg; Calcium 141mg; Fibre 0.7g; Sodium 102mg.
Raspberry Layer Energy 114kcal/483kJ; Protein 5.5g; Carbohydrate 20.4g, of which sugars 11.7g; Fat 2g, of which saturates 0.5g; Cholesterol 1mg; Calcium 142mg; Fibre 2.6g; Sodium 120mg.

Cherry Clafoutis

This favourite dessert has been reproduced with all manner of fruit, but you simply can't beat the traditional version, which uses slightly tart black cherries. These tasty fruits are at their best late into the spring and into the summer months, but be on your toes as the season is sadly all too short.

Serves 6
25g/1oz/2 tbsp butter, for greasing
450g/1lb/2 cups black cherries, pitted
25g/1oz/¼ cup plain (all-purpose) flour
50g/2oz/½ cup icing (confectioners') sugar, plus extra for dusting
4 eggs, beaten
250ml/8fl oz/1 cup creamy milk
30ml/2 tbsp Kirsch (see Cook's Tip)

1 Preheat the oven to 180°C/350°F/Gas 4. Use the butter to thickly grease a 1.2 litre/2 pint/5 cup gratin dish. Sprinkle the cherries over the base.

2 Sift the flour and icing sugar together into a large mixing bowl and gradually whisk in the eggs until the mixture is smooth. Whisk in the milk until blended, then stir in the Kirsch.

3 Pour the batter carefully over the cherries, then bake for 35–45 minutes or until just set and lightly golden.

4 Allow the pudding to cool for about 15 minutes. Dust liberally with icing sugar just before serving.

> **Cook's Tip**
> Kirsch, also known as kirschwasser (meaning cherry water), is a clear brandy distilled from cherry juice and stones (pits).

> **Variation**
> Try other liqueurs in this dessert. Almond-flavoured liqueur is delicious teamed with cherries. Hazelnut, raspberry or orange liqueur would also work nicely.

Cherry Strudel

There are many varieties of strudel filling, ranging from poppy seed, raisin and honey to sweet cheese. The spring glut of cherries means this strudel is among the most popular at this time of year.

Serves 8–10
250g/9oz/2¼ cups strong flour
75g/3oz/⅔ cup plain (all-purpose) flour
1 egg, beaten
150g/5oz/10 tbsp butter, melted
100ml/3½fl oz/½ cup warm water
sifted icing (confectioners') sugar, for dredging

For the filling
65g/2½oz/generous ½ cup walnuts, roughly chopped
115g/4oz/generous ½ cup caster (superfine) sugar
675g/1½lb cherries, pitted
40g/1½oz/scant 1 cup day-old breadcrumbs

1 Preheat the oven to 200°C/400°F/Gas 6. Sift the flour in a warm bowl. Make a well in the centre, add the egg, 115g/4oz/½ cup of the melted butter and the water. Mix to a smooth dough, adding extra flour if required. Leave wrapped in clear film (plastic wrap) for 30 minutes to rest.

2 Meanwhile, in a large bowl, mix together the chopped walnuts, sugar, cherries and breadcrumbs.

3 Lay out a clean dish towel and sprinkle it with flour. Carefully roll out the dough until it covers the towel. The dough should be as thin as possible, so that you can see the design on the cloth through it.

4 Dampen the edges with water. Spread the cherry filling over the pastry, leaving a gap all the way round the edge, about 2.5cm/1in wide. Roll up the pastry carefully with the side edges folded in over the filling to prevent it coming out. Use the dish towel to help you roll the pastry.

5 Brush the strudel with the remaining melted butter. Place on a baking sheet and curl into a horseshoe shape. Cook for 30–40 minutes, or until golden brown. Dredge with icing sugar; serve warm or cold.

Cherry Clafoutis Energy 201kcal/843kJ; Protein 6.7g; Carbohydrate 23.8g, of which sugars 20.7g; Fat 8.9g, of which saturates 4.3g; Cholesterol 142mg; Calcium 89mg; Fibre 0.8g; Sodium 91mg.
Cherry Strudel Energy 370kcal/1553kJ; Protein 3.2g; Carbohydrate 51.2g, of which sugars 33.2g; Fat 18.4g, of which saturates 11.4g; Cholesterol 47mg; Calcium 57mg; Fibre 1.2g; Sodium 197mg.

Noodle Pudding with Cherries and Nuts

This is an unusual dessert but one that is very popular in parts of Europe, and takes full advantage of the local seasonal fruits in spring.

Serves 6
900ml/1½ pints/3¾ cups milk
450g/1lb/4 cups medium
  egg noodles

350g/12oz/1½ cups butter
90ml/6 tbsp sugar
7 egg yolks
7.5ml/1½ tsp vanilla extract
75g/3oz/¾ cup ground walnuts
675g/1½lb pitted fresh cherries
50g/2oz/¼ cup caster
  (superfine) sugar
50ml/2fl oz/¼ cup cherry
  brandy (optional)

1 Preheat the oven to 180°C/350°F/Gas 4. Grease and base-line a 23–25cm/9–10in square cake tin (pan).

2 Bring the milk to the boil in a large pan and add the noodles. Reduce the heat and cook until the noodles have absorbed the milk, stirring all the time.

3 Carefully, stir the butter into the pan of noodles until melted and combined with the milk and noodles. Remove the pan from the heat and set aside to cool.

4 Beat the sugar in a large mixing bowl with the egg yolks and vanilla extract. Very carefully add the ground walnuts to the noodles, then stir the egg yolk mixture into the noodles.

5 Spread about one-third of the noodles in the bottom of the prepared cake tin and level the surface using the back of a large spoon or metal spatula.

6 Top the noodles with half of the cherries, sugar and cherry brandy, if using. Add another layer of noodles, followed by the remaining cherries, sugar and cherry brandy.

7 Finish with a final layer of noodles, smoothing down the surface, then place the tin in the preheated oven and bake for 40–45 minutes, until golden. Cut into six portions and serve.

Ice Cream with Hot Black Cherry Sauce

The sauce, made from black cherries, transforms ice cream into a delicious dessert for any occasion.

Serves 4
425g/15oz can pitted black
  cherries in juice
10ml/2 tsp cornflour (cornstarch)
finely grated rind of 1 lemon,
  plus 10ml/2 tsp juice

15ml/1 tbsp caster
  (superfine) sugar
2.5ml/½ tsp ground cinnamon
30ml/2 tbsp brandy or Kirsch
400ml/14fl oz/1⅔ cups dark
  (bittersweet) chocolate ice cream
400ml/14fl oz/1⅔ cups vanilla
  ice cream
drinking chocolate powder,
  for dusting

1 Drain the cherries, reserving the canned juice. Spoon the cornflour into a small pan and blend to a paste with a little of the reserved juice.

2 Stir in the remaining canned juice with the lemon rind and juice, sugar and cinnamon. Bring to the boil, stirring, until smooth and glossy.

3 Add the cherries, with the brandy or Kirsch. Stir gently to combine, then cook for 1 minute.

4 Scoop the chocolate and vanilla ice creams into shallow individual bowls. Spoon the hot cherry sauce around the edges and over the ice cream, dust each portion with drinking chocolate powder and serve immediately.

> **Variation**
> The hot cherry sauce also makes a delicious filling for pancakes. For a speedy dessert, use heated, ready-made sweet pancakes – just spread a little sauce in the centre of each pancake and fold into a triangle shape or roll up. Then arrange on a serving dish and spoon the rest of the sauce over the top. Finish with spoonfuls of thick yogurt or whipped cream.

Ice Cream Energy 529kcal/2213kJ; Protein 8.4g; Carbohydrate 59.5g, of which sugars 57g; Fat 30.2g, of which saturates 18.1g; Cholesterol 0mg; Calcium 218mg; Fibre 0.7g; Sodium 130mg.
Noodle Pudding Energy 1095kcal/4572kJ; Protein 20.7g; Carbohydrate 99g, of which sugars 46.6g; Fat 71.4g, of which saturates 37.3g; Cholesterol 401mg; Calcium 276mg; Fibre 3.6g; Sodium 669mg.

Devilish Chocolate Roulade

Indulge yourself with this
wickedly rich roulade when
strawberries are in season.

Serves 6–8
175g/6oz plain (semisweet)
 chocolate, chopped into
 small pieces
4 eggs, separated
115g/4oz/generous $^1/_2$ cup caster
 (superfine) sugar
unsweetened cocoa powder,
 for dusting

chocolate-dipped strawberries,
 to decorate

For the filling
225g/8oz plain (semisweet)
 chocolate, chopped into
 small pieces
45ml/3 tbsp brandy
2 eggs, separated
250g/9oz/generous 1 cup
 mascarpone

1 Preheat the oven to 180°C/350°F/Gas 4. Grease a 33 x 23cm/
13 x 9in Swiss roll tin (jelly roll pan) and line with baking
parchment. Melt the chocolate in a bowl over a pan of hot water.

2 Whisk the egg yolks and sugar in a bowl until pale and thick,
then stir in the melted chocolate. Place the egg whites in a
clean, grease-free bowl. Whisk them to soft peaks, then fold
lightly and evenly into the egg and chocolate mixture.

3 Scrape into the tin and spread to the corners. Bake for
15–20 minutes, until well risen and firm to the touch. Dust a
sheet of baking parchment with cocoa. Turn the sponge out on
to the paper, cover with a clean dish towel and cool.

4 Make the filling. Melt the chocolate with the brandy in a
heatproof bowl over a pan of simmering water. Remove from
the heat. Beat the egg yolks together, then beat into the
chocolate mixture. In a separate bowl, whisk the whites to
soft peaks, then fold them lightly and evenly into the filling.

5 Uncover the roulade, remove the paper and spread with the
mascarpone. Spread the chocolate mixture over the top, then
roll up from a long side to enclose the filling. Transfer to a
serving plate with the join underneath, top with fresh
chocolate-dipped strawberries and chill before serving.

Cheese Tart

This light, creamy tart is
perfect as an accompaniment
to coffee but, when topped
with any of the many
berries that appear in late
spring, it can also be served
as a fine dessert.

Makes 1 tart
150g/5oz/10 tbsp unsalted
 (sweet) butter, softened, plus
 extra for greasing
150g/5oz/$^3/_4$ cup caster
 (superfine) sugar
2 eggs, beaten
5ml/1 tsp vanilla extract

grated rind of 1 lemon and
 15ml/1 tbsp lemon juice
250g/9oz/generous $^3/_4$ cup
 cream cheese
mixed berries, to decorate
 (optional)

For the pastry
500g/1$^1/_4$lb/4$^1/_2$ cups plain
 (all-purpose) flour
5ml/1 tsp baking powder
30ml/2 tbsp caster
 (superfine) sugar
150g/5oz/10 tbsp unsalted butter
1 egg, beaten

1 Preheat the oven to 180°C/350°F/Gas 4. Grease a deep,
loose-bottomed 23cm/9in cake tin (pan) with butter.

2 To make the pastry, sift the flour and baking powder into a
large bowl and add the sugar. Cut the butter into small pieces,
add to the flour and rub in until the mixture resembles fine
breadcrumbs. Alternatively, put the flour, baking powder and
sugar in a food processor, add the butter and, using a pulsating
action, blend to form fine breadcrumbs.

3 Add the beaten egg to the flour mixture and mix lightly
together to form a dough. Pat the dough into the bottom and
up the sides of the tin.

4 Cream the butter and sugar in a large mixing bowl, then add
the eggs, one at a time, and beat until smooth. Add the vanilla
extract, lemon juice and rind, and the cream cheese, and mix
gently to combine.

5 Pour the mixture into the pastry-lined cake tin and bake in
the oven for about 40 minutes, until set. Leave to cool in the tin
before serving and decorating with mixed berries, if liked.

Devilish Roulade Energy 486kcal/2022kJ; Protein 10.2g; Carbohydrate 32.8g, of which sugars 32.4g; Fat 34.5g, of which saturates 19.9g; Cholesterol 189mg; Calcium 41mg; Fibre 1.3g; Sodium 143mg.
Tart Energy 5891kcal/24,582kJ; Protein 70g; Carbohydrate 578.4g, of which sugars 197.4g; Fat 382.9g, of which saturates 234.6g; Cholesterol 1258mg; Calcium 1151mg; Fibre 15.5g; Sodium 2734mg.

Spring Cheesecake with Cinnamon

This cheesecake is made with fragrant Greek honey and the fresh, unsalted local cheese, called myzithra. It is similar to Italian ricotta, which makes a good substitute if necessary.

Serves 6–8
225g/8oz/2 cups plain (all-purpose) flour sifted with a pinch of salt
30ml/2 tbsp caster (superfine) sugar
115g/4oz/¹/₂ cup unsalted butter, cubed
45–60ml/3–4 tbsp cold water

For the filling
4 eggs
50g/2oz/¹/₄ cup caster (superfine) sugar
15ml/1 tbsp plain (all-purpose) flour
500g/1¹/₄lb/2¹/₂ cups fresh myzithra or ricotta cheese
60ml/4 tbsp Greek thyme-scented honey
2.5ml/¹/₂ tsp ground cinnamon

1 Mix the flour and sugar in a bowl, then rub in the butter until the mixture resembles breadcrumbs. Add the water, a little at a time, until the mixture clings together and forms a dough. It should not be too wet. Draw it into a ball, wrap it in clear film (plastic wrap) and chill for 30 minutes.

2 Preheat the oven to 180°C/350°F/Gas 4. Put a baking sheet in the oven to heat. Roll out the pastry thinly on a lightly floured surface and use to line a 25cm/10in round springform tin (pan). Carefully trim off any excess pastry.

3 To make the filling, beat the eggs in a bowl, add the sugar and flour and beat until fluffy. Add the cheese, honey and half the cinnamon and beat until well mixed. Pour into the pastry case and level the surface. Place the tart on the hot baking sheet and cook for 50–60 minutes, until light golden. Sprinkle with the remaining cinnamon while still hot.

> **Cook's Tip**
> Save time by using a 500g/1¹/₄lb packet of ready-made shortcrust pastry instead of making your own.

Rhubarb and Ginger Trifles

Nothing signals the coming of spring quite like a big bunch of rhubarb. Ginger is the perfect partner for the rhubarb in this delicious and simple dessert.

50ml/2fl oz/¹/₄ cup rhubarb compote
450ml/³/₄ pint/scant 2 cups extra thick double (heavy) cream

Serves 4
12 ginger nut biscuits (gingersnaps)

1 Put the ginger biscuits in a plastic bag and seal the opening. Press the biscuits with a rolling pin until they are all roughly and evenly crushed.

2 Set aside 30ml/2 tbsp of the crushed biscuits to use as a topping and divide the rest evenly among four dessert glasses or bowls.

3 Spoon the rhubarb compote on top of the crushed biscuits, then top with the double cream. Place the dessert glasses in the refrigerator and chill for about 30 minutes.

4 To serve, sprinkle the reserved crushed biscuits over the top of the trifles and serve immediately.

> **Variation**
> You could use other biscuits (cookies) for this dessert, if you prefer. Try chocolate cookies or amaretti, or a plainer type such as digestive biscuits (graham crackers).

> **Cook's Tip**
> Choose a jar of good-quality rhubarb compote for this speedy recipe. It will improve the finished result. You could always make your own at home, if you prefer.

Cheesecake Energy 453kcal/1894kJ; Protein 15.7g; Carbohydrate 38.1g, of which sugars 16.7g; Fat 27.6g, of which saturates 16.9g; Cholesterol 170mg; Calcium 287mg; Fibre 0.9g; Sodium 1024mg.
Rhubarb Trifles Energy 695kcal/2874kJ; Protein 3.6g; Carbohydrate 27.1g, of which sugars 14.1g; Fat 64.3g, of which saturates 39.4g; Cholesterol 154mg; Calcium 98mg; Fibre 0.6g; Sodium 124mg.

One-crust Rhubarb Pie

This method can be used for whatever fruits are in season and is really foolproof. It doesn't matter how rough the pie looks when it goes into the oven; it always comes out looking absolutely fantastic.

Serves 6
350g/12oz shortcrust pastry,
  thawed if frozen
1 egg yolk, beaten

25g/1oz/3 tbsp semolina
25g/1oz/¼ cup hazelnuts,
  coarsely chopped
30ml/2 tbsp golden sugar

For the filling
450g/1lb rhubarb, cut into
  2.5cm/1in pieces
75g/3oz/6 tbsp caster
  (superfine) sugar
1–2 pieces preserved stem
  ginger in syrup, drained and
  finely chopped

1 Preheat the oven to 200°C/400°F/Gas 6. Roll out the pastry to a circle 35cm/14in across. Lay it over the rolling pin and transfer it to a large baking sheet. Brush a little egg yolk over the pastry. Sprinkle the semolina over the centre, leaving a wide rim all round the edge.

2 Make the filling. Place the rhubarb pieces, caster sugar and chopped ginger in a large bowl and mix well.

3 Pile the rhubarb mixture into the middle of the pastry. Fold the rim roughly over the filling so that it almost covers it. Some of the fruit will remain visible in the centre.

4 Brush the pastry rim with any remaining egg yolk to glaze, then sprinkle the hazelnuts and golden sugar over the top. Bake the pie for 30–35 minutes or until the pastry is golden brown. Serve hot or warm.

> **Cook's Tip**
> *Egg yolk glaze brushed on to pastry gives it a nice golden sheen. However, be careful not to drip the glaze on the baking sheet, or it will burn and be difficult to remove.*

Rhubarb Meringue Pie

Tangy rhubarb is a welcome feature of spring. It contrasts beautifully with meringue.

Serves 6
675g/1½lb rhubarb, chopped
250g/9oz/1¼ cup caster
  (superfine) sugar
grated rind and juice of 3 oranges
3 eggs, separated
75ml/5 tbsp cornflour (cornstarch)

For the pastry
200g/7oz/1¾ cups plain
  (all-purpose) flour
25g/1oz/¼ cup ground walnuts
115g/4oz/½ cup butter, diced
30ml/2 tbsp sugar
1 egg yolk, beaten with
  15ml/1 tbsp water

1 To make the pastry, sift the flour into a bowl and add the walnuts. Rub in the butter until the mixture resembles very fine breadcrumbs. Stir in the sugar and egg yolk mixture to make a firm dough. Knead lightly, wrap and chill for 30 minutes.

2 Preheat the oven to 190°C/375°F/Gas 5. Roll out the pastry on a lightly floured surface and use to line a 23cm/9in fluted flan tin (tart pan). Prick the base all over with a fork. Line the pastry with foil and baking beans, then bake for 15 minutes.

3 Meanwhile, to make the filling, put the chopped rhubarb in a large pan with 75g/3oz/6 tbsp of the sugar. Add the orange rind. Cover and cook over a low heat until tender.

4 Remove the foil and beans from the pastry case, then brush all over with a little egg yolk. Bake the pastry case for about 15 minutes, or until the pastry is crisp and golden.

5 Mix together the cornflour and the orange juice in a mixing bowl. Remove the rhubarb from the heat, stir in the cornflour mixture, then return the pan to the heat and bring to the boil, stirring constantly. Cook for 1–2 minutes more. Cool slightly, then beat in the remaining egg yolks. Pour into the pastry case.

6 Whisk the egg whites until they form soft peaks, then whisk in the remaining sugar, 15ml/1 tbsp at a time. Swirl over the filling and bake for 25 minutes until the meringue is golden.

Rhubarb Pie Energy 567kcal/2388kJ; Protein 8.4g; Carbohydrate 89.5g, of which sugars 52.6g; Fat 22.1g, of which saturates 11.1g; Cholesterol 136mg; Calcium 202mg; Fibre 2.8g; Sodium 168mg.
One-crust Pie Energy 389kcal/1633kJ; Protein 5.6g; Carbohydrate 49.7g, of which sugars 19.6g; Fat 20.1g, of which saturates 5.6g; Cholesterol 42mg; Calcium 139mg; Fibre 2.5g; Sodium 239mg.

Red Alert

This juice is perfect for those times when you're not thinking straight or you need to concentrate. Beetroot, carrots and spinach all contain folic acid, which is known to help maintain a healthy brain, while the addition of fresh orange juice will give your body a natural vitamin boost. This delicious and vibrant blend is guaranteed to set your tastebuds tingling.

Serves 1–2
200g/7oz raw beetroot (beets)
1 carrot
1 large orange
50g/2oz spinach

1 Using a sharp knife, cut the raw beetroot into wedges. Roughly chop the carrot, then cut away the skin from the orange and roughly slice the flesh.

2 Push the orange, beetroot and carrot pieces alternately through a juicer, then add the spinach. Pour into glasses and serve immediately.

Variation
You could make this drink with a blood orange, if they are available, rather than the normal orange.

Cook's Tips
• *Only use fresh, raw, firm beetroot (beet) for juicing, rather than the cooked variety – and most definitely avoid the pickled type that comes in jars. Beetroot juice is a stunning, vibrant red and is surprisingly sweet, especially when mixed with carrot and orange juice.*
• *Make this drink early in the spring season when beetroot are still available and oranges are plentiful and at their best.*

Green Devil

Choose a well-flavoured avocado, such as a knobbly, dark-skinned Haas, for this slightly spicy, hot and sour smoothie. Cucumber adds a refreshing edge, while lemon and lime juice zip up the flavour, and the chilli sauce adds an irresistible fiery bite. This is one little devil that is sure to liven up even the most lethargic days.

Serves 2–3
1 small ripe avocado
½ cucumber
30ml/2 tbsp lemon juice
30ml/2 tbsp lime juice
10ml/2 tsp caster (superfine) sugar
pinch of salt
250ml/8fl oz/1 cup apple juice or mineral water
10–20ml/2–4 tsp sweet chilli sauce
ice cubes
red chilli curls, to decorate

1 Halve the avocado and use a sharp knife to remove the stone (pit). Scoop the flesh from both halves into a blender or food processor.

2 Peel and roughly chop the cucumber and add to the blender or food processor, then add the lemon and lime juice, the caster sugar and a little salt.

3 Process the ingredients until smooth and creamy, then add the apple juice or mineral water and a little of the chilli sauce. Blend once more to lightly mix the ingredients together.

4 Pour the smoothie into serving glasses over ice cubes. Decorate with red chilli curls and serve with stirrers and extra chilli sauce.

Cook's Tips
• *To make chilli curls, core and seed a fresh red chilli and cut it into very fine strips. Put the strips in a bowl of iced water and leave to stand for 20 minutes or until the strips curl. Use them to decorate this smoothie.*
• *Seductively smooth avocados are as good for you as they taste. Their fresh vitamin- and mineral-rich flesh is reputed to be fantastic for healthy hair and skin.*

Green Devil Energy 143kcal/598kJ; Protein 1.3g; Carbohydrate 13.2g, of which sugars 12.5g; Fat 9.8g, of which saturates 2.1g; Cholesterol 0mg; Calcium 19mg; Fibre 1.9g; Sodium 6mg.
Red Alert Energy 65kcal/273kJ; Protein 2.8g; Carbohydrate 13.2g, of which sugars 12.4g; Fat 0.5g, of which saturates 0.1g; Cholesterol 0mg; Calcium 75mg; Fibre 1.4g; Sodium 113mg.

Kiwi and Stem Ginger Spritzer

The delicate, refreshingly tangy flavour of kiwi fruit becomes sweeter and more intense when the flesh is juiced. Choose plump, unwrinkled fruits that give a little when gently pressed as under-ripe fruits will produce a slightly bitter taste. A single kiwi fruit contains more than the recommended daily intake of vitamin C, so this juice will boost the system.

Serves 1
2 kiwi fruit
1 piece preserved stem ginger, plus 15ml/1 tbsp syrup from the ginger jar
sparkling mineral water

1 Using a sharp knife, roughly chop the kiwi fruit and the piece of preserved stem ginger. (For a better colour, you may wish to peel the kiwi fruit before chopping, but this is not essential.)

2 Push the pieces of stem ginger and kiwi fruit through a juicer and pour the juice into a large jug (pitcher). Add the ginger syrup and stir to combine.

3 Pour the juice into a tall glass, then top up with plenty of sparkling mineral water and serve immediately.

> **Variation**
> If you prefer, you can use still mineral water for this smoothie rather than the sparkling variety, although the added fizz makes the drink more refreshing.

> **Cook's Tip**
> Kiwis are a subtropical fruit, not a tropical one, so it is best to store them in the refrigerator before using. If you want them to ripen quickly, store in a closed plastic bag with an apple, pear or banana.

Simply Strawberry

Nothing evokes a sense of wellbeing more than the scent and flavour of sweet, juicy strawberries. By late spring, local berries should be appearing in the stores so grab them while you can.

30–45ml/2–3 tbsp icing (confectioners') sugar
200g/7oz/scant 1 cup Greek (US strained plain) yogurt
60ml/4 tbsp single (light) cream

Serves 2
400g/14oz/3½ cups strawberries, plus extra to decorate

1 Hull the strawberries and place them in a blender or food processor with 30ml/2 tbsp of the icing sugar.

2 Blend to a smooth purée, scraping the mixture down from the side of the bowl with a rubber spatula, if necessary.

3 Add the yogurt and cream and blend again until smooth and frothy.

4 Check the sweetness, adding a little more sugar if you find the flavour too sharp. Pour into glasses and serve decorated with extra strawberries.

> **Cook's Tip**
> This recipe uses an abundance of fragrant strawberries so, if possible, make it when the season is right and local ones are at their most plentiful.

> **Variation**
> You can replace the strawberries with other fruits if you wish. Try using raspberries, or fresh bananas instead to make another very popular milkshake.

Kiwi Spritzer Energy 104kcal/439kJ; Protein 1.4g; Carbohydrate 24.6g, of which sugars 24.2g; Fat 0.6g, of which saturates 0g; Cholesterol 0mg; Calcium 32mg; Fibre 2.3g; Sodium 45mg.
Simply Strawberry Energy 286kcal/1195kJ; Protein 9.1g; Carbohydrate 30.4g, of which sugars 30.4g; Fat 16.2g, of which saturates 8.9g; Cholesterol 17mg; Calcium 217mg; Fibre 2.2g; Sodium 93mg.

Classic Gazpacho

A wonderful, traditional chilled soup from the kitchens of Spain – ideal for a hot summer's day.

Serves 6

900g/2lb ripe tomatoes, peeled and seeded
1 cucumber, peeled and chopped
2 red (bell) peppers, seeded and roughly chopped
2 garlic cloves, crushed
1 large onion, roughly chopped
30ml/2 tbsp white wine vinegar
120ml/4fl oz/½ cup olive oil
250g/9oz/4½ cups fresh white breadcrumbs
450ml/¾ pint/scant 2 cups iced water
salt and ground black pepper
ice cubes, to serve

For the garnish

30–45ml/2–3 tbsp olive oil
4 thick slices bread, crusts removed, and cut into cubes
2 tomatoes, peeled, seeded and finely diced
1 small green (bell) pepper, seeded and finely diced
1 small onion, very finely sliced
small bunch of fresh flat leaf parsley, chopped

1 In a large bowl, mix the tomatoes, cucumber, peppers, garlic and onion. Stir in the vinegar, oil, breadcrumbs and water until well mixed.

2 Purée the mixture in a food processor or blender until almost smooth and pour into a large bowl. If the soup is too thick, add a little cold water. Stir in salt and black pepper to taste and chill.

3 To make the garnish, heat the oil in a frying pan and add the bread cubes. Cook over medium heat for 5–6 minutes, stirring occasionally to brown evenly.

4 Drain the cubes on kitchen paper and put into a small bowl. Place the remaining garnishing ingredients into separate bowls or on to a serving plate.

5 Ladle the gazpacho into individual bowls and add ice cubes to each, then serve immediately. Pass around the bowls of garnishing ingredients with the soup so that they can be added to each diner's taste.

Chilled Pepper Soup

The secret is to serve this soup very cold, but not over-chilled.

Serves 4

1 onion, quartered
4 garlic cloves, unpeeled
2 red (bell) peppers, seeded and quartered
2 yellow (bell) peppers, seeded and quartered
30–45ml/2–3 tbsp olive oil
grated rind and juice of 1 orange
200g/7oz can chopped tomatoes
600ml/1 pint/2½ cups cold water
salt and ground black pepper
30ml/2 tbsp snipped fresh chives, to garnish (optional)

For the hot Parmesan toast

1 medium baguette
50g/2oz/¼ cup butter
175g/6oz Parmesan cheese

1 Preheat the oven to 200°C/400°F/Gas 6. Put the onion, garlic and peppers in a roasting tin. Drizzle the oil over the vegetables and mix well, then turn the pieces of pepper skin sides up. Roast for 25–30 minutes, until slightly charred. Cool slightly.

2 Squeeze the garlic flesh into a food processor or blender. Add the roasted vegetables, orange rind and juice, tomatoes and water. Process until smooth, then press through a sieve (strainer) into a bowl. Season well and chill for 30 minutes.

3 Make the Parmesan toasts when you are ready to serve the soup. Preheat the grill (broiler) to high. Tear the baguette in half lengthways, then tear or cut it across to give four large pieces. Spread the pieces of bread with butter.

4 Pare most of the Parmesan into thin slices or shavings using a swivel-bladed vegetable knife or a small paring knife, then finely grate the remainder. Arrange the sliced Parmesan on the toasts, then dredge with the grated cheese. Transfer to a large baking sheet or grill rack and toast under the grill for a few minutes, until the topping is well browned.

5 Ladle the chilled soup into large, shallow bowls and sprinkle with snipped fresh chives, if using, and plenty of freshly ground black pepper. Serve the hot Parmesan toast with the chilled soup.

Gazpacho Energy 356kcal/1494kJ; Protein 7.6g; Carbohydrate 41.9g, of which sugars 21.5g; Fat 18.8g, of which saturates 2.9g; Cholesterol 0mg; Calcium 90mg; Fibre 6.7g; Sodium 346mg.
Pepper Soup Energy 678kcal/2842kJ; Protein 28.7g; Carbohydrate 71.2g, of which sugars 17.1g; Fat 32.9g, of which saturates 16.8g; Cholesterol 70mg; Calcium 671mg; Fibre 5.9g; Sodium 1182mg.

Cold Somen Noodles

At the height of summer, cold somen noodles served immersed in ice cold water and accompanied by sauces and relishes make a refreshing and exotic meal.

Serves 4
300g/11oz dried somen or
  soba noodles

For the dipping sauce
105ml/7 tbsp mirin
2.5ml/½ tsp sea salt
105ml/7 tbsp shoyu
20g/¾oz kezuri-bushi
400ml/14fl oz/1⅔ cups water

For the relishes
2 spring onions (scallions),
  trimmed and finely chopped
2.5cm/1in fresh root ginger,
  peeled and finely grated
2 shiso or basil leaves, finely
  chopped (optional)
30ml/2 tbsp toasted sesame seeds

For the garnishes
10cm/4in cucumber
5ml/1 tsp sea salt
ice cubes or a block of ice
ice-cold water
115g/4oz cooked, peeled small
  prawns (shrimp)
orchid flowers or nasturtium
  flowers and leaves (optional)

1 To make the dipping sauce, put the mirin in a pan and bring to the boil to evaporate the alcohol. Add the salt and shoyu and shake the pan gently to mix. Add the kezuri-bushi and mix with the liquid. Add the water to the pan and bring to the boil. Cook over vigorous heat for 3 minutes without stirring. Remove from the heat and strain through a muslin (cheesecloth) bag. Leave to cool, then chill for at least an hour.

2 Prepare the cucumber garnish. If the cucumber is bigger than 4cm/1½in in diameter, cut in half and scoop out the seeds, then slice thinly. For a smaller cucumber, cut into 5cm/2in lengths, then use a vegetable peeler to remove the seeds and make a hole in the centre. Slice thinly. Sprinkle with the salt and leave in a sieve (strainer) for 20 minutes, then rinse in water and drain.

3 Bring at least 1.5 litres/2½ pints/6¼ cups water to the boil in a large pan. Meanwhile, untie the bundle of somen. Have 75ml/2½fl oz/⅓ cup cold water to hand. Somen only take 2 minutes to cook. Put the somen in the rapidly boiling water. When it foams again, pour the glass of water in. When the water boils again, the somen are ready. Drain into a colander. Rinse under cold running water, and rub the somen with your hands to remove the starch. Drain well.

4 Put some ice cubes or a block of ice in the centre of a chilled, large glass bowl, and add the somen. Gently pour on enough ice-cold water to cover the somen, then arrange cucumber slices, prawns and flowers, if using, on top.

5 Prepare all the relishes separately in small dishes or small sake cups. Divide approximately one-third of the dipping sauce among four small cups. Put the remaining sauce in a jug (pitcher) or gravy boat.

6 Serve the noodles cold with the relishes. The guests are invited to put any combination of relishes into their dipping-sauce cup. Hold the cup over the somen bowl, pick up a mouthful of somen, then dip them into the sauce and eat. Add more dipping sauce from the jug and more relishes as required.

Tomato and Peach Jus with Prawns

American-style soups, made from the clear juices extracted from vegetables or fruits and referred to as 'water' soups by chefs, provide the inspiration for this summery recipe.

Serves 6
1.3–1.6kg/3–3½lb ripe peaches,
  peeled, stoned (pitted) and cut
  into chunks
1.2kg/2½lb beefsteak tomatoes,
  peeled and cut into chunks
30ml/2 tbsp white wine vinegar

1 lemon grass stalk, crushed
  and chopped
2.5cm/1in fresh root
  ginger, grated
1 bay leaf
150ml/¼ pint/⅔ cup water
18 tiger prawns (shrimp), shelled
  with tails on and deveined
olive oil, for brushing
salt and ground black pepper
handful of fresh coriander
  (cilantro) leaves and 2 vine-
  ripened tomatoes, peeled,
  seeded and diced, to garnish

1 Purée the peaches and tomatoes in a food processor. Stir in the vinegar and seasoning. Line a large bowl with muslin (cheesecloth). Pour the purée into the bowl, gather up the ends of the muslin and tie tightly. Suspend over the bowl and leave at room temperature for 3 hours or until about 1.2 litres/2 pints/5 cups juice have drained through.

2 Meanwhile, put the lemon grass, ginger and bay leaf into a pan with the water, and simmer for 5–6 minutes. Set aside to cool. Strain the mixture into the tomato and peach juice and chill for at least 4 hours.

3 Using a sharp knife, slit the prawns down their curved sides, cutting about three-quarters of the way through and keeping their tails intact. Open them out flat.

4 Heat a griddle or frying pan and brush with a little oil. Sear the prawns for 1–2 minutes on each side, until tender and slightly charred. Pat dry on kitchen paper to remove any remaining oil. Cool, but do not chill.

5 Ladle the soup into bowls and place three prawns in each. Add some coriander leaves and diced tomato to each bowl.

Somen Noodles Energy 445kcal/1885kJ; Protein 16.3g; Carbohydrate 79.2g, of which sugars 23.7g; Fat 9.2g, of which saturates 0.7g; Cholesterol 56mg; Calcium 109mg; Fibre 2.9g; Sodium 2420mg.
Tomato and Peach Energy 188kcal/797kJ; Protein 12.7g; Carbohydrate 25.2g, of which sugars 25.2g; Fat 4.8g, of which saturates 0.8g; Cholesterol 98mg; Calcium 71mg; Fibre 5.8g; Sodium 116mg.

Creamy Aubergine Soup with Mozzarella and Gremolata

Gremolata, a classic Italian mixture of garlic, lemon and parsley, adds a flourish of fresh flavour to this rich cream soup.

Serves 6
30ml/2 tbsp olive oil
2 shallots, chopped
2 garlic cloves, chopped
1kg/2¼lb aubergines (eggplants), trimmed and roughly chopped
1 litre/1¾ pints/4 cups chicken stock
150ml/¼ pint/⅔ cup double (heavy) cream
30ml/2 tbsp chopped fresh parsley
175g/6oz buffalo mozzarella, thinly sliced
salt and ground black pepper

For the gremolata
2 garlic cloves, finely chopped
grated rind of 2 lemons
15ml/1 tbsp chopped fresh parsley

1 Heat the oil in a large pan and add the shallots and garlic. Cook for 4–5 minutes, until softened.

2 Add the aubergines to the pan and cook for about 25 minutes, stirring occasionally, until the vegetables are very soft and browned.

3 Pour in the chicken stock and cook for about 5 minutes. Leave the soup to cool slightly.

4 Purée the soup in a food processor or blender until smooth. Return to the rinsed-out pan and season. Add the cream and parsley, and bring to the boil.

5 Mix the ingredients for the gremolata. Ladle the soup into bowls and lay the mozzarella on top. Sprinkle with gremolata and serve.

Cook's Tip
There is no need these days to follow the tradition of salting aubergines to take out their bitterness.

Cream of Tomato Soup with Black Olive Ciabatta Toasts

This version of the popular soup is a revelation – fresh, but wonderfully warming and with an earthy richness hidden in its depths.

Serves 6
450g/1lb very ripe tomatoes (preferably fresh rather than canned plum tomatoes)
30ml/2 tbsp olive oil
1 onion, chopped
1 garlic clove, crushed
30ml/2 tbsp sherry vinegar
30ml/2 tbsp tomato purée (paste)
15ml/1 tbsp cornflour (cornstarch) or potato flour
300ml/½ pint/1¼ cups passata (bottled strained tomatoes)
1 bay leaf
900ml/1½ pints/3¾ cups vegetable or chicken stock
200ml/7fl oz/scant 1 cup crème fraîche
salt and ground black pepper
basil leaves, to garnish

For the black olive ciabatta toast
1 plain or black olive ciabatta
1 small red (bell) pepper
3 whole garlic cloves, skins on
225g/8oz black olives
30–45ml/2–3 tbsp salted capers or capers in vinegar
12 drained canned anchovy fillets or 1 small can tuna, drained
about 150ml/¼ pint/⅔ cup good quality olive oil
fresh lemon juice and ground black pepper, to taste
45ml/3 tbsp chopped fresh basil

1 Make the toasts first. Preheat the oven to 200°C/400°F/Gas 6. Split the bread in half and cut each half into nine fingers. Arrange on a baking sheet and bake for 10–15 minutes until golden. Place the whole pepper and cloves under a hot grill (broiler) for 15 minutes, turning, until charred all over. Put the garlic and pepper in a plastic bag, seal and leave to cool for 10 minutes.

2 Lightly rub the skin off the pepper (do not wash) and remove the stalk and seeds. Peel the skin from the garlic. Pit the olives. Rinse the capers under running water, to remove the salt. Place the prepared ingredients in a food processor with the anchovies or tuna and process until roughly chopped. With the machine running, slowly add the oil until a fairly smooth dark paste forms. Season to taste with lemon juice and pepper. Stir in the basil. Spread the paste on the finger toasts.

3 Make the soup. If using fresh tomatoes, cut them in half and remove the seeds and pulp using a lemon squeezer. Press the pulp through a sieve (strainer) and reserve. Retain the tomato halves. Heat the oil in a pan and add the onion, garlic, sherry vinegar, tomato purée and the tomato halves or canned tomatoes, if using. Stir, then cover the pan and cook over low heat for 1 hour until very soft. Stir from time to time. When done, pour the soup into a blender or food processor and process until smooth, then pass through a sieve to remove any pieces of skin. Return to the pan.

4 Mix the cornflour or potato flour with the reserved tomato pulp or 30ml/2 tbsp water until very smooth, then stir into the hot tomato soup with the passata, bay leaf and stock. Simmer for 30 minutes. Taste and adjust the seasoning. Stir in the crème fraîche and garnish with the basil leaves. Serve piping hot, with the ciabatta toasts.

Aubergine Soup Energy 261kcal/1079kJ; Protein 7.5g; Carbohydrate 4.9g, of which sugars 4.3g; Fat 23.7g, of which saturates 13.1g; Cholesterol 51mg; Calcium 137mg; Fibre 3.5g; Sodium 124mg.
Tomato Soup Energy 107kcal/447kJ; Protein 2.3g; Carbohydrate 11.4g, of which sugars 10.9g; Fat 6.1g, of which saturates 3.5g; Cholesterol 13mg; Calcium 50mg; Fibre 3.9g; Sodium 71mg.

Chunky Courgette and Tomato Soup

This brightly coloured, fresh-tasting tomato soup makes the most of summer vegetables in season. Add lots of sweet, ripe red and yellow peppers to make a sweeter version.

Serves 4
450g/1lb ripe plum tomatoes
225g/8oz ripe yellow tomatoes
45ml/3 tbsp olive oil
1 large onion, finely chopped
15ml/1 tbsp sun-dried tomato purée (paste)
225g/8oz courgettes (zucchini), trimmed and roughly chopped
225g/8oz yellow courgettes (zucchini), trimmed and roughly chopped
3 waxy new potatoes, diced
2 garlic cloves, crushed
about 1.2 litres/2 pints/5 cups vegetable stock or water
60ml/4 tbsp chopped fresh basil
50g/2oz/²/₃ cup freshly grated Parmesan cheese
salt and ground black pepper

1 Plunge all the tomatoes in boiling water for 30 seconds. Then drain, peel and chop them finely.

2 Heat the oil in a large pan, add the onion and cook gently for about 5 minutes, stirring constantly, until softened.

3 Stir in the sun-dried tomato purée, chopped tomatoes, courgettes, diced potatoes and garlic. Mix well and cook gently for 10 minutes, shaking the pan often.

4 Pour in the stock or water. Bring to the boil, lower the heat, half cover the pan and simmer for 15 minutes or until the vegetables are tender. Add more stock or water if necessary.

5 Remove the soup from the heat. Stir in the chopped basil, half the cheese and seasoning. Serve immediately, sprinkled with the remaining cheese.

> **Variation**
> Any summer squash or pumpkin can be used in this soup instead of, or with, the courgettes (zucchini).

Soup Niçoise with Seared Tuna

The summer season ingredients for the famous French salad are transformed into a simple soup by adding a hot garlic-infused stock.

Serves 4
12 bottled anchovy fillets, drained
30ml/2 tbsp milk
115g/4oz French (green) beans, halved
4 plum tomatoes, peeled, halved and seeded
16 black olives, pitted
1 litre/1³/₄ pints/4 cups good vegetable stock
3 garlic cloves, crushed
30ml/2 tbsp lemon juice
15ml/1 tbsp olive oil
4 tuna steaks, about 75g/3oz each
small bunch of spring onions (scallions), shredded lengthways
handful of fresh basil leaves, chopped
salt and ground black pepper
fresh crusty bread, to serve

1 Soak the anchovies in the milk for 10 minutes. Drain well and dry on kitchen paper. Cook the French beans in boiling salted water for 2–3 minutes. Drain, refresh under cold running water and drain. Cut the tomatoes into thin wedges. Wash the olives, then cut into quarters. Set all the prepared ingredients aside.

2 Bring the stock and garlic to the boil in a pan. Reduce the heat, simmer for 10 minutes, season and add the lemon juice.

3 Meanwhile, brush a griddle pan with the oil and heat until very hot. Season the tuna and cook for about 2 minutes each side. Do not overcook the tuna or it will become dry.

4 Gently toss the French beans, tomatoes, spring onions, anchovies, black olives and basil leaves. Put the seared tuna into four bowls and pile the vegetables on top. Ladle the stock around the ingredients. Serve immediately, with crusty bread.

> **Cook's Tip**
> Buy anchovy fillets that have been bottled in extra virgin olive oil if you can, as they have a far superior flavour.

Courgette Soup: Energy 277kcal/1157kJ; Protein 10.7g; Carbohydrate 29.3g, of which sugars 12.7g; Fat 13.7g, of which saturates 4.1g; Cholesterol 13mg; Calcium 215mg; Fibre 4.8g; Sodium 166mg.
Soup Niçoise Energy 217kcal/909kJ; Protein 27.4g; Carbohydrate 3g, of which sugars 2.7g; Fat 10.7g, of which saturates 2.2g; Cholesterol 34mg; Calcium 76mg; Fibre 2g; Sodium 829mg.

Summer Pea and Chive Soup

This quick and simple soup is light and refreshing. Using fresh garden peas that have just been shelled gives a wonderful flavour to this soup. Simply add them straight to the pan with the hot stock and herbs. Fresh peas are much loved because they are deliciously sweet and tender.

Serves 6

25g/1oz/2 tbsp butter
1 leek, sliced
1 garlic clove, crushed

450g/1lb/4 cups fresh young peas
1.2 litres/2 pints/5 cups vegetable stock
small bunch of fresh chives, coarsely chopped
300ml/½ pint/1¼ cups double (heavy) cream
90ml/6 tbsp Greek (US strained plain) yogurt
4 slices prosciutto, roughly chopped
salt and ground black pepper
fresh chives, to garnish

1 Melt the butter in a pan. Add the leek and garlic, cover and cook gently for 4–5 minutes, until softened. Stir in the fresh peas, stock and chives. Bring slowly to the boil, then simmer for 5 minutes. Cool slightly.

2 Process the soup in a food processor or blender until thick and smooth. Pour into a bowl, stir in the cream and season. Chill for at least 2 hours.

3 Ladle the soup into bowls and add a spoon of Greek yogurt to the centre of each. Sprinkle the chopped prosciutto over the top and garnish with chives before serving.

Cook's Tips

• Use kitchen scissors to trim and cut prosciutto – for best results do this straight into the soup, so that the pieces fall neatly rather than sticking together.

• For a clever garnish, cut five lengths of chives to about 6cm/2½in, then use another chive to tie them together. Lay this on top of the soup.

Chilled Cucumber and Prawn Soup

If you've never served a chilled soup before, this is the perfect one to try. Delicious, attractive and light, it's the perfect way to celebrate summer.

Serves 4

25g/1oz/2 tbsp butter
2 shallots, finely chopped
2 garlic cloves, crushed
1 cucumber, peeled, seeded and diced
300ml/½ pint/1¼ cups milk

225g/8oz/2 cups cooked peeled prawns (shrimp)
15ml/1 tbsp each finely chopped fresh mint, dill, chives and chervil
300ml/½ pint/1¼ cups whipping cream
salt and ground white pepper

For the garnish

30ml/2 tbsp crème fraîche (optional)
4 large, cooked prawns (shrimp), peeled with tail intact
fresh dill and chives

1 Melt the butter in a pan and cook the shallots and garlic over a low heat until soft but not coloured. Add the cucumber and cook gently, stirring frequently, until tender.

2 Stir in the milk, bring almost to boiling point, then lower the heat and simmer for 5 minutes. Transfer the soup into a blender or food processor and process until very smooth. Season the soup to taste with salt and ground white pepper.

3 Pour the soup into a large bowl and leave to cool. When cool, stir in the prawns, chopped herbs and cream. Cover, transfer to the refrigerator and chill for at least 2 hours.

4 To serve, ladle the soup into individual bowls, top each portion with a spoonful of crème fraîche, if using, and place a prawn over the edge of each dish. Sprinkle a little extra dill over each bowl and tuck two or three chives under the prawns on the edge of the bowls to garnish. Serve immediately.

Cook's Tip

If you prefer hot soup, reheat it gently until hot but not boiling. Do not boil, or the delicate flavour will be spoilt.

Summer Pea Soup Energy 386kcal/1610kJ; Protein 20.6g; Carbohydrate 32.8g, of which sugars 4.5g; Fat 20.1g, of which saturates 6.9g; Cholesterol 53mg; Calcium 47mg; Fibre 5.3g; Sodium 682mg.
Cucumber Soup Energy 439kcal/1817kJ; Protein 18.9g; Carbohydrate 7.5g, of which sugars 7.1g; Fat 37.2g, of which saturates 23.1g; Cholesterol 255mg; Calcium 212mg; Fibre 0.5g; Sodium 245mg.

Yogurt Soup with Chilli Salsa

The refreshing flavours of cucumber and yogurt in this soup fuse with the cool salsa and the smoky flavour of the charred salmon topping to bring a taste of summer to the table.

Serves 4
3 medium cucumbers
300ml/½ pint/1¼ cups Greek (US strained plain) yogurt
250ml/8fl oz/1 cup vegetable stock, chilled
120ml/4fl oz/½ cup crème fraîche
15ml/1 tbsp chopped fresh chervil
15ml/1 tbsp chopped fresh chives
15ml/1 tbsp chopped fresh flat leaf parsley
1 small red chilli, seeded and very finely chopped
a little oil, for brushing
225g/8oz salmon fillet, skinned and cut into eight thin slices
salt and ground black pepper
fresh chervil or chives, to garnish

1 Peel two of the cucumbers and halve them lengthways. Scoop out and discard the seeds, then roughly chop the flesh. Purée in a food processor or blender, then add the yogurt, stock, crème fraîche, chervil, chives and seasoning, and process until smooth. Chill.

2 Peel, halve and seed the remaining cucumber. Cut the flesh into small neat dice. Mix with the chopped parsley and chilli. Chill until required.

3 Brush a griddle or frying pan with oil and heat until very hot. Sear the salmon slices for 1–2 minutes on each side, until tender and charred.

4 Ladle the chilled soup into soup bowls. Top with two slices of the salmon, then pile a portion of salsa into the centre of each. Garnish with the chervil or chives and serve.

Variation
• Fresh tuna can be used instead of salmon.
• For a vegetarian alternative, make this soup with brown halved cherry tomatoes and diced halloumi cheese.

Vichyssoise

This classic, chilled potato soup was first created in the 1920s by Louis Diat, chef at the New York Ritz-Carlton. He named it after Vichy, near his home in France.

Serves 4–6
50g/2oz/¼ cup unsalted butter
450g/1lb leeks, white parts only, thinly sliced
3 large shallots, sliced
250g/9oz floury potatoes (such as King Edward or Maris Piper), peeled and cut into chunks
1 litre/1¾ pints/4 cups light chicken stock or water
300ml/½ pint/1¼ cups double (heavy) cream
iced water (optional)
a little lemon juice (optional)
salt and ground black pepper
chopped fresh chives, to garnish

1 Melt the butter in a heavy pan and cook the leeks and shallots gently, covered, for about 15–20 minutes, until soft but not browned.

2 Add the potatoes and cook, uncovered, for a few minutes. Stir in the stock or water with 5ml/1 tsp salt and pepper to taste. Bring to the boil, then reduce the heat and partly cover the pan. Simmer for 15 minutes, or until the potatoes are soft.

3 Cool, then process the mixture until smooth in a blender or food processor. Strain the soup into a bowl and stir in the cream. Taste and adjust the seasoning and add a little iced water if the consistency of the soup seems too thick.

4 Chill the soup for at least 4 hours or until very cold. Before serving taste the chilled soup for seasoning and add a squeeze of lemon juice, if required. Pour the soup into bowls and sprinkle with chopped chives. Serve immediately.

Variations
• Add about 50g/2oz/1 cup shredded sorrel to the soup at the end of cooking. Finish and chill as in the main recipe, then serve the soup garnished with a little pile of finely shredded sorrel.
• The same amount of watercress can be used in the same way.

Vichyssoise Energy 547Kcal/2260kJ; Protein 4.6g; Carbohydrate 17.7g, of which sugars 6.8g; Fat 51.4g, of which saturates 31.7g; Cholesterol 129mg; Calcium 79mg; Fibre 3.6g; Sodium 103mg.
Yogurt Soup Energy 226Kcal/942kJ; Protein 15.8g; Carbohydrate 9.1g, of which sugars 5.9g; Fat 14.4g, of which saturates 2.3g; Cholesterol 29mg; Calcium 177mg; Fibre 0.6g; Sodium 91mg.

Classic Tomato Salsa

A classic Mexican salsa, full of fiery summer flavour. Use three chillies for a mild taste; six if you like it hot.

Serves 6
3–6 fresh serrano chillies
1 large white onion, finely chopped
grated rind and juice of 2 limes, plus pared lime rind, to garnish
8 ripe, firm tomatoes
large bunch of fresh coriander (cilantro), chopped finely
1.5ml/¼ tsp caster (superfine) sugar
salt

1 To peel the chillies, spear them on a long-handled metal skewer and roast them over the flame of a gas burner until the skins blister and darken. Do not let the flesh burn. Alternatively, dry-fry them in a griddle pan until the skins are scorched.

2 Place the roasted chillies in a strong plastic bag and tie the top of the bag. Set aside for about 20 minutes. Meanwhile, put the onion in a bowl with the lime rind and juice. The lime juice will soften the onion.

3 Remove the chillies from the bag and peel off the skins. Cut off the stalks, then slit the chillies and scrape out the seeds. Chop the flesh roughly and set aside.

4 Make a cut in the top of the tomatoes, then plunge into boiling water for 30 seconds. Refresh in cold water. Remove the skins completely. Dice the tomato flesh and put in a bowl.

5 Add the softened onion and lime juice mixture to the tomatoes, together with the coriander, chillies and the sugar. Mix gently until the sugar has dissolved. Cover and chill for 2–3 hours to allow the flavours to blend. Garnish with lime and serve immediately.

> **Variations**
> • Use spring onions (scallions) instead of white onion.
> • For a smoky flavour use chipotle instead of serrano chillies.

Mixed Melon and Orange Salsa

A combination of two very different melons gives this salsa an exciting flavour and texture. It is ideal for a hot summer's day in the garden. Try it with some thinly sliced Parma ham or smoked salmon.

Serves 10
1 small orange-fleshed melon, such as Charentais
1 large wedge watermelon
2 oranges
Parma ham or smoked salmon, to serve

1 Quarter the orange-fleshed melon and scoop out all the seeds. Use a large, sharp knife to cut off the skin. Dice the melon flesh.

2 Pick out the seeds from the watermelon, then remove the skin. Dice the flesh into small chunks.

3 Use a zester to pare long strips of rind from both oranges. Halve the oranges and squeeze out all their juice, using a hand juicer if you have one.

4 Mix both types of melon and the orange rind and juice together in a large bowl. Chill in the refrigerator for about 30 minutes and serve.

> **Cook's Tips**
> • When buying melons, avoid any with soft spots, lacerations or other blemishes on the skin.
> • Store whole melons in the refrigerator if possible and use within a week. If the melon is too large for your refrigerator, keep it in a cool, dark place.
> • Wrap cut pieces of melon, refrigerate and use within a day or so.

> **Variation**
> Other melons can be used for this salsa. Try cantaloupe, Galia or Ogen.

Mixed Melon Salsa Energy 58kcal/250kJ; Protein 1.1g; Carbohydrate 13.5g, of which sugars 13.5g; Fat 0.4g, of which saturates 0.1g; Cholesterol 0mg; Calcium 30mg; Fibre 0.9g; Sodium 25mg.
Classic Tomato Salsa Energy 45kcal/190kJ; Protein 2.2g; Carbohydrate 8.2g, of which sugars 7g; Fat 0.7g, of which saturates 0.1g; Cholesterol 0mg; Calcium 43mg; Fibre 2.3g; Sodium 16mg.

Creamy Aubergine Dip

Spread this velvet-textured dip thickly on to toasted bread, then top them with slivers of sun-dried tomato to make wonderful, Italian-style crostini.

Serves 4
1 large aubergine (eggplant)
30ml/2 tbsp olive oil

1 small onion, finely chopped
2 garlic cloves, finely chopped
60ml/4 tbsp chopped fresh
  parsley, plus extra to garnish
75ml/5 tbsp crème fraîche
red Tabasco sauce, to taste
juice of 1 lemon, to taste
salt and ground black pepper
sun-dried tomato, to garnish
toasted bread, to serve

1 Preheat the grill (broiler) to medium. Place the whole aubergine on a non-stick baking sheet and grill (broil) it for 20–30 minutes under medium-high heat, turning occasionally, until the skin is blackened and wrinkled, and the aubergine feels soft when squeezed.

2 Cover the aubergine with a clean dish towel and leave it to cool for about 5 minutes.

3 Heat the olive oil in a frying pan. Add the onion and garlic, and cook for about 5–7 minutes, stirring frequently, until it is softened but not browned.

4 Peel the skin from the cooled aubergine and discard. Mash the flesh in a mixing bowl with a large fork or potato masher until it becomes a pulpy purée.

5 Stir in the onion and garlic, parsley and crème fraîche. Add Tabasco, lemon juice, and salt and pepper to taste.

6 Transfer the dip to a serving bowl and serve warm or leave to cool and serve at room temperature.

> **Cook's Tip**
> *The aubergine (eggplant) can be roasted in the oven at 200°C/400°F/Gas 6 for about 20 minutes, or until tender.*

Sour Cream Cooler

This cooling dip makes the perfect accompaniment to spicy dishes. Alternatively, serve it at a summer picnic with the fieriest tortilla chips you can find.

150ml/¼ pint/⅔ cup sour cream
30ml/2 tbsp chopped fresh
  parsley, plus extra to garnish
salt and ground black pepper
grated lemon rind, to garnish

Serves 2
1 small yellow (bell) pepper
2 small tomatoes

1 Cut the pepper in half lengthways. With a sharp knife, remove the core and scoop out the seeds, then cut the flesh into tiny dice.

2 Cut the tomatoes in half, then use a teaspoon to scoop out and discard the seeds. Cut the tomato flesh into tiny dice.

3 Place the sour cream into a mixing bowl. Stir the pepper and tomato dice and the chopped fresh parsley into the sour cream. Mix well until the all the ingredients are combined.

4 Spoon the dip into a serving bowl and chill. Garnish with grated lemon rind and more chopped parsley before serving.

> **Cook's Tip**
> *If you prefer, you can peel the tomatoes first. Cut a cross into the bottom of each and place them in a bowl of very hot water for 2 minutes. Remove from the bowl and, when cool enough to handle, peel them from where the skin is coming away at the crosses.*

> **Variation**
> *Use finely diced avocado or cucumber in place of the pepper or tomato, if you like.*

Creamy Aubergine Dip Energy 137kcal/566kJ; Protein 1.4g; Carbohydrate 3.1g, of which sugars 2.5g; Fat 13.4g, of which saturates 5.9g; Cholesterol 21mg; Calcium 42mg; Fibre 1.8g; Sodium 9mg.
Sour Cream Cooler Energy 204kcal/845kJ; Protein 4.2g; Carbohydrate 12g, of which sugars 11.7g; Fat 15.8g, of which saturates 9.6g; Cholesterol 45mg; Calcium 114mg; Fibre 3.2g; Sodium 48mg.

Kefalotyri Cubes Spiked with Bay Leaves

These are delicious with a really cold resinous wine, plenty of excellent olives, fruity olive oil and rustic bread for dipping. They take only minutes to cook and make the perfect pre-dinner snack for a crowd. The lemon and bay leaves are the ideal complement to the hard, salty cheese.

Serves 6

18 large bay leaves or mixed bay and lemon leaves
275g/10oz Kefalotyri or Kasseri cheese, cut into 18 cubes
20ml/4 tsp extra virgin olive oil
ground black pepper
18 short wooden skewers

1 Soak the wooden skewers in cold water for 30 minutes. Add the bay and/or lemon leaves to the water to prevent them from burning when cooked in the griddle.

2 Put the cheese cubes in a dish large enough to hold the skewers. Pour over the olive oil. Sprinkle over a little black pepper and toss.

3 Drain the skewers, then thread them with the cheese and drained bay leaves and/or lemon leaves. Put the skewers of cheese back in the oil.

4 Heat a griddle until a few drops of water sprinkled on to the surface evaporate instantly. Lower the heat a little and place the skewers on the griddle, evenly spacing them.

5 Cook the cheese skewers for about 5 seconds on each side. The pieces of cheese should have golden brown lines, and should just be starting to melt. Serve immediately.

> **Cook's Tip**
> *Kefalotyri is a hard, salty cheese made from sheep's milk and/or goat's milk.*

Summer Green Beans in a Light Batter

Summer is the best time for tasty, fresh French green beans. Here they are coated in a light tempura batter, before being deep-fried. They make great finger food at a drinks party or barbecue.

100g/3¾oz/scant 1 cup plain (all-purpose) flour
1 egg
vegetable oil, for deep-frying
salt

Serves 4
400g/14oz French green beans

1 Trim the beans and blanch them in a large pan of boiling water for about 1 minute. Drain and refresh in iced water, then drain again well.

2 Sift the flour into a bowl and stir in enough cold water to make a medium paste. Add the egg and beat well, then season with salt.

3 Heat the vegetable oil in a large pan or deep-fryer to 170°C/340°F or until a cube of day-old bread browns in 40 seconds.

4 Dip the beans in the batter, ensuring they are evenly coated in the mixture. Carefully add the beans to the hot oil and deep-fry until crisp and golden brown. Cook the beans in batches if necessary, rather than over-crowding the pan.

5 Drain the beans thoroughly on a sheet of kitchen paper and serve immediately.

> **Variation**
> *You can prepare other vegetables in the same way, if you prefer. Try mushrooms, red (bell) pepper strips or carrots cut into thin batons.*

Kefalotyri Cubes Energy 213kcal/880kJ; Protein 11.8g; Carbohydrate 0g, of which sugars 0g; Fat 18.4g, of which saturates 10.6g; Cholesterol 48mg; Calcium 316mg; Fibre 0g; Sodium 307mg.
Summer Green Beans Energy 227Kcal/945kJ; Protein 5.8g; Carbohydrate 22.6g, of which sugars 2.7g; Fat 13.2g, of which saturates 1.8g; Cholesterol 48mg; Calcium 78mg; Fibre 3g; Sodium 18mg.

Courgette Tempura

This is a twist on the classic Japanese tempura, using gram flour in the batter. Also known as besan, gram flour is more commonly used in Indian cuisine and gives a wonderfully crisp texture to the tender courgettes, which are plentiful in the summer months.

Serves 4

600g/1lb 5oz courgettes
   (zucchini)
90g/3½oz/¾ cup gram flour
5ml/1 tsp baking powder
2.5ml/½ tsp turmeric
10ml/2 tsp ground coriander
5ml/1 tsp ground cumin
5ml/1 tsp chilli powder
250ml/8fl oz/1 cup beer
sunflower oil, for frying
salt
steamed basmati rice, natural
   (plain) yogurt and pickles,
   to serve

1 Cut the courgettes into thick, finger-sized batons and set aside. Sift the gram flour, baking powder, turmeric, ground coriander, cumin and chilli powder into a large bowl.

2 Season the mixture with salt and gradually add the beer, mixing to make a thick batter – do not overmix.

3 Fill a large wok one-third full with sunflower oil and heat to 180°C/350°F (or until a cube of bread, dropped into the oil, browns in 15 seconds).

4 Working in batches, dip the courgette batons in the spiced batter and then deep-fry for 1–2 minutes, or until crisp and golden. Lift out of the wok using a slotted spoon and drain on kitchen paper.

5 Serve the courgettes immediately with steamed basmati rice, yogurt, pickles and chutney.

> **Variation**
> You can cook all kinds of vegetables in this way. Try using onion rings, aubergine (eggplant) slices, or even whole mild chillies.

Crispy Seven-spice Aubergines

Seven-spice powder is the key ingredient that gives these aubergines a lovely warm flavour, perfect for a summer garden party – or enjoy them cold on a picnic.

Serves 4

2 egg whites
90ml/6 tbsp cornflour
   (cornstarch)
5ml/1 tsp salt
15ml/1 tbsp Thai or Chinese
   seven-spice powder
15ml/1 tbsp mild chilli powder
500g/1¼lb aubergines
   (eggplants), thinly sliced
sunflower oil, for deep-frying
fresh mint leaves, to garnish
steamed rice or noodles and hot
   chilli sauce, to serve

1 Put the egg whites in a large grease-free bowl and beat them with an electric whisk until light and foamy, but not dry.

2 In a separate bowl, combine the cornflour, salt, seven-spice powder and chilli powder. Spread this spice mixture evenly on to a large plate.

3 Fill a wok one-third full of oil and heat to 180°C/350°F or until a cube of day-old bread, dropped into the oil, browns in about 40 seconds.

4 Dip the aubergine slices in the egg white and then into the spiced flour mixture to coat. Deep-fry, in batches, for 3–4 minutes, or until crisp and golden.

5 Drain the slices on kitchen paper and transfer to a platter to keep hot, while you cook the remaining slices.

6 Serve the aubergines garnished with mint leaves and with hot chilli sauce on the side for dipping.

> **Cook's Tip**
> Seven-spice powder is a commercial blend of spices, usually comprising coriander, cumin, cinnamon, star anise, chilli, cloves and lemon peel.

Courgette Tempura Energy 241Kcal/999kJ; Protein 7.3g; Carbohydrate 15.3g, of which sugars 4.6g; Fat 15.6g, of which saturates 1.9g; Cholesterol 0mg; Calcium 83mg; Fibre 3.8g; Sodium 15mg.
Crispy Seven-spice Aubergines Energy 203Kcal/850kJ; Protein 2.7g; Carbohydrate 23.5g, of which sugars 2.5g; Fat 11.7g, of which saturates 1.4g; Cholesterol 0mg; Calcium 17mg; Fibre 2.5g; Sodium 45mg.

Tapenade and Quail's Eggs

Tapenade is a purée made from capers, olives and anchovies. It is popularly used in Mediterranean cooking. It complements the taste of eggs perfectly, especially quail's eggs, which look very pretty on open sandwiches.

45ml/3 tbsp tapenade
curly endive leaves
3 small tomatoes, sliced
black olives
4 canned anchovy fillets, drained
    and halved lengthways
parsley sprigs, to garnish

Serves 8
8 quail's eggs
1 small baguette

1 Boil the quail's eggs for 3 minutes, then plunge them straight into cold water to cool. Crack the shells gently and remove them very carefully.

2 Cut the baguette into slices on the diagonal and spread each one with some of the tapenade.

3 Arrange a little curly endive, torn to fit, and the tomato slices on top of the tapenade.

4 Halve the quail's eggs and place them on top of the tomato slices. Finish with a little more tapenade, the olives and finally the anchovies. Garnish with small parsley sprigs.

Cook's Tip
To make 300ml/½ pint/1¼ cups of tuna tapenade, put a 90g/3½oz canned drained tuna in a food processor with 25g/1oz/2 tbsp capers, 10 canned anchovy fillets and 75g/3oz/¾ cup pitted black olives and blend until smooth, scraping down the sides as necessary. Gradually add 60ml/ 4 tbsp olive oil through the feeder tube. This purée can be used for filling hard-boiled eggs. Blend the tapenade with the egg yolks then pile into the whites.

Griddled Tomatoes on Soda Bread

Nothing could be simpler than this summer brunch dish, transformed into something special by adding a drizzle of olive oil, balsamic vinegar and shavings of Parmesan cheese to griddled tomatoes and serving them on toast.

Serves 4
olive oil, for brushing and drizzling
6 tomatoes, thickly sliced
4 thick slices soda bread
balsamic vinegar, for drizzling
salt and ground black pepper
shavings of Parmesan cheese,
    to serve

1 Brush a griddle pan with olive oil and heat over high heat. Add the tomato slices and cook for about 4–6 minutes, turning once, until softened and slightly blackened on both sides. Alternatively, heat a grill (broiler) to high and line the rack with foil. Grill (broil) the tomato slices for about 4–6 minutes, turning once, until softened.

2 While the tomatoes are cooking, lightly toast the soda bread. Place the tomatoes on top of the toast and drizzle each portion with a little olive oil and vinegar. Season to taste and serve immediately with thin shavings of Parmesan.

Variation
A dish like this one tastes perfect on its own, but if you prefer something more substantial, add slices of bacon, grilled (broiled) until crisp, or some herby sausage. When cooking the sausage, don't prick it first, as this allows juices to flow out and tends to make the sausage dry. If you grill (broil) the sausage under low to medium heat, and turn it often, it will be unlikely to burst.

Cook's Tip
Using a griddle pan reduces the amount of oil required for cooking the tomatoes and gives them a barbecued flavour. The ridges on the pan brand the tomatoes, which gives them an attractive appearance.

Tapenade and Eggs Energy 157kcal/666kJ; Protein 6.3g; Carbohydrate 28.4g, of which sugars 1.8g; Fat 2.8g, of which saturates 0.6g; Cholesterol 37mg; Calcium 76mg; Fibre 1.5g; Sodium 523mg.
Griddled Tomatoes Energy 178kcal/751kJ; Protein 4.2g; Carbohydrate 26.3g, of which sugars 6.9g; Fat 7g, of which saturates 1g; Cholesterol 0mg; Calcium 66mg; Fibre 2.7g; Sodium 175mg.

Courgette Fritters with Chilli Jam

Chilli jam is hot, sweet and sticky – rather like a thick chutney. It adds a delicious piquancy to these light courgette fritters which are always a popular summertime snack.

Makes 12

450g/1lb/3½ cups coarsely grated courgettes (zucchini)
50g/2oz/⅔ cup freshly grated Parmesan cheese

2 eggs, beaten
60ml/4 tbsp plain (all-purpose) flour
vegetable oil, for frying
salt and ground black pepper

For the chilli jam
75ml/5 tbsp olive oil
4 large onions, diced
4 garlic cloves, chopped
1–2 green chillies, seeded and sliced
30ml/2 tbsp soft dark brown sugar

1 First make the chilli jam. Heat the oil in a frying pan until hot, then add the onions and the garlic. Cook for 20 minutes, stirring frequently, until the onions are very soft.

2 Leave the onion mixture to cool, then transfer to a food processor or blender. Add the chillies and sugar and blend until smooth, then return the mixture to the pan. Cook for a further 10 minutes, stirring frequently, until the liquid evaporates and the mixture has the consistency of jam. Cool slightly.

3 To make the fritters, squeeze the courgettes in a dish towel to remove any excess liquid, then combine with the Parmesan, eggs, flour and salt and pepper.

4 Heat enough oil to cover the base of a large frying pan. Add 30ml/2 tbsp of the mixture for each fritter and cook three fritters at a time. Cook for 2–3 minutes on each side until golden, then keep warm while you cook the rest. Drain on kitchen paper and serve warm with a spoonful of the chilli jam.

> **Cook's Tip**
> Stored in an airtight jar in the refrigerator, the chilli jam will keep for up to 1 week.

Tomato and Courgette Timbales

Timbales are baked savoury custards, mainly made with light vegetables. This combination is delicious as a summery appetizer. It can be served warm or cool. Try other combinations if you like and choose different herbs as well.

Serves 4
a little butter
2 courgettes (zucchini), about 175g/6oz

2 firm, ripe vine tomatoes, sliced
2 eggs plus 2 egg yolks
45ml/3 tbsp double (heavy) cream
15ml/1 tbsp fresh tomato sauce or passata (bottled strained tomatoes)
10ml/2 tsp chopped fresh basil or oregano or 5ml/1 tsp dried
salt and ground black pepper
salad leaves, to serve

1 Preheat the oven to 180°C/350°F/Gas 4. Lightly butter four large ramekins. Top and tail the courgettes, then cut them into thin slices.

2 Place the courgette slices into a steamer and steam over a pan of boiling water for 4–5 minutes. Drain well in a colander, then layer the courgettes in the ramekins, alternating with the sliced tomatoes.

3 In a large mixing bowl, whisk together the eggs, cream, tomato sauce or passata, herbs and seasoning. Pour the egg mixture into the ramekins.

4 Place the ramekins in a roasting pan and half fill with hot water. Bake for 20–30 minutes until the custard is just firm.

5 Cool slightly, then run a knife round the rims and carefully turn out on to small plates. Serve with salad leaves.

> **Cook's Tip**
> Don't overcook the timbales or the texture of the savoury custard will become rubbery.

Courgette Fritters Energy 157kcal/652kJ; Protein 4.4g; Carbohydrate 11.1g, of which sugars 6.1g; Fat 10.8g, of which saturates 2.2g; Cholesterol 36mg; Calcium 85mg; Fibre 1.2g; Sodium 59mg.
Tomato Timbales Energy 72kcal/299kJ; Protein 5.1g; Carbohydrate 2.7g, of which sugars 2.5g; Fat 4.7g, of which saturates 1.3g; Cholesterol 146mg; Calcium 35mg; Fibre 1g; Sodium 55mg.

Roast Pepper Terrine

This terrine is perfect for a summertime dinner party because it tastes better if made ahead. Prepare the salsa on the day of serving.

Serves 8

8 whole (bell) peppers, red, yellow and orange
675g/1½lb mascarpone cheese
3 eggs, separated
30ml/2 tbsp each chopped flat leaf parsley and basil
2 large garlic cloves, chopped
2 red, yellow or orange (bell) peppers, seeded and chopped
30ml/2 tbsp extra virgin olive oil
10ml/2 tsp balsamic vinegar
a few basil sprigs
salt and ground black pepper

1 Place the whole peppers under a hot grill (broiler) for about 8–10 minutes, turning frequently. Then put into a plastic bag until cold before skinning and seeding them. Chop seven of the peppers lengthways into thin strips.

2 Put the cheese in a bowl with the egg yolks, herbs and half the garlic. Season and beat well. In a separate bowl, whisk the egg whites to a soft peak, then fold into the cheese mixture.

3 Preheat the oven to 180°C/350°F/Gas 4. Line the base of a lightly oiled 900g/2lb loaf tin (pan). Put one-third of the cheese mixture in the tin and spread level. Arrange half the pepper strips on top in an even layer. Repeat until all the cheese and peppers are used, ending with a layer of the cheese mixture.

4 Cover the tin with foil and place in a roasting pan. Pour in boiling water to come halfway up the sides of the pan. Bake for 1 hour. Cool in the pan, then lift out and chill overnight.

5 A few hours before serving, make the salsa. Place the remaining skinned pepper and fresh peppers in a food processor. Add the remaining garlic, oil and vinegar. Set aside a few basil leaves for garnishing and add the rest to the processor. Process until finely chopped. Place the mixture into a bowl, season to taste and mix well. Cover and chill until ready to serve.

6 Turn out the terrine, peel off the lining and slice thickly. Garnish with the basil leaves and serve with the pepper salsa.

Grilled Vegetable Terrine

This colourful, layered terrine uses vegetables that are associated with long, balmy summer evenings.

Serves 6

2 large red (bell) peppers, quartered, cored and seeded
2 large yellow (bell) peppers, quartered, cored and seeded
1 large aubergine (eggplant), sliced lengthways
2 large courgettes (zucchini), sliced lengthways
90ml/6 tbsp olive oil
1 large red onion, thinly sliced
75g/3oz/½ cup raisins
15ml/1 tbsp tomato purée (paste)
15ml/1 tbsp red wine vinegar
400ml/14fl oz tomato juice
15g/½oz/2 tbsp powdered gelatine
fresh basil leaves, to garnish

For the dressing

90ml/6 tbsp extra virgin olive oil
30ml/2 tbsp red wine vinegar
salt and ground black pepper

1 Place the peppers skin side up under a hot grill (broiler) until the skins are blackened. Place in a bowl, cover and leave to cool.

2 Arrange the aubergine and courgettes on baking sheets. Brush with oil and grill (broil) until they are tender and golden.

3 Heat the remaining oil in a pan and cook the onion, raisins, tomato purée and vinegar until soft and syrupy. Leave to cool.

4 Pour half the tomato juice into a pan and sprinkle with the gelatine. Dissolve gently, stirring to prevent lumps forming.

5 Line a 1.75 litre/3 pint/7½ cup terrine with clear film (plastic wrap), leaving a little hanging over the sides of the container. Place a layer of red peppers in the base of the terrine, and pour in enough of the tomato juice with gelatine to cover.

6 Continue layering, pouring tomato juice over each layer. Finish with red peppers. Add the remaining tomato juice to the pan and pour into the terrine. Cover and chill until set.

7 Whisk the dressing ingredients and season. Turn out the terrine and remove the clear film. Serve in thick slices, drizzled with dressing and garnished with basil leaves.

Pepper Terrine Energy 276kcal/1145kJ; Protein 12.5g; Carbohydrate 16.8g, of which sugars 16.1g; Fat 18g, of which saturates 8.9g; Cholesterol 107mg; Calcium 41mg; Fibre 3.8g; Sodium 37mg.
Vegetable Terrine Energy 296kcal/1229kJ; Protein 3.5g; Carbohydrate 20.2g, of which sugars 19.7g; Fat 22.9g, of which saturates 3.4g; Cholesterol 0mg; Calcium 42mg; Fibre 3.8g; Sodium 169mg.

Butterfly Prawn Skewers with Chilli and Raspberry Dip

Filo Cigars Stuffed with Creamy Prawns

These tasty snacks feature spring onions, which are available throughout the summer months.

Makes about 24
175g/6oz filo pastry sheets
40g/1½oz/3 tbsp butter, melted
sunflower oil, for frying
1 spring onion (scallion) and fresh
    coriander (cilantro) leaves,
    to garnish
ground cinnamon and icing
    (confectioners') sugar,
    to serve

For the prawn (shrimp) filling
15ml/1 tbsp olive oil
15g/½oz/1 tbsp butter
2–3 spring onions (scallions),
    finely chopped
15g/½oz/2 tbsp plain
    (all-purpose) flour
300ml/½ pint/1¼ cups milk
2.5ml/½ tsp paprika
350g/12oz cooked peeled prawns
    (shrimp), chopped
salt and white pepper

1 First make the filling. Heat the olive oil and butter in a pan and fry the spring onions over very gentle heat for 2–3 minutes until soft.

2 Stir in the flour, and then gradually add the milk. Heat gently, stirring constantly, until the sauce is thickened and smooth. Simmer gently for 2–3 minutes, stirring. Season the sauce with paprika, salt and pepper and stir in the prawns.

3 Halve a sheet of filo pastry widthways, to make a rectangle about 18 × 14cm/7 × 5½in. Cover the remaining pastry with clear film (plastic wrap) to prevent it drying out. Brush the pastry with melted butter and then place a heaped teaspoon of filling at one end. Roll up like a cigar, tucking in the sides as you go. Continue this way until you have used the pastry and filling.

4 Heat about 1cm/½in oil in a heavy pan and fry the cigars, in batches if necessary, for 2–3 minutes until golden, turning occasionally. Drain on kitchen paper, arrange on a serving plate and then serve garnished with spring onion and coriander leaves, and sprinkled with cinnamon and icing sugar, if liked.

The success of this dish stems from the quality of the prawns, so it is worth getting really good ones, such as Mediterranean prawns. A fruity, slightly spicy dip is such an easy but fabulous accompaniment.

Serves 6
30 raw Mediterranean prawns
    (jumbo shrimp), peeled, with
    heads removed but tails left on

15ml/1 tbsp sunflower oil
sea salt
30 wooden skewers

For the chilli and raspberry dip
30ml/2 tbsp raspberry vinegar
15ml/1 tbsp sugar
115g/4oz/⅔ cup raspberries
1 large fresh red chilli, seeded and
    finely chopped

1 Prepare the barbecue. Soak the skewers in cold water for 30 minutes. Make the dip by mixing the vinegar and sugar in a small pan. Heat gently until the sugar has dissolved, then add the raspberries.

2 When the raspberry juices start to flow, tip the mixture into a sieve (strainer) set over a bowl. Push the raspberries through the sieve using the back of a ladle. Discard the seeds. Stir the chilli into the raspberry purée. When the dip is cool, cover and place in a cool place until needed.

3 Butterfly each prawn by making an incision down the curved back, just as you would when deveining. Use a piece of kitchen paper to wipe away the dark spinal vein.

4 Mix the oil with a little sea salt in a bowl. Add the prawns and toss to coat, then thread them on to the drained skewers, spearing them head first. Once the flames have died down, position a lightly oiled grill rack over the coals to heat.

5 When the coals are hot, or with a light coating of ash, grill the prawns for about 5 minutes, depending on size, turning them over once. Serve hot, with the dip.

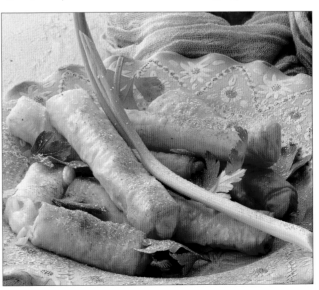

Butterfly Prawn Skewers Energy 82kcal/345kJ; Protein 12g; Carbohydrate 3.5g, of which sugars 3.5g; Fat 2.3g, of which saturates 0.3g; Cholesterol 130mg; Calcium 59mg; Fibre 0.5g; Sodium 127mg.
Filo Cigars Energy 77kcal/320kJ; Protein 4.3g; Carbohydrate 5.5g, of which sugars 0.7g; Fat 4.3g, of which saturates 1.6g; Cholesterol 17mg; Calcium 47mg; Fibre 0.2g; Sodium 251mg.

Salt and Pepper Prawns

These succulent and piquant shellfish beg to be eaten with the fingers, so provide finger bowls or hot cloths for your guests.

Serves 3–4
15–18 large raw prawns (shrimp), in the shell, about 450g/1lb
vegetable oil, for deep-frying
3 shallots or 1 small onion, very finely chopped
2 garlic cloves, crushed
1cm/½in piece fresh root ginger, peeled and very finely grated
1–2 fresh red chillies, seeded and finely sliced
2.5ml/½ tsp sugar, or to taste
3–4 spring onions (scallions), shredded, to garnish

For the fried salt
10ml/2 tsp salt
5ml/1 tsp Sichuan peppercorns

1 Make the fried salt by dry-frying the ingredients in a heavy frying pan over medium heat until the peppercorns begin to release their aroma. Set aside the pan to cool the mixture, then transfer into a mortar and crush with a pestle.

2 Carefully remove the heads and legs from the raw prawns and discard. Leave the body shells and the tails in place. Pat the prepared prawns dry with sheets of kitchen paper.

3 Heat the oil in a karahi, wok or deep-fryer to a temperature of 190°C/375°F, or until a cube of bread dropped in the oil browns in about 45 seconds. Fry the prawns for 1 minute, then lift them out and drain thoroughly on kitchen paper.

4 Spoon about 30ml/2 tbsp of the hot oil from the deep-frying pan into a large frying pan, leaving the rest of the oil to one side to cool.

5 Heat the oil in the frying pan. Add the fried salt, with the shallots or onion, garlic, ginger, chillies and sugar. Toss the mixture together for 1 minute.

6 Add the prawns to the frying pan and toss them over the heat for 1 minute more until they are coated and the shells are impregnated with the seasonings. Serve immediately, garnished with the spring onions.

Tomatoes Stuffed with Grey Shrimp

This elegant dish is served in summer, when tomatoes are abundant and at their peak. It also features top-quality grey shrimp, which fishermen have for centuries caught and cooked at sea. Serve this as a first course to whet the appetite or as a satisfying lunch with crispy fries. An ice-cold ale will balance the saltiness of the shrimp.

Serves 4
4 medium unblemished tomatoes
grated rind of 1 organic lemon
15ml/1 tbsp chopped fresh parsley or chopped chives
60ml/4 tbsp mayonnaise, preferably home-made
200g/7oz peeled cooked grey shrimp or pink salad shrimp
salt and ground black pepper

To garnish
2 slices of lemon, halved
4 small sprigs of parsley

To serve
lettuce leaves, mixed greens or watercress
baby green peas, raw or lightly cooked radishes
alfalfa sprouts
grated carrots

1 Slice the top off each tomato and set aside as lids. Using a spoon or melon baller, carefully scoop out the flesh, and either discard it or save it for making a soup or sauce. Season the inside of each tomato with salt. Stand upside-down on paper towels to drain.

2 Mix the lemon rind and herbs with the mayonnaise and season with salt and pepper to taste. Fold in the shrimp carefully, so as not to break them.

3 Spoon the shrimp mixture into each tomato and replace the caps, setting them slightly askew to reveal the filling.

4 Line a platter or individual plates with lettuce, watercress or mixed greens. Arrange the stuffed tomatoes on top and garnish each one with a twist of lemon and a sprig of parsley.

5 Surround the serving platter with the remaining vegetables and serve immediately.

Salt Prawns Energy 206kcal/856kJ; Protein 20.2g; Carbohydrate 2.7g, of which sugars 2.4g; Fat 12.7g, of which saturates 1.6g; Cholesterol 219mg; Calcium 97mg; Fibre 0.3g; Sodium 1197mg.
Tomatoes Energy 186kcal/776kJ; Protein 13.2g; Carbohydrate 4.2g, of which sugars 4.2g; Fat 13.1g, of which saturates 2.1g; Cholesterol 76mg; Calcium 182mg; Fibre 1.5g; Sodium 1998mg.

Fish and Chermoula Mini Pies

The filling of these pies is flavoured with chermoula, a mixture of spices and fresh coriander and parsley.

Makes 8
500g/1¼lb firm white fish fillets
225g/8oz uncooked king prawns
   (jumbo shrimp)
16 sheets filo pastry
60–75ml/4–5 tbsp sunflower oil
1 egg yolk, mixed with a few
   drops of water
salt

For the chermoula
75ml/5 tbsp olive oil
juice of 1 lemon
5ml/1 tsp ground cumin
5–10ml/1–2 tsp paprika
2–3 garlic cloves, crushed
1 red chilli, seeded
   and chopped
large bunch of fresh flat leaf
   parsley, chopped
large bunch of fresh coriander
   (cilantro), chopped

1 Prepare the chermoula. Combine all the ingredients in a bowl and set aside. Place the fish in a frying pan and add just enough water to cover the fillets.

2 Season the fish with a little salt and heat until just simmering, then cook gently for 3 minutes, until the fish just begins to flake. Remove from the liquid and break it up, removing all the bones.

3 Poach the prawns in the fish liquor for 10 minutes, then drain and shell. Toss the prawns and fish in the chermoula, cover and set aside for 1 hour. Preheat the oven to 180°C/350°F/Gas 4. Grease two baking sheets.

4 To make the pies, lay the filo pastry under a damp cloth. Take two sheets of filo: brush one with oil, lay the second one on top, then brush it with oil. Place some filling in the middle of the length of the sheet but to one side. Fold the edge of the pastry over the filling, then fold the long side over to cover the filling. Wrap the ends around the filling like a collar to make a neat package with the edges tucked in, then brush with egg yolk.

5 Continue as before with the rest of the fish and chermoula mixture. Bake the pies for about 20 minutes, until the pastry is crisp and golden brown. Serve hot or warm.

Lettuce Parcels

This dish makes the most of the abundance of lettuce in summer and is a popular 'assemble-it-yourself' snack.

Serves 6
2 chicken breast fillets
4 Chinese dried mushrooms,
   soaked for 30 minutes in
   warm water to cover
30ml/2 tbsp vegetable oil
2 garlic cloves, crushed
6 drained canned water
   chestnuts, thinly sliced
30ml/2 tbsp light soy sauce
5ml/1 tsp Sichuan peppercorns,
   dry fried and crushed
4 spring onions (scallions),
   finely chopped
5ml/1 tsp sesame oil
vegetable oil, for deep-frying
50g/2oz cellophane noodles
salt and ground black pepper
1 crisp lettuce and 60ml/4 tbsp
   hoisin sauce, to serve

1 Remove the skin from the chicken fillets, pat dry and set aside. Chop the chicken into thin strips. Drain the soaked mushrooms. Cut off and discard the mushroom stems; slice the caps finely and set aside.

2 Heat the oil in a wok or large frying pan. Add the garlic, then add the chicken. Stir-fry until the pieces are cooked through.

3 Add the sliced mushrooms, water chestnuts, soy sauce and peppercorns. Toss for 2–3 minutes, then season, if needed. Stir in half of the spring onions, then the sesame oil. Remove from the heat and set aside.

4 Cut the chicken skin into strips, deep fry in hot oil until very crisp and drain on kitchen paper. Deep fry the noodles until they are crisp. Drain on kitchen paper.

5 Crush the cellophane noodles and place in a serving dish. Top the noodles with the chicken skin, chicken mixture and the remaining spring onions. Arrange the lettuce leaves on a platter. Toss the chicken and noodles to mix. Invite guests to take a lettuce leaf, spread the inside with hoisin sauce and add a spoonful of filling, turning in the sides of the leaf and rolling it into a parcel before eating it.

Fish Mini Pies Energy 236kcal/984kJ; Protein 18.2g; Carbohydrate 10g, of which sugars 0.4g; Fat 13.9g, of which saturates 2g; Cholesterol 109mg; Calcium 67mg; Fibre 0.9g; Sodium 96mg.
Lettuce Parcels Energy 237kcal/984kJ; Protein 15.3g; Carbohydrate 7.6g, of which sugars 1.1g; Fat 16.1g, of which saturates 2g; Cholesterol 41mg; Calcium 24mg; Fibre 0.6g; Sodium 41mg.

Summer Salad with Capers and Olives

Make this refreshing salad in the summer when tomatoes are at their sweetest and full of flavour. Serve with warm ciabatta or walnut bread.

Serves 4

4 tomatoes
½ cucumber
1 bunch spring onions (scallions), trimmed and chopped
1 bunch watercress
8 stuffed olives
30ml/2 tbsp drained capers

For the dressing
30ml/2 tbsp red wine vinegar
5ml/1 tsp paprika
2.5ml/½ tsp ground cumin
1 garlic clove, crushed
75ml/5 tbsp extra virgin olive oil
salt and ground black pepper

1 Using a sharp knife, make a small cross on the top of the tomatoes, then plunge into a bowl of boiling water for about 1–2 minutes. Peel off the skin, then finely dice the flesh. Place in a salad bowl.

2 Peel the cucumber, dice finely and add to the tomatoes. Add half the spring onions to the salad bowl and mix lightly.

3 Break the watercress into sprigs. Add them to the tomato mixture, with the olives and capers and mix well.

4 To make the dressing, mix the wine vinegar, paprika, cumin and garlic in a bowl. Whisk in the oil and add salt and black pepper to taste.

5 Pour the dressing over the salad and toss lightly. Serve immediately with the remaining spring onions.

Variation
If you cannot find any watercress, you can use other leaves in its place. Rocket (arugula) has a similar peppery taste and texture to watercress and is therefore ideal as a substitute in this recipe.

Cucumber and Tomato Salad with Yogurt Dressing

Luxurious Greek yogurt, olive oil and sweet summer tomatoes combine deliciously in this recipe.

Serves 4

450g/1lb firm ripe tomatoes
½ cucumber
1 onion
1 small fresh red or green chilli, seeded and chopped, or fresh chives, chopped into 2.5cm/1in lengths, to garnish
crusty bread or pitta breads, to serve

For the dressing
60ml/4 tbsp olive or vegetable oil
90ml/6 tbsp Greek (US strained plain) yogurt
30ml/2 tbsp chopped fresh parsley or chives
2.5ml/½ tsp vinegar
salt and ground black pepper

1 Cut a small cross in the bottom of each tomato and plunge them into a pan of boiling water for about 1 minute, then transfer them to a bowl of cold water. Drain, then slip off and discard their skins. Halve the tomatoes, remove and discard the seeds and cores and chop the flesh into even pieces. Put them into a salad bowl.

2 Chop the cucumber and onion into pieces of a similar size to the tomatoes and put them in the bowl.

3 Mix all the dressing ingredients together and season to taste. Pour the dressing over the salad and toss all the ingredients together thoroughly.

4 Season with black pepper and garnish with the chilli or chives. Serve with crusty bread or pile into pitta pockets.

Cook's Tip
If you have time, before assembling the salad salt the chopped cucumber lightly and leave it in a colander for 30 minutes to drain. This will avoid making the salad watery.

Summer Salad Energy 172kcal/712kJ; Protein 2.5g; Carbohydrate 5g, of which sugars 4.3g; Fat 16g, of which saturates 2.4g; Cholesterol 0mg; Calcium 71mg; Fibre 2.2g; Sodium 305mg.
Cucumber Salad Energy 156kcal/646kJ; Protein 3g; Carbohydrate 5.8g, of which sugars 5.4g; Fat 13.9g, of which saturates 2.9g; Cholesterol 0mg; Calcium 75mg; Fibre 2.1g; Sodium 32mg.

Tomato Salad with Marinated Peppers and Oregano

This refreshing appetizer is perfect for when tomatoes are at their best in summer with maximum flavour and sweetness. They combine superbly with marinated peppers, which, because they have been well roasted before soaking, are sweeter and more digestible than raw ones.

Serves 4–6
*2 marinated (bell)
   peppers, drained
6 ripe tomatoes, sliced
15ml/1 tbsp chopped
   fresh oregano
75ml/5 tbsp olive oil
30ml/2 tbsp white wine vinegar
sea salt*

1 If the marinated peppers are in large pieces, cut them into even strips. Arrange the tomato slices and pepper strips on a serving dish, sprinkle with the fresh oregano and season to taste with sea salt.

2 Whisk together the olive oil and white wine vinegar in a jug (pitcher) and pour the dressing over the salad. Serve the salad immediately or cover the dish and chill in the refrigerator until required.

Cook's Tips
• *Marinated (bell) peppers are widely available in jars, often labelled as pimentos. However, they are much tastier when prepared yourself. To do this, wrap one green and one red pepper in foil and place on a baking sheet. Cook in a preheated oven at 180°C/350°F/Gas 4, or under a preheated grill (broiler), turning occasionally, for 20–30 minutes, until tender. Unwrap and when cool, peel the peppers, then halve and seed. Cut the flesh into strips and pack into a screw-top jar. Add olive oil to cover, close and store in the refrigerator for up to 6 days.*
• *You can preserve marinated peppers by cooking them in a closed jar in boiling water for about 30 minutes. They can then be kept for approximately 6 weeks.*

Tomato and Mozzarella Salad

Sweet, naturally ripened tomatoes and fresh basil leaves capture the essence of summer in this simple Mediterranean salad. Choose ripe plum or beefsteak tomatoes for this dish – whatever is available at the grocery store.

Serves 4
*5 ripe tomatoes
2 x 225g/8oz buffalo mozzarella
   cheese, drained
1 small red onion, chopped*

For the dressing
½ small garlic clove, peeled

*15g/½ oz/½ cup fresh
   basil leaves
30ml/2 tbsp chopped fresh flat
   leaf parsley
25ml/1½ tbsp small salted
   capers, rinsed
2.5ml/½ tsp mustard
75–90ml/5–6 tbsp extra virgin
   olive oil
5–10ml/1–2 tsp balsamic vinegar
ground black pepper*

For the garnish
*fresh basil leaves
fresh parsley sprigs*

1 First make the dressing. Put the garlic, basil, parsley, half the capers and the mustard in a food processor or blender and process briefly to chop.

2 Then, with the motor running, gradually pour in the olive oil through the feeder tube to make a smooth purée with a dressing consistency.

3 Add the balsamic vinegar to the dressing to taste. Season with plenty of ground black pepper.

4 Slice the tomatoes and the mozzarella. Arrange the tomato and cheese slices alternately on a serving plate. Sprinkle the chopped red onion over the top and season with a little ground black pepper.

5 Drizzle the dressing over the salad, then sprinkle a few basil leaves, parsley sprigs and the remaining capers over the top as a garnish. Set aside and leave for about 10–15 minutes before serving.

Tomato Salad Energy 119kcal/494kJ; Protein 1.4g; Carbohydrate 6.9g, of which sugars 6.7g; Fat 9.7g, of which saturates 1.5g; Cholesterol 0mg; Calcium 17mg; Fibre 2.1g; Sodium 12mg.
Tomato and Mozzarella Energy 261kcal/1080kJ; Protein 11.2g; Carbohydrate 3.1g, of which sugars 3.1g; Fat 22.7g, of which saturates 9.4g; Cholesterol 33mg; Calcium 211mg; Fibre 1g; Sodium 231mg.

Quinoa Salad with Citrus Dressing

Quinoa is a type of grain grown in the Andes. A staple food of the region, it has been cultivated since the time of the Incas and Aztecs. Quinoa is packed with protein and is also gluten free, so it is ideal for vegetarians and those who are gluten intolerant.

Serves 6

175g/6oz/1 cup quinoa
½ cucumber, peeled
1 large tomato, seeded and cubed
4 spring onions (scallions), sliced
30ml/2 tbsp chopped fresh mint
15ml/1 tbsp chopped fresh flat
    leaf parsley
salt and ground black pepper

For the dressing
90ml/6 tbsp olive oil
juice of 2 limes
juice of 1 large orange
2 fresh green chillies, seeded and
    finely chopped
2 garlic cloves, crushed

1 Put the quinoa in a sieve (strainer), rinse thoroughly under cold water, then transfer into a large pan. Pour in cold water to cover and bring to the boil.

2 Lower the heat under the quinoa and simmer for about 10–12 minutes, until just tender. Drain well and leave to cool.

3 Make the dressing by whisking the olive oil with the lime and orange juices. Stir in the chopped chillies and garlic and season with salt.

4 Cut the cucumber in half lengthways and, using a teaspoon, scoop out and discard the seeds. Cut into 5mm/¼in slices and add to the cooled quinoa with the tomato, spring onions and herbs. Toss well to combine.

5 Pour the dressing over the salad and toss again until well mixed. Check the seasoning and serve.

Cook's Tip
Quinoa can also be eaten plain as an accompaniment to meat or fish dishes.

Chargrilled Pepper Salad

The ingredients of this colourful salad are simple and few, but the overall flavour is quite intense.

Serves 4

1 large red (bell) pepper, halved
    and seeded
1 large green (bell) pepper, halved
    and seeded
250g/9oz/2¼ cups dried fusilli
    tricolore or other pasta shapes
1 handful fresh basil leaves
1 handful fresh coriander
    (cilantro) leaves
1 garlic clove
salt and ground black pepper

For the dressing
30ml/2 tbsp pesto
juice of ½ lemon
60ml/4 tbsp extra virgin olive oil

1 Place the red and green pepper halves, skin side up, on a grill (broiler) rack and grill (broil) until the skins have blistered and are beginning to char. Transfer the peppers to a large bowl, cover with crumpled kitchen paper and leave to cool slightly. When the peppers are cool enough to handle, rub off the skins and discard.

2 Bring a large pan of salted water to the boil, add the pasta and cook according to the packet instructions, until al dente.

3 Meanwhile, whisk together the pesto, lemon juice and olive oil in a large bowl. Season to taste with salt and pepper.

4 Drain the cooked pasta well and add to the bowl of dressing. Toss thoroughly to mix and set aside to cool.

5 Chop the pepper flesh and add to the pasta. Put most of the basil and coriander and all the garlic on a board and chop them. Add the herb mixture to the pasta and toss, then season to taste, if necessary, and serve, garnished with the herb leaves.

Cook's Tip
Serve the salad at room temperature or lightly chilled, whichever you prefer.

Pepper Salad Energy 379kcal/1593kJ; Protein 11.7g; Carbohydrate 52.3g, of which sugars 7.7g; Fat 15.1g, of which saturates 3.3g; Cholesterol 8mg; Calcium 138mg; Fibre 3.9g; Sodium 91mg.
Quinoa Salad Energy 213kcal/885kJ; Protein 3.4g; Carbohydrate 24.3g, of which sugars 2g; Fat 11.6g, of which saturates 1.6g; Cholesterol 0mg; Calcium 26mg; Fibre 0.5g; Sodium 5mg.

Caesar Salad

This much-enjoyed summery salad was created by Caesar Cordoni in Tijuana in 1924. Be sure to use crisp lettuce and add the eggs and garlic croûtons at the last minute.

Serves 6

175ml/6fl oz/¾ cup salad oil, preferably olive oil
115g/4oz/2 cups French or Italian bread, cut in 2.5cm/ 1in cubes
1 large garlic clove, crushed with the flat side of a knife
1 cos or romaine lettuce
2 eggs, boiled for 1 minute
120ml/4fl oz/½ cup lemon juice
50g/2oz/⅔ cup freshly grated Parmesan cheese
6 anchovy fillets, drained and finely chopped (optional)
salt and ground black pepper

1 Heat 50ml/2fl oz/¼ cup of the salad oil in a frying pan. Add the bread cubes and garlic and cook, stirring constantly, until the cubes are golden brown. Drain on kitchen paper and discard the garlic.

2 Tear any large lettuce leaves into smaller pieces. Put all the lettuce in a large salad bowl.

3 Add the remaining olive oil to the salad leaves and season with salt and ground black pepper. Toss to coat well.

4 Break the soft-boiled eggs on top of the leaves. Sprinkle with the lemon juice and toss to combine the ingredients.

5 Add the grated Parmesan cheese and anchovies to the bowl, if using, then toss again. Sprinkle the croûtons on top of the salad and serve immediately.

> **Cook's Tip**
> To make a tangier dressing, mix the olive oil with 30ml/2 tbsp white wine vinegar, 2.5ml/½ tsp mustard, 5ml/1 tsp sugar, and salt and pepper.

Warm Dressed Salad with Eggs

Soft poached eggs, chilli, hot croûtons and cool, crisp salad leaves make a lively and unusual combination. This simple salad is perfect for a summer supper. Poached eggs are delicious with salad leaves as the yolk runs out when the eggs are pierced and combines with the dressing in the most delightful way.

Serves 2

½ small loaf wholemeal (whole-wheat) bread
45ml/3 tbsp chilli oil
2 eggs
115g/4oz mixed salad leaves
45ml/3 tbsp extra virgin olive oil
2 garlic cloves, crushed
15ml/1 tbsp balsamic or sherry vinegar
50g/2oz Parmesan cheese, shaved
ground black pepper

1 Carefully cut the crust from the wholemeal loaf and discard. Cut the bread into neat slices and then cut each slice into 2.5cm/1in cubes.

2 Heat the chilli oil in a large frying pan. Add the bread cubes and cook for about 5 minutes, tossing the cubes occasionally, until they are crisp and golden brown all over.

3 Meanwhile, bring a pan of water to the boil. Break each egg into a measuring jug (cup) and carefully slide into the water, one at a time.

4 Gently poach the eggs in the simmering water for about 4 minutes until they are lightly cooked.

5 Meanwhile, divide the salad leaves between two plates. Using a slotted spoon, remove the croûtons from the pan and arrange them over the leaves.

6 Wipe the pan clean with kitchen paper. Then heat the olive oil in the pan, add the garlic and vinegar and cook over high heat for about 1 minute. Pour the warm dressing evenly over the salads.

7 Place a poached egg on each salad. Top with thin Parmesan shavings and a little ground black pepper. Serve immediately.

Caesar Salad Energy 307kcal/1272kJ; Protein 8g; Carbohydrate 11.7g, of which sugars 1.4g; Fat 25.7g, of which saturates 5.4g; Cholesterol 84mg; Calcium 149mg; Fibre 0.7g; Sodium 230mg.
Warm Dressed Salad Energy 697kcal/2907kJ; Protein 25.9g; Carbohydrate 41.3g, of which sugars 2.8g; Fat 49g, of which saturates 11.5g; Cholesterol 215mg; Calcium 408mg; Fibre 6.3g; Sodium 914mg.

Peppery Egg, Watercress and Chilli Salad

Chillies and eggs may seem unlikely partners, but actually work very well together. The peppery flavour of the watercress makes it the perfect foundation for this tasty salad.

Serves 2

15ml/1 tbsp groundnut (peanut) oil
1 garlic clove, thinly sliced
4 eggs
2 shallots, thinly sliced
2 small fresh red chillies, seeded and thinly sliced
1/2 small cucumber, finely diced
1cm/1/2in piece fresh root ginger, peeled and grated
juice of 2 limes
30ml/2 tbsp soy sauce
5ml/1 tsp caster (superfine) sugar
small bunch coriander (cilantro)
bunch watercress or rocket (arugula), coarsely chopped

1 Heat the oil in a frying pan. Add the garlic and cook over low heat until it starts to turn golden.

2 Crack the eggs into the pan. Break the yolks with a wooden spatula, then fry until the eggs are almost firm. Remove from the pan and set aside.

3 In a bowl, mix together the shallots, chillies, cucumber and ginger until well blended.

4 In a separate bowl, whisk the lime juice with the soy sauce and sugar. Pour this dressing over the vegetables and toss lightly.

5 Set aside a few coriander sprigs for the garnish. Chop the rest and add them to the salad. Toss it again.

6 Reserve a few watercress or rocket sprigs and arrange the remainder on two serving plates. Cut the fried eggs into slices and divide them between the watercress or rocket mounds.

7 Spoon the shallot mixture over the eggs and serve immediately, garnished with the reserved coriander and watercress or rocket.

Salad Niçoise

Made with the freshest of ingredients, this classic salad makes a simple yet unbeatable summer dish.

Serves 4

115g/4oz French (green) beans, trimmed and cut in half
115g/4oz mixed salad leaves
1/2 small cucumber, thinly sliced
4 ripe tomatoes, quartered
50g/2oz can anchovies, drained and halved lengthways
4 eggs, hard-boiled
1 tuna steak, about 175g/6oz
olive oil, for brushing
1/2 bunch small radishes, trimmed
50g/2oz/1/2 cup small black olives
salt and ground black pepper

For the dressing
90ml/6 tbsp extra virgin olive oil
2 garlic cloves, crushed
15ml/1 tbsp white wine vinegar

1 To make the dressing, whisk together the oil, garlic and vinegar and season to taste with salt and pepper. Set aside.

2 Cook the French beans in a pan of boiling water for 2 minutes until just tender, then drain.

3 Mix together the salad leaves, sliced cucumber, tomatoes and French beans in a large, shallow bowl. Halve the anchovies lengthways and shell and quarter the eggs.

4 Preheat the grill (broiler). Brush the tuna steak with olive oil and sprinkle with salt and ground black pepper. Cook under the grill for 3–4 minutes on each side until cooked through. Cool, then flake.

5 Sprinkle the flaked tuna, anchovies, quartered eggs, radishes and olives over the salad. Pour over the dressing and toss together lightly to combine. Serve immediately.

> **Variation**
> *Opinions vary on whether salad Niçoise should include potatoes but, if you like, include a few small cooked new potatoes and some chopped celery.*

Peppery Egg Salad Energy 215kcal/894kj; Protein 14.2g; Carbohydrate 2.4g; of which sugars 2.2g; Fat 16.9g; of which saturates 4.2g; Cholesterol 381mg; Calcium 112mg; Fibre 0.8g; Sodium 1223mg.
Salad Niçoise Energy 351kcal/1457kj; Protein 21.7g; Carbohydrate 5.3g, of which sugars 5g; Fat 27.3g, of which saturates 5g; Cholesterol 210mg; Calcium 114mg; Fibre 2.6g; Sodium 876mg.

Roasted Pepper Salad

This is the Moroccan cousin of gazpacho – roasting the peppers adds a sweet richness to the salad, which contrasts superbly with the tangy flavour of preserved lemons.

Serves 4
3 green (bell) peppers, quartered
4 large tomatoes
2 garlic cloves, finely chopped
30ml/2 tbsp olive oil
30ml/2 tbsp lemon juice
good pinch of paprika
pinch of ground cumin
1/4 preserved lemon
salt and ground black pepper
fresh coriander (cilantro) and flat leaf parsley, to garnish

1 Heat the grill (broiler) until very hot. Grill (broil) the peppers skin side up until the skins are blistered and charred. Place the peppers in a plastic bag and tie the ends. Leave for about 10 minutes, or until the peppers are cool enough to handle, then peel off the skins.

2 Cut the peppers into small pieces, discarding the seeds and core, and place in a serving dish.

3 Plunge the tomatoes into a pan of boiling water for about 30 seconds, then refresh in cold water. Peel off the skins and remove the seeds and cores. Chop coarsely and add to the peppers. Sprinkle the garlic on top and chill for 1 hour.

4 In a bowl, blend together the olive oil, lemon juice, paprika and cumin and pour over the salad. Season with salt and ground black pepper.

5 Rinse the preserved lemon in cold water and remove the flesh and pith. Cut the peel into slivers and sprinkle them over the salad. Garnish with coriander and flat leaf parsley.

Cook's Tip
It is always better to use fresh, rather than bottled lemon juice; as a guide, 30ml/2 tbsp is the average yield from half a lemon.

Aubergine, Lemon and Caper Salad

This cooked vegetable relish is delicious served as an accompaniment to a selection of cold meats or with pasta for a tasty summer buffet or barbecue in the garden.

Serves 4
1 large aubergine (eggplant), about 675g/1 1/2lb
60ml/4 tbsp olive oil
grated rind and juice of 1 lemon, plus extra rind to garnish
30ml/2 tbsp capers, rinsed
12 pitted green olives
30ml/2 tbsp chopped fresh flat leaf parsley
salt and ground black pepper

1 Cut the aubergine into 2.5cm/1in cubes. Heat the olive oil in a large frying pan and cook the aubergine cubes over medium heat for about 10 minutes, tossing regularly, until golden and soft. You may need to do this in two batches. Drain on kitchen paper and sprinkle with a little salt.

2 Place the aubergine cubes in a large serving bowl. Toss thoroughly with the lemon rind and juice, capers, olives and chopped fresh parsley,

3 Season to taste with salt and ground black pepper. Serve the salad at room temperature, garnished with a few strands of grated lemon rind.

Cook's Tips
• This salad will taste even better when made the day before. It will store, covered, in the refrigerator for up to 4 days.
• Ensure that the capers are well rinsed, otherwise they will make the salad too salty.

Variation
You can replace the lemon rind and juice with that of an orange, if you prefer.

Aubergine Salad Energy 141kcal/585kJ; Protein 2g; Carbohydrate 4.1g, of which sugars 3.7g; Fat 13.2g, of which saturates 2g; Cholesterol 0mg; Calcium 50mg; Fibre 4.4g; Sodium 289mg.
Roasted Pepper Salad Energy 113kcal/469kJ; Protein 2.2g; Carbohydrate 12.3g, of which sugars 11.9g; Fat 6.4g, of which saturates 1g; Cholesterol 0mg; Calcium 19mg; Fibre 3.3g; Sodium 15mg.

Yellow Courgette Wraps with Spinach and Mozzarella

This is a good first course or accompaniment, especially useful for gardeners with a glut of courgettes in the summer. You need the large ones that have been growing sneakily under the leaves. They should measure about 19cm/7¼in. A barbecue with an adjustable grill is ideal for this recipe.

Serves 6
2 large yellow courgettes (zucchini), total weight about 675g/1½lb

45ml/3 tbsp olive oil
250g/9oz baby leaf spinach
250g/9oz mini mozzarella balls
salt and ground black pepper
salad burnet, rocket (arugula) and mizuna leaves, to garnish (optional)

For the dressing
2 whole, unpeeled garlic cloves
30ml/2 tbsp white wine vinegar
30ml/2 tbsp olive oil
15ml/1 tbsp extra virgin olive oil
45ml/3 tbsp walnut oil

1 Prepare the barbecue. To make the dressing, place the garlic in a small pan with water to cover. Bring to the boil, lower the heat and simmer for 5 minutes. Drain the garlic. When cool enough to handle, pop the garlic cloves out of their skins and crush to a smooth paste with a little salt. Scrape into a bowl and add the vinegar. Whisk in the oils and season to taste with salt and ground black pepper.

2 Slice each courgette lengthways into six or more broad strips, about 3mm/⅛in wide. Lay them on a tray. Set aside 5ml/1 tsp of the oil and brush the rest over the courgette strips, evenly coating them with the oil.

3 Place a wok over a high heat. When it starts to smoke, add the reserved oil and stir-fry the spinach for 30 seconds, or until just wilted. Tip into a sieve (strainer) and drain well, then pat dry the leaves with kitchen paper. Tear or slice the mozzarella balls in half and place on kitchen paper to drain.

4 Once the flames have died down, position a lightly oiled grill rack over the coals to heat. When the coals are medium-hot, or with a moderate coating of ash, lay the courgettes on the rack. Grill on one side only for 2–3 minutes, or until striped golden. As each strip cooks, return it to the tray, grilled-side up.

5 Place small heaps of spinach towards one end of each courgette strip. Lay two pieces of mozzarella on each pile of spinach. Season well.

6 Using a metal spatula, carefully transfer the topped strips, a few at a time, back to the barbecue rack and grill for about 2 minutes, or until the underside of each is striped with golden-brown grill marks.

7 When the cheese starts to melt, fold the plain section of each courgette over the filling to make a wrap. Lift off carefully and drain on kitchen paper. Serve with the garnish of salad leaves, if you like, and drizzle the dressing over the top.

Courgettes with Cheese and Green Chillies

This is a very tasty way to serve courgettes, often a rather bland vegetable, and the dish looks good too. Serve it as a vegetarian main dish or an unusual side dish.

Serves 6
30ml/2 tbsp vegetable oil
½ onion, thinly sliced
2 garlic cloves, crushed

5ml/1 tsp dried oregano
2 tomatoes
500g/1¼lb courgettes (zucchini)
50g/2oz/⅓ cup drained pickled jalapeño chilli slices, chopped
115g/4oz/½ cup cream cheese
salt and ground black pepper
fresh oregano sprigs, to garnish
crusty bread to serve, optional

1 Heat the oil in a frying pan. Add the onion, garlic and dried oregano. Fry for 3–4 minutes, stirring occasionally, until the onion is soft and translucent.

2 Cut a cross in the base of each tomato. Place in a heatproof bowl and cover with boiling water. Leave in the water for 3 minutes, then lift out on a slotted spoon and plunge into a bowl of cold water. Drain. The skins will have begun to peel back from the crosses. Remove the skins and cut the tomatoes in half and squeeze out the seeds. Chop the flesh into strips.

3 Top and tail the courgettes, then cut them lengthways into 1cm/½in wide strips. Slice the strips into matchsticks.

4 Stir the courgettes into the onion mixture and fry for about 10 minutes, stirring occasionally, until just tender. Add the tomatoes and chopped jalapeños to the pan and cook for 2–3 minutes more.

5 Add the cheese and reduce the heat to very low. As the cheese melts, stir gently to coat the courgettes and season.

6 Pile into a heated dish and serve, garnished with fresh oregano. If serving as a main course, rustic crusty bread makes a good accompaniment.

Courgettes with Cheese Energy 143kcal/587kJ; Protein 2.7g; Carbohydrate 3.3g, of which sugars 3g; Fat 13.3g, of which saturates 6.2g; Cholesterol 18mg; Calcium 47mg; Fibre 1.2g; Sodium 62mg.
Courgette Wraps Energy 237kcal/977kJ; Protein 10.9g; Carbohydrate 2.7g, of which sugars 2.5g; Fat 20.2g, of which saturates 7.4g; Cholesterol 24mg; Calcium 250mg; Fibre 1.9g; Sodium 224mg.

Courgette Roulade

This makes an impressive buffet supper or dinner party dish, or can be served chilled for a picnic.

Serves 6
40g/1½oz/3 tbsp butter
50g/2oz/½ cup plain (all-purpose) flour
300ml/½ pint/1¼ cups milk
4 eggs, separated
3 courgettes (zucchini), grated
25g/1oz/⅓ cup freshly grated Parmesan cheese

salt and ground black pepper
herb and green leaf salad, to serve

For the filling
75g/3oz/⅔ cup soft goat's cheese
60ml/4 tbsp fromage frais
225g/8oz/2 cups cooked rice, such as Thai fragrant rice or Japanese short grain
15ml/1 tbsp chopped mixed fresh herbs
15ml/1 tbsp olive oil
15g/½oz/1 tbsp butter
75g/3oz/generous 1 cup button (white) mushrooms, chopped

1 Preheat the oven to 200°C/400°F/Gas 6. Line a 33 × 23cm/ 13 × 9in Swiss roll tin (jelly roll pan) with baking parchment.

2 Melt the butter in a pan, stir in the flour and cook for about 1–2 minutes, stirring all the time. Gradually add the milk, stirring until the mixture forms a smooth sauce. Remove from the heat and cool for a few minutes. Stir in the egg yolks, one at a time. Add the courgettes and Parmesan, and check the seasoning.

3 Whisk the egg whites until stiff, fold them into the courgette mixture and spread evenly into the tin, smoothing the surface. Bake for 10–15 minutes until the roulade is firm and golden.

4 Turn the roulade out on to baking parchment sprinkled with 30ml/2 tbsp grated Parmesan. Peel away the parchment. Roll the roulade up, using the paper as a guide, and leave it to cool.

5 To make the filling, mix the goat's cheese, fromage frais, rice and the herbs in a bowl. Season with salt and pepper. Heat the oil and butter in a small pan and fry the mushrooms until soft.

6 Unwrap the roulade, spread with the filling and the mushrooms along the centre. Roll up again. Serve warm.

Courgettes and Tofu with Tomato Sauce

This dish is great hot or cold in the summer, and its flavour improves if it is kept for a day or two, covered, in the refrigerator. It makes the perfect accompaniment to a nut or meat roast.

Serves 4
30ml/2 tbsp olive oil
2 garlic cloves, finely chopped
4 large courgettes (zucchini), thinly sliced on the diagonal

250g/9oz firm tofu, drained and cubed
1 lemon
sea salt and ground black pepper

For the tomato sauce
10ml/2 tsp balsamic vinegar
5ml/1 tsp sugar
300ml/½ pint/1¼ cups passata (bottled strained tomatoes)
small bunch of fresh mint or parsley, chopped

1 First, make the tomato sauce. Place all the ingredients in a small pan and heat through gently, stirring occasionally.

2 Meanwhile, heat the olive oil in a large non-stick wok or frying pan until very hot, then add the garlic and stir-fry for about 30 seconds, until golden. Add the courgettes and stir-fry over high heat for about 5–6 minutes, or until golden around the edges. Remove from the pan.

3 Add the tofu to the pan and brown on one side for a few minutes. Turn gently, then brown again. Grate the rind from half the lemon and reserve for the garnish. Squeeze the lemon juice over the tofu.

4 Season to taste with sea salt and pepper, then leave to sizzle until all the lemon juice has evaporated. Gently stir the courgettes into the tofu until well combined, then remove the wok or pan from the heat.

5 Transfer the courgettes and tofu to a warm serving dish and pour the tomato sauce over the top. Sprinkle with the grated lemon rind, taste and season with more salt and pepper, if necessary, and serve immediately.

Courgettes and Tofu Energy 141kcal/585kJ; Protein 8.8g; Carbohydrate 6.8g, of which sugars 6.3g; Fat 8.9g, of which saturates 1.3g; Cholesterol 0mg; Calcium 389mg; Fibre 2.4g; Sodium 181mg.
Roulade Energy 322kcal/1343kJ; Protein 14g; Carbohydrate 22.3g, of which sugars 4.2g; Fat 20.2g, of which saturates 10.5g; Cholesterol 166mg; Calcium 194mg; Fibre 1g; Sodium 250mg.

Grilled Aubergine Parcels

These summery bundles feature tomatoes, mozzarella cheese and basil, wrapped in slices of aubergine.

Serves 4

2 large aubergines (eggplants)
225g/8oz mozzarella cheese
2 plum tomatoes
16 large basil leaves
30ml/2 tbsp olive oil
salt and ground black pepper

For the dressing

60ml/4 tbsp olive oil
5ml/1 tsp balsamic vinegar
15ml/1 tbsp sun-dried tomato paste
15ml/1 tbsp lemon juice

For the garnish

30ml/2 tbsp toasted pine nuts
torn basil leaves

1 Remove the stalks from the aubergines and cut them lengthways into 16 thin slices – about 5mm/¼in thick.

2 Bring a large pan of salted water to the boil and cook the aubergine slices for about 2 minutes, until just softened. Drain the sliced aubergines, then dry on kitchen paper.

3 Cut the mozzarella cheese into eight slices. Cut each tomato into eight slices, not counting the first and last slices.

4 Take two aubergine slices and place on a dish, in a cross. Place a slice of tomato in the centre, season with salt and pepper, then add a basil leaf, followed by a slice of mozzarella, another basil leaf, a slice of tomato and more seasoning.

5 Fold the ends of the aubergine slices around the mozzarella and tomato filling to make a neat parcel. Repeat with the rest of the assembled ingredients to make eight parcels. Chill the parcels for about 20 minutes.

6 To make the dressing, whisk together the olive oil, balsamic vinegar, sun-dried tomato paste and lemon juice. Season to taste.

7 Preheat the grill (broiler). Brush the parcels with olive oil and cook for about 5 minutes on each side, until golden. Serve hot, with the dressing, sprinkled with pine nuts and basil.

Aubergine Rolls

As well as making an original appetizer, these little rolls of aubergine wrapped around a filling of ricotta and rice are tasty served as part of a buffet or for a Turkish-style meze.

Serves 4

2 aubergines (eggplants)
olive oil, for shallow frying
75g/3oz/scant ½ cup ricotta cheese
75g/3oz/scant ½ cup soft goat's cheese
225g/8oz/2 cups cooked white long grain rice
15ml/1 tbsp chopped fresh basil
5ml/1 tsp chopped fresh mint, plus mint sprigs, to garnish
salt and ground black pepper

For the tomato sauce

15ml/1 tbsp olive oil
1 red onion, finely chopped
1 garlic clove, crushed
400g/14oz can chopped tomatoes
120ml/4fl oz/½ cup chicken stock or white wine or a mixture
15ml/1 tbsp chopped fresh parsley

1 Preheat the oven to 190°C/375°F/Gas 5. Make the tomato sauce. Heat the oil in a small pan and fry the onion and garlic for 3–4 minutes until softened.

2 Add the tomatoes, chicken stock and wine, if using, and sprinkle in the parsley. Season with salt and pepper. Bring to the boil, then lower the heat and simmer for 10–12 minutes until slightly thickened, stirring.

3 Meanwhile, cut the aubergines lengthways into four or five slices. Heat the oil in a large frying pan and fry the aubergine in batches until the slices are golden brown on both sides. Drain on kitchen paper.

4 Mix the ricotta, goat's cheese, rice, basil and mint in a bowl. Season well with salt and pepper.

5 Place a generous spoonful of the filling at one end of each aubergine slice and roll up. Arrange the rolls side by side in a baking dish. Pour the sauce over the top. Bake for 10–15 minutes until heated through. Garnish with the mint sprigs and serve.

Aubergine Parcels Energy 350kcal/1449kJ; Protein 12.7g; Carbohydrate 5g, of which sugars 4.7g; Fat 31.2g, of which saturates 10.5g; Cholesterol 33mg; Calcium 223mg; Fibre 3.6g; Sodium 230mg.
Aubergine Rolls Energy 283kcal/1185kJ; Protein 8.9g; Carbohydrate 24.7g, of which sugars 6.7g; Fat 17.3g, of which saturates 6.6g; Cholesterol 25mg; Calcium 56mg; Fibre 3.3g; Sodium 125mg.

Roasted Garlic and Aubergine Custards with Red Pepper Dressing

These elegant little moulds make a rather splendid main course for a special dinner.

Serves 6

2 large heads of garlic
6–7 fresh thyme sprigs
60ml/4 tbsp extra virgin olive oil, plus extra for greasing
350g/12oz aubergines (eggplants), cut into 1cm/½in dice
2 large red (bell) peppers, halved and seeded
pinch of saffron strands
300ml/½ pint/1¼ cups whipping cream

2 large eggs
pinch of caster (superfine) sugar
30ml/2 tbsp shredded fresh basil leaves
salt and ground black pepper

For the dressing

90ml/6 tbsp extra virgin oil
25ml/1½ tbsp balsamic vinegar
pinch of caster (superfine) sugar
115g/4oz tomatoes, peeled, seeded and finely diced
½ small red onion, finely chopped
generous pinch of ground toasted cumin seeds
handful of fresh basil leaves

1 Preheat the oven to 190°C/375°F/Gas 5. Place the garlic on a piece of foil with the thyme, sprinkle with 15ml/1 tbsp of the oil and wrap up. Bake for 35–45 minutes, then cool slightly. Reduce the oven temperature to 180°C/350°F/Gas 4.

2 Meanwhile, heat the remaining oil in a pan. Add the aubergine and fry over medium heat, stirring frequently, for 5–8 minutes.

3 Grill the peppers, skin sides up, until they are black. Place the peppers in a bowl, cover and leave for 10 minutes. When they are cool enough to handle, peel and dice them. Soak the saffron in 15ml/1 tbsp hot water for 10 minutes.

4 Unwrap the roasted garlic and pop it out of its skin into a blender or food processor. Discard the thyme. Add the oil from cooking, the cream and eggs to the garlic. Process until smooth. Add the soaked saffron with its liquid, season and add a pinch of sugar. Stir in half the diced red pepper and the basil.

5 Lightly grease six large ovenproof ramekins and line the base of each with a circle of greased baking parchment.

6 Divide the aubergines among the dishes. Pour the egg mixture into the ramekins, then place them in a roasting pan. Cover each dish with foil and make a little hole in the centre of the foil to allow steam to escape. Pour hot water into the tin to come halfway up the outsides of the ramekins. Bake for 25–30 minutes, until the custards are just set in the centre.

7 Make the dressing while the custards are cooking. Whisk the oil and vinegar with salt, pepper and a pinch of sugar. Stir in the tomatoes, red onion, remaining red pepper and cumin. Set aside some basil leaves for garnishing, then chop the rest and add to the dressing.

8 Leave the custards to cool for about 5 minutes, then turn them out on to warmed serving plates. Spoon the dressing around the custards and garnish each with the reserved fresh basil leaves. Serve immediately.

Stewed Aubergine with Tomatoes and Red Wine

Stewing aubergines with tomatoes, red wine and garlic really brings out the best in this delectable summer vegetable.

Serves 4

1 large aubergine (eggplant)
60–90ml/4–6 tbsp olive oil

2 shallots, thinly sliced
2 garlic cloves, thinly sliced
4 tomatoes, quartered
60ml/4 tbsp red wine
30ml/2 tbsp chopped fresh parsley, plus extra to garnish
30–45ml/2–3 tbsp virgin olive oil (if serving cold)
salt and ground black pepper

1 Slice the aubergine into 1cm/½in rounds. Layer the aubergine slices in a colander, sprinkling each layer with a little salt. Leave to drain over a sink or plate for about 20 minutes.

2 Rinse the aubergine slices well, then press between several layers of kitchen paper to remove any excess liquid.

3 Heat 30ml/2 tbsp of the oil in a large frying pan until smoking. Add one layer of aubergine slices and fry, turning once, until golden brown. Transfer to a plate covered with kitchen paper. Heat more oil and fry the second batch in the same way.

4 Heat 15ml/1 tbsp of oil in a pan and cook the shallots for 5 minutes until golden. Cut the aubergine into strips and add to the shallots with the tomatoes, garlic and wine. Cover and simmer for 30 minutes.

5 Stir in the parsley and check the seasonings. Sprinkle with a little more parsley and serve hot. To serve cold, dribble a little virgin olive oil over the dish before it goes on the table.

Cook's Tip
Heat the oil before adding the aubergine (eggplant) slices and do not be tempted to add more oil once the aubergines are cooking as they will absorb cold oil, resulting in a greasy dish.

Aubergine Custards Energy 425kcal/1754kJ; Protein 5.1g; Carbohydrate 9.8g, of which sugars 8.1g; Fat 40.9g, of which saturates 15.9g; Cholesterol 116mg; Calcium 55mg; Fibre 2.8g; Sodium 42mg.
Stewed Aubergine Energy 135kcal/560kJ; Protein 1.4g; Carbohydrate 5.2g, of which sugars 4.7g; Fat 11.6g, of which saturates 1.7g; Cholesterol 0mg; Calcium 17mg; Fibre 2.5g; Sodium 10mg.

Tomato and Black Olive Tart

This delicious tart has a fresh, rich Mediterranean flavour and is perfect for summer picnics. If you are taking this tart on a picnic, use a rectangular tin, which makes it easier to transport and cut into portions at the picnic destination.

3 eggs, beaten
300ml/½ pint/1¼ cups milk
30ml/2 tbsp chopped fresh herbs, such as parsley, marjoram or basil
6 firm plum tomatoes
75g/3oz ripe Brie cheese
about 16 black olives, pitted
salt and ground black pepper

Serves 8
375g/13oz shortcrust pastry, at room temperature

1 Preheat the oven to 190°C/375°F/Gas 5. Roll out the pastry thinly on a lightly floured surface. Line a 28 × 18cm/11 × 7in loose-based rectangular flan tin (pan), trimming off any overhanging edges.

2 Line the pastry case (pie shell) with baking parchment and baking beans, and bake blind for 15 minutes. Remove the baking parchment and beans and bake for a further 5 minutes until the base is crisp.

3 Meanwhile, mix together the eggs, milk, seasoning and herbs. Slice the tomatoes, cube the cheese, and slice the olives. Place the prepared flan case on a baking sheet, arrange the tomatoes, cheese and olives in the bottom of the case, then pour in the egg mixture. Transfer carefully to the oven and bake for about 40 minutes until just firm and turning golden. Slice hot or cool in the tin, then serve.

Onion Tart

This tart also makes a delicious main course when served warm with a fresh, summery salad.

Serves 4–6
175g/6oz/1½ cups plain (all-purpose) flour
75g/3oz/6 tbsp butter, chilled
30–45ml/2–3 tbsp iced water

For the filling
50g/2oz/¼ cup butter
900g/2lb Spanish (Bermuda) onions, thinly sliced
1 egg plus 2 egg yolks
250ml/8fl oz/1 cup double (heavy) cream
1.5ml/¼ tsp freshly grated nutmeg
salt and ground black pepper

1 Process the flour, a pinch of salt and the chilled butter in a food processor until reduced to fine crumbs. Add the iced water and process briefly to form a dough. Wrap in clear film (plastic wrap) and chill for 40 minutes.

2 For the filling, melt the butter in a pan and add the onions and a pinch of salt. Turn them in the butter. Cover and cook very gently, stirring frequently, for 30–40 minutes. Cool slightly.

3 Preheat the oven to 190°C/375°F/Gas 5. Roll out the dough thinly and use to line a 23–25cm/9–10in loose-based flan tin (pan). Line with foil or baking parchment and baking beans, then bake blind for 10 minutes.

4 Remove the foil or parchment and baking beans, and bake for another 4–5 minutes, until the pastry is lightly cooked to a pale brown colour (blonde is a good description). Reduce the oven temperature to 180°C/350°F/Gas 4.

5 Beat the egg, egg yolks and cream together. Season with salt, lots of black pepper and the grated nutmeg. Place half the onions in the pastry shell and add half the egg mixture. Add the remaining onions, then pour in as much of the remaining custard as you can.

6 Place on a baking sheet and bake on the middle shelf for 40–50 minutes, or until the custard is risen, browned and set in the centre. Serve warm rather than piping hot.

Variations
• This tart is delicious made with other cheeses. Try slices of Gorgonzola or Camembert for a slightly stronger flavour.
• Alternatively, sprinkle a few strips of anchovy fillet over the tart before baking.

Onion Tart Energy 548kcal/2271kJ; Protein 7.4g; Carbohydrate 35.4g, of which sugars 9.7g; Fat 42.9g, of which saturates 25.6g; Cholesterol 200mg; Calcium 115mg; Fibre 3g; Sodium 156mg.
Tomato and Olive Tart Energy 315kcal/1316kJ; Protein 9.3g; Carbohydrate 26.1g, of which sugars 4.6g; Fat 19.9g, of which saturates 7.2g; Cholesterol 90mg; Calcium 151mg; Fibre 1.7g; Sodium 505mg.

Baked Tomatoes with Mint

This is a dish for the height of the summer when the tomatoes are falling off the vines and are very ripe, juicy and full of flavour. Mint flourishes in sunny or shady places, as well as growing well in pots. This tomato dish goes especially well with lamb.

Serves 4

6 large ripe tomatoes
300ml/½ pint/1¼ cups double
   (heavy) cream
2 sprigs of fresh mint
olive oil, for brushing
a few pinches of caster
   (superfine) sugar
30ml/2 tbsp grated Bonnet cheese
salt and ground black pepper

1 Preheat the oven to 220°C/425°F/Gas 7. Bring a pan of water to the boil and have a bowl of iced water ready. Cut the cores out of the tomatoes and make a cross at the base. Plunge the tomatoes into the boiling water for 10 seconds and then straight into the iced water. Leave to cool completely.

2 Put the cream and mint in a small pan and bring to the boil. Reduce the heat and allow to simmer until it has reduced by about half.

3 When the tomatoes have cooled enough to handle, peel and slice them thinly.

4 Brush a shallow gratin dish lightly with a little olive oil. Layer the sliced tomatoes in the dish, overlapping slightly, and season with salt and ground black pepper. Sprinkle a little sugar over the top.

5 Strain the reduced cream evenly over the top of the tomatoes. Sprinkle on the cheese and bake in the preheated oven for 15 minutes, or until the top is browned and bubbling. Serve immediately in the gratin dish.

> **Cook's Tip**
> Bonnet is a hard goat's cheese but any hard, well-flavoured cheese will do.

Rocket and Tomato Pizza

Peppery rocket and aromatic basil add both colour and lots of summery flavour to this crisp pizza.

Serves 2

10ml/2 tsp olive oil, plus extra
   for drizzling
1 garlic clove, crushed
150g/5oz/1 cup canned
   chopped tomatoes
2.5ml/½ tsp sugar
30ml/2 tbsp torn fresh basil leaves
2 tomatoes, seeded and chopped

150g/5oz/²⁄₃ cup mozzarella
   cheese, sliced
20g/³⁄₄oz/1 cup rocket
   (arugula) leaves
rock salt and ground black pepper

For the pizza base

225g/8oz/2 cups strong white
   flour, sifted
5ml/1 tsp salt
2.5ml/½ tsp easy-blend
   (rapid-rise) dried yeast
15ml/1 tbsp olive oil

1 To make the pizza base, place the flour, salt and yeast in a bowl. Add the oil and 150ml/¼ pint/²⁄₃ cup warm water to a well in the centre. Mix to form a soft dough.

2 Turn out the dough on to a floured work surface and knead for 5 minutes. Cover with the upturned bowl or a dish towel and leave for 5 minutes. Knead for a further 5 minutes until the dough is smooth and elastic. Place in an oiled bowl and cover. Leave in a warm place for 45 minutes until doubled in bulk.

3 Preheat the oven to 220°C/425°F/Gas 7. Make the topping. Heat the oil in a frying pan and fry the garlic for 1 minute. Add the tomatoes and sugar, and cook for 5–7 minutes until thickened. Stir in the basil and seasoning, then set aside.

4 Knead the risen dough lightly, then roll out to form a rough 30cm/12in round. Place on a lightly oiled baking sheet and push up the edges of the dough to form a shallow, even rim.

5 Spoon the tomato mixture over the base, then top with fresh tomatoes. Arrange the mozzarella on top. Season with rock salt and pepper and drizzle with a little olive oil. Bake in the top of the oven for 10–12 minutes until crisp and golden. Sprinkle the rocket over the pizza just before serving.

Baked Tomatoes Energy 443kcal/1831kJ; Protein 5g; Carbohydrate 6.7g, of which sugars 6.7g; Fat 44.1g, of which saturates 27.4g; Cholesterol 113mg; Calcium 123mg; Fibre 1.8g; Sodium 105mg.
Rocket Pizza Energy 683kcal/2874kJ; Protein 26.1g; Carbohydrate 92.3g, of which sugars 6.5g; Fat 25.8g, of which saturates 11.9g; Cholesterol 44mg; Calcium 494mg; Fibre 5.7g; Sodium 1312mg.

Grilled Vegetable Pizza

You really can't go too far wrong with this classic mixture of Mediterranean grilled vegetables on home-made pizza dough. It is filling and healthy, and is a favourite in summer.

Serves 6

1 courgette (zucchini), sliced
2 baby aubergines (eggplants) or
  1 small aubergine, sliced
30ml/2 tbsp olive oil
1 yellow (bell) pepper, seeded
  and sliced

115g/4oz/1 cup cornmeal
50g/2oz/¹⁄₂ cup potato flour
50g/2oz/¹⁄₂ cup soya flour
5ml/1 tsp baking powder
2.5ml/¹⁄₂ tsp sea salt
50g/2oz/¹⁄₄ cup non-
  hydrogenated margarine
about 105ml/7 tbsp milk
4 plum tomatoes, skinned
  and chopped
30ml/2 tbsp chopped fresh basil
115g/4oz buffalo mozzarella
  cheese, sliced
sea salt and ground black pepper
fresh basil sprigs, to garnish

1 Preheat the grill (broiler). Brush the courgette and aubergine slices with a little oil and place on a grill rack with the pepper slices. Cook under the grill until lightly browned, turning once.

2 Meanwhile, preheat the oven to 200°C/400°F/Gas 6. Place the cornmeal, potato flour, soya flour, baking powder and salt in a mixing bowl and stir to mix. Lightly rub in the margarine until the mixture resembles coarse breadcrumbs, then stir in enough of the milk to make a soft but not sticky dough.

3 Place the pizza dough on a sheet of baking parchment on a baking sheet and roll or gently press it out to form a 25cm/10in round, making the edges slightly thicker than the centre.

4 Lightly brush the pizza dough with any remaining oil, then spread the chopped plum tomatoes evenly over the dough.

5 Sprinkle with the basil and seasoning. Arrange the grilled (broiled) vegetables over the tomatoes and top with the cheese.

6 Bake for about 25–30 minutes until crisp and golden brown. Garnish the pizza with fresh basil sprigs and serve immediately, cut into slices.

Conchiglie with Roasted Vegetables

Nothing could be simpler – or more delicious – than tossing freshly cooked pasta with roasted summer vegetables. The flavour is absolutely superb.

Serves 4–6

1 red (bell) pepper, seeded and
  cut into 1cm/¹⁄₂in squares
1 yellow or orange (bell) pepper,
  seeded and cut into
  1cm/¹⁄₂in squares
1 small aubergine (eggplant),
  roughly diced

2 courgettes (zucchini),
  roughly diced
75ml/5 tbsp extra virgin olive oil
15ml/1 tbsp chopped fresh
  flat leaf parsley
5ml/1 tsp dried oregano
  or marjoram
250g/9oz baby Italian plum
  tomatoes, hulled and
  halved lengthways
2 garlic cloves, roughly chopped
350–400g/12–14oz/3–3¹⁄₂ cups
  dried conchiglie
salt and ground black pepper
4–6 fresh marjoram or oregano
  flowers, to garnish

1 Preheat the oven to 190°C/375°F/Gas 5. Rinse the prepared peppers, aubergine and courgettes in a sieve (strainer) or colander under cold running water, drain, then transfer the vegetables into a large roasting pan.

2 Pour about 45ml/3 tbsp of the olive oil over the vegetables and sprinkle with the fresh and dried herbs. Add salt and pepper to taste and stir well.

3 Roast the vegetables in the preheated oven for about 30 minutes, stirring two or three times during the cooking.

4 Stir the tomatoes and garlic into the vegetable mixture, then roast for 20 minutes more, stirring once or twice.

5 Meanwhile, cook the pasta according to the instructions on the packet. Drain the pasta and transfer it into a warmed bowl.

6 Add the roasted vegetables and the remaining oil to the pasta and toss well. Serve the pasta and vegetables hot in warmed individual bowls, sprinkling each portion with a few herb flowers.

Vegetable Pizza Energy 400kcal/1666kJ; Protein 11.9g; Carbohydrate 34.6g, of which sugars 9.6g; Fat 23.9g, of which saturates 5.3g; Cholesterol 18mg; Calcium 166mg; Fibre 4.4g; Sodium 240mg.
Conchiglie with Vegetables Energy 277kcal/1171kJ; Protein 9.5g; Carbohydrate 50.3g, of which sugars 8.7g; Fat 5.5g, of which saturates 0.8g; Cholesterol 0mg; Calcium 52mg; Fibre 4.6g; Sodium 11mg.

Roasted Vegetable Quesadillas with Melted Mozzarella

Barbecuing gives these vegetables a wonderful smoky flavour, enhanced by the bite of green chillies.

Serves 4

8 long baby aubergines
  (eggplants), total weight about
  175g/6oz, halved lengthways
2 red onions, cut into wedges,
  leaving the roots intact
2 red (bell) peppers, quartered
1 yellow and 1 orange (bell)
  pepper, quartered
30ml/2 tbsp olive oil
400g/14oz block
  mozzarella cheese
2 fresh green chillies, seeded and
  sliced into rounds
15ml/1 tbsp tomato sauce
8 corn or wheat flour tortillas
handful of fresh basil leaves
salt and ground black pepper

1 Toss the aubergines, onions and peppers in the oil on a large baking sheet. Place the peppers, skin side down, on the griddle or directly on the grill rack of a medium hot barbecue and cook until seared and browned underneath. If the food starts to char, remove the rack until the coals cool down.

2 Put the peppers in a bowl, cover with clear film (plastic wrap) and set aside. Grill (broil) the onions and aubergines until they have softened slightly and are branded with brown grill marks, then set aside. Rub the skins off the peppers with your fingers, cut each piece in half and add to the other vegetables.

3 Cut the mozzarella into 20 slices. Place them, together with the roasted vegetables, in a large bowl and add the sliced chillies and the tomato sauce. Stir well to mix, and season with salt and pepper.

4 Place a griddle over the heat. When it is hot, lay a tortilla on the griddle and pile a quarter of the vegetable mixture into the centre. Sprinkle over some basil leaves. When the tortilla has browned underneath, put another tortilla on top, cooked side down. Turn the quesadilla over and continue to cook until the underside has browned. Keep warm while you cook the remaining quesadillas. Serve immediately.

Sweet Romanos Stuffed with Two Cheeses and Cherry Peppers

Romanos are wonderful Mediterranean peppers. They are long, pointy and slightly gnarled, and look a little like a large poblano chilli. Not hot but delightfully sweet, their flavour is nicely balanced by the ricotta salata.

Serves 4

4 sweet romano peppers,
  preferably in mixed colours,
  total weight about 350g/12oz
90ml/6 tbsp extra virgin olive oil
200g/7oz mozzarella cheese
10 drained bottled sweet cherry
  peppers, finely chopped
115g/4oz ricotta salata
30ml/2 tbsp chopped fresh
  oregano leaves
24 black olives
2 garlic cloves, crushed
salt and ground black pepper
dressed mixed salad leaves and
  bread, to serve

1 Prepare the barbecue. Split the peppers lengthways and remove the seeds and membrane. Rub 15ml/1 tbsp of the oil all over the peppers. Place them hollow-side uppermost.

2 Slice the mozzarella and divide equally among the pepper halves. Sprinkle over the chopped cherry peppers, season lightly and crumble the ricotta salata over the top, followed by the oregano leaves and olives. Mix the garlic with the remaining oil and add a little salt and pepper. Spoon about half the mixture over the filling in the peppers.

3 Once the flames have died down, rake the coals to one side. Position a lightly oiled grill rack over the coals to heat. When the coals are medium-hot, or with a moderate coating of ash, place the filled peppers on the section of grill rack that is not over the coals. Cover with a lid, or improvise with a wok lid or tented heavy-duty foil. Grill for 6 minutes.

4 Spoon the remaining oil mixture over the filling, replace the lid and continue to grill for 6–8 minutes more, or until the peppers are lightly charred and the cheese has melted. Serve the peppers immediately with a dressed green or leafy salad and bread.

Vegetable Quesadillas Energy 233kcal/971kJ; Protein 11.8g; Carbohydrate 17.1g, of which sugars 8.5g; Fat 13.6g, of which saturates 7.4g; Cholesterol 29mg; Calcium 214mg; Fibre 2.7g; Sodium 268mg.
Sweet Romanos Energy 95kcal/399kJ; Protein 5.6g; Carbohydrate 12.8g, of which sugars 12g; Fat 2.8g, of which saturates 0.7g; Cholesterol 48mg; Calcium 53mg; Fibre 4.5g; Sodium 301mg.

Roasted Mixed Pepper and Parmesan Risotto

This makes an excellent and colourful vegetarian lunch or supper dish.

Serves 3–4
1 red (bell) pepper
1 yellow (bell) pepper
15ml/1 tbsp olive oil
25g/1oz/2 tbsp butter
1 onion, chopped
2 garlic cloves, crushed
275g/10oz/1½ cups risotto rice
1 litre/1¾ pints/4 cups
    simmering vegetable stock
50g/2oz/⅔ cup freshly grated
    Parmesan cheese
salt and ground black pepper
freshly grated Parmesan cheese,
    to serve (optional)

1 Preheat the grill (broiler). Cut the peppers in half, remove the seeds and pith and arrange, cut side down, on a baking sheet. Place under the grill for 5–6 minutes until the skin is charred. Put the peppers in a plastic bag, tie the ends and leave for 4–5 minutes.

2 Peel the peppers when they are cool enough to handle and the steam has loosened the skin. Cut into thin strips.

3 Heat the oil and butter in a pan and cook the onion and garlic for 4–5 minutes over low heat until the onion begins to soften. Add the peppers and cook the mixture for 3–4 minutes more, stirring occasionally.

4 Stir in the rice. Cook over medium heat for 3–4 minutes, stirring constantly all the time, until the rice is evenly coated in oil and the outer part of each grain has become translucent.

5 Add a ladleful of stock. Cook, stirring, until all the liquid has been absorbed. Continue to add the stock, a ladleful at a time, making sure each quantity has been absorbed before adding the next.

6 When the rice is tender but retains a little 'bite', stir in the Parmesan, and add seasoning to taste. Cover and leave to stand for 4 minutes, then serve, with extra Parmesan, if using.

Summer Vegetable Kebabs with Harissa and Yogurt Dip

This simple and tasty vegetarian dish is delicious served with couscous and a fresh, crispy green salad. It also makes an excellent side dish to accompany meat-based main courses. Vegetable and fish kebabs are becoming increasingly popular in Morocco.

Serves 4
2 aubergines (eggplants), part-
    peeled and cut into chunks
2 courgettes (zucchini), cut
    into chunks
2–3 red or green (bell) peppers,
    cut into chunks
12–16 cherry tomatoes
4 small red onions, quartered
60ml/4 tbsp olive oil
juice of ½ lemon
1 garlic clove, crushed
5ml/1 tsp ground coriander
5ml/1 tsp ground cinnamon
10ml/2 tsp clear honey
5ml/1 tsp salt

For the harissa and yogurt dip
450g/1lb/2 cups natural
    (plain) yogurt
30–60ml/2–4 tbsp harissa
small bunch of fresh coriander
    (cilantro), finely chopped
small bunch of mint,
    finely chopped
salt and ground black pepper

1 Preheat the grill (broiler) on the hottest setting. Put all the vegetables in a bowl.

2 Mix the olive oil, lemon juice, garlic, ground coriander, cinnamon, honey and salt and pour the mixture over the vegetables. Turn the vegetables gently in the marinade, then thread them on to metal skewers. Cook the kebabs under the grill, turning them occasionally until the vegetables are nicely browned all over.

3 To make the dip, put the yogurt in a bowl and beat in the harissa, making it as fiery as you like by adding more harissa.

4 Add most of the coriander and mint, reserving a little to garnish, and season well with salt and pepper. While they are still hot, slide the vegetables off the skewers. Garnish with the reserved herbs and serve with the yogurt dip.

Pepper Risotto Energy 555kcal/2312kJ; Protein 16.1g; Carbohydrate 80.1g, of which sugars 10g; Fat 18g, of which saturates 8.4g; Cholesterol 34mg; Calcium 238mg; Fibre 2.6g; Sodium 241mg.
Summer Kebabs Energy 274kcal/1144kJ; Protein 11.1g; Carbohydrate 28.8g, of which sugars 26.2g; Fat 13.7g, of which saturates 2.5g; Cholesterol 1mg; Calcium 303mg; Fibre 5.9g; Sodium 111mg.

Roasted Ratatouille Moussaka

Roasting brings out the deep rich flavours of the summer vegetables, which contrast with the light egg-and-cheese topping.

Serves 4–6
2 red (bell) peppers, cut into
    large chunks
2 yellow (bell) peppers, cut into
    large chunks
2 aubergines (eggplants), cut into
    large chunks
3 courgettes (zucchini), cut into
    thick slices
45ml/3 tbsp olive oil
3 garlic cloves, crushed
400g/14oz can
    chopped tomatoes

30ml/2 tbsp sun-dried
    tomato paste
45ml/3 tbsp chopped fresh basil
15ml/1 tbsp balsamic vinegar
1.5ml/¼ tsp soft brown sugar
salt and ground black pepper
basil leaves, to garnish

For the topping
25g/1oz/2 tbsp butter
25g/1oz/¼ cup plain
    (all-purpose) flour
300ml/½ pint/1¼ cups milk
1.5ml/¼ tsp freshly
    grated nutmeg
250g/9oz ricotta cheese
3 eggs, beaten
25g/1oz/⅓ cup freshly grated
    Parmesan cheese

1 Preheat the oven to 230°C/450°F/Gas 8. Arrange the chunks of peppers, aubergines and courgettes in an even layer in a large roasting pan. Season with salt and ground black pepper.

2 Mix together the oil and crushed garlic cloves and pour them over the vegetables. Shake the pan to coat the vegetables thoroughly in the garlic mixture.

3 Roast in the oven for 15–20 minutes, until slightly charred, tossing once during cooking. Remove the pan from the oven and set aside. Reduce the temperature to 200°C/400°F/Gas 6.

4 Put the chopped tomatoes, sun-dried tomato paste, basil, balsamic vinegar and brown sugar in a large, heavy pan and heat gently to boiling point. Reduce the heat and simmer, uncovered, for about 10–15 minutes, until reduced, stirring occasionally. Season with salt and pepper to taste.

5 Carefully transfer the roasted vegetables out of their pan and into the tomato sauce. Mix well, coating the vegetables thoroughly. Spoon into an ovenproof dish.

6 To make the topping, melt the butter in a large, heavy pan over a gentle heat. Stir in the flour and cook for 1 minute. Pour in the milk, stirring constantly, then whisk until blended. Add the nutmeg and continue whisking over a gentle heat until thickened. Cook for a further 2 minutes, then remove from the heat and leave to cool slightly.

7 Mix the ricotta cheese and beaten eggs thoroughly into the sauce. Season with salt and plenty of freshly ground black pepper to taste.

8 Level the surface of the roasted vegetable mixture with the back of a spoon. Spoon the moussaka topping over the vegetables and sprinkle with the Parmesan cheese. Bake for 30–35 minutes, until the topping is golden brown. Serve immediately, garnished with basil leaves.

Kan Shao Green Beans

The slim green beans that appear in stores in summer are ideal for use in this quick and tasty recipe.

Serves 6
450/1lb fresh green beans
175ml/6fl oz/¾ cup sunflower oil

5cm/2in piece fresh root ginger,
    peeled and cut into matchsticks
5ml/1 tsp sugar
10ml/2 tsp light soy sauce
salt and ground black pepper

1 Top and tail the beans. Heat the oil in a wok and stir-fry the beans for 1–2 minutes until just tender.

2 Lift out the green beans on to a plate lined with kitchen paper. Remove all but 30ml/2 tbsp oil from the wok.

3 Reheat the oil in the wok, add the ginger and stir-fry for a minute or two to flavour the oil.

4 Return the green beans to the wok, stir in the sugar, soy sauce and salt and pepper, and toss together to ensure the beans are well coated. Transfer into a heated bowl and serve.

Penne with Tomatoes and Basil

This pasta dish is fresh, healthy and ready in a matter of minutes. It is the perfect way to use up a glut of ripe, flavoursome tomatoes during the summer season.

Serves 4
500g/1¼lb dried penne
5 very ripe plum tomatoes
1 small bunch of fresh basil
60ml/4 tbsp extra virgin olive oil
salt and ground black pepper

1 Cook the pasta in a pan of salted, boiling water according to the instructions on the packet. Meanwhile, chop the tomatoes, pull the basil leaves from their stems and tear the leaves.

2 Drain the pasta and toss with the tomatoes, basil and olive oil. Season with salt and black pepper and serve immediately.

Moussaka Energy 570kcal/2367kJ; Protein 22.1g; Carbohydrate 27.5g, of which sugars 21.7g; Fat 42.1g, of which saturates 20.3g; Cholesterol 223mg; Calcium 339mg; Fibre 7.1g; Sodium 447mg.
Kan Shao Green Beans Energy 223kcal/917kJ; Protein 1.4g; Carbohydrate 3.1g, of which sugars 2.4g; Fat 22.9g, of which saturates 2.8g; Cholesterol 0mg; Calcium 27mg; Fibre 1.7g; Sodium 0mg.
Penne with Tomatoes Energy 552kcal/2336kJ; Protein 16.3g; Carbohydrate 96.9g, of which sugars 8.3g; Fat 13.8g, of which saturates 2g; Cholesterol 0mg; Calcium 65mg; Fibre 5.5g; Sodium 19mg.

Farfalle with Courgettes and Prawns

In this modern recipe, pink prawns and green courgettes combine prettily with cream and pasta bows to make a substantial main course for summer. Serve with crusty Italian rolls or warm ciabatta bread.

Serves 4

50g/2oz/¼ cup butter
2–3 spring onions (scallions), very thinly sliced on the diagonal
350g/12oz courgettes (zucchini), thinly sliced on the diagonal
60ml/4 tbsp dry white wine
300g/11oz/2¾ cups dried farfalle
75ml/5 tbsp crème fraîche
225g/8oz/1⅓ cups peeled cooked prawns (shrimp), thawed and thoroughly dried if frozen
15ml/1 tbsp finely chopped fresh marjoram or flat leaf parsley, or a mixture
salt and ground black pepper

1 Melt the butter in a large pan, add the spring onions and cook over a low heat, stirring frequently, for about 5 minutes until softened. Add the courgettes, with salt and pepper to taste, and stir-fry for 5 minutes. Pour over the wine and let it bubble, then cover and simmer for 10 minutes.

2 Cook the pasta in a pan of salted boiling water according to the instructions on the packet. Meanwhile, add the crème fraîche to the courgette mixture and simmer for about 10 minutes until well reduced.

3 Add the prawns to the courgette mixture, heat through gently and taste for seasoning. Drain the pasta and transfer it into a warmed bowl. Add the sauce and chopped herbs and toss well. Serve immediately.

> **Variation**
> Use penne instead of the farfalle, and asparagus tips instead of the courgettes (zucchini), if you like.

Light and Fragrant Tiger Prawns with Cucumber and Dill

This simple, elegant dish has a fresh, light flavour full of the tastes of summer. It is equally good for a simple supper or a dinner party.

Serves 4

500g/1¼lb raw tiger prawns (jumbo shrimp), peeled with tail on
500g/1¼lb cucumber
30ml/2 tbsp butter
15ml/1 tbsp olive oil
15ml/1 tbsp finely chopped garlic
45ml/3 tbsp chopped fresh dill
juice of 1 lemon
salt and ground black pepper
steamed rice or noodles, to serve

1 Using a small, sharp knife, carefully make a shallow slit along the back of each prawn and use the point of the knife to remove the black vein. Set the prawns aside.

2 Peel the cucumber and slice in half lengthways. Using a small teaspoon, gently scoop out all the seeds and discard. Cut the cucumber into 4 × 1cm/1½ × ½in sticks.

3 Heat a wok over a high heat, then add the butter and oil. When the butter has melted, add the cucumber and garlic and stir-fry over a high heat for 2–3 minutes.

4 Add the prepared prawns to the wok and continue to stir-fry over a high heat for 3–4 minutes, or until the prawns turn pink and are just cooked through, then remove from the heat.

5 Add the fresh dill and lemon juice to the wok and toss to combine. Season well with salt and ground black pepper and serve immediately with steamed rice or noodles.

> **Variation**
> The delicate flavour of prawns (shrimp) goes really well with cucumber and fragrant dill, but if you prefer a more robust dish, toss in a handful of chives as well.

Farfalle Energy 490kcal/2058kJ; Protein 21.1g; Carbohydrate 57.9g, of which sugars 4.7g; Fat 19.8g, of which saturates 11.9g; Cholesterol 158mg; Calcium 102mg; Fibre 3.1g; Sodium 191mg.
Fragrant Prawns Energy 165kcal/691kJ; Protein 15.7g; Carbohydrate 10.5g, of which sugars 10.1g; Fat 7g, of which saturates 0.9g; Cholesterol 171mg; Calcium 78mg; Fibre 0.3g; Sodium 167mg.

Fried Eel with Creamy Potatoes

This dish is a great way to enjoy fried eel. Served with these delicious potatoes and accompanied by a cold beer, this seasonal dish is a summer speciality.

Serves 4
about 1kg/2¼lb eel, skinned and cleaned
1 egg
5ml/1 tsp water
25g/1oz/½ cup fine breadcrumbs, toasted
10ml/2 tsp salt
2.5ml/½ tsp white pepper

40g/1½oz/3 tbsp butter
2 lemons, sliced into wedges, to garnish

For the potatoes
800g/1¾lb potatoes, peeled
5ml/1 tsp salt
40g/1½oz/3 tbsp butter
20g/¾oz/4 tbsp plain (all-purpose) flour
475ml/16fl oz/2 cups single (light) cream
salt and white pepper, to taste
45ml/3 tbsp chopped fresh parsley, to garnish

1 Using a sharp knife, cut the skinned eel into 10cm/4in lengths. Whisk together the egg and water in a shallow dish. Place the breadcrumbs in a second shallow dish. Dip the eel first into the egg mixture, then into the breadcrumbs to coat both sides evenly. Sprinkle with salt and pepper. Leave the fish aside to rest for at least 10 minutes.

2 Melt the butter in a large pan over medium-high heat. Add the eel pieces and cook, turning once, for around 10 minutes on each side, depending on thickness, until the coating is golden brown and the eel is tender. Remove from the pan and drain on kitchen paper. Keep warm.

3 Meanwhile, boil the potatoes in salted water for about 20 minutes. Drain, slice and keep warm. Melt the butter in a pan and stir in the flour. Cook, stirring, for 5 minutes until the roux is pale beige. Slowly stir in the cream and cook for about 5 minutes, stirring constantly, until the sauce has thickened. Season to taste.

4 Stir the potato slices into the cream sauce. Serve with the fried eel on warmed plates, garnished with the parsley, lemon wedges and accompanied by fresh vegetables, if you wish.

Salted and Grilled Sardines

Grilled sardines are classic Mediterranean beach food. Nothing beats grilling these fresh fish on a barbecue at the coast on a hot summer's day. Serve with focaccia or fresh crusty bread.

Serves 4–8
8 sardines, about 800g/1¾lb total weight, scaled and gutted
50g/2oz/¼ cup salt
oil, for brushing

focaccia or fresh crusty bread, to serve (optional)

For the herb salsa
5ml/1 tsp sea salt flakes
60ml/4 tbsp chopped fresh tarragon leaves
40g/1½oz/generous 1 cup chopped flat leaf parsley
1 small red onion, very finely chopped
105ml/7 tbsp extra virgin olive oil
60ml/4 tbsp lemon juice

1 Make the herb salsa by grinding the salt in a mortar and adding the other salsa ingredients one at a time.

2 Wash the sardines inside and out. Pat dry with kitchen paper and rub them inside and out with salt. Cover and put in a cool place for 30–45 minutes. Meanwhile, prepare the barbecue.

3 Rinse the salt off the sardines. Pat them dry with kitchen paper, then leave to air-dry for 15 minutes.

4 When the coals have a thick coating of ash, brush the fish with olive oil and cook directly on the oiled grill.

5 Cook the fish for about 3 minutes on one side and about 2½ minutes on the other. Serve immediately with the herb salsa and bread.

Cook's Tip
Fresh sardines are only available for a very limited season during the summer months, usually close to where they have been caught. Sardine is a slightly generic term for young, small fish – usually it refers to young pilchards but canned sardines may be sprats or herring as well.

Fried Eel Energy 978kcal/4074kJ; Protein 50.2g; Carbohydrate 43.7g, of which sugars 5.6g; Fat 68.2g, of which saturates 32.3g; Cholesterol 483mg; Calcium 184mg; Fibre 2.3g; Sodium 448mg.
Salted Sardines Energy 423kcal/1,754kJ; Protein 31.5g; Carbohydrate 1.8g, of which sugars 1.4g; Fat 32.1g, of which saturates 6.4g; Cholesterol 0mg; Calcium 187mg; Fibre 1g; Sodium 667mg.

Sardine 'Cutlets'

Fresh sardines are readily available in the summer, and one of the most popular ways to cook them is to simply deep-fry them. Serve the fish with a seasonal tomato salad, potatoes and olive oil. If you are at an informal summer barbecue, they are equally delicious eaten on a slice of bread.

Serves 4
12 medium sardines
juice of 2 lemons
1 garlic clove, finely
    chopped (optional)
3 eggs
50g/2oz/½ cup plain
    (all-purpose) flour
50g/2oz/1 cup breadcrumbs
vegetable oil, for deep-frying
salt

1 To scale the sardines, hold each fish by the tail and scrape off the scales with a fish scaler or serrated knife held at an angle, working from head to tail. Rinse well under cold running water. Slit open the belly of each fish with a sharp knife and pull out the intestines with your fingers. Rinse well again. If you want to remove the bones, open out the fish, skin side uppermost, and press along the backbone with your thumb. Turn the fish over and ease out the bones.

2 Place the sardines in a non-metallic dish and pour the lemon juice over them. Sprinkle them with salt and garlic, if using. Leave to marinate for 30 minutes.

3 Beat the eggs in a shallow dish. Spread out the flour in another shallow dish and the breadcrumbs in a third. Heat the oil in a large pan or deep-fryer to 180°C/350°F or until a cube of day-old bread browns in 40 seconds.

4 Dip the sardines in the flour, shaking off any excess, then in the egg and then in the breadcrumbs. Deep-fry in batches for 5 minutes, until cooked through. Drain on kitchen paper and serve.

Cook's Tip
For a cleaner dinner table, remove the sardine heads, along with the backbones, at the end of step 1.

Sardines in Summer Marinade

Sardines are a welcome catch in the summer months for many people and this marinated dish is an especially good way to enjoy them. The basic marinade consists of sliced onion, garlic, bay leaves and plenty of good-quality white wine vinegar, to which tomatoes or other vegetables may be added.

Serves 4–6
12 sardines, cleaned
plain (all-purpose) flour, for dusting
150ml/¼ pint/⅔ cup olive oil
2 onions, halved and thinly sliced
3 bay leaves
2 garlic cloves, chopped
150ml/¼ pint/⅔ cup white
    wine vinegar
2 ripe tomatoes, diced
sea salt
crusty bread, to serve

1 Dust the sardines with flour, shaking off any excess. Heat 75ml/5 tbsp of the olive oil in a heavy frying pan.

2 Add the sardines to the frying pan, in batches of three or four, and cook them over medium heat, for about 1 minute each side. Remove each fish with a slotted spatula and drain on kitchen paper.

3 In a clean pan, cook the onions, bay leaves and garlic with the rest of the olive oil over low heat, stirring occasionally, for about 5 minutes, until softened. Add the vinegar and the tomatoes, and season with sea salt to taste.

4 Return the sardines to the pan. If they are not completely covered, add a little water or some more vinegar. Cook for a few minutes.

5 Transfer the mixture to a deep plate, allow to cool and leave to marinate in the refrigerator for about 3 days. Serve with crusty bread.

Cook's Tip
Leave the sardine marinade for some days and don't be shy with the vinegar, as it will be absorbed.

Sardine 'Cutlets' Energy 489kcal/2042kJ; Protein 38.2g; Carbohydrate 19.4g, of which sugars 0.5g; Fat 29.4g, of which saturates 6.5g; Cholesterol 143mg; Calcium 181mg; Fibre 0.7g; Sodium 328mg.
Sardines in Marinade Energy 335kcal/1392kJ; Protein 21.2g; Carbohydrate 4.3g, of which sugars 1.1g; Fat 26g, of which saturates 5.1g; Cholesterol 0mg; Calcium 92mg; Fibre 0.5g; Sodium 123mg.

Herrings in Oatmeal

Herrings have a wonderfully strong flavour and are ideal for simple summer recipes. In this traditional recipe, the herrings are first coated in rolled oats before being grilled and served with a mustard sauce. The fish make for a hearty meal, and they are also easy to prepare and cook.

Serves 4
175ml/6fl oz/³⁄₄ cup thick
   mayonnaise
15ml/1 tbsp Dijon mustard
7.5ml/1¹⁄₂ tsp tarragon vinegar
4 herrings, approximately
   225g/8oz each
juice of 1 lemon
115g/4oz/generous 1 cup
   medium rolled oats
salt and ground black pepper

1 Place the mayonnaise in a small mixing bowl and add the Dijon mustard and tarragon vinegar. Mix thoroughly and then chill for a few minutes.

2 Place one fish at a time on a chopping board, cut side down, and open out. Press gently along the backbone with your thumbs. Turn the fish over and carefully lift away the backbone.

3 Squeeze lemon juice over both sides of the fish, then season with salt and ground black pepper. Fold the fish in half, skin side outwards.

4 Preheat the grill (broiler) to medium hot. Place the rolled oats on a plate, then coat each herring evenly in the oats, pressing it in gently.

5 Place the herrings on a grill rack and grill (broil) the fish for 3–4 minutes on each side, until the skin is golden brown and crisp and the flesh flakes easily when the fish is cut into. Serve immediately on warmed plates with the mustard sauce handed round in a separate dish or bowl.

> **Cook's Tip**
> Use the best-quality mayonnaise you can find for this dish. It will taste even better if you use a home-made version.

Mackerel with Rhubarb Sauce

Mackerel are really at their best in early summer, just when rhubarb is growing strongly. The tartness of rhubarb offsets the richness of the oily fish to perfection.

Serves 4
4 whole mackerel, cleaned
25g/1oz/2 tbsp butter
1 onion, finely chopped
90ml/6 tbsp fresh white
   breadcrumbs
15ml/1 tbsp chopped fresh parsley
finely grated rind of 1 lemon

freshly grated nutmeg
1 egg, lightly beaten
melted butter or olive oil,
   for brushing
sea salt and ground black pepper

For the sauce
225g/8oz rhubarb (trimmed
   weight), cut in 1cm/¹⁄₂in lengths
25–50g/1–2oz/2–4 tbsp caster
   (superfine) sugar
25g/1oz/2 tbsp butter
15ml/1 tbsp chopped fresh
   tarragon (optional), to garnish

1 Ask the fishmonger to bone the mackerel, or do it yourself: open out the body of the fish, turn flesh side down and run your thumb firmly down the backbone – when you turn the fish over, the bones should lift out in a complete section.

2 Melt the butter in a pan and cook the onion gently for 5–10 minutes, until softened but not browned. Add the breadcrumbs, parsley, lemon rind, salt, pepper and grated nutmeg. Mix well, and then add the beaten egg to bind.

3 Divide the mixture among the four fish, wrap the fish over and secure with cocktail sticks (toothpicks). Brush with melted butter or olive oil. Preheat the grill (broiler) and cook under medium heat for about 8 minutes on each side.

4 Meanwhile, make the sauce: put the rhubarb into a pan with 75ml/2¹⁄₂fl oz/¹⁄₃ cup water, 25g/1oz/2 tbsp of the sugar and the butter. Cook over low heat until the rhubarb is tender. Taste for sweetness and add extra sugar if necessary, bearing in mind that the sauce needs to be quite sharp.

5 Serve the stuffed mackerel with the hot rhubarb sauce, garnished with a little of the fresh tarragon.

Herrings in Oatmeal Energy 755kcal/3143kJ; Protein 36.7g; Carbohydrate 32.6g, of which sugars 0.6g; Fat 54g, of which saturates 9.3g; Cholesterol 98mg; Calcium 149mg; Fibre 3g; Sodium 459mg.
Mackerel with Rhubarb Energy 728kcal/3034kJ; Protein 48.2g; Carbohydrate 27.5g, of which sugars 9.8g; Fat 48g, of which saturates 14.3g; Cholesterol 193mg; Calcium 129mg; Fibre 1.8g; Sodium 398mg.

Mackerel with Nutty Bacon Stuffing

The mackerel are stuffed, tied with raffia and then grilled. They taste just as good cold so, when mackerel are at their peak in the summer, make extra for lunch next day.

Serves 6
45ml/3 tbsp olive oil
2 onions, finely chopped
2 garlic cloves, crushed
6 rindless smoked bacon rashers (strips), diced
50g/2oz/1/2 cup pine nuts
45ml/3 tbsp chopped fresh sweet marjoram
6 mackerel, about 300g/11oz each, cleaned but with heads left on
salt and ground black pepper
lemon wedges, to serve
raffia, soaked in water

1 Heat the oil in a large frying pan and sweat the onion and garlic over medium heat for 5 minutes. Increase the heat and add the bacon and pine nuts. Fry for 5–7 minutes, stirring occasionally, until golden. Transfer into a bowl to cool. Gently fold in the marjoram, season lightly, cover and chill until needed.

2 To prepare each fish, snip the backbone at the head end. Extend the cavity opening at the tail end so you can reach the backbone more easily. Turn the fish over and, with the heel of your hand, press firmly along the entire length of the backbone to loosen it. Snip the bone at the tail end and it will lift out surprisingly easily. Season the insides lightly.

3 Stuff the cavity in each mackerel with some of the chilled onion mixture, then tie the mackerel along its entire length with raffia to hold in the stuffing. Chill the fish for at least 15 minutes. They can be chilled for up to 2 hours, but if so, allow them to come to room temperature for about 15 minutes before grilling.

4 Prepare the barbecue. Once the flames have died down, position a lightly oiled grill rack over the coals to heat. When the coals are medium-hot, or with a moderate coating of ash, transfer the mackerel to the rack and cook for 8 minutes on each side, or until cooked and golden. If your barbecue has a lid, use it. This will help you achieve an even golden skin without moving the fish. Serve the mackerel immediately with lemon wedges and black pepper.

Stuffed Horse Mackerel

Horse mackerel, also known as scad, is a member of the fish family that also includes jacks, pompanos, trevallys, kingfish and queenfish. This is a delicious dish, which is absolutely perfect for the summer months.

Serves 4
8 small horse mackerel, about 10cm/4in long, gutted
30ml/2 tbsp olive oil
1 small onion, chopped
1 green (bell) pepper, seeded and cut in small cubes
1 garlic clove, chopped
15ml/1 tbsp paprika paste
1 tomato, peeled and diced
2 slices day-old bread, crusts removed
10ml/2 tsp white wine vinegar
30ml/2 tbsp chopped fresh parsley
25g/1oz/1/4 cup pitted green olives, cut into small strips
vegetable oil, for deep-frying
cornflour (cornstarch), for dusting
salt

1 Cut off and discard the fish heads. To scale them, hold each fish by the tail and scrape off the scales with a fish scaler or serrated knife held at an angle, working from head to tail. Rinse well under cold running water. Open out the fish, skin side uppermost – you may need to extend the slit in the bellies. Press along the backbones with your thumb. Turn the fish over and ease out the bones. Remove small bones with tweezers.

2 Heat the oil in a frying pan. Add the onion and green pepper and cook over a low heat, stirring occasionally, for 5 minutes, until softened. Add the garlic, paprika paste and tomato and cook for a few minutes, then remove the pan from the heat.

3 Tear the bread into pieces and mash to a paste with water. Stir the paste into the pan and season to taste with salt and vinegar. Stir in the parsley and olives.

4 Heat the oil for deep-frying to 180°C/350°F or until a cube of day-old bread browns in 40 seconds. Meanwhile, divide the filling among four of the fish. Place the remaining fish on top and secure with wooden cocktail sticks (toothpicks). Dust each pair of fish with cornflour, shaking off any excess, add to the hot oil and deep-fry for about 5 minutes, until golden brown and cooked through. Drain on kitchen paper and serve immediately.

Mackerel with Stuffing Energy 858kcal/3561kJ; Protein 64.5g; Carbohydrate 5.8g, of which sugars 4.3g; Fat 64.1g, of which saturates 12.9g; Cholesterol 175mg; Calcium 69mg; Fibre 1.5g; Sodium 641mg.
Stuffed Mackerel Energy 558kcal/2316kJ; Protein 30.4g; Carbohydrate 15.2g, of which sugars 4.9g; Fat 42.1g, of which saturates 7.2g; Cholesterol 81mg; Calcium 70mg; Fibre 2.2g; Sodium 316mg.

Mackerel in Lemon Samfaina

Samfaina is a sauce from the east coast of Spain and the Costa Brava. It shares the same ingredients as the French dish ratatouille and is rather like a chunky summer vegetable stew. This version is particularly lemony, to offset the richness of the mackerel.

Serves 4
2 large mackerel, filleted, or 4 fillets
plain (all-purpose) flour,
  for dusting

30ml/2 tbsp olive oil
lemon wedges, if serving cold

For the samfaina sauce
1 large aubergine (eggplant)
60ml/4 tbsp olive oil
1 large onion, chopped
2 garlic cloves, finely chopped
1 large courgette (zucchini), sliced
1 red and 1 green (bell) pepper,
  cut into squares
800g/1¾lb ripe tomatoes,
  roughly chopped
1 bay leaf
salt and ground black pepper

1 To make the sauce, peel the aubergine, cut the flesh into cubes, sprinkle with salt and leave to stand in a colander for 30 minutes.

2 Heat half the oil in a flameproof casserole large enough to fit the fish. Fry the onion over a medium heat until it colours. Add the garlic, then the courgette and peppers, and stir-fry. Add the tomatoes and bay leaf, partially cover and simmer gently, letting the tomatoes just soften.

3 Rinse the salt off the aubergine and squeeze dry in kitchen paper. Heat the remaining oil in a frying pan until smoking. Put in one handful of aubergine cubes, then the next, stirring and cooking over a high heat until the cubes are brown on all sides. Stir into the tomato sauce.

4 Cut each mackerel fillet into three, and dust the filleted side with flour. Heat the oil over high heat and fry the fish, floured side down, for 3 minutes. Turn and cook for another 1 minute, then slip the fish into the sauce and simmer, covered, for 5 minutes. Serve immediately.

> **Variation**
> The fish can also be served cold. Present the mackerel skin-side up, surrounded by the vegetables, with lemon wedges.

Halibut with Peppers and Coconut

This aromatic dish from Brazil is full of the tastes of the sun. Cooked and served in an earthenware dish, it is usually accompanied by white rice and cassava flour to soak up the delicious sauce.

Serves 6
6 halibut, cod, haddock or monkfish
  fillets, each about 115g/4oz
juice of 2 limes
8 fresh coriander (cilantro) sprigs
2 fresh red chillies, seeded
  and chopped
3 tomatoes, sliced into thin rounds

1 red (bell) pepper, seeded and
  sliced into thin rounds
1 green (bell) pepper, seeded and
  sliced into thin rounds
1 small onion, sliced into thin rounds
200ml/7fl oz/scant 1 cup
  coconut milk
60ml/4 tbsp palm oil
salt
cooked white rice, to serve

For the flavoured cassava flour
30ml/2 tbsp palm oil
1 medium onion, thinly sliced
250g/9oz/2¼ cups cassava flour

1 Place the fish fillets in a large, shallow dish and pour over water to cover. Pour in the lime juice and set aside for 30 minutes. Drain the fish thoroughly and pat dry with kitchen paper. Arrange the fish in a single layer in a heavy pan which has a tight-fitting lid.

2 Sprinkle the coriander and chillies over the fish, then top with a layer each of tomatoes, peppers and onion. Pour the coconut milk over, cover and leave to stand for 15 minutes before cooking.

3 Season with salt, then place the pan over high heat and cook until the coconut milk comes to the boil. Lower the heat and simmer for 5 minutes. Remove the lid, pour in the palm oil, cover again and simmer for 10 minutes.

4 Meanwhile, make the flavoured cassava flour. Heat the oil in a large frying pan over very low heat. Stir in the onion slices and cook for 8–10 minutes until soft and golden. Stir in the cassava flour and cook, stirring constantly, for 1–2 minutes until lightly toasted and evenly coloured by the oil. Season with salt. Serve the halibut and peppers with the rice and cassava flour.

Mackerel in Samfaina Energy 621kcal/2591kJ; Protein 34.3g; Carbohydrate 32.4g, of which sugars 29.4g; Fat 40.6g, of which saturates 7.6g; Cholesterol 66mg; Calcium 134mg; Fibre 19.4g; Sodium 111mg.
Halibut with Peppers Energy 207kcal/868kJ; Protein 21.8g; Carbohydrate 6.7g, of which sugars 6.2g; Fat 10.6g, of which saturates 3.8g; Cholesterol 58mg; Calcium 46mg; Fibre 1.6g; Sodium 140mg.

Plaice Fillets with Sorrel and Lemon Butter

Sorrel is a wild herb that is now grown commercially. It is very good in salads and, roughly chopped, it partners this slightly sweet-fleshed fish very well. Plaice – such a pretty fish with its orange spots and fern-like frills – is a delicate fish that works well with this sauce. Cook the fish simply like this to get the full natural flavours of the ingredients.

Serves 4
200g/7oz/scant 1 cup butter
500g/1¼lb plaice fillets, skinned and patted dry
30ml/2 tbsp chopped fresh sorrel
90ml/6 tbsp dry white wine
a little lemon juice

1 Heat half the butter in a large frying pan and, just as it is melted, place the fillets skin side down. Cook briefly, just to firm up, reduce the heat and turn the fish over. The fish will be cooked in less than 5 minutes. Try not to let the butter brown or allow the fish to colour.

2 Carefully remove the fish fillets from the pan with a metal spatula and keep them warm between two plates. Cut the remaining butter into chunks.

3 Add the chopped sorrel to the pan and stir. Add the wine, then, as it bubbles, add the butter, swirling it in piece by piece and not allowing the sauce to boil. Stir in a little lemon juice.

4 Serve the fish with the sorrel and lemon butter spooned over, with some crunchy green beans and perhaps some new potatoes, if you like.

> **Variation**
> Instead of using sorrel, you could try this recipe with fresh tarragon or thyme.

Fried Plaice with Tomato and Basil Sauce

This simple summer dish is perennially popular with children. It works equally well with lemon sole or dabs (these do not need skinning), or fillets of haddock and whiting.

Serves 4
25g/1oz/¼ cup plain (all-purpose) flour
2 eggs, beaten
75g/3oz/¾ cup dried breadcrumbs, preferably home-made

4 small plaice or flounder, skinned
15g/½oz/1 tbsp butter
15ml/1 tbsp sunflower oil
salt and ground black pepper
1 lemon, quartered, to serve
fresh basil leaves, to garnish

For the tomato sauce
30ml/2 tbsp olive oil
1 red onion, finely chopped
1 garlic clove, finely chopped
400g/14oz can chopped tomatoes
15ml/1 tbsp tomato purée (paste)
15ml/1 tbsp torn fresh basil leaves

1 First make the tomato sauce. Heat the olive oil in a large pan, add the finely chopped onion and garlic and cook gently for about 5 minutes, until softened and pale golden. Stir in the chopped tomatoes and tomato purée and simmer for 20–30 minutes, stirring occasionally. Season with salt and pepper and stir in the basil.

2 Spread out the flour in a shallow dish, pour the beaten eggs into another and spread out the breadcrumbs in a third. Season the fish with salt and pepper.

3 Hold a fish in your left hand and dip it first in flour, then in egg and finally, in the breadcrumbs, patting the crumbs on with your dry right hand.

4 Heat the butter and oil in a frying pan until foaming. Fry the fish one at a time in the hot fat for about 5 minutes on each side, until golden brown and cooked through, but still juicy in the middle. Drain on kitchen paper and keep hot while you fry the rest. Serve with lemon wedges and the tomato sauce, garnished with basil leaves.

Plaice Fillets Energy 494kcal/2047kJ; Protein 25.7g; Carbohydrate 0.5g, of which sugars 0.5g; Fat 43.3g, of which saturates 26.4g; Cholesterol 170mg; Calcium 98mg; Fibre 0.3g; Sodium 501mg.
Fried Plaice Energy 333kcal/1390kJ; Protein 22.5g; Carbohydrate 14.2g, of which sugars 3.9g; Fat 21.1g, of which saturates 2.5g; Cholesterol 0mg; Calcium 90mg; Fibre 1.3g; Sodium 279mg.

Baked Cod with Beer and Lemon

Cod is one of the most popular types of fish, as it has a mild flavour and plenty of dense, meaty white flesh that can be cooked in a variety of ways during its peak season in the summer.

Serves 4
90g/3½oz/7 tbsp butter
1 small onion or 3 shallots, very finely chopped
handful of chopped fresh parsley

drizzle of vegetable oil or olive oil
4 cod fillets, each about 175g/6oz
1 bay leaf
300ml/½ pint/1¼ cups white beer, such as Hoegaarden, or dry white wine
8 lemon slices
4 thyme sprigs
60ml/4 tbsp soft white breadcrumbs
chopped fresh parsley and lemon wedges, to garnish
boiled or steamed potatoes, to serve

1 Preheat the oven to 180°C/350°F/Gas 4. Using half the butter, grease a flameproof casserole. Add the onion or shallots and parsley. Drizzle with the oil. Transfer the casserole to the oven and cook the onion for about 4 minutes.

2 Season the cod fillets on both sides. Place on top of the onion and parsley mix. Add the bay leaf and pour in the beer or wine to almost cover the fish. Top each fillet with two lemon slices and a thyme sprig.

3 Return the casserole to the oven and bake for 15–20 minutes, depending on the thickness of the fillets, until the fish flakes when tested with the tip of a sharp knife. Transfer the fillets to a platter, cover with foil and keep warm.

4 Put the casserole over medium heat on top of the stove. Cook for 4–5 minutes until the juices have reduced by about three quarters. Add the breadcrumbs and stir until they have been absorbed.

5 Cut the remaining butter into small cubes and add to the sauce, a little at a time. Stir until thick and creamy. If is too thick, add more beer or wine to thin it. Check the seasoning and pour the sauce over the fish. Garnish with the parsley and lemon wedges, and serve with the potatoes.

Marinated Sea Trout

Sea trout has a superb texture and a flavour like that of wild salmon. It is best served with strong but complementary flavours, such as chillies and lime, that cut the richness of its flesh.

Serves 6
6 sea trout cutlets, each about 115g/4oz, or wild or farmed salmon

2 garlic cloves, chopped
1 fresh long red chilli, seeded and chopped
45ml/3 tbsp chopped Thai basil
15ml/1 tbsp sugar or palm sugar (jaggery)
3 limes
400ml/14fl oz/1⅔ cups coconut milk
15ml/1 tbsp fish sauce

1 Place the sea trout or salmon cutlets side by side in a shallow dish. Using a pestle, pound the chopped garlic and chilli in a large mortar to break them both up roughly. Add about 30ml/2 tbsp of the Thai basil with the sugar and continue to pound to a rough paste.

2 Grate the rind from 1 lime and squeeze the juice. Mix the rind and juice into the chilli paste, with the coconut milk. Pour the mixture over the cutlets. Cover and chill for about 1 hour. Cut the remaining limes into wedges.

3 Take the fish out of the refrigerator so that it can return to room temperature. Remove the cutlets from the marinade. Either cook on a barbecue, in an oiled hinged wire fish basket, or under a hot grill (broiler). Cook the fish for 4 minutes on each side, trying not to move them. They may stick to the grill rack if not seared first.

4 Strain the remaining marinade into a pan, reserving the contents of the sieve (strainer). Bring the marinade to the boil, then simmer gently for 5 minutes, stirring. Stir in the contents of the sieve and continue to simmer for 1 minute more. Add the fish sauce and the remaining Thai basil.

5 Lift each fish cutlet on to a warmed serving plate, pour over the sauce and serve immediately with the lime wedges.

Baked Cod Energy 407kcal/1695kJ; Protein 27.5g; Carbohydrate 13g, of which sugars 1.4g; Fat 25.3g, of which saturates 12.5g; Cholesterol 111mg; Calcium 44mg; Fibre 0.6g; Sodium 339mg.
Marinated Sea Trout Energy 157kcal/662kJ; Protein 23.1g; Carbohydrate 5.9g, of which sugars 5.9g; Fat 4.7g, of which saturates 0.1g; Cholesterol 0mg; Calcium 46mg; Fibre 0.4g; Sodium 141mg.

Spatchcock Poussins with Herbes de Provence Butter

Spatchcock is said to be a distortion of an 18th-century Irish expression 'dispatch cock' for providing an unexpected guest with a quick and simple meal. A young summer chicken was prepared without frills or fuss by being split, flattened and fried or grilled.

Serves 2
2 poussins, each weighing about 450g/1lb
1 shallot, finely chopped
2 garlic cloves, crushed
45ml/3 tbsp chopped mixed fresh herbs, such as flat leaf parsley, sage, rosemary and thyme
75g/3oz/6 tbsp butter, softened
salt and ground black pepper

1 To spatchcock a poussin, place it breast down on a chopping board and split it along the back. Open out the bird and turn it over, so that the breast side is uppermost.

2 Press the poussin as flat as possible on to the chopping board, then thread two metal skewers through it, across the breast and thigh, to keep it flat.

3 Repeat the spatchcocking process with the second poussin. Place the skewered birds on a large grill (broiler) pan.

4 Place the chopped shallot, crushed garlic and chopped mixed herbs in a large bowl. Add the butter with plenty of seasoning, and then beat until well combined. Dot the butter over the spatchcock poussins.

5 Preheat the grill to high and cook the poussins for about 30 minutes, turning them over halfway through. Turn again and baste with the cooking juices, then cook for a further 5–7 minutes on each side. Serve immediately.

> **Variation**
> Add some finely chopped chilli or a little grated lemon rind to the butter.

Pandanus-flavoured Chicken Satay with Hot Cashew Nut Sambal

Pandanus leaves are frequently used in South-east Asian cooking, in both savoury and sweet dishes. They are very versatile, and in this recipe they give the chicken a delicate flavour.

Serves 6
about 1kg/2¼lb skinless chicken breast fillets
30ml/2 tbsp olive oil
5ml/1 tsp ground coriander
2.5ml/½ tsp ground cumin
2.5cm/1in piece fresh root ginger, finely grated
2 garlic cloves, crushed

5ml/1 tsp caster (superfine) sugar
2.5ml/½ tsp salt
18 long pandanus leaves, each halved to give 20cm/8in lengths
36 bamboo or wooden skewers

For the cashew nut sambal
2 garlic cloves, roughly chopped
4 small fresh hot green chillies (not tiny birdseye chillies), seeded and sliced
50g/2oz/⅓ cup cashew nuts
10ml/2 tsp sugar, preferably palm sugar (jaggery)
75ml/5 tbsp light soy sauce
juice of ½ lime
30ml/2 tbsp coconut cream

1 To make the sambal, place the garlic and chillies in a mortar and grind them quite finely with a pestle. Add the nuts and continue to grind until the mixture is almost smooth, with just a bit of texture. Pound in the remaining ingredients, cover and leave in a cool place until needed.

2 Soak the skewers in water for 30 minutes. Slice the chicken horizontally into thin pieces and then into strips about 2.5cm/1in wide. Toss in the oil. Mix the coriander, cumin, ginger, garlic, sugar and salt together. Rub this mixture into the strips of chicken. Leave to marinate while you prepare the barbecue.

3 Thread a strip of leaf and a piece of chicken lengthways on to each skewer. Position an oiled grill rack over the coals to heat.

4 Cook over medium-hot coals, meat-side down, covered with a lid or tented heavy-duty foil for 5–7 minutes. Once the meat has seared, move the satays around so that the leaves don't scorch. Serve hot, with the sambal.

Poussins Energy 621kcal/2583kJ; Protein 50.1g; Carbohydrate 0.3g, of which sugars 0.3g; Fat 46.8g, of which saturates 16.4g; Cholesterol 288mg; Calcium 21mg; Fibre 0g; Sodium 256mg.
Pandanus Chicken Energy 197kcal/835kJ; Protein 42.5g; Carbohydrate 2.4g, of which sugars 2g; Fat 2g, of which saturates 0.5g; Cholesterol 123mg; Calcium 15mg; Fibre 0.4g; Sodium 640mg.

Grilled Skewered Chicken

These fabulous little skewers, cooked on the barbecue, make the ideal finger food for a summer's day gathering.

Serves 4
8 chicken thighs with skin, boned
8 large, thick spring onions (scallions), trimmed
oil, for greasing
lemon wedges, to serve

For the yakitori sauce
60ml/4 tbsp sake
75ml/5 tbsp shoyu
15ml/1 tbsp mirin
15ml/1 tbsp unrefined caster (superfine) sugar

1 First, make the yakitori sauce. Mix all the ingredients together in a small pan. Bring to the boil, then reduce the heat and simmer for 10 minutes.

2 Cut the chicken into 2.5cm/1in cubes. Cut the spring onions into 2.5cm/1in long sticks. To cook the chicken on a barbecue, soak eight bamboo skewers overnight in water. This prevents the skewers from burning during cooking. Prepare the barbecue. Thread about four pieces of chicken and three spring onion pieces on to each of the skewers. Place the yakitori sauce in a small bowl and have a brush ready.

3 Cook the skewered chicken on the barbecue. Keep the skewer handles away from the fire, turning them frequently. Brush the chicken with sauce. Return to the coals and repeat this process twice more until the chicken is well cooked.

4 Alternatively, to grill (broil), preheat the grill (broiler) to high. Oil the wire rack and spread out the chicken cubes on it. Grill both sides of the chicken until the juices drip, then dip the pieces in the sauce and put back on the rack. Grill for 30 seconds on each side, repeating the dipping process twice more.

5 Set aside and keep warm. Gently grill the spring onions until soft and slightly brown outside. Do not dip. Thread the chicken and spring onion pieces on to skewers as above. Arrange the skewered chicken and spring onions on a serving platter and serve accompanied by lemon wedges.

Tandoori Drumsticks with Kachumbar

This classic tandoori dish can be barbecued, if the weather permits, or baked in the oven. Kachumbar, a cool salad laced with chillies, is a perfect accompaniment. Use sweet white onions if you can't find pink ones.

Serves 6
12 skinless chicken drumsticks
3 garlic cloves, crushed to a paste with a pinch of salt
150ml/¼ pint/⅔ cup strained natural (plain) yogurt
10ml/2 tsp ground coriander
5ml/1 tsp ground cumin
5ml/1 tsp ground turmeric
1.5ml/¼ tsp cayenne pepper
2.5ml/½ tsp garam masala
15ml/1 tbsp curry paste
juice of ½ lemon
salt
warmed naan breads, to serve

For the kachumbar
2 pink onions, halved and thinly sliced
10ml/2 tsp salt
4cm/1½in piece of fresh root ginger, finely shredded
2 fresh long green chillies, seeded and finely chopped
20ml/4 tsp sugar, preferably palm sugar (jaggery)
juice of ½ lemon
60ml/4 tbsp chopped fresh coriander (cilantro)

1 Place the drumsticks in a non-metallic bowl. Put the garlic, yogurt, spices, curry paste and lemon juice in a food processor and whizz until smooth. Pour the mixture over the drumsticks to coat, cover and chill overnight.

2 Two hours before serving, make the kachumbar. Put the onion slices in a bowl, sprinkle them with the salt, cover and leave to stand for 1 hour. Transfer into a sieve (strainer), rinse well under cold running water, then drain and pat dry. Roughly chop the slices and put them in a serving bowl. Add the remaining ingredients and mix well. About 30 minutes before cooking, drain the drumsticks in a sieve set over a bowl.

3 Prepare the barbecue, if using, or preheat the oven to 190°C/375°F/Gas 5. Salt the drumsticks, wrap the tips with strips of foil to prevent them from burning, then place on the grill rack so that they are not directly over the coals. Cover with a lid or tented heavy-duty foil and grill or roast for 15–20 minutes, turning. Serve with the kachumbar and naan bread.

Skewered Chicken Energy 165kcal/695kJ; Protein 22g; Carbohydrate 9g, of which sugars 8.8g; Fat 2.9g, of which saturates 0.8g; Cholesterol 105mg; Calcium 24mg; Fibre 0.4g; Sodium 1429mg.
Tandoori Drumsticks Energy 423kcal/1771kJ; Protein 30g; Carbohydrate 58g, of which sugars 8.5g; Fat 7.8g, of which saturates 0.7g; Cholesterol 70mg; Calcium 63mg; Fibre 1.2g; Sodium 1210mg.

Chicken Fillets with Serrano Ham

This modern dish is light and very easy to make. It looks fabulous, too. Serve with a summer salad for a delicious light lunch, or with vegetables for a main meal.

Serves 4
4 skinless chicken breast fillets
4 slices Serrano ham

75g/3oz/6 tbsp butter
30ml/2 tbsp chopped capers
30ml/2 tbsp fresh thyme leaves
1 large lemon, cut lengthways
   into 8 slices
a few small fresh thyme sprigs
salt and ground black pepper

1 Preheat the oven to 200°C/400°F/Gas 6. Wrap each chicken breast fillet loosely in clear film (plastic wrap) and beat with a rolling pin until slightly flattened.

2 Arrange the chicken breast fillets in a large, shallow ovenproof dish, then top each with a slice of Serrano ham.

3 Beat the butter with the capers, thyme and seasoning until well mixed. Divide the butter into quarters and shape each into a neat portion, then place on each ham-topped chicken fillet.

4 Arrange two lemon slices on the butter and sprinkle with small sprigs of fresh thyme leaves. Bake the fillets in the preheated oven for 25 minutes, or until the chicken is tender and cooked through.

5 To serve, transfer the chicken portions to a warmed serving platter or individual plates and spoon the piquant, buttery juices over the top. Serve immediately, with boiled new potatoes and steamed broccoli or mangetouts. Discard the lemon slices before serving, if you prefer.

Variation
This dish tastes just as good with other thinly sliced cured ham, such as the Italian prosciutto or Parma ham, in place of the Serrano ham.

Apricot and Almond Stuffed Chicken

Couscous makes a light and simple base for this summery slow-cooker dish.

Serves 4
50g/2oz/¼ cup ready-to-eat
   dried apricots
150ml/¼ pint/⅔ cup orange juice
4 skinned chicken breast fillets
50g/2oz/⅓ cup instant couscous

150ml/¼ pint/⅔ cup boiling
   chicken stock
25g/1oz/¼ cup chopped
   toasted almonds
1.5ml/¼ tsp dried tarragon
1 egg yolk
30ml/2 tbsp orange marmalade
salt and ground black pepper
boiled or steamed basmati and
   wild rice, to serve

1 Put the apricots in a bowl and pour over the orange juice. Leave to soak while you prepare the remaining ingredients.

2 Cut a deep pocket horizontally in each chicken breast fillet, taking care not to cut all the way through. Put the fillets between two sheets of oiled clear film (plastic wrap), then gently beat with a rolling pin or mallet until slightly thinner.

3 Put the couscous in a bowl and spoon over 50ml/2fl oz/¼ cup of the stock. Leave to stand until all the stock has been absorbed.

4 Drain the apricots, reserving the juice, then stir them into the couscous along with the almonds and tarragon. Season with salt and pepper, then stir in enough egg yolk to bind the mixture.

5 Divide the stuffing between the chicken fillets, securing with cocktail sticks (toothpicks). Place the stuffed chicken fillets in the base of the ceramic cooking pot.

6 Stir the orange marmalade into the remaining hot stock until dissolved, then stir in the orange juice. Season with salt and pepper and pour over the chicken. Cover the pot and cook on high for 3–5 hours, or until the chicken is tender.

7 Remove the chicken from the sauce and keep warm. Transfer the sauce to a wide pan and boil rapidly until reduced by half. Carve the chicken into slices and arrange on plates. Spoon over the sauce and serve with basmati and wild rice.

Chicken Fillets Energy 227kcal/952kJ; Protein 33.5g; Carbohydrate 0.3g, of which sugars 0.3g; Fat 10.2g, of which saturates 5.8g; Cholesterol 120mg; Calcium 9mg; Fibre 0g; Sodium 361mg.
Apricot Stuffed Chicken Energy 379kcal/1604kJ; Protein 40.2g; Carbohydrate 38g, of which sugars 27g; Fat 8.5g, of which saturates 1.3g; Cholesterol 155mg; Calcium 61mg; Fibre 1.6g; Sodium 117mg.

Chicken Flautas

Crisp fried tortillas with a chicken and cheese filling make a delicious light meal on a summer's day, especially when served with a spicy tomato salsa.

Serves 4
2 skinless chicken breast fillets
1 onion
2 garlic cloves
15ml/1 tbsp vegetable oil
90g/3½ oz feta cheese, crumbled
12 corn tortillas

oil, for frying
salt and ground black pepper

For the salsa
3 tomatoes, peeled, seeded and chopped
juice of ½ lime
small bunch of fresh coriander (cilantro), chopped
½ small onion, finely chopped
3 fresh fresno chillies or similar fresh green chillies, seeded and chopped

1 Start by making the salsa. Mix the tomatoes, lime juice, coriander, onion and chillies in a bowl. Season with salt to taste and set aside.

2 Put the chicken breast fillets in a large pan, add water to cover and bring to the boil. Lower the heat and simmer for 15–20 minutes or until the chicken is cooked. Remove the chicken from the pan and let it cool a little. Using two forks, shred the chicken into small pieces. Set it aside.

3 Chop the onion finely and crush the garlic. Heat the oil in a frying pan, add the onion and garlic and fry over low heat for about 5 minutes, or until the onion has softened but not coloured. Add the shredded chicken, with salt and ground black pepper to taste. Mix until well combined, remove from the heat and stir in the feta.

4 Before they can be rolled, soften the tortillas by steaming three or four at a time on a plate over boiling water for a few moments until they are pliable. Alternatively, wrap them in microwave-safe film and then heat them in a microwave oven on full power for about 30 seconds.

5 Place a spoonful of the chicken filling on one tortilla. Roll the tortilla tightly around the filling to make a neat cylinder. Secure with a cocktail stick (toothpick). Cover the roll with clear film (plastic wrap) to prevent the tortilla from drying out and splitting. Fill and roll the remaining tortillas in the same way.

6 Pour oil into a frying pan to a depth of 2.5cm/1in. Heat it until a small cube of bread, added to the oil, rises to the surface and bubbles at the edges before turning golden. Remove the cocktail sticks, then add the flutes to the pan, a few at a time.

7 Fry the flutes for 2–3 minutes until golden, turning frequently. Drain on kitchen paper and serve immediately, with the salsa.

Cook's Tip
You might find it easier to keep the cocktail sticks (toothpicks) in place until after the flutes have been fried, in which case remove them before serving.

Chicken Fajitas

The perfect dish for casual summer entertaining, fajitas are a self-assembly dish: warm flour tortillas are brought to the table and everyone adds their fillings.

Serves 6
3 skinless, chicken breast fillets
finely grated rind and juice of 2 limes

30ml/2 tbsp caster (superfine) sugar
10ml/2 tsp dried oregano
2.5ml/½ tsp cayenne pepper
5ml/1 tsp ground cinnamon
2 onions
3 (bell) peppers, 1 red, 1 yellow or orange and 1 green
45ml/3 tbsp vegetable oil
12 ready-made fajitas or soft tortillas, guacamole, salsa and sour cream, to serve

1 Slice the chicken into 2cm/¾in wide strips and place them in a large bowl. Add the lime rind and juice, caster sugar, oregano, cayenne and cinnamon. Mix thoroughly. Set aside to marinate for at least 30 minutes.

2 Cut the onions in half and slice them thinly. Cut the peppers in half, remove the cores and seeds, then slice the flesh into 1cm/½in wide strips.

3 Heat a large frying pan or griddle and warm each tortilla in turn for about 30 seconds on each side, or until the surface starts to colour and begins to blister. Keep the heated tortillas warm and pliable by wrapping them in a clean, dry dish towel while you warm the remainder.

4 Heat the oil in a large frying pan. Stir-fry the marinated chicken for 5–6 minutes, then add the peppers and onions and cook for 3–4 minutes more, until the chicken strips are cooked through and the vegetables are soft and tender, but still juicy. Spoon the chicken mixture into a serving bowl and take it to the table with the warm tortillas and bowls of guacamole, salsa and sour cream.

5 To eat, take a tortilla, spread it with a little tomato salsa, add a spoonful of guacamole and pile some of the chicken mixture into the centre. The final touch is to add a small dollop of sour cream. The tortilla is then folded and ready to eat.

Chicken Flautas Energy 131kcal/553kJ; Protein 9.6g; Carbohydrate 16.8g, of which sugars 1.9g; Fat 3.3g, of which saturates 1.4g; Cholesterol 23mg; Calcium 73mg; Fibre 1.2g; Sodium 209mg.
Chicken Fajitas Energy 485kcal/2044kJ; Protein 26g; Carbohydrate 67.4g, of which sugars 15.3g; Fat 14.2g, of which saturates 3.8g; Cholesterol 60mg; Calcium 118mg; Fibre 4g; Sodium 53mg.

Arroz con Pollo

Many Spanish families eat rice once a week, referring to it as arroz unless it is paella. Rice with chicken is a casserole, with more liquid than a paella. It is a perfect summer dish; seasonal vegetables are included and even peas and corn can be used.

Serves 4

60ml/4 tbsp olive oil
6 chicken thighs, free-range if possible, halved along the bone
5ml/1 tsp paprika
1 large Spanish onion, roughly chopped
2 garlic cloves, finely chopped
1 chorizo sausage, sliced
115g/4oz Serrano or cooked ham or gammon, diced
1 red (bell) pepper, seeded and roughly chopped
1 yellow (bell) pepper, seeded and roughly chopped
225g/8oz/1 generous cup paella rice, washed and drained
2 large tomatoes, chopped or 200g/7oz can chopped tomatoes
120ml/4fl oz/1/2 cup amontillado sherry
750ml/1 1/4 pints/3 cups chicken stock
5ml/1 tsp dried oregano or thyme
1 bay leaf
salt and ground black pepper
15 green olives and chopped fresh flat leaf parsley, to garnish

1 Heat the oil in a wide flameproof casserole. Season the chicken pieces with salt and paprika. Fry until nicely brown all over, then reserve on a plate.

2 Add the onion and garlic to the pan and fry gently until beginning to soften. Add the chorizo and ham or gammon and stir-fry. Add the chopped peppers. Cook until they begin to soften.

3 Sprinkle in the drained rice and cook, stirring, for 1–2 minutes. Add the tomatoes, sherry, chicken stock and dried herbs and season well. Arrange the chicken pieces deep in the mixture, and tuck in the bay leaf.

4 Cover and cook over a very low heat for 30–40 minutes, until the chicken and rice are done. Stir, then garnish and serve.

Chicken with Prawns

This gorgeous dish features a sauce that is thickened with a picada of ground toasted almonds, which is easier than making a roux with butter and flour at the last moment. Enjoy in the summer with a spinach salad.

Serves 4

1.3kg/3lb free-range chicken
75–90ml/5–6 tbsp olive oil
1 large onion, chopped
2 garlic cloves, finely chopped
400g/14oz tomatoes, peeled and seeded then chopped or 400g/14oz can tomatoes, drained
1 bay leaf
150ml/1/4 pint/2/3 cup dry white wine
450g/1lb large raw prawns (shrimp), or 16 large shelled prawn tails
15ml/1 tbsp oil
15g/1/2oz/1 tbsp butter
30ml/2 tbsp anis spirit, such as Ricard or Pernod
75ml/2 1/2 fl oz/1/3 cup double (heavy) cream
1.5ml/1/4 tsp cayenne pepper
salt, paprika and ground black pepper
fresh flat leaf parsley, to garnish
boiled rice or raw spinach salad, to serve

For the picada

25g/1oz/1/4 cup blanched almonds
15g/1/2oz/1 tbsp butter
1 garlic clove, finely chopped
3 Marie, Rich Tea or plain all-butter biscuits (cookies), broken
90ml/6 tbsp chopped fresh parsley

1 Cut the chicken into eight serving portions, then separate the small fillet from the back of each breast portion. Rub salt and paprika into the chicken.

2 Heat 30ml/2 tbsp oil in a wide flameproof casserole and fry the onion and garlic until soft. Put in the chicken pieces, skin downwards, and fry over a medium heat, turning until they are golden on all sides.

3 Meanwhile, make the picada. Dry-fry the almonds in a small pan and then place them in a blender. Add 15g/1/2oz/1 tbsp butter to the pan and gently fry the garlic, then add it to the blender, with the broken biscuits. Reduce the biscuits to crumbs, then add the chopped parsley and blend to a purée, adding a little of the wine intended for the casserole.

4 Add the tomatoes to the casserole, tuck in the bay leaf and cook down to a sauce, stirring occasionally. Pour in the remaining wine, season to taste with salt and ground black pepper, and leave to simmer gently.

5 Check the shelled prawn tails, if using: if they have a black thread along the back, nick it out with a knife. Heat the oil and the butter in the frying pan and add the prawns. Cook over a medium heat for 2 minutes on each side.

6 Pour the anis into a ladle and set light to it. Off the heat pour this over the prawns and let it burn off. Stir in the juices from the casserole, then add the pan contents to the casserole.

7 Remove the bay leaf from the pan and stir in the picada, then the cream. Add cayenne to taste and check the seasonings, adding more if necessary. Heat through gently and serve garnished with more parsley.

Arroz con Pollo Energy 654kcal/2736kJ; Protein 49.7g; Carbohydrate 59.3g, of which sugars 11.2g; Fat 20.6g, of which saturates 5g; Cholesterol 132mg; Calcium 52mg; Fibre 2.8g; Sodium 651mg.
Chicken with Prawns Energy 881kcal/3655kJ; Protein 52.5g; Carbohydrate 9.8g, of which sugars 4.1g; Fat 65.8g, of which saturates 22g; Cholesterol 368mg; Calcium 110mg; Fibre 1.7g; Sodium 934mg.

Chicken with Tomatoes, Cinnamon and Honey

Cooking the tomatoes very slowly with the aromatic spices gives the sauce for this unusual chicken dish a wonderfully intense summery flavour, which mellows when the honey is stirred in.

Serves 4
30ml/2 tbsp sunflower oil
25g/1oz/2 tbsp butter
4 chicken quarters or 1 whole chicken, quartered
1 onion, grated or very finely chopped
1 garlic clove, crushed
5ml/1 tsp ground cinnamon
good pinch of ground ginger
1.3–1.6kg/3–3½lb tomatoes, skinned, cored and roughly chopped
30ml/2 tbsp clear honey
50g/2oz/⅓ cup blanched almonds
15ml/1 tbsp sesame seeds
salt and ground black pepper
corn bread, to serve

1 Heat the oil and butter in a large, flameproof casserole. Add the chicken quarters and cook over medium heat for about 3 minutes, until browned.

2 Add the onion, garlic, cinnamon, ginger, tomatoes and seasoning, and heat gently until the tomatoes begin to bubble.

3 Lower the heat, cover and simmer very gently for 1 hour, stirring and turning the chicken occasionally, until it is completely cooked through.

4 Transfer the chicken pieces to a plate and then increase the heat and cook the tomatoes until the sauce is reduced to a thick purée, stirring frequently.

5 Stir in the honey, cook for 1 minute and then return the chicken to the pan and cook for 2–3 minutes to heat through. Dry-fry the almonds and sesame seeds.

6 Transfer the chicken and sauce to a warmed serving dish and sprinkle with the almonds and sesame seeds. Serve immediately with corn bread.

Roast Chicken with Summer Vegetables and Potatoes

A whole chicken is oven-roasted with a medley of sweet-tasting summer vegetables.

Serves 4
1.8–2.25kg/4–5lb roasting chicken
150ml/¼ pint/⅔ cup extra virgin olive oil
½ lemon
a few sprigs of fresh thyme
450g/1lb small new potatoes
1 aubergine (eggplant), cut into 2.5cm/1in cubes
1 red or yellow (bell) pepper, seeded and quartered
1 fennel bulb, trimmed and quartered
8 large garlic cloves, unpeeled
coarse sea salt and ground black pepper

1 Preheat the oven to 200°C/400°F/Gas 6. Rub the chicken all over with olive oil and season with pepper. Place the lemon half inside the bird, with a sprig or two of thyme. Put the chicken breast side down in a large roasting pan. Roast for 30 minutes.

2 Remove the chicken from the oven and season with salt. Turn the chicken right side up and baste with juices from the pan.

3 Arrange the potatoes around the chicken and roll them in the cooking juices until they are thoroughly coated. Return the roasting pan to the oven to continue roasting.

4 After 30 minutes, add the aubergine, pepper, fennel and garlic cloves to the pan. Drizzle the vegetables with the remaining oil, and season to taste with salt and pepper.

5 Add the remaining sprigs of thyme to the roasting pan, tucking the sprigs in among the vegetables. Return the chicken and vegetables to the oven and cook for 30–50 minutes more, basting and turning the vegetables occasionally during cooking.

6 To find out if the chicken is cooked, push the tip of a sharp knife between the thigh and breast – the juices should run clear, rather than pink. The vegetables should be tender and tinged brown. Serve the chicken and vegetables from the pan.

Chicken with Tomatoes Energy 610kcal/2539kJ; Protein 37.7g; Carbohydrate 16.8g, of which sugars 16.4g; Fat 44g, of which saturates 11.4g; Cholesterol 206mg; Calcium 92mg; Fibre 4.5g; Sodium 211mg.
Roast Chicken Energy 798kcal/3310kJ; Protein 43.3g; Carbohydrate 23.7g, of which sugars 6.1g; Fat 59.3g, of which saturates 13.5g; Cholesterol 208mg; Calcium 45mg; Fibre 4.2g; Sodium 183mg.

Pan-fried Ham and Mediterranean Vegetables with Eggs

Little vegetable dishes, and ones that contain ham or eggs, or both, are the backbone of the Spanish summer scene. This delicious dish is incredibly simple to make and is hearty enough to serve as a meal in itself. Unlike tortilla, the eggs are not beaten, but are broken into the vegetable mixture and cooked whole.

Serves 4

30ml/2 tbsp olive oil
1 onion, roughly chopped
2 garlic cloves, finely chopped
175g/6oz cooked ham
225g/8oz courgettes (zucchini)
1 red (bell) pepper, seeded and
    thinly sliced
1 yellow (bell) pepper, seeded
    and thinly sliced
10ml/2 tsp paprika
400g/14oz can chopped tomatoes
15ml/1 tbsp sun-dried tomato
    purée (paste)
4 large (US extra large) eggs
115g/4oz/1 cup coarsely grated
    Cheddar cheese
salt and ground black pepper
crusty bread, to serve

1 Heat the olive oil in a deep frying pan. Add the onion and garlic and cook for 4 minutes, stirring frequently.

2 Meanwhile, cut the cooked ham and the courgettes into 5cm/2in batons.

3 Add the courgettes and peppers to the pan and cook over medium heat for 3–4 minutes.

4 Stir the paprika, tomatoes, tomato purée, ham and seasoning into the pan. Bring to a simmer and cook gently for 15 minutes.

5 Reduce the heat to low. Make four wells in the tomato mixture, break an egg into each and season with salt and pepper.

6 Cook over low heat until the white begins to set. Preheat the grill (broiler). Sprinkle the cheese over and grill (broil) for about 5 minutes until the eggs are set. Serve immediately.

Lamb Burgers with Red Onion and Tomato Relish

A sharp-sweet red onion relish works well with spicy lamb burgers. Serve with pitta bread and tabbouleh or a green summery salad.

Serves 4

25g/1oz/3 tbsp bulgur wheat
500g/1¼lb minced (ground) lamb
1 small red onion, finely chopped
2 garlic cloves, finely chopped
1 green chilli, seeded and chopped
5ml/1 tsp ground cumin seeds
2.5ml/½ tsp ground sumac
15g/½oz chopped fresh parsley
30ml/2 tbsp chopped fresh mint
olive oil, for frying
salt and ground black pepper

For the relish
2 red (bell) peppers, halved
2 red onions, cut into 5mm/¼in
    thick slices
75–90ml/5–6 tbsp virgin olive oil
350g/12oz cherry
    tomatoes, chopped
½–1 fresh red or green chilli,
    seeded and finely chopped
30ml/2 tbsp chopped mint
30ml/2 tbsp chopped parsley
15ml/1 tbsp chopped oregano
2.5–5ml/½–1 tsp each ground
    toasted cumin and sumac
juice of ½ lemon
caster (superfine) sugar, to taste

1 Pour 150ml/¼ pint/⅔ cup hot water over the bulgur wheat and leave to stand for 15 minutes, then drain.

2 Place the bulgur in a bowl and add the lamb, onion, garlic, chilli, cumin, sumac, parsley and mint. Mix together, then season with 5ml/1 tsp salt and plenty of pepper. Form the mixture into eight burgers and set aside while you make the relish.

3 Grill (broil) the peppers, until the skin chars and blisters. Peel off the skin, dice and place in a bowl. Brush the onions with oil and grill until browned. Chop. Add the onions, tomatoes, chilli, mint, parsley, oregano and 2.5ml/½ tsp each of the cumin and sumac to the peppers. Stir in 60ml/4 tbsp oil, 15ml/1 tbsp of the lemon juice and salt, pepper and sugar to taste. Set aside.

4 Heat a frying pan over high heat and grease with olive oil. Cook the burgers for about 5–6 minutes on each side. Serve immediately with the relish.

Pan-fried Ham Energy 365kcal/1522kJ; Protein 25g; Carbohydrate 14.7g, of which sugars 13.2g; Fat 22.9g, of which saturates 9.3g; Cholesterol 244mg; Calcium 286mg; Fibre 3.7g; Sodium 827mg.
Lamb Burgers Energy 537kcal/2228kJ; Protein 27.2g; Carbohydrate 19g, of which sugars 13.4g; Fat 39.6g, of which saturates 11.1g; Cholesterol 96mg; Calcium 83mg; Fibre 4.2g; Sodium 105mg.

Lamb with Tomatoes and Peppers

Lamb continues through spring and into the summer months. Use lean lamb from the leg for this spiced curry.

Serves 6

2.5cm/1in piece fresh root ginger
1.5kg/3¼lb boneless lamb, cubed
250ml/8fl oz/1 cup natural (plain) yogurt
30ml/2 tbsp sunflower oil
3 onions

2 red (bell) peppers, seeded and cut into chunks
3 garlic cloves, finely chopped
1 fresh red chilli, chopped
30ml/2 tbsp mild curry paste
2 × 400g/14oz cans chopped tomatoes
large pinch of saffron threads
800g/1¾lb plum tomatoes, halved, seeded and chopped
salt and ground black pepper
chopped fresh coriander (cilantro)

1 Peel the fresh root ginger, then grate the peeled root finely. Set aside. Mix the lamb with the yogurt in a bowl. Cover and chill for about 1 hour.

2 Heat the oil in a large pan. Drain the lamb and reserve the yogurt, then cook the lamb in batches until it is golden all over. Remove from the pan using a slotted spoon and set aside.

3 Cut two of the onions into six wedges each and add to the pan. Fry the onions over medium heat for 10 minutes, or until they soften. Add the peppers for 5 minutes. Use a slotted spoon to remove the vegetables from the pan and set aside.

4 Meanwhile, chop the remaining onion. Add it to the pan with the garlic, chilli and grated ginger, and cook for 4–5 minutes, stirring frequently, until the onion has softened.

5 Stir in the curry paste and chopped tomatoes with the reserved yogurt. Return the lamb to the pan, season and stir well. Bring to the boil, then simmer for 30 minutes.

6 Pound the saffron to a powder in a mortar, then add a little hot water to dissolve the saffron. Add to the curry and stir well. Stir the onion and pepper mixture and the fresh tomatoes into the curry. Simmer for 15 minutes. Garnish with fresh coriander and serve hot.

Moussaka

This slow-cooker classic is delicious in summer, served with a leafy salad.

Serves 6

900g/2lb small or medium aubergines (eggplants), sliced
60ml/4 tbsp olive oil
1 onion, finely chopped
2 garlic cloves, crushed
450g/1lb lean minced (ground) lamb
400g/14oz can chopped tomatoes
5ml/1 tsp dried oregano

pinch of ground cinnamon
salt and ground black pepper

For the topping
50g/2oz/¼ cup butter
50g/2oz/½ cup plain (all-purpose) flour
600ml/1 pint/2½ cups milk
pinch of freshly grated nutmeg
75g/3oz/¾ cup grated mature (sharp) Cheddar cheese
1 egg yolk
30ml/2 tbsp white breadcrumbs

1 Layer the aubergine slices in a colander, sprinkling each layer with salt. Place the colander over a bowl for 20 minutes. Rinse the slices under cold running water and dry with kitchen paper.

2 Brush the slices with oil, then arrange on a baking sheet. Place under a grill (broiler) and cook, turning once, until softened and golden. Arrange half the slices in the bottom of the ceramic cooking pot and switch to high. Set aside the remaining slices.

3 Heat the remaining oil in a heavy pan. Cook the onion for 10 minutes, then add the garlic and lamb and cook, stirring, until the meat is browned. Stir in the tomatoes, oregano and cinnamon, season and bring to the boil. Spoon into the slow cooker over the aubergine. Arrange the remaining slices on top, cover and cook for 2 hours.

4 Meanwhile, make the topping. Melt the butter in a pan, stir in the flour and cook for 1 minute. Stir in the milk, bring to the boil and stir until thickened. Season, then stir in the nutmeg and two-thirds of the cheese. Leave to cool for 5 minutes, then beat in the egg. Pour over the aubergine. Cover and cook for 2 hours.

5 Sprinkle the remaining cheese and the breadcrumbs over the top and cook under a grill (broiler) until golden brown. Leave to stand for 5–10 minutes before serving.

Spiced Lamb Energy 559kcal/2343kJ; Protein 54.4g; Carbohydrate 20.5g, of which sugars 18.8g; Fat 29.6g, of which saturates 13.5g; Cholesterol 191mg; Calcium 139mg; Fibre 4.6g; Sodium 278mg.
Moussaka Energy 444kcal/1850kJ; Protein 24.1g; Carbohydrate 1.5g, of which sugars 11.2g; Fat 31g, of which saturates 14g; Cholesterol 93.5mg; Calcium 268mg; Fibre 4.1g; Sodium 266mg.

Beef Meatballs in a Tomato and Wine Sauce

These tasty meatballs in tomato sauce are usually served in tapas bars in individual casserole dishes, accompanied by crusty bread. They make a good summer supper, too, with a green salad or pasta.

Serves 4

225g/8oz minced (ground) beef
4 spring onions (scallions), thinly sliced
2 garlic cloves, finely chopped
30ml/2 tbsp grated Parmesan cheese
10ml/2 tsp fresh thyme leaves
15ml/1 tbsp olive oil
3 tomatoes, chopped
30ml/2 tbsp red or dry white wine
10ml/2 tsp chopped fresh rosemary
pinch of sugar
salt and ground black pepper
fresh thyme, to garnish

1 Put the minced beef in a bowl. Add the spring onions, garlic, Parmesan and thyme and plenty of salt and pepper. Stir the mixture well to combine. Using your hands, shape the mixture into 12 small firm meatballs.

2 Heat the olive oil in a large, heavy frying pan and cook the meatballs for 5–8 minutes, turning often, until evenly browned.

3 Add the chopped tomatoes, wine, rosemary and sugar to the pan, with salt and ground black pepper to taste.

4 Cover the pan and cook gently for about 15 minutes until the tomatoes are pulpy and the meatballs are cooked through. Check the sauce for seasoning and serve the meatballs hot, garnished with the thyme.

Variation

If you prefer to make larger beefburgers, shape the meat mixture into four wide patties and fry. Serve the patties on a slice of grilled (broiled) beefsteak tomato, or surrounded by tomato sauce. Top with a fried egg, if you like.

Polpettes with Mozzarella and Tomato

These Italian meatballs are made with beef and topped with slices of mozzarella cheese and tomato.

Serves 6

½ slice white bread, crusts removed
45ml/3 tbsp milk
675g/1½lb minced (ground) beef
1 egg, beaten
50g/2oz/½ cup dry breadcrumbs
vegetable oil for frying
2 beefsteak or other large tomatoes, sliced
15ml/1 tbsp chopped fresh oregano
1 mozzarella cheese, cut into 6 slices
6 drained canned anchovies, cut in half lengthways
salt and ground black pepper

1 Preheat the oven to 200°C/ 400°F/Gas 6. Put the bread and milk into a small pan and heat very gently, until the bread absorbs all the milk.

2 Mash the soaked bread to a pulp with a fork or potato masher. Set aside to cool.

3 Put the minced beef into a large bowl with the bread mixture and the egg. Season with salt and black pepper. Mix well, then shape the mixture into six patties.

4 Sprinkle the breadcrumbs on to a plate and dredge the patties, coating them thoroughly.

5 Heat about 5mm/¼in oil in a large frying pan. Add the patties and fry for 2 minutes on each side, until brown. Transfer to a greased ovenproof dish, in a single layer.

6 Lay a slice of tomato on top of each patty, sprinkle with oregano and season with salt and pepper. Place the mozzarella slices on top. Arrange two strips of anchovy, placed in a cross on top of each slice of mozzarella.

7 Bake for about 10–15 minutes, until the mozzarella has melted. Serve hot, straight from the dish.

Meatballs Energy 206kcal/857kJ; Protein 14.7g; Carbohydrate 2.5g, of which sugars 2.5g; Fat 14.6g, of which saturates 5.9g; Cholesterol 41mg; Calcium 105mg; Fibre 0.9g; Sodium 135mg.
Polpettes Energy 230kcal/960kJ; Protein 8.4g; Carbohydrate 20.9g, of which sugars 2.3g; Fat 13.1g, of which saturates 5.3g; Cholesterol 68mg; Calcium 122mg; Fibre 1.4g; Sodium 446mg.

Spicy Beefburgers

The coconut used in these burgers, which may seem an unusual ingredient, gives them a rich and succulent flavour. They taste wonderful accompanied by a sharp yet sweet mango chutney and can be eaten in mini naan or pitta breads.

Serves 8

500g/1¼lb/2½ cups minced (ground) beef
5ml/1 tsp anchovy paste
10ml/2 tsp tomato purée (paste)
10ml/2 tsp ground coriander
5ml/1 tsp ground cumin
7.5ml/1½ tsp finely grated fresh root ginger
2 garlic cloves, crushed
1 egg white
75g/3oz solid creamed coconut or 40g/1½oz desiccated (dry unsweetened shredded) coconut
45ml/3 tbsp chopped fresh coriander (cilantro)
salt and ground black pepper
8 fresh vine leaves (optional), to serve
mango chutney and mini naan or pitta breads, to serve

1 Mix the minced beef, anchovy paste, tomato purée, coriander, cumin, ginger and garlic in a bowl. Add the egg white, with salt and pepper to taste. Using your hands, mix well.

2 Grate the block of coconut and work it gently into the meat mixture so that it doesn't melt, with the fresh coriander. Form the mixture into eight burgers, about 7.5cm/3in in diameter. Chill for 30 minutes.

3 Prepare the barbecue. Once the flames have died down, rake the hot coals to one side and insert a drip tray flat beside them. Position a lightly oiled grill rack over the coals to heat.

4 When the coals are medium-hot, or with a moderate coating of ash, place the chilled burgers on the rack over the drip tray. Cook for 10–15 minutes, turning them over once or twice. Check that they are cooked by breaking off a piece of one of the burgers.

5 If you are using vine leaves, wash them and pat dry with kitchen paper. Wrap one around each burger. Serve with mango chutney and mini naan or pitta breads.

Steak Ciabatta with Hummus

This family favourite tastes all the better when enjoyed on a sunny beach after a day spent battling the surf.

Serves 4

3 garlic cloves, crushed to a paste with enough salt to season the steaks
30ml/2 tbsp extra virgin olive oil
4 sirloin steaks, 2.5cm/1in thick, total weight about 900g/2lb
2 romaine lettuce hearts
4 small ciabatta breads, split
salt and ground black pepper

For the dressing

10ml/2 tsp Dijon mustard
5ml/1 tsp cider or white wine vinegar
15ml/1 tbsp olive oil

For the hummus

400g/14oz can chickpeas, drained and rinsed
45ml/3 tbsp tahini
2 garlic cloves, crushed
juice of 1 lemon
30ml/2 tbsp water
60ml/4 tbsp extra virgin olive oil

1 To make the hummus, process the chickpeas in a food processor to form a paste. Add the tahini, garlic, lemon juice and seasoning. Pour in the water and pulse to mix. Scrape into a jar and pour the oil over. Cover, then put in a cool place.

2 Make a dressing for the salad by mixing the mustard and vinegar in a small jar. Gradually whisk in the oil, then season.

3 Mix the crushed garlic and oil together in a shallow dish. Add the steaks and rub the mixture into both surfaces. Cover and leave in a cool place until ready to cook.

4 Prepare the barbecue. Once the flames have died down, position a lightly oiled grill rack over the coals to heat. When the coals are ready, cook the steaks. For rare steaks, cook for 2 minutes on one side, then 3 minutes on the other. Medium steaks will take 4 minutes each side. Leave to rest for 2 minutes.

5 Separate and dress the romaine leaves. Place the ciabatta cut side down on the rack for a minute. Spread the hummus, with any oil, on the bottom half of each ciabatta. Slice the steaks and arrange on top of the hummus, with some of the leaves. Replace the lids and cut each filled ciabatta in half to serve.

Spicy Burgers Energy 177kcal/734kJ; Protein 13.4g; Carbohydrate 0.8g, of which sugars 0.7g; Fat 13.4g, of which saturates 7g; Cholesterol 38mg; Calcium 22mg; Fibre 1.1g; Sodium 90mg.
Steak Ciabatta Energy 765kcal/3210kJ; Protein 69.8g; Carbohydrate 55.2g, of which sugars 2.8g; Fat 30.8g, of which saturates 7.4g; Cholesterol 115mg; Calcium 222mg; Fibre 6.7g; Sodium 783mg.

Strawberry and Lavender Sorbet

Delicately perfumed with just a hint of lavender, this delightful pastel pink sorbet is perfect for a summer dinner party.

Serves 6
150g/5oz/³/₄ cup caster
  (superfine) sugar

300ml/¹/₂ pint/1¹/₄ cups water
6 fresh lavender flowers
500g/1¹/₄lb/5 cups
  strawberries, hulled
1 egg white
lavender flowers, to decorate

1 Bring the sugar and water to the boil in a pan, stirring until the sugar has dissolved.

2 Take the pan off the heat, add the lavender flowers and leave to infuse (steep) for 1 hour. Chill the syrup before using.

3 Purée the strawberries in a food processor or blender, then press the purée through a sieve (strainer) into a bowl.

4 BY HAND: Pour the purée into a plastic tub, strain in the syrup then freeze for 4 hours until mushy. Transfer to a food processor and process until smooth. Whisk the egg white until frothy, and stir into the sorbet. Spoon the sorbet back into the tub and freeze until firm.
USING AN ICE CREAM MAKER: Pour the strawberry purée into the bowl and strain in the lavender syrup. Churn until thick. Add the whisked egg white to the ice cream maker and continue to churn until the sorbet is firm enough to scoop.

5 Serve in scoops, piled into tall glasses, and decorate with sprigs of lavender flowers.

> **Cook's Tip**
> *The size of the lavender flowers can vary; if they are very small you may need to use eight. To check, taste a little of the cooled lavender syrup. If you think the flavour is a little mild, add two or three more flowers, reheat and cool again before using.*

Sponge Cake with Fruit and Cream

Called Génoise, this is the French cake used as the base for both simple and elaborate creations. You could simply dust it with icing sugar, or layer it with seasonal fruits and serve the cake as a dessert.

Serves 6
115g/4oz/1 cup plain
  (all-purpose) flour
pinch of salt
4 eggs, at room temperature

115g/4oz/scant ²/₃ cup caster
  (superfine) sugar
2.5ml/¹/₂ tsp vanilla extract
50g/2oz/4 tbsp butter, melted or
  clarified and cooled

For the filling
450g/1lb fresh strawberries or
  raspberries
30–60ml/2–4 tbsp caster
  (superfine) sugar
475ml/16fl oz/2 cups
  whipping cream
5ml/1 tsp vanilla extract

1 Preheat the oven to 180°C/350°F/Gas 4. Lightly butter a 23cm/9in springform tin (pan) or deep cake tin. Line the base with baking parchment, and dust lightly with flour. Sift the flour and salt together twice.

2 Half-fill a medium pan with hot water and set over a low heat (do not allow the water to boil). Put the eggs in a heatproof bowl, which just fits into the pan without touching the water. Using an electric mixer, beat the eggs at medium-high speed, gradually adding the sugar, for 8–10 minutes until the mixture is very thick and pale and leaves a ribbon trail when the beaters are lifted. Remove the bowl from the pan, add the vanilla extract and continue beating until the mixture is cool.

3 Fold in the flour mixture in three batches, using a balloon whisk or metal spoon. Before the third addition of flour, stir a large spoonful of the mixture into the melted or clarified butter to lighten it, then fold the butter into the remaining mixture with the last addition of flour. Work quickly, but gently, so the mixture does not deflate. Pour into the prepared tin, smoothing the top so the sides are slightly higher than the centre.

4 Bake in the oven for about 25–30 minutes until the top of the cake springs back when touched and the edge begins to shrink away from the sides of the tin. Place the cake in its tin on a wire rack to cool for 5–10 minutes, then invert the cake on to the rack to cool completely. Peel off the baking parchment.

5 To make the filling, slice the strawberries, place in a bowl, sprinkle with 15–30ml/1–2 tbsp of the sugar and set aside. Beat the cream with 15–30ml/1–2 tbsp of the sugar and the vanilla extract until it holds soft peaks.

6 To assemble the cake (up to 4 hours before serving), split the cake horizontally, using a serrated knife. Place the top, cut side up, on a serving plate. Spread with a third of the cream and cover with an even layer of sliced strawberries.

7 Place the bottom half of the cake, cut side down, on top of the filling and press lightly. Spread the remaining cream over the top and sides of the cake. Chill until ready to serve. Serve the remaining strawberries with the cake.

Strawberry Sorbet Energy 123kcal/523kJ; Protein 1.3g; Carbohydrate 31.1g, of which sugars 31.1g; Fat 0.1g, of which saturates 0g; Cholesterol 0mg; Calcium 27mg; Fibre 0.9g; Sodium 17mg.
Sponge Cake Energy 592kcal/2466kJ; Protein 8.8g; Carbohydrate 45.8g, of which sugars 31.2g; Fat 42.9g, of which saturates 25.5g; Cholesterol 228mg; Calcium 125mg; Fibre 2.5g; Sodium 121mg.

Watermelon Granita

Pastel pink flakes of ice, subtly blended with the citrus freshness of lime and the delicate flavour of watermelon, make this granita the perfect summer treat for the eye as well as the tastebuds.

150ml/¼ pint/¾ cup water
1 whole watermelon, about
   1.75kg/4–4½lb
finely grated rind and juice of
   2 limes, plus lime wedges,
   for serving

Serves 6
150g/5oz/⅔ cup caster
   (superfine) sugar

1 Bring the sugar and water to the boil in a pan, stirring until all of the sugar has dissolved. Pour into a bowl. Cool, then chill. Cut the watermelon into quarters.

2 Discard most of the seeds, scoop the flesh into a food processor and process briefly until smooth. Alternatively, use a blender, and process the watermelon quarters in small batches.

3 Strain the purée into a large plastic container. Discard the seeds. Pour in the chilled syrup, lime rind and juice and mix well.

4 Cover and freeze for 2 hours until the mixture around the sides of the container is mushy. Mash the ice finely with a fork and return the granita to the freezer.

5 Freeze for 2 hours more, mashing every 30 minutes, until it has a fine slushy consistency. Serve in dishes with extra lime.

Variation
To serve this granita cocktail-style, dip the rim of each glass serving dish in a little water or beaten egg white, then dip it into sugar. Spoon in the granita, pour over a little Cointreau, Tequila or white rum and decorate with lime wedges or thin strips of lime rind removed with a cannelle knife and twisted around a cocktail stick.

Frozen Melon

Freezing sorbet in hollowed-out fruit, which is then cut into icy wedges, is an excellent idea. This dessert is irresistible on a hot summer's day.

30ml/2 tbsp clear honey
15ml/1 tbsp lemon juice
60ml/4 tbsp water
1 medium cantaloupe melon
   or Charentais melon,
   about 1kg/2¼lb
crushed ice, cucumber slices and
   borage flowers, to decorate

Serves 6
50g/2oz/¼ cup unrefined caster
   (superfine) sugar

1 Put the sugar, honey, lemon juice and water in a heavy pan and heat gently until the sugar dissolves. Bring to the boil and boil for 1 minute, without stirring, to make a syrup. Leave to cool.

2 Cut the cantaloupe or Charentais melon in half and discard the seeds. Carefully scoop out the flesh using a metal spoon or melon baller and place in a food processor, taking care to keep the halved shells intact.

3 Blend the melon flesh until very smooth, then transfer to a mixing bowl. Stir in the cooled sugar syrup and chill until very cold. Invert the melon shells and leave them to drain on kitchen paper for a few minutes, then transfer them to the freezer.

4 BY HAND: Pour the mixture into a container and freeze for 3–4 hours, beating well twice with a fork, a whisk or in a food processor, to break up the ice crystals and produce a smooth texture.
USING AN ICE CREAM MAKER: Churn the melon mixture in the ice cream maker until the sorbet holds its shape.

5 Pack the sorbet into the melon shells and level the surface. Use a dessertspoon to scoop out the centre of each filled shell to simulate the seed cavity. Freeze overnight until firm.

6 To serve, cut each melon half into three wedges. Serve on a bed of ice on a large platter or individual serving plates, and decorate with the cucumber slices and borage flowers.

Watermelon Granita Energy 189kcal/808kJ; Protein 1.6g; Carbohydrate 46.8g, of which sugars 46.8g; Fat 0.9g, of which saturates 0.3g; Cholesterol 0mg; Calcium 34mg; Fibre 0.3g; Sodium 7mg.
Frozen Melon Energy 101kcal/432kJ; Protein 0.9g; Carbohydrate 24.9g, of which sugars 24.9g; Fat 0.5g, of which saturates 0.2g; Cholesterol 0mg; Calcium 18mg; Fibre 0.2g; Sodium 4mg.

Peach and Cardamom Ice Cream

The velvety texture of this smooth peach ice cream spiced with cardamom suggests it is made with cream rather than yogurt.

Serves 4

8 cardamom pods

6 peaches, about 500g/1¼lb total, halved, and stoned (pitted)
75g/3oz/6 tbsp caster (superfine) sugar
30ml/2 tbsp water
200ml/7fl oz/scant 1 cup natural bio (plain) yogurt

1 Put the cardamom pods on a board and crush them with the bottom of a ramekin, or in a mortar and pestle.

2 Chop the peaches roughly and put them in a pan. Add the crushed cardamom pods, with their black seeds, and the sugar and water. Cover and simmer for 10 minutes or until the fruit is tender. Leave to cool.

3 Transfer the peach mixture into a food processor or blender, process until smooth, then press through a sieve (strainer) placed over a bowl.

4 BY HAND: Add the yogurt to the sieved (strained) purée and mix together in the bowl. Pour into a plastic tub and freeze for 5–6 hours until firm, beating once or twice with a fork, electric whisk or in a processor to break up the ice crystals.
USING AN ICE CREAM MAKER: Churn the purée until thick, then scrape it into a plastic tub or similar container. Stir in the yogurt and freeze until firm enough to hold a scoop shape.

5 Scoop the ice cream into balls and place on to a large platter, and serve immediately.

> **Cook's Tip**
> Use bio natural (plain) yogurt for its extra mild taste. Greek (US strained plain) yogurt or non-bio natural yogurt are both sharper and more acidic and tend to overwhelm the delicate taste of the peaches.

Apricot and Amaretti Ice Cream

Prolong the very short summer season of fresh apricots by transforming them into this superb ice cream with crushed amaretti cream.

Serves 4–6

500g/1¼lb fresh apricots, halved and stoned (pitted)

juice of 1 orange
50g/2oz/¼ cup caster (superfine) sugar
300ml/½ pint/1¼ cups whipping cream
50g/2oz amaretti

1 Place the apricots, orange juice and sugar in a pan. Cover and simmer for 5 minutes until the fruit is tender. Leave to cool.

2 Lift out one third of the fruit and set it aside on a plate. Transfer the remaining contents of the pan into a food processor or blender and process to a smooth purée.

3 BY HAND: Whip the cream until it is just thick but still soft enough to fall from a spoon. Gradually add the fruit purée, folding it into the mixture. Pour into a plastic tub or similar freezerproof container and freeze for 4 hours, beating once with a fork, electric mixer or in a food processor.
USING AN ICE CREAM MAKER: Churn the apricot purée until it is slushy, then gradually add the cream. Continue to churn until the ice cream is thick, but not firm enough to scoop.

4 BY HAND: Beat for a second time. Crumble in the amaretti.
USING AN ICE CREAM MAKER: Scrape the ice cream into a tub. Crumble in the amaretti.

5 Add the reserved apricots and gently fold into the ice cream. Freeze for 2–3 hours or until firm enough to scoop.

> **Cook's Tip**
> Chill the fruit purée if you have time; this will speed up the churning or freezing process.

Peach Ice Cream Energy 69kcal/296kJ; Protein 3.8g; Carbohydrate 13.3g, of which sugars 13.3g; Fat 0.6g, of which saturates 0.3g; Cholesterol 1mg; Calcium 104mg; Fibre 1.9g; Sodium 43mg.
Apricot Ice Cream Energy 289kcal/1202kJ; Protein 2.3g; Carbohydrate 23.4g, of which sugars 19.8g; Fat 21.3g, of which saturates 13.1g; Cholesterol 53mg; Calcium 58mg; Fibre 1.6g; Sodium 43mg.

Gooseberry and Clotted Cream Ice Cream

Often a rather neglected fruit, gooseberries conjure up images of the tired grey-looking crumble that used to be served at school or in the works canteen. This indulgent ice cream puts gooseberries in a totally different class. Its delicious, slightly tart flavour goes particularly well with tiny, melt-in-the-mouth meringues.

Serves 4–6
500g/1¼lb/4 cups gooseberries, topped and tailed
60ml/4 tbsp water
75g/3oz/6 tbsp caster (superfine) sugar
150ml/¼ pint/⅔ cup whipping cream
a few drops of green food colouring (optional)
120ml/4fl oz/½ cup clotted cream
fresh mint sprigs, to decorate
meringues, to serve

1 Put the gooseberries in a pan and add the water and sugar. Cover and simmer for 10 minutes or until soft. Transfer into a food processor or blender and process to a smooth purée. Press through a sieve (strainer) over a bowl. Cool, then chill.

2 BY HAND: Chill the purée in a plastic tub or similar container. Whip the cream until it is thick but still falls from a spoon. Fold into the purée with the green food colouring, if using. Freeze for 2 hours, then beat with a fork, electric mixer or in a food processor, to break up. Return to the freezer for 2 hours.

3 BY HAND: Beat the ice cream again, then fold in the clotted cream. Freeze for 2–3 hours.
USING AN ICE CREAM MAKER: Mix the chilled purée with the whipping cream, add a few drops of green food colouring if using and churn until thickened and semi-frozen. Add the clotted cream and continue to churn the mixture until thick enough to scoop.

4 To serve, scoop the ice cream into dishes or small plates, decorate with fresh mint sprigs and add a few small meringues to each serving.

Strawberry and Ricotta Cheese Semi-freddo

Serve this quick strawberry and ricotta dessert semi-frozen to enjoy the flavour at its best. The contrasting texture of crisp dessert biscuits makes the perfect accompaniment.

Serves 4–6
250g/9oz/generous 2 cups strawberries
115g/4oz/scant ½ cup strawberry jam
250g/9oz/generous 1 cup ricotta cheese
200g/7oz/scant 1 cup Greek (US strained plain) yogurt
5ml/1 tsp natural vanilla extract
40g/1½oz/3 tbsp caster (superfine) sugar
extra strawberries and mint or lemon balm, to decorate

1 Put the strawberries in a bowl and mash them with a fork until broken into small pieces but not completely puréed. Stir in the strawberry jam. Drain off any whey from the ricotta.

2 Transfer the ricotta to a large bowl and stir in the Greek yogurt, vanilla extract and sugar. Using a dessertspoon, gently fold the mashed strawberries into the ricotta mixture to create a rippled effect.

3 Spoon into individual freezerproof dishes and freeze for at least 2 hours until almost solid. Alternatively, freeze until completely solid, then transfer the ice cream to the refrigerator for about 45 minutes to soften before serving.

4 Serve in small bowls with extra strawberries and decorated with mint or lemon balm.

> **Cook's Tip**
> *Don't mash the strawberries too much in step 1 otherwise they'll become too liquid. Freeze the strawberry pulp in a large freezer container if you don't have suitable small dishes. Transfer the fruit pulp to the refrigerator to thaw slightly, then scoop into glasses to serve.*

Gooseberry Ice Cream Energy 278kcal/1152kJ; Protein 1.8g; Carbohydrate 16.7g, of which sugars 16.7g; Fat 23.1g, of which saturates 14.3g; Cholesterol 60mg; Calcium 52mg; Fibre 2g; Sodium 12mg.
Strawberry Semi-freddo Energy 181kcal/764kJ; Protein 5.8g; Carbohydrate 29.6g, of which sugars 29.6g; Fat 5.3g, of which saturates 3.2g; Cholesterol 15mg; Calcium 91mg; Fibre 0.9g; Sodium 43mg.

Blueberry and Vanilla Crumble

In this heavenly dessert, vanilla ice cream is packed into a buttery crumble case with summer berries and baked until the ice cream melts over the crumble.

Serves 8
225g/8oz/2 cups plain
  (all-purpose) flour
5ml/1 tsp baking powder
175g/6oz/¾ cup unsalted
  butter, diced
150g/5oz/¾ cup caster
  (superfine) sugar
1 egg
75g/3oz/¾ cup ground almonds
10ml/2 tsp natural vanilla extract
5ml/1 tsp ground mixed spice
500ml/17fl oz/2¼ cups vanilla
  ice cream
175g/6oz/1½ cups blueberries
icing (confectioners') sugar,
  for dusting

1 Preheat the oven to 180°C/350°F/Gas 4. Put the flour and baking powder in a food processor. Add the butter and process briefly to mix. Add the sugar and process briefly again until the mixture is crumbly. Remove about 175g/6oz/1½ cups of the crumble mixture and set this aside.

2 Add the egg, ground almonds, vanilla extract and mixed spice to the remaining crumble mixture and blend to a paste. Scrape the paste into a 20cm/8in springform tin (pan). Press it firmly on to the base and halfway up the sides to make an even case. Line the case with baking parchment and fill with baking beans.

3 Sprinkle the crumble mixture on to a baking sheet. Bake the crumble for 20 minutes and the case for 30 minutes until pale golden. Remove the paper and beans and bake the case for 5 minutes. Leave both the crumble and the case to cool.

4 Pack the ice cream into the almond pastry case and level the surface. Sprinkle with the blueberries and then the baked crumble mixture. Freeze overnight.

5 About 25 minutes before serving, preheat the oven to 180°C/350°F/Gas 4. Bake the crumble for 10–15 minutes, until the ice cream has started to soften. Dust with icing sugar and serve in wedges.

Strawberry Cream Shortbreads

Simple to assemble, these pretty strawberry desserts are always popular in the summer season. Serve them as soon as they are ready because the shortbread biscuits will lose their lovely crisp texture if left to stand for too long.

Serves 3
150g/5oz/generous 1 cup
  strawberries
450ml/¾ pint/scant 2 cups
  double (heavy) cream
6 round shortbread biscuits
fresh mint sprigs, to
  decorate (optional)

1 Reserve three strawberries for decoration. Hull the remaining strawberries and cut them in half.

2 Put the halved strawberries in a bowl and gently crush using the back of a fork. (Only crush the berries lightly; they should not be reduced to a purée.)

3 Put the cream in a large, clean bowl and whip to form soft peaks. Add the crushed strawberries and gently fold in to combine – do not overmix.

4 Halve the reserved strawberries, then spoon the strawberry and cream mixture on top of the shortbread biscuits. Decorate each one with half a strawberry and a mint sprig, if you like. Serve immediately.

Cook's Tip
Use whole strawberries for the decoration and give them a pretty frosted effect by painting with whisked egg white, then dipping in caster (superfine) sugar. Leave to dry before serving.

Variation
You can use any other berry you like for this dessert – try raspberries or blueberries. Two ripe, peeled peaches will also give great results.

Strawberry Shortbreads Energy 890kcal/3673kJ; Protein 4.4g; Carbohydrate 22g, of which sugars 9.6g; Fat 87.8g, of which saturates 54.8g; Cholesterol 225mg; Calcium 105mg; Fibre 1g; Sodium 106mg.
Blueberry Crumble Energy 522kcal/2183kJ; Protein 8.1g; Carbohydrate 57.7g, of which sugars 34.4g; Fat 29.7g, of which saturates 15.9g; Cholesterol 86mg; Calcium 142mg; Fibre 2g; Sodium 182mg.

Chocolate Redcurrant Torte

A sumptuously rich cake that will be the centrepiece of any summer table.

Serves 8–10
115g/4oz/½ cup unsalted
 (sweet) butter, softened
115g/4oz/½ cup dark
 muscovado (molasses) sugar
2 eggs
150ml/¼ pint/⅔ cup sour cream
150g/5oz/1¼ cups self-raising
 (self-rising) flour
5ml/1 tsp baking powder

50g/2oz/½ cup unsweetened
 cocoa powder
75g/3oz/¾ cup stemmed
 redcurrants, plus 115g/4oz/1 cup
 redcurrant sprigs, to decorate

For the icing
150g/5oz plain (semisweet)
 chocolate, chopped into
 small pieces
45ml/3 tbsp redcurrant jelly
30ml/2 tbsp dark rum
120ml/4fl oz/½ cup double
 (heavy) cream

1 Preheat the oven to 180°C/350°F/Gas 4. Grease a 1.2 litre/ 2 pint/5 cup ring tin (pan) and dust lightly with flour. Cream the butter with the sugar in a mixing bowl until pale and fluffy. Beat in the eggs and sour cream until thoroughly mixed.

2 Sift the flour, baking powder and cocoa over the mixture, then fold in evenly. Fold in the stemmed redcurrants. Spoon into the tin and level the surface. Bake for 40–50 minutes, or until well risen. Turn out on to a wire rack to cool completely.

3 Make the icing. Mix the chocolate, redcurrant jelly and rum in a heatproof bowl over a pan of simmering water. Stir until melted. Remove from the heat and cool to room temperature, then add the cream, stirring until the mixture is well blended.

4 Transfer the cake to a serving plate. Spoon the icing over, drizzling it down the sides. Decorate with redcurrant sprigs.

> **Cook's Tip**
> Use a decorative gugelhupf tin, if you have one. Add a little cocoa powder to the flour used for dusting the greased tin, as this will prevent the cake from being streaked with white.

Summer Pudding

Unbelievably simple to make and totally delicious, this is a real warm-weather classic featuring mixed summer fruits. It's also a productive way of using up any leftover bread you may have.

Serves 4
about 8 slices white bread, at
 least one day old
800g/1¾lb mixed summer fruits
about 25g/1oz/2 tbsp sugar
30ml/2 tbsp water

1 Remove the crusts from the bread. Cut a round from one slice of bread to fit in the base of a 1.2 litre/2 pint/5 cup round ovenproof bowl and place in position. Cut strips of bread about 5cm/2in wide and use to line the sides of the bowl, overlapping the strips as you work.

2 Gently heat the fruit, sugar and the water in a large heavy pan, shaking the pan occasionally, until the juices begin to run.

3 Reserve about 45ml/3 tbsp fruit juice, then spoon the fruit and remaining juice into the prepared bowl, taking care not to dislodge the bread lining.

4 Cut the remaining bread to fit entirely over the fruit. Stand the bowl on a plate and cover with a saucer or small plate that will just fit inside the top of the bowl. Place a heavy weight on top of the plate. Chill the pudding and the reserved fruit juice overnight in the refrigerator.

5 Run a knife carefully around the inside of the bowl rim, then invert the pudding on to a cold serving plate. Pour over the reserved juice, making sure that all the bread is completely covered, and serve.

> **Cook's Tips**
> • Use a good mix of summer fruits for this pudding – red- and blackcurrants, raspberries, strawberries and loganberries.
> • Summer pudding freezes well so make an extra one to enjoy during the winter.

Chocolate Torte Energy 347kcal/1444kJ; Protein 3.7g; Carbohydrate 26.5g, of which sugars 25.9g; Fat 25.2g, of which saturates 15.3g; Cholesterol 89mg; Calcium 50mg; Fibre 1.2g; Sodium 138mg.
Summer Pudding Energy 211kcal/893kJ; Protein 6.2g; Carbohydrate 46.5g, of which sugars 21.3g; Fat 1.2g, of which saturates 0g; Cholesterol 0mg; Calcium 96mg; Fibre 3g; Sodium 293mg.

Raspberry and White Chocolate Cheesecake

Summer raspberries and white chocolate are an irresistible combination.

Serves 8

50g/2oz/4 tbsp unsalted butter
225g/8oz/2⅓ cups ginger nut biscuits (gingersnaps), crushed
50g/2oz/½ cup chopped pecan nuts or walnuts

For the filling

275g/10oz/1¼ cups mascarpone cheese
175g/6oz/¾ cup fromage frais

2 eggs, beaten
45ml/3 tbsp caster (superfine) sugar
250g/9oz white chocolate, broken into squares
225g/8oz/1⅓ cups fresh or frozen raspberries

For the topping

115g/4oz/½ cup mascarpone cheese
75g/3oz/⅓ cup fromage frais
white chocolate curls and raspberries, to decorate

1 Preheat the oven to 150°C/300°F/Gas 2. Melt the butter in a pan, then stir in the crushed biscuits and nuts. Press into the base of a 23cm/9in springform cake tin (pan).

2 Make the filling. Beat the mascarpone and fromage frais in a large bowl, then beat in the eggs and caster sugar until evenly mixed.

3 Melt the white chocolate gently in a heatproof bowl set over a pan of hot water. Stir the chocolate into the cheese mixture with the raspberries.

4 Transfer into the prepared tin and spread evenly, then bake for about 1 hour or until just set. Switch off the oven, but do not remove the cheesecake. Leave it until cold and completely set.

5 Release the tin and lift the cheesecake on to a plate. Make the topping by mixing the mascarpone and fromage frais in a bowl and spread over the cheesecake. Decorate with chocolate curls and raspberries.

Wild Berry Tart

Make this tart in the summer when wild berries, such as blackberries and redcurrants are abundant.

Serves 6–8

500g/1¼lb fresh or frozen mixed wild berries
200g/7oz/1 cup caster (superfine) sugar
whipped double (heavy) cream, to serve

For the pastry

300g/10oz/2½ cups plain (all-purpose) flour
115g/4oz/½ cup unsalted butter, diced
50g/2oz/¼ cup caster (superfine) sugar
1 egg, beaten

1 To make the pastry, put the flour in a food processor. Add the butter to the flour and then, using a pulsating action, mix together until the mixture resembles fine breadcrumbs.

2 Stir in the sugar and add the egg. Combine to form a dough. Wrap in baking parchment and chill for 1 hour.

3 Preheat the oven to 180°C/350°F/Gas 4. On a floured surface, roll out the pastry thinly and use to line a 20cm/8in flan tin (pan). Put a circle of baking parchment in the case and fill with baking beans. Bake in the oven for 10–15 minutes until the pastry has set. Remove the paper and beans and bake for 5 minutes more.

4 Fill the tart with the berries and sugar. Then return the tart to the oven and bake for a further 5–10 minutes until the pastry is golden brown. Serve warm with whipped cream.

Cook's Tip

Instead of cooking the fruit in the tart, you can make the tart and then fill it with uncooked fresh berries. Bake the pastry case for a further 10 minutes, leave it to cool and then brush the base with melted plain (semisweet) chocolate. Leave to set and then fill with fresh berries. The chocolate will stop the berries from softening the pastry before the tart is served.

Raspberry Cheesecake Energy 551kcal/2305kJ; Protein 12.8g; Carbohydrate 53.9g, of which sugars 41.4g; Fat 33.1g, of which saturates 17g; Cholesterol 88mg; Calcium 170mg; Fibre 1.4g; Sodium 195mg.
Wild Berry Tart Energy 618kcal/2601kJ; Protein 8g; Carbohydrate 98.1g, of which sugars 43.3g; Fat 24.2g, of which saturates 14.9g; Cholesterol 60mg; Calcium 141mg; Fibre 3.8g; Sodium 177mg.

Caramelized Apricots with Pain Perdu

Pain perdu is a French invention that literally translates as 'lost bread'. Americans call it French toast, while a British version is known as Poor Knights.

Serves 4

75g/3oz/6 tbsp unsalted
   butter, clarified
450g/1lb apricots, stoned (pitted)
   and thickly sliced
115g/4oz/½ cup caster
   (superfine) sugar
150ml/¼ pint/⅔ cup double
   (heavy) cream
30ml/2 tbsp apricot brandy

For the pain perdu
600ml/1 pint/2½ cups milk
1 vanilla pod (bean)
50g/2oz/¼ cup caster
   (superfine) sugar
4 large eggs, beaten
115g/4oz/½ cup unsalted
   butter, clarified
6 brioche slices, diagonally halved
2.5ml/½ tsp ground cinnamon

1 Heat a heavy frying pan and melt a quarter of the butter. Add the apricot slices and cook for 2–3 minutes until golden. Using a slotted spoon, transfer them to a bowl. Heat the rest of the butter with the sugar, stirring, until golden.

2 Pour in the cream and brandy and cook gently until a smooth sauce forms. Boil for 2–3 minutes until thickened, then pour the sauce over the apricots and set aside.

3 To make the pain perdu, pour the milk into a pan and add the vanilla pod and half the sugar. Heat gently until almost boiling, then set aside to cool. Remove the vanilla pod and pour the milk into a shallow dish. Whisk in the eggs.

4 Heat a sixth of the butter in the clean frying pan. Dip a slice of brioche into the milk mixture and fry until golden brown on both sides. Add the remaining butter as needed. As the pain perdu is cooked, remove the slices and keep hot.

5 Warm the apricot sauce and spoon it on to the pain perdu. Mix the remaining sugar with the cinnamon and sprinkle a little over each portion.

Summer Parcels with Apricots and Honey Glaze

These summery parcels can be made with dried apricots that have been poached in syrup before being stuffed with the almond mixture, but fresh fruit is the better option when available. It has a juicy tartness that cuts through the sweetness of the honey. Roll the filo parcels into any shape, but leave them open so that both fruit and pastry benefit from the glaze.

Serves 6

200g/7oz/1¾ cups blanched
   almonds, ground
115g/4oz/⅔ cup sugar
30–45ml/2–3 tbsp orange flower
   water or rose water
12 fresh apricots, slit and
   stoned (pitted)
3–4 sheets of filo pastry, cut into
   12 circles or squares
30ml/2 tbsp clear honey
cream, crème fraîche or Greek
   (US strained plain) yogurt,
   to serve

1 Preheat the oven to 180°C/350°F/Gas 4. Using your hands or a blender or food processor, bind the almonds, sugar and orange flower or rose water to a soft paste.

2 Take walnut-size lumps of the paste and roll into balls. Press a ball of paste into each slit apricot and squeeze the fruit closed.

3 Place a stuffed apricot on a piece of filo pastry, fold up the sides to secure the fruit and twist the ends to form an open boat shape. Repeat with the remaining apricots and filo pastry.

4 Place the filo parcels in a shallow ovenproof dish and drizzle the honey over them. Bake for 20–25 minutes, until the pastry is crisp and the fruit has browned on top. Serve hot or cold with cream, crème fraîche or a spoonful of Greek yogurt.

> **Cook's Tip**
> *Apricots thrive in the hot Mediterranean climate where they are widely cultivated. They are abundantly available after the summer harvest.*

Caramelized Apricots Energy 1071kcal/4471kJ; Protein 18.5g; Carbohydrate 92.1g, of which sugars 69.2g; Fat 70.9g, of which saturates 41.6g; Cholesterol 353mg; Calcium 343mg; Fibre 3.3g; Sodium 634mg.
Apricot Parcels Energy 347kcal/1455kJ; Protein 9g; Carbohydrate 37.8g, of which sugars 27.4g; Fat 18.9g, of which saturates 1.5g; Cholesterol 0mg; Calcium 120mg; Fibre 4.2g; Sodium 8mg.

Peach Cobbler

A satisfying pudding that is ideal for the summer when peaches are plentiful. Here fresh peaches are topped with a hearty almond-flavoured pastry.

Serves 6
about 1.5kg/3lb peaches, peeled and sliced
45ml/3 tbsp caster (superfine) sugar
30ml/2 tbsp peach brandy
15ml/1 tbsp freshly squeezed lemon juice
15ml/1 tbsp cornflour (cornstarch)
ice cream or crème fraîche, to serve

For the topping
115g/4oz/1 cup plain (all-purpose) flour
7.5ml/1½ tsp baking powder
1.5ml/¼ tsp salt
40g/1½oz/¼ cup finely ground almonds
50g/2oz/¼ cup caster (superfine) sugar
50g/2oz/¼ cup butter or margarine
85ml/3fl oz/⅓ cup milk
1.5ml/¼ tsp almond extract

1 Preheat the oven to 220°C/425°F/Gas 7. Place the peaches in a bowl and add the sugar, peach brandy, lemon juice and cornflour. Toss together, then spoon the peach mixture into a 2 litre/3½ pint/8 cup baking dish.

2 Now make the topping. Sift the flour, baking powder and salt into a mixing bowl. Stir in the ground almonds and all but 15ml/1 tbsp of the sugar. With two knives, or a pastry blender, cut in the butter or margarine until the mixture resembles coarse breadcrumbs.

3 Add the milk and almond extract and stir until the topping mixture is just combined.

4 Carefully drop the topping in spoonfuls on to the peaches in the baking dish. Sprinkle the top with the remaining sugar.

5 Bake for 30–35 minutes until the cobbler topping is browned. Serve hot with ice cream or crème fraîche, if you prefer.

Strawberry Snow

Strawberries have a delicate, fragrant taste and most desserts made from them are best eaten soon after they are made. Dishes like this are generally made from fresh berries in the summer months, such as strawberries and raspberries, but can also be made with apples in the autumn.

Serves 4
120ml/4fl oz/½ cup water
15ml/1 tbsp powdered gelatine
300g/11oz/2¾ cups strawberries, crushed lightly
250ml/8fl oz/1 cup double (heavy) cream
4 egg whites
90g/3½oz/½ cup caster (superfine) sugar
halved strawberries, to decorate

1 Put the water in a small heatproof bowl and sprinkle in the gelatine. Stand the bowl over a pan of hot water and heat gently until dissolved. Remove the bowl from the pan and leave to cool slightly.

2 Put half the crushed strawberries in a pan and bring to the boil. Remove from the heat, then stir in the dissolved gelatine. Chill in the refrigerator for about 2 hours until syrupy.

3 Pour the cream into a bowl and whisk until it holds its shape. Whisk the egg whites until stiff, gradually adding the sugar as they rise.

4 Fold the egg whites into the cooled strawberry mixture, then fold in the remaining crushed strawberries followed by the whipped cream.

5 Turn into individual serving dishes and serve immediately or chill until required. Serve decorated with halved strawberries.

> **Cook's Tip**
> Strawberry Snow freezes well and can then be served as an iced strawberry parfait. All you have to do to make this is spoon the mixture into a loaf tin (pan) lined with clear film (plastic wrap) and freeze for a couple of hours, until it is firm.

Strawberry Snow Energy 443kcal/1841kJ; Protein 7.8g; Carbohydrate 29.1g, of which sugars 29.1g; Fat 33.7g, of which saturates 20.9g; Cholesterol 86mg; Calcium 56mg; Fibre 0.8g; Sodium 81mg.
Peach Cobbler Energy 299kcal/1265kJ; Protein 4.9g; Carbohydrate 53.5g, of which sugars 36.6g; Fat 7.6g, of which saturates 4.5g; Cholesterol 19mg; Calcium 72mg; Fibre 4.4g; Sodium 62mg.

Mango Wontons with Raspberry Sauce

These crisp, golden parcels filled with meltingly sweet, hot mango are perfect for a summertime supper or a sophisticated dinner. The sweet raspberry sauce looks stunning drizzled over the wontons and adds a taste of summer to the dessert. Serve any extra raspberry sauce in a jug at the table so that your dinner guests can add more.

Serves 4

2 firm, ripe mangoes
24 fresh wonton wrappers
　(approximately 7.5cm/3in
　square)
oil, for frying
icing (confectioners') sugar, to dust

For the sauce
400g/14oz/3$\frac{1}{2}$ cups raspberries
45ml/3 tbsp icing
　(confectioners') sugar
a squeeze of lemon juice

1 First make the sauce. Place the raspberries and icing sugar in a food processor and blend until smooth. Press the raspberry purée through a sieve (strainer) to remove the seeds, then stir a squeeze of lemon juice into the sauce. Cover and place in the refrigerator until ready to serve.

2 Peel the mango, then carefully slice the flesh away from one side of the flat stone (pit). Repeat on the second side, then trim off any remaining flesh from around the stone. Cut the mango flesh into 1cm/½in dice.

3 Lay 12 wonton wrappers on a clean work surface and place 10ml/2 tsp of the chopped mango in the centre of each one. Brush the edges with water and top with the remaining wonton wrappers. Press the edges to seal.

4 Heat the oil in a wok to 180°C/350°F (or until a cube of bread, dropped into the oil, browns in 15 seconds). Deep-fry the wontons, 2 or 3 at a time, for about 2 minutes, or until crisp and golden. Remove from the oil using a slotted spoon and drain on kitchen paper.

5 Dust the wontons with icing sugar and serve on individual plates. Drizzle the raspberry sauce over each serving or pour it into small individual bowls on the side.

Mangoes with Sticky Rice

Sticky rice is just as good in desserts as in savoury dishes, and mangoes, with their delicate fragrance and velvety flesh, complement it especially well. You need to start preparing this dish the day before you intend to serve it.

Serves 4
175ml/6fl oz/ $\frac{3}{4}$ cup thick
　coconut milk
115g/4oz/ $\frac{2}{3}$ cup white
　glutinous rice
45ml/3 tbsp sugar
pinch of salt
2 ripe mangoes
strips of pared lime rind, to decorate

1 Pour the coconut milk into a bowl and leave to stand until the cream rises to the top.

2 Rinse the glutinous rice thoroughly in several changes of cold water until it runs clear, then leave to soak overnight in a bowl of fresh cold water.

3 Drain the rice well and spread it out evenly in a steamer lined with muslin (cheesecloth). Cover and steam over a double boiler or a pan of simmering water for about 20 minutes, or until the rice is tender.

4 Reserve 45ml/3 tbsp of the cream from the top of the coconut milk. Pour the remainder into a pan and add the sugar and salt. Heat, stirring constantly, until the sugar has dissolved, then bring to the boil. Remove the pan from the heat, pour the coconut milk into a bowl and leave to cool.

5 Transfer the cooked rice into a bowl and pour over the cooled coconut milk mixture. Stir well, then leave the rice mixture to stand for 10–15 minutes.

6 Meanwhile, peel the mangoes, cut the flesh away from the central stones (pits) and cut into slices.

7 Spoon the rice on to individual serving plates. Arrange the mango slices on one side, then drizzle with the reserved coconut cream. Decorate with strips of lime rind and serve.

Mango Wontons Energy 314kcal/1331kJ; Protein 5.5g; Carbohydrate 56.1g, of which sugars 27.3g; Fat 9.2g, of which saturates 1.2g; Cholesterol 0mg; Calcium 93mg; Fibre 5.6g; Sodium 6mg.
Mangoes with Rice Energy 200kcal/846kJ; Protein 3.1g; Carbohydrate 46g, of which sugars 24.3g; Fat 0.8g, of which saturates 0.2g; Cholesterol 0mg; Calcium 32mg; Fibre 2g; Sodium 51mg.

Grilled Mango Cheeks with Lime Syrup and Sorbet

If you can locate them, use Alphonso mangoes. They have a heady scent and silky texture, which is balanced by the tart lime sorbet and syrup. They ripen in early summer and are available from specialist greengrocers.

Serves 6

250g/9oz/1¼ cups sugar
juice of 6 limes
3 star anise
6 small or 3 medium to
    large mangoes
groundnut (peanut) oil,
    for brushing

1 Place the sugar in a pan and add 250ml/8fl oz/1 cup water. Heat gently until the sugar has dissolved. Increase the heat and boil for 5 minutes. Cool completely. Add the lime juice and any pulp that has collected in the squeezer. Strain the mixture and reserve 200ml/7fl oz/scant 1 cup in a bowl with the star anise.

2 Pour the remaining liquid into a measuring jug or cup and make up to 600ml/1 pint/2½ cups with cold water. Mix well and pour into a freezerproof container. Freeze for 1½ hours, stir well and return to the freezer for another hour until set.

3 Transfer the sorbet mixture to a processor and pulse to a smooth icy purée. Freeze for 1 hour or longer. Alternatively, make the sorbet in an ice cream maker; it will take 20 minutes, and should then be frozen for at least 30 minutes before serving.

4 Pour the reserved syrup into a pan and boil for 2–3 minutes, or until thickened. Leave to cool. Cut the cheeks from either side of the stone (pit) on each unpeeled mango, and score the flesh on each in a diamond pattern. Brush with a little oil. Heat a griddle until very hot and a few drops of water sprinkled on the surface evaporate instantly. Lower the heat a little and grill (broil) the mango halves, cut side down, for 30–60 seconds until branded with golden grill marks.

5 Invert the mango cheeks on individual plates and serve hot or cold with the syrup drizzled over and a scoop or two of sorbet. Decorate with the reserved star anise.

Honey-seared Melon with Lavender and Raspberries

This fabulously simple dessert is perfect for enjoying on a summer's evening, with the lavender in flower and a bowl of strongly scented raspberries to hand. The honeycomb is a delicious partner for the melon and raspberries.

200g/7oz honeycomb
5ml/1 tsp water
a bunch of lavender, plus extra
    flowers for decoration
300g/11oz/2 cups raspberries

Serves 6

1.3kg/3lb melon, preferably
    Charentais

1 Cut the melon in half, scoop out the seeds using a spoon then cut each half into three slices.

2 Put about a third of the honey into a bowl and dilute it by stirring in the water. Make a brush with the lavender and dip it in the honey.

3 Heat a griddle until a few drops of water sprinkled on to the surface evaporate instantly. Lightly brush the melon with the honey mixture.

4 Grill the melon slices for about 30 seconds on each side. Serve with the raspberries, honeycomb and lavender flowers.

Variations
• Other soft summer fruits can be used in this dessert, if you prefer. Choose whatever is in season and looks best in the store. Strawberries, blueberries or redcurrants will all be delicious in this recipe.
• You can grill (broil) the melon slices on a barbecue, if you prefer, and if the weather permits.

Grilled Mango Cheeks Energy 63kcal/272kJ; Protein 2g; Carbohydrate 14.5g, of which sugars 14.3g; Fat 0.2g, of which saturates 0.1g; Cholesterol 0mg; Calcium 12mg; Fibre 2g; Sodium 32mg.
Honey-seared Melon Energy 161kcal/685kJ; Protein 1.9g; Carbohydrate 39.9g, of which sugars 39.9g; Fat 0.4g, of which saturates 0.1g; Cholesterol 0mg; Calcium 42mg; Fibre 2.1g; Sodium 72mg.

Meringue Cake with Raspberries

This summer dessert uses a basic meringue mixture. For the best results avoid very fresh eggs, and ensure they are at room temperature.

Serves 8–10
4 egg whites
225g/8oz/generous 1 cup
  caster (superfine) sugar

For the filling
300ml/½ pint/1¼ cups
  whipping cream
caster (superfine) sugar, to taste
*3–4 drops of vanilla extract or
  2.5ml/½ tsp liqueur, such as
  Kirsch or Crème de Framboise*
450g/1lb/2¾ cups raspberries
*icing (confectioners) sugar,
  for dusting*

1 Preheat the oven to 150°C/300°F/Gas 2. Line two baking sheets with baking parchment and draw two circles: one 23cm/9in in diameter and the other 20cm/8in. Fit a piping (icing) bag with a 1cm/½in star nozzle.

2 Whisk the egg whites until stiff peaks form. Add half of the sugar, 15ml/1 tbsp at a time; keep whisking until the mixture stands in stiff peaks. Using a metal spoon, carefully fold in the remaining sugar to mix thoroughly without the loss of volume.

3 Use most of the mixture to pipe inside the prepared circles, then put the remaining meringue into the piping bag and use to pipe nine mini meringues on to the surrounding parchment.

4 Cook in the preheated oven for 50–60 minutes, until lightly coloured and quite dry (the small ones will take less time). Peel off the parchment, cool the meringues on wire racks and, when cold, store immediately in airtight containers.

5 Whip the cream until soft peaks form, sweeten with caster sugar and flavour with a few drops of vanilla extract or liqueur.

6 Lay the larger meringue circle on a serving dish. Spread with three-quarters of the cream and three-quarters of the raspberries, reserving the best berries for the top. Add the smaller meringue circle, spread with the remaining cream, and arrange the small meringues around the edge. Decorate the top with the remaining fruit. Dust lightly with icing sugar.

Simple Strawberry Ice Cream

Capture the essence of childhood summers with this easy-to-make ice cream. Whipping cream is better than double cream for this recipe as it doesn't overwhelm the taste of the fresh fruit.

Serves 4–6
*500g/1¼lb/4 cups
  strawberries, hulled*
*50g/2oz/½ cup icing
  (confectioners') sugar*
juice of ½ lemon
*300ml/½ pint/1¼ cups
  whipping cream*
extra strawberries, to decorate

1 Purée the strawberries in a food processor or blender until smooth, then add the icing sugar and lemon juice and process again to mix. Press the purée through a sieve (strainer) into a bowl. Chill until very cold.

2 BY HAND: Whip the cream until it is just thickened but still falls from a spoon. Fold into the purée, then pour into a plastic tub or similar freezerproof container. Freeze for 6 hours until firm, beating twice with a fork, electric whisk or in a food processor to break up the ice crystals.
USING AN ICE CREAM MAKER: Churn the purée until mushy, then pour in the cream and churn until thick enough to scoop.

3 Scoop the ice cream into serving dishes and decorate each with a few extra strawberries.

Variation
Raspberry or any other summer berry fruit can be used to make this ice cream, in the same way as strawberry. Keep your eye out for any berries growing wild in your neighbourhood.

Cook's Tip
If possible, taste the strawberries before buying them – or picking them, if you are lucky to have a strawberry producer nearby where you can gather your own berries.

Strawberry Ice Cream Energy 244kcal/1012kJ; Protein 2.4g; Carbohydrate 12.2g, of which sugars 10.4g; Fat 20.4g, of which saturates 12.1g; Cholesterol 51mg; Calcium 73mg; Fibre 0.7g; Sodium 32mg.
Meringue Cake Energy 298kcal/1252kJ; Protein 3.2g; Carbohydrate 39.5g, of which sugars 39.5g; Fat 15.3g, of which saturates 9.5g; Cholesterol 39mg; Calcium 55mg; Fibre 1.4g; Sodium 44mg.

Gazpacho Juice

This is a light version of the classic Spanish soup, made without the usual bread, but making the most of the summer supply of tomatoes. It is the perfect refreshment after a day spent in the sunshine,

Serves 4–5
½ fresh red chilli
800g/1¾lb tomatoes, skinned

½ cucumber, roughly sliced
1 red (bell) pepper, seeded and
    cut into chunks
1 celery stick, chopped
1 spring onion (scallion),
    roughly chopped
a small handful of fresh coriander
    (cilantro), stalks included, plus
    extra to decorate
juice of 1 lime
salt
ice cubes

1 Using a sharp knife, seed the chilli. Add to a blender or food processor with the tomatoes, cucumber, red pepper, celery, spring onion and coriander.

2 Blend the mixture well until smooth, scraping the vegetable mixture down from the side of the bowl, if necessary, and blending again.

3 Add the lime juice and a little salt and blend. Pour into glasses or small bowls. Add ice cubes and a few coriander leaves and serve immediately.

Variation
If fresh chillies aren't available, soak 2 dried chillies in a little warm water for 20–30 minutes until they are rehydrated. Chop them and add to the juice as with the fresh variety above.

Cook's Tip
Ensure that you do not touch your eyes after chopping the fresh chilli. The oil from the chilli will aggravate your eyes. Make sure that you wash your hands in plenty of soapy water after preparing the chilli.

Red Defender

Boost your body's defences with this delicious blend of red fruits. Watermelon and strawberries are a good source of vitamin C and the black watermelon seeds, like all other seeds, are rich in essential nutrients. If you really don't like the idea of blending the seeds, remove them first.

Serves 2
200g/7oz/1¾ cups strawberries
small bunch red grapes,
    about 90g/3½oz
1 small wedge of watermelon

1 Hull the strawberries. Cut any berries in half if they are particularly large.

2 Pull the red grapes from their stalks. Cut away the skin from the watermelon using a knife or a vegetable peeler and chop into a few pieces.

3 Put the watermelon in a blender or food processor and blend until the seeds are broken up.

4 Add the strawberries and grapes and blend the mixture until completely smooth, scraping the mixture down from the side of the bowl, if necessary. Serve in tall glasses.

Variations
• Try this drink with other red summer fruits such as raspberries or redcurrants.
• Use green grapes, if you prefer, although the colour of the drink won't be quite as dramatic.

Cook's Tip
Decorate this juice with chunks of watermelon or strawberry halves, if you like.

Gazpacho Juice Energy 43kcal/183kJ; Protein 1.8g; Carbohydrate 7.9g, of which sugars 7.8g; Fat 0.7g, of which saturates 0.2g; Cholesterol 0mg; Calcium 24mg; Fibre 2.5g; Sodium 21mg.
Red Defender Energy 85kcal/362kJ; Protein 1.5g; Carbohydrate 20.1g, of which sugars 20.1g; Fat 0.5g, of which saturates 0.1g; Cholesterol 0mg; Calcium 29mg; Fibre 1.5g; Sodium 9mg.

Sparkling Peach Melba

Serve this delightfully fresh and fruity drink during the summer months when raspberries and peaches are at their sweetest and best. Traditional cream soda gives this drink a really smooth flavour and a lovely fizz, while the optional shot of Drambuie or brandy gives it a definite kick. Serve with long spoons for scooping up any fruit left in the glasses.

Serves 2
300g/11oz/scant 2 cups
  raspberries
2 large ripe peaches
30ml/2 tbsp Drambuie or
  brandy (optional)
15ml/1 tbsp icing
  (confectioners') sugar
cream soda, to serve

1 Pack a few raspberries into six tiny shot glasses, or into six sections of an ice cube tray, and pour over water to cover. Freeze for several hours.

2 Using a small, sharp knife, halve and stone (pit) the peaches and cut one half into thin slices. Reserve 115g/4oz/⅔ cup of the raspberries and divide the rest, along with the peach slices, between two tall stemmed glasses. Drizzle with the Drambuie or brandy, if using.

3 Push the reserved raspberries and the remaining peach flesh through the juicer. Stir the icing sugar into the juice and pour the juice over the fruits.

4 Turn the raspberry-filled ice cubes out of the shot glasses or ice cube tray and add three to each glass. Top up with cream soda and serve immediately.

> **Cook's Tip**
> *If using shot glasses, dip these into a bowl of warm water for a few seconds to loosen the blocks of frozen raspberries. If using ice cube trays, turn these upside down and hold under warm running water for a few seconds. The ice cubes should then pop out easily.*

Purple Haze

Thick, dark blueberry purée swirled into pale and creamy vanilla-flavoured buttermilk looks stunning and tastes simply divine. Despite its creaminess, the buttermilk gives this sumptuous smoothie a delicious sharp tang. If you do not like buttermilk or cannot find it in your local supermarket, you could use a mixture of half natural yogurt and half milk instead.

Serves 2
250g/9oz/2¼ cups blueberries
50g/2oz/¼ cup caster
  (superfine) sugar
15ml/1 tbsp lemon juice
300ml/½ pint/1¼ cups
  buttermilk
5ml/1 tsp vanilla extract
150ml/¼ pint/⅔ cup full cream
  (whole) milk

1 Push the blueberries through a juicer and stir in 15ml/1 tbsp of the sugar and the lemon juice.

2 Stir the blueberry mixture well and divide it between two tall glasses.

3 Put the buttermilk, vanilla extract, milk and remaining sugar in a blender or food processor and blend until really frothy. (Alternatively, use a hand-held electric blender and blend until the mixture froths up.)

4 Pour the buttermilk mixture over the blueberry juice so the mixtures swirl together naturally – there is no need to stir them together as it tastes and looks better if they remain separate to a certain degree. Serve immediately.

> **Cook's Tip**
> *The deep violet blueberry juice in this drink makes a fantastic contrast in both colour and flavour to the buttermilk. If you cannot get hold of blueberries, other slightly tart summer fruits such as raspberries or blackberries would also work in this creamy combination.*

Purple Haze Energy 274kcal/1157kJ; Protein 9.1g; Carbohydrate 54.2g, of which sugars 49.2g; Fat 3.9g, of which saturates 2.4g; Cholesterol 13mg; Calcium 283mg; Fibre 2.5g; Sodium 99mg.
Sparkling Peach Melba Energy 100kcal/432kJ; Protein 3.2g; Carbohydrate 22.4g, of which sugars 22.4g; Fat 0.6g, of which saturates 0.2g; Cholesterol 0mg; Calcium 49mg; Fibre 5.3g; Sodium 6mg.

Spinach and Rice Soup

Use very young spinach leaves from the autumn harvest to prepare this light and fresh-tasting soup.

Serves 4
675g/1½lb fresh spinach
   leaves, washed
45ml/3 tbsp extra virgin olive oil
1 small onion, finely chopped
2 garlic cloves, finely chopped
1 small fresh red chilli, seeded
   and finely chopped
225g/8oz/generous 1 cup risotto
   rice, such as arborio
1.2 litres/2 pints/5 cups
   vegetable stock
salt and ground black pepper
Parmesan or Pecorino cheese
   shavings, to serve

1 Place the spinach in a large pan with just the water that clings to its leaves after washing. Add a large pinch of salt. Heat gently until the spinach has wilted, then remove the pan from the heat and drain, reserving any liquid.

2 Either chop the spinach finely using a large kitchen knife or place in a food processor or blender and process the leaves to a fairly coarse purée.

3 Heat the oil in a large pan and gently cook the onion, garlic and chilli for 4–5 minutes, until softened.

4 Stir in the rice until well coated with the oil, then pour in the stock and reserved spinach liquid. Bring to the boil, lower the heat and simmer for 10 minutes.

5 Add the spinach, with salt and ground black pepper to taste. Cook for 5–7 minutes, until the rice is tender. Check the seasoning. Serve immediately in heated bowls, topped with the shavings of cheese.

> **Cook's Tip**
> Buy Parmesan or Pecorino cheese as a small block from a reputable supplier, as it will be full of flavour and easy to grate or shave with a vegetable peeler. The hard cheeses will keep for a long time if well wrapped and refrigerated.

Parsnip and Apple Soup

Choose a sharp apple juice to complement the sweetness of the parsnips and the warmth of the spices in this tempting soup, which combines two favourite autumn ingredients.

Serves 4–6
25g/1oz/2 tbsp butter
1 onion, finely chopped
1 garlic clove, finely chopped
500g/1¼lb parsnips, thinly sliced
5ml/1 tsp curry paste or powder
300ml/½ pint/1¼ cups
   apple juice
600ml/1 pint/2½ cups
   vegetable stock
300ml/½ pint/1¼ cups milk
salt and ground black pepper
chopped fresh herbs such as mint
   or parsley, to garnish
thick natural (plain) yogurt,
   to serve

1 Melt the butter in a large pan and add the onion, garlic and parsnips. Cook gently for about 10 minutes, stirring often.

2 Add the curry paste or powder and cook, stirring, for 1 minute. Pour in the apple juice and stock and bring to the boil. Reduce the heat, cover the pan and simmer gently for about 20 minutes or until the parsnips are soft.

3 Process or blend the soup until smooth and return it to the rinsed-out pan. Stir in the milk and season to taste with salt and pepper. Reheat the soup gently, without boiling, and serve topped with a spoonful of yogurt and a sprinkling of herbs.

> **Variations**
> • Omit the curry paste or powder and season the soup with a little cinnamon and freshly grated nutmeg, adding it at the beginning of cooking to give an integrated, mellow flavour.
> • Instead of apple juice, peel, core and finely chop 4 eating apples and cook them with the onion. Replace the juice with extra stock.
> • Add a fruity garnish to the soup – core and thinly slice a red-skinned eating apple and sprinkle over the soup before adding the chives.
> • Garnish with toasted cashew nuts and chives.

Spinach Soup Energy 293kcal/1215kJ; Protein 13g; Carbohydrate 26.8g, of which sugars 3.4g; Fat 14.7g, of which saturates 4.4g; Cholesterol 15mg; Calcium 476mg; Fibre 3.8g; Sodium 400mg.
Parsnip and Apple Soup Energy 130kcal/548kJ; Protein 3.4g; Carbohydrate 18.5g, of which sugars 12.6g; Fat 5.3g, of which saturates 2.9g; Cholesterol 12mg; Calcium 101mg; Fibre 4g; Sodium 56mg.

Curried Parsnip Soup

The mild sweetness of autumn parsnips and mango chutney is given an exciting lift with a blend of spices in this simple soup.

Serves 4
30ml/2 tbsp olive oil
1 onion, chopped
1 garlic clove, crushed
1 small green chilli, seeded and finely chopped
15ml/1 tbsp grated fresh root ginger
5 large parsnips, diced
5ml/1 tsp cumin seeds

5ml/1 tsp ground coriander
2.5ml/½ tsp ground turmeric
30ml/2 tbsp mango chutney
1.2 litres/2 pints/5 cups water
juice of 1 lime
salt and ground black pepper
chopped fresh coriander (cilantro), to garnish (optional)
60ml/4 tbsp natural (plain) yogurt and mango chutney, to serve

For the sesame naan croûtons
45ml/3 tbsp olive oil
1 large naan, cut into small dice
15ml/1 tbsp sesame seeds

1 Heat the oil in a large pan and add the onion, garlic, chilli and ginger. Cook for 4–5 minutes, until the onion has softened. Add the parsnips and cook for 2–3 minutes. Sprinkle in the cumin seeds, coriander and turmeric, and cook for 1 minute, stirring.

2 Add the chutney and the water. Season well and bring to the boil. Reduce the heat, cover and simmer for 15 minutes, until the parsnips are soft.

3 Cool the soup slightly, then purée it in a food processor or blender and return it to the pan. Stir in the lime juice.

4 To make the naan croûtons, heat the oil in a large frying pan and cook the diced naan for 3–4 minutes, stirring, until golden all over. Remove from the heat and drain off any excess oil. Add the sesame seeds and return the pan to the heat for no more than 30 seconds, until the seeds are pale golden.

5 Ladle the soup into bowls. Spoon a little yogurt into each portion, then top with a little mango chutney and some of the sesame naan croûton mixture. Garnish with chopped fresh coriander, if you like.

Squash Soup with Horseradish

The partnering of squash and apple in this curried soup gives it a real taste of autumn. For fans of horseradish, the cream topping is an absolute must.

900ml/1½ pints/3¾ cups vegetable stock
5ml/1 tsp chopped fresh sage
150ml/¼ pint/⅔ cup apple juice
salt and ground black pepper
lime shreds, to garnish

Serves 6
1 butternut squash
1 cooking apple
25g/1oz/2 tbsp butter
1 onion, finely chopped
5–10ml/1–2 tsp curry powder, plus extra to garnish

For the horseradish cream (optional)
60ml/4 tbsp double (heavy) cream
10ml/2 tsp horseradish sauce
2.5ml/½ tsp curry powder

1 Peel the squash, remove the seeds and chop the flesh. Peel, core and chop the apple.

2 Heat the butter in a large pan. Add the onion and cook, stirring occasionally, for 5 minutes until soft. Stir in the curry powder. Cook to bring out the flavour, stirring constantly, for about 2 minutes.

3 Add the stock, squash, apple and sage. Bring to the boil, lower the heat, cover and simmer for 20 minutes until the squash and apple are soft.

4 If making the horseradish cream, whip the cream in a bowl until stiff, then stir in the horseradish sauce and curry powder. Cover and chill until required.

5 Purée the soup in a food processor or blender. Return to the clean pan and add the apple juice, with salt and pepper to taste. Reheat gently, without boiling.

6 Ladle the soup into warmed individual bowls, and top each with a spoonful of horseradish cream, if using, and a dusting of curry powder. Garnish each serving with a few lime shreds and serve immediately.

Curried Parsnip Soup Energy 150kcal/623kJ; Protein 4.7g; Carbohydrate 7.8g, of which sugars 6.8g; Fat 11.4g, of which saturates 7g; Cholesterol 32mg; Calcium 170mg; Fibre 0.8g; Sodium 112mg.
Squash Soup Energy 118kcal/489kJ; Protein 1.3g; Carbohydrate 7.7g, of which sugars 6.7g; Fat 9.3g, of which saturates 5.7g; Cholesterol 23mg; Calcium 50mg; Fibre 1.7g; Sodium 44mg.

Mixed Mushroom Soup

Mushrooms are one of the great joys of the autumn kitchen and this intensely flavoured soup is truly delicious. Serve little boiled potatoes on the side, to cut up and add as desired. The tart flavours of pickled cucumber, capers and lemon add extra bite to this rich mushroom medley.

25ml/1½ tbsp tomato
  purée (paste)
1 pickled cucumber, or
  dill pickle, chopped
1 bay leaf
15ml/1 tbsp capers in
  brine, drained
pinch of salt
6 peppercorns, crushed
675g/1½lb small potatoes
a little butter

Serves 4
2 onions, chopped
1.2 litres/2 pints/5 cups
  vegetable stock
450g/1lb mixed mushrooms, sliced

For the garnish
lemon rind curls
green olives
spring onions (scallions)
sprigs of flat leaf parsley

1 Put the onions in a large pan with 50ml/2fl oz/¼ cup of the stock. Cook, stirring occasionally, until the liquid has evaporated. Add the remaining vegetable stock with the sliced mushrooms. Bring to the boil, reduce the heat and cover the pan. Then simmer gently for 30 minutes.

2 In a small bowl, blend the tomato purée to a smooth, thin paste with about 30ml/2 tbsp of stock from the soup. Then stir the tomato mixture into the soup.

3 Add the pickled cucumber, bay leaf, capers, salt and peppercorns. Simmer the soup gently for another 10 minutes.

4 Meanwhile, place the potatoes in a pan and add water to cover. Bring to the boil, reduce the heat slightly and cook for about 10 minutes or until tender. Drain, place in a serving bowl and top with a little butter.

5 Ladle the soup into bowls. Sprinkle lemon rind curls, a few olives, sliced spring onions and a sprig of flat leaf parsley over each portion. Serve with the potatoes on the side.

Sweet Potato and Parsnip Soup

The sweetness of two of the most popular root vegetables – which are used in both the main part of the dish and the garnish – comes through beautifully in this delicious soup. It is the ideal way to enjoy these typically autumn vegetables.

2 celery sticks, chopped
450g/1lb sweet potatoes, diced
225g/8oz parsnips, diced
900ml/1½ pints/3¾ cups
  vegetable stock
salt and ground black pepper

For the garnish
15ml/1 tbsp chopped
  fresh parsley
roasted strips of sweet potatoes
  and parsnips

Serves 6
15ml/1 tbsp sunflower oil
1 large leek, sliced

1 Heat the oil in a large pan and add the leek, celery, sweet potatoes and parsnips. Cook gently for about 5 minutes, stirring to prevent them browning or sticking to the pan.

2 Stir in the vegetable stock and bring to the boil, then cover and simmer gently for about 25 minutes, or until the vegetables are tender, stirring occasionally. Season to taste with salt and ground black pepper. Remove the pan from the heat and allow the soup to cool slightly.

3 Purée the soup in a food processor or blender until smooth, then return the soup to the pan and reheat gently.

4 Ladle the soup into warmed soup bowls to serve and sprinkle over the chopped parsley and roasted strips of sweet potatoes and parsnips.

Cook's Tip
Making and freezing soup is a practical way of preserving a glut of root vegetables that are unlikely to keep well. Not only can excess raw vegetables be used this way, but leftover boiled, mashed or roasted root vegetables can all be added to soup, puréed, cooled or frozen.

Sweet Potato Soup Energy 113kcal/479kJ; Protein 2.1g; Carbohydrate 21.6g, of which sugars 7.2g; Fat 2.6g, of which saturates 0.4g; Cholesterol 0mg; Calcium 45mg; Fibre 4.3g; Sodium 40mg.
Mixed Mushroom Soup Energy 54kcal/224kJ; Protein 3.4g; Carbohydrate 8.9g, of which sugars 6.4g; Fat 0.8g, of which saturates 0.1g; Cholesterol 0mg; Calcium 33mg; Fibre 2.8g; Sodium 18mg.

Curried Pumpkin and Leek Soup

Ginger and cumin give this pumpkin soup a terrifically warm and spicy flavour. It makes a hearty, full-flavoured meal for a cold autumn night.

Serves 4

900g/2lb pumpkin, peeled and seeds removed
30ml/2 tbsp extra virgin olive oil
2 leeks, sliced
1 garlic clove, crushed
5ml/1 tsp ground ginger
5ml/1 tsp ground cumin
900ml/1½ pints/3¾ cups chicken stock
salt and ground black pepper
60ml/4 tbsp Greek (US strained plain) yogurt, to serve

1 Cut the pumpkin flesh into even chunks. Heat the oil in a large pan and add the leeks and garlic. Cover and cook gently, stirring occasionally, for about 15 minutes, until the vegetables are softened.

2 Add the ground ginger and cumin and cook, stirring, for a further 1 minute. Add the pumpkin chunks and the chicken stock and season with salt and pepper. Bring the mixture to the boil, reduce the heat and cover the pan. Then simmer for 30 minutes, or until the pumpkin is tender.

3 Process the soup, in batches if necessary, in a food processor or blender until smooth. Then return it to the rinsed-out pan.

4 Reheat the soup gently, and ladle out into four warmed individual bowls. Add a spoonful of Greek yogurt on the top of each and swirl it through the top layer of soup. Season with more ground black pepper, if you wish.

Variations
• Use marrow (large zucchini) instead of pumpkin and replace half the stock with coconut milk.
• For a slightly spicy twist, add a seeded and chopped fresh green chilli to the yogurt before swirling it into the soup.
• Use double the ginger and omit the cumin.

Pumpkin and Coconut Soup

This simple, yet punchy, autumn soup is rich with coconut balanced by an intriguing hint of sugar and spice. Just firm, but still fluffy, white rice provides an unusual garnish, but it is the perfect contrast for the silken texture of this soup. Following the amount given here, you should have just enough left over to serve as an accompaniment.

Serves 4

about 1.1kg/2lb 7oz pumpkin
750ml/1¼ pints/3 cups vegetable stock
750ml/1¼ pints/3 cups coconut milk
10–15ml/2–3 tsp sugar
115g/4oz/1 cup white rice
salt and ground black pepper
5ml/1 tsp ground cinnamon, to garnish

1 Remove any seeds or strands of fibre from the pumpkin, cut off the peel and chop the flesh. Put the prepared pumpkin in a pan and add the stock, coconut milk, sugar and seasoning.

2 Bring the soup to the boil, reduce the heat and cover. Simmer for about 20 minutes, until the pumpkin is tender. Purée the soup in a food processor or blender. Return it to the rinsed-out pan.

3 Place the rice in a pan and rinse it in several changes of cold water. Then drain in a sieve (strainer) and return it to the pan. Add plenty of fresh cold water to cover and bring to the boil. Stir once, reduce the heat and simmer for 15 minutes, until the grains are tender. Drain in a sieve (strainer).

4 Reheat the soup and taste it for seasoning, then ladle into bowls. Spoon a little rice into each portion and dust with cinnamon. Serve immediately, offering more rice at the table.

Variation
Use butternut squash in place of pumpkin, and brown rice in place of white rice, if you prefer. Both the butternut squash and the pumpkin are at their best in the autumn months.

Curried Pumpkin Soup Energy 98kcal/409kJ; Protein 3g; Carbohydrate 7.5g, of which sugars 5.8g; Fat 6.4g, of which saturates 1.1g; Cholesterol 0mg; Calcium 86mg; Fibre 4.2g; Sodium 2mg.
Pumpkin Soup Energy 148kcal/627kJ; Protein 8.8g; Carbohydrate 20.7g, of which sugars 13.5g; Fat 4g, of which saturates 2.3g; Cholesterol 11mg; Calcium 308mg; Fibre 2.8g; Sodium 81mg.

Pear and Roquefort Soup

Like most fruity soups, this is served in small portions. It makes an unusual and seasonal appetizer for an autumn dinner party.

2.5ml/½ tsp paprika
juice of ½ lemon
175g/6oz Roquefort cheese
salt and ground black pepper
watercress sprigs, to garnish

Serves 4
30ml/2 tbsp sunflower oil
1 onion, chopped
3 pears, peeled, cored and chopped
400ml/14fl oz/1⅔ cups
   vegetable stock

For the caramelized pears
50g/2oz/¼ cup butter
2 pears, halved, cored and cut
   into wedges

1 Heat the oil in a large pan. Add the onion and cook for about 4–5 minutes until softened but not browned. Add the pears and stock, then bring to the boil. Cook for 8–10 minutes, until the pears are very soft. Stir in the paprika, lemon juice, cheese and seasoning.

2 Cool the soup slightly before puréeing it in a food processor or blender until smooth. Pass the soup through a fine sieve (strainer) and return it to the pan.

3 To make the caramelized pears, melt the butter in a frying pan and add the pears. Cook for 8–10 minutes, turning occasionally, until golden and beginning to caramelize.

4 Reheat the soup gently, then ladle into small, shallow bowls. Add a few caramelized pear wedges to each portion. Garnish with tiny sprigs of watercress and serve immediately.

> **Cook's Tip**
> Pears discolour quickly when peeled, so prepare them at the last minute. Adding the peeled fruit to a bowl of cold water with a little lemon juice helps to prevent them from turning brown. This is not so important for the soup but the caramelized pears should not be discoloured before cooking.

Simple Cream of Onion Soup

This wonderfully soothing soup has a deep, buttery flavour that is complemented by crisp croûtons or chopped chives.

105ml/7 tbsp dry white vermouth
1 litre/1¾ pints/4 cups good
   chicken or vegetable stock
150ml/¼ pint/⅔ cup double
   (heavy) cream
a little lemon juice (optional)
salt and ground black pepper
croûtons or chopped fresh chives,
   to garnish

Serves 4
115g/4oz/½ cup unsalted butter
1kg/2¼lb yellow onions, sliced
1 fresh bay leaf

1 Melt 75g/3oz/6 tbsp of the butter in a large heavy pan. Set about 200g/7oz of the onions aside and add the rest to the pan with the bay leaf. Stir to coat in the butter, then cover and cook very gently for about 30 minutes. The onions should be very soft and tender, but not browned.

2 Add the vermouth, increase the heat and boil rapidly until the liquid has evaporated. Add the stock, 5ml/1 tsp salt and pepper to taste. Bring to the boil, lower the heat and simmer for 5 minutes, then remove from the heat. Leave to cool, then discard the bay leaf and process the soup in a blender or food processor. Return the soup to the rinsed pan.

3 Meanwhile, melt the remaining butter in another pan and cook the remaining onions slowly, covered, until soft but not browned. Uncover and continue to cook gently until golden.

4 Add the cream to the soup and reheat it gently until hot, but do not allow it to boil. Taste and adjust the seasoning, adding a little lemon juice if liked. Add the buttery onions and stir for 1–2 minutes, then ladle the soup into bowls. Sprinkle with croûtons or chopped chives and serve.

> **Cook's Tip**
> Adding the second batch of onions gives texture and a buttery flavour to this soup. Make sure they do not brown.

Pear Soup Energy 381kcal/1579kJ; Protein 10.1g; Carbohydrate 21.8g, of which sugars 20.9g; Fat 28.7g, of which saturates 15.6g; Cholesterol 59mg; Calcium 246mg; Fibre 4.7g; Sodium 616mg.
Cream of Onion Soup Energy 519kcal/2139kJ; Protein 3.8g; Carbohydrate 21.4g, of which sugars 15.6g; Fat 44.3g, of which saturates 27.5g; Cholesterol 113mg; Calcium 88mg; Fibre 3.5g; Sodium 193mg.

Mushroom Soup with Croûtes

This classic soup is still a favourite in the autumn when mushrooms are popping up everywhere.

Serves 6
1 onion, chopped
1 garlic clove, chopped
25g/1oz/2 tbsp butter
450g/1lb/6 cups chestnut or brown cap mushrooms, roughly chopped
15ml/1 tbsp plain (all-purpose) flour
45ml/3 tbsp dry sherry
900ml/1½ pints/3¾ cups vegetable stock
150ml/¼ pint/⅔ cup double (heavy) cream
salt and ground black pepper
sprigs of fresh chervil, to garnish

For the crostini
15ml/1 tbsp olive oil, plus extra for brushing
1 shallot, chopped
115g/4oz/1½ cups button mushrooms, finely chopped
15ml/1 tbsp chopped fresh parsley
6 brown cap mushrooms
6 slices baguette
1 small garlic clove
115g/4oz/1 cup soft goat's cheese

1 Cook the onion and garlic in the butter for 5 minutes. Add the mushrooms, cover and cook for 10 minutes, stirring often.

2 Stir the flour into the pan and cook for 1 minute. Stir in the sherry and stock and bring to the boil, then simmer for about 15 minutes. Cool slightly, then purée it in a food processor or blender.

3 For the crostini, heat the oil in a small pan. Add the shallot and button mushrooms, and cook for 8–10 minutes, until softened. Drain well and transfer to a food processor. Add the parsley and process until finely chopped.

4 Preheat the grill (broiler). Brush the brown cap mushrooms with oil and grill (broil) for 5–6 minutes. Toast the baguette, rub with the garlic and top with goat's cheese. Add the grilled (broiled) mushrooms and fill these with the mushroom mixture.

5 Return the soup to the pan and stir in the cream. Season, then reheat gently. Ladle the soup into six bowls. Float a croûte in the centre of each and garnish with chervil.

Spicy Roasted Pumpkin Soup

The pumpkin is roasted whole, then split open and scooped out to make this delicious soup.

Serves 6–8
1.5kg/3–3½lb pumpkin
90ml/6 tbsp olive oil
2 onions, chopped
3 garlic cloves, chopped
7.5cm/3in piece fresh root ginger, grated
5ml/1 tsp ground coriander
2.5ml/½ tsp ground turmeric
pinch of cayenne pepper
1 litre/1¾ pints/4 cups vegetable stock
salt and ground black pepper
15ml/1 tbsp sesame seeds and fresh coriander (cilantro) leaves, to garnish

For the pumpkin crisps
wedge of fresh pumpkin, seeded
120ml/4fl oz/½ cup olive oil

1 Preheat the oven to 200°C/400°F/Gas 6. Prick the pumpkin around the top with a fork. Brush with plenty of the oil and bake for 45 minutes or until tender. Set aside to cool slightly.

2 When the pumpkin is cool enough to handle, scoop out and discard the seeds. Scoop out and chop the flesh.

3 Heat 60ml/4 tbsp of the remaining oil in a large pan and add the onions, garlic and ginger, then cook gently for 4–5 minutes. Add the coriander, turmeric and cayenne, and cook for about 2 minutes. Stir in the pumpkin flesh and stock. Bring to the boil, reduce the heat and simmer for 20 minutes.

4 Cool the soup slightly, then purée it in a food processor or blender until smooth. Return the soup to the rinsed pan and season well.

5 Meanwhile, prepare the pumpkin crisps. Using a swivel-blade potato peeler, pare off long thin strips. Heat the oil in a small pan and fry the strips in batches for 2–3 minutes, until crisp. Drain on kitchen paper.

6 Reheat the soup and ladle it into bowls. Top with the pumpkin crisps and garnish each portion with sesame seeds and coriander leaves.

Mushroom with Croûtes: Energy 368kcal/1533kJ; Protein 10.3g; Carbohydrate 25.1g, of which sugars 3.1g; Fat 25g, of which saturates 14.5g; Cholesterol 61mg; Calcium 99mg; Fibre 2.4g; Sodium 399mg.
Spicy Pumpkin Soup Energy 271kcal/1119kJ; Protein 3.1g; Carbohydrate 11.1g, of which sugars 8.2g; Fat 24.1g, of which saturates 3.6g; Cholesterol 0mg; Calcium 110mg; Fibre 3.8g; Sodium 3mg.

Roasted Garlic and Butternut Squash Soup with Tomato Salsa

This is a wonderful, richly flavoured soup, given bite by the spicy tomato salsa.

Serves 6

2 garlic bulbs, outer papery
   skin removed
a few fresh thyme sprigs
75ml/5 tbsp olive oil
1 large butternut squash, halved
2 onions, chopped
5ml/1 tsp ground coriander
1.2 litres/2 pints/5 cups vegetable
   or chicken stock

30–45ml/2–3 tbsp fresh oregano
   or marjoram, stems removed,
   leaves chopped
salt and ground black pepper

For the salsa

4 large ripe tomatoes, halved
   and seeded
1 red (bell) pepper
1 large fresh red chilli, seeded
30ml/2 tbsp extra virgin
   olive oil
15ml/1 tbsp balsamic vinegar
pinch of caster (superfine) sugar

1 Preheat the oven to 220°C/425°F/Gas 7. Wrap the garlic bulbs in foil with the thyme and 7.5ml/1½ tsp of the oil. Put the parcel on a baking sheet with the squash and the tomatoes, pepper and fresh chilli for the salsa. Brush the squash with 10ml/2 tsp of the remaining oil. Roast for 25 minutes, then remove the tomatoes, pepper and chilli. Reduce the oven temperature to 190°C/375°F/Gas 5 and roast the squash and garlic for a further 20–25 minutes, or until tender.

2 Heat the remaining oil in a large non-stick pan and cook the onions and ground coriander gently for about 10 minutes.

3 Meanwhile, skin the pepper and chilli, then process them with the tomatoes and the oil for the salsa. Stir in the vinegar and seasoning to taste, adding a pinch of sugar if necessary.

4 Squeeze the roasted garlic out of its skin into the onions and add the squash, scooped out of its skin. Add the stock, season with salt and pepper, and simmer for 10 minutes. Stir in half the chopped fresh herbs then process or strain the soup. Reheat and taste for seasoning. Serve in warmed bowls topped with a spoonful of salsa and sprinkled with the remaining herbs.

Butternut Squash and Blue Cheese Risotto Soup

This is, in fact, a very wet risotto, but it bears more than a passing resemblance to soup and makes a very smart first course for an autumnal dinner party. The combination of blue cheese and creamy rice is irresistible, and the perfect base for the nutty squash.

Serves 4

25g/1oz/2 tbsp butter
30ml/2 tbsp olive oil
2 onions, finely chopped
½ celery stick, finely sliced

1 small butternut squash,
   peeled, seeded and cut into
   small cubes
15ml/1 tbsp chopped sage
300g/11oz/1½ cups risotto or
   arborio rice
1.2 litres/2 pints/5 cups hot
   chicken stock
30ml/2 tbsp double
   (heavy) cream
115g/4oz blue cheese,
   finely diced
30ml/2 tbsp olive oil
salt and ground black pepper
4 large fresh sage leaves

1 Place the butter in a large pan with the oil and heat gently. Add the onions and celery, and cook for 4–5 minutes, until softened.

2 Stir in the butternut squash and cook for a further 3–4 minutes, then add the sage.

3 Add the rice and cook for 1–2 minutes, stirring, until the grains are slightly translucent. Add the chicken stock a ladleful at a time.

4 Cook until each ladleful of the stock has been absorbed by the rice before adding the next. Continue adding the stock in this way until you have a very wet rice mixture. Season with salt and pepper and stir in the cream.

5 Meanwhile, heat the oil in a frying pan and fry the sage leaves for a few seconds until crisp. Drain. Stir the blue cheese into the risotto soup and ladle it into bowls. Garnish with fried sage leaves.

Garlic and Squash Soup Energy 238kcal/986kJ; Protein 2.9g; Carbohydrate 11.9g, of which sugars 10.3g; Fat 20.2g, of which saturates 3.1g; Cholesterol 0mg; Calcium 79mg; Fibre 4.1g; Sodium 11mg.
Butternut Squash Soup Energy 505kcal/2100kJ; Protein 9.2g; Carbohydrate 63.7g, of which sugars 5.7g; Fat 23g, of which saturates 8.3g; Cholesterol 26mg; Calcium 110mg; Fibre 2.7g; Sodium 91mg.

Cream of Duck Soup

This rich soup is full of glorious autumnal flavours and will go down perfectly at a dinner party.

Serves 4
2 duck breast fillets
4 rindless streaky (fatty) bacon
   rashers (strips), chopped
1 onion, chopped
1 garlic clove, chopped
2 carrots, diced
2 celery sticks, chopped
4 large mushrooms, chopped
15ml/1 tbsp tomato purée (paste)
2 duck legs, chopped into pieces
15ml/1 tbsp plain
   (all-purpose) flour

45ml/3 tbsp brandy
150ml/$\frac{1}{4}$ pint/$\frac{2}{3}$ cup port
300ml/$\frac{1}{2}$ pint/1$\frac{1}{4}$ cups red wine
900ml/1$\frac{1}{2}$ pints/ 3$\frac{3}{4}$ cups
   chicken stock
1 bay leaf
2 sprigs fresh thyme
15ml/1 tbsp redcurrant jelly
150ml/$\frac{1}{4}$ pint/$\frac{2}{3}$ cup double
   (heavy) cream
salt and ground black pepper

For the blueberry relish
150g/5oz/1$\frac{1}{4}$ cups blueberries
15ml/1 tbsp caster (superfine) sugar
grated rind and juice of 2 limes
15ml/1 tbsp chopped fresh parsley
15ml/1 tbsp balsamic vinegar

1 Score the skin and fat on the duck breast fillets. Brown in a hot heavy pan, skin down, for 8–10 minutes. Turn and cook for 5–6 minutes, until tender. Remove the duck. Drain off some of the duck fat, leaving about 45ml/3 tbsp in the pan.

2 Add the bacon, onion, garlic, carrots, celery and mushrooms and cook for 10 minutes, stirring. Stir in the tomato purée and cook for 2 minutes. Remove the skin and bones from the duck legs and chop the flesh. Add to the pan and cook for 5 minutes.

3 Stir in the flour, then the brandy, port, wine and stock. Boil, stirring. Stir in the bay, thyme and jelly. Reduce the heat and simmer for 1 hour. Strain the soup and simmer for 10 minutes.

4 In a bowl, mix together all the ingredients for the relish, crushing some berries as you stir.

5 Discard the skin and fat from the duck breasts. Cut the meat into thin strips and add to the soup with the cream. Season and reheat, then ladle into bowls and serve topped with relish.

Mussel Soup with Pumpkin

This delicious soup is a fine way to enjoy two of best foods on offer over the autumn months.

Serves 4
1kg/2$\frac{1}{4}$lb mussels, cleaned
300ml/$\frac{1}{2}$ pint/1$\frac{1}{4}$ cups dry
   white wine
1 large lemon
1 bay leaf

15ml/1 tbsp olive oil
1 onion, chopped
1 garlic clove, crushed
675g/1$\frac{1}{2}$lb pumpkin, seeded,
   peeled and roughly chopped
900ml/1$\frac{1}{2}$ pints/3$\frac{3}{4}$ cups
   vegetable stock
30ml/2 tbsp chopped fresh dill
salt and ground black pepper
lemon wedges, to serve

1 Discard any open mussels that do not shut when tapped sharply, and put the rest into a large pan. Pour in the wine.

2 Pare large pieces of rind from the lemon and squeeze the juice, then add both to the mussels with the bay leaf. Cover and bring to the boil, then cook for 4–5 minutes, shaking the pan occasionally until all the mussels have opened. Drain the mussels in a colander over a large bowl. Reserve the liquid.

3 Discard the lemon rind and bay leaf, and any mussel shells that have not opened. Set aside a few mussels in their shells for the garnish. Remove the shells from the remaining mussels. Strain the reserved cooking liquid through a muslin- (cheesecloth) lined sieve (strainer).

4 Heat the oil in a large, clean pan. Add the onion and garlic and cook for 4–5 minutes, until softened. Add the pumpkin flesh and the strained mussel cooking liquid. Bring to the boil and simmer, uncovered, for 5–6 minutes. Pour in the stock and cook for 25–30 minutes, until the pumpkin is very tender.

5 Cool the soup slightly, then process it in a food processor or blender until smooth. Return the soup to the rinsed-out pan and season well. Stir in the chopped dill and the shelled mussels, then bring just to the boil. Ladle the soup into warmed bowls. Garnish with the reserved mussels in shells. Serve lemon wedges with the soup.

Mussel with Pumpkin Energy 126kcal/532kJ; Protein 13g; Carbohydrate 7.5g, of which sugars 4g; Fat 5g, of which saturates 0.8g; Cholesterol 40mg; Calcium 113mg; Fibre 2.5g; Sodium 245mg.
Cream of Duck Soup Energy 642kcal/2673kJ; Protein 39.2g; Carbohydrate 14.2g, of which sugars 13.6g; Fat 35g, of which saturates 17.2g; Cholesterol 252mg; Calcium 83mg; Fibre 2.8g; Sodium 384mg.

Lemon, Chilli and Garlic Relish

This powerful relish is flavoured with North African spices and punchy preserved lemons, which are widely available in Middle Eastern stores. It is great served with Moroccan tagines.

Makes 1 small jar

45ml/3 tbsp olive oil
3 large red onions, sliced
2 heads of garlic, separated into
cloves and peeled
10ml/2 tsp coriander
seeds, crushed
10ml/2 tsp light muscovado
(brown) sugar, plus a little extra
pinch of saffron threads
5cm/2in piece cinnamon stick
2–3 small whole dried red
chillies (optional)
2 fresh bay leaves
30–45ml/2–3 tbsp sherry vinegar
juice of ½ small orange
30ml/2 tbsp chopped
preserved lemon
salt and ground black pepper

1 Gently heat the oil in a large heavy pan. Add the onions and stir, then cover and cook on the lowest setting for 10–15 minutes, stirring occasionally, until soft.

2 Add the garlic cloves and the coriander seeds. Cover and cook for 5–8 minutes, until soft.

3 Add a pinch of salt, lots of ground black pepper and the sugar to the onions and cook, uncovered, for a further 5 minutes.

4 Soak the saffron in about 45ml/3 tbsp warm water for 5 minutes, then add to the onions, together with the soaking water. Add the cinnamon, dried chillies, if using, and bay leaves. Stir in 30ml/2 tbsp of the sherry vinegar and the orange juice.

5 Cook very gently, uncovered, until the onions are very soft and most of the liquid has evaporated. Stir in the preserved lemon and cook gently for 5 minutes.

6 Taste the relish and adjust the seasoning, adding more salt, sugar and/or vinegar to taste.

7 Serve warm or cold (not hot or chilled). The relish tastes best if left to stand for 24 hours.

Papaya and Lemon Relish

This chunky relish is best made with a firm, unripe papaya. The long, gentle simmering in the slow cooker allows plenty of time for all the flavours to mellow. Serve the relish with roast meats, or with cheese and crackers.

Makes 450g/1lb

1 large unripe papaya
1 onion, very thinly sliced
175ml/6fl oz/generous ¾ cup
red wine vinegar
juice of 2 lemons
165g/5½oz/¾ cup golden caster
(superfine) sugar
1 cinnamon stick
1 bay leaf
2.5ml/½ tsp hot paprika
2.5ml/½ tsp salt
150g/5oz/1 cup sultanas
(golden raisins)

1 Peel the papaya and cut it in half lengthways. Remove the seeds and discard, then cut the flesh into small chunks of a roughly similar size.

2 Place the papaya chunks in the ceramic cooking pot, add the onion slices and stir in the red wine vinegar. Switch the slow cooker to the high setting, cover with the lid and cook for 2 hours.

3 Add the lemon juice, golden caster sugar, cinnamon stick, bay leaf, paprika, salt and sultanas to the ceramic cooking pot. Gently stir the mixture thoroughly until all of the sugar has completely dissolved.

4 Cook the chutney for a further 1 hour. Leave the cover of the slow cooker off to allow some of the liquid to evaporate and the mixture to reduce slightly. The relish should be fairly thick and syrupy.

5 Ladle the chutney into hot sterilized jars. Seal the jars and store the chutney for 1 week before using to allow it to mature a little and for the flavours to further develop. The chutney should be used within 1 year of making it. However, once a jar has been opened, the chutney should be stored in the refrigerator and consumed within 2 weeks.

Lemon and Chilli Relish Energy 102kcal/422kJ; Protein 1.9g; Carbohydrate 11.4g, of which sugars 7.8g; Fat 5.7g, of which saturates 0.8g; Cholesterol 0mg; Calcium 28mg; Fibre 1.7g; Sodium 4mg.
Papaya Relish Energy 1294kcal/5511kJ; Protein 8.4g; Carbohydrate 332.7g, of which sugars 332.7g; Fat 1.4g, of which saturates 0g; Cholesterol 0mg; Calcium 272mg; Fibre 16.1g; Sodium 1111mg.

Toffee Onion Relish

Slow, gentle cooking reduces the onions to a soft, caramelized golden brown mixture in this recipe. This relish adds a sweet flavour to a mature cheese or toasted goat's cheese, and it is ideal to serve with flans and quiches.

Serves 4
3 large onions
50g/2oz/¼ cup butter
30ml/2 tbsp olive oil
30ml/2 tbsp light muscovado
   (brown) sugar
30ml/2 tbsp pickled capers
30ml/2 tbsp chopped fresh parsley
salt and ground black pepper

1 Peel the onions and cut them in half vertically through the core, then slice them thinly.

2 Heat the butter and oil together in a large, heavy pan. Add the sliced onions and sugar and cook very gently for about 30 minutes over a low heat, stirring occasionally, until the onions are reduced to a soft rich-brown, toffee-like mixture.

3 Roughly chop the capers and stir them into the browned onion mixture. Allow the mixture to cool completely and then transfer to a bowl.

4 Stir the chopped fresh parsley into the dip, and add salt and ground black pepper to taste. Cover the bowl and chill until ready to serve.

Cook's Tip
Choose a pan with a heavy base in which to cook the relish. This will ensure you get an evenly browned toffee mixture without the risk of burning.

Variation
Try making this recipe with red onions in place of the normal white onions for a subtle variation in flavour. You could even use the same weight of shallots, if you like.

Apple and Cider Relish

This relish couldn't be simpler to make. It tastes great with roast pork, duck or goose. It is an ideal way to use cooking apples that appear in the stores in the autumn.

2.5ml/½ tsp cider vinegar
25g/1oz/2 tbsp butter
2 whole cloves
a few sprigs of fresh thyme
15ml/1 tbsp clear honey
10ml/2 tsp Dijon mustard

Makes 450g/1lb
450g/1lb Bramley apples
150ml/¼ pint/⅔ cup sweet cider

1 Peel the apples with a sharp knife or vegetable peeler. Remove the cores and discard, then slice the flesh.

2 Place the apple slices in a large pan. Pour in the sweet cider, cider vinegar, butter, cloves and sprigs of fresh thyme.

3 Bring the mixture to the boil, then reduce the heat and simmer over low heat, stirring occasionally, for about 10 minutes or until the apples are soft and pulpy.

4 Increase the heat and cook over medium heat until most of the liquid has evaporated.

5 Remove the cloves and thyme sprigs and beat in the honey and mustard. Taste and add more honey if necessary, but the sauce is best when slightly tart.

Variation
Other fresh herbs will work as well: try parsley, rosemary or dill.

Cook's Tip
You can press the apple sauce through a sieve (strainer) using a wooden spoon if you prefer it to be perfectly smooth rather than lumpy.

Toffee Onion Relish Energy 239kcal/992kJ; Protein 2.6g; Carbohydrate 22.1g, of which sugars 18g; Fat 16.3g, of which saturates 7.3g; Cholesterol 27mg; Calcium 75mg; Fibre 3.1g; Sodium 86mg.
Apple and Cider Relish Energy 453kcal/1909kJ; Protein 2.2g; Carbohydrate 56.4g, of which sugars 56.2g; Fat 21.7g, of which saturates 13.6g; Cholesterol 58mg; Calcium 42mg; Fibre 7.2g; Sodium 504mg.

Cheese Pies with Raisins and Nuts

These delicious small pies always dazzle people. In Crete, where they are very popular, there are several variations, including one with a filling of sautéed wild greens. These little treats can be offered with drinks or presented as part of a large meze table.

Serves 4–6
1 large (US extra large) egg, plus
   1 egg yolk for glazing
150g/5oz feta cheese

30ml/2 tbsp milk
30ml/2 tbsp chopped fresh
   mint leaves
15ml/1 tbsp raisins
15ml/1 tbsp pine nuts,
   lightly toasted
a little vegetable oil, for greasing

For the pastry
225g/8oz/2 cups self-raising
   (self-rising) flour
45ml/3 tbsp extra virgin olive oil
15g/½oz/1 tbsp butter, melted
90g/3½oz Greek (US strained
   plain) yogurt

1 To make the pastry, put the flour in a bowl and mix in the oil, butter and yogurt by hand. Cover the bowl with cling film (plastic wrap) and leave it to rest in the refrigerator for about 15 minutes.

2 Meanwhile, make the filling. Beat the egg lightly in a bowl. Crumble in the cheese, then mix in the milk, mint, raisins and pine nuts.

3 Preheat the oven to 190°C/375°F/Gas 5. Cover half of the pastry with a clean dish cloth, thinly roll out the remainder and cut out 7.5cm/3in rounds.

4 Place a heaped teaspoon of filling on each round and fold the pastry over to make a half-moon shape. Press the edges to seal, then place the pies on a greased baking sheet.

5 Repeat the rolling and filling process with the remaining pastry. Brush the pies with egg yolk.

6 Place the pies in the preheated oven and bake for about 20 minutes, or until they are golden brown and crisp all over. Serve immediately.

Confit of Slow-cooked Onions and Prunes

Onions are caramelized in the slow cooker in sweet-sour balsamic vinegar. It makes a fantastic seasonal accompaniment to cold meats or cheese and chunks of crusty bread.

Serves 6
30ml/2 tbsp extra virgin olive oil
15g/½oz/1 tbsp butter

500g/1¼lb onions, thinly sliced
3–5 fresh thyme sprigs
1 bay leaf
30ml/2 tbsp light muscovado
   (brown) sugar, plus a little extra
30ml/2 tbsp balsamic vinegar,
   plus a little extra
120ml/4fl oz/½ cup red wine
50g/2oz/¼ cup ready-to-eat
   prunes, chopped
salt and ground black pepper

1 Put the oil and butter in the ceramic cooking pot and heat on high for 15 minutes.

2 Add the onions to the pot and stir to coat the slices in the butter. Cover the cooker with the lid, then place a folded dish towel on top to help retain the heat. Cook the onions for 5 hours, stirring the mixture occasionally.

3 Season with salt and pepper, then add the thyme, bay leaf, sugar, vinegar and wine. Stir until the sugar has dissolved, then stir in the prunes.

4 Cover and cook for 1½–2 hours, until thickened. Adjust the seasoning, adding sugar and/or vinegar to taste.

Cook's Tip
Chopping onions causes tears because of sulfuric compounds in the raw flesh. Most cause this to some extent – ranging from a little sniffle to a torrential downpour. Putting the onion in the freezer for about 20 minutes before chopping helps. If you suffer considerably when chopping onions, you may want to consider safety goggles, although you may look a little silly wearing them while chopping vegetables.

Confit of Onions Energy 133kcal/556kJ; Protein 1.2g; Carbohydrate 16.5g, of which sugars 14.6g; Fat 5.9g, of which saturates 1.8g; Cholesterol 5mg; Calcium 26mg; Fibre 1.6g; Sodium 20mg.
Cheese Pies Energy 160kcal/669kJ; Protein 5.1g; Carbohydrate 16.4g, of which sugars 2.5g; Fat 8.8g, of which saturates 3.4g; Cholesterol 31mg; Calcium 129mg; Fibre 0.7g; Sodium 270mg.

Chickpea Rissoles

This inexpensive yet delicious dish is a family favourite. Serve it with two ingredients that are widely available in autumn: radishes and rocket.

Serves 4

300g/11oz/scant 1½ cups chickpeas, soaked overnight in water to cover
105ml/7 tbsp extra virgin olive oil
2 large onions, chopped
15ml/1 tbsp ground cumin
2 garlic cloves, crushed
3–4 fresh sage leaves, chopped
45ml/3 tbsp chopped flat leaf parsley
1 egg, lightly beaten
45ml/3 tbsp self-raising (self-rising) flour
50g/2oz/½ cup plain (all-purpose) flour
salt and ground black pepper
radishes, rocket (arugula) and olives, to serve

1 Drain the chickpeas, rinse under cold water and drain again. Transfer them into a large pan, cover with plenty of cold water and bring them to the boil. Skim the froth from the surface of the water with a slotted spoon until the liquid is clear.

2 Cover the pan and cook for 1¼–1½ hours, or until the chickpeas are very soft. Set aside a few tablespoons of cooking liquid, then strain the chickpeas, discarding the rest of the liquid. Transfer them to a food processor, add 30–45ml/2–3 tbsp of the reserved liquid and process to a velvety mash.

3 Heat 45ml/3 tbsp of the olive oil in a large frying pan, add the onions, and sauté until they are light golden. Add the cumin and the garlic and stir for a few seconds until their aroma rises. Stir in the chopped sage leaves and the parsley, and set aside.

4 Scrape the chickpea mash into a large bowl and add the egg, the self-raising flour, and the fried onion and herb mixture. Season and mix well. Take large walnut-size pieces and flatten them so that they look like thick, round mini-hamburgers.

5 Coat the rissoles lightly in the plain flour. Heat the remaining olive oil in a large frying pan and fry them in batches until they are crisp and golden on both sides. Drain on kitchen paper and serve hot with the radishes, rocket and olives.

Spiced Onion Pakoras

These delicious Indian onion fritters are made with chickpea flour, otherwise known as gram flour or besan. Serve with chutney or a yogurt dip.

Serves 4–5

675g/1½lb onions, halved and thinly sliced
5ml/1 tsp salt
5ml/1 tsp ground coriander
5ml/1 tsp ground cumin
2.5ml/½ tsp ground turmeric
1–2 green chillies, seeded and finely chopped
45ml/3 tbsp chopped fresh coriander (cilantro)
90g/3½oz/¾ cup gram flour
2.5ml/½ tsp baking powder
vegetable oil, for deep-frying

To serve

lemon wedges (optional)
fresh coriander (cilantro) sprigs
yogurt and cucumber dip

1 Place the onions in a colander, add the salt and toss. Place on a plate and leave to stand for 45 minutes, tossing once or twice. Rinse the onions, then squeeze out any excess moisture.

2 Transfer the onions to a bowl. Add the ground coriander, cumin, turmeric, chillies and fresh coriander. Mix well.

3 Add the gram flour and baking powder, then use your hands to mix the ingredients thoroughly. Shape the mixture by hand into 12–15 pakoras, about the size of golf balls.

4 Heat the oil for deep-frying to 180–190°C/350–375°F or until a cube of day-old bread browns in 30–45 seconds. Fry the pakoras, 4–5 at a time, until they are deep golden brown all over. Drain each batch on kitchen paper and keep warm until all the pakoras are cooked. Serve with lemon wedges, if using, coriander sprigs and a yogurt dip.

> **Cook's Tip**
> For a cucumber dip, stir half a diced cucumber and 1 seeded and chopped fresh green chilli into 250ml/8fl oz/1 cup natural (plain) yogurt. Season with salt and cumin.

Chickpea Rissoles Energy 532kcal/2231kJ; Protein 19.7g; Carbohydrate 63.6g, of which sugars 8.1g; Fat 23.9g, of which saturates 3.2g; Cholesterol 0mg; Calcium 222mg; Fibre 10.7g; Sodium 77mg.
Onion Pakoras Energy 207kcal/861kJ; Protein 5.4g; Carbohydrate 19.8g, of which sugars 8.2g; Fat 12.3g, of which saturates 1.4g; Cholesterol 0mg; Calcium 84mg; Fibre 4.3g; Sodium 14mg.

Cheese-stuffed Pears

These autumn pears, made in the slow cooker, make a sublime dish with their scrumptious creamy topping. If you don't have a large slow cooker, choose short squat pears rather than long, tapering ones, so that they will fit in one layer.

Serves 4

50g/2oz/¼ cup ricotta cheese
50g/2oz/¼ cup dolcelatte cheese

15ml/1 tbsp honey
½ celery stick, finely sliced
8 green olives, pitted and
　roughly chopped
4 dates, pitted and cut into
　thin strips
pinch of paprika
2 medium barely ripe pears
150ml/¼ pint/⅔ cup fresh
　apple juice
mixed salad leaves, to serve
　(optional)

1 Place the ricotta cheese in a bowl and crumble in the dolcelatte. Add the honey, celery, olives, dates and paprika and mix together well until creamy and thoroughly blended.

2 Halve the pears lengthways. Use a melon baller or teaspoon to remove the cores and make a hollow for the filling.

3 Divide the ricotta filling equally between the pears, packing it into the hollow, then arrange the fruit in a single layer in the ceramic cooking pot.

4 Pour the apple juice around the pears, then cover with the lid. Cook on high for 1½–2 hours, or until the fruit is tender. (The cooking time will depend on the ripeness of the pears.)

5 Remove the pears from the slow cooker and brown them under a hot grill (broiler) for a few minutes. Serve with mixed salad leaves, if you like.

Cook's Tip
These pears go particularly well with slightly bitter and peppery leaves, such as chicory and rocket (arugula). Try them tossed in a walnut oil dressing.

Mushroom Caviar

The name caviar refers to the dark colour and texture of this dish of chopped mushrooms. Serve the mixture in individual serving dishes accompanied by toasted rye bread rubbed with cut garlic cloves. Chopped hard-boiled egg, spring onion, and parsley, which are the traditional garnishes for caviar, can be added just before serving.

Serves 4

45ml/3 tbsp olive or
　vegetable oil
450g/1lb mushrooms,
　coarsely chopped
5–10 shallots, chopped
4 garlic cloves, chopped
15ml/1 tbsp chopped fresh
　parsley, to garnish
chopped hard-boiled egg and a
　handful of chopped spring
　onion (scallion), to serve

1 Heat the olive or vegetable oil in a large pan. Add the mushrooms, shallots and garlic, and cook, stirring occasionally, for 3–4 minutes until browned.

2 Season with a little salt, then continue cooking over medium heat until the mushrooms give up their liquor.

3 Continue cooking, stirring frequently, until the liquor has evaporated and the mushrooms are brown and dry. This will take about 10–15 minutes. Ensure that you stir the mixture regularly, otherwise they may burn when the liquid has gone.

4 Put the mixture in a food processor or blender and process briefly until a chunky paste is formed. Spoon the mushroom caviar into dishes and serve with the chopped hard-boiled egg and spring onion. Garnish with parsley.

Variation
For a rich wild mushroom caviar, soak 10–15g/¼–½oz dried porcini in about 120ml/4fl oz/½ cup water for about 30 minutes. Add the porcini and their soaking liquid to the browned mushrooms in step 3. Continue as in the recipe. Serve with wedges of lemon, for their tangy juice.

Cheese-stuffed Pears Energy 236kcal/992kJ; Protein 6.9g; Carbohydrate 35.6g, of which sugars 35.6g; Fat 8.2g, of which saturates 5.0g; Cholesterol 24mg; Calcium 141mg; Fibre 4.1g; Sodium 261mg.
Mushroom Caviar Energy 68kcal/283kJ; Protein 3.3g; Carbohydrate 6.4g, of which sugars 3.8g; Fat 3.5g, of which saturates 0.5g; Cholesterol 0mg; Calcium 24mg; Fibre 2.4g; Sodium 8mg.

Garlic Mushrooms

Everybody loves garlic mushrooms and autumn is the best time of year to enjoy them. This recipe has been made a little more sophisticated by using big, juicy flat mushrooms instead of the usual bland buttons. The wine deepens the flavour even further.

Serves 4

4 large slices of country
   (preferably sourdough) bread

75g/3oz/6 tbsp butter, plus extra
   melted butter
3 shallots, finely chopped
2 garlic cloves, finely chopped
675g/1½lb field (portabello) or
   chestnut mushrooms,
   thickly sliced
75ml/5 tbsp dry white wine
45ml/3 tbsp chopped
   fresh parsley
salt and ground black pepper

1 Toast the bread on both sides on a hot ridged griddle. This will create a striped charred effect as if it had been grilled on a barbecue. Brush the toasted bread with the extra melted butter and keep warm.

2 Melt the butter in a frying pan, add the shallots and garlic, and cook for 5 minutes until golden.

3 Add the mushrooms and toss well. Fry over high heat for about 1 minute. Pour over the wine and season well with salt and ground black pepper.

4 Keep the heat high under the pan and continue to cook the mushroom mixture, stirring occasionally, until the wine evaporates. Lightly stir in the parsley. Pile the mushrooms on to the toasted bread and serve immediately.

> **Cook's Tip**
> The ridged griddle must be heated until very hot or the bread will take ages to colour and will just dry out. If you don't have a griddle, toast the bread under a hot grill (broiler) on both sides until quite dark.

Mushroom and Bean Pâté

Making pâté in the slow cooker results in this light and tasty version. It is delicious served on triangles of wholemeal toast for an autumnal appetizer, or with crusty French bread as a light lunch served with salad.

Serves 8
450g/1lb/6 cups mushrooms, sliced
1 onion, finely chopped
2 garlic cloves, crushed

1 red (bell) pepper, seeded
   and diced
30ml/2 tbsp vegetable stock
30ml/2 tbsp dry white wine
400g/14oz can red kidney beans,
   rinsed and drained
1 egg, beaten
50g/2oz/1 cup fresh wholemeal
   (whole-wheat) breadcrumbs
10ml/2 tsp chopped fresh thyme
10ml/2 tsp chopped fresh rosemary
salt and ground black pepper
salad leaves, fresh herbs and
   tomato wedges, to garnish

1 Put the mushrooms, onion, garlic, red pepper, stock and wine in the ceramic cooking pot. Cover and cook on high for 2 hours, then set aside for about 10 minutes to cool.

2 Transfer the mixture to a food processor or blender and add the kidney beans. Process to make a smooth purée, stopping the machine once or twice to scrape down the sides.

3 Lightly grease and line a 900g/2lb loaf tin (pan). Put an inverted saucer or metal pastry ring in the bottom of the ceramic cooking pot. Pour in about 2.5cm/1in of hot water, and set to high.

4 Transfer the vegetable mixture to a bowl. Add the egg, breadcrumbs and herbs, and season. Mix thoroughly, then spoon into the loaf tin and cover with cling film (plastic wrap) or foil.

5 Put the tin in the slow cooker and pour in enough boiling water to come just over halfway up the sides of the tin. Cover with the lid and cook on high for 4 hours, or until lightly set.

6 Remove the tin and place on a wire rack until cool. Chill for several hours, or overnight. Turn the pâté out of the tin, remove the lining paper and serve garnished with salad leaves, herbs and tomato wedges.

Garlic Mushrooms Energy 131kcal/542kJ; Protein 6.7g; Carbohydrate 1.8g, of which sugars 1.5g; Fat 11.3g, of which saturates 2.8g; Cholesterol 7mg; Calcium 65mg; Fibre 1.9g; Sodium 136mg.
Mushroom and Bean Pâté Energy 85kcal/358kJ; Protein 5.5g; Carbohydrate 12.3g, of which sugars 3.8g; Fat 1.6g, of which saturates 0.4g; Cholesterol 28mg; Calcium 47mg; Fibre 3.7g; Sodium 187mg.

Garlic with Goat's Cheese Pâté

The combination of sweet roasted garlic and goat's cheese is a classic one. The pâté is flavoured with herbs and walnuts, which are hitting their peak in autumn.

Serves 4
4 large garlic bulbs
4 fresh rosemary sprigs
8 fresh thyme sprigs
60ml/4 tbsp olive oil
sea salt and ground black pepper

thyme sprigs, to garnish
4–8 slices sourdough bread and walnuts, to serve

For the pâté
200g/7oz/scant 1 cup soft goat's cheese
5ml/1 tsp finely chopped fresh thyme
15ml/1 tbsp chopped fresh parsley
50g/2oz/⅓ cup walnuts, chopped
15ml/1 tbsp walnut oil (optional)
fresh thyme, to garnish

1 Preheat the oven to 180°C/350°F/Gas 4. Strip the papery skin from the garlic bulbs. Place them in an ovenproof dish large enough to hold them snugly. Tuck in the fresh rosemary sprigs and fresh thyme sprigs, drizzle the olive oil over and season with a little sea salt and plenty of ground black pepper.

2 Cover the garlic tightly with foil and bake in the oven for 50–60 minutes, opening the parcel and basting once halfway through the cooking time. Set aside and leave to cool.

3 Preheat the grill (broiler). To make the pâté, cream the cheese with the thyme, parsley and chopped walnuts. Beat in 15ml/1 tbsp of the cooking oil from the garlic and season to taste with plenty of ground black pepper. Transfer the pâté to a serving bowl and chill until ready to serve.

4 Brush the sourdough bread slices on one side with the remaining cooking oil from the garlic bulbs, then grill (broil) until lightly toasted.

5 Divide the pâté among four plates. Drizzle the walnut oil, if using, over the goat's cheese pâté and grind some pepper over it. Place some garlic on each plate and serve with the pâté and some toasted bread. Garnish the pâté with a little fresh thyme and serve a few freshly shelled walnuts with each portion.

Marinated Mussels

Large, ultra-fresh mussels are one of the most eagerly awaited treats of autumn each year. Here they are served raw on the half shell in a flavoursome vinaigrette.

Serves 4–6
24 large live mussels, scrubbed and bearded
7.5ml/1½ tsp red wine vinegar or lemon juice

30ml/2 tbsp vegetable or olive oil
1 shallot, finely chopped
1 spring onion (scallion), finely chopped
1 medium ripe but firm tomato, finely chopped
salt and ground white pepper
30ml/2 tbsp freshly chopped parsley and 4–6 lemon wedges, to garnish
crusty bread, to serve

1 Discard any mussels that are not tightly closed, or which do not snap shut when tapped. Holding a mussel firmly between the thumb and index finger of one hand, carefully lever it open from the side with a sharp, short-bladed knife.

2 Insert the knife blade in the cavity and cut the muscle to which the mussel meat is attached. Work the knife blade around to free the mussel. Put it in a non-reactive bowl. Repeat the process with the remaining mussels. Wash and dry the mussel shells and save them.

3 In a separate bowl, whisk the vinegar or lemon juice with the oil. Season, then drizzle over the mussels. Fold in the shallot, spring onion and tomato. Cover and marinate in the refrigerator for at least 1 hour.

4 To serve, arrange half the mussel shells on a large platter and place a marinated mussel on each. Garnish with parsley and lemon wedges and serve with crusty bread.

> **Cook's Tips**
> • Mussels for serving raw must be bought from a reputable fishmonger so they are guaranteed to be fresh.
> • Marinated mussels can be kept in the refrigerator for 4 days.

Goat's Cheese Pâté Energy 371kcal/1534kJ; Protein 14.5g; Carbohydrate 5.1g, of which sugars 1.3g; Fat 32.7g, of which saturates 11.3g; Cholesterol 47mg; Calcium 91mg; Fibre 1.7g; Sodium 304mg.
Marinated Mussels Energy 59kcal/246kJ; Protein 3.5g; Carbohydrate 1.8g, of which sugars 1.1g; Fat 4.3g, of which saturates 0.6g; Cholesterol 11mg; Calcium 14mg; Fibre 0.4g; Sodium 81mg.

Shelled Mussels with Garlic and Herbs

These mussels are served without their shells, in a delicious paprika-flavoured sauce. Eat them with cocktail sticks.

Serves 4
900g/2lb fresh mussels
1 lemon slice
90ml/6 tbsp olive oil
2 shallots, finely chopped
1 garlic clove, finely chopped
15ml/1 tbsp chopped
   fresh parsley
2.5ml/½ tsp sweet paprika
1.5ml/¼ tsp dried chilli flakes

1 Scrub the mussels, discarding any damaged ones that do not close when tapped sharply with a knife. Place the mussels in a large pan, with about 250ml/8fl oz/1 cup water and the slice of lemon.

2 Bring the mixture to the boil and cook the mussels for about 3–4 minutes, removing the mussels as they open. Discard any that remain closed. Take the mussels out of the shells and drain on kitchen paper.

3 Heat the oil in a sauté pan, add the mussels and cook, stirring, for 1 minute. Remove from the pan.

4 Add the shallots and garlic and cook, covered, over low heat for about 5 minutes or until soft. Remove from the heat and stir in the parsley, paprika and chilli.

5 Return to the heat and stir in the mussels. Cook briefly. Remove from the heat and cover for a minute or two, to let the flavours mingle, before serving.

> **Cook's Tip**
> *If you prefer a little more heat in your food, then you can simply add a little more dried chilli flakes and paprika to the shallots and garlic in step 4.*

Deep-fried Layered Shiitake and Scallop

A wok does double duty for making these delicate mushroom and seafood treats, first for steaming and then for deep-frying.

Serves 4
4 scallops
8 large fresh shiitake mushrooms
225g/8oz long yam, unpeeled
20ml/4 tsp miso
50g/2oz/1 cup fresh breadcrumbs
cornflour (cornstarch), for dusting
2 eggs, beaten
vegetable oil, for deep-frying
salt
4 lemon wedges, to serve

1 Slice the scallops in two horizontally, then sprinkle with salt. Remove the stalks from the shiitake mushrooms and discard them. Cut shallow slits on the top of the shiitake to form a 'hash' symbol. Sprinkle with a little salt.

2 Heat a steamer and steam the long yam for 10–15 minutes, or until soft. Test with a skewer. Leave to cool, then remove the skin. Mash the flesh in a bowl, add the miso and mix well. Take the breadcrumbs into your hands and break them down finely. Mix half into the mashed long yam, keeping the rest on a small plate.

3 Fill the underneath of the shiitake caps with a scoop of mashed long yam. Smooth down with the flat edge of a knife and dust the mash with cornflour. Add a little mash to a slice of scallop and place on top.

4 Spread another 5ml/1 tsp mashed long yam on to the scallop and shape to completely cover. Make sure all the ingredients are clinging together. Repeat to make eight little mounds.

5 Place the beaten eggs in a shallow container. Dust the shiitake and scallop mounds with cornflour, then dip into the egg. Handle with care as the mash and scallop are quite soft. Coat well with the remaining breadcrumbs and deep-fry in hot oil until golden. Drain well on kitchen paper. Serve hot on individual plates with a wedge of lemon.

Mussels with Herbs Energy 214kcal/888kJ; Protein 12g; Carbohydrate 1.3g, of which sugars 0.9g; Fat 17.9g, of which saturates 2.6g; Cholesterol 27mg; Calcium 145mg; Fibre 0.4g; Sodium 144mg.
Shiitake and Scallop Energy 812kcal/3396kJ; Protein 45.8g; Carbohydrate 54g, of which sugars 12.6g; Fat 47.8g, of which saturates 7.5g; Cholesterol 428mg; Calcium 279mg; Fibre 7g; Sodium 741mg.

Pan-fried Baby Squid with Spices

You need to work quickly to cook this dish, then serve it immediately, so that the squid is just cooked and tender. Baby squid are widely available ready prepared. The flavours of turmeric, ginger and harissa are fabulous with the contrasting sweetness of the squid, which is reinforced by the addition of a spoonful of honey, and the whole dish is sharpened up by the zesty lemon juice.

Serves 4
8 baby squid, prepared,
   with tentacles
5ml/1 tsp ground turmeric
15ml/1 tbsp olive oil
2 garlic cloves, finely chopped
15g/ oz fresh root ginger, peeled
   and finely chopped
5–10ml/1–2 tsp honey
juice of 1 lemon
10ml/2 tsp harissa
salt
small bunch of fresh coriander
   (cilantro), roughly chopped,
   to serve

1 Pat dry the squid bodies, inside and out with kitchen paper (paper towels), and dry the tentacles. Sprinkle the squid and tentacles with the ground turmeric.

2 Heat the olive oil in a large heavy frying pan and stir in the garlic and ginger. Cook, stirring constantly, for 2–3 minutes.

3 Just as the ginger and garlic begin to colour, add the squid and tentacles to the pan and fry quickly on both sides over a high heat. (Be careful not to overcook the squid, otherwise it will become rubbery.)

4 Add the honey, lemon juice and harissa and stir to form a thick, spicy, caramelized sauce. Season with salt, sprinkle with the chopped coriander and serve immediately.

Cook's Tip
Harissa, the fiery red paste used in the cuisines of Tunisia, Algeria and Morocco, is made from chillies, olive oil and garlic. The chillies are often smoked, and other flavourings include coriander and cumin.

Chicken Bitki

This is a popular dish and makes an attractive appetizer. Serve them with deep red beetroot, whose season is in full swing at this time of year, and seasonal green salad leaves.

Serves 4
15g/½oz/1 tbsp butter, melted
115g/4oz flat mushrooms,
   finely chopped
50g/2oz/1 cup fresh white
   breadcrumbs

350g/12oz skinless chicken
   breast fillets or guinea
   fowl, minced (ground) or
   finely chopped
2 eggs, separated
1.5ml/¼ tsp grated nutmeg
30ml/2 tbsp plain
   (all-purpose) flour
45ml/3 tbsp oil
salt and ground black pepper
salad leaves and grated pickled
   beetroot (beet), to serve

1 Melt the butter in a large frying pan and fry the mushrooms for about 5 minutes until soft and the juices have evaporated. Allow to cool.

2 In a large bowl, mix together the cooled mushrooms and the breadcrumbs. Stir in the minced or chopped chicken or guinea fowl, egg yolks and nutmeg. Season with salt and ground black pepper and mix thoroughly.

3 Whisk the egg whites until stiff. Stir half into the chicken mixture to slacken it, then fold in the remainder.

4 Shape into 12 even-size meatballs, about 7.5cm/3in long and 2.5cm/1in wide. Roll in the flour to coat.

5 Heat the oil in a frying pan and fry the bitki for about 10 minutes, turning until evenly golden brown and cooked through. Serve hot with salad leaves and pickled beetroot.

Cook's Tip
Guinea fowl has a mild gamey flavour and is popular in the autumn. Hens are usually more tender than the males.

Pan-fried Baby Squid Energy 154kcal/647kJ; Protein 19.8g; Carbohydrate 5.8g, of which sugars 4.3g; Fat 5.9g, of which saturates 1g; Cholesterol 281mg; Calcium 54mg; Fibre 1g; Sodium 144mg.
Chicken Bitki Energy 102kcal/426kJ; Protein 9g; Carbohydrate 5.2g, of which sugars 0.2g; Fat 5.2g, of which saturates 1.3g; Cholesterol 55mg; Calcium 16mg; Fibre 0.3g; Sodium 69mg.

Pâté with Bacon and Mushrooms

Liver pâté demonstrates its flavoursome versatility paired with crisp bacon rashers and sautéed seasonal mushrooms.

Serves 4
40g/1½oz/3 tbsp salted
   butter, softened
4 button (white)
   mushrooms, sliced

4 cooked unsmoked streaky
   (fatty) bacon rashers (strips)
300g/11oz block of liver pâté
2 slices rye bread
2 leaves round
   (butterhead) lettuce
2 slices pickled beetroot (beet),
   cut into matchsticks
parsley, to garnish

1 Melt 15g/½oz/1 tbsp of the butter in a frying pan over medium heat. Add the mushrooms and cook, stirring occasionally, for 4–5 minutes, until lightly browned. Remove from the pan and leave to cool.

2 Place the bacon in a frying pan over a medium heat. Cook until browned and crisp. Drain on kitchen paper.

3 Cut the liver pâté into slices with a sharp knife. How thick you cut the slice depends on how much you want, but aim for a thickness of around 5mm/¼in.

4 Spread the slices of bread to the edges with the remaining butter. Place a lettuce leaf on each slice and cut the slices in half. Leaving one curl of lettuce visible, arrange two slices of liver pâté on the lettuce on each slice.

5 Place two slices of bacon over the pâté. Garnish each sandwich with two or three sticks of beetroot and chopped fresh parsley.

Cook's Tip
Garnish with small pickled gherkins to accent the sandwich's textures and flavours. Small, whole beetroot (beet) slices can also be used as a garnish.

Bacon with Apples

Apples are a familiar autumn ingredient and they appear in many savoury dishes at this time of year. In this open sandwich, the sweet combination of apples and onions mixed with crisp, salty bacon is both rich and satisfying.

Serves 4
8 unsmoked streaky (fatty) bacon
   rashers (strips)

75g/3oz/1 cup finely
   chopped onion
2 firm apples, peeled
   and chopped
25g/1oz/2 tbsp salted
   butter, softened
2 slices rye bread
2 leaves round
   (butterhead) lettuce
4 parsley sprigs

1 Fry the bacon over medium-high heat until crisp; drain on kitchen paper, leaving the fat in the pan.

2 Cook the onion in the reserved bacon fat for 5–7 minutes, until transparent but not browned.

3 Add the apples to the pan, and continue cooking for about 5 minutes, until tender. Crumble half the bacon into the apple mixture in the pan.

4 Butter the slices of bread to the edges, top each with the lettuce leaves and cut each slice in half. Leaving one curl of lettuce visible on each piece of bread, spoon the apple and bacon mixture on to the lettuce, dividing it evenly among the four sandwiches.

5 Break the four reserved bacon rashers in half, and place two pieces on each sandwich. Garnish with parsley sprigs, and serve warm.

Cook's Tip
Crisp, tart eating apples are the best to use for this recipe, rather than the cooking variety.

Liver Pâté Energy 418kcal/1731kJ; Protein 15g; Carbohydrate 7.8g, of which sugars 1.7g; Fat 36.6g, of which saturates 13.5g; Cholesterol 157mg; Calcium 35mg; Fibre 2.2g; Sodium 868mg.
Bacon with Apples Energy 215kcal/895kJ; Protein 9.8g; Carbohydrate 13.9g, of which sugars 8g; Fat 13.7g, of which saturates 6.4g; Cholesterol 40mg; Calcium 21mg; Fibre 2g; Sodium 883mg.

Papaya, Lime and Ginger Salad

This refreshing, fruity salad makes a lovely light breakfast, perfect for the autumn months when these ingredients are at their best. When buying, choose really ripe, fragrant papayas for the best flavour.

Serves 4
2 large ripe papayas
juice of 1 fresh lime
2 pieces preserved stem ginger, finely sliced

1 Cut both the papayas in half lengthways and scoop out the seeds using a teaspoon.

2 Using a sharp knife, cut the papaya flesh into thin slices and arrange on a platter.

3 Squeeze the lime juice over the papaya and sprinkle with the sliced stem ginger. Serve immediately.

Cook's Tips
• Papaya are large fruits, approximately 15cm/6in long, and weigh anything from 450g/1lb to 900g/2lb, and they are pear shaped. They have a golden yellow skin when ripe, and the similarly coloured flesh is juicy and silky smooth, with a sweet-tart flavour. When buying, look for richly coloured specimens that give slightly when squeezed gently. If they are a little green, they will ripen quickly at room temperature, if placed in a paper bag. Chill ripe fruit in the refrigerator and use them as soon as possible.
• Instead of discarding the papaya seeds, you can add them to a salad dressing – they have a pleasant peppery flavour.

Variation
This refreshing fruit salad is delicious made with other tropical fruit. Try using two ripe peeled stoned (pitted) mangoes in place of the papayas.

Pears with Cashel Blue Cream and Walnuts

The cheese Cashel Blue is the perfect partner to the ripe, juicy pears that start to appear in grocery stores in autumn – and it is now widely available from specialist cheese suppliers.

6 ripe pears
15ml/1 tbsp lemon juice
mixed salad leaves, such as frisée, oakleaf lettuce and radicchio
6 cherry tomatoes
sea salt and ground black pepper
walnut halves and sprigs of fresh flat leaf parsley, to garnish

Serves 6
115g/4oz fresh cream cheese
75g/3oz Cashel Blue cheese
30–45ml/2–3 tbsp single (light) cream
115g/4oz/1 cup roughly chopped walnuts

For the dressing
juice of 1 lemon
a little finely grated lemon rind
pinch of caster (superfine) sugar
60ml/4 tbsp olive oil

1 Mash the cream cheese and Cashel Blue cheese together in a mixing bowl with a good grinding of black pepper, then blend in the cream to make a smooth mixture. Add 25g/1oz/½ cup chopped walnuts and mix to distribute evenly. Cover and chill.

2 Peel and halve the pears and scoop out the core. Put them into a bowl of water with the lemon juice to prevent them from browning. To make the dressing, whisk the lemon juice, lemon rind, caster sugar and olive oil together in a bowl and season with salt and pepper to taste.

3 Arrange a bed of salad leaves on six plates – shallow soup plates are ideal – add a tomato to each and sprinkle over the remaining chopped walnuts.

4 Drain the pears well and pat dry with kitchen paper, then turn them in the prepared dressing and arrange, hollow side up, on the salad leaves. Divide the Cashel Blue mixture between the six halved pears and spoon the rest of the dressing over the top. Garnish each pear with a walnut half and a sprig of fresh flat leaf parsley.

Papaya Salad Energy 55kcal/233kJ; Protein 0.8g; Carbohydrate 13.4g, of which sugars 13.4g; Fat 0.2g, of which saturates 0g; Cholesterol 0mg; Calcium 35mg; Fibre 3.3g; Sodium 8mg.
Pears with Cashel Blue Cream Energy 331kcal/1373kJ; Protein 6.7g; Carbohydrate 16.3g, of which sugars 16.1g; Fat 27g, of which saturates 9.8g; Cholesterol 30mg; Calcium 120mg; Fibre 4.1g; Sodium 219mg.

Roquefort and Walnut Salad

This delicious, fresh-tasting salad makes a wonderful light lunch dish. The combination of luxurious fresh figs with the tangy blue cheese and crunchy autumnal walnuts is exquisite.

Serves 4

45ml/3 tbsp walnut oil
juice of 1 lemon
mixed salad leaves
4 fresh figs
115g/4oz Roquefort cheese, cut into small chunks
75g/3oz/³/₄ cup walnut halves
salt and ground black pepper

1 Whisk together the walnut oil and lemon juice in a bowl until emulsified, then season with salt and pepper.

2 Wash and dry the salad leaves, then tear them gently into bitesize pieces. Place in a large mixing bowl and toss with the salad dressing. Transfer to a large serving dish or divide among four individual plates, ensuring a good balance of colour and texture on each plate.

3 Cut the figs into quarters and add to the salad leaves. Sprinkle the cheese over the salad, crumbling it slightly. Then sprinkle over the walnuts, breaking them up roughly in your fingers as you work. Serve immediately.

Cook's Tip
Look for dark green salad leaves, such as lamb's lettuce and rocket (arugula), and reds, such as lollo rosso, as well as some crunchy leaves, such as Little Gem (Bibb), to add interest.

Variation
The figs may be replaced with ripe nectarines or peaches if you prefer. Wash and cut in half, discard the stone (pit), then cut each half into three or four slices. If the skin is very tough, you may need to remove it completely.

Halloumi and Grape Salad

Firm salty halloumi cheese makes a tasty lunch or supper dish. In this recipe it is tossed with sweet, juicy grapes, a popular autumn fruit that complements the distinctive sweet and salty flavour of the cheese.

Serves 4

150g/5oz mixed green salad leaves
75g/3oz seedless green and black grapes
250g/9oz halloumi cheese
45ml/3 tbsp olive oil
fresh young thyme leaves or dill, to garnish

For the dressing
60ml/4 tbsp olive oil
15ml/1 tbsp lemon juice
2.5ml/¹/₂ tsp caster (superfine) sugar
salt and ground black pepper
5ml/1 tsp chopped fresh thyme or dill

1 To make the dressing, mix together the olive oil, lemon juice and sugar. Season with salt and ground black pepper. Stir in the thyme or dill and set aside.

2 Toss together the salad leaves and the green and black grapes, then transfer to a large serving plate.

3 Thinly slice the cheese. Heat the oil in a frying pan. Add the cheese slices and fry briefly until turning golden on the underside. Turn with a fish slice or metal spatula and cook the other side.

4 Arrange the cheese over the salad. Pour over the dressing and garnish with thyme or dill.

Variations
• Add a few fresh mint leaves to the salad leaves, or some young sorrel leaves. Sorrel has a lovely lemony flavour but is high in oxalic acid, so don't use too much.
• Substitute physalis for the grapes. These little golden fruits have a delicious sweet-sour flavour which would be an excellent foil for the salty halloumi cheese.

Roquefort Salad Energy 415kcal/1726kL; Protein 10.6g; Carbohydrate 26.6g, of which sugars 26.4g; Fat 30.3g, of which saturates 7.3g; Cholesterol 22mg; Calcium 286mg; Fibre 4.5g; Sodium 383mg.
Halloumi Salad Energy 215kcal/889kJ; Protein 10.2g; Carbohydrate 1.8g, of which sugars 1.7g; Fat 18.6g, of which saturates 8.1g; Cholesterol 29mg; Calcium 205mg; Fibre 2.4g; Sodium 209mg.

Warm Halloumi and Fennel Salad

The firm texture of halloumi cheese makes it perfect for the barbecue, as it keeps its shape very well. Combined with the delicate flavour of seasonal fennel, it makes a lovely chargrilled salad.

2 fennel bulbs, trimmed
 and thinly sliced
30ml/2 tbsp roughly chopped
 fresh oregano
45ml/3 tbsp lemon-infused
 olive oil
salt and ground black pepper

Serves 4
200g/7oz halloumi cheese,
 thickly sliced

1 Place the halloumi, fennel and oregano in a mixing bowl and drizzle over the lemon-infused oil. Season with salt and black pepper to taste. Mix together the ingredients until they are thoroughly combined.

2 Cover the bowl with a piece of clear film (plastic wrap) and chill in the refrigerator for about 2 hours to allow all the flavours to develop.

3 Heat a griddle pan on the stove until very hot, or light a barbecue and wait until there is a coating of ash on the coals.

4 Place the halloumi and fennel on a griddle pan or over the barbecue, reserving the marinade, and cook for about 3 minutes on each side, until charred.

5 Divide the halloumi and fennel among four serving plates and drizzle over the reserved marinade. Serve immediately.

> **Cook's Tips**
> • Fennel is often on its way out of season as autumn comes to an end and winter begins, so make the most of this tasty, underrated vegetable.
> • Halloumi is a fairly salty cheese, so be very careful when adding extra salt.

Grilled Fennel Salad

Fennel has many fans, but is often used only in its raw state or lightly braised, making this griddle recipe a delightful discovery for ways to treat this delicious autumn vegetable.

30ml/2 tbsp olive oil
15ml/1 tbsp cider or white
 wine vinegar
45ml/3 tbsp extra virgin olive oil
24 small Niçoise olives
2 long sprigs of fresh savory,
 leaves removed
salt and ground black pepper

Serves 6
3 sweet baby orange
 (bell) peppers
5 fennel bulbs with green tops,
 about 900g/2lb total weight

1 Heat a griddle until a few drops of water sprinkled on to the surface evaporate instantly. Grill (broil) the baby peppers, turning them every few minutes until charred all over. Remove the pan from the heat, place the peppers in a bowl and cover with clear film (plastic wrap).

2 Remove the green fronds from the fennel and reserve. Slice the fennel lengthways into five roughly equal pieces. If the root looks a little tough, cut it out. Place the fennel pieces in a flat dish, coat with the olive oil and season with salt and pepper. Rub off the charred skin from the grilled peppers, remove the seeds and cut the flesh into small dice.

3 Re-heat the griddle and test the temperature again, then lower the heat slightly and grill (broil) the fennel slices in batches for about 8–10 minutes, turning frequently, until they are branded with golden grill marks. Monitor the heat so they cook through without over charring. As each batch cooks, transfer it to a flat serving dish.

4 Whisk the vinegar and extra virgin olive oil together in a small bowl, then pour over the fennel. Gently fold in the diced baby orange peppers and the Niçoise olives. Roughly tear the savory leaves and fennel fronds and sprinkle over the salad. Serve warm.

Warm Halloumi Salad Energy 215kcal/889kJ; Protein 10.2g; Carbohydrate 1.8g, of which sugars 1.7g; Fat 18.6g, of which saturates 8.1g; Cholesterol 29mg; Calcium 205mg; Fibre 2.4g; Sodium 209mg.
Grilled Fennel Salad Energy 139kcal/574kJ; Protein 2.4g; Carbohydrate 8.7g, of which sugars 8.3g; Fat 10.8g, of which saturates 1.6g; Cholesterol 0mg; Calcium 49mg; Fibre 5.3g; Sodium 208mg.

Marinated Button Mushrooms with Sherry

This Spanish dish makes a refreshing alternative to the ever-popular mushrooms fried in garlic.

Serves 4

30ml/2 tbsp extra virgin olive oil
1 small onion, very finely chopped
1 garlic clove, finely chopped
15ml/1 tbsp tomato
  purée (paste)
50ml/2fl oz/¼ cup
  amontillado sherry
50ml/2fl oz/¼ cup water
2 cloves
225g/8oz/3 cups button (white)
  mushrooms, trimmed
salt and ground black pepper
chopped fresh parsley,
  to garnish

1 Heat the oil in a pan. Add the onion and garlic and cook until soft. Stir in the tomato purée, sherry, water and the cloves and season with salt and black pepper.

2 Bring the mixture to the boil, cover the pan and simmer gently for about 45 minutes, adding more water if the mixture becomes too dry.

3 Add the mushrooms to the pan, then cover and allow to simmer for about 5 minutes. Remove from the heat and allow to cool, still covered.

4 Chill the mushrooms in the refrigerator overnight so that they take on the flavours. Serve the salad cold, sprinkled with the chopped parsley.

Cook's Tip
One of the joys of autumn is the plentiful supply of mushrooms. You can use free wild mushrooms for this dish if you are lucky enough to live near a woodland where you can go and pick your own. When picking wild mushrooms, remember to carry them in a basket so that their spores can drop on to the ground as you wander around the area.

Fragrant Mushrooms in Lettuce Leaves

This quick and easy autumn salad is a perfect way to enjoy the abundance of mushrooms at this time of year. Served on leaves, they make great finger food.

Serves 2

30ml/2 tbsp vegetable oil
2 garlic cloves, finely chopped
2 baby cos or romaine lettuces,
  or 2 Little Gem (Bibb) lettuces
1 lemon grass stalk, finely chopped
2 kaffir lime leaves, rolled in
  cylinders and thinly sliced
200g/7oz/3 cups oyster or
  chestnut mushrooms, sliced
1 small fresh red chilli, seeded
  and finely chopped
juice of ½ lemon
30ml/2 tbsp light soy sauce
5ml/1 tsp palm sugar (jaggery) or
  light muscovado (brown) sugar
1 small bunch fresh mint, leaves
  removed from the stalks

1 Heat the oil in a wok or frying pan. Add the garlic and cook over medium heat, stirring occasionally, until golden. Do not let it burn or it will taste bitter.

2 Meanwhile, divide up the lettuces into separate, individual leaves and set aside.

3 Increase the heat under the wok or pan and add the lemon grass, lime leaves and mushrooms. Stir-fry for about 2 minutes.

4 Add the chilli, lemon juice, soy sauce and sugar to the wok or pan. Toss the mixture over the heat to combine the ingredients together, then stir-fry for a further 2 minutes.

5 Arrange the lettuce leaves on a large plate. Spoon a little mushroom mixture on to each leaf, top with a mint leaf and serve immediately.

Cook's Tip
If you can't find kaffir leaves, you can use freshly grated lime rind instead.

Marinated Mushrooms Energy 80kcal/329kJ; Protein 1.4g; Carbohydrate 2.1g, of which sugars 1.7g; Fat 5.8g, of which saturates 0.9g; Cholesterol 0mg; Calcium 9mg; Fibre 0.9g; Sodium 14mg.
Fragrant Mushrooms Energy 162kcal/672kJ; Protein 4.6g; Carbohydrate 7.9g, of which sugars 6.3g; Fat 12.7g, of which saturates 1.6g; Cholesterol 0mg; Calcium 117mg; Fibre 2.9g; Sodium 549mg.

Pumpkin Salad with Red Onion and Parsley

Red wine vinegar brings out the sweetness of the pumpkin. No salad leaves are used, just plenty of fresh parsley. This is a great dish to serve at a cold buffet during the autumn.

Serves 4

1 large red onion, peeled and very thinly sliced into rings
200ml/7fl oz/scant 1 cup olive oil
60ml/4 tbsp red wine vinegar
675g/1½lb pumpkin, peeled and cut into 4cm/1½ in pieces
40g/1½oz/¾ cup fresh flat leaf parsley leaves, chopped
salt and ground black pepper
fresh flat leaf parsley sprigs, to garnish (optional)

1 Mix the onion, olive oil and vinegar in a large bowl. Season with salt and pepper, then stir well to combine.

2 Put the pumpkin pieces in a large pan of cold salted water. Bring to the boil, then lower the heat and simmer gently for 15–20 minutes. Drain.

3 Immediately add the drained pumpkin to the bowl containing the dressing and toss lightly with your hands. Leave to cool. Stir in the chopped parsley, cover with clear film (plastic wrap) and chill until needed.

4 Allow the salad to come back to room temperature before serving. Garnish with fresh parsley sprigs, if you like.

Cook's Tip
Pumpkins are a popular vegetable when their season begins in the autumn. They are crucial for two festivals at this time of year: Thanksgiving with its pumpkin pie; and Halloween, when the large gourd is hollowed out to make a spooky lantern. The flesh from the smaller sizes tends to be more tender and succulent. Choose ones that have no blemishes or dents and are heavy for their size. Store at room temperature for a month.

Roasted Shallot and Butternut Squash Salad

This autumn salad is especially good served with a grain or starchy salad, based on rice or couscous, for example. Serve with plenty of home-made organic bread to mop up the juices. Autumn is also a good time for walnuts, which combine well with the other ingredients in this salad.

Serves 4–6

75ml/5 tbsp olive oil
15ml/1 tbsp balsamic vinegar, plus a little extra, if you like
15ml/1 tbsp sweet soy sauce
350g/12oz shallots, peeled but left whole
3 fresh red chillies
1 butternut squash, peeled, seeded and cut into chunks
5ml/1 tsp finely chopped fresh thyme
15g/½oz flat leaf parsley
1 small garlic clove, finely chopped
75g/3oz/¾ cup walnuts, chopped
150g/5oz feta cheese
sea salt and ground black pepper

1 Preheat the oven to 200°C/400°F/Gas 6. Beat the olive oil, balsamic vinegar and soy sauce together in a large bowl, then season with a little salt and plenty of ground black pepper.

2 Toss the shallots and two of the chillies in the oil mixture and transfer into a large roasting pan or ovenproof dish. Roast for 15 minutes, stirring once or twice.

3 Add the butternut squash chunks and roast for a further 30–35 minutes, stirring once, until the squash is tender and browned. Remove from the oven, stir in the chopped fresh thyme and set the vegetables aside to cool.

4 Chop the parsley and garlic together and mix with the walnuts. Seed and finely chop the remaining chilli.

5 Stir the parsley, garlic and walnut mixture into the vegetables. Add chopped chilli to taste and adjust the seasoning, adding a little extra balsamic vinegar, if you like. Crumble the feta and add to the salad. Transfer to a serving dish and serve immediately.

Pumpkin Salad Energy 404kcal/1663kJ; Protein 1.7g; Carbohydrate 5.2g, of which sugars 4g; Fat 42g, of which saturates 6.1g; Cholesterol 0mg; Calcium 73mg; Fibre 2.4g; Sodium 4mg.
Shallot Salad Energy 275kcal/1136kJ; Protein 7.7g; Carbohydrate 9.3g, of which sugars 7g; Fat 23.2g, of which saturates 5.6g; Cholesterol 18mg; Calcium 165mg; Fibre 2.9g; Sodium 541mg.

Duck Salad with Poached Eggs

Golden duck skewers look and taste wonderful, and they are combined here with chanterelle mushrooms to ensure the dish is packed with the flavours of autumn.

Serves 4
3 skinless duck breast portions, thinly sliced
30ml/2 tbsp soy sauce
30ml/2 tbsp balsamic vinegar
30ml/2 tbsp groundnut (peanut) oil
1 shallot, finely chopped
115g/4oz/1½ cups chanterelle mushrooms
4 eggs
50g/2oz mixed salad leaves
salt and ground black pepper
30ml/2 tbsp extra virgin olive oil, to serve

1 Put the duck in a shallow dish and toss with the soy sauce and balsamic vinegar. Cover and chill for 30 minutes. Meanwhile, soak 12 bamboo skewers (about 13cm/5in long) in water to help prevent them from burning during cooking.

2 Preheat the grill (broiler). Thread the marinated duck slices on to the skewers, pleating them neatly. Place the skewers on a grill pan and cook for about 3–5 minutes, then turn the skewers over and cook for a further 3 minutes, or until the duck is golden brown.

3 Meanwhile, heat the groundnut oil in a frying pan (skillet) and cook the chopped shallot until softened. Add the mushrooms and cook over a high heat for 5 minutes, stirring occasionally.

4 While the chanterelles are cooking, half fill a frying pan with water, add a little salt and heat until simmering. Break the eggs one at a time into a cup, then gently transfer each one into the water. Poach the eggs gently for about 3 minutes, or until the whites are set. Use a slotted spoon to transfer the eggs to a warm plate, pat them dry with kitchen paper, then trim off any untidy white.

5 Arrange the salad leaves on four individual plates, then add the chanterelles and skewered duck. Place the poached eggs on the plates. Drizzle the salad with olive oil, season with pepper and serve immediately.

Beetroot and Potato Salad

A brightly coloured salad, perfect for the autumn when beetroot is at its peak. The sweetness of the beetroot contrasts perfectly with the tangy dressing. Ideal with a selection of cold meats.

Serves 4
4 medium beetroot (beets)
4 potatoes, peeled and diced
1 red onion, finely chopped
150ml/¼ pint/⅔ cup natural (plain) yogurt
10ml/2 tsp cider vinegar
2 small sweet and sour cucumbers, finely chopped
10ml/2 tsp creamed horseradish
salt and ground black pepper
fresh parsley sprigs, to garnish

1 Trim the leafy stalks of the beetroot down to about 2.5cm/1in of the root. Wash the beetroot but do not peel. Boil the unpeeled beetroot in a large pan of water for 40 minutes or until tender.

2 Meanwhile, boil the diced potatoes in a separate pan for 20 minutes until just tender.

3 When the beetroot are cooked, rinse and remove the skins. Chop into rough pieces and place in a bowl. Drain the potatoes and add to the bowl, together with the onions.

4 Mix the yogurt, vinegar, cucumbers and horseradish. Reserve a little for a garnish and pour the remainder over the salad. Toss and serve with parsley sprigs and remaining dressing.

> **Cook's Tip**
> If you are short of time, buy vacuum-packed ready-cooked and peeled beetroot (beet), available in most supermarkets.

> **Variation**
> Add toasted chopped walnuts to the yogurt dressing, if you like.

Beetroot Salad Energy 141kcal/597kJ; Protein 5.8g; Carbohydrate 28.8g, of which sugars 12.9g; Fat 1.2g, of which saturates 0.3g; Cholesterol 1mg; Calcium 107mg; Fibre 3.4g; Sodium 144mg.
Duck Salad Energy 271kcal/1132kJ; Protein 29.2g; Carbohydrate 1.5g, of which sugars 1.1g; Fat 18.6g, of which saturates 3.9g; Cholesterol 314mg; Calcium 51mg; Fibre 0.7g; Sodium 196mg.

Husk-grilled Corn on the Cob

You can barbecue, grill or oven-bake corn on the cob in this way. Keeping the husks on the corn protects the kernels and encloses the butter, so the flavours are contained. Fresh cobs with husks intact are perfect, but banana leaves or a double layer of foil will also work as a protective layer.

Serves 6

3 dried chipotle chillies
250g/9oz/generous 1 cup
    butter, softened
7.5ml/1½ tsp lemon juice
45ml/3 tbsp chopped fresh flat
    leaf parsley
6 corn on the cob, with
    husks intact
salt and ground black pepper

1 Heat a heavy frying pan. Roast the dried chillies in the pan by stirring them constantly for 1 minute without letting them scorch. Put them in a bowl with almost boiling water to cover. Use a saucer to keep them submerged, and leave them to rehydrate for up to 1 hour.

2 Drain, remove the seeds and chop the chillies finely. Place the butter in a bowl and add the chillies, lemon juice and parsley. Season to taste and mix well.

3 Peel back the husks from each cob without tearing them. Remove the silk. Smear about 30ml/2 tbsp of the chilli butter over each cob. Pull the husks back over the cobs, ensuring that the butter is well hidden.

4 Put the rest of the butter in a pot, smooth the top and chill in the refrigerator to use later. Place the cobs in a bowl of cold water and leave in a cool place for 1–3 hours; longer if that suits your work plan better.

5 Prepare the barbecue. Remove the corn cobs from the water and wrap in pairs in foil. Once the flames have died down, position a lightly oiled grill rack over the coals to heat. When the coals are medium-hot, or have a moderate coating of ash, grill the corn for 15–20 minutes. Remove the foil and cook them for about 5 minutes more, turning them often to char the husks a little. Serve hot, with the rest of the butter.

Stuffed Baby Squash

It is worth making the most of baby squash while they are in season. Use any varieties you can find and do not worry too much about choosing vegetables of uniform size, as an assortment of different types and sizes looks attractive. The baked vegetables can easily be shared out at the table. Serve with warm sun-dried tomato bread and a ready-made spicy tomato sauce for a hearty autumn supper.

Serves 4

4 small squash, each about
    350g/12oz
200g/7oz/1 cup mixed wild and
    basmati rice
60ml/4 tbsp chilli and garlic oil
150g/5oz/1¼ cups grated
    Gruyère cheese
sun-dried tomato bread and
    a ready-made tomato sauce,
    to serve (optional)

1 Preheat the oven to 190°C/375°F/Gas 5. Pierce the squash in several places with the tip of a knife.

2 Bake the squash in the preheated oven for approximately 30–40 minutes, until the squash are tender. Leave until cool enough to handle.

3 Meanwhile, cook the rice in plenty of salted, boiling water for about 12 minutes, until tender, then drain thoroughly.

4 Slice a lid off the top of each cooked squash and scoop out the seeds with a spoon and discard. Scoop out the flesh and chop into small pieces.

5 Heat the oil in a frying pan and cook the chopped squash for 5 minutes, stirring occasionally. Reserve 60ml/4 tbsp of the cheese, add the remainder to the pan with the rice and a little salt. Mix well.

6 Pile the mixture into the squash shells and place in an ovenproof dish. Add the rest of the cheese and bake for 20 minutes. Serve immediately, with bread and a sauce, if liked.

Husk-grilled Corn Energy 435kcal/1805kJ; Protein 3.4g; Carbohydrate 27.1g, of which sugars 10g; Fat 35.6g, of which saturates 21.9g; Cholesterol 89mg; Calcium 28mg; Fibre 1.8g; Sodium 525mg.
Stuffed Squash Energy 483kcal/2011kJ; Protein 15.9g; Carbohydrate 48.2g, of which sugars 6.4g; Fat 24.3g, of which saturates 10.1g; Cholesterol 36mg; Calcium 396mg; Fibre 3.8g; Sodium 271mg.

Winter Squash in Tomato Sauce

This dish is Italian Jewish in origin and a favourite of the Jews of Northern Italy, from around Mantua, where the most magnificent squash grow. Squash is a very versatile ingredient and lights up many an autumn dinner table.

Serves 4–6

45–75ml/3–5 tbsp olive oil
1kg/2¹⁄₂lb pumpkin or orange
   winter squash, peeled and sliced

1 onion, chopped
3–5 garlic cloves, chopped
2 x 400g/14oz cans
   chopped tomatoes
pinch of sugar
2–3 sprigs of fresh rosemary,
   stems removed and
   leaves chopped
salt and ground black pepper

1 Preheat the oven to 160°C/325°F/Gas 3. Heat 45ml/3 tbsp of the oil in a pan and fry the pumpkin slices in batches until golden brown, removing them from the pan as they are cooked.

2 In the same pan, add the onion, with more oil if necessary, and fry for about 5 minutes until softened.

3 Add the garlic to the pan and cook for 1 minute, then add the tomatoes and sugar and cook over a medium-high heat until the mixture is of a sauce consistency. Stir in the rosemary and season with salt and pepper to taste.

4 Layer the pumpkin slices and tomato sauce in an ovenproof dish, ending with a layer of sauce.

5 Bake in the oven for 35 minutes, or until the top is glazed and beginning to brown, and the pumpkin is tender. Serve.

Variation
Acorn, butternut or Hubbard squash can all be used in this recipe. Choose whichever is available, although they are all varieties that are available during the autumn months.

Barley Risotto with Roasted Squash

This is more like a pilaff made with slightly chewy pearl barley than a classic risotto. Leeks and roasted squash are superb with this earthy, autumn dish.

Serves 4–5

200g/7oz/1 cup pearl barley
1 butternut squash, peeled,
   seeded and cut into chunks
10ml/2 tsp chopped fresh thyme
60ml/4 tbsp olive oil
25g/1oz/2 tbsp butter
4 leeks, cut into fairly thick
   diagonal slices

2 garlic cloves, finely chopped
175g/6oz/2¹⁄₂ cups chestnut
   mushrooms, sliced
2 carrots, coarsely grated
about 120ml/4fl oz/¹⁄₂ cup
   vegetable stock
30ml/2 tbsp chopped fresh flat
   leaf parsley
50g/2oz/²⁄₃ cup Parmesan cheese
   or premium Italian-style
   vegetarian cheese, grated
   or shaved
45ml/3 tbsp pumpkin seeds,
   toasted, or chopped
   walnuts, optional
sea salt and ground black pepper

1 Rinse the barley, then cook it in simmering water, keeping the pan part-covered, for 35–45 minutes, or until tender. Drain. Preheat the oven to 200°C/400°F/Gas 6.

2 Place the squash in a roasting pan with half the thyme. Season with pepper and toss with half the oil. Roast, stirring once, for 30–35 minutes, until the squash is tender and beginning to brown.

3 Heat half the butter with the remaining olive oil in a large frying pan. Cook the leeks and garlic gently for 5 minutes. Add the mushrooms and remaining thyme, then cook until the liquid from the mushrooms evaporates and they begin to fry.

4 Stir in the carrots and cook for 2 minutes, then add the barley and most of the stock. Season well and part-cover the pan. Cook for 5 minutes. Pour in the remaining stock if it is dry.

5 Stir in the parsley, the remaining butter and half the cheese, then stir in the squash. Add seasoning to taste and serve immediately, sprinkled with the toasted pumpkin seeds or walnuts, if using, and the remaining cheese.

Winter Squash Energy 97kcal/407kJ; Protein 2.2g; Carbohydrate 8.6g, of which sugars 7.5g; Fat 6.3g, of which saturates 1.1g; Cholesterol 0mg; Calcium 60mg; Fibre 3.1g; Sodium 12mg.
Barley Risotto Energy 498kcal/2089kJ; Protein 15.6g; Carbohydrate 55.6g, of which sugars 11.2g; Fat 25.2g, of which saturates 5.2g; Cholesterol 13mg; Calcium 287mg; Fibre 7.6g; Sodium 156mg.

Pumpkin with Spices

Roasted pumpkin has a wonderful, rich flavour redolent of autumn. Eat it straight from the skin, eat the skin too, or scoop out the cooked flesh, add a spoonful of a spicy tomato salsa and wrap it in a warm tortilla. It is also good for making flavoursome soups and tasty sauces.

Serves 6
1kg/2¹/₄lb pumpkin
50g/2oz/¹/₄ cup butter
10ml/2 tsp hot chilli sauce
2.5ml/¹/₂ tsp salt
2.5ml/¹/₂ tsp ground allspice
5ml/1 tsp ground cinnamon
chopped fresh herbs, to garnish
spicy tomato salsa and crème
  fraîche, to serve

1 Preheat the oven to 220°C/425°F/Gas 7. Cut the pumpkin into large pieces. Scoop out and discard the fibre and seeds, then put the pumpkin pieces in a roasting pan.

2 Melt the butter in a pan over low heat, or in a heatproof bowl in the microwave. Mix together the melted butter and chilli sauce and drizzle the mixture evenly over the pumpkin pieces in the roasting pan.

3 Put the salt in a small bowl and add the ground allspice and cinnamon. Mix together well and sprinkle the mixture over the pumpkin pieces.

4 Place the roasting pan in the oven and roast for 25 minutes, turning halfway through the cooking. The pumpkin flesh should yield when pressed gently, if it is ready.

5 Transfer the spiced pumpkin pieces to a warmed serving dish and serve. Offer the salsa and crème fraîche separately.

Cook's Tip
Green, grey or orange-skinned pumpkins all roast well and would work in this recipe. The orange-fleshed varieties are, however, the most vibrantly coloured and will look wonderful when used in this dish.

Sweet Pumpkin and Peanut Curry

Rich, sweet, spicy and fragrant, the flavours of this Thai-style curry really come together during the long simmering in the slow cooker. Serve with rice or noodles for a supper dish on a cold autumn night.

Serves 4
30ml/2 tbsp vegetable oil
4 garlic cloves, crushed
4 shallots, finely chopped
30ml/2 tbsp yellow curry paste
2 kaffir lime leaves, torn
15ml/1 tbsp chopped
  fresh galangal

450g/1lb pumpkin, peeled, seeded
  and diced
225g/8oz sweet potatoes, diced
400ml/14fl oz/1²/₃ cups
  near-boiling vegetable stock
300ml/¹/₂ pint/1¹/₄ cups
  coconut milk
90g/3¹/₂oz/1¹/₂ cups chestnut
  mushrooms, sliced
15ml/1 tbsp soy sauce
90g/3¹/₂oz/scant 1 cup peanuts,
  roasted and chopped
50g/2oz/¹/₃ cup pumpkin seeds,
  toasted, and fresh green chilli
  flowers, to garnish

1 Heat the oil in a frying pan. Add the garlic and shallots and cook over medium heat, stirring occasionally, for 10 minutes, until softened and beginning to turn golden.

2 Add the yellow curry paste to the pan and stir-fry over medium heat for 30 seconds, until fragrant. Transfer the mixture to the ceramic cooking pot.

3 Add the lime leaves, galangal, pumpkin and sweet potatoes to the cooking pot. Pour the hot vegetable stock and about 150ml/¹/₄ pint/²/₃ cup of the coconut milk over the vegetables, and stir to combine. Cover with the lid and cook on the high setting for 1¹/₂ hours.

4 Stir the mushrooms and soy sauce into the curry, then add the chopped peanuts and pour in the remaining coconut milk. Cover and cook on high for a further 3 hours, or until the vegetables are very tender.

5 Spoon the curry into warmed serving bowls, garnish with the pumpkin seeds and chillies, and serve immediately.

Pumpkin with Spices Energy 84kcal/347kJ; Protein 1.2g; Carbohydrate 3.7g, of which sugars 2.9g; Fat 7.2g, of which saturates 4.5g; Cholesterol 18mg; Calcium 50mg; Fibre 1.7g; Sodium 214mg.
Sweet Pumpkin Curry Energy 337kcal/1404kJ; Protein 10.3g; Carbohydrate 21.7g, of which sugars 10.8g; Fat 23.8g, of which saturates 4g; Cholesterol 0mg; Calcium 168mg; Fibre 5.1g; Sodium 554mg.

Pumpkin Gnocchi with Chanterelle Parsley Cream

Pumpkin adds a sweetness to these potato gnocchi, which are superb on their own or served with meat.

Serves 4
450g/1lb pumpkin, peeled, seeded and chopped
450g/1lb potatoes, boiled
2 egg yolks
200g/7oz/1¾ cups plain (all-purpose) flour, plus more if necessary
pinch of ground allspice
1.5ml/¼ tsp cinnamon
pinch of freshly grated nutmeg

finely grated rind of ½ orange
salt and ground black pepper

For the sauce
30ml/2 tbsp olive oil
1 shallot, finely chopped
175g/6oz fresh chanterelles, sliced, or 15g/½oz dried, soaked in warm water for 20 minutes, then drained
10ml/2 tsp almond butter
150ml/¼ pint/⅔ cup crème fraîche
75ml/5 tbsp chopped fresh parsley
50g/2oz/½ cup Parmesan cheese, freshly grated

1 Wrap the pumpkin in foil and bake at 180°C/350°F/Gas 4 for 30 minutes. Pass the pumpkin and cooked potatoes through a food mill into a bowl. Add the egg yolks, flour, spices, orange rind and seasoning and mix well to make a soft dough. If the mixture is too loose add a little flour to stiffen it.

2 To make the sauce, heat the oil in a pan and fry the shallot until soft. Add the chanterelles and cook briefly, then add the almond butter. Stir to melt and stir in the crème fraîche. Simmer briefly, add the parsley and season to taste. Keep hot.

3 Flour a work surface. Spoon the gnocchi dough into a piping (pastry) bag fitted with a 1cm/½in plain nozzle. Pipe on to the flour to make a 15cm/6in sausage. Roll in flour and cut crossways into 2.5cm/1in pieces. Repeat. Mark each piece lightly with a fork and drop into a pan of fast boiling salted water.

4 The gnocchi are done when they rise to the surface, after 3–4 minutes. Drain and turn into bowls. Spoon the sauce over, sprinkle with Parmesan, and serve immediately.

Spiced Couscous with Halloumi and Courgette Ribbons

Couscous forms the foundation of this dish and is topped with griddled, sliced courgettes and halloumi.

Serves 4
275g/10oz/1⅔ cups couscous
1 bay leaf
1 cinnamon stick
30ml/2 tbsp olive oil, plus extra for brushing
1 large red onion, chopped
2 garlic cloves, chopped
5ml/1 tsp mild chilli powder

5ml/1 tsp ground cumin
5ml/1 tsp ground coriander
5 cardamom pods, bruised
50g/2oz/¼ cup whole almonds, toasted
1 peach, stoned (pitted) and diced
25g/1oz/2 tbsp butter
3 courgettes (zucchini), sliced lengthways into ribbons
225g/8oz halloumi cheese, sliced
salt and ground black pepper
chopped fresh flat leaf parsley, to garnish

1 Place the couscous in a bowl and pour over 500ml/17fl oz/generous 2 cups boiling water. Add the bay leaf and cinnamon stick and season with salt. Leave the couscous for 10 minutes until the water is absorbed, then fluff up the grains with a fork.

2 Meanwhile, heat the oil in a large heavy pan, add the onion and garlic and cook, stirring, for about 7 minutes until soft.

3 Stir in the chilli powder, cumin, coriander and cardamom pods, and cook for 3 minutes. Add the couscous, almonds, diced peach and butter, and heat through for 2 minutes.

4 Brush a griddle pan with oil and heat until very hot. Turn down the heat to medium, then place the courgettes on the griddle and cook for 5 minutes until tender and slightly charred. Turn the courgettes over, add the halloumi and continue cooking for 5 minutes, turning the halloumi halfway through.

5 Remove the cinnamon stick, bay leaf and cardamom pods from the couscous, then arrange it on a plate and season well. Top with the halloumi and courgettes. Sprinkle the parsley over the top and serve.

Pumpkin Gnocchi Energy 553kcal/2317kJ; Protein 15.6g; Carbohydrate 61.7g, of which sugars 5.9g; Fat 28.8g, of which saturates 14.7g; Cholesterol 156mg; Calcium 299mg; Fibre 4.5g; Sodium 166mg.
Spiced Couscous Energy 515kcal/2138kJ; Protein 19.9g; Carbohydrate 42.7g, of which sugars 6.1g; Fat 30.3g, of which saturates 12.5g; Cholesterol 46mg; Calcium 290mg; Fibre 2.9g; Sodium 264mg.

Braised Artichokes with Fresh Peas

This artichoke dish can be made in the early autumn when the seasons for peas and artichokes coincide. Shelling fresh peas is a little time-consuming but their matchless flavour makes the task very worthwhile. Sit on a step outside in the autumn sunshine, and what at first seems a chore will be positively therapeutic.

Serves 4

4 globe artichokes
juice of 1½ lemons

150ml/¼ pint/⅔ cup
    extra virgin olive oil
1 onion, thinly sliced
4–5 spring onions (scallions),
    roughly chopped
2 carrots, sliced in rounds
1.2kg/2½lb fresh peas in pods,
    shelled (this will give you about
    500–675g/1¼–1½lb peas)
450ml/¾ pint/scant 2 cups
    hot water
60ml/4 tbsp finely chopped
    fresh dill
salt and ground black pepper

1 To prepare the artichokes, trim the stalks of the artichokes close to the base, cut the very tips off the leaves and then divide them into quarters. Remove the inedible hairy choke (the central part), carefully scraping the hairs away from the heart at the base of the artichoke. Drop them into a bowl of water acidulated with about one-third of the lemon juice.

2 Heat the olive oil in a wide, shallow pan and add the onion and spring onions, and then a minute later, add the carrots. Sauté the mixture, stirring constantly, for a few seconds, then add the peas and stir for 1–2 minutes to coat them in the oil.

3 Pour in the remaining lemon juice. Let it bubble and evaporate for a few seconds, then add the hot water and bring to the boil. Drain the artichokes and add them to the pan, with salt and pepper to taste. Cover and cook gently for about 40–45 minutes, stirring occasionally.

4 Add the dill to the pan and cook for a further 5 minutes, or until the vegetables are tender. Serve either hot or at room temperature.

Broccoli and Cheese Mina

A mina is a type of pie, with matzos and a savoury sauce, topped with egg. This mina features broccoli, which holds its season through summer and into autumn.

Serves 4

1 large broccoli head
pinch of salt
pinch of sugar
8 matzo squares
50g/2oz/½ cup butter, plus extra
    for greasing

1 onion, chopped
250g/9oz/2¼ cups grated
    Cheddar cheese
250g/9oz/generous 1 cup
    cottage cheese
65g/2½oz/¾ cup freshly grated
    Parmesan cheese
2 spring onions (scallions), chopped
30–45ml/2–3 tbsp chopped
    fresh dill
4 eggs
30ml/2 tbsp water
8 garlic cloves, chopped

1 Preheat the oven to 190°C/375°F/Gas 5. Remove the tough stem from the broccoli, then cut it into even florets. Cook the broccoli by either steaming or boiling in water to which you have added a pinch of salt and sugar. Cook until bright green, then remove with a slotted spoon.

2 Wet four matzos and leave to soak for 2–3 minutes. Butter a baking sheet that is large enough to hold four matzo pieces in a single layer. If necessary, use two baking sheets.

3 Place the dampened matzos on the baking sheet, then top evenly with the broccoli, onion, Cheddar cheese, cottage cheese, Parmesan cheese, spring onions and dill.

4 Beat together the eggs and water, then pour about half the egg over the cheese and broccoli mixture. Wet the remaining matzos and place on top of the broccoli. Pour the remaining egg over the top, dot with half the butter and half the garlic.

5 Bake the mina for 20 minutes. Dot the remaining butter on top and sprinkle over the remaining chopped garlic. Return to the oven and bake for about 10 minutes more, or until the mina is golden brown and crisp on top. Serve hot or warm.

Braised Artichokes Energy 363kcal/1499kJ; Protein 10.3g; Carbohydrate 20.1g, of which sugars 8.3g; Fat 27.5g, of which saturates 4g; Cholesterol 0mg; Calcium 121mg; Fibre 9.2g; Sodium 91mg.
Broccoli Mina Energy 687kcal/2852kJ; Protein 42.4g; Carbohydrate 23g, of which sugars 4.2g; Fat 45.6g, of which saturates 26.6g; Cholesterol 304mg; Calcium 816mg; Fibre 2.8g; Sodium 969mg.

Marinated Tofu and Broccoli with Crispy Fried Shallots

This meltingly tender tofu flavoured with spices and served with broccoli makes a perfect autumn lunch. To give the recipe that little bit extra, deep-fry some crispy shallots to serve on the side, if you like.

Serves 4
6 shallots, peeled and sliced
oil for frying
500g/1¼lb block of firm
   tofu, drained

45ml/3 tbsp kecap manis
30ml/2 tbsp sweet chilli sauce
45ml/3 tbsp soy sauce
5ml/1 tsp sesame oil
5ml/1 tsp finely grated fresh
   root ginger
400g/14oz tenderstem broccoli,
   halved lengthways
45ml/3 tbsp roughly chopped
   coriander (cilantro), and
   30ml/2 tbsp toasted
   sesame seeds, to garnish

1 Make the crispy shallots. Add the shallot rings to a wok one-third full of hot oil, then lower the heat and stir constantly until crisp. Lift out and spread on kitchen paper to drain.

2 Cut the tofu into four triangular pieces: slice the block in half widthways, then diagonally. Place in a heatproof dish.

3 In a small bowl, combine the kecap manis, chilli sauce, soy sauce, sesame oil and ginger, then pour over the tofu. Leave the tofu to marinate for at least 30 minutes, turning occasionally.

4 Place the broccoli on a heatproof plate and place on a trivet in the wok. Cover and steam for 4–5 minutes, until tender. Remove and keep warm.

5 Place the dish of tofu on the trivet in the wok, cover and steam for 4–5 minutes. Divide the broccoli among four warmed serving plates and top each one with a triangle of tofu.

6 Spoon the remaining juices over the tofu and broccoli, then sprinkle with the coriander and toasted sesame seeds. Serve immediately with steamed white rice or noodles.

Spaghetti with Broccoli and Red Chilli

The contrast in this recipe between the hot chilli pieces and the mild, earthy flavour of the broccoli is wonderful and goes perfectly with spaghetti. To add extra flavour and texture to the dish, try sprinkling the spaghetti and broccoli with toasted pine nuts and freshly grated or shaved Parmesan cheese just before serving.

Serves 4
350g/12oz dried spaghetti
450g/1lb broccoli, cut into
   small florets
150ml/¼ pint/⅔ cup
   garlic-infused olive oil
1 fat red chilli, seeded and
   finely chopped
salt and ground black pepper
freshly grated Parmesan cheese,
   to garnish

1 Bring a large pan of lightly salted water to the boil. Add the spaghetti and broccoli and cook for 8–10 minutes, until both are tender. Drain thoroughly.

2 Using the back of a fork, crush the broccoli roughly in the pan, taking care not to mash any of the spaghetti strands at the same time.

3 Meanwhile, warm the garlic oil and finely chopped chilli in a small pan over low heat. Cook very gently, stirring occasionally, for 5 minutes.

4 Pour the chilli and oil over the spaghetti and broccoli and toss together to combine. Season to taste with salt and ground black pepper. Divide between four warmed pasta bowls and serve immediately with the garnish.

> **Variation**
> To make this dish even more seasonal, you could garnish it with some toasted and chopped walnut pieces in place of the toasted pine nuts or Parmesan cheese.

Marinated Tofu Energy 202kcal/840kJ; Protein 16.5g; Carbohydrate 6.9g, of which sugars 5.6g; Fat 12.1g, of which saturates 1.7g; Cholesterol 0mg; Calcium 750mg; Fibre 3.5g; Sodium 938mg.
Spaghetti with Broccoli Energy 396kcal/1678kJ; Protein 17.3g; Carbohydrate 68.3g, of which sugars 6g; Fat 7.9g, of which saturates 0.8g; Cholesterol 0mg; Calcium 114mg; Fibre 5.6g; Sodium 24mg.

Fusilli with Wild Mushrooms

A very rich dish with an earthy flavour and lots of garlic, this makes an ideal main course for vegetarians, especially if it is followed by a crisp green salad.

Serves 4
½ x 275g/10oz jar wild
    mushrooms in olive oil
25g/1oz/2 tbsp butter
225g/8oz/2 cups fresh wild
    mushrooms, sliced if large
5ml/1 tsp finely chopped
    fresh thyme
5ml/1 tsp finely chopped fresh
    marjoram or oregano, plus
    extra herbs to serve
4 garlic cloves, crushed
350g/12oz/3 cups fresh or
    dried fusilli
200ml/7fl oz/scant 1 cup panna
    da cucina or double
    (heavy) cream
salt and ground black pepper

1 Drain about 15ml/1 tbsp of the oil from the mushrooms into a medium pan. Slice or chop the bottled mushrooms into bitesize pieces, if they are large.

2 Add the butter to the oil in the pan and place over a low heat until sizzling. Add the bottled and the fresh mushrooms, the chopped herbs and the garlic, with salt and ground black pepper to taste. Simmer over medium heat, stirring frequently, for about 10–12 minutes or until the fresh mushrooms are soft and tender.

3 Meanwhile, cook the pasta in salted boiling water according to the instructions on the packet.

4 As soon as the mushrooms are cooked, increase the heat to high and toss the mixture with a wooden spoon to drive off any excess liquid.

5 Pour the cream into the pan and mix in. Bring the mixture to the boil, stirring, then taste and add more salt and black pepper if needed.

6 Drain the pasta and transfer it into a warmed bowl. Pour the sauce over the pasta and toss well. Serve immediately, sprinkled with extra fresh herb leaves.

Braised Tofu with Mushrooms

Autumn brings with it a plentiful supply of mushrooms. Four different kinds of mushrooms combine beautifully with tofu in this sophisticated and substantial recipe.

Serves 4
350g/12oz firm tofu
2.5ml/½ tsp sesame oil
10ml/2 tsp light soy sauce
15ml/1 tbsp vegetable oil
2 garlic cloves, finely chopped
2.5ml/½ tsp grated fresh
    root ginger
115g/4oz/scant 2 cups fresh
    shiitake mushrooms,
    stalks removed
175g/6oz/scant 2 cups fresh
    oyster mushrooms
115g/4oz/scant 2 cups canned
    straw mushrooms, drained
115g/4oz/scant 2 cups button
    (white) mushrooms, halved
15ml/1 tbsp dry sherry
15ml/1 tbsp dark soy sauce
90ml/6 tbsp vegetable stock
5ml/1 tsp cornflour (cornstarch)
15ml/1 tbsp cold water
ground white pepper
salt
2 shredded spring onions
    (scallions), to garnish

1 Put the tofu in a dish. Sprinkle with the sesame oil, light soy sauce and a large pinch of pepper. Marinate for 10 minutes, then drain and cut into 2.5 × 1cm/1 × ½in pieces.

2 Heat the vegetable oil in a large non-stick frying pan or wok. Add the garlic and ginger and stir-fry for a few seconds. Add all the mushrooms and stir-fry for a further 2 minutes.

3 Stir in the dry sherry, dark soy sauce and stock. Season to taste. Lower the heat and simmer gently for 4 minutes.

4 Place the cornflour in a bowl with the water. Mix to make a smooth paste. Stir the cornflour mixture into the pan or wok and cook, stirring constantly to prevent lumps, until thickened.

5 Carefully add the pieces of tofu, toss gently to coat thoroughly in the sauce and simmer for 2 minutes.

6 Sprinkle the shredded spring onions over the top of the mixture to garnish and serve immediately.

Braised Tofu Energy 118kcal/491kJ; Protein 9.3g; Carbohydrate 2.9g, of which sugars 1.1g; Fat 7.4g, of which saturates 0.9g; Cholesterol 0mg; Calcium 456mg; Fibre 1.2g; Sodium 455mg.
Fusilli with Mushrooms Energy 656kcal/2741kJ; Protein 13g; Carbohydrate 66.1g, of which sugars 4g; Fat 39.5g, of which saturates 21g; Cholesterol 82mg; Calcium 53mg; Fibre 3.6g; Sodium 56mg.

Wild Mushroom and Fontina Tarts

Fontina cheese gives these tarts a creamy, nutty flavour. Serve them warm with rocket, which is in abundance in the autumn.

Serves 4
25g/1oz/½ cup dried wild
  mushrooms
30ml/2 tbsp olive oil
1 red onion, chopped
2 garlic cloves, chopped
30ml/2 tbsp medium-dry sherry
1 egg

120ml/4fl oz/½ cup single
  (light) cream
25g/1oz Fontina cheese, sliced
salt and ground black pepper
rocket (arugula) leaves, to serve

For the pastry
115g/4oz/1 cup wholemeal
  (whole-wheat) flour
50g/2oz/4 tbsp unsalted butter
25g/1oz/¼ cup walnuts, roasted
  and ground
1 egg, lightly beaten

1 To make the pastry, rub the flour and butter together until the mixture resembles fine breadcrumbs, then stir in the walnuts. Add the egg and mix to form a soft dough. Wrap in clear film (plastic wrap) and chill for about 30 minutes.

2 Meanwhile, soak the dried mushrooms in 300ml/½ pint/ 1¼ cups boiling water for 30 minutes. Drain and reserve the liquid. Heat the oil in a frying pan. Add the onion and fry for 5 minutes, then add the garlic and fry for 2 minutes, stirring.

3 Add the mushrooms and cook over high heat until the edges become crisp. Add the sherry and the reserved liquid. Cook for 10 minutes until the liquid evaporates. Season and leave to cool.

4 Preheat the oven to 200°C/400°F/Gas 6. Lightly grease four 10cm/4in tart tins (pans). Roll out the pastry on a lightly floured work surface and use to line the tart tins. Prick the pastry, line with baking parchment and baking beans and bake blind for 10 minutes. Remove the paper and beans.

5 Whisk the egg and cream to mix, add to the mushroom mixture, then season to taste. Spoon into the pastry cases (pie shells), top with cheese slices and bake for 18 minutes until the filling is set. Serve warm with rocket.

Mushrooms with Hot Garlic Sauce

When you are planning a feast for guests, it can be tricky finding something really special for the vegetarians in the party. These tasty mushroom kebabs are ideal because they look, smell and taste absolutely wonderful. Cook them on a barbecue if the autumn weather permits, otherwise cook them under a grill indoors.

Serves 4
12 field (portabello), chestnut or
  oyster mushrooms or a mixture

4 garlic cloves, coarsely chopped
6 coriander (cilantro) roots,
  coarsely chopped
15ml/1 tbsp granulated
  (white) sugar
30ml/2 tbsp light soy sauce
ground black pepper

For the dipping sauce
15ml/1 tbsp sugar
90ml/6 tbsp rice vinegar
5ml/1 tsp salt
1 garlic clove, crushed
1 small fresh red chilli, seeded
  and finely chopped

1 If using wooden skewers, soak them in cold water for at least 30 minutes before using to prevent them burning over the barbecue or under the grill (broiler). You will need eight skewers.

2 Make the dipping sauce by heating the sugar, rice vinegar and salt in a small pan, stirring occasionally until the sugar and salt have dissolved. Add the garlic and chilli, pour into a serving dish and keep warm.

3 Halve the mushrooms and thread them on to each skewer. Lay the filled skewers side by side in a shallow dish.

4 In a mortar or spice grinder, pound or blend the garlic and coriander roots. Scrape into a bowl and mix with the sugar, soy sauce and a little pepper. Brush the soy sauce mixture over the mushrooms and leave to marinate for 15 minutes.

5 Prepare the barbecue or preheat the grill (broiler). When the coals have a light coating of grey ash, cook the mushrooms for about 2–3 minutes on each side. Serve immediately, accompanied by the dipping sauce.

Mushroom Tarts Energy 409kcal/1701kJ; Protein 10.2g; Carbohydrate 21.9g, of which sugars 2.3g; Fat 31g, of which saturates 13.4g; Cholesterol 143mg; Calcium 121mg; Fibre 2.3g; Sodium 199mg.
Mushrooms with Garlic Energy 51kcal/215kJ; Protein 2.5g; Carbohydrate 9.7g, of which sugars 8.7g; Fat 0.5g, of which saturates 0.1g; Cholesterol 0mg; Calcium 12mg; Fibre 1.3g; Sodium 1031mg.

Mushroom Stroganoff

This creamy mixed mushroom sauce tastes great and is ideal for an autumn dinner party. Serve it with toasted buckwheat, brown rice or a mix of wild rices. Ribbon noodles also make a good accompaniment. Cook them in boiling water or stock then toss them in a little olive oil.

Serves 8

25g/1oz/2 tbsp butter
900g/2lb/8 cups mixed
  mushrooms, cut into
  bitesize pieces
350g/12oz/1¾ cups white long
  grain rice
350ml/12fl oz/1½ cups white
  wine sauce
250ml/8fl oz/1 cup sour cream
salt and ground black pepper
chopped chives, to garnish

1 Melt the butter in a large pan and cook the mushrooms over medium heat until they give up their liquid. Cook until they are tender and beginning to reabsorb the pan juices and brown.

2 Meanwhile, bring a large pan of lightly salted water to the boil. Add the rice, partially cover the pan and cook over medium heat for 13–15 minutes until the rice is just tender.

3 Add the wine sauce to the cooked mushrooms in the pan and bring to the boil, stirring. Stir in the sour cream and season to taste with salt and pepper.

4 Drain the rice well, spoon on to warm plates, top with the sauce and garnish with chives. Serve immediately.

Cook's Tip
Although you can make this with regular button (white) mushrooms, it is especially delicious with wild mushrooms such as ceps or oyster mushrooms. When wild fungi are plentiful, in the autumn, farmers' markets are a good source. You may even be able to find more unusual specimens such as chicken of the woods, chanterelles, cauliflower fungus, morels or wood blewits. If you pick wild mushrooms yourself, make sure you know exactly what you are doing – mistakes can be deadly.

Garlic Chive Rice with Mushrooms

A wide range of mushrooms is readily available in the autumn. They combine well with rice and garlic chives to make a tasty dish.

Serves 4

350g/12oz/generous 1¾ cups
  long grain rice, washed
60ml/4 tbsp groundnut (peanut) oil
1 small onion, finely chopped
2 green chillies, seeded and chopped

25g/1oz garlic chives, chopped
15g/½oz fresh coriander (cilantro)
600ml/1 pint/2½ cups vegetable
  or mushroom stock
2.5ml/½ tsp sea salt
250g/9oz mixed mushrooms,
  thickly sliced
50g/2oz cashew nuts, fried in
  15ml/1 tbsp olive oil until
  golden brown
ground black pepper

1 Drain the rice. Heat half the oil in a pan and cook the onion and chillies over low heat, stirring, for 10–12 minutes until soft.

2 Set half the chives aside. Cut the stalks off the coriander and set the leaves aside. Purée the remaining chives and the coriander stalks with the stock in a food processor or blender.

3 Add the rice to the onions and fry over low heat, stirring frequently, for 4–5 minutes. Pour in the stock mixture, then add the salt and some black pepper. Bring to the boil, stir well and reduce the heat to very low. Cover with a lid and cook for 15–20 minutes, or until the rice has absorbed all the liquid.

4 Remove the pan from the heat and lay a clean, folded dish towel over the pan, under the lid, and press on the lid to wedge it firmly in place. Leave the rice to stand for a further 10 minutes, allowing the towel to absorb the steam while the rice becomes completely tender.

5 Meanwhile, heat the remaining oil in a frying pan and cook the mushrooms for 5–6 minutes until tender and browned. Stir in the remaining garlic chives and cook for 1–2 minutes.

6 Stir the mushroom and chive mixture and coriander leaves into the rice. Adjust the seasoning, then transfer to a warmed serving dish, sprinkled with the fried cashew nuts.

Stroganoff Energy 556kcal/2316kJ; Protein 13.3g; Carbohydrate 80.4g, of which sugars 7.2g; Fat 21.7g, of which saturates 11.4g; Cholesterol 51mg; Calcium 96mg; Fibre 2.5g; Sodium 897mg.
Garlic Chive Rice Energy 504kcal/2100kJ; Protein 10.4g; Carbohydrate 73.8g, of which sugars 1.8g; Fat 18.2g, of which saturates 2.6g; Cholesterol 0mg; Calcium 41mg; Fibre 1.6g; Sodium 533mg.

Spicy Root Vegetable Gratin

Subtly spiced, this rich gratin is slowly baked in the oven and is substantial enough to serve on its own for lunch or supper. It is also perfect as a tasty side dish to accompany grilled meats.

Serves 4

2 large potatoes, total weight
   about 450g/1lb
2 sweet potatoes, total weight
   about 275g/10oz
175g/6oz celeriac

15ml/1 tbsp unsalted butter
5ml/1 tsp curry powder
5ml/1 tsp ground turmeric
2.5ml/½ tsp ground coriander
5ml/1 tsp mild chilli powder
3 shallots, chopped
150ml/¼ pint/⅔ cup single
   (light) cream
150ml/¼ pint/⅔ cup milk
salt and ground black pepper
chopped fresh flat leaf parsley,
   to garnish

1 Peel the potatoes, sweet potatoes and celeriac and cut into thin, even slices using a sharp knife or the slicing attachment on a food processor. Immediately place the vegetables in a bowl of cold water to prevent them from discolouring.

2 Preheat the oven to 180°C/350°F/Gas 4. Heat half the butter in a heavy pan, add the curry powder, ground turmeric and coriander and half the chilli powder. Cook for 2 minutes, then leave to cool slightly.

3 Drain the vegetables, then pat them dry with kitchen paper. Place in a bowl, add the spice mixture and the shallots, and mix well. Arrange the vegetables in a shallow baking dish, seasoning well with salt and pepper between the layers.

4 In a bowl, mix together the cream and milk until well blended. Pour the mixture over the vegetables in the dish, then sprinkle the remaining chilli powder on top.

5 Cover the dish with baking parchment and bake for about 45 minutes. Remove the baking parchment, dot the vegetables with the remaining butter and bake for a further 50 minutes, or until the top is golden brown. Serve the gratin garnished with chopped parsley.

Onions Stuffed with Goat's Cheese

Long, gentle cooking is the best way to get maximum flavour from onions, so the slow cooker is the natural choice for this delicious stuffed-onion dish.

Serves 4

2 large onions, unpeeled
30ml/2 tbsp olive oil (or use oil
   from the sun-dried tomatoes)
150g/5oz/⅔ cup firm goat's
   cheese, crumbled or cubed

50g/2oz/1 cup fresh
   white breadcrumbs
8 sun-dried tomatoes in olive oil,
   drained and chopped
1 garlic clove, finely chopped
2.5ml/½ tsp fresh thyme
30ml/2 tbsp chopped fresh parsley
1 small egg, beaten
45ml/3 tbsp pine nuts
150ml/¼ pint/⅔ cup near-boiling
   vegetable stock
salt and ground black pepper
chopped fresh parsley, to garnish

1 Bring a large pan of water to the boil. Add the whole onions in their skins and boil for 10 minutes.

2 Drain the onions and leave until cool enough to handle, then cut each onion in half horizontally and peel. Using a teaspoon, remove the centre of each onion, leaving a thick shell.

3 Very finely chop the flesh from one of the scooped-out onion halves and place in a bowl. Stir in 5ml/1 tsp of the olive oil or oil from the sun-dried tomatoes, then add the goat's cheese, breadcrumbs, sun-dried tomatoes, garlic, thyme, parsley, egg and pine nuts. Season with salt and pepper and mix well.

4 Divide the stuffing among the onions and cover each one with a piece of oiled foil. Brush the base of the ceramic cooking pot with 15ml/1 tbsp of oil, then pour in the stock. Put the onions in the base of the cooking pot, cover with the lid and cook on high for 4 hours, or until the onions are tender but still hold their shape.

5 Remove the onions from the slow cooker and transfer them to a grill (broiler) pan. Remove the foil and drizzle with the remaining oil. Brown the tops of the onions under the grill for 3–4 minutes, taking care not to burn the nuts. Serve immediately, garnished with parsley.

Spicy Gratin Energy 268kcal/1129kJ; Protein 5.8g; Carbohydrate 37.7g, of which sugars 9.8g; Fat 11.6g, of which saturates 7.1g; Cholesterol 31mg; Calcium 127mg; Fibre 3.6g; Sodium 117mg.
Onions Stuffed Energy 330kcal/1370kJ; Protein 13.8g; Carbohydrate 14.3g, of which sugars 11.3g; Fat 24.7g, of which saturates 8.4g; Cholesterol 83.7mg; Calcium 98mg; Fibre 1.9g; Sodium 349mg.

Mussels in a Cider and Cream Broth

Mussels are delicious in the autumn when steamed and lifted out of their shells, and quickly fried with bacon. Here they are cooked with a broth of cider, garlic and cream. Serve the mussels in large shallow bowls with a chunk of bread to mop up the juices. Don't forget to provide finger bowls for cleaning sticky fingers.

Serves 4
1.8kg/4lb mussels in their shells
40g/1½oz/3 tbsp butter
1 leek, washed and finely chopped
1 garlic clove, finely chopped
150ml/¼ pint/⅔ cup dry
   (hard) cider
30–45ml/2–3 tbsp double
   (heavy) cream
a handful of fresh
   parsley, chopped
ground black pepper

1 Scrub the mussels and scrape off any barnacles. Discard those with broken shells or that refuse to close when given a sharp tap with a knife. Pull off the hairy beards from the mussels with a sharp tug.

2 Melt the butter in a very large pan and add the leek and garlic. Cook over medium heat for about 5 minutes, stirring frequently, until very soft but not browned. Season with pepper.

3 Add the cider and immediately tip in the mussels. Cover with a lid and cook quickly, shaking the pan occasionally, until the mussels have just opened (take care not to overcook and toughen them).

4 Remove the lid, add the cream and parsley and bubble gently for a minute or two. Serve immediately in shallow bowls.

Cook's Tips
Eat mussels the fun way! Use an empty shell as pincers to pick out the mussels from the other shells. Don't try to eat any whose shells have not opened during cooking or you risk food poisoning. Provide an empty bowl for the mussel shells.

Steamed Mussels with Onions and Celery

One of the best ways of preparing this dish is to simply steam the mussels in their own juices with celery and onions. This allows the delectable flavour of the mussels to shine through.

2 onions, roughly chopped
3–4 celery sticks, roughly chopped
salt and ground white pepper
chopped fresh parsley, to garnish
fries or crusty bread and
   pickles or mayonnaise,
   to serve

Serves 4
4kg/9lb live mussels
40g/1½oz/3 tbsp
   butter, softened

1 Scrub the mussels until the shells are shiny black and smooth. Remove beards, if present. If any of the shells are cracked or broken, discard them, along with any mussels that are open and that do not snap shut if tapped.

2 Melt the butter in a large heavy pan over medium heat. Add the onions and sauté for 5 minutes until softened and glazed. Add the celery and sauté for 5 minutes more. Add the mussels and season generously with salt and pepper.

3 Cover the pan and cook over high heat for 3–4 minutes or until the mussels open, shaking the pan occasionally to distribute the steam. Discard any mussels that do not open. Taste the liquid in the pan and adjust the seasoning if necessary, then spoon the mussels and the liquid into bowls or pots.

4 Sprinkle with parsley and serve with fries or crusty bread. Offer pickles, mayonnaise or mustard vinaigrette on the side.

Variation
A splash of white wine, poured over the mussels before cooking, improves the dish, and a little hot mustard can also be added.

Mussel Risotto

The addition of freshly cooked mussels, aromatic coriander and a little cream to a packet of instant risotto can turn a simple meal into a decadent treat. Serve with a side salad for a splendid autumnal supper. Other types of cooked shellfish, such as clams or prawns, can be used instead of mussels.

Serves 3–4
900g/2lb fresh mussels
275g/10oz packet risotto
30ml/2 tbsp chopped fresh
 coriander (cilantro)
30ml/2 tbsp double
 (heavy) cream

1 Scrub the mussels, discarding any that do not close when sharply tapped. Place in a large pan. Add 120ml/4fl oz/½ cup water and seasoning, then bring to the boil. Cover the pan and cook the mussels, shaking the pan occasionally, for 4–5 minutes, until they have opened. Drain, reserving the liquid and discarding any that have not opened. Shell most of the mussels, reserving a few in their shells for garnish. Strain the mussel liquid.

2 Make up the packet risotto according to the instructions, using the cooking liquid from the mussels and making it up to the required volume with water.

3 When the risotto is about three-quarters cooked, add the mussels to the pan. Add the coriander and re-cover the pan without stirring in these ingredients.

4 Remove the risotto from the heat, stir in the cream, cover and leave to rest for a few minutes. Spoon into a warmed serving dish, garnish with the reserved mussels in their shells, and serve.

Cook's Tip
For a super-quick mussel risotto, use cooked mussels in their shells – the type sold vacuum packed ready to reheat. Just reheat them according to the packet instructions and add to the made risotto with the coriander and cream.

Clams and Mussels in Banana Leaves

Autumn is the perfect time for these tasty, pretty parcels. It is the ideal dish to make the most of the clams and mussels during the season.

Serves 6
15ml/1 tbsp olive oil
1 large onion, finely chopped
2 garlic cloves, crushed
1.5ml/¼ tsp saffron threads
60ml/4 tbsp Noilly Prat or other
 dry vermouth
30ml/2 tbsp water
30ml/2 tbsp chopped fresh flat
 leaf parsley
500g/1¼lb clams, scrubbed
900g/2lb cleaned mussels
6 banana leaves
salt and ground black pepper
raffia, for tying
bread sticks, for serving

1 Heat the oil in a pan and cook the onion and garlic with the saffron threads over low heat for 4 minutes. Add the vermouth and water, and simmer for 2 minutes. Stir in the parsley, with seasoning to taste. Transfer to a bowl and leave to cool.

2 Tap the clam and mussel shells and discard any that stay open. Stir them into the bowl containing the onion mixture. Trim the hard edge from each banana leaf and discard it. Cut the leaves in half lengthways. Soak in hot water for 10 minutes, then drain. Rinse, then pour over boiling water to soften.

3 Top a sheet of foil with a piece of banana leaf, placing it smooth-side up. Place another piece of leaf on top, at right angles, so that the leaves form a cross.

4 Pile one-sixth of the seafood mixture into the centre, then bring up the leaves and tie them into a money-bag shape, using lengths of raffia. Do the same with the foil, scrunching slightly to seal the top. Make the remaining parcels in the same way, then chill the parcels until needed.

5 Prepare the barbecue. Once the flames have died down, position a lightly oiled grill rack over the coals to heat. When the coals are medium-hot, or with a moderate coating of ash, cook the parcels for 15 minutes. Remove the outer layer of foil from each and put the parcels back on the grill rack for 1 minute. Transfer to plates and serve with bread sticks.

Mussel Risotto Energy 439kcal/1833kJ; Protein 17.2g; Carbohydrate 56.6g, of which sugars 1.4g; Fat 11.3g, of which saturates 3.5g; Cholesterol 37mg; Calcium 159mg; Fibre 0.2g; Sodium 146mg.
Clams and Mussels Energy 116kcal/488kJ; Protein 14g; Carbohydrate 6.2g, of which sugars 4g; Fat 3.1g, of which saturates 0.5g; Cholesterol 40mg; Calcium 131mg; Fibre 0.9g; Sodium 498mg.

Clams with Tomato Sauce

This recipe combines tomatoes and shellfish to make a dish that is perfect for a cold autumn's evening.

Serves 4

1kg/2¼lb fresh clams
250ml/8fl oz/1 cup dry white
   wine, or vegetable stock
2 garlic cloves, bruised
1 handful fresh flat leaf parsley
30ml/2 tbsp extra virgin olive oil
1 small onion, finely chopped
8 ripe plum tomatoes, peeled,
   seeded and finely chopped
1 red chilli, seeded and chopped
350g/12oz dried vermicelli
salt and ground black pepper

1 Scrub the clams thoroughly with a brush under cold running water and discard any that are open or do not close their shells when sharply tapped against the work surface.

2 Pour the white wine or vegetable stock into a large, heavy pan and add the garlic. Shred half the parsley finely, add to the wine or stock, then add the clams. Cover the pan tightly with the lid and bring to the boil. Cook for 5 minutes, shaking the pan frequently, until the clams have opened.

3 Transfer the clams into a large colander set over a bowl and let the liquid drain through. Leave the clams until cool enough to handle, then remove about two-thirds of them from their shells, tipping the clam liquor into the bowl of cooking liquid. Discard any clams that have failed to open. Set both shelled and unshelled clams aside, keeping the unshelled clams warm.

4 Heat the oil in a pan, add the onion and cook, stirring, for 5 minutes, until softened. Add the tomatoes, then strain in the clam cooking liquid. Add the chilli, and seasoning. Bring to the boil, half cover the pan and simmer for 15–20 minutes.

5 Meanwhile, cook the pasta according to the packet instructions. Chop the remaining parsley finely. Add the shelled clams to the tomato sauce, stir well and heat through for 2–3 minutes.

6 Transfer the pasta into a warmed bowl. Pour the sauce over the pasta and toss together. Garnish with the reserved clams, sprinkle the parsley over the pasta and serve immediately.

Seafood Spaghetti Parcels

In this recipe, the cooking is finished in a paper parcel. When the parcel is opened, the most wonderful aroma wafts out.

Serves 4

500g/1¼ lb fresh mussels,
   scrubbed and bearded
500g/1¼lb small clams, scrubbed
105ml/7 tbsp dry white wine
60ml/4 tbsp olive oil
2 fat garlic cloves, chopped
2 dried red chillies, crumbled
200g/7oz squid, cut into rings
200g/7oz raw peeled
   prawns (shrimp)
400g/14oz dried spaghetti
30ml/2 tbsp chopped
   fresh parsley
5ml/1 tsp chopped fresh oregano
   or 2.5ml/½ tsp dried
salt and ground black pepper

For the tomato sauce

30ml/2 tbsp olive oil
1 red onion, finely chopped
1 garlic clove, finely chopped
400g/14oz can
   chopped tomatoes
15ml/1 tbsp tomato
   purée (paste)
15ml/1 tbsp torn fresh
   basil leaves

1 Make the tomato sauce. Heat the oil in a pan and cook the onion and garlic over low heat for 5 minutes. Stir in the tomatoes and tomato purée and simmer for 20–30 minutes, stirring occasionally. Season and add the basil.

2 Put the mussels, clams and wine in a large pan and bring to the boil. Put on the lid and shake the pan until all the shells have opened. Discard any that remain closed. Remove most of the mussels and clams from the shells, leaving about a dozen of each in the shell. Strain the juices and set aside.

3 Heat the olive oil in a frying pan, add the garlic and cook until lightly coloured. Add the chillies, then add the squid and prawns and sauté for 2–3 minutes, until the squid is opaque and the prawns have turned pink. Add the shellfish and their reserved juices, then stir in the tomato sauce. Set aside.

4 Preheat the oven to 240°C/475°F/Gas 9 or the grill (broiler) to hot. Cook the spaghetti in a pan of lightly salted, boiling water for about 12 minutes, or until it is just tender.

5 Drain the pasta very thoroughly, then return to the clean pan and stir in the shellfish sauce, tossing to coat all the strands of spaghetti. Stir in the parsley and oregano, with some salt and black pepper.

6 Cut out four 25cm/10in square pieces of baking parchment. Put a quarter of the spaghetti mixture into the middle of one piece and fold up the edges, pleating them to make a secure bag. Seal the sides first, then blow gently into the top to fill the bag with air. Fold over the top to seal. Make another three parcels with the rest of the spaghetti mixture.

7 Place the parcels on a baking sheet and cook in the hot oven or under the grill until the paper is browned and slightly charred at the edges.

8 Transfer the parcels to individual serving plates and open them at the table so that you can enjoy the wonderful aromas that emerge.

Clams Energy 500kcal/2091kJ; Protein 21.6g; Carbohydrate 77.3g, of which sugars 6.9g; Fat 7.1g, of which saturates 1.1g; Cholesterol 50mg; Calcium 134mg; Fibre 2.9g; Sodium 932mg.
Seafood Parcels Energy 681kcal/2875kJ; Protein 44.4g; Carbohydrate 80.5g, of which sugars 7.6g; Fat 20.6g, of which saturates 3g; Cholesterol 259mg; Calcium 201mg; Fibre 3.9g; Sodium 881mg.

Scallop Risotto

Buy fresh scallops for this dish, when they are in season in the autumn – they taste much better than frozen ones. Fresh scallops come with the coral attached, which adds flavour, texture and colour.

Serves 3–4
about 12 scallops, with their corals
50g/2oz/4 tbsp butter
15ml/1 tbsp olive oil
30ml/2 tbsp Pernod
2 shallots, finely chopped
275g/10oz/1½ cups risotto rice
1 litre/1¾ pints/4 cups
    simmering fish stock
pinch of saffron strands, dissolved
    in 15ml/1 tbsp warm milk
30ml/2 tbsp chopped fresh parsley
60ml/4 tbsp double
    (heavy) cream
salt and ground black pepper

1 Separate the scallops from their corals. Cut the white flesh in half or into 2cm/¾in slices. Melt half the butter with 5ml/1 tsp oil. Fry the white parts of the scallops for 2–3 minutes. Pour over the Pernod, heat for a few seconds, then ignite and allow to flame for a few seconds. When the flames have died down, remove the pan from the heat.

2 Heat the remaining butter and olive oil in a pan and fry the shallots for about 3–4 minutes, until soft but not browned. Add the rice and cook for a few minutes, stirring, until the rice is coated with oil and is beginning to turn translucent around the edges.

3 Gradually add the hot stock, a ladleful at a time, stirring constantly and waiting for each ladleful of stock to be absorbed before adding the next.

4 When the rice is very nearly cooked, add the scallops and all the juices from the pan, together with the corals, the saffron milk, parsley and seasoning. Stir well to mix. Continue cooking, adding the remaining stock and stirring occasionally, until the risotto is thick and creamy.

5 Remove the pan from the heat, stir in the cream and cover. Leave the risotto to rest for about 3 minutes to complete the cooking, then pile it into a warmed bowl and serve.

Tagliatelle with Scallops

Scallops and brandy make this a relatively expensive dish, but it is so delicious that you will find it well worth the cost. Make it in the autumn when scallops are at their best.

Serves 4
200g/7oz scallops
30ml/2 tbsp plain
    (all-purpose) flour
40g/1½oz/3 tbsp butter
2 spring onions (scallions), cut into
    thin rings
½–1 small fresh red chilli, seeded
    and very finely chopped
30ml/2 tbsp finely chopped fresh
    flat leaf parsley
60ml/4 tbsp brandy
105ml/7 tbsp fish stock
275g/10oz fresh spinach-
    flavoured tagliatelle
salt and ground black pepper

1 Remove the corals from the scallops if they have them, and slice the white part of each one horizontally into 2 or 3 pieces. Toss the scallops in the flour. Bring a large pan of salted water to the boil, ready for cooking the pasta.

2 Meanwhile, melt the butter in a large pan. Add the spring onions, finely chopped chilli and half the parsley and fry, stirring frequently, for 1–2 minutes over medium heat. Add the scallops and toss over the heat for 1–2 minutes.

3 Pour the brandy over the scallops, then set it alight with a match. As soon as the flames have died down, stir in the fish stock and salt and pepper to taste. Mix well. Simmer for 2–3 minutes, then cover the pan and remove it from the heat.

4 Add the pasta to the boiling water and cook it according to the instructions on the packet. Drain, add to the sauce and toss over medium heat until mixed. Serve immediately, in warmed bowls sprinkled with the remaining parsley.

> **Cook's Tip**
> *Buy fresh scallops, with their corals if possible. Fresh scallops always have a better texture and flavour than frozen ones, which tend to be watery.*

Tagliatelle Energy 429kcal/1809kJ; Protein 20.7g; Carbohydrate 58.7g, of which sugars 2.6g; Fat 10.3g, of which saturates 5.6g; Cholesterol 45mg; Calcium 46mg; Fibre 2.3g; Sodium 153mg.
Scallop Risotto Energy 550kcal/2290kJ; Protein 23g; Carbohydrate 58.9g, of which sugars 1.2g; Fat 22.5g, of which saturates 12.2g; Cholesterol 82mg; Calcium 48mg; Fibre 0.2g; Sodium 215mg.

Scallops with Fennel, Mascarpone and Bacon

This dish is a delicious combination of succulent seasonal scallops and crispy bacon, served on a bed of tender fennel and melting mascarpone. If you can't get large scallops (known as king scallops), buy the smaller queen scallops and serve a dozen per person. If you buy scallops in the shell, wash and keep the pretty fan-shaped shells to serve a range of fish dishes in.

Serves 2

2 small fennel bulbs
130g/4½oz/generous ½ cup mascarpone cheese
8 large scallops, shelled
75g/3oz thin smoked streaky (fatty) bacon rashers (strips)
salt and ground black pepper

1 Trim, halve and slice the fennel, reserving and chopping any feathery tops. Blanch in boiling water for 3 minutes. Drain.

2 Preheat the grill (broiler) to moderate. Place the fennel in a shallow flameproof dish and season with salt and pepper. Dot with the mascarpone and grill (broil) for about 5 minutes, until the cheese has melted and the fennel is lightly browned.

3 Meanwhile, pat the scallops dry on kitchen paper and season lightly. Cook the bacon in a large, heavy frying pan, until crisp and golden, turning once. Drain and keep warm. Fry the scallops in the pan for 1–2 minutes on each side, until cooked through.

4 Transfer the fennel to serving plates and crumble or snip the bacon into bitesize pieces over the top. Pile the scallops on the bacon and sprinkle with any reserved fennel tops.

Cook's Tip
Choose fresh rather than frozen scallops as the frozen ones tend to exude water on cooking. Have the pan very hot as scallops need only the briefest cooking at high heat – just until they turn opaque and brown on each side.

Scallops and Tiger Prawns

Serve this light, delicate dish for lunch or supper accompanied by aromatic steamed rice or fine rice noodles and stir-fried pak choi or broccoli. Scallops are particularly good with ingredients such as fresh ginger and soy sauce.

Serves 4

15ml/1 tbsp stir-fry oil or sunflower oil
500g/1¼lb raw tiger prawns (jumbo shrimp), peeled
1 star anise
225g/8oz scallops, halved horizontally if large
2.5cm/1in piece fresh root ginger, peeled and grated
2 garlic cloves, thinly sliced
1 red (bell) pepper, seeded and cut into thin strips
115g/4oz/1¾ cups shiitake or button (white) mushrooms, thinly sliced
juice of 1 lemon
5ml/1 tsp cornflour (cornstarch), mixed to a paste with 30ml/2 tbsp cold water
30ml/2 tbsp light soy sauce
salt and ground black pepper
chopped fresh chives, to garnish

1 Heat the oil in a wok until very hot. Put in the prawns and star anise and stir-fry over a high heat for 2 minutes.

2 Add the scallops, ginger and garlic and stir-fry for 1 minute more, by which time the prawns should have turned pink and the scallops will be opaque. Season with a little salt and plenty of pepper and then remove from the wok using a slotted spoon. Transfer the scallops to a bowl and discard the star anise.

3 Add the red pepper and mushrooms to the wok and stir-fry for 1–2 minutes. Pour in the lemon juice, cornflour paste and soy sauce, bring to the boil and bubble this mixture for 1–2 minutes, stirring all the time, until the sauce is smooth and slightly thickened.

4 Stir the prawns and scallops into the sauce, cook for a few seconds until heated through, then season with salt and ground black pepper. Spoon on to individual plates and serve garnished with the chives.

Scallops with Fennel Energy 362kcal/1512kJ; Protein 36.9g; Carbohydrate 9g, of which sugars 5.4g; Fat 20.1g, of which saturates 9.4g; Cholesterol 99mg; Calcium 79mg; Fibre 4.8g; Sodium 675mg.
Scallops and Prawns Energy 212kcal/892kJ; Protein 36.3g; Carbohydrate 6.6g, of which sugars 3.3g; Fat 4.6g, of which saturates 0.8g; Cholesterol 270mg; Calcium 122mg; Fibre 1g; Sodium 877mg.

Steamed Scallops with Ginger

It helps to have two woks when making this dish. Borrow an extra one from a friend, or use a large, heavy pan with a trivet for steaming the second plate of scallops. Take care not to overcook the tender seafood.

Serves 4
24 king scallops in their
  shells, cleaned
15ml/1 tbsp very finely shredded
  fresh root ginger
5ml/1 tsp very finely
  chopped garlic
1 large fresh red chilli, seeded
  and very finely chopped
15ml/1 tbsp light soy sauce
15ml/1 tbsp Chinese rice wine
a few drops of sesame oil
2–3 spring onions (scallions),
  very finely shredded
15ml/1 tbsp very finely chopped
  fresh chives
noodles or rice, to serve

1 Remove the scallops from their shells, then remove the membrane and hard white muscle from each one. Arrange the scallops on two plates. Rinse the shells, dry and set aside.

2 Fill two woks with 5cm/2in water and place a trivet in the base of each one. Bring to the boil.

3 Meanwhile, mix together the ginger, garlic, chilli, soy sauce, rice wine, sesame oil, spring onions and chives.

4 Spoon the flavourings over the scallops. Lower a plate into each of the woks. Turn the heat to low, cover and steam for 10–12 minutes.

5 Divide the scallops among four, or eight, of the reserved shells and serve immediately with noodles or rice.

> **Cook's Tip**
> Use the freshest scallops you can find. If you ask your fishmonger to shuck them, remember to ask for the shells so that you can use them for serving the scallops.

Spiced Scallops and Sugar Snaps

This is a great dish for special-occasion entertaining.

Serves 4
45ml/3 tbsp oyster sauce
10ml/2 tsp soy sauce
5ml/1 tsp sesame oil
5ml/1 tsp golden caster
  (superfine) sugar
30ml/2 tbsp sunflower oil
2 fresh red chillies, finely sliced
4 garlic cloves, finely chopped
10ml/2 tsp finely chopped fresh
  root ginger
250g/9oz sugar snap
  peas, trimmed
500g/1¼lb king scallops, cleaned
  and halved, roes discarded
3 spring onions (scallions),
  finely shredded

For the noodle cakes
250g/9oz fresh thin egg noodles
10ml/2 tsp sesame oil
120ml/4fl oz/½ cup sunflower oil

1 Cook the noodles in boiling water until tender. Drain, toss with the sesame oil and 15ml/1 tbsp of the sunflower oil and spread out on a large baking sheet. Leave to dry in a warm place for 1 hour.

2 Heat 15ml/1 tbsp of the sunflower oil in a wok. Add a quarter of the noodle mixture, flatten it and shape it into a cake.

3 Cook the cake for about 5 minutes on each side until crisp and golden. Drain on kitchen paper and keep hot while you make the remaining three noodle cakes in the same way.

4 Mix the oyster sauce, soy sauce, sesame oil and sugar, stirring until the sugar has dissolved completely.

5 Heat a wok, add the sunflower oil, then stir-fry the chillies, garlic, ginger and sugar snaps for 1–2 minutes. Add the scallops and spring onions and stir-fry for 1 minute, then add the sauce mixture and cook for 1 minute.

6 Place a noodle cake on each plate, top with the scallop mixture and serve immediately.

Spiced Scallops Energy 689kcal/2888kJ; Protein 41.4g; Carbohydrate 59.9g, of which sugars 6.2g; Fat 33.3g, of which saturates 5.4g; Cholesterol 78mg; Calcium 73mg; Fibre 5g; Sodium 700mg.
Scallops with Ginger Energy 392kcal/1621kJ; Protein 13.6g; Carbohydrate 4.5g, of which sugars 2.5g; Fat 34.1g, of which saturates 22.4g; Cholesterol 115mg; Calcium 63mg; Fibre 0.4g; Sodium 168mg.

Lobster Thermidor

One of the classic French dishes, Lobster Thermidor makes a little lobster go a long way. It is best to use one big rather than two small lobsters, as a larger lobster will contain a higher proportion of flesh and the meat will be sweeter.

Serves 2

1 large lobster, about
    800g–1kg/1¾–2¼lb, boiled
25g/1oz/2 tbsp butter
2 shallots, finely chopped
115g/4oz/1½ cups button
    (white) mushrooms, thinly sliced
15ml/1 tbsp plain
    (all-purpose) flour
105ml/7 tbsp fish or shellfish stock
120ml/4fl oz/½ cup double
    (heavy) cream
5ml/1 tsp Dijon mustard
2 egg yolks, beaten
45ml/3 tbsp dry white wine
45ml/3 tbsp brandy
45ml/3 tbsp freshly
    grated Parmesan
salt, ground black pepper and
    cayenne pepper
steamed rice and mixed salad
    leaves, to serve

1 Split the lobster in half lengthways; crack the claws. Discard the stomach sac; keep the coral for another dish. Keeping each half-shell intact, extract the meat from the tail and claws, then cut into large dice. Place in a shallow dish; sprinkle over the brandy. Cover and set aside. Wipe and dry the half-shells and set them aside.

2 Melt the butter in a pan and cook the shallots over low heat until soft. Add the mushrooms and cook until just tender. Stir in the flour and a pinch of cayenne; cook, stirring, for 2 minutes. Gradually add the stock, stirring until the sauce boils and thickens.

3 Stir in the cream and mustard and continue to cook until the sauce is smooth and thick. Season to taste with salt, black pepper and cayenne. Pour half the sauce on to the egg yolks, stir well and return the mixture to the pan. Stir in the wine; adjust the seasoning, being generous with the cayenne.

4 Preheat the grill (broiler) to medium-high. Stir the diced lobster and the brandy into the sauce. Arrange the lobster half-shells in a grill pan and divide the mixture among them.

Vegetable-stuffed Squid

Squid joins other seafood such as mussels, clams and lobsters in making the fishmongers a busy place in the autumn. Small cuttlefish can be prepared in the same way. Serve with saffron rice.

Serves 4

4 medium squid, or 12 small
    squid, skinned and cleaned
75g/3oz/6 tbsp butter
50g/2oz/1 cup fresh
    white breadcrumbs
2 shallots, chopped
4 garlic cloves, chopped
1 leek, finely diced
2 carrots, finely diced
150ml/¼ pint/⅔ cup fish stock
30ml/2 tbsp olive oil
30ml/2 tbsp chopped fresh parsley
salt and ground black pepper
rosemary sprigs, to garnish
saffron rice, to serve

1 Preheat the oven to 220°C/425°F/Gas 7. Cut off the tentacles and side flaps from the squid and chop these finely. Set the squid aside. Melt half the butter in a large frying pan that can be used in the oven. Add the breadcrumbs and cook until they are golden brown, stirring frequently. Using a slotted spoon, transfer the breadcrumbs to a bowl and set aside.

2 Heat the remaining butter in the frying pan and add the chopped and diced vegetables. Cook until softened but not browned, then stir in the stock and cook until it has reduced and the vegetables are very soft. Season with salt and pepper and transfer to the bowl with the breadcrumbs. Mix lightly.

3 Heat half the olive oil in the frying pan, add the chopped squid and cook over high heat for 1 minute. Remove the squid with a slotted spoon; stir into the vegetable mixture. Stir in the parsley.

4 Use a teaspoon to stuff the squid tubes with the mixture. Do not overfill them. Secure with cocktail sticks (toothpicks). Heat the remaining oil in the frying pan and cook the stuffed squid until they are sealed on all sides and golden brown. Transfer the pan to the oven and roast for 20 minutes.

5 Unless the squid are very small, cut them into three or four slices and arrange on a bed of rice. Spoon the cooking juices over and serve immediately, garnished with rosemary.

Lobster Thermidor Energy 859kcal/3573kJ; Protein 56g; Carbohydrate 9.8g, of which sugars 2g; Fat 59.6g, of which saturates 33.8g; Cholesterol 536mg; Calcium 488mg; Fibre 1.2g; Sodium 976mg.
Stuffed Squid Energy 356kcal/1486kJ; Protein 21.8g; Carbohydrate 15.2g, of which sugars 3.6g; Fat 23.6g, of which saturates 11.1g; Cholesterol 321mg; Calcium 55mg; Fibre 1.9g; Sodium 352mg.

Seared Swordfish with Citrus Dressing

This contemporary Japanese dish takes conventional salad ingredients and mixes them with shoyu, dashi and sesame oil for a bright, new taste. Fresh, seasonal fish is sliced thinly and seared or marinated, then served with salad leaves and vegetables.

Serves 4
75g/3oz mooli (daikon), peeled
50g/2oz carrot, peeled
1 Japanese or salad cucumber
10ml/2 tsp vegetable oil

300g/11oz skinned fresh
    swordfish steak, cut against
    the grain
2 cartons salad cress
15ml/1 tbsp toasted sesame seeds

For the dressing
105ml/7 tbsp shoyu
105ml/7 tbsp second dashi stock,
    or the same amount of water
    and 5ml/1 tsp dashi-no-moto
30ml/2 tbsp toasted sesame oil
juice of ½ lime
rind of ½ lime, shredded into
    thin strips

1 Make the garnishes first. Use either a very sharp knife, mandolin or vegetable slicer with a julienne blade to make very thin (about 4cm/1½in long) strands of mooli, carrot and cucumber.

2 Soak the mooli and carrot in ice-cold water for 5 minutes, then drain well and keep in the refrigerator. Mix together the ingredients for the dressing and stir well, then chill.

3 Heat the oil in a small frying pan until smoking hot. Sear the fish for 30 seconds on all sides. Plunge it into cold water in a bowl to stop the cooking. Dry on kitchen paper and wipe off as much oil as possible.

4 Cut the swordfish steak in half lengthways before slicing it into even 5mm/¼in thick pieces in the other direction, against the grain.

5 Arrange the fish slices in a ring on individual plates. Mix the vegetable strands, salad cress and sesame seeds. Fluff up with your hands, then shape them into a sphere. Gently place it in the centre of the plate, on the swordfish. Pour the dressing around the plate's edge and serve immediately.

Squid Stuffed with Garlic Pork

This recipe calls for tender baby squid to be stuffed with a dill-flavoured pork mixture. The squid can be grilled or fried.

Serves 4
3 dried cloud ear (wood
    ear) mushrooms
10 dried tiger lily buds
25g/1oz bean thread
    (cellophane) noodles
8 baby squid, cleaned

350g/12oz minced (ground) pork
3–4 shallots, finely chopped
4 garlic cloves, finely chopped
1 bunch dill fronds, finely chopped
30ml/2 tbsp nuoc mam
5ml/1 tsp palm sugar (jaggery)
ground black pepper
vegetable or groundnut (peanut)
    oil, for frying
coriander (cilantro) leaves,
    to garnish
nuoc cham, for drizzling

1 Soak the mushrooms, tiger lily buds and bean thread noodles in lukewarm water for about 15 minutes, until softened. Rinse the squid and pat dry with kitchen paper. Chop the tentacles.

2 Drain the mushrooms, tiger lily buds and bean thread noodles. Squeeze them in kitchen paper to get rid of any excess water, then chop them finely and put them in a bowl. Add the chopped tentacles, minced pork, shallots, garlic and three-quarters of the dill. In a small bowl, stir the nuoc mam with the sugar, until it dissolves completely. Add it to the mixture in the bowl and mix well. Season with black pepper.

3 Using your fingers, stuff the pork mixture into each squid, packing it in firmly. Leave a little gap at the end to sew together with a needle and cotton thread or to skewer with a cocktail stick (toothpick) so that the filling doesn't spill out on cooking.

4 Heat some oil in a large wok or heavy pan, and fry the squid for about 5 minutes, turning them from time to time. Pierce each one several times to release any excess water – this will cause the oil to spit, so take care when doing this; you may wish to use a spatterproof lid. Continue cooking for a further 10 minutes, until the squid are nicely browned. Serve whole or thinly sliced, garnished with the remaining dill and coriander, and drizzled with nuoc cham.

Seared Swordfish Energy 192kcal/799kJ; Protein 15.6g; Carbohydrate 4.1g, of which sugars 3.7g; Fat 12.7g, of which saturates 2g; Cholesterol 31mg; Calcium 53mg; Fibre 1.1g; Sodium 1887mg.
Squid with Pork Energy 315kcal/1311kJ; Protein 25g; Carbohydrate 7.9g, of which sugars 1.9g; Fat 20.4g, of which saturates 4.6g; Cholesterol 170mg; Calcium 18mg; Fibre 0.2g; Sodium 110mg.

Roasted Chicken with Grapes and Fresh Root Ginger

Oven-roasted chicken with a delicious blend of spices and sweet autumn fruit.

Serves 4

115–130g/4–4¹/₂oz fresh root
  ginger, grated
6–8 garlic cloves, roughly chopped
juice of 1 lemon
about 30ml/2 tbsp olive oil

2–3 large pinches of
  ground cinnamon
1–1.6kg/2¹/₄–3¹/₂lb chicken
500g/1¹/₄lb seeded red and
  green grapes
500g/1¹/₄lb seedless green grapes
5–7 shallots, chopped
about 250ml/8fl oz/1 cup
  chicken stock
salt and ground black pepper

1 Mix together half the ginger, the garlic, half the lemon juice, the oil, cinnamon and seasoning. Rub over the chicken and set aside.

2 Meanwhile, cut the red and green seeded grapes in half, remove the seeds and set aside. Add the whole green seedless grapes to the halved ones.

3 Preheat the oven to 180°C/350°F/Gas 4. Heat a heavy frying pan or flameproof casserole until hot. Remove the chicken from the marinade and cook in the pan until browned on all sides.

4 Put a few shallots into the chicken cavity with the garlic and ginger from the marinade and as many of the red and green grapes as will fit. Roast for 40–60 minutes, or until cooked.

5 Remove the chicken from the pan and keep warm. Pour off any oil from the pan, reserving any sediment in the base. Add the remaining shallots and cook for 5 minutes until softened.

6 Add half the remaining red and green grapes, the remaining ginger, the stock and any juices from the chicken and cook over medium-high heat until the grapes have reduced to a thick sauce. Season with salt, pepper and the remaining lemon juice.

7 Serve the chicken on a warmed serving dish, surrounded by the sauce and the reserved grapes.

Chicken and Mushroom Donburi

'Donburi' means a one-dish meal, and its name comes from the eponymous Japanese porcelain food bowl. This dish is ideal for using the mushrooms that are abundant in autumn.

Serves 4

10ml/2 tsp groundnut (peanut) oil
50g/2oz/4 tbsp butter
2 garlic cloves, crushed
2.5cm/1in piece of fresh root
  ginger, grated
5 spring onions, diagonally sliced
1 green chilli, seeded and sliced

3 skinless chicken breast fillets,
  cut into thin strips
150g/5oz tofu, cut into small cubes
115g/4oz/1³/₄ shiitake
  mushrooms, stalks discarded
  and cups sliced
15ml/1 tbsp Japanese rice wine
30ml/2 tbsp light soy sauce
10ml/2 tsp sugar
400ml/14fl oz/1²/₃ cups hot
  chicken stock

For the rice
225–275g/8–10oz/generous
  1–1¹/₂ cups Japanese rice or
  Thai fragrant rice

1 Cook the rice by the absorption method or by following the instructions on the packet.

2 While the rice is cooking, heat the oil and half the butter in a large frying pan. Stir-fry the garlic, ginger, spring onions and chilli for 1–2 minutes until slightly softened. Add the strips of chicken and fry, in batches if necessary, until all the pieces are browned.

3 Transfer the chicken mixture to a plate and add the tofu to the pan. Stir-fry for a few minutes, then add the mushrooms. Stir-fry for 2–3 minutes over a medium heat until the mushrooms are tender.

4 Stir in the rice wine, soy sauce and sugar and cook briskly for 1–2 minutes, stirring all the time. Return the chicken to the pan, toss over the heat for about 2 minutes, then pour in the stock. Stir well and cook over low heat for about 5–6 minutes until the stock is bubbling.

5 Spoon the rice into individual serving bowls and pile the chicken mixture on top, making sure that each portion gets a generous amount of chicken sauce.

Roasted Chicken Energy 454kcal/1891kJ; Protein 31.6g; Carbohydrate 19.5g, of which sugars 19.5g; Fat 28.1g, of which saturates 7.1g; Cholesterol 165mg; Calcium 28mg; Fibre 1g; Sodium 116mg.
Chicken Donburi Energy 408kcal/1709kJ; Protein 35.2g; Carbohydrate 46.3g, of which sugars 1.1g; Fat 8.8g, of which saturates 1.2g; Cholesterol 79mg; Calcium 216mg; Fibre 0.5g; Sodium 605mg.

Coq au Vin

This rustic, one-pot casserole contains chunky pieces of chicken, slowly simmered in a rich red wine sauce until tender, making it a welcome meal on a cold autumn's night.

Serves 6
45ml/3 tbsp light olive oil
12 shallots
225g/8oz rindless streaky (fatty)
   bacon rashers (strips), chopped
3 garlic cloves, finely chopped
225g/8oz small mushrooms, halved
6 boneless chicken thighs
3 chicken breast fillets, halved
1 bottle red wine
salt and ground black pepper
45ml/3 tbsp chopped fresh
   parsley, to garnish
boiled potatoes, to serve

For the bouquet garni
3 sprigs each parsley, thyme, sage
1 bay leaf
4 peppercorns

For the beurre manié
25g/1oz/2 tbsp butter, softened
25g/1oz/¼ cup plain
   (all-purpose) flour

1 Heat the oil in a flameproof casserole and cook the shallots for 5 minutes until golden. Increase the heat, then add the bacon, garlic and mushrooms and cook, stirring, for 10 minutes.

2 Transfer the cooked ingredients to a plate, then brown the chicken pieces in the oil remaining in the pan, turning them until golden brown all over. Return the shallots, garlic, mushrooms and bacon to the casserole and pour in the red wine.

3 Tie the ingredients for the bouquet garni in a bundle in a small piece of muslin (cheesecloth) and add to the casserole. Bring to the boil. Reduce the heat, cover and simmer for 30–40 minutes.

4 To make the beurre manié, cream the butter and flour together in a bowl using your fingers to make a smooth paste. Add small lumps of the paste to the casserole, stirring well until each piece has melted. When all the paste has been added, bring the casserole back to the boil and simmer for 5 minutes.

5 Season the casserole to taste with salt and pepper. Serve immediately, garnished with chopped fresh parsley and accompanied by boiled potatoes.

Chicken and Pork in Peanut Sauce

This traditional dish is made with dried potatoes, which break up when cooked to thicken the sauce. The same effect is achieved here by using floury potatoes, which are widely available in the autumn as the maincrop season hits full swing.

Serves 6
75g/3oz/¾ cup unsalted peanuts
60ml/4 tbsp olive oil
3 chicken breast portions, halved
500g/1¼lb boneless pork loin,
   cut into 2cm/¾in pieces
1 large onion, chopped
3 garlic cloves, crushed
5ml/1 tsp paprika
5ml/1 tsp ground cumin
500g/1¼lb floury potatoes,
   peeled and thickly sliced
550ml/18fl oz/scant 2½ cups
   vegetable stock
salt and ground black pepper
cooked rice, to serve

For the garnish
2 hard-boiled eggs, sliced
50g/2oz/½ cup pitted black olives
chopped fresh flat leaf parsley

1 Place the peanuts in a large dry frying pan over low heat. Toast for 2–3 minutes, until golden. Leave to cool, then process in a food processor until finely ground.

2 Heat half the oil in a heavy pan. Add the chicken pieces, season and cook for 10 minutes, until golden brown all over.

3 Transfer the pieces of chicken to a plate, using a slotted spoon. Heat the remaining oil and cook the pork for about 3–4 minutes, until brown. Transfer to the plate with the cooked chicken pieces.

4 Lower the heat, add the onion and fry for 5 minutes. Add the garlic, paprika and cumin and fry for 1 minute. Stir in the sliced potatoes, cover the pan and cook for a further 3 minutes. Mix in the peanuts and stock. Simmer for 30 minutes.

5 Return the meat to the pan and bring to the boil. Lower the heat, replace the lid and simmer for 6–8 minutes.

6 Garnish the stew with the egg slices, black olives and chopped parsley. Serve with the rice.

Coq au Vin Energy 538kcal/2240kJ; Protein 43.5g; Carbohydrate 7g, of which sugars 2.8g; Fat 28.2g, of which saturates 8.9g; Cholesterol 170mg; Calcium 50mg; Fibre 1.1g; Sodium 610mg.
Chicken in Peanut Sauce Energy 394kcal/1651kJ; Protein 39.3g; Carbohydrate 16.7g, of which sugars 2.4g; Fat 19.4g, of which saturates 4.1g; Cholesterol 85mg; Calcium 33mg; Fibre 1.8g; Sodium 123mg.

Duck Sausages with Plum Sauce

Rich duck sausages are best baked in their own juices for 30 minutes. Creamy mashed sweet potatoes and spicy plum sauce are the perfect seasonal complements and contrast with the richness of the sausages.

Serves 4

8–12 duck sausages

For the sweet potato mash
1.5kg/3¼lb sweet potatoes, cut
   into chunks

25g/1oz/2 tbsp butter
60ml/4 tbsp milk
salt and ground
   black pepper

For the plum sauce
30ml/2 tbsp olive oil
1 small onion, chopped
1 small red chilli, seeded and
   finely chopped
450g/1lb plums, stoned
   and chopped
30ml/2 tbsp red wine vinegar
45ml/3 tbsp clear honey

1 Preheat the oven to 190°C/375°F/Gas 5. Arrange the duck sausages in a single layer in a large, shallow ovenproof dish and bake, uncovered, for 25–30 minutes, turning the sausages two or three times during cooking, to ensure that they brown and cook evenly.

2 Meanwhile, put the sweet potatoes in a pan and pour in enough water to cover them. Bring to the boil, reduce the heat and simmer for 20 minutes, or until tender.

3 Drain and mash the sweet potatoes, then place the pan over a low heat. Stir frequently for about 5 minutes to dry out the mashed potatoes. Beat in the butter and milk, and season with salt and pepper.

4 Heat the oil in a frying pan and fry the onion and chilli gently for 5 minutes until the onion is soft and translucent. Stir in the plums, vinegar and honey, then simmer gently for 10 minutes.

5 Divide the freshly cooked sausages among four plates and serve immediately with the sweet potato mash and piquant plum sauce.

Duck with Plum Sauce

This is a great autumn meal featuring a number of ingredients that are at their best this season: plums, celeriac and duck. The sharp plums cut the rich flavour of duck wonderfully well in this updated version of an old English dish. Duck is often considered to be a fatty meat but modern breeding methods have made leaner ducks widely available. For an easy dinner party main course, serve the duck with creamy mashed potatoes and seasonal celeriac and steamed broccoli.

Serves 4
4 duck quarters
1 large red onion, finely chopped
500g/1¼ lb ripe plums, stoned
   (pitted) and quartered
30ml/2 tbsp redcurrant jelly
creamy mashed potato, celeriac
   and broccoli, to serve (optional)
salt and ground black pepper

1 Prick the duck skin all over with a fork to release the fat during the cooking process and help give a crisp result, then place the portions in a heavy frying pan, skin side down.

2 Cook the duck pieces for about 8–10 minutes on each side, or until golden brown and cooked right through. Remove the duck from the frying pan using a slotted spoon and keep warm while you prepare the rest.

3 Pour away all but 30ml/2 tbsp of the duck fat, then stir-fry the onion for about 5 minutes, or until soft and golden. Add the plums and cook for another 5 minutes, stirring frequently. Add the jelly and mix well.

4 Replace the duck portions in the pan and cook for a further 5 minutes, or until thoroughly reheated. Season to taste with salt and pepper before serving.

Cook's Tip
It is important that the plums used in this dish are very ripe, otherwise the mixture will be too dry and the sauce will be extremely sharp.

Duck Sausages Energy 894kcal/3755kJ; Protein 17.8g; Carbohydrate 110.8g, of which sugars 42.9g; Fat 45.5g, of which saturates 17.9g; Cholesterol 67mg; Calcium 170mg; Fibre 11.6g; Sodium 1052mg.
Duck with Plum Energy 894kcal/3755kJ; Protein 17.8g; Carbohydrate 110.8g, of which sugars 42.9g; Fat 45.5g, of which saturates 17.9g; Cholesterol 67mg; Calcium 170mg; Fibre 11.6g; Sodium 1052mg.

Roast Duck with Prunes and Apples

This autumn dish features a roast duck stuffed with seasonal apples and prunes. Serve with roast potatoes, and braised red cabbage, or serve more simply with steamed cauliflower – another autumn favourite.

Serves 4

1 duck, about 1.8–2.5kg/4–5½lb, with giblets

150g/5oz pitted prunes, sliced
2 medium dessert apples, peeled and chopped
20g/3/4oz fine breadcrumbs
475ml/16fl oz/2 cups hot chicken stock
small bay leaf
30ml/2 tbsp plain (all-purpose) flour
15ml/1 tbsp single (light) cream
salt and white pepper

1 Preheat the oven to 240°C/475°F/Gas 9. Rinse the duck and pat dry. Score the breast with a crosshatch pattern. Season well.

2 Toss the prunes and apples with the breadcrumbs in a bowl and spoon this mixture into the duck cavity, packing it firmly. Close the opening with skewers or sew up with fine string.

3 Pour 250ml/8fl oz/1 cup of the chicken stock into a roasting pan. Place the duck on a rack in the pan, breast side down, and cook for 20 minutes.

4 Put the giblets in a pan with 475ml/16fl oz/2 cups water and the bay leaf. Bring to a rolling boil for 20–30 minutes until reduced. Strain and set aside.

5 Lower the oven to 180°C/350°F/Gas 4. Turn the duck breast side up. Pour the remaining stock into the pan. Continue to cook for 40 minutes per kg/20 minutes per lb, until the juices run clear when the thickest part of the leg is pierced. Transfer to a serving dish and leave in a warm place for 10 minutes.

6 To make the gravy, pour off the fat from the roasting pan and whisk the flour into the remaining juices. Cook over medium heat for 2–3 minutes until light brown. Gradually whisk in the giblet stock and stir in the cream. Cook the gravy, stirring, for 3 minutes, pour into a sauceboat and serve with the duck.

Farm Pigeon with Elderberry Wine

Elderberry wine is just one of many things that can be enjoyed in autumn. The berries are bitter on their own but make a deep, rich, almost port-like wine. Pigeons are also best in the autumn months.

Serves 4

4 pigeons
15ml/1 tbsp plain (all-purpose) flour

30ml/2 tbsp olive oil, plus extra if needed
1 onion, chopped
225g/8oz button (white) mushrooms, sliced
250ml/8fl oz/1 cup dark stock
100ml/3½fl oz/scant ½ cup elderberry wine
salt and ground black pepper
kale, to serve (optional)

1 Preheat the oven to 170°C/325°F/Gas 3. Season the pigeons inside and out with salt and black pepper and roll liberally in the flour. Heat a heavy pan over medium heat, add the olive oil and wait for it to bubble slightly. Brown the pigeons lightly all over, then transfer them to a casserole dish.

2 Brown the onion and then the mushrooms in the same pan, still over a medium heat, adding more oil if necessary. Add the vegetables to the casserole with the pigeon and mix well.

3 Pour in the stock, elderberry wine and just enough water to cover. Bring to the boil, cover tightly with a lid and cook in the preheated oven for 2 hours, until the pigeons are tender.

4 Remove the birds from the casserole and keep warm. Boil the cooking liquor rapidly to thicken slightly. Return the pigeons to the pan and heat through. Serve with kale, if you like.

> **Variation**
> *This recipe suits most game birds, so if you can't find pigeon, or it is the wrong season, you can use partridge, woodcock, pheasant or even wild duck or goose.*

Roast Duck Energy 663kcal/2757kJ; Protein 31.6g; Carbohydrate 24g, of which sugars 14.6g; Fat 49.6g, of which saturates 14g; Cholesterol 100mg; Calcium 55mg; Fibre 2.8g; Sodium 222mg.
Braised Farm Pigeon Energy 296kcal/1237kJ; Protein 31g; Carbohydrate 6.8g, of which sugars 2.5g; Fat 14.3g, of which saturates 0.1g; Cholesterol 0mg; Calcium 35mg; Fibre 1g; Sodium 117mg.

Roast Grouse with Rowanberry and Wine Sauce

Autumn is the best time of year for enjoying game meats of all descriptions, particularly the various game birds on offer. As with venison, rowan jelly goes well with this autumn bird. Young grouse have very little fat on them so bacon is used in this recipe to protect the breasts during the initial roasting.

Serves 2

2 young grouse
6 rashers (strips) bacon
2 sprigs of rowanberries or
   1 lemon, quartered, plus
   30ml/2 tbsp extra
   rowanberries (optional)
50g/2oz/¼ cup butter
150ml/¼ pint/⅔ cup red wine
150ml/¼ pint/⅔ cup water
5ml/1 tsp rowan jelly
salt and ground black pepper

1 Preheat the oven to 200°C/400°F/Gas 6. Wipe the grouse with kitchen paper and place in a roasting pan. Lay the bacon over the breasts.

2 If you have rowanberries, place one sprig in the cavity of each grouse as well as a little butter. Otherwise put a lemon quarter in each cavity.

3 Roast the grouse in the preheated oven for 10 minutes, then remove the bacon and pour in the wine. Return to the oven for 10 minutes.

4 Baste the birds with the juices and cook for a further 5 minutes. Remove the birds from the pan and keep warm. Add the water and rowan jelly to the pan and simmer gently until the jelly melts. Strain into another pan, add the rowanberries, if using, and simmer until the sauce just begins to thicken. Season with salt and ground black pepper.

Cook's Tip
Grouse is traditionally served with bread sauce and game chips but the Scottish oatmeal dish skirlie is excellent too.

Pork Escalopes with Apple and Potato Rösti

The juices from the pork cook into the seasonal apples and potatoes, giving the dish a wonderfully autumnal flavour.

Serves 4

2 large potatoes, finely grated
1 medium Bramley apple, grated
2 garlic cloves, crushed
1 egg, beaten
butter, for greasing
15ml/1 tbsp olive oil
4 large slices prosciutto
4 pork escalopes, about
   175g/6oz each
4 sage leaves
1 medium Bramley apple,
   cut into thin wedges
25g/1oz/2 tbsp unsalted
   butter, diced
salt and ground black pepper
caramelized apple wedges,
   to serve

1 Preheat the oven to 200°C/400°F/Gas 6. Squeeze out all the excess liquid from the grated potatoes and apple. Thoroughly mix the grated ingredients together with the garlic, egg and seasoning.

2 Divide the potatoes into four portions and spoon each quarter on to a baking sheet that has been lined with foil and greased. Form a circle with the potatoes and flatten out slightly with the back of a spoon. Drizzle with a little olive oil. Bake for 10 minutes.

3 Meanwhile, lay the prosciutto on a clean surface and place a pork escalope on top. Lay a sage leaf and a quarter of the apple wedges over each escalope and top each piece with the butter. Wrap the prosciutto around each piece of meat, making sure it is covered completely.

4 Remove the potatoes from the oven, place each pork parcel on top of the potatoes and return the pan to the oven for about 20 minutes.

5 Carefully lift the pork and potatoes off the foil and serve at once with caramelized wedges of apple and any cooking juices on the side.

Roast Grouse Energy 423kcal/1763kJ; Protein 43.8g; Carbohydrate 1.5g, of which sugars 1.5g; Fat 24g, of which saturates 10.8g; Cholesterol 51mg; Calcium 43mg; Fibre 0g; Sodium 902mg.
Pork Escalopes Energy 396kcal/1659kJ; Protein 42.7g; Carbohydrate 19.2g, of which sugars 4.4g; Fat 16.9g, of which saturates 6.7g; Cholesterol 177mg; Calcium 29mg; Fibre 1.5g; Sodium 310mg.

Roast Pork, Apples and Glazed Potatoes

For this pork and potato recipe, select a bone-in pork loin with the skin left on for the crackling.

Serves 8–10
2.25kg/5lb bone-in pork loin,
10ml/2 tsp mustard powder
15 whole cloves
2 bay leaves
900ml/1½ pints/3¾ cups water
175ml/6fl oz/¾ cup single (light)
   cream (optional)
salt and white pepper
braised red cabbage, to serve

For the glazed potatoes
900g/2lb small potatoes
50g/2oz/¼ cup caster
   (superfine) sugar
65g/2½ oz/5 tbsp butter

For the apples with redcurrant jelly
750ml/1¼ pints/3 cups water
115g/4oz/generous ½ cup soft
   light brown sugar
5ml/1 tsp lemon juice
4–5 tart apples, peeled, cored
   and halved
60–75ml/4–5 tbsp redcurrant jelly

1 Preheat the oven to 200°C/400°F/Gas 6. Score the pork skin and rub with the salt, pepper and mustard powder. Push the cloves and bay leaves into the skin. Place the pork, skin side up, on a rack in a roasting pan and cook for 1 hour, until the skin is crisp. Pour the water into the pan and cook for 30 minutes.

2 Boil the potatoes in salted water for 15–20 minutes, or until soft. Drain, peel and keep warm. Melt the sugar in a frying pan over low heat until it turns light brown. Add the potatoes and butter and cook for 6–8 minutes. Keep warm.

3 Bring the water for the apples to the boil in a pan and stir in sugar, lemon juice and apple halves. Lower the heat and simmer until the apples are just tender. Remove the apples and spoon 7.5ml/1½ tsp jelly into the hollow of each half. Keep warm.

4 Transfer the pork to a serving dish and rest for 15 minutes before carving. Make the gravy: pour the roasting pan juices into a pan and reduce over medium heat. Whisk in a little cream if you wish, and season. Remove the crackling. Serve the pork with the gravy, potatoes, apples and crackling.

Caramelized Onion and Sausage Tarte Tatin

Toulouse sausages have a garlicky flavour and meaty texture that is delicious with fried onions. Serve this simple autumn dish with a green salad of bitter seasonal leaves, such as rocket or watercress.

450g/1lb Toulouse sausages
2 large onions, sliced
250g/9oz ready-made puff
   pastry, thawed if frozen
salt and ground black pepper
salad of bitter leaves, such as
   rocket (arugula) or watercress
   to serve (optional)

Serves 4
45ml/3 tbsp sunflower oil

1 Heat the oil in a 23cm/9in non-stick frying pan with an ovenproof handle so that it can be used in the oven, and add the sausages.

2 Cook the sausages over low heat, turning occasionally, for 7–10 minutes, or until golden and cooked through. Remove from the pan and set aside.

3 Preheat the oven to 190°C/375°F/Gas 5. Pour the remaining oil into the frying pan and add the onions. Season with salt and pepper and cook over a gentle heat for 10 minutes, stirring occasionally, until caramelized and tender.

4 Slice each sausage into four or five chunks and stir into the onions. Remove from the heat and set aside.

5 Roll out the puff pastry on a lightly floured surface and cut out a circle slightly larger than the frying pan.

6 Lay the pastry over the sausages and onions, tucking the edges in all the way around.

7 Bake for 20 minutes, or until the pastry is risen and golden. Turn out on to a board, pastry side down, cut into wedges and serve immediately.

Roast Pork Energy 654kcal/2735kJ; Protein 36.9g; Carbohydrate 39.5g, of which sugars 26.2g; Fat 39.9g, of which saturates 16.1g; Cholesterol 124mg; Calcium 36mg; Fibre 1.5g; Sodium 152mg.
Onion Tarte Energy 765kcal/3176kJ; Protein 17g; Carbohydrate 43.7g, of which sugars 9.4g; Fat 59.9g, of which saturates 14.7g; Cholesterol 53mg; Calcium 114mg; Fibre 2.3g; Sodium 1053mg.

Hunter's Stew

Hearty and sustaining, this cabbage and meat stew is an ideal dish as the autumn nights get longer.

Serves 6–8

1kg/2¼lb fresh cabbage, shredded
10 dried mushrooms
2 onions, chopped
500g/1¼lb smoked sausage, sliced
1kg/2¼lb sauerkraut, drained
2 cooking apples, peeled, cored and diced
10 prunes
10 juniper berries, crushed
3–4 bay leaves
10 peppercorns
2.5ml/½ tsp salt
750ml/1¼ pints/3 cups boiling water
500g/1¼lb roast pork, diced
500g/1¼lb roast beef, diced
500g/1¼lb boiled ham, diced
150ml/¼ pint/¾ cup dry red wine
5ml/1 tsp honey
wholemeal (whole-wheat) or rye bread and chilled vodka, to serve

1 Place the cabbage in a heatproof colander and wilt the leaves by carefully pouring boiling water over them. Rinse the mushrooms, then place them in a bowl with enough warm water to cover. Leave to soak for 15 minutes, then transfer to a pan and cook in the soaking liquid for 30 minutes. Strain, reserving the cooking liquid, then cut the mushrooms into strips.

2 Put the onions and smoked sausage in a small frying pan and fry gently, until the onions have softened. Remove the sausage from the pan and set aside.

3 Put the wilted cabbage and drained sauerkraut in a large pan, then add the cooked onions, along with the mushrooms, mushroom cooking liquid, apples, prunes, juniper berries, bay leaves, peppercorns and salt. Pour over the boiling water, then cover and simmer gently for 1 hour.

4 Add the cooked sausage to the pan with the other cooked, diced meats. Pour in the wine and add the honey. Cook, uncovered, for a further 40 minutes, stirring frequently. Adjust the seasoning as required. Remove from the heat. Allow to cool, then cover it and chill overnight. Simmer for 10 minutes to heat through before serving with bread and a glass of vodka.

Stuffed Cabbage Leaves

This is a great dish for making in the autumn when cabbages are at their peak. The leaves are stuffed with delicious beef and then baked in a tomato sauce.

Serves 6–8

1kg/2¼lb lean minced (ground) beef
75g/3oz/scant ½ cup long grain rice
4 onions, 2 chopped and 2 sliced
5–8 garlic cloves, chopped
2 eggs
45ml/3 tbsp water
1 large head of white or green cabbage
2 x 400g/14oz cans chopped tomatoes
45ml/3 tbsp demerara (raw) sugar
45ml/3 tbsp white wine vinegar, cider vinegar or lemon juice
pinch of ground cinnamon
salt and ground black pepper
lemon wedges, to serve

1 Put the beef, rice, 5ml/1 tsp salt, pepper, chopped onions and garlic in a bowl. Beat the eggs with the water, and combine with the meat mixture. Chill in the refrigerator until needed.

2 Cut the core from the cabbage in a cone shape and discard. Bring a large pan of water to the boil, lower the cabbage into the water and blanch for 1–2 minutes, then remove from the pan. Peel one or two layers of leaves off, then re-submerge the cabbage. Repeat until all the leaves are removed.

3 Preheat the oven to 150°C/300°F/Gas 2. Form the beef mixture into ovals, the size of small lemons, and wrap each in one or two cabbage leaves, folding and overlapping the leaves so that the mixture is completely enclosed.

4 Lay the cabbage rolls in the base of a large ovenproof dish, alternating with the sliced onions. Pour the tomatoes over and add the sugar, vinegar or lemon juice, salt, pepper and cinnamon. Cover and bake for 2 hours.

5 During cooking, remove the parcels from the oven and baste them with the tomato juices two or three times. After 2 hours, uncover the dish and cook for a further 30–60 minutes, or until the tomato sauce has thickened and is lightly browned on top. Serve hot with wedges of lemon.

Hunter's Stew Energy 546kcal/2279kJ; Protein 50.4g; Carbohydrate 24.6g, of which sugars 19.8g; Fat 26.4g, of which saturates 9.7g; Cholesterol 149mg; Calcium 213mg; Fibre 7.7g; Sodium 2122mg.
Stuffed Cabbage Energy 425kcal/1773kJ; Protein 29.7g; Carbohydrate 27.5g, of which sugars 17.6g; Fat 22.3g, of which saturates 9.2g; Cholesterol 123mg; Calcium 86mg; Fibre 3.7g; Sodium 134mg.

Steak and Mushroom Pudding with a Herby Suet Crust

This dish can seem like a lot of work, but the results are heaven on an autumn night.

Serves 6

25g/1oz/½ cup dried porcini
    mushrooms, soaked in warm
    water for 20 minutes
1.3kg/3lb rump (round) steak
30ml/2 tbsp plain (all-purpose) flour
30ml/2 tbsp olive or sunflower oil
1 large onion, chopped
225g/8oz chestnut or open cup
    mushrooms, halved if large
300ml/½ pint/1¼ cups red wine
300ml/½ pint/1¼ cups beef stock
45ml/3 tbsp mushroom ketchup
1 bay leaf

For the herby suet crust

275g/10oz/2½ cups self-raising
    (self-rising) flour
5ml/1 tsp baking powder
15ml/1 tbsp each finely chopped
    fresh parsley, sage, rosemary
    and thyme
finely grated rind of 1 lemon
75g/3oz/1½ cups beef or
    vegetable suet (US chilled,
    grated shortening)
50g/2oz/¼ cup butter, chilled
    and grated
1 egg, beaten
juice of ½ lemon
150ml/¼ pint/⅔ cup cold water
salt and ground black pepper

1 Preheat the oven to 180°C/350°F/Gas 4. Drain the porcini mushrooms, reserving the soaking liquid, and roughly chop. Cut the steak into large cubes, then toss with the flour and seasoning.

2 Heat the oil in a large frying pan until very hot. Add the onion and cook, stirring frequently until golden brown. Using a slotted spoon, transfer the onions to an ovenproof casserole. Fry the floured steak in batches until well browned on all sides.

3 Add the meat to the casserole with all the mushrooms. Pour in the reserved soaking liquid, wine and stock, add the ketchup, if using, and the bay leaf. Cover and cook for 1½ hours, until the meat is tender. Allow the mixture to cool completely.

4 To make the crust, butter a deep 1.7 litre/3 pint/7 cup ovenproof bowl. Sift the flour, baking powder and 2.5ml/½ tsp salt into a large mixing bowl. Stir in the herbs and lemon rind and season with pepper. Stir in the suet and butter. Make a well in the centre, add the egg, lemon juice and enough of the cold water to mix and gather into a soft but manageable dough.

5 Knead the dough lightly on a well-floured work surface. Cut off a quarter of the dough and wrap in cling film (plastic wrap). Shape the rest into a ball and roll out into a large round, big enough to line the bowl. Lift up the dough and drop it into the bowl, pressing against the sides to line the bowl evenly. Roll out the reserved pastry to a round large enough to use as a lid.

6 Spoon in the beef filling to within 1cm/½in of the rim. Top up with the gravy. (Keep the rest to serve with the pudding later.) Dampen the edges of the pastry and fit the lid. Press the edges to seal and trim away the excess. Cover with pleated, buttered baking parchment, then with pleated foil. Tie string under the lip of the basin to hold the paper in place, then take it over the top to form a handle. Place in a large pan of simmering water, cover and steam for 1½ hours, topping up with boiling water as necessary. Bring the bowl to the table to serve.

Beef with Chanterelle Mushrooms in a Cream Sauce

The trick here is to use really good beef with no fat and to fry the dried pieces quickly in the hot oil so the outside is well browned and the inside very rare. Chanterelle mushrooms are the most delicious wild mushrooms, yellowy orange in colour and with a shape like inverted umbrellas. Enjoy them throughout the autumn months.

Serves 4

115g/4oz chanterelle mushrooms
2 rump (round) steaks, 175g/6oz
    each, cut into strips
45ml/3 tbsp olive oil
1 garlic clove, crushed
1 shallot, finely chopped
60ml/4 tbsp dry white wine
60ml/4 tbsp double (heavy) cream
25g/1oz/2 tbsp butter
salt and ground black pepper
chopped fresh parsley, to garnish

1 Clean the mushrooms. If you have collected them from the wild, cut off the ends where they have come from the ground and, using kitchen paper, wipe off any leaf matter or moss. Trim the mushrooms, then halve them through the stalk and cap.

2 Dry the beef thoroughly on kitchen paper. Heat a large frying pan over a high heat, then add 30ml/2 tbsp olive oil. Working in batches, add the meat to the hot oil in the pan and quickly brown the strips on all sides.

3 Remove the meat, which should still be very rare, from the pan, set aside and keep warm. Add the remaining olive oil to the pan and reduce the heat. Stir in the garlic and shallot and cook, stirring, for about 1 minute.

4 Increase the heat and add the mushrooms. Season and cook until they start to soften. Add the wine, bring to the boil and add the cream. As the liquid thickens, return the beef to the pan and heat through.

5 Remove the pan from the heat and swirl in the butter. Serve on warmed plates, garnished with the parsley.

Steak Pudding Energy 823kcal/3437kJ; Protein 56.2g; Carbohydrate 46.7g, of which sugars 4.9g; Fat 43.8g, of which saturates 19.5g; Cholesterol 187mg; Calcium 125mg; Fibre 3g; Sodium 224mg.
Beef with Mushrooms Energy 415kcal/1725kJ; Protein 29.9g; Carbohydrate 0.7g, of which sugars 0.6g; Fat 31g, of which saturates 14.2g; Cholesterol 122mg; Calcium 21mg; Fibre 0.4g; Sodium 124mg.

Spicy Pumpkin and Orange Bombe

Pumpkin has a subtle flavour that is transformed with the addition of fruits and spices.

Serves 8
For the sponge
115g/4oz/½ cup unsalted butter
115g/4oz/½ cup caster
   (superfine) sugar
115g/4oz/1 cup self-raising
   (self-rising) flour
2.5ml/½ tsp baking powder
2 eggs

For the ice cream
juice and pared rind of 1 orange
300g/11oz/scant 1½ cups golden
   granulated sugar
300ml/½ pint/1¼ cups water
2 cinnamon sticks, halved
10ml/2 tsp whole cloves
30ml/2 tbsp orange flower water
400g/14oz can unsweetened
   pumpkin purée
300ml/½ pint/1¼ cups extra
   thick double (heavy) cream
2 pieces stem ginger, grated
icing (confectioners') sugar, to dust

1 Preheat the oven to 180°C/350°F/Gas 4. Grease and line a 450g/1lb loaf tin (pan). Beat the butter, caster sugar, flour, baking powder and eggs until creamy. Turn into the tin, level the surface and bake for 30 minutes, until firm in the centre. Leave to cool.

2 Make the ice cream. Cut the pared orange rind into very fine shreds. Heat the sugar and water in a heavy pan until the sugar dissolves, then boil rapidly for 3 minutes. Stir in the orange shreds, juice, cinnamon and cloves and heat gently for 5 minutes. Strain, reserving the rind and spices. Measure 300ml/½ pint/ 1½ cups of the syrup and reserve. Return the spices to the remaining syrup with the orange flower water.

3 Beat the pumpkin purée with 175ml/6fl oz/¾ cup of the measured syrup, the cream and ginger. Pour the mixture into a shallow container and freeze until firm.

4 Line a 1.5 litre/2½ pint/6¼ cup bowl with clear film (plastic wrap). Cut the cake into 1cm/½in slices. Dip them briefly in the remaining strained syrup and use to line the bowl, trimming the pieces to fit. Chill, then fill with the ice cream, level the surface and freeze until firm, preferably overnight. To serve, invert the ice cream on to a serving plate and peel away the film. Dust with icing sugar and serve in wedges with the spiced syrup.

Pear and Sauternes Sorbet

Based on a traditional sorbet that would have been served between savoury courses, this fruity ice is delicately flavoured with the honied bouquet of Sauternes wine, spiked with brandy.

Serves 6
675g/1½lb ripe pears
50g/2oz/¼ cup caster
   (superfine) sugar
250ml/8fl oz/1 cup water
   plus 60ml/4 tbsp extra
250ml/8fl oz/1 cup Sauternes
   wine, plus extra to serve
30ml/2 tbsp brandy
juice of ½ lemon
1 egg white
fresh mint sprigs, dusted with
   icing (confectioners') sugar,
   to decorate

1 Quarter the pears, peel them and cut out the cores. Slice them into a pan and add the sugar and 60ml/4 tbsp of the measured water. Cover and simmer for 10 minutes, or until the pears are just tender.

2 Transfer the pear mixture into a food processor or blender and process until smooth, then scrape into a bowl. Leave to cool, then chill.

3 Stir the wine, brandy and lemon juice into the chilled pear purée with the remaining water.

4 BY HAND: Pour the mixture into a plastic tub or similar freezerproof container, freeze for about 4 hours, then beat it in a food processor or blender until smooth. Return the sorbet to the tub.
USING AN ICE CREAM MAKER: Simply churn the pear mixture in an ice cream maker until thick.

5 Lightly whisk the egg white with a fork until just frothy. Either add to the sorbet in the ice cream maker, or stir into the sorbet in the tub. Churn or return to the freezer until the sorbet is firm.

6 Serve the sorbet in small dessert glasses, with a little extra Sauternes poured over each portion. Decorate with the sugared mint sprigs.

Spicy Pumpkin Bombe Energy 571kcal/2387kJ; Protein 4.2g; Carbohydrate 67g, of which sugars 56.1g; Fat 33.6g, of which saturates 20.5g; Cholesterol 130mg; Calcium 122mg; Fibre 1g; Sodium 168mg.
Pear and Sauternes Sorbet Energy 130kcal/549kJ; Protein 1g; Carbohydrate 22.4g, of which sugars 22.4g; Fat 0.1g, of which saturates 0g; Cholesterol 0mg; Calcium 23mg; Fibre 2.5g; Sodium 20mg.

Pear and Gingerbread Sundaes

The best sundaes do not consist solely of ice cream, but are a feast of flavours that melt into each other, rather like a trifle. Poach the seasonal pears and chill them in advance, so that the dessert can be assembled in minutes. As a finishing touch, serve with wafers.

Serves 4

65g/2½oz/5 tbsp light
  muscovado (brown) sugar
90ml/6 tbsp water
30ml/2 tbsp lemon juice
40g/1½oz/⅓ cup sultanas
  (golden raisins) or raisins
1.5ml/¼ tsp mixed
  (apple pie) spice
4 small pears
150g/5oz moist gingerbread or
  ginger cake
250ml/8fl oz/1 cup vanilla
  ice cream

1 Heat the sugar and water in a heavy pan until the sugar has dissolved. Add the lemon juice, sultanas or raisins and spice. Peel, quarter and core the pears, then add them to the pan. Cover the pan and simmer very gently for 5–10 minutes until the pears are just tender.

2 Leave the pears to cool in the syrup. Using a slotted spoon, lift them out of the syrup and put them in a bowl. Pour the syrup into a jug (pitcher). Chill both the pears and the syrup in the refrigerator.

3 Cut the gingerbread or ginger cake into four pieces and arrange in four glass dishes. Divide the pears among the glasses, then pile vanilla ice cream in the centre of each portion. Pour a little of the syrup over each sundae and serve.

Variation
This extremely quick and easy dessert can be made just as successfully with tart dessert apples in the autumn months. Peel, quarter and core the apples, then cook as for the pears, until just tender. Replace some of the water with clear apple juice to make the apple flavour more intense.

Apple and Cider Sorbet

This dessert has a subtle apple flavour with just a hint of cider. Because the apple purée is very pale, almost white, you can add just a few drops of green food colouring to echo the pale green of the apple skin.

Serves 6

500g/1¼lb green-skinned
  eating apples
150g/5oz/¾ cup caster
  (superfine) sugar
300ml/½ pint/1¼ cups water
250ml/8fl oz/1 cup strong
  dry (hard) cider
few drops of green food
  colouring (optional)
strips of pared lime rind,
  to decorate

1 Quarter, core and roughly chop the apples. Put them in a pan. Add the caster sugar and half the water. Cover and simmer for 10 minutes or until the apples are soft.

2 Press the mixture through a sieve (strainer) placed over a bowl. Discard the apple skins. Stir the cider and the remaining water into the purée. Add a little green colouring, if you like.

3 Pour into a shallow freezer container and freeze for 6 hours, beating with a fork once or twice to break up the ice crystals. Alternatively, churn in an ice cream maker until firm. Scoop into dishes and decorate with strips of lime rind before serving.

Variation
Put 500g/1¼lb/5 cups strawberries in a food processor or blender and process to a purée, then press through a sieve (strainer) into a bowl. Stir in 150g/5oz/¾ cup caster (superfine) sugar and 350ml/12fl oz/1½ cups champagne or sparkling white wine, mixing well until the sugar has dissolved. Pour into a shallow freezer container and freeze for 3 hours. Stiffly whisk an egg white in a grease-free bowl. Remove the ice from the freezer and beat well with a fork, then fold in the egg white. Return to the freezer for 3 hours more. Serve decorated with mint sprigs.

Pear Sundaes Energy 404kcal/1706kJ; Protein 5.2g; Carbohydrate 75.6g, of which sugars 63.7g; Fat 10.3g, of which saturates 3.8g; Cholesterol 15mg; Calcium 125mg; Fibre 4g; Sodium 120mg.
Apple Sorbet Energy 143kcal/610kJ; Protein 0.4g; Carbohydrate 34.6g, of which sugars 34.6g; Fat 0.1g, of which saturates 0g; Cholesterol 0mg; Calcium 20mg; Fibre 1.3g; Sodium 6mg.

Old-fashioned Apple Cake

This old-fashioned dessert is not really a cake at all, but an easy-to-make layered confection of sweetened breadcrumbs, stewed apples and whipped cream. Use a glass bowl to show the different layers, and assemble about an hour before serving so the breadcrumbs stay crisp. The seasonal apples in this dish are complemented by the deep, warm spices, adding to the autumnal feel of this delicious dessert.

Serves 6

1kg/2¼lb tart eating apples

90g/3½oz/½ cup sugar, or to taste
5ml/1 tsp cinnamon
1.5ml/¼ tsp nutmeg
1.5ml/¼ tsp ground cloves (optional)
25g/1oz/2 tbsp butter
175g/6oz/3 cups fresh breadcrumbs
25g/1oz/2 tbsp soft brown sugar
250ml/8fl oz/1 cup double (heavy) cream
10ml/2 tsp icing (confectioners') sugar
5ml/1 tsp vanilla sugar
chopped nuts or grated plain (semisweet) chocolate, to decorate

1 Peel and core the apples and cut them into chunks. Place them in a heavy pan with 250ml/8fl oz/1 cup of water, the sugar, cinnamon, nutmeg and cloves (if using).

2 Cover the pan and cook over low heat, stirring occasionally, for about 25 minutes, until soft but still chunky. Remove from the heat and leave to cool.

3 Melt the butter in a frying pan. Stir in the breadcrumbs and brown sugar, tossing to coat the crumbs evenly with the butter. Cook, stirring constantly, for about 4–5 minutes until the crumbs are lightly browned and toasted. Remove from the heat and set aside.

4 Beat the double cream until soft peaks form and stir in the icing and vanilla sugars. Place a thin layer of breadcrumbs in the bottom of six serving glasses or bowls, cover the breadcrumbs with a layer of apple, then a layer of cream. Repeat the layers, ending with cream. Chill, then decorate before serving.

Mini Toffee Apples

Crunchy apple wedges are fried until crisp in a light batter, then dipped in caramel, to make a sweet, sticky dessert that is perfect for an autumn festival such as Bonfire Night or Halloween.

Serves 4

115g/4oz/1 cup plain (all-purpose) flour

10ml/2 tsp baking powder
60ml/4 tbsp cornflour (cornstarch)
4 firm apples
sunflower oil, for deep-frying
200g/7oz/1 cup caster (superfine) sugar

1 In a large mixing bowl, combine the flour, baking powder, cornflour and 175ml/6fl oz/¾ cup water. Stir to make a smooth batter and set aside.

2 Peel and core the apples, then cut each one into 8 thick wedges. Fill a large bowl with ice cubes and chilled water.

3 Fill a wok one-third full of sunflower oil and heat to 180°C/350°F or until a cube of bread, dropped into the oil, browns in 45 seconds. Working quickly, in batches, dip the apple wedges in the batter, drain off any excess and deep-fry for 2 minutes, or until golden brown. Remove with a slotted spoon and place on kitchen paper to drain.

4 Reheat the oil to 180°C/350°F and fry the wedges for a second time, again giving them about 2 minutes. Drain well on kitchen paper and set aside.

5 Very carefully, pour off all but 30ml/2 tbsp of the oil from the wok and stir in the caster sugar. Heat gently until the sugar melts and starts to caramelize. When the mixture is a light brown colour, add a few pieces of apple at a time and toss to coat evenly.

6 Plunge the coated pieces briefly into the bowl of iced water to set the caramel, then remove from the pan with a slotted spoon and serve immediately.

Apple Cake Energy 498kcal/2090kJ; Protein 4.7g; Carbohydrate 64.3g, of which sugars 42.5g; Fat 26.5g, of which saturates 16.1g; Cholesterol 66mg; Calcium 79mg; Fibre 3.3g; Sodium 261mg.
Toffee Apples Energy 457kcal/1940kJ; Protein 3.4g; Carbohydrate 97.3g, of which sugars 61.6g; Fat 8.8g, of which saturates 1.1g; Cholesterol 0mg; Calcium 73mg; Fibre 2.5g; Sodium 14mg.

Baked Stuffed Apples

The amaretti and apples in this slow-cooker dessert gives a lovely almondy and autumnal flavour. Dried cranberries and glacé fruit add sweetness and colour. Choose apples that will stay firm during cooking.

Serves 4
75g/3oz/6 tbsp butter, softened
45ml/3 tbsp orange or apple juice
75g/3oz/scant ½ cup light
  muscovado (brown) sugar
grated rind and juice of ½ orange
1.5ml/¼ tsp ground cinnamon
30ml/2 tbsp crushed amaretti
25g/1oz/¼ cup pecan
  nuts, chopped
25g/1oz/¼ cup dried cranberries
  or sour cherries
25g/1oz/¼ cup luxury mixed
  glacé (candied) fruit, chopped
4 large cooking apples, such
  as Bramleys
cream, crème fraîche or vanilla
  ice cream, to serve

1 Grease the ceramic cooking pot with 15g/½oz/1 tbsp of the butter, then pour in the fruit juice and switch the slow cooker to the high setting.

2 Put the remaining butter, the sugar, orange rind and juice, cinnamon and amaretti crumbs in a bowl and mix well.

3 Add the nuts and dried cranberries or sour cherries and glacé fruit to the bowl and mix well, then set aside the filling while you prepare the apples.

4 Wash and dry the apples. Remove the cores using an apple corer, then carefully enlarge each core cavity to twice its size, using the corer to shave out more flesh. Using a sharp knife, score each apple around its equator.

5 Divide the filling among the apples, packing it into the hole, then piling it on top. Stand the apples in the cooking pot and cover with the lid. Reduce the temperature to low and cook for 4 hours, or until tender.

6 Transfer the apples to warmed serving plates and spoon the sauce over the top. Serve immediately, with cream, crème fraîche or vanilla ice cream.

Apple Charlottes

These tempting little fruit Charlottes are a wonderful way to use windfalls in the autumn months.

Serves 4
175g/6oz/¾ cup butter
450g/1lb cooking apples
225g/8oz eating apples
60ml/4 tbsp water
130g/4½oz/scant ⅔ cup caster
  (superfine) sugar
2 egg yolks
pinch of grated nutmeg
9 thin slices white bread,
  crusts removed
extra thick double (heavy) cream
  or custard, to serve

1 Preheat the oven to 190°C/375°F/Gas 5. Put a knob (pat) of the butter in a pan. Peel and core the apples, dice them finely and put them in the pan with the water. Cover and cook for 10 minutes or until the cooking apples have pulped down.

2 Stir 115g/4oz/½ cup of the caster sugar into the pan. Boil, uncovered, until any liquid has evaporated and what remains is a thick pulp. Remove from the heat, beat in the egg yolks and nutmeg and set aside.

3 Melt the remaining butter in a separate pan over a low heat until the white curds start to separate from the clear yellow liquid. Remove from the heat. Leave to stand for a few minutes, then strain the clear clarified butter through a sieve (strainer) lined with muslin (cheesecloth), discarding the curds.

4 Brush four 150ml/¼ pint/⅔ cup individual Charlotte moulds or round tins (pans) with a little of the clarified butter; sprinkle with the remaining caster sugar. Cut the bread slices into 2.5cm/1in strips. Dip the strips into the remaining clarified butter; use to line the moulds or tins. Overlap the strips on the base to give the effect of a swirl and let the excess bread overhang the tops of the moulds or tins.

5 Fill each bread case with apple pulp. Fold the excess bread over the top of each mould or tin to make a lid and press down lightly. Bake for 45–50 minutes until golden. Run a knife between each Charlotte and its mould or tin, then turn out on to dessert plates. Serve immediately with cream or custard.

Baked Stuffed Apples Energy 347kcal/1457kJ; Protein 1.6g; Carbohydrate 42.4g, of which sugars 41.3g; Fat 20.3g, of which saturates 10.3g; Cholesterol 40mg; Calcium 27mg; Fibre 3g; Sodium 131mg.
Apple Charlottes Energy 686kcal/2874kJ; Protein 7.5g; Carbohydrate 79.2g, of which sugars 50.8g; Fat 40g, of which saturates 23.6g; Cholesterol 194mg; Calcium 111mg; Fibre 3.6g; Sodium 591mg.

Noodle Kugel Flavoured with Apple and Cinnamon

This blissfully buttery noodle kugel, which is fragrant with cinnamon and apples and oozing autumnal charm, was brought to North America from Russia. Use flat egg noodles that are at least 1cm/½in wide.

Serves 4–6
350–500g/12oz–1¼lb egg noodles
130g/4½oz/generous ½ cup plus 15ml/1 tbsp unsalted butter

2 well-flavoured cooking apples
250g/9oz/generous 1 cup cottage cheese
3–4 eggs, lightly beaten
10ml/2 tsp ground cinnamon
250g/9oz/1¼ cups sugar
2–3 handfuls of raisins
2.5ml/½ tsp bicarbonate of soda (baking soda)
salt

1 Preheat the oven to 180°C/350°C/Gas 4. Cook the noodles in salted boiling water according to the directions on the packet, or until just tender, then drain.

2 Melt the butter in a pan, then add it to the noodles and toss together well so the noodles are well buttered.

3 Coarsely grate the apples and add to the noodles, then stir in the cottage cheese, eggs, cinnamon, sugar, raisins, bicarbonate of soda and a tiny pinch of salt.

4 Transfer the noodle mixture into a deep rectangular ovenproof dish, measuring about 38 × 20cm/15 × 8in. Bake in the preheated oven for about 1–1¼ hours, until browned and crisp. Serve immediately.

Cook's Tip
This kugel is also good served cold. Serve any leftovers the next day, as a snack.

Poached Pears in Red Wine

In this recipe, the pears take on a red blush from the wine and make a very pretty dessert. For best results, use a small slow cooker, which ensures that the pears stay submerged during cooking.

Serves 4
1 bottle fruity red wine
150g/5oz/¾ cup caster (superfine) sugar

45ml/3 tbsp clear honey
1 cinnamon stick
1 vanilla pod (bean), split lengthways
large strip of lemon or orange rind
2 whole cloves
2 black peppercorns
4 firm ripe pears
juice of ½ lemon
mint leaves, to decorate
whipped cream or sour cream, to serve

1 Pour the red wine into the ceramic cooking pot. Add the sugar, honey, cinnamon stick, vanilla pod, lemon or orange rind, cloves and peppercorns. Cover with the lid and cook on high for 30 minutes, stirring occasionally.

2 Meanwhile, peel the pears using a vegetable peeler, leaving the stem intact. Take a very thin slice off the base of each pear so it will stand square and upright. As each pear is peeled, toss it in the lemon juice to prevent the flesh browning when exposed to the air.

3 Place the pears in the spiced wine mixture in the cooking pot. Cover with the lid and cook for 2–4 hours, turning the pears occasionally, until they are just tender; be careful not to overcook them.

4 Transfer the pears to a bowl, using a slotted spoon. Continue to cook the wine mixture, uncovered, for a further hour, until reduced and thickened a little, then turn off the slow cooker and leave to cool. Alternatively, to save time, pour the cooking liquor into a pan and boil briskly for 10–15 minutes.

5 Strain the cooled liquid over the pears and chill for at least 3 hours. Divide the pears between four individual serving dishes and spoon a little of the wine syrup over each one. Garnish with fresh mint and serve with whipped or sour cream.

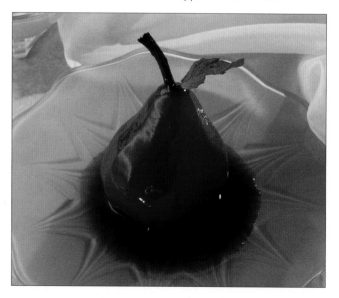

Noodle Kugel Energy 686kcal/2889kJ; Protein 16.2g; Carbohydrate 100.6g, of which sugars 59.9g; Fat 27.1g, of which saturates 14.4g; Cholesterol 165mg; Calcium 118mg; Fibre 2.4g; Sodium 409mg.
Poached Pears in Red Wine Energy 87kcal/367kJ; Protein 0.5g; Carbohydrate 16.6g, of which sugars 16.6g; Fat 0.2g, of which saturates 0g; Cholesterol 0mg; Calcium 19mg; Fibre 3.3g; Sodium 7mg.

Pears in Chocolate Fudge Blankets

Warm poached pears coated in a rich chocolate fudge sauce – nobody can resist this autumn treat.

Serves 6
6 ripe eating pears
30ml/2 tbsp fresh lemon juice
75g/3oz/6 tbsp caster
    (superfine) sugar
300ml/½ pint/1¼ cups water
1 cinnamon stick

For the sauce
200ml/7fl oz/scant 1 cup double
    (heavy) cream
150g/5oz/scant 1 cup light
    muscovado (brown) sugar
25g/1oz/2 tbsp unsalted butter
60ml/4 tbsp golden
    (light corn) syrup
120ml/4fl oz/½ cup milk
200g/7oz plain (semisweet)
    chocolate, broken into squares

1 Peel the pears thinly, leaving the stalks on. Scoop out the cores from the base. Brush the cut surfaces with lemon juice to prevent browning.

2 Place the sugar and water in a large pan. Heat gently until the sugar dissolves. Add the pears and cinnamon stick with any remaining lemon juice, and, if necessary, a little more water, so that the pears are almost covered.

3 Bring to the boil, then lower the heat, cover the pan and simmer the pears gently for 15–20 minutes.

4 Meanwhile, make the sauce. Place the cream, sugar, butter, golden syrup and milk in a heavy pan. Heat gently until the sugar has dissolved and the butter and syrup have melted, then bring to the boil. Boil, stirring constantly, for about 5 minutes or until thick and smooth.

5 Remove the pan from the heat and stir in the chocolate, a few squares at a time, stirring until it has all melted.

6 Using a slotted spoon, transfer the poached pears to a dish. Keep hot. Boil the syrup rapidly to reduce to 45–60ml/ 3–4 tbsp. Remove the cinnamon stick and gently stir the syrup into the chocolate sauce. Serve the pears with the sauce spooned over.

Pear and Almond Tart

This tart is equally successful made with other kinds of fruit – variations can be seen in almost every good French pâtisserie.

Serves 6
350g/12oz shortcrust or sweet
    shortcrust pastry
3 firm pears
lemon juice
15ml/1 tbsp peach brandy
    or water

60ml/4 tbsp peach
    preserve, strained

For the almond cream filling
115g/4oz/¾ cup blanched
    whole almonds
50g/2oz/¼ cup caster
    (superfine) sugar
65g/2½oz/5 tbsp butter
1 egg, plus 1 egg white
few drops almond extract

1 Roll out the pastry thinly and use to line a 23cm/9in flan tin (tart pan). Chill the pastry case (pie shell). Meanwhile, make the filling. Put the almonds and sugar in a food processor and pulse until finely ground (not a paste). Add the butter and process until creamy. Add the egg, egg white and almond extract and mix well.

2 Place a baking sheet in the oven and preheat to 190°C/ 375°F/Gas 5. Peel the pears, halve them, remove the cores and rub with lemon juice. Put the pear halves, cut-side down, on a board and slice thinly crossways, keeping the slices together.

3 Pour the almond cream filling into the pastry case. Slide a metal spatula under one pear half and press the top with your fingers to fan out the slices. Transfer to the tart, placing the fruit on the filling like spokes of a wheel. If you like, remove a few slices from each half before arranging and use to fill in any gaps in the centre.

4 Place on the baking sheet and bake for 50–55 minutes until the filling is set and well browned. Cool on a rack.

5 Meanwhile, heat the brandy or water and the preserve in a small pan, then brush over the top of the hot tart to glaze. Serve the tart warm, or at room temperature.

Pears in Chocolate Energy 613kcal/2570kJ; Protein 3.6g; Carbohydrate 84.8g, of which sugars 84.5g; Fat 31.2g, of which saturates 19.1g; Cholesterol 58mg; Calcium 90mg; Fibre 4.1g; Sodium 77mg.
Pear Tart Energy 558kcal/2326kJ; Protein 8.6g; Carbohydrate 50.3g, of which sugars 24.4g; Fat 37.2g, of which saturates 6.8g; Cholesterol 55mg; Calcium 92mg; Fibre 4.2g; Sodium 189mg.

Quince Mousse with Almond Biscuits

Quinces and ginger are perfectly matched flavour partners in the autumn.

Serves 4

450g/1lb quinces, peeled and cored
75g/3oz/⅓ cup caster
   (superfine) sugar
grated rind of ½ lemon
90ml/6 tbsp water
2 pieces stem ginger in syrup,
   finely chopped, plus 15ml/
   1 tbsp syrup from the jar
15ml/1 tbsp powdered gelatine

150ml/¼ pint/⅔ cup double
   (heavy) cream
2 egg whites
mint leaves and blackberries
   dusted with caster (superfine)
   sugar, to decorate

For the biscuits (cookies)
50g/2oz/¼ cup butter
30ml/2 tbsp caster (superfine) sugar
50g/2oz/½ cup plain
   (all-purpose) flour
50g/2oz/½ cup ground almonds
a few drops of almond extract

1 Grease four ramekins and line with baking parchment. Put the quinces in a pan with the sugar, lemon rind and 60ml/4 tbsp of the water. Cover and simmer for 10 minutes or until soft. Remove the lid and cook until the liquid has almost evaporated.

2 Cool the quinces slightly, then purée in a food processor or blender. Press the purée through a sieve (strainer) into a large bowl, then stir in the ginger and syrup and set aside.

3 Pour the remaining 30ml/2 tbsp water into a bowl and sprinkle the gelatine on top. Leave for 5 minutes. Stand the bowl in a pan of hot water until the gelatine has dissolved.

4 Whip the cream. Stir the gelatine into the quince purée, then fold in the cream. Whisk the egg whites to stiff peaks and fold into the quince mixture. Divide among the ramekins, level the tops and chill until firm. Preheat the oven to 190°C/375°F/Gas 5.

5 Make the biscuits. Line a baking sheet with baking parchment. Cream the butter and sugar. Add the flour, almonds and extract and mix to a dough. Roll out and cut into rounds with a 7.5cm/ 3in cutter. Chill on the sheet for 10 minutes. Bake for 12 minutes. Cool slightly on the paper, then lift on to a wire rack to cool. Turn out the mousse on to plates. Decorate and serve.

Hot Quince Soufflés

These delicious fruits are more often picked in the autumn than purchased as they are seldom found in stores or markets. You can use pears instead in the autumn months, but the flavour will not be as intense as the quinces.

Serves 6

2 quinces, peeled and cored
60ml/4 tbsp water
115g/4oz/½ cup caster (superfine)
   sugar, plus extra for sprinkling

5 egg whites
melted butter, for greasing
icing (confectioners') sugar,
   for dusting

For the pastry cream
250ml/8fl oz/1 cup milk
1 vanilla pod (bean)
3 egg yolks
75g/3oz/⅓ cup caster
   (superfine) sugar
25g/1oz/¼ cup plain
   (all-purpose) flour
15ml/1 tbsp Poire William liqueur

1 Cut the quinces into cubes. Place in a pan with the water. Stir in half the sugar. Bring to the boil, lower the heat, cover and simmer for 10 minutes or until tender. Remove the lid; boil until most of the liquid has evaporated.

2 Cool the quince mixture slightly, then purée the fruit in a blender or food processor. Press through a sieve (strainer) into a bowl; set aside.

3 Make the pastry cream. Pour the milk into a small pan. Add the vanilla pod and bring to the boil over low heat. Meanwhile, beat the egg yolks, caster sugar and flour in a bowl until smooth.

4 Gradually strain the hot milk on to the eggs and sugar in the bowl, whisking frequently until the mixture is smooth.

5 Discard the vanilla pod. Return the mixture to the clean pan and heat gently, stirring until thickened. Cook for a further 2 minutes, whisking constantly, to ensure that the sauce is smooth and the flour is cooked.

6 Remove the pan from the heat and stir in the quince purée and liqueur. Cover the surface of the pastry cream with clear film (plastic wrap) to prevent it from forming a skin. Allow to cool slightly, while you prepare the ramekins.

7 Preheat the oven to 220°C/425°F/Gas 7. Place a large baking sheet in the oven to heat up. Generously butter six 150ml/¼ pint/⅔ cup ramekins and sprinkle the inside of each with caster sugar.

8 In a grease-free bowl, whisk the egg whites to stiff peaks. Gradually whisk in the remaining caster sugar, then fold the egg whites into the pastry cream.

9 Divide the mixture among the prepared ramekins and level the surface of each. Carefully run a sharp knife between the side of each ramekin and the mixture, then place the ramekins on the hot baking sheet and bake for 8–10 minutes until the tops of the soufflés are well risen and golden. Generously dust the tops with icing sugar and serve the soufflés immediately.

Quince Mousse Energy 534kcal/2226kJ; Protein 6.4g; Carbohydrate 50.3g, of which sugars 40.4g; Fat 37.6g, of which saturates 18.6g; Cholesterol 78mg; Calcium 95mg; Fibre 3.8g; Sodium 145mg.
Quince Soufflés Energy 218kcal/926kJ; Protein 5.9g; Carbohydrate 43.4g, of which sugars 40.2g; Fat 3.6g, of which saturates 1.2g; Cholesterol 103mg; Calcium 91mg; Fibre 1.2g; Sodium 82mg.

Figs and Pears in Honey with Cardamom

Fresh figs picked straight from the tree are so delicious that it seems almost sacrilege to cook them – unless you have so many during the fruit's season that you fancy a change – when you can try this superb recipe.

Serves 4
1 lemon
90ml/6 tbsp clear honey
1 cinnamon stick
1 cardamom pod
350ml/12fl oz/1 1/2 cups water
2 pears
8 fresh figs, halved

1 Pare the rind from the lemon using a cannelle knife (zester) or vegetable peeler and cut the rind into very thin strips.

2 Place the lemon rind, honey, cinnamon stick, cardamom pod and the water in a pan and boil, uncovered, for about 10 minutes, until the liquid is reduced by about half.

3 Cut the pears into eighths, discarding the core. Leave the peel on or discard, as preferred.

4 Place the pear pieces in the syrup; add the figs. Bring the mixture to just near boiling point, then reduce the heat and simmer for about 5 minutes, until the fruit is tender.

5 Transfer the fruit from the pan to a serving bowl with a slotted spoon. Cook the liquid until syrupy, discard the cinnamon stick and pour the sauce over the figs and pears. Serve warm or cold.

> **Cook's Tip**
> The season for fresh figs reaches its peak in September and October, so make this dish earlier in the autumn rather than later. Figs are extremely perishable and should be used as soon after purchase as possible. Store fresh figs in the refrigerator for about 2 to 3 days.

Honey Baked Figs with Hazelnut Ice Cream

Figs baked in a lemon grass-scented honey syrup have the most wonderful flavour, especially when served with a good-quality ice cream dotted with roasted hazelnuts. If you prefer to avoid nuts, because you don't like them or because a guest has an allergy, use plain rich vanilla or toffee ice cream instead.

Serves 4
1 lemon grass stalk, finely chopped
1 cinnamon stick, roughly broken
60ml/4 tbsp clear honey
200ml/7fl oz/scant 1 cup water
75g/3oz/3/4 cup hazelnuts
8 large ripe dessert figs
400ml/14fl oz/1 2/3 cups good-quality vanilla ice cream
30ml/2 tbsp hazelnut liqueur (optional)

1 Preheat the oven to 190°C/375°F/Gas 5. Make the syrup by mixing the lemon grass, cinnamon stick, honey and measured water in a small pan. Heat gently, stirring until the honey has dissolved, then bring to the boil. Simmer for 2 minutes.

2 Meanwhile, spread out the hazelnuts on a baking sheet and grill (broil) under medium heat until golden brown. Shake the sheet occasionally, so that they are evenly toasted.

3 Cut the figs into quarters, leaving them intact at the bases. Stand the figs in a baking dish and pour the syrup over. Cover the dish tightly with foil and bake for 13–15 minutes until the figs are tender.

4 While the figs are baking, remove the ice cream from the freezer and let it soften slightly. Chop the hazelnuts roughly and beat the softened ice cream briefly with an electric beater, then fold in the toasted hazelnuts until evenly distributed.

5 To serve, puddle a little of the syrup from the figs on to each individual dessert plate. Arrange the figs on top and add a spoonful of the nutty ice cream. At the very last moment before serving, spoon a little hazelnut liqueur over the ice cream, if you like.

Figs and Pears Energy 143kcal/606kJ; Protein 1.7g; Carbohydrate 34.4g, of which sugars 34.4g; Fat 0.7g, of which saturates 0g; Cholesterol 0mg; Calcium 109mg; Fibre 4.7g; Sodium 28mg.
Honey Baked Figs Energy 433kcal/1816kJ; Protein 7.8g; Carbohydrate 53.6g, of which sugars 52.1g; Fat 21.2g, of which saturates 7g; Cholesterol 24mg; Calcium 227mg; Fibre 4.2g; Sodium 88mg.

Fig and Walnut Torte

This recipe is a sweet, delicious treat for the autumn months.

Makes 20–25 pieces
75g/3oz/⅓ cup butter, melted, plus extra for greasing
175g/6oz/1½ cups walnuts, finely chopped
115g/4oz/1 cup ground almonds
75g/3oz/⅓ cup caster (superfine) sugar
10ml/2 tsp ground cinnamon

9 sheets of filo pastry, thawed if frozen, each cut into two 30 x 20cm/12 x 8in rectangles
4 fresh figs, sliced
Greek (US strained plain) yogurt, to serve

For the syrup
350g/12oz/1½ cups caster (superfine) sugar
4 whole cloves
1 cinnamon stick
2 strips of lemon rind

1 Preheat the oven to 160°C/325°F/Gas 3. Grease a 30 × 20cm/12 × 8in shallow baking tin (pan) with melted butter. Mix the walnuts, ground almonds, sugar and cinnamon and set aside.

2 Fit a sheet of filo pastry in the base of the tin. Brush with some melted butter and place a sheet of filo on top. Repeat this until you have layered up eight sheets. Spoon half the nut mixture over the pastry to the edges, and top with the fig slices. Place two filo sheets on top of the figs, brushing each with more melted butter as before, then evenly spoon over the remaining nut mixture.

3 Layer the remaining filo sheets on top, buttering each one. Brush melted butter over the top of the torte, then score the surface in a diamond pattern. Bake for 1 hour until golden.

4 Meanwhile, make the syrup. Place all the ingredients in a pan and mix well. Heat, stirring, until the sugar has dissolved. Bring to the boil, lower the heat and simmer for 10 minutes until syrupy, stirring occasionally.

5 Allow the syrup to cool for about 15 minutes, then strain it evenly over the hot torte. Allow to cool and leave to soak for 2–3 hours, then cut the torte into diamonds or squares and serve with Greek yogurt.

Papaya Baked with Ginger

Ginger enhances the flavour of papaya in this recipe, which takes no more than ten minutes to prepare. Don't overcook the papaya or the flesh will become very watery.

Serves 4
2 ripe papayas
2 pieces stem ginger in syrup, drained, plus 15ml/1 tbsp syrup from the jar

8 amaretti or other dessert biscuits (cookies), coarsely crushed
45ml/3 tbsp raisins
shredded, finely pared rind and juice of 1 lime
25g/1oz/¼ cup pistachio nuts, chopped
15ml/1 tbsp light muscovado (brown) sugar
60ml/4 tbsp crème fraîche, plus extra to serve

1 Preheat the oven to 200°C/400°F/Gas 6. Cut the papayas in half and scoop out their seeds. Place the halves in a baking dish and set aside. Cut the stem ginger into fine matchsticks.

2 Make the filling. Combine the crushed amaretti biscuits, stem ginger matchsticks and raisins in a bowl. Stir in the lime rind and juice, two-thirds of the nuts, then add the sugar and the crème fraîche. Mix well.

3 Fill the papaya halves and drizzle with the ginger syrup. Sprinkle with the remaining nuts. Bake for about 25 minutes or until tender. Serve with extra crème fraîche.

Cook's Tip
If crème fraîche is not available, make your own version. Combine 250ml/8fl oz/1 cup whipping cream and 30ml/2 tbsp buttermilk in a glass bowl. Cover at room temperature for 8 to 24 hours, or until thick. Stir well, cover and refrigerate for up to 10 days.

Variation
You can use almonds or walnuts instead of pistachio nuts.

Fig Torte Energy 218kcal/915kJ; Protein 3.5g; Carbohydrate 29.2g, of which sugars 22.2g; Fat 10.5g, of which saturates 2.3g; Cholesterol 15mg; Calcium 59mg; Fibre 1.4g; Sodium 32mg.
Papaya with Ginger Energy 292kcal/1228kJ; Protein 3.6g; Carbohydrate 44.6g, of which sugars 35.7g; Fat 12.3g, of which saturates 5.7g; Cholesterol 17mg; Calcium 84mg; Fibre 4.2g; Sodium 127mg.

Butternut Squash and Maple Pie

This American-style autumn pie has a crisp pastry case and a creamy filling, sweetened with maple syrup and flavoured with fresh ginger and a dash of brandy.

Serves 10
1 small butternut squash
60ml/4 tbsp water
2.5cm/1in piece fresh root ginger, peeled and grated
275g/10oz shortcrust pastry
120ml/4fl oz/½ cup double (heavy) cream
90ml/6 tbsp maple syrup
40g/1½oz/3 tbsp light muscovado (brown) sugar
3 eggs, lightly beaten
30ml/2 tbsp brandy
1.5ml/¼ tsp grated nutmeg
beaten egg, to glaze

1 Halve the squash, peel and scoop out the seeds. Cut the flesh into cubes and put in a pan with the water. Cover and cook gently for 15 minutes. Uncover, stir in the ginger and cook for a further 5 minutes until the liquid has evaporated and the squash is tender. Cool slightly, then purée in a food processor.

2 Roll out the pastry and use to line a 23cm/9in flan tin (pan). Re-roll the trimmings, then cut into maple leaf shapes. Brush the edge of the pastry case with beaten egg and attach the leaf shapes at regular intervals to make a decorative rim. Cover with clear film (plastic wrap) and chill for 30 minutes.

3 Put a heavy baking sheet in the oven and preheat to 200°C/400°F/Gas 6. Prick the pastry base, line with foil and fill with baking beans. Bake blind on the baking sheet for 12 minutes.

4 Remove the foil and beans and bake for a further 5 minutes. Brush the base of the pastry case with beaten egg and return to the oven for about 3 minutes. Lower the oven temperature to 180°C/350°F/Gas 4.

5 Mix 200g/7oz/scant 1 cup of the butternut purée with the cream, syrup, sugar, eggs, brandy and nutmeg. (Discard any remaining purée.) Pour into the pastry case. Bake for about 30 minutes, until the filling is lightly set. Leave to cool slightly and serve immediately.

Blackberry Ice Cream

There could scarcely be fewer ingredients in this delicious, vibrant ice cream. Blackberries are a feature of early autumn and can often be picked wild on hedges at the side of roads and country paths. Use store-bought cookies or make your own.

Serves 4–6
500g/1¼lb/5 cups blackberries, hulled, plus extra, to decorate
75g/3oz/6 tbsp caster (superfine) sugar
30ml/2 tbsp water
300ml/½ pint/1¼ cups whipping cream
crisp dessert biscuits (cookies), to serve

1 Put the blackberries into a pan, and add the sugar and water. Cover and simmer for 5 minutes until just soft. Place the fruit in a sieve (strainer) over a bowl and press it through using a wooden spoon. Leave to cool, then chill.

2 BY HAND: Whip the cream until it is just thick but still soft enough to fall from a spoon, then mix it with the chilled fruit purée. Pour the mixture into a plastic tub or similar freezerproof container and freeze for 2 hours.
USING AN ICE CREAM MAKER: Churn the chilled purée for 10–15 minutes until it is thick, then gradually pour in the cream. There is no need to whip the cream first.

3 BY HAND: Mash the mixture with a fork, or beat it in a food processor to break up the ice crystals. Return it to the freezer for 4 hours more, beating the mixture again after 2 hours.
USING AN ICE CREAM MAKER: Continue to churn the ice cream until it is firm enough to scoop.

4 Scoop into dishes and decorate with extra blackberries. Serve with crisp dessert biscuits.

Variation
- *Frozen blackberries can be used for the purée. You will need to increase the cooking time to 10 minutes.*
- *Blackcurrants can be used instead of blackberries.*

Butternut Pie Energy 266kcal/1109kJ; Protein 4g; Carbohydrate 26.2g, of which sugars 13.7g; Fat 16.1g, of which saturates 4.6g; Cholesterol 74mg; Calcium 56mg; Fibre 1.4g; Sodium 92mg.
Blackberry Ice Energy 261kcal/1081kJ; Protein 1.8g; Carbohydrate 18.7g, of which sugars 18.7g; Fat 20.3g, of which saturates 12.6g; Cholesterol 53mg; Calcium 70mg; Fibre 2.6g; Sodium 15mg.

Cinnamon Squash

Lightly cooked butternut squash makes a delicious smoothie. It has a wonderfully rich, rounded flavour that is lifted perfectly by the addition of tart citrus juice and warm, spicy cinnamon. Imagine pumpkin pie as a gorgeous smooth drink and you're halfway to experiencing the flavours of this lusciously sweet and tantalizing treat.

Serves 2–3

1 small butternut squash, total weight about 600g/1lb 6oz
2.5ml/½ tsp ground cinnamon
3 large lemons
1 grapefruit
60ml/4 tbsp light muscovado (brown) sugar
ice cubes

1 Cut the squash in half, scoop out the seeds using a spoon and discard. Cut the flesh into chunks. Using a sharp knife, cut away the skin and discard.

2 Steam or boil the squash for 10–15 minutes until just tender. Drain well and leave to stand until cool.

3 Put the cooled squash in a blender or food processor and add the ground cinnamon.

4 Squeeze the lemons and grapefruit and pour the juice over the squash, then add the muscovado sugar.

5 Process the ingredients until they are smooth. If necessary, pause to scrape down the side of the processor or blender.

6 Put a few ice cubes in two or three short glasses and pour over the smoothie. Serve immediately.

Cook's Tip
If you can only buy a large squash, cook it all and add the leftovers to stew or soup.

Sweet Dream

A soothing blend guaranteed to wake you up slowly, this fruity threesome is naturally sweet so there is no need for any additional sugar. Fresh grapefruit juice marries brilliantly with the dried fruits, and rich creamy yogurt makes a delicious contrast of colour and flavour – simply perfect to sip over a leisurely breakfast while reading the newspaper.

Serves 2

25g/1oz/scant ¼ cup dried figs or dates, stoned (pitted)
50g/2oz/¼ cup ready-to-eat prunes
25g/1oz/scant ¼ cup sultanas (golden raisins)
1 grapefruit
350ml/12fl oz/1½ cups full cream (whole) milk
30ml/2 tbsp Greek (US strained plain) yogurt

1 Put the dried fruits in a blender or food processor. Squeeze out the grapefruit juice and add to the machine. Blend until smooth, scraping the mixture down from the side of the bowl, if necessary.

2 Pour the milk into the blender or processor. Blend the mixture until it is completely smooth, scraping down the sides as before.

3 Using a teaspoon, tap a spoonful of the yogurt around the inside of each of two tall glasses so that it runs up in a spiral pattern – don't worry if it isn't too neat. Pour in the fruit mixture and serve immediately.

Variations
• To make a dairy-free version of this drink, omit the Greek (US strained plain) yogurt and use soya or rice milk instead of ordinary milk. The consistency of the smoothie will not be as creamy but it will still be delicious – and perhaps better for those who prefer a lighter drink in the morning. It will also be drinkable by those on a dairy-free diet.
• Other dried fruits can be used as well: try raisins, currants or ready-to-eat dried apricots.

Cinnamon Squash Energy 121kcal/513kJ; Protein 1.9g; Carbohydrate 28.9g, of which sugars 27.9g; Fat 0.5g, of which saturates 0.2g; Cholesterol 0mg; Calcium 81mg; Fibre 2.7g; Sodium 3mg.
Sweet Dream Energy 246kcal/1033kJ; Protein 8.6g; Carbohydrate 38.3g, of which sugars 38.3g; Fat 7.4g, of which saturates 4.5g; Cholesterol 25mg; Calcium 301mg; Fibre 3.7g; Sodium 103mg.

Sweet Sharp Shock

The taste-tingling combination of sweet red grape and tart apple is quite delicious. Grapes are full of natural sugars and, mixed with apple juice, they'll create a seasonal juice that's full of pep and zing. Grapes are also renowned for their cleansing properties, making this an ideal addition to any detox regime. For a longer drink, top up with sparkling mineral water.

Serves I

150g/5oz/1¼ cups red grapes
1 green-skinned eating apple
1 small cooking apple
crushed ice

1 Slice some grapes and a sliver or two of the eating apple and set aside to use later for the decoration.

2 Chop the remainder of the eating apple and the cooking apple. Push the pieces through a juicer, followed by the grapes.

3 Pour over crushed ice, decorate with the sliced fruit and serve immediately.

Variation
If you can't find red grapes or green eating apples, then choose another coloured variety of both fruits. The colour may be different but the taste of the drink will be just as delicious.

Cook's Tip
The simplest flavour combinations are often the most delicious. Sugary grapes together with mouth-puckeringly tart apples is one of those perfect pairings that simply cannot be beaten. The fact that the seasons for the fruits coincide in the autumn months makes this drink an absolute must at this time of year.

Pink and Perky

This deliciously refreshing, rose-tinged blend of grapefruit and pear juice will keep you bright-eyed and bushy-tailed. It's perfect for a quick breakfast drink or as a pick-me-up later in the day when energy levels are flagging. If the grapefruit is particularly tart, serve with a little bowl of brown sugar to sweeten, or use brown sugar stirrers.

Serves 2

1 pink and 1 white grapefruit, halved
2 ripe pears
ice cubes

1 Take a thin slice from one grapefruit half and cut a few thin slices of pear. Roughly chop the remaining pear and push through a juicer.

2 Squeeze all the juice from the grapefruit halves. Mix the fruit juices together and serve over ice. Decorate with the grapefruit and pear slices.

Variation
You can use tart, ripe eating apples instead of pears.

Cook's Tip
Pears are a popular fruit throughout the autumn months. Unlike most fruit, pears improve in texture and flavour after they have been plucked from the tree. This means they can be picked and transported while still hard, preventing damage to this easily bruised fruit. Ripe pears are juicy and, depending on the variety, can range in flavour from spicy to sweet to tart-sweet. When buying, choose specimens that are fragrant and free of any blemishes. Store pears at room temperature until they are ripe but refrigerate any ripe fruit.

Sweet Sharp Shock Energy 178kcal/763kJ; Protein 1.4g; Carbohydrate 45.4g, of which sugars 45.4g; Fat 0.4g, of which saturates 0g; Cholesterol 0mg; Calcium 30mg; Fibre 5.1g; Sodium 8mg.
Pink and Perky Energy 216kcal/910kJ; Protein 3.5g; Carbohydrate 51.8g, of which sugars 51.8g; Fat 0.6g, of which saturates 0g; Cholesterol 0mg; Calcium 107mg; Fibre 10.8g; Sodium 19mg.

Curried Cauliflower Soup

This spicy, creamy soup is perfect for lunch on a cold winter's day served with crusty bread and garnished with fresh coriander.

Serves 4
750ml/1¼ pints/3 cups milk
1 large cauliflower
15ml/1 tbsp garam masala
salt and ground black pepper

1 Pour the milk into a large pan and place over medium heat. Cut the cauliflower into florets and add to the milk with the garam masala. Season with salt and pepper.

2 Bring the milk to the boil, then reduce the heat, partially cover the pan with a lid and simmer for about 20 minutes, or until the cauliflower is tender.

3 Let the mixture cool for a few minutes, then transfer to a food processor or blender and process until smooth (you may have to do this in two batches).

4 Return the purée to the rinsed-out pan and heat through gently, checking and adjusting the seasoning. Ladle into warm bowls and serve immediately.

Variation
Cauliflower lends itself beautifully to mildly curried recipes, but you can also make broccoli soup in the same way, using the same weight of broccoli in place of the cauliflower.

Cook's Tip
There is no need to discard all the outer leaves from a cauliflower when making soup. Trim off any wilted or badly damaged green parts and stalks, and any very tough stalk. Then cut off the florets and dice the larger parts of the stalk. Thinly slice the leafy parts from around the sides. Add all these to the pan and they will bring excellent flavour to the soup. When they are cut smaller they cook as quickly as florets.

Roast Vegetable Medley

This soup recipe for chunky roasted roots makes the most of winter vegetables. Serve it with bread baked with a hint of added summer flavour in the form of sun-dried tomatoes.

few sprigs of fresh thyme
1 bulb garlic, broken into cloves, unpeeled
1 litre/1¾ pints/4 cups vegetable stock
salt and ground black pepper
fresh thyme sprigs, to garnish

Serves 4
4 parsnips, quartered lengthways
2 red onions, cut into thin wedges
4 carrots, thickly sliced
2 leeks, thickly sliced
1 small swede (rutabaga), cut into chunks
4 potatoes, cut into chunks
60ml/4 tbsp olive oil

For the sun-dried tomato bread
1 ciabatta loaf
75g/3oz/6 tbsp butter, softened
1 garlic clove, crushed
4 sun-dried tomatoes, finely chopped
30ml/2 tbsp chopped fresh parsley

1 Preheat the oven to 200°C/400°F/Gas 6. Cut the thick ends of the parsnip quarters into four, then place them in a large roasting pan. Add the onions, carrots, leeks, swede and potatoes, and spread them in an even layer.

2 Drizzle the olive oil over the vegetables. Add the thyme and unpeeled garlic cloves. Toss well and roast for 45 minutes, until all the vegetables are tender and slightly charred.

3 To make the sun-dried tomato bread, slice the loaf, without cutting right through. Mix the butter, garlic, sun-dried tomatoes and parsley. Spread the butter between the slices. Wrap in foil. Bake for 15 minutes, opening the foil for the last 4–5 minutes.

4 Discard the thyme from the vegetables. Squeeze the garlic from its skins over the vegetables and purée half the mixture with the stock. Pour into a pan. Add the remaining vegetables. Bring to the boil and season well.

5 Ladle the soup into bowls and garnish with fresh thyme leaves. Serve the hot bread with the soup.

Cauliflower Soup Energy 136kcal/575kJ; Protein 11.5g; Carbohydrate 13.3g, of which sugars 12g; Fat 4.6g, of which saturates 2.2g; Cholesterol 11mg; Calcium 259mg; Fibre 3.1g; Sodium 100mg.
Vegetable Medley: Energy 511kcal/2146kJ; Protein 13.9g; Carbohydrate 72.6g, of which sugars 18.9g; Fat 20.4g, of which saturates 10.6g; Cholesterol 40mg; Calcium 218mg; Fibre 12.1g; Sodium 521mg.

Peanut and Potato Soup

In this Latin-American soup, the peanuts are used as a thickening agent, with delicious results.

Serves 6
60ml/4 tbsp groundnut
   (peanut) oil
1 onion, finely chopped
2 garlic cloves, crushed
1 red (bell) pepper, seeded
   and chopped
250g/9oz potatoes, peeled and diced

2 fresh red chillies, seeded
   and chopped
200g/7oz canned
   chopped tomatoes
150g/5oz/1¼ cups
   unsalted peanuts
1.5 litres/2½ pints/6¼ cups
   vegetable stock
salt and ground black pepper
30ml/2 tbsp chopped fresh
   coriander (cilantro), to garnish

1 Heat the oil in a large heavy pan over low heat. Stir in the onion and cook for 5 minutes. Add the garlic, pepper, potatoes, chillies and tomatoes. Stir well, cover and cook for 5 minutes.

2 Meanwhile, toast the peanuts by gently cooking them in a large dry frying pan. Turn and stir the peanuts until they are evenly golden. Take care not to burn them.

3 Set 30ml/2 tbsp of the peanuts aside for garnish. Grind the remaining nuts in a food processor or blender. Add the vegetables and process until smooth.

4 Return the mixture to the pan and stir in the stock. Boil, lower the heat and simmer for 10 minutes.

5 Pour the soup into heated individual bowls. Garnish with a generous sprinkling of coriander and the remaining peanuts and serve immediately.

> **Cook's Tip**
> *Replace the unsalted peanuts with peanut butter, if you like. Use equal quantities of chunky and smooth peanut butter for the ideal texture.*

Winter Farmhouse Soup

Root vegetables are in abundance in winter and form the base of this chunky, minestrone-style main meal soup. Always choose seasonal vegetables and vary according to what you have to hand.

Serves 4
30ml/2 tbsp olive oil
1 onion, roughly chopped
3 carrots, cut into large chunks
175–200g/6–7oz turnips, cut into
   large chunks
about 175g/6oz swede (rutabaga),
   cut into large chunks
400g/14oz can chopped
   Italian tomatoes

15ml/1 tbsp tomato purée (paste)
5ml/1 tsp dried mixed herbs
5ml/1 tsp dried oregano
50g/2oz dried (bell)
   peppers, washed and
   thinly sliced (optional)
1.5 litres/2½ pints/6¼ cups
   vegetable stock or water
50g/2oz/½ cup dried macaroni
400g/14oz can red kidney beans,
   rinsed and drained
30ml/2 tbsp chopped fresh flat
   leaf parsley
sea salt and ground black pepper
freshly grated Parmesan cheese or
   premium Italian-style vegetarian
   cheese, to serve

1 Heat the olive oil in a large pan, add the onion and cook over a low heat for about 5 minutes until softened. Add the carrot, turnip and swede chunks, canned chopped tomatoes, tomato purée, dried mixed herbs, dried oregano and dried peppers, if using. Stir in a little salt and pepper to taste.

2 Pour in the vegetable stock or water and bring to the boil. Stir well, cover the pan, then lower the heat and simmer for 30 minutes, stirring occasionally.

3 Add the pasta to the pan and bring quickly to the boil, stirring. Lower the heat and simmer, uncovered, for about 8 minutes until the pasta is only just tender, or according to the instructions on the packet. Stir frequently.

4 Stir in the kidney beans. Heat through for 2–3 minutes, then remove the pan from the heat and stir in the parsley. Taste the soup for seasoning. Serve hot in warmed soup bowls, with grated cheese handed separately.

Peanut Soup Energy 260kcal/1079kJ; Protein 8g; Carbohydrate 14.7g, of which sugars 6.2g; Fat 19.2g, of which saturates 3.6g; Cholesterol 0mg; Calcium 30mg; Fibre 3g; Sodium 20mg.
Winter Soup Energy 257kcal/1081kJ; Protein 10.8g; Carbohydrate 39.7g, of which sugars 15.9g; Fat 7.2g, of which saturates 1.1g; Cholesterol 0mg; Calcium 165mg; Fibre 11.4g; Sodium 436mg.

Smoked Haddock Chowder

Based on a traditional Scottish recipe, this soup combines the sweetness of sweet potatoes and butternut squash with aromatic Thai basil.

Serves 6

400g/14oz sweet potatoes (pink-fleshed variety), diced
225g/8oz peeled butternut squash, cut into 1cm/½in slices

50g/2oz/¼ cup butter
1 onion, chopped
450g/1lb Finnan haddock fillets, skinned
300ml/½ pint/1¼ cups water
600ml/1 pint/2½ cups milk
small handful of Thai basil leaves
60ml/4 tbsp double (heavy) cream
salt and ground black pepper

1 Cook the sweet potatoes and butternut squash separately in a large pan of boiling salted water for 15 minutes or until tender. Drain well.

2 Meanwhile, melt half the butter in a large, heavy pan. Add the onion and cook for 4–5 minutes, until softened but not browned. Add the haddock fillets and water.

3 Bring to the boil, reduce the heat and simmer for 10 minutes, until the fish is cooked. Use a draining spoon to lift the fish out of the pan and leave to cool. Set the liquid aside.

4 When cool enough to handle, carefully break the flesh into large flakes, discarding the skin and bones. Set the fish aside.

5 Press the sweet potatoes through a sieve (strainer) and beat in the remaining butter with seasoning to taste.

6 Strain the reserved fish cooking liquid and return it to the rinsed-out pan, then whisk in the sweet potato. Stir in the milk and bring to the boil. Simmer for about 2–3 minutes.

7 Stir the butternut squash, fish, Thai basil leaves and cream into the soup. Season the soup to taste and heat through without boiling. Ladle the soup into six warmed soup bowls and serve immediately.

Chicken Soup

This versatile chicken soup should be an essential part of every cook's winter repertoire. In this version, a rich stock is prepared using a whole chicken.

Serves 8–10

1 chicken, about 2kg/4½lb
350g/12oz beef bone
2 bay leaves
3 large leeks, sliced
1 parsnip, thinly sliced

4 carrots, thinly sliced
6 celery sticks, sliced
salt
75ml/5 tbsp chopped fresh parsley, to garnish

For the dumplings

350g/12oz/3 cups plain (all-purpose) flour
125g/4oz/½ cup butter
4 eggs
5ml/1 tsp sugar
salt

1 Bring 3 litres/5 pints/12½ cups water to the boil in a large pan. Add the chicken, beef bone and bay leaves to the pot, and return to the boil. Skim, lower the heat and simmer for 1 hour.

2 Add the leeks, parsnip, carrots and celery to the chicken stock and season with salt. Simmer for about 20 minutes, until the vegetables are tender.

3 Meanwhile, make the dumplings. Place the flour in a bowl. Bring 250ml/8fl oz/1 cup water to the boil in a pan, add the butter and return to the boil. Stir the mixture into the flour, beating vigorously with a fork to blend smoothly. Leave to cool.

4 Beat in the eggs, one at a time, to make a soft dough. Stir in the sugar and salt to taste. Leave to rest for 20 minutes.

5 Bring a large pan of lightly salted water to the boil. Use a teaspoon to form small, unevenly shaped balls of dough, and drop them one at a time into the water. They will sink to the bottom, then rise to the top when cooked, in 3–5 minutes. Lift out the dumplings and set aside until needed.

6 Remove the beef bone from the soup. Carve the chicken to serve separately, or pull the meat from the bones and return to the soup. Add the dumplings to warm through, and serve.

Haddock Chowder Energy 285kcal/1196kJ; Protein 19.1g; Carbohydrate 20.7g, of which sugars 9.9g; Fat 14.7g, of which saturates 8.9g; Cholesterol 64mg; Calcium 166mg; Fibre 2.1g; Sodium 173mg.
Chicken Soup Energy 266kcal/1115kJ; Protein 25.7g; Carbohydrate 24g, of which sugars 6.6g; Fat 7.5g, of which saturates 1.2g; Cholesterol 109mg; Calcium 48mg; Fibre 2.7g; Sodium 86mg.

Kale, Chorizo and Potato Soup

This hearty winter soup has a spicy kick from the chorizo sausage. The soup becomes more potent if chilled overnight. It is worth buying the best possible chorizo sausage to achieve superior flavour.

Serves 6–8
225g/8oz kale, stems removed
225g/8oz chorizo sausage
675g/1½lb potatoes, cut
   into chunks
1.75 litres/3 pints/7½ cups
   vegetable stock
5ml/1 tsp ground black pepper
pinch of cayenne pepper (optional)
12 slices French bread, toasted on
   both sides
salt and ground black pepper

1 Place the kale in a food processor or blender and process for a few seconds to chop it finely. Alternatively, shred it finely by hand.

2 Prick the sausages and place in a pan with enough water to cover. Bring just to boiling point, then reduce the heat immediately before the water boils too rapidly and simmer for 15 minutes. Drain and cut into thin slices.

3 Boil the potatoes for about 15 minutes or until the slices are just tender. Drain, and place in a bowl, then mash adding a little of the cooking liquid to form a thick paste.

4 Bring the vegetable stock to the boil and add the kale. Bring back to the boil. Reduce the heat and add the chorizo, then simmer for 5 minutes. Gradually add the potato paste, stirring it into the soup, then simmer for 20 minutes. Season with black pepper and cayenne.

5 Divide the freshly made toast among serving bowls. Pour the soup over and serve immediately, sprinkled with pepper.

Cook's Tip
Select seasonal maincrop, floury potatoes for this soup rather than new potatoes or waxy salad potatoes.

Hare Soup

This soup can be made with any other game that is available in the winter months, such as wild duck, goose or guinea fowl.

Serves 6
1 hare or rabbit
2 carrots
75ml/5 tbsp olive oil
75ml/5 tbsp dry white port
1 onion, sliced
1 leek, sliced
1 garlic clove, chopped
6 black peppercorns
1 bay leaf
15ml/1 tbsp cornflour
   (cornstarch)
1 turnip, diced
3 heads pak choi (bok choy), cut
   into strips
200g/7oz oyster
   mushrooms, sliced
300g/11oz/2¼ cups cooked
   haricot (navy) beans
1 small bunch of fresh
   peppermint, chopped
salt

1 Cut the hare into pieces. Wash well and pat dry with kitchen paper. Slice one carrot and dice the other. Heat 45ml/3 tbsp of the oil in a large pan. Add the pieces of hare and cook, turning occasionally, for about 10 minutes, until golden brown all over.

2 Drain off the oil from the pan. Add the port, onion, leek, sliced carrot, garlic, peppercorns and bay leaf, and pour in enough water to cover. Bring to the boil, then lower the heat and simmer gently for 1½ hours.

3 Strain the stock into a bowl and reserve the meat. Remove the bones from the meat and cut the meat into small pieces. Return the stock to the rinsed-out pan and set over a low heat.

4 Mix the cornflour to a paste with 30ml/2 tbsp water. Stir it into the stock and season to taste with salt.

5 Cook the remaining carrot, the turnip and pak choi in separate pans of boiling water until just tender, then add to the stock.

6 Meanwhile, heat the remaining oil in another pan, add the mushrooms and cook over a low heat, stirring occasionally, for 5–7 minutes. Add them to the stock with the beans. Stir in the reserved meat and the peppermint, heat through and serve.

Kale Soup Energy 411kcal/1740kJ; Protein 13.2g; Carbohydrate 69.3g, of which sugars 6.2g; Fat 11g, of which saturates 4.1g; Cholesterol 15mg; Calcium 140mg; Fibre 4g; Sodium 812mg.
Hare Soup Energy 297kcal/1242kJ; Protein 24g; Carbohydrate 18.7g, of which sugars 8.5g; Fat 12.9g, of which saturates 2.9g; Cholesterol 69mg; Calcium 159mg; Fibre 6.4g; Sodium 299mg.

Onion and Red Chilli Relish

This popular relish, known as *cebollas en escabeche*, is typical of the Yucatan region of Mexico and is often served alongside chicken, fish or turkey dishes. It is also delicious served with savoury crackers and cheese – it will add a lovely spicy, tangy taste and won't contribute any additional fat or sugar.

Makes 1 small jar
2 fresh red fresno chillies
5ml/1 tsp allspice berries
2.5ml/½ tsp black peppercorns
5ml/1 tsp dried oregano
2 white onions
2 garlic cloves, peeled
100ml/3½fl oz/⅓ cup white wine vinegar
200ml/7fl oz/scant 1 cup cider vinegar
salt

1 Spear the fresno chillies on a long-handled metal skewer and roast them over the flame of a gas burner until the skins blister. Do not let the flesh burn. Alternatively, dry-fry them in a griddle pan until the skins are scorched. Place the roasted chillies in a strong plastic bag and tie the top to keep the steam in. Set aside for 20 minutes.

2 Meanwhile, place the allspice, black peppercorns and oregano in a mortar or food processor. Grind the herbs and spices slowly by hand with a pestle or blend in the processor until coarsely ground.

3 Cut the onions in half and slice them thinly. Put them in a bowl. Dry-roast the garlic in a heavy frying pan until golden. Do not let it burn, otherwise it will taste bitter. Crush the roasted garlic and add to the onions in the bowl.

4 Remove the chillies from the bag and peel off the skins. Slit the chillies, scrape out the seeds with a small sharp knife and discard. Chop the chillies roughly.

5 Add the ground spices to the onion mixture, followed by the chopped chillies. Add both vinegars and stir well. Add salt to taste and mix thoroughly.

6 Cover the bowl and chill for at least 1 day before serving.

Beetroot Relish

Beetroot is often eaten pickled or used to make bortscht soup. However, this delicious winter vegetable makes a wonderfully tangy relish and is a perfect accompaniment to cold meats, such as ham and sausage. The fresh, sweet and nutty flavour of beetroot makes an ideal partner for horseradish. Beetroot is believed to have beauty-enhancing and aphrodisiac properties.

Serves 4
4–5 medium-sized raw beetroot (beets)
15ml/1 tbsp sugar
60–75ml/4–5 tbsp freshly grated horseradish
juice of 1 lemon
1 glass dry red wine
2.5ml/1/2 tsp salt
cold meats, to serve

1 Put the beetroot, in their skins, in a large pan, and pour over enough cold water to cover.

2 Bring to the boil and cook the beetroot for about 1 hour, or until the beetroots are tender when pierced with a sharp knife. Remove from the heat, drain, and leave to cool.

3 Rub the skins from the beetroot, or peel them, then shred them finely. Put the shredded beetroot in a large jar with the sugar, horseradish, lemon juice, red wine and salt.

4 Cover tightly and store in a cool place for up to 4 months to mature. Serve the beetroots with a range of cold meats.

Cook's Tips
• *Beetroot, once cooked, should be eaten within two to three days and should be stored in a refrigerator. Uncooked beetroot which still has leaves and roots can be stored in a cool, dark cupboard for a few days.*
• *If the beetroot is young, the leaves can also be eaten; they are cooked and served as you would any green leafy vegetable.*

Beetroot Relish Energy 60kcal/253kJ; Protein 1.5g; Carbohydrate 9g, of which sugars 8.5g; Fat 0.1g, of which saturates 0g; Cholesterol 0mg; Calcium 20mg; Fibre 1.6g; Sodium 221mg.
Onion and Red Chilli Relish Energy 151kcal/629kJ; Protein 5.8g; Carbohydrate 31.8g, of which sugars 22.6g; Fat 1g, of which saturates 0g; Cholesterol 0mg; Calcium 111mg; Fibre 5.6g; Sodium 14mg.

Piquant Pineapple Relish

Pineapples are in abundance during the winter and this is one way of enjoying this delicious fruit. This recipe uses canned pineapples so can be made all year, but ensure you use fresh fruit when in season.

Serves 4

400g/14oz can crushed
  pineapple in natural juice

30ml/2 tbsp light muscovado
  (brown) sugar
30ml/2 tbsp wine vinegar
1 garlic clove, finely chopped
4 spring onions (scallions),
  finely chopped
2 red chillies, seeded and chopped
10 fresh basil leaves,
  finely shredded
salt and ground black pepper

1 Drain the canned pineapple and reserve about 60ml/4 tbsp of the juice.

2 Place the reserved juice in a small pan with the sugar and vinegar, then heat gently, stirring frequently, until all of the sugar has completely dissolved. Remove the pan from the heat and set aside to cool a little. Season with salt and ground black pepper to taste.

3 Place the drained pineapple, chopped garlic, spring onions and chillies in a medium bowl. Mix well and stir in the sugary juice. Allow to cool for about 5 minutes, then stir in the basil and serve immediately.

Cook's Tip
This fruity sweet-and-sour relish is excellent served with grilled (broiled) chicken, gammon (smoked or cured ham) or bacon.

Variation
This relish tastes extra special when made with fresh pineapple. Look out for them in your grocery store or supermarket during the winter months when they are particularly delicious.

Christmas Chutney

This savoury mixture of spices and dried fruit takes its inspiration from mincemeat, and makes a delicious traditional addition to the Boxing Day buffet. Nothing could be more fitting on the winter table.

**Makes about
1–1.6kg/2¼–3½ lb**

450g/1lb cooking apples, peeled,
  cored and chopped

500g/1¼ lb/3⅓ cups luxury
  mixed dried fruit
grated rind of 1 orange
30ml/2 tbsp mixed spice
150ml/¼ pint/⅔ cup
  cider vinegar
350g/12oz/1½ cups light
  muscovado (brown) sugar

1 Place the chopped apples, dried fruit and grated orange rind in a large, heavy pan.

2 Stir the mixed spice, cider vinegar and sugar into the pan. Heat the ingredients gently, stirring constantly until all the sugar has dissolved.

3 Bring the mixture to the boil, then lower the heat and simmer for about 40–45 minutes, stirring occasionally, until it has thickened.

4 Ladle the chutney into warm, sterilized jars, cover and seal. Keep for 1 month before using.

Cook's Tips
• Watch the chutney carefully toward the end of the cooking time, as it has a tendency to catch on the bottom of the pan. Stir frequently at this stage.
• Store jars of the chutney in the refrigerator after opening.
• This chutney is delicious served with cold meats, such as a special ham for the festive season. It also tastes delicious served with a chunk of cheese, some crusty bread and wedges of fresh, seasonal apple.

Piquant Pineapple Relish Energy 81kcal/343kJ; Protein 0.7g; Carbohydrate 20.5g, of which sugars 20.4g; Fat 0.1g, of which saturates 0g; Cholesterol 0mg; Calcium 26mg; Fibre 0.9g; Sodium 4mg.
Christmas Chutney Energy 2876kcal/12283kJ; Protein 14.6g; Carbohydrate 746.3g, of which sugars 746.3g; Fat 2.4g, of which saturates 0g; Cholesterol 0mg; Calcium 569mg; Fibre 18.2g; Sodium 270mg.

Beetroot Patties

In the days before air-freighted vegetables, beetroot was a staple ingredient in Finland, and was the basis for a wide variety of imaginative recipes. These delicious patties can be served with a dollop of sour cream as an appetizer or alongside grilled meat or fish to provide a different texture and flavour. They are also often served in conjunction with fried onions.

Serves 4
2 cooked beetroot (beets)
1 egg, beaten
100g/3¾oz/2 cups fine
    fresh breadcrumbs
vegetable oil, for shallow frying
salt and ground black pepper

1 Peel the outer skin from the cooked beetroot using a sharp knife, then cut the flesh into 1cm/½in slices.

2 Break the egg on a plate and beat lightly. Spread the breadcrumbs on a separate plate and season with salt and black pepper.

3 Dip the beetroot slices in the egg and then the breadcrumbs, to coat both sides.

4 Heat the oil in a large frying pan, add the coated beetroot and fry for about 5 minutes, turning once, until golden brown on both sides. Drain on kitchen paper and serve hot.

> **Cook's Tip**
> To prepare and cook beetroot: trim the leafy stalks from the beetroot down to within about 2.5cm/1in of the root. Gently wash the beetroot but do not peel, otherwise the colour and nutrients will leach out during cooking. Boil the unpeeled beetroot in a large pan of water for about 40–50 minutes or until they are tender.

Leek Fritters

Leeks are at their best during the winter months and these crispy fried morsels are the perfect way to enjoy them during the season. These fritters are best served at room temperature, with a good squeeze of fresh lemon juice, a sprinkling of sea salt and freshly grated nutmeg.

Serves 4
4 large leeks, total weight about
    1kg/2¼ lb, thickly sliced
120–175ml/4–6fl oz/½–¾ cup
    coarse matzo meal
2 eggs, lightly beaten
olive oil or vegetable oil, for
    shallow frying
sea salt
lemon wedges and a sprinkling of
    nutmeg, to serve (optional)

1 Cook the leeks in salted boiling water for 5 minutes, or until just tender and bright green. Drain well and leave to cool.

2 Chop the leeks coarsely. Put in a bowl and combine with the matzo meal, eggs and seasoning.

3 Heat 5mm/¼in oil in a frying pan. Using two tablespoons, carefully spoon the leek mixture into the hot oil. Cook over medium-high heat until golden brown on the underside, then turn and cook the second side.

4 Drain the cooked fritters on kitchen paper. Add more oil if needed, and heat before cooking the rest of the mixture. Serve at room temperature with lemon wedges and a little nutmeg.

> **Cook's Tip**
> Matzo meal, a traditional Jewish ingredient, is used in these fritters: it is made from crumbled matzo, an unleavened bread, similar to water biscuits.

> **Variation**
> Matzo meal is used in a similar way to breadcrumbs, which can also be used to make these fritters.

Beetroot Patties Energy 174kcal/734kJ; Protein 5.3g; Carbohydrate 23.2g, of which sugars 4.2g; Fat 7.4g, of which saturates 1g; Cholesterol 48mg; Calcium 50mg; Fibre 1.5g; Sodium 241mg.
Leek Fritters Energy 326kcal/1356kJ; Protein 10g; Carbohydrate 29.2g, of which sugars 5.5g; Fat 18.8g, of which saturates 2.6g; Cholesterol 95mg; Calcium 75mg; Fibre 6.2g; Sodium 40mg.

Leek Soufflé

Some people think of a soufflé as a dinner party dish, and a rather tricky one at that. However, others frequently serve them for family meals because they are quick and easy to make. This version makes the most of tasty winter leeks.

Serves 2–3

15ml/1 tbsp sunflower oil
40g/1½oz/3 tbsp butter

2 leeks, thinly sliced
about 300ml/½ pint/
  1¼ cups milk
25g/1oz/¼ cup plain
  (all-purpose) flour
4 eggs, separated
75g/3oz Gruyère or Emmenthal
  cheese, grated
salt and ground black pepper

1 Preheat the oven to 180°C/350°F/Gas 4 and butter a large soufflé dish. Heat the sunflower oil and 15g/½oz/1 tbsp of the butter in a pan or flameproof casserole and fry the leeks over low heat for about 4–5 minutes until softened but not browned, stirring occasionally.

2 Stir in the milk and bring to the boil. Cover and simmer for 4–5 minutes until the leeks are tender. Strain the liquid through a sieve (strainer) into a measuring jug (cup).

3 Melt the remaining butter in a pan, stir in the flour and cook for 1 minute. Remove the pan from the heat. Make up the reserved liquid with milk to 300ml/½ pint/1¼ cups.

4 Gradually stir the milk into the pan to make a smooth sauce. Return to the heat and bring to the boil, stirring. When thickened, remove from the heat. Cool slightly and then beat in the egg yolks, and add the cheese and the leeks.

5 In a large, grease-free bowl, whisk the egg whites until stiff peaks form. Using a large metal spoon, fold the eggs into the leek and egg mixture.

6 Pour into the prepared soufflé dish and bake in the oven for about 30 minutes until golden and puffy. Serve immediately.

Leek and Onion Tartlets

These winter tartlets look great in individual tins.

Serves 6

25g/1oz/2 tbsp butter
1 onion, thinly sliced
2.5ml/½ tsp dried thyme
450g/1lb leeks, thinly sliced
50g/2oz Gruyère cheese, grated
3 eggs
300ml/½ pint/1¼ cups single
  (light) cream

pinch of freshly grated nutmeg
salt and ground black pepper
mixed salad leaves, to serve

For the pastry
175g/6oz/1⅓ cup plain
  (all-purpose) flour
75g/3oz/6 tbsp cold butter
1 egg yolk
30–45ml/2–3 tbsp cold water
2.5ml/½ tsp salt

1 Make the pastry. Sift the flour into a bowl and add the butter. Rub the butter into the flour until it resembles breadcrumbs. Make a well in the centre of the mixture. Beat together the egg yolk, water and salt, pour into the well and combine the flour and liquid until it begins to stick together. Form into a ball. Wrap and chill for 30 minutes.

2 Butter six 10cm/4in tartlet tins (muffin pans). Roll out the dough until 3mm/⅛in thick, then cut out rounds with a 12.5cm/5in cutter. Press the rounds into the tins. Re-roll the trimmings and line the remaining tins. Prick the bases and chill.

3 Preheat the oven to 190°C/375°F/Gas 5. Line the cases with foil and fill with baking beans. Place on a baking sheet and bake for 6–8 minutes until golden. Remove the foil and beans and bake for 2 minutes. Transfer to a wire rack to cool. Reduce the oven temperature to 180°C/350°F/Gas 4.

4 In a large pan, melt the butter. Cook the onion and thyme for 3–5 minutes, then add the leeks for 10–12 minutes. Divide the mixture among the cases and sprinkle each with cheese.

5 Beat together the eggs, cream, nutmeg and seasoning. Place the cases on a baking sheet and pour in the mixture. Bake for 15–20 minutes until golden. Cool on a wire rack slightly, then serve warm or at room temperature with salad leaves.

Leek Soufflé Energy 409kcal/1702kJ; Protein 20.6g; Carbohydrate 14.4g, of which sugars 7.3g; Fat 30.4g, of which saturates 14.8g; Cholesterol 310mg; Calcium 388mg; Fibre 2.5g; Sodium 506mg.
Leek Tartlets Energy 422kcal/1755kJ; Protein 11.5g; Carbohydrate 26.8g, of which sugars 3.9g; Fat 30.4g, of which saturates 17.7g; Cholesterol 200mg; Calcium 189mg; Fibre 2.7g; Sodium 215mg.

Gruyère and Potato Soufflés

This potato recipe can be prepared in advance, if you are entertaining, and given its second baking just before you serve it up.

Serves 4
225g/8oz floury potatoes
2 eggs, separated

175g/6oz/1½ cups Gruyère
 cheese, grated
50g/2oz/½ cup self-raising
 (self-rising) flour
50g/2oz spinach leaves
butter, for greasing
salt and ground black pepper
salad leaves, to serve

1 Preheat the oven to 200°C/400°F/Gas 6. Cook the potatoes in lightly salted boiling water for around 20 minutes until very tender. Drain the potatoes and mash thoroughly before adding the two egg yolks and mixing to combine.

2 Stir in half of the Gruyère cheese and all of the flour. Season to taste with salt and pepper.

3 Finely chop the spinach leaves and gently fold into the potato and egg yolk mixture.

4 Whip the egg whites until they form soft peaks. Fold a little of the egg white into the mixture to loosen it slightly. Using a large metal spoon, then fold the remaining egg white into the mixture.

5 Butter four large ramekin dishes. Pour the mixture in, place on a baking sheet and bake for 20 minutes. Remove from the oven and leave to cool.

6 Turn the soufflés out on to a baking sheet and sprinkle with the remaining cheese. Bake again for 5 minutes and serve immediately with salad leaves.

Variation
For a different flavouring, try replacing the Gruyère with a crumbled blue cheese, such as Stilton or Shropshire Blue cheeses, which have a more intense taste than the Gruyère.

Potato Skins with Cajun Dip

Divinely crisp, these potato skins are great on their own, or served with this piquant dip as a garnish or to the side. They are delicious as a snack, or as a tasty accompaniment to a winter feast.

Serves 2
2 large baking potatoes
vegetable oil, for deep frying

For the dip
120ml/4fl oz/½ cup natural
 (plain) yogurt
1 garlic clove, crushed
5ml/1 tsp tomato purée (paste)
2.5ml/½ tsp green chilli purée or
 ½ small green chilli, chopped
1.5ml/¼ tsp celery salt
salt and ground black pepper

1 Preheat the oven to 180°C/350°F/Gas 4. Bake the potatoes for 45–50 minutes until tender. Remove from the oven and set aside to cool slightly.

2 When the potatoes have cooled down enough to handle, cut them in half and scoop out the flesh, leaving a thin layer on the skins. Keep the flesh for another meal.

3 To make the dip, mix together all the ingredients and chill in the refrigerator until the skins are ready.

4 Heat a 1cm/½in layer of oil in a large pan or deep-fat fryer. Cut each potato half in half again, then fry them until crisp and golden on both sides.

5 Drain on kitchen paper, sprinkle with salt and black pepper and serve with a bowl of dip or a dollop of dip in each skin.

Cook's Tips
• *If you prefer, you can microwave the potatoes to save time. This will take about 10 minutes.*
• *The scooped-out flesh from the potatoes is delicious if mixed with leftover winter vegetables such as leeks or cabbage, then formed into small cakes and fried in a little oil until golden.*

Gruyère Soufflés Energy 304kcal/1270kJ; Protein 16.7g; Carbohydrate 19g, of which sugars 1.2g; Fat 17.5g, of which saturates 10.4g; Cholesterol 138mg; Calcium 380mg; Fibre 1.2g; Sodium 376mg.
Potato Skins Energy 211kcal/873kJ; Protein 2.7g; Carbohydrate 12.5g, of which sugars 3.3g; Fat 17g, of which saturates 2.2g; Cholesterol 0mg; Calcium 62mg; Fibre 0.7g; Sodium 35mg.

Idaho Potato Slices

This unusual and tasty dish is made from a layered ring of potatoes, cheese and herbs. Cooking the ingredients together gives them a very rich flavour.

Serves 4
3 large potatoes
butter, for greasing

1 small onion, finely sliced
    into rings
200g/7oz/1¾ cups red Leicester
    or mature (sharp) Cheddar
    cheese, grated
fresh thyme sprigs
150ml/¼ pint/⅔ cup single
    (light) cream
salt and ground black pepper
salad leaves, to serve

1 Preheat the oven to 200°C/400°F/Gas 6. Peel the potatoes and cook in boiling water for 10 minutes until they are just starting to soften. Remove from the water and pat dry with kitchen paper.

2 Finely slice the potatoes, using the straight edge of a grater or a mandoline. Grease the base and sides of an 18cm/7in cake tin (pan) with butter and lay some of the potatoes on the base to cover it completely. Season with salt and pepper.

3 Sprinkle some of the onion rings over the potatoes and top with a little of the cheese. Sprinkle over some of the thyme and then continue to layer the ingredients, finishing with a layer of cheese and a little more seasoning.

4 Press the potato layers right down. (The mixture may seem quite high at this point but it will cook down.)

5 Pour over the cream and bake for 35–45 minutes. Remove from the oven and cool. Invert on to a plate and cut into wedges. Serve immediately with a few salad leaves.

> **Variation**
> *If you want to make this dish more substantial, top the potato wedges with slices of crispy bacon, or strips of roasted red or yellow (bell) peppers.*

Swiss Soufflé Potatoes

A combination of rich and satisfying ingredients – cheese, eggs, cream, butter and potatoes. This is perfect for cold-weather eating.

Serves 4
4 floury baking potatoes
115g/4oz/1 cup Gruyère
    cheese, grated

115g/4oz/8 tbsp herb-
    flavoured butter
60ml/4 tbsp double
    (heavy) cream
2 eggs, separated
salt and ground black pepper
fresh chives, to garnish
mayonnaise, to serve

1 Preheat the oven to 220°C/425°F/Gas 7. Prick the potatoes all over with a fork. Bake in the oven for 1–1½ hours until tender. Remove them from the oven and reduce the temperature to 180°C/350°F/Gas 4.

2 Cut each potato in half and scoop out the flesh into a bowl. Return the shells to the oven to crisp them up for 5 minutes.

3 Mash the potato flesh using a fork, then add the Gruyère, herb-flavoured butter, cream, egg yolks and seasoning. Beat well until smooth.

4 Whisk the egg whites in a separate bowl until they hold stiff but not dry peaks, then carefully fold into the potato mixture.

5 Pile the mixture back into the potato shells and place on a baking sheet. Bake in the oven for 20–25 minutes until risen and golden brown.

6 Serve the potatoes hot, sprinkled with fresh, chopped chives, if wished, and a bowl of mayonnaise to the side.

> **Variation**
> *Use other cheeses, if you like. Mature (sharp) Cheddar would work well, or go for another blue cheese such as Stilton or Dolcelatte, if you prefer.*

Swiss Soufflé Potatoes Energy 576kcal/2394kJ; Protein 14.2g; Carbohydrate 32.6g, of which sugars 3g; Fat 44.3g, of which saturates 27.2g; Cholesterol 209mg; Calcium 251mg; Fibre 2g; Sodium 486mg.
Idaho Potato Slices Energy 408kcal/1706kJ; Protein 17.1g; Carbohydrate 30.2g, of which sugars 4g; Fat 24.1g, of which saturates 15.6g; Cholesterol 69mg; Calcium 417mg; Fibre 2g; Sodium 392mg.

Potato and Onion Cakes with Beetroot Relish

These grated potato cakes are utterly irresistible. In winter, they are delicious with the sweet-sharp beetroot relish.

Serves 4
500g/1¼lb potatoes (such as King Edward, Estima or Desirée)
1 small cooking apple, peeled, cored and coarsely grated
1 small onion, finely chopped
50g/2oz/½ cup plain (all-purpose) flour
2 large eggs, beaten
30ml/2 tbsp chopped chives
vegetable oil, for shallow frying
salt and ground black pepper

fresh dill sprigs and fresh chives or chive flowers, to garnish
250ml/8fl oz/1 cup sour cream or crème fraîche, to serve

For the beetroot relish
250g/9oz beetroot (beets), cooked, peeled and diced
1 large dessert apple, cored and finely diced
15ml/1 tbsp finely chopped red onion
15–30ml/1–2 tbsp tarragon vinegar
15ml/1 tbsp chopped fresh dill
15–30ml/1–2 tbsp light olive oil
pinch of caster (superfine) sugar (optional)

1 To make the relish, mix the beetroot with the apple and onion. Add 15ml/1 tbsp of the vinegar, the dill and 15ml/1 tbsp of oil. Season, adding more vinegar and oil, and a pinch of sugar to taste.

2 Coarsely grate the potatoes, then rinse, drain and dry them on a clean dish towel. Mix the potatoes, apple and onion in a bowl. Stir in the flour, eggs and chives. Season and mix again.

3 Heat about 5mm/¼ in depth of oil in a frying pan and fry spoonfuls of the mixture. Flatten them to make pancakes 7.5–10cm/3–4in across and cook for 3–4 minutes on each side, until browned. Drain on kitchen paper and keep warm until the mixture is used up.

4 Serve a stack of cakes with spoonfuls of sour cream or crème fraîche, and relish. Garnish with dill sprigs and chives or chive flowers and season with black pepper just before serving.

Oysters Rockefeller on the Half Shell

This is the perfect dish for those who prefer to eat their oysters lightly cooked. Mussels or scallops can be given the same treatment; they will also taste delicious.

Serves 6
450g/1lb/3 cups coarse sea salt, plus extra to serve
24 oysters, opened
115g/4oz/½ cup butter
2 shallots, finely chopped

500g/1¼lb spinach leaves, finely chopped
60ml/4 tbsp chopped fresh parsley
60ml/4 tbsp chopped celery leaves
90ml/6 tbsp fresh white or wholemeal (whole-wheat) breadcrumbs
10–20ml/2–4 tsp vodka
cayenne pepper
sea salt and ground black pepper
lemon or lime wedges, to serve

1 Preheat the oven to 220°C/425°F/Gas 7. Make a bed of coarse sea salt on two large baking sheets. Set the oysters in the half-shell in the bed of salt to keep them steady. Set aside.

2 Melt the butter in a large frying pan. Add the chopped shallots and cook them over a low heat for 2–3 minutes until they are softened. Stir in the spinach and let it wilt.

3 Add the parsley, celery leaves and breadcrumbs to the pan and fry gently for 5 minutes. Season with salt, pepper and cayenne pepper.

4 Divide the stuffing among the oysters. Drizzle a few drops of vodka over each oyster, then bake for about 5 minutes until bubbling and golden brown. Serve on a heated platter on a shallow salt bed with lemon or lime wedges.

> **Cook's Tip**
> Frozen chopped spinach can be used when the fresh variety is out of season. Thaw it in a colander over a bowl and press out as much liquid as possible.

Potato Cakes Energy 471kcal/1964kJ; Protein 10.3g; Carbohydrate 42.1g, of which sugars 13.4g; Fat 30.2g, of which saturates 10.6g; Cholesterol 152mg; Calcium 118mg; Fibre 3.7g; Sodium 125mg.
Oysters Rockefeller Energy 210kcal/867kJ; Protein 6.4g; Carbohydrate 3.4g, of which sugars 2.1g; Fat 17g, of which saturates 10.1g; Cholesterol 60mg; Calcium 211mg; Fibre 2.3g; Sodium 406mg.

Merguez Sausages with Iced Oysters

This is a truly wonderful taste sensation – revel in the French Christmas tradition of munching on a little hot sausage, then quelling the burning sensation with an ice-cold oyster. Merguez sausages come from North Africa and owe their flavour and colour to harissa, a hot chilli paste with subtle hints of spices such as coriander and caraway, and garlic.

Serves 6
675g/1½lb merguez sausages
crushed ice for serving
24 oysters
2 lemons, cut into wedges, for squeezing

1 Prepare the barbecue. Once the flames have died down, position a lightly oiled grill rack over the coals to heat. When the coals are medium-hot, or with a moderate coating of ash, place the sausages on the rack. Grill them for 8 minutes, or until cooked through and golden, turning often.

2 Meanwhile, spread out the crushed ice on a platter and keep it chilled while you ready the oysters. Make sure all the oysters are tightly closed, and discard any that aren't. Place them on the grill rack, a few at a time, with the deep side down, so that as they open the juices will be retained in the lower shell. They will begin to ease open after 3–5 minutes and must be removed from the heat immediately, so they don't start to cook.

3 Lay the oysters on the ice. When they have all eased open, get to work with a sharp knife, opening them fully if need be. Remove the oysters from the flat side of the shell and place them with the juices on the deep half shells. Discard any oysters that fail to open. Serve the oysters immediately, accompanied by the hot, cooked sausages, and the lemon wedges for squeezing over the oysters.

> **Cook's Tip**
> *This recipe can also be cooked on a griddle if the weather is particularly wintry. The sausages will take 1–2 minutes more. Remove them, and increase the heat to open the oysters.*

Three-fish Terrine

This striped terrine uses three fish available in winter: haddock, salmon and turbot. Serve with a small salad, brown bread or Melba toast and butter.

Serves 8–10
450g/1lb spinach
350–450g/12oz–1lb haddock, cod or other white fish, skinned and chopped
3 eggs
115g/4oz/2 cups fresh breadcrumbs
300ml/½ pint/1¼ cups fromage blanc or low-fat cream cheese
a little freshly grated nutmeg
350–450g/12oz–1lb salmon fillet
350–450g/12oz–1lb fresh turbot fillet, or other flat fish
oil, for greasing
salt and ground black pepper
lemon wedges and rocket, to serve

1 Preheat the oven to 160°C/325°F/Gas 3. Remove the stalks from the spinach and cook the leaves briskly in a pan without any added water, shaking the pan occasionally, until the spinach is just tender. Drain and squeeze out the water.

2 Put the spinach into a food processor or blender with the haddock or other white fish, eggs, breadcrumbs, fromage blanc or cream cheese, salt, pepper and nutmeg to taste. Process until smooth. Skin and bone the salmon fillet and cut into long thin strips. Repeat with the turbot.

3 Oil a 900g/2lb loaf tin (pan) and line the base with baking parchment or foil. Make layers from the spinach mixture and the strips of salmon and turbot, starting and finishing with spinach.

4 Press down carefully and cover with oiled baking parchment. Prick a few holes in it, then put the terrine into a roasting pan and pour boiling water around it to come two-thirds of the way up the sides.

5 Bake in the preheated oven for 1–1½ hours, or until risen, firm and set. Leave to cool, then chill well before serving.

6 To serve, ease a sharp knife down the sides to loosen the terrine and turn out on to a flat serving dish. Slice the terrine and serve with lemon wedges and fresh rocket.

Merguez Sausages Energy 439kcal/1820kJ; Protein 16.3g; Carbohydrate 11.8g, of which sugars 1.6g; Fat 36.6g, of which saturates 13.8g; Cholesterol 76mg; Calcium 102mg; Fibre 0.6g; Sodium 1059mg.
Three-fish Terrine Energy 290kcal/1216kJ; Protein 32.5g; Carbohydrate 13.7g, of which sugars 2.8g; Fat 12.1g, of which saturates 3.9g; Cholesterol 112mg; Calcium 203mg; Fibre 1.5g; Sodium 306mg.

Hare and Calf's Liver Terrine

For tender meat and a good flavour, use young hare that has been hung for at least a week. However, you can use slightly older animals for this terrine, since the meat is minced finely and then combined with other winter ingredients.

Serves 4–6

5 dried mushrooms, rinsed and
  soaked in warm water for
  30 minutes
saddle, thighs, liver, heart and
  lungs of 1 hare
2 onions, cut into wedges
1 carrot, chopped
1 parsnip, chopped
4 bay leaves
10 allspice berries
300g/11oz calf's liver
165g/5½oz unsmoked streaky
  (fatty) bacon rashers (strips)
75g/3oz/1½ cups soft white
  breadcrumbs
4 eggs
105ml/7 tbsp vodka
5ml/1 tsp freshly grated nutmeg
10ml/2 tsp dried marjoram
10g/¼oz juniper berries
4 garlic cloves, crushed
150g/5oz smoked streaky (fatty)
  bacon rashers (strips)
butter, to grease
salt and ground black pepper,
  to taste
redcurrant jelly and salad, to serve

1 Drain the mushrooms and slice into strips. Put the pieces of hare in a large pan and pour in enough water to just cover. Add the onions, carrot, parsnip, mushrooms, bay leaves and allspice. Bring to the boil, then cover and simmer gently for 1 hour. Add a pinch of salt and allow the meat to cool in the stock.

2 Slice the liver and 50g/2oz unsmoked bacon into small pieces and put in a medium pan. Add a ladleful of the stock and simmer for 15 minutes.

3 Preheat the oven to 180°C/350°F/Gas 4. Put two ladlefuls of the stock in a small bowl, add the breadcrumbs and leave to soak for 15 minutes.

4 Remove the hare pieces, liver and bacon from the stock and chop finely with a large knife. Transfer to a large bowl, then add the soaked breadcrumbs, eggs, vodka, nutmeg, marjoram, juniper berries and crushed garlic. Season to taste and mix well to combine thoroughly.

5 Line a 1.2 litre/2 pint/5 cup ovenproof dish with the smoked and remaining unsmoked bacon rashers, making sure they overhang the edges. Spoon in the meat mixture and bring the excess bacon over the top. Cover with buttered baking parchment, then cover with a lid or foil.

6 Place the dish in a roasting pan containing boiling water, then put in the oven and bake for 1½ hours, or until a skewer pushed into the centre comes out clean and the juices that emerge run clear. Remove the baking parchment and lid or foil about 15 minutes before the end of cooking to allow the terrine to brown.

7 Remove from the oven and take the dish out of the roasting pan. Cover the terrine with baking parchment and a board and weight down with a 900g/2lb weight (such as two cans). Leave to cool, then turn out on to a serving dish. Serve in slices with redcurrant jelly and a green salad.

Hare Pâté

One of the culinary joys of winter is the sheer abundance and variety of game meats on offer. Hare meat is dark, with a sweet flavour and is often compared to venison, another game meat that is at its best in the winter.

Serves 6–8

40g/1½oz/3 tbsp butter
3 bay leaves
250g/9oz chicken livers, trimmed
15ml/1 tbsp fresh thyme
120ml/4fl oz/½ cup port
1 oven-ready hare
500g/1¼lb unsmoked
  bacon, cubed
200ml/7fl oz/scant 1 cup double
  (heavy) cream
2 eggs
15ml/1 tbsp plain
  (all-purpose) flour
1 garlic clove, crushed
15ml/1 tbsp brandy
pinch of grated nutmeg
ground black pepper
brown bread, toasted, to serve

1 Preheat the oven to 140°C/275°F/Gas 1. Butter a 20cm/8in loaf tin (pan) with 15g/½oz of the butter and put two bay leaves in the bottom.

2 Melt the remaining butter in a frying pan, add the chicken livers, thyme and remaining bay leaf and, stirring all the time, fry for about 4 minutes until browned. Transfer the livers and their cooking juices to a bowl. Pour over the port and leave to cool.

3 Meanwhile, cut the hare into small cubes. Using a food processor or mincer, mince (grind) half of the meat. Put all the meat in a bowl, add the bacon, cream, eggs, flour, garlic, brandy, nutmeg and pepper and mix together.

4 When the chicken livers have cooled, put the livers and port in a pan and boil until the port has reduced by half to make a sauce. Add the chicken livers and port sauce to the meat mixture and mix together.

5 Place the mixture into the prepared loaf tin and cook in the preheated oven for about 2 hours. Leave to cool in the tin before turning out on to a plate and serving with toasted brown bread.

Hare Pâté Energy 470kcal/1950kJ; Protein 34.5g; Carbohydrate 3.7g, of which sugars 2.3g; Fat 33g, of which saturates 16.6g; Cholesterol 298mg; Calcium 46mg; Fibre 0.1g; Sodium 1091mg.
Hare Terrine Energy 370kcal/1544kJ; Protein 25g; Carbohydrate 14.1g, of which sugars 2.5g; Fat 18.1g, of which saturates 6.4g; Cholesterol 291mg; Calcium 52mg; Fibre 1.3g; Sodium 851mg.

Chicken Wings with Blood Oranges

The rub that gives the chicken wings their fiery flavour is based on a classic spice mix called harissa. It is often used in Middle Eastern or African dishes. Sweet-tart blood oranges are in season during the winter and their bright red flesh gives a splash of vibrant colour to this dish. The juicy oranges also help to balance the heat of the spicy wings. Serve the oranges separately or on skewers with the chicken.

Serves 4
60ml/4 tbsp fiery harissa
30ml/2 tbsp olive oil
16–20 chicken wings
4 blood oranges, quartered
icing (confectioners') sugar
small bunch of fresh coriander
(cilantro), chopped, to garnish
salt

1 Preheat the grill (broiler) to its hottest setting. Put the harissa in a small bowl with the olive oil and mix to form a loose paste. Add a little salt and stir to combine.

2 Brush the harissa mixture over the chicken wings so that they are well coated on all sides. Grill (broil) the wings over a medium heat for 5–8 minutes on each side, until cooked and a dark golden brown.

3 Once the wings begin to cook, dip the orange quarters lightly in icing sugar and grill them for a few minutes, until they are slightly burnt but take care they do not become black and charred. Serve the chicken wings immediately with the oranges, sprinkled with a little chopped fresh coriander.

> **Variations**
> If you prefer, you can use cherry tomatoes in place of the blood oranges in this recipe.
> When blood oranges are out of season and not available, normal oranges can be used instead.

Golden Beef and Potato Puffs

These crisp, golden pillows of pastry filled with spiced beef and potatoes are delicious served straight from the wok. The light pastry puffs up in the hot oil and contrasts enticingly with the fragrant spiced beef.

Serves 4
15ml/1 tbsp sunflower oil
½ small onion, finely chopped
3 garlic cloves, crushed
5ml/1 tsp fresh root ginger, grated
1 red chilli, seeded and chopped
30ml/2 tbsp hot curry powder
75g/3oz minced (ground) beef
115g/4oz mashed potato
60ml/4 tbsp chopped fresh
coriander (cilantro)
2 sheets ready-rolled, fresh
puff pastry
1 egg, lightly beaten
vegetable oil, for frying
salt and ground black pepper
fresh coriander (cilantro) leaves,
to garnish
tomato ketchup, to serve

1 Heat the oil in a wok, then add the onion, garlic, ginger and chilli. Stir-fry over a medium heat for 2–3 minutes. Add the curry powder and beef and stir-fry over a high heat for a further 4–5 minutes, or until the beef is browned and just cooked through, then remove from the heat.

2 Transfer the beef mixture to a large bowl and add the mashed potato and chopped fresh coriander. Stir well, then season and set aside.

3 Lay the pastry sheets on a clean, dry surface and cut out eight rounds, using a 7.5cm/3in pastry (cookie) cutter. Place a large spoonful of the beef mixture in the centre of each pastry round. Brush the edges of the pastry with the beaten egg and fold each round in half to enclose the filling. Press and crimp the edges with the tines of a fork to seal.

4 Fill a wok one-third full of oil and heat to 180°C/350°F (or until a cube of bread, dropped into the oil, browns in 15 seconds).

5 Deep-fry the puffs, in batches, for about 2–3 minutes until they turn a golden brown colour. Drain on kitchen paper and serve garnished with fresh coriander leaves. Offer tomato ketchup to diners for dipping.

Chicken Wings Energy 500kcal/2077kJ; Protein 44.8g; Carbohydrate 0g, of which sugars 0g; Fat 35.6g, of which saturates 8.9g; Cholesterol 196mg; Calcium 14mg; Fibre 0g; Sodium 132mg.
Golden Beef Puffs Energy 408kcal/1695kJ; Protein 9g; Carbohydrate 24.2g, of which sugars 1.8g; Fat 31.8g, of which saturates 4.2g; Cholesterol 67mg; Calcium 46mg; Fibre 0.5g; Sodium 202mg.

Pineapple with Ginger and Chilli

This fruity seasonal salad is delicious when served alongside spicy dishes.

Serves 4

30ml/2 tbsp groundnut (peanut) oil
2 garlic cloves, finely shredded
40g/1½oz fresh root ginger, peeled and finely shredded
2 red Thai chillies, seeded and finely shredded
1 pineapple, trimmed, peeled, cored and cut into chunks
15ml/1 tbsp Thai fish sauce
30ml/2 tbsp soy sauce
15ml–30ml/1–2 tbsp sugar
30ml/2 tbsp roasted unsalted peanuts, finely chopped
1 lime, cut into quarters, to serve

1 Heat a large wok or heavy pan and add the oil. Stir in the garlic, ginger and chilli. Stir-fry until they begin to colour. Add the pineapple and stir-fry until the edges turn golden.

2 Stir in the fish sauce, soy sauce and sugar to taste and stir-fry until the pineapple begins to caramelize. Transfer to a serving dish, sprinkle with the peanuts and serve with lime wedges.

Beetroot with Fresh Mint

For adding a splash of colour to a cold wintry day, this salad is hard to beat. The dressing brings out the earthy flavour of beetroot.

Serves 4

4–6 cooked beetroot (beets), peeled and diced
5–10ml/1–2 tsp sugar
15–30ml/1–2 tbsp balsamic vinegar
juice of ½ lemon
30ml/2 tbsp extra virgin olive oil
1 bunch fresh mint, leaves stripped and thinly sliced
salt

1 Put the cooked beetroot in a bowl. Add the sugar, balsamic vinegar, lemon juice, olive oil and a pinch of salt and toss together.

2 Add half the thinly sliced fresh mint to the salad and toss lightly. Chill the salad for about 1 hour. Serve garnished with the remaining thinly sliced mint leaves.

Curried Red Cabbage Slaw

A variation on a classic, this spicy coleslaw is excellent for adding flavour and colour to a meal on a winter's day. Quick and easy to make, it is a useful dish for a last-minute gathering.

Serves 4–6

½ red cabbage, thinly sliced
1 red (bell) pepper, chopped or very thinly sliced
½ red onion, chopped
60ml/4 tbsp red or white wine vinegar or cider vinegar
60ml/4 tbsp sugar, or to taste
120ml/4fl oz/½ cup Greek (US strained plain) yogurt or natural (plain) yogurt
120ml/4fl oz/½ cup mayonnaise, preferably home-made
1.5ml/¼ tsp curry powder
2–3 handfuls of raisins
salt and ground black pepper

1 Put the cabbage, red pepper and red onions in a bowl and toss to combine thoroughly.

2 Heat the vinegar and sugar in a small pan until the sugar has dissolved, then pour over the vegetables. Leave to cool slightly.

3 Mix together the yogurt and mayonnaise, then stir into the cabbage mixture. Season to taste with curry powder, salt and ground black pepper, then mix in the raisins.

4 Chill the salad in the refrigerator for at least 2 hours before serving. Just before serving, drain off any excess liquid and briefly stir the slaw again.

Cook's Tip
If you have the time, it is worth making your own mayonnaise at home. If not, buy the best quality you can find.

Variation
To ring the changes, add extra ingredients to the basic slaw. Choose sliced celery, olives, raisins, chopped red (bell) pepper, chopped cooked potatoes and chopped spring onions (scallions).

Pineapple with Ginger Energy 203kcal/844kJ; Protein 2.7g; Carbohydrate 16g, of which sugars 15.4g; Fat 14.7g, of which saturates 1.9g; Cholesterol 0mg; Calcium 31mg; Fibre 1.8g; Sodium 810mg.
Beetroot with Fresh Mint Energy 90kcal/378kJ; Protein 1.7g; Carbohydrate 8.9g, of which sugars 8.3g; Fat 5.6g, of which saturates 0.8g; Cholesterol 0mg; Calcium 21mg; Fibre 1.9g; Sodium 66mg.
Red Cabbage Slaw Energy 286kcal/1194kJ; Protein 3.5g; Carbohydrate 31.6g, of which sugars 31g; Fat 17g, of which saturates 2.6g; Cholesterol 17mg; Calcium 108mg; Fibre 3.1g; Sodium 134mg.

Winter Coleslaw

A delicious and nutritious mixture of crunchy, seasonal vegetables, fruit and nuts, tossed together in a mayonnaise dressing.

Serves 6
225g/8oz white cabbage
1 large carrot
175g/6oz/ ¾ cup ready-to-eat
   dried apricots
50g/2oz/ ½ cup walnuts
50g/2oz/ ½ cup hazelnuts
115g/4oz/ ⅔ cup raisins
30ml/2 tbsp chopped
   fresh parsley
105ml/7 tbsp mayonnaise
75ml/5 tbsp natural (plain) yogurt
salt and ground black pepper
fresh chives, to garnish (optional)

1 Finely shred the cabbage, removing any tough core pieces, and coarsely grate the carrot. Place both in a large mixing bowl.

2 Roughly chop the dried apricots, walnuts and hazelnuts. Stir them into the cabbage and carrot mixture with the raisins and chopped parsley.

3 In a separate bowl, mix together the mayonnaise and yogurt and season to taste with salt and pepper.

4 Add the mayonnaise dressing to the cabbage mixture and toss together to mix. Cover the bowl with cling film (plastic wrap) and set aside in a cool place for at least 30 minutes before serving, to allow the flavours to mingle. Garnish with a few fresh chives and serve.

Variations
• For a salad that is lower in fat, use low-fat natural (plain) yogurt and reduced-calorie mayonnaise.
• Instead of walnuts and hazelnuts, use flaked almonds and chopped pistachios.
• Omit the dried apricots and add a cored and chopped, unpeeled eating apple.
• Substitute other dried fruit or a mixture for the apricots – try nectarines, peaches or prunes.

Chicory Salad with Roquefort

The distinctive flavour and creamy richness of Roquefort cheese perfectly complements the slightly bitter taste of the salad leaves in this palate-tingling salad. Chicory, also known as Belgian endive, and celery are both in season during the winter months. Warmed crusty bread makes the ideal accompaniment.

Serves 4
30ml/2 tbsp red wine vinegar
5ml/1 tsp Dijon mustard
60ml/2fl oz/¼ cup walnut oil
15–30ml/1–2 tbsp sunflower oil
2 chicory (Belgian endive) heads,
   white or red
1 celery heart or 4 celery sticks,
   peeled and cut into
   julienne strips
75g/3oz/1 cup walnut halves,
   lightly toasted
30ml/2 tbsp chopped fresh parsley
115g/4oz Roquefort
   cheese, crumbled
fresh parsley sprigs, to garnish

1 Whisk together the vinegar and mustard in a small bowl, then whisk in salt and pepper to taste. Slowly whisk in the walnut oil, then the sunflower oil.

2 Divide the chicory heads into leaves and arrange decoratively on individual plates. Sprinkle over the celery julienne strips, walnut halves and chopped parsley.

3 Crumble equal amounts of Roquefort cheese over each serving and drizzle a little vinaigrette over each. Garnish with parsley sprigs and serve immediately.

Cook's Tip
Roquefort is a rich, blue cheese with a soft, crumbly texture and quite a sharp flavour. Good for salads or cooking, it is made in the village of Roquefort in France and is produced from ewe's milk. The good sheep-grazing land and limestone caves in this district contribute to giving the cheese its unique flavour. Roquefort is widely available in larger supermarkets, but if you have difficulty in finding it, you could use another well-flavoured blue cheese, such as Gorgonzola or Stilton.

Winter Coleslaw Energy 309kcal/1285kJ; Protein 4.3g; Carbohydrate 19.1g, of which sugars 18.8g; Fat 24.5g, of which saturates 2.9g; Cholesterol 13mg; Calcium 72mg; Fibre 2.5g; Sodium 103mg.
Chicory Salad Energy 361kcal/1488kJ; Protein 9.4g; Carbohydrate 1.5g, of which sugars 1.3g; Fat 35.3g, of which saturates 7.9g; Cholesterol 22mg; Calcium 204mg; Fibre 1.8g; Sodium 423mg.

Potato Salad with Capers and Black Olives

A dish from southern Italy, this salad is a perfect combination of olives, capers and anchovies.

Serves 4–6
900g/2lb large white potatoes
50ml/2fl oz/¼ cup white
    wine vinegar
75ml/5 tbsp olive oil

30ml/2 tbsp chopped flat
    leaf parsley
30ml/2 tbsp capers,
    finely chopped
50g/2oz/½ cup pitted black
    olives, chopped in half
3 garlic cloves, finely chopped
50g/2oz marinated anchovies
    (unsalted)
salt and ground black pepper

1 Boil the potatoes in their skins in a large pan for 20 minutes or until just tender. Remove from the pan using a slotted spoon and place them in a separate bowl.

2 When the potatoes are cool enough to handle, carefully peel off the skins. Cut the peeled potatoes into even chunks and place in a large, flat earthenware dish.

3 In a bowl, mix together the white wine vinegar and the olive oil. Season to taste with salt and ground black pepper.

4 Add the fresh parsley, capers, black olives and garlic to the dressing. Toss carefully to combine all the ingredients thoroughly and then pour over the potato chunks in the dish. The potatoes will absorb more of the dressing if they are still a little warm at this stage.

5 Lay the anchovies on top of the salad. Cover with a cloth and leave the salad to settle for 30 minutes or so before serving to allow the flavours to penetrate.

> **Variation**
> If you want to serve this dish to vegetarians, simply omit the anchovies, it tastes delicious even without them.

Black and Orange Salad with a Spicy Dressing

This dramatically colourful winter salad is dressed with a mildly spiced vinaigrette. It is ideal for serving with plainly grilled seasonal meat and fish.

Serves 4
3 oranges
115g/4oz/1 cup pitted black olives

15ml/1 tbsp chopped fresh
    coriander (cilantro)
15ml/1 tbsp chopped fresh parsley

For the dressing
30ml/2 tbsp olive oil
15ml/1 tbsp lemon juice
2.5ml/½ tsp paprika
2.5ml/½ tsp ground cumin

1 Cut a slice off the top and bottom of one orange to reveal the flesh. Place the orange upright on a board and, using a small sharp knife, cut off the skin, taking care to remove all the bitter white pith. Repeat with the remaining oranges, then cut between the membranes to release the segments.

2 Place the orange segments in a salad bowl and add the black olives, coriander and parsley.

3 To make the dressing, blend together the olive oil, lemon juice, paprika and cumin.

4 Pour the dressing over the salad and toss gently until all the ingredients are thoroughly mixed. Chill for about 30 minutes before serving.

> **Variation**
> The strong flavours and vivid colours of this salad work brilliantly with couscous. Adapt the recipe by chopping the orange segments and olives quite finely. Mix the finely chopped olives and oranges with the herbs and dressing into a bowl of cooked couscous while it is still warm. Either chill the salad or serve it immediately. It's delicious cold or warm – and perfect for a picnic with cold chicken or smoked ham.

Black and Orange Salad Energy 129kcal/537kJ; Protein 1.8g; Carbohydrate 11.1g, of which sugars 10.6g; Fat 9g, of which saturates 1.3g; Cholesterol 0mg; Calcium 79mg; Fibre 3g; Sodium 654mg.
Potato Salad Energy 282kcal/1174kJ; Protein 5g; Carbohydrate 24.4g, of which sugars 2.2g; Fat 18.9g, of which saturates 2.8g; Cholesterol 5mg; Calcium 54mg; Fibre 2g; Sodium 347mg.

Winter Cabbage Salad with Coconut and Lime Dressing

This is a simple and delicious way of serving a somewhat mundane winter vegetable. Classic Thai flavours permeate this colourful warm salad.

Serves 4–6
30ml/2 tbsp vegetable oil
2 large fresh red chillies, seeded and cut into thin strips
6 garlic cloves, thinly sliced
6 shallots, thinly sliced
1 small cabbage, shredded
30ml/2 tbsp coarsely chopped roasted peanuts, to garnish

For the dressing
30ml/2 tbsp Thai fish sauce
grated rind of 1 lime
30ml/2 tbsp fresh lime juice
120ml/4fl oz/½ cup coconut milk

1 To make the dressing, mix the fish sauce, lime rind and juice and coconut milk in a bowl. Whisk well, then set aside.

2 Heat the oil in a wok. Stir-fry the chillies, garlic and shallots over medium heat for 3–4 minutes, until the shallots are brown and crisp. Remove with a slotted spoon and set aside.

3 Bring a large pan of lightly salted water to the boil. Add the cabbage and blanch for 2–3 minutes. Turn into a colander, drain well and transfer to a bowl.

4 Whisk the dressing again, add it to the warm cabbage and toss to mix. Transfer the salad to a serving dish. Sprinkle with the fried shallot mixture and the peanuts. Serve immediately.

Cook's Tip
Buy coconut milk in cans from supermarkets and ethnic stores.

Variation
Other seasonal vegetables, such as cauliflower, broccoli and Chinese leaves (Chinese cabbage), can be cooked in this way.

Roasted Beetroot with Horseradish Dressing

Fresh beetroot is enjoying a well-deserved renaissance. Roasting gives it a delicious sweet flavour, which contrasts wonderfully with this sharp, tangy dressing.

Serves 4
450g/1lb baby beetroot (beet), preferably with leaves
15ml/1 tbsp olive oil

For the dressing
30ml/2 tbsp lemon juice
30ml/2 tbsp mirin or saké
120ml/8 tbsp olive oil
30ml/2 tbsp creamed horseradish
salt and ground black pepper

1 Cook the unpeeled beetroot in boiling salted water for 30 minutes. Drain, add the olive oil and toss gently. Preheat the oven to 200°C/400°F/Gas 6.

2 Place the beetroot on a baking sheet and roast in the preheated oven for about 40 minutes or until tender when pierced with a knife.

3 Meanwhile, make the dressing. Whisk together the lemon juice, mirin or saké, olive oil and horseradish until smooth and creamy. Season with salt and pepper to taste.

4 Peel the beetroot, cut them in half, place in a bowl and add the dressing. Toss gently and serve immediately.

Cook's Tips
• *This salad is probably at its best served warm, but you can make it in advance, if you wish, and serve it at room temperature. Add the dressing just before serving.*
• *Beetroot has a reputation for containing cancer-fighting compounds and is thought to enhance the immune system. It is a powerful blood-purifier and is rich in iron, vitamins C and A, and folates, which are essential for healthy cells.*

Cabbage Salad Energy 798kcal/3334kJ; Protein 38.5g; Carbohydrate 131.8g, of which sugars 127.7g; Fat 14.3g, of which saturates 1.4g; Cholesterol 0mg; Calcium 1259mg; Fibre 53.7g; Sodium 461mg.
Roasted Beetroot Energy 254kcal/1052kJ; Protein 2.1g; Carbohydrate 10g, of which sugars 9.1g; Fat 22.2g, of which saturates 3.2g; Cholesterol 1mg; Calcium 26mg; Fibre 2.3g; Sodium 143mg.

Beetroot, Apple and Potato Salad

This salad is from Finland, where it is known as rosolli. It is served on Christmas Eve, just as the festive excitement mounts. The sweet apple and beetroot are the perfect partner for potatoes, pickled gherkins and eggs.

Serves 4

1 apple
3 cooked potatoes, finely diced
2 large gherkins, finely diced
3 cooked beetroot (beet), finely diced
3 cooked carrots, finely diced
1 onion, finely chopped
500ml/17fl oz/generous 2 cups double (heavy) cream
3 hard-boiled eggs, roughly chopped
15ml/1 tbsp chopped fresh parsley
salt and ground white pepper

1 Cut the apple into small dice. Place the pieces into a large bowl and add the diced potatoes, gherkins, beetroot, carrots and onion. Season the ingredients with plenty of salt and ground black pepper.

2 Carefully mix together all the ingredients in the bowl until they are well combined. Spoon the mixture into individual serving bowls.

3 Place the double cream into a separate bowl. Add any juice from the diced beetroot into the cream to give it additional flavour and an attractive pinkish colour. Stir well until the juice and cream are thoroughly combined.

4 Spoon the beetroot cream over the chopped vegetables and apple. Sprinkle the chopped eggs and parsley over the top of each portion before serving.

Variation
Stir in 1/2 finely chopped salted herring fillet or 2 finely chopped anchovy fillets to the mixture with the parsley to add an extra dimension to the dish. Omit the added salt if you add the fish, as they will be salty themselves.

Baked Sweet Potato Salad

This salad has a tropical taste and is ideal served with Asian dishes to brighten up a dull wintry day.

Serves 4–6

1kg/2¼lb sweet potatoes
1 red (bell) pepper, seeded and finely diced
3 celery sticks, finely diced
¼ red onion, finely chopped
1 fresh red chilli, finely chopped
salt and ground black pepper
coriander (cilantro) leaves, to garnish

For the dressing
45ml/3 tbsp chopped fresh coriander (cilantro)
juice of 1 lime
150ml/¼ pint/⅔ cup natural (plain) yogurt

1 Preheat the oven to 200°C/400°F/Gas 6. Wash the potatoes, and pierce them all over with a fork. Place in the oven and bake for about 40 minutes, or until tender.

2 Meanwhile, make the dressing. Whisk together the coriander, lime juice and yogurt in a small bowl and season to taste with salt and pepper. Chill in the refrigerator while you prepare the remaining salad ingredients.

3 In a large bowl, mix the diced red pepper, celery, chopped onion and chilli together.

4 Remove the potatoes from the oven. As soon as they are cool enough to handle, peel them and cut them into cubes. Add them to the bowl.

5 Drizzle the dressing over and toss gently to combine. Taste and adjust the seasoning, if necessary. Serve, garnished with coriander leaves.

Cook's Tip
It is generally thought that the seeds are the hottest part of a chilli. In fact, they contain no capsaicin – the hot element – but it is intensely concentrated in the flesh surrounding them. Removing the seeds usually removes this extra-hot flesh.

Beetroot Potato Salad Energy 717kcal/2959kJ; Protein 8.5g; Carbohydrate 11g, of which sugars 10.2g; Fat 71.5g, of which saturates 42.9g; Cholesterol 314mg; Calcium 114mg; Fibre 2.3g; Sodium 132mg.
Baked Sweet Potato Salad Energy 176kcal/750kJ; Protein 4g; Carbohydrate 40.4g, of which sugars 14.1g; Fat 1g, of which saturates 0.3g; Cholesterol 0mg; Calcium 116mg; Fibre 5.2g; Sodium 103mg.

Beef and Sweet Potato Salad

This delicious salad makes an attractive main dish for a winter buffet or party, especially if the beef has been cut into strips.

Serves 6–8
800g/1¾lb fillet of beef
5ml/1 tsp black
    peppercorns, crushed
10ml/2 tsp chopped fresh thyme
60ml/4 tbsp olive oil
450g/1lb orange-fleshed sweet
    potato, peeled and sliced
salt and ground black pepper

For the dressing
1 garlic clove, chopped
15g/½oz flat leaf parsley
30ml/2 tbsp chopped fresh
    coriander (cilantro)
15ml/1 tbsp small salted
    capers, rinsed
½–1 fresh green chilli, seeded
    and chopped
10ml/2 tsp Dijon mustard
10–15ml/2–3 tsp white
    wine vinegar
75ml/5 tbsp extra virgin olive oil
2 shallots, finely chopped

1 Roll the beef fillet in the crushed peppercorns and thyme, then set aside to marinate for a few hours. Preheat the oven to 200°C/400°F/Gas 6.

2 Heat half the olive oil in a frying pan. Add the beef and brown it all over, turning frequently, to seal it. Place on a baking sheet and cook in the oven for 10–15 minutes. Remove from the oven, and cover with foil, then leave to rest for 10–15 minutes.

3 Meanwhile, preheat the grill (broiler). Brush the sweet potato with the remaining olive oil, season to taste with salt and pepper, and grill (broil) for about 5–6 minutes on each side, until browned. Cut into strips and place them in a bowl. Cut the beef into slices or strips and toss with the sweet potato.

4 To make the dressing, process the garlic, parsley, coriander, capers, chilli, mustard and 10ml/2 tsp of the vinegar in a food processor until chopped. With the motor still running, gradually pour in the oil to make a smooth dressing. Season and add more vinegar, to taste. Stir in the shallots.

5 Toss the dressing into the sweet potatoes and beef and mix until the ingredients are well coated. Leave to stand for up to 2 hours before serving.

Seared Mixed Onion Salad

This unusual and delicious salad is brilliant served as an accompaniment to a winter meal of grilled meat and fish. It can also be served simply alongside fresh crusty bread and a selection of cold meats and cheeses, making it ideal for a buffet.

Serves 4
6 red spring onions
    (scallions), trimmed
6 green salad onions, trimmed
    and split lengthwise
250g/9oz small or baby (pearl)
    onions, peeled and left whole

2 pink onions, sliced horizontally
    into 5mm/4in rounds
2 red onions, sliced into wedges
2 small yellow onions, sliced
    into wedges
4 banana shallots, halved
    lengthways
200g/7oz shallots
45ml/3 tbsp olive oil, plus extra
    for drizzling
juice of 1 lemon
45ml/3 tbsp chopped fresh flat
    leaf parsley
30ml/2 tbsp balsamic vinegar
salt and ground black pepper

1 Preheat the grill (broiler). Spread the onions and shallots in a large flat dish.

2 Whisk the oil and lemon juice together and pour over. Turn the onions and shallots in the dressing to coat them evenly. Season to taste.

3 Put the onions and shallots on a griddle or a grill pan placed under the hot grill. Cook for 5–7 minutes, turning occasionally. Alternatively, cook the onions on a preheated barbecue, once the coals are coated in ash.

4 Just before serving, add the parsley and gently toss to mix, then drizzle over the balsamic vinegar and extra olive oil.

Cook's Tip
The proportions of onions in this dish aren't set in stone, so feel free to mix and match the quantities of the different varieties depending on what is available in the store.

Beef Salad Energy 300kcal/1253kJ; Protein 21.9g; Carbohydrate 12g, of which sugars 3.2g; Fat 18.6g, of which saturates 4.6g; Cholesterol 61mg; Calcium 18mg; Fibre 1.4g; Sodium 67mg.
Seared Onion Salad Energy 183kcal/762kJ; Protein 4.5g; Carbohydrate 22.6g, of which sugars 16.7g; Fat 9.1g, of which saturates 1.2g; Cholesterol 0mg; Calcium 100mg; Fibre 5g; Sodium 17mg.

Stir-fried Cauliflower with Garlic Crumbs

Brussels Sprouts with Bacon and Caraway Seeds

Brussels sprouts are not usually associated with stir-frying, but this style of cooking helps to retain their crunchy texture. Shredding the sprouts and cooking them briefly guarantees that there will not be a single soggy sprout in sight.

Serves 4

*450g/1lb Brussels sprouts,
    trimmed and washed*
30ml/2 tbsp sunflower oil
*2 streaky (fatty) bacon rashers
    (strips), finely chopped*
*10ml/2 tsp caraway seeds,
    lightly crushed*
salt and ground black pepper

1 Using a sharp knife, cut the Brussels sprouts into fine shreds and set aside. Heat the oil in a wok or large frying pan and add the bacon. Cook for 1–2 minutes, or until the bacon is beginning to turn golden.

2 Add the shredded sprouts to the wok or pan and stir-fry for 1–2 minutes, or until lightly cooked.

3 Season the sprouts with salt and ground black pepper to taste and stir in the caraway seeds. Cook for a further 30 seconds, then serve immediately.

> **Variation**
> *Add a few sliced water chestnuts to the stir-fry to introduce an extra crunchy texture. Cook fresh chestnuts for about 5 minutes, canned for 2 minutes to retain their crispness.*

> **Cook's Tips**
> • *The sulphurous flavour that many people dislike in Brussels sprouts is produced when they are overcooked. Briefly stir-frying them avoids this problem.*
> • *Caraway seeds have a flavour rather like aniseed and are much used in central and eastern European cookery.*

This method of cooking cauliflower is very simple and it makes a great accompaniment to any meat or dairy meal. The garlic breadcrumbs add bite and flavour. If you are not keen on garlic it can be omitted and the cauliflower can be topped with grated cheese. Brown the cheese topping under a hot grill.

Serves 4–6

*1 large cauliflower, cut into
    bitesize florets*
pinch of sugar
*90–120ml/6-8 tbsp olive or
    vegetable oil*
*130g/4½ oz/2¼ cups dry white
    or wholemeal (whole-wheat)
    breadcrumbs*
*3–5 garlic cloves, thinly sliced
    or chopped*
salt and ground black pepper

1 Steam or boil the cauliflower in a pan of water, to which you have added the sugar and a pinch of salt, until just tender. Drain the cauliflower in a colander and leave to cool.

2 Heat 60–75ml/4–5 tbsp of the olive or vegetable oil in a pan, add the breadcrumbs and cook over medium heat, tossing and turning, until browned and crisp. Add the garlic, turn once or twice, then remove from the pan and set aside.

3 Heat the remaining oil in the pan, then add the cauliflower, mashing and breaking it up a little as it lightly browns in the oil. (Do not overcook but just cook lightly in the oil.)

4 Add the garlic breadcrumbs to the pan and cook them, stirring, until well combined and some of the cauliflower is still holding its shape. Season with salt and pepper and spoon into a heated dish. Serve hot or warm.

> **Cook's Tip**
> *In Israel, where this dish is popular, it is often eaten with meat or fish wrapped in filo pastry, since the textures and flavours complement each other perfectly.*

Stir-fried Cauliflower Energy 204kcal/852kJ; Protein 5.5g; Carbohydrate 19.3g, of which sugars 2.7g; Fat 12.2g, of which saturates 1.7g; Cholesterol 0mg; Calcium 46mg; Fibre 2g; Sodium 172mg.
Brussels Sprouts Energy 131kcal/545kJ; Protein 5.9g; Carbohydrate 4.6g, of which sugars 3.5g; Fat 10g, of which saturates 2g; Cholesterol 8mg; Calcium 30mg; Fibre 4.6g; Sodium 164mg.

Kale with Mustard Dressing

Sea kale is used for this dish, available in many regions between January and March. Use curly kale if you can't get sea kale, although you should boil it briefly for a few minutes.

Serves 4

250g/9oz sea kale or curly kale
45ml/3 tbsp light olive oil
5ml/1 tsp wholegrain mustard
15ml/1 tbsp white wine vinegar
pinch of caster (superfine) sugar
salt and ground black pepper

1 Wash the sea kale, drain thoroughly, then trim it and cut in two. Whisk the oil into the mustard. When it is blended completely, whisk in the wine vinegar. It should begin to thicken.

2 Season the dressing to taste with sugar, salt and pepper. Toss the sea kale in the dressing and serve immediately.

Spiced Greens

Here is a really good way to enliven your winter greens, great for cabbage but also good for kale.

Serves 4

1 medium cabbage
15ml/1 tbsp groundnut (peanut) oil
5ml/1 tsp grated fresh root ginger
2 garlic cloves, grated
2 shallots, finely chopped
2 red chillies, seeded and sliced
salt and ground black pepper

1 Remove any tough outer leaves from the cabbage, then quarter it and remove the core. Shred the leaves.

2 Pour the groundnut oil into a large pan and as it heats stir in the ginger and garlic. Add the shallots and as the pan becomes hotter add the chillies.

3 Add the greens and toss to mix. Cover the pan and reduce the heat to create some steam. Cook, shaking the pan occasionally, for about 3 minutes. Remove the lid and increase the heat to dry off the steam, season with salt and pepper and serve immediately in a heated bowl.

Colcannon

This traditional Irish dish is especially associated with Halloween, when it is likely to be made with seasonal curly kale and would have a ring hidden in it – predicting marriage during the coming year for the person who found it. At other times during the winter green cabbage is more often used.

Serves 3–4

450g/1lb potatoes, peeled and boiled
450g/1lb curly kale or cabbage, cooked
milk, if necessary
50g/2oz/¼ cup butter, plus extra for serving
1 large onion, finely chopped
salt and ground black pepper

1 Mash the potatoes and spoon them into a large bowl. Chop the kale or cabbage, add it to the potatoes and mix. Stir in a little milk if the mash is too stiff, and season with salt and ground black pepper.

2 Melt a little butter in a frying pan over a medium heat and add the onion. Cook for 3–4 minutes until softened. Remove and mix well with the potato and kale or cabbage.

3 Add the remainder of the butter to the hot pan. When it is very hot, turn the potato mixture on to the pan and spread it out in an even layer.

4 Fry the potato mixture until golden brown, then cut it roughly into pieces and continue frying until these are crisp and brown.

5 Spoon the colcannon into a large serving bowl or individual bowls, and add a generous knob of butter to each. Serve immediately. As the butter melts, guests can fork it in to the cabbage mixture.

Cook's Tip
This winter dish is delicious when served as an accompaniment to pork chops or sausages for a substantial meal, or you can serve it simply with fried eggs.

Kale with Mustard Dressing Energy 99kcal/409kJ; Protein 2.1g; Carbohydrate 1.9g, of which sugars 1.9g; Fat 9.3g, of which saturates 1.3g; Cholesterol 0mg; Calcium 82mg; Fibre 2g; Sodium 27mg.
Spiced Greens Energy 77kcal/322kJ; Protein 2.6g; Carbohydrate 9.9g, of which sugars 9.4g; Fat 3.1g, of which saturates 0.5g; Cholesterol 0mg; Calcium 90mg; Fibre 3.9g; Sodium 13mg.
Colcannon Energy 1224kcal/5124kJ; Protein 21.6g; Carbohydrate 162.4g, of which sugars 54.4g; Fat 58.4g, of which saturates 35.2; Cholesterol 144mg; Calcium 416mg; Fibre 23.6g; Sodium 508mg.

Crispy Winter Cabbage

Like so many wintertime brassicas, this winter staple is lovely when crisp, yet utterly horrible when soggy. In this recipe the balance is just right.

Serves 4–6
1 medium green or small white cabbage
30–45ml/2–3 tbsp oil
salt and ground black pepper

1 Remove the central core from the cabbage as well as any coarse outside leaves and the central rib from the larger remaining leaves.

2 Place the cabbage on a board and shred the leaves finely. Wash under cold running water, drain in a colander, shake well and blot on kitchen paper to dry thoroughly.

3 Heat a wok or wide-based flameproof casserole over fairly high heat. Heat the oil and add the cabbage. Stir-fry for 2–3 minutes, using one or two wooden spoons to keep the cabbage moving so that it cooks evenly but is still crunchy. Season with salt and plenty of ground black pepper and serve immediately.

Cook's Tip
Don't throw away the coarse outer leaves and central rib from the cabbage. They can be used with other vegetables such as onions and carrots to make vegetable stock. As long as the cabbage doesn't dominate, the flavour will be very good.

Variation
For cabbage with a bacon dressing, fry 225g/8oz diced streaky (fatty) bacon in a pan. Set aside while cooking the cabbage. Remove the cabbage from the pan and keep warm with the bacon. Boil 15ml/1 tbsp wine or cider vinegar with the juices remaining in the pan. Bring to the boil and season with ground black pepper. Pour over the cabbage and bacon. This makes a versatile side dish, and is especially good with chicken.

Braised Red Cabbage

Sweet, tangy red cabbage is a wintertime favourite in many regions. It is outstanding when paired with roast pork. It is also served as the traditional accompaniment for a Christmas goose or duck. If the blend of sweet, sour and fruity flavours weren't enticing enough, the vivid violet colour would captivate anyone. This vegetable dish looks as good as it tastes.

Serves 6
1.3kg/3lb red cabbage
50ml/2fl oz/¼ cup distilled white vinegar
25g/1oz/2 tbsp butter
1 medium onion, finely chopped
2 tart apples, peeled, cored and thinly sliced
50g/2oz/¼ cup sugar
120ml/4fl oz/½ cup blackcurrant juice or jam
1.5ml/¼ tsp ground allspice
6 whole cloves salt

1 Remove the outer leaves and core of the red cabbage and cut it into quarters. Thinly chop or shred the cabbage, and place in a large pan.

2 Add 120ml/4fl oz/½ cup water and the vinegar and bring to the boil. Reduce the heat, cover and simmer for 1 hour, stirring occasionally to prevent scorching.

3 Meanwhile, melt the butter in a large frying pan over a medium heat. Stir in the onion and apple and cook for 5–7 minutes until soft.

4 Stir the apples and onions into the cabbage with the sugar, blackcurrant juice or jam, allspice and cloves, and season with salt. Simmer gently for a further 1½ hours. Adjust the seasoning to taste before serving.

Cook's Tip
If blackcurrant juice or jam are not available, you can substitute apple juice or redcurrant jelly, if you like. The cabbage will be just as delicious.

Crispy Cabbage Energy 56kcal/230kJ; Protein 1.2g; Carbohydrate 4.2g, of which sugars 4.1g; Fat 3.8g, of which saturates 0.5g; Cholesterol 0mg; Calcium 41mg; Fibre 1.8g; Sodium 6mg.
Braised Red Cabbage Energy 90kcal/381kJ; Protein 3.1g; Carbohydrate 19.4g, of which sugars 18g; Fat 0.5g, of which saturates 0g; Cholesterol 0mg; Calcium 98mg; Fibre 5g; Sodium 14mg.

Sauerkraut Pie

This winter pie uses shortcrust pastry, and is filled with a mixture of sauerkraut, two types of cabbage and chunks of ham.

Serves 4

300g/11oz sauerkraut
20g/¾oz/1½ tbsp butter
5ml/1 tsp sugar
100ml/3½fl oz/scant ½ cup white wine
150g/5oz white cabbage, shredded
150g/5oz Savoy cabbage, shredded
150g/5oz boiled ham, cubed
1 egg yolk
5ml/1 tsp water

For the pastry

275g/10oz/2½ cups plain (all-purpose) flour
5ml/1 tsp salt
150g/5oz/10 tbsp unsalted butter
45ml/3 tbsp vegetable oil
25ml/1½ tbsp water

1 To make the pastry, put the flour and salt in a large bowl. Cut the butter into small pieces, add to the flour and rub in until the mixture resembles fine breadcrumbs. Alternatively, put the flour and salt in a food processor, add the butter and, using a pulsing action, blend to form fine breadcrumbs. Add the oil and water and mix to form a dough. Shape into a ball, cover with a clean dish towel, then leave to rest in the refrigerator for 1 hour.

2 Rinse the sauerkraut in cold running water if necessary, then put in a pan with the butter and sugar and heat for 1–2 minutes. Add the wine, cover the pan, bring the mixture to the boil, then remove from the heat.

3 Cook the shredded white and the Savoy cabbage in boiling salted water for about 5 minutes until tender, then drain, refresh under cold running water, and drain again. Put in a bowl and add the sauerkraut and ham. Mix together well and transfer to a deep, ovenproof pie dish.

4 Preheat the oven to 180°C/350°F/Gas 4. Roll out the pastry on a lightly floured surface so that it is large enough to cover the dish, and place it over the dish. Combine the egg yolk and water and brush over the pie to glaze. Bake in the oven for 20 minutes or until the pastry is golden brown. Serve hot.

Swede Pudding

A traditional Finnish Christmas dish, this baked pudding combines mashed swede with butter and cream to make a delicious vegetable accompaniment. The texture of swede is quite dense compared, for example, with parsnip, so you will need to cut it into relatively small dice or allow for extra cooking time.

Serves 4

1 large swede (rutabaga), diced
40g/1½oz/3 tbsp butter, plus extra for greasing
200ml/7fl oz/scant 1 cup double (heavy) cream
50g/2oz/1 cup fine fresh breadcrumbs
2.5ml/½ tsp grated nutmeg
5ml/1 tsp salt
2 eggs, beaten

1 Put the diced swede in a large pan and cover generously with water. Bring to the boil, lower the heat and simmer for about 20 minutes until tender.

2 Remove the pan from the heat and leave the swede to cool in the water for about 30 minutes. Drain well through a sieve (strainer) and mash the swede.

3 Preheat the oven to 180°C/350°F/Gas 4. Grease a deep, ovenproof dish with butter. Pour the cream into a bowl, add the breadcrumbs, nutmeg and salt and mix together. Add the beaten eggs.

4 Add the cream mixture to the mashed swede and mix together. Spoon the mixture into the prepared dish and dot the surface with the butter. Bake in the oven for about 30 minutes until lightly browned. Serve hot.

Cook's Tips
• Swede (rutabaga) is generally available throughout the whole winter.
• Unlike potato, it contains no gluten, so it will not turn sticky if puréed in a food processor. The other ingredients can then be added to the processing bowl as soon as the swede is blended.

Sauerkraut Pie Energy 728kcal/3032kJ; Protein 16.3g; Carbohydrate 59.8g, of which sugars 7.4g; Fat 46.8g, of which saturates 24.1g; Cholesterol 163mg; Calcium 190mg; Fibre 5.4g; Sodium 1652mg.
Swede Pudding Energy 434kcal/1794kJ; Protein 6.3g; Carbohydrate 16.9g, of which sugars 7.4g; Fat 38.5g, of which saturates 22.7g; Cholesterol 185mg; Calcium 123mg; Fibre 2.7g; Sodium 712mg.

Clapshot

This root vegetable dish is perfect in winter, and is an excellent accompaniment to haggis or used on top of a shepherd's pie in place of mashed potato. Turnips give a delicious earthy flavour, and swede introduces a sweet accent. It is also less heavy than mashed potato, which makes it good for a lighter meal or supper.

Serves 4
450g/1lb potatoes
450g/1lb turnips or
  swede (rutabaga)
50g/2oz/1/4 cup butter
50ml/2fl oz/1/4 cup milk
5ml/1 tsp freshly grated nutmeg
30ml/2 tbsp chopped
  fresh parsley
salt and ground black pepper

1 Peel the potatoes and turnips or swede, then cut them into even small chunks. You will need a large sharp knife for the turnips.

2 Place the chopped vegetables in a pan and cover with cold water. Bring to the boil over a medium heat, then reduce the heat and simmer until both vegetables are cooked, which will take about 15–20 minutes. Test the vegetables by pushing the point of a sharp knife into one of the cubes; if it goes in easily and the cube begins to break apart, then it is cooked.

3 Drain the vegetables through a colander. Return to the pan and allow them to dry out for a few minutes over a low heat, stirring occasionally to prevent any from sticking to the base of the pan.

4 Place the butter and the milk in a small pan over a low heat. Gently heat until the butter has melted, stirring constantly to combine it with the milk.

5 Mash the dry potato and turnip or swede mixture with a potato masher, then add the milk mixture.

6 Grate in the nutmeg, add the chopped parsley, mix thoroughly and season to taste with salt and pepper. Serve immediately with roast meat or game.

Jerusalem Artichokes with Garlic

The slightly smoky and earthy flavour of Jerusalem artichokes is excellent with garlic, shallots and smoked bacon. They are generally available throughout the winter months.

Serves 4
50g/2oz/1/4 cup butter or
  50ml/3 1/2 tbsp olive oil
115g/4oz smoked bacon, chopped
800g/1 3/4 lb Jerusalem artichokes
8–12 garlic cloves, peeled
115g/4oz shallots, chopped
75ml/5 tbsp water
30ml/2 tbsp olive oil
25g/1oz/1/2 cup fresh white or
  wholemeal (whole-wheat)
  breadcrumbs
30–45ml/2–3 tbsp chopped
  fresh parsley
sea salt and ground black pepper

1 Melt half the butter or heat half the olive oil in a heavy frying pan, add the chopped bacon and cook until it is brown and just beginning to crisp. Remove half the bacon from the frying pan and set aside.

2 Add the artichokes, garlic and shallots to the pan, and cook, stirring frequently, for 5–6 minutes or until the artichokes and garlic begin to brown slightly.

3 Season with salt and ground black pepper to taste and stir in the water. Cover and cook for a further 8–10 minutes, shaking the pan occasionally.

4 Uncover the pan, increase the heat and cook for 5 minutes, or until all the moisture has evaporated and the artichokes are tender.

5 In another frying pan, heat the remaining butter or oil with the 30ml/2 tbsp olive oil. Add the white or wholemeal breadcrumbs and fry over a moderate heat, stirring frequently with a wooden spoon, until crisp and golden. Stir in the chopped parsley and the reserved cooked bacon.

6 Combine the artichokes with the crispy breadcrumb and bacon mixture, mixing well. Season to taste with a little salt and plenty of ground black pepper, if necessary. Transfer to a warmed serving dish and serve immediately.

Clapshot Energy 204kcal/852kJ; Protein 3.4g; Carbohydrate 24.1g, of which sugars 7.2g; Fat 11.2g, of which saturates 6.8g; Cholesterol 27mg; Calcium 78mg; Fibre 3.8g; Sodium 111mg.
Jerusalem Artichokes Energy 377kcal/1575kJ; Protein 9.3g; Carbohydrate 39.4g, of which sugars 4.5g; Fat 21.3g, of which saturates 9.3g; Cholesterol 42mg; Calcium 31mg; Fibre 2.6g; Sodium 589mg.

Roasted Jerusalem Artichokes

Jerusalem artichokes grow easily in many parts of the world, and this wintry vegetable conceals a deliciously sweet white flesh inside the knobbly brown exterior. While they are best known for soups, their natural sweetness enables them to glaze easily and they make a delicious side vegetable with many foods, but have a special affinity with game – of which many meats are available in the winter season.

Serves 6
*675g/1½lb Jerusalem
    artichokes
15ml/1 tbsp lemon juice
    or vinegar
salt
50g/2oz/¼ cup unsalted butter
seasoned flour, for dusting*

1 Peel the artichokes, dropping them straight into a bowl of water acidulated with lemon juice or vinegar to prevent browning. Cut up the artichokes so that the pieces are matched for size, otherwise they will cook unevenly.

2 Preheat the oven to 180°C/350°F/Gas 4. Bring a pan of salted water to the boil, drain the artichokes from the acidulated water and boil them for 5 minutes, or until just tender. Watch them carefully, as they break up easily.

3 Melt the butter in a roasting pan, coat the artichokes in the seasoned flour and roll them around in the butter in the pan.

4 Cook the butter and flour coated artichokes in the preheated oven for 20–30 minutes, or until golden brown. Serve immediately.

Variation
Puréeing is a useful fall-back if the artichokes break up during cooking: simply blend or mash the drained boiled artichokes with salt and freshly ground black pepper to taste and a little single (light) cream, if you like. Puréed artichokes are especially good served with game, which tends to be dry.

Cheesy Creamy Leeks

Serve this rich dish as a meal in itself with brown rice.

Serves 4
*4 large leeks or 12 baby leeks,
    trimmed and washed
15ml/1 tbsp olive oil
150ml/¼ pint/⅔ cup double
    (heavy) cream
75g/3oz mature (sharp) Cheddar
    or Monterey Jack cheese, grated
salt and ground black pepper*

1 Preheat the grill (broiler) to high. If using large leeks, slice them lengthways. Heat the oil in a frying pan and add the leeks. Season and cook for 4 minutes, stirring, until turning golden.

2 Pour the cream into the pan and stir until well combined. Allow to bubble gently for a few minutes.

3 Transfer the creamy leeks to a shallow ovenproof dish and sprinkle with the cheese. Grill for 4–5 minutes, or until the cheese is golden brown and bubbling and serve immediately.

Jerusalem Artichokes au Gratin

This dish is a lovely accompaniment to roast meat or fried fish.

Serves 4
*250ml/8fl oz/1 cup sour cream
50ml/2fl oz/¼ cup single
    (light) cream
675g/1½lb Jerusalem artichokes,
    coarsely chopped
40g/1½oz/½ cup grated
    Danbo or Cheddar cheese
60ml/4 tbsp fresh breadcrumbs
salt*

1 Preheat the oven to 190°C/375°F/Gas 5. Grease an ovenproof dish. Mix the sour cream and single cream and season with salt.

2 Add the artichokes to the cream and toss to coat evenly. Spread the artichokes over the bottom of the prepared dish.

3 Sprinkle evenly with the cheese, then the breadcrumbs. Bake for 30 minutes, until the cheese melts and the top is bubbling.

Roasted Artichokes Energy 101kcal/419kJ; Protein 0.7g; Carbohydrate 8.9g, of which sugars 8.4g; Fat 7.2g, of which saturates 4.5g; Cholesterol 18mg; Calcium 30mg; Fibre 2.7g; Sodium 242mg.
Cheesy Leeks Energy 322kcal/1330kJ; Protein 7.8g; Carbohydrate 5g, of which sugars 4g; Fat 29.8g, of which saturates 17.1g; Cholesterol 70mg; Calcium 193mg; Fibre 3.3g; Sodium 147mg.
Jerusalem Artichokes Energy 296kcal/1230kJ; Protein 6.9g; Carbohydrate 27.6g, of which sugars 15.5g; Fat 18.1g, of which saturates 11.1g; Cholesterol 52mg; Calcium 186mg; Fibre 4.4g; Sodium 240mg.

Baked Leek and Potato Gratin

Potatoes baked in a creamy cheese sauce make the ultimate comfort dish for a cold winter's day, whether served as an accompaniment to pork or fish or, as here, with plenty of leeks and cheese as a main course.

Serves 4–6
900g/2lb medium potatoes, thinly sliced
2 large leeks, trimmed
200g/7oz ripe Brie cheese, sliced
450ml/³⁄₄ pint/scant 2 cups single (light) cream
salt and ground black pepper

1 Preheat the oven to 180°C/350°F/Gas 4. Cook the potatoes in plenty of lightly salted, boiling water for 3 minutes, until slightly softened, then drain.

2 Cut the leeks into 1cm/½in slices and blanch them in a pan of boiling water for 1–2 minutes, until softened, then drain.

3 Place half the potatoes into a lightly greased ovenproof dish and spread them out. Cover the potatoes with about two-thirds of the leeks, then add the remaining potatoes on top.

4 Tuck the cheese and the remaining leeks in among the potatoes. Season with salt and pepper and pour the cream over.

5 Bake for 1 hour, until tender and golden. Cover with foil if the top starts to overbrown before the potatoes are tender.

Cook's Tip
When preparing leeks, separate the leaves and rinse them thoroughly under cold running water, as soil and grit often get caught between the layers.

Variation
This dish can be made with vegetable stock in place of the cream if you are concerned about calories.

Carrot Bake

Carrots and rice are surprisingly well-suited partners. The characteristic stickiness of the short grain pudding rice binds all the other ingredients together to make a satisfying and comforting winter's dish.

Serves 4
500g/1¼lb carrots, sliced
500ml/17fl oz/generous 2 cups water

5ml/1 tsp salt
100g/3³⁄₄oz/½ cup short grain rice
100ml/3½fl oz/scant ½ cup milk
25g/1oz/2 tbsp butter, softened, for greasing
30ml/2 tbsp demerara (raw) sugar
2 eggs, beaten
2.5ml/½ tsp ground white pepper
25g/1oz/½ cup fine fresh breadcrumbs

1 Put the carrots in a large pan and cover generously with water. Bring the water to the boil, lower the heat and simmer for about 20 minutes until the carrots are tender. Remove the carrots with a slotted spoon and mash in a clean pan.

2 Bring the liquid the carrots were cooked in to the boil, then add the salt and the rice and simmer for 25 minutes. Add the milk and simmer until it has been absorbed.

3 Preheat the oven to 200°C/400°F/Gas 6. Use the butter to grease a deep, ovenproof dish. Transfer the cooked rice to a bowl. Add the mashed carrots, sugar and eggs and mix together. Season the mixture with salt and the ground white pepper.

4 Spoon the carrot mixture into the prepared dish and sprinkle the breadcrumbs over the top. Place in the preheated oven and bake for about 40 minutes or until golden brown. Serve immediately.

Cook's Tip
Cooking rice for a savoury dish in water first helps to speed up the cooking time. Milk can then be added halfway through to give a creamier texture to the finished dish.

Carrot and Parsnip Purée

This purée features two of the favourite winter vegetables. The creaminess of purées appeals to all ages, and they are ideal partners for crisp, seasonal vegetables such as lightly cooked Savoy cabbage or pan-fried kale. If serving the purée directly on to plates, mould it by using two spoons.

Serves 6–8
350g/12oz carrots
450g/1lb parsnips
a pinch of freshly grated nutmeg
　or ground mace
15g/¹/₂oz/1 tbsp butter
about 15ml/1 tbsp single (light)
　cream or crème fraîche
a small bunch of parsley,
　chopped, plus extra to garnish
salt and ground black pepper

1 Peel the carrots and slice fairly thinly. Peel the parsnips and cut into bitesize chunks.

2 Boil the carrots and parsnips in separate pans of lightly salted water until tender. Drain them well, then purée them together in a food processor, with the grated nutmeg or mace, a generous seasoning of salt and ground black pepper, and the butter. Whizz until smooth.

3 Transfer the purée to a mixing bowl and beat in the single cream or crème fraîche. Add the fresh parsley for extra flavour.

4 Transfer the carrot and parsnip purée to a warmed serving bowl, sprinkle with the remaining parsley to garnish, and serve immediately, as vegetable purées tend to lose their heat rapidly.

Cook's Tips
Any leftover purée can be thinned to taste with good-quality chicken or vegetable stock and heated to make a quick home-made soup. Add more seasoning if needed.

Variation
Use diced sweet potato instead of the carrots.

Parsnip and Chickpea Stew

Sweet parsnips go very well with the spices in this Indian-style winter stew, made in the slow cooker.

Serves 4
5 garlic cloves, finely chopped
1 small onion, chopped
5cm/2in piece fresh root ginger,
　finely chopped
2 green chillies, seeded and chopped
75ml/5 tbsp cold water
60ml/4 tbsp groundnut (peanut) oil
5ml/1 tsp cumin seeds
10ml/2 tsp coriander seeds
5ml/1 tsp ground turmeric

2.5ml/¹/₂ tsp chilli powder
　or mild paprika
50g/2oz/¹/₂ cup cashew nuts,
　toasted and ground
225g/8oz tomatoes, peeled
　and chopped
400g/14oz can chickpeas, drained
　and rinsed
900g/2lb parsnips, cut into chunks
350ml/12fl oz/1¹/₂ cups boiling
　vegetable stock
juice of 1 lime, to taste
salt and ground black pepper
chopped fresh coriander (cilantro)
　leaves, toasted cashew nuts and
　natural (plain) yogurt, to serve

1 Reserve 10ml/2 tsp of the garlic, then place the remainder in a food processor or blender with the onion, ginger and half the chillies. Add the water and process to a smooth paste.

2 Heat the oil in a large frying pan, add the cumin seeds and cook for 30 seconds. Stir in the coriander seeds, turmeric, chilli powder or paprika and the ground cashew nuts. Add the ginger and chilli paste and cook, stirring frequently, until the paste starts to bubble and the water begins to evaporate.

3 Add the tomatoes to the pan and cook for 1 minute. Transfer the mixture to the ceramic cooking pot and switch the slow cooker to high. Add the chickpeas and parsnips to the pot and stir to coat in the spicy tomato mixture, then stir in the stock and season with salt and pepper. Cover with the lid and cook on high for 4 hours, or until the parsnips are tender.

4 Stir half the lime juice, the reserved garlic and green chillies into the stew. Re-cover and cook for 30 minutes more, then taste and add more lime juice if needed. Spoon on to plates and sprinkle with fresh coriander leaves and toasted cashew nuts. Serve immediately, with a generous spoonful of natural yogurt.

Carrot and Parsnip Purée Energy 71kcal/298kJ; Protein 1.5g; Carbohydrate 10.7g, of which sugars 6.6g; Fat 2.7g, of which saturates 1.4g; Cholesterol 5mg; Calcium 49mg; Fibre 4g; Sodium 31mg.
Parsnip Stew Energy 453kcal/1899kJ; Protein 14.8g; Carbohydrate 50.1g, of which sugars 16.6g; Fat 23g, of which saturates 4.3g; Cholesterol 0mg; Calcium 148mg; Fibre 15.8g; Sodium 394mg.

Creamy Potato and Parsnip Bake

As the potatoes and parsnips cook, they gradually absorb the garlic-flavoured cream, while the cheese on top browns to a crispy finish.

Serves 4–6
3 large potatoes, total weight about 675g/1½lb
350g/12oz parsnips

200ml/7fl oz/scant 1 cup single (light) cream
105ml/7 tbsp milk
2 garlic cloves, crushed
5ml/1 tsp freshly grated nutmeg
butter, for greasing
75g/3oz/¾ cup coarsely grated Gruyère cheese
salt and ground black pepper

1 Peel the potatoes and parsnips and cut them into thin slices, using a sharp knife. Place them in a pan of salted boiling water and cook for 5 minutes. Drain and leave to cool slightly.

2 Meanwhile, pour the cream and milk into a heavy pan, add the garlic and bring to the boil. Remove the pan from the heat and leave to stand for about 10 minutes.

3 Lightly grease a 25cm/10in rectangular earthenware baking dish. Preheat the oven to 180°C/350°F/Gas 4.

4 Layer the potatoes and parsnips in the prepared dish, seasoning each layer with salt, pepper and a little grated nutmeg.

5 Pour the garlic-flavoured cream and milk mixture into the dish and press the sliced potatoes and parsnips down into the liquid. The liquid should come to just underneath the top layer. Cover with lightly buttered foil and bake for 45 minutes.

6 Remove the dish from the oven and remove the foil from the dish. Sprinkle the grated Gruyère cheese over the vegetables in an even layer.

7 Return the dish to the oven and bake, uncovered, for a further 20–30 minutes, or until the potatoes and parsnips are both tender and the topping has turned golden brown. Serve immediately.

Potato Gnocchi

Gnocchi are little dumplings made either with potato and flour, or with semolina.

Serves 4–6
1kg/2¼lb waxy potatoes
250–300g/9–11oz/2¼–2¾ cups plain (all-purpose) flour, plus more if necessary

1 egg
pinch of freshly grated nutmeg
25g/1oz/2 tbsp butter
salt
fresh basil leaves, to garnish
Parmesan cheese cut in shavings, to garnish

1 Cook the potatoes in their skins in a large pan of boiling salted water until tender but not falling apart. Drain and peel while the potatoes are still hot.

2 Spread a layer of flour on a work surface. Pass the hot potatoes through a food mill, dropping them directly on to the flour. Sprinkle with about half of the remaining flour and mix in very lightly. Break the egg into the mixture.

3 Finally, add the nutmeg to the dough and knead lightly, adding more flour if the mixture is too loose. When the dough is light to the touch and no longer moist it is ready to be rolled. Divide the dough into four pieces. On a lightly floured surface, form each into a roll about 2cm/¾in in diameter. Cut the rolls crossways into equally-sized pieces of about 2cm/¾in in length.

4 Hold an ordinary table fork with tines sideways, leaning on the board. Then one by one, press and roll the gnocchi lightly along the tines of the fork towards the points, making ridges on one side, and a depression from your thumb on the other.

5 Bring a large pan of salted water to the boil, then drop in about half the gnocchi. When they rise to the surface, after about 3–4 minutes, they are done. Lift them out of the pan with a slotted spoon, drain well, and place in a warmed serving bowl. Dot with knobs of butter. Cover to keep warm while cooking the remainder. As soon as they are cooked, toss the gnocchi with the butter, garnish with Parmesan and basil leaves, and serve immediately.

Potato Bake Energy 241kcal/1009kJ; Protein 7.8g; Carbohydrate 27g, of which sugars 6.4g; Fat 11.7g, of which saturates 7.2g; Cholesterol 31mg; Calcium 174mg; Fibre 3.8g; Sodium 126mg.
Potato Gnocchi Energy 296kcal/1254kJ; Protein 7.8g; Carbohydrate 59.2g, of which sugars 2.8g; Fat 4.7g, of which saturates 2.3g; Cholesterol 39mg; Calcium 74mg; Fibre 3g; Sodium 52mg.

Grated Potato Casserole

This recipe comes from Finland. The floury, maincrop potatoes available throughout winter will produce the best results.

Serves 4

a small knob (pat) of butter
2 eggs
250ml/8floz/1 cup full-fat (whole) milk
30ml/2 tbsp plain (all-purpose) flour
5ml/1 tsp salt
2 potatoes
15ml/1 tbsp chopped fresh parsley, to garnish (optional)

1 Preheat the oven to 180°C/350°F/Gas 4. Melt the butter gently in a pan and use it to grease an ovenproof dish.

2 Beat the eggs together in a large mixing bowl, then add the milk and mix together.

3 Add the flour and salt to the eggs and milk and mix with your hands until the mixture forms a smooth batter.

4 Peel the potatoes, then grate them using a hand grater and add them to the batter.

5 Transfer the potato mixture to the prepared dish, then bake in the oven for about 50 minutes, until the potatoes are cooked. Serve hot, sprinkled with chopped parsley, if using.

Cook's Tip
Fresh parsley is simple to grow yourself. Buy a plant and keep it on a windowsill in your kitchen. Ensure it is kept moist but don't over-water it, and pull off the leaves as and when you need them. They will regrow in a matter of days.

Variation
To make a richer, creamier version, substitute half the milk with single (light) cream, if you like.

Roasted Sweet Potatoes, Onions and Beetroot in Coconut Paste

Sweet potatoes and beetroot become wonderfully sweet when slowly roasted. They work well with savoury onions and an aromatic coconut, ginger and garlic paste.

Serves 4

30ml/2 tbsp groundnut (peanut) or mild olive oil
450g/1lb sweet potatoes, peeled and cut into strips or chunks
4 beetroot (beets), cooked, peeled and cut into wedges
450g/1lb small onions, halved
5ml/1 tsp coriander seeds, crushed
3–4 small whole fresh red chillies
salt and ground black pepper
chopped fresh coriander (cilantro), to garnish

For the paste
2 large garlic cloves, chopped
1–2 green chillies, seeded and chopped
15ml/1 tbsp chopped fresh root ginger
45ml/3 tbsp chopped fresh coriander (cilantro)
75ml/5 tbsp coconut milk
30ml/2 tbsp groundnut (peanut) or mild olive oil
grated rind of ½ lime
2.5ml/½ tsp soft light brown sugar

1 To make the paste, process the garlic, chillies, ginger, coriander and coconut milk in a food processor or blender. Transfer the paste into a small bowl and beat in the oil, grated lime rind and light brown sugar. Preheat the oven to 200°C/400°F/Gas 6.

2 Heat the oil in a large roasting pan in the oven for 5 minutes. Add the sweet potatoes, beetroot, onions and coriander seeds, tossing them in the hot oil. Roast the vegetables for 10 minutes.

3 Stir in the paste and the whole red chillies. Season well with salt and pepper, and shake the pan to toss the vegetables and coat them thoroughly with the paste.

4 Return the vegetables to the oven and cook for a further 25–35 minutes, or until the vegetables are tender. During cooking, stir the mixture two or three times to prevent the coconut and ginger paste from sticking to the roasting pan. Serve the vegetables immediately, garnished with a little chopped fresh coriander.

Potato Casserole Energy 215kcal/894kJ; Protein 8.7g; Carbohydrate 13g, of which sugars 3.3g; Fat 14.7g, of which saturates 7.7g; Cholesterol 123mg; Calcium 277mg; Fibre 3g; Sodium 297mg.
Sweet Potatoes Energy 272kcal/1143kJ; Protein 4.4g; Carbohydrate 39.8g, of which sugars 19.2g; Fat 11.8g, of which saturates 1.7g; Cholesterol 0mg; Calcium 98mg; Fibre 6.3g; Sodium 122mg.

Halibut with Leek and Ginger

Generally fish needs to be absolutely fresh, but halibut needs to mature for a day or two to bring out the flavour. Sometimes the catch is so fresh the fish needs to be refrigerated for a day or so before cooking.

Serves 4
2 leeks
50g/2oz piece fresh root ginger
4 halibut steaks, approximately 175g/6oz each (see Cook's Tip)
15ml/1 tbsp olive oil
75g/3oz/6 tbsp butter
salt and ground black pepper
mashed potato, to serve

1 Trim the leeks, discarding the coarse outer leaves, the very dark green tops and the root end. Cut them into 5cm/2in lengths, then slice into thin matchsticks. Wash thoroughly.

2 Peel the fresh ginger as best you can, then slice it very thinly and cut the slices into thin sticks.

3 Dry the halibut on kitchen paper. Heat a large pan with the oil and add 50g/2oz/¼ cup of the butter. As it begins to bubble, place the steaks carefully in the pan, skin side down. Allow the halibut to colour – about 3–4 minutes. Then turn the steaks over, reduce the heat and cook for about a further 10 minutes.

4 Remove the fish from the pan, set aside and keep warm. Add the leeks and ginger to the pan, stir to mix, then allow the leeks to soften (they may colour slightly but this is fine). Once softened, season with a little salt and ground black pepper. Cut the remaining butter into small pieces then, off the heat, gradually stir into the pan.

5 Serve the halibut steaks topped with the leek and ginger mixture. Accompany with mashed potato, if you like.

Cook's Tip
Ask your fishmonger for flattish halibut steaks that are not too thick as you want to cook them in a pan on the stove and not in the oven. Also ask him or her to skin them for you.

Fillets of Turbot with Oysters

This luxurious dish is perfect in winter as the main ingredients are at their best.

Serves 4
12 Pacific (rock) oysters
115g/4oz/½ cup butter
2 carrots, cut into julienne strips
200g/7oz celeriac, cut into julienne strips
the white parts of 2 leeks, cut into julienne strips
375ml/13fl oz/generous 1½ cups Champagne or dry white sparkling wine (about ½ bottle)
105ml/7 tbsp whipping cream
1 turbot, about 1.75kg/4–4½lb, filleted and skinned
salt and ground white pepper

1 Using an oyster knife, open the oysters over a bowl to catch the juices, then carefully remove them, discarding the shells, and place them in a separate bowl. Set aside until required.

2 Melt 25g/1oz/2 tbsp of the butter in a shallow pan, add the vegetable julienne and cook over a low heat until tender but not coloured. Pour in half the Champagne or sparkling wine and cook very gently until all the liquid has evaporated. Keep the heat low so that the vegetables do not colour.

3 Strain the oyster juices into a small pan and add the cream and the remaining Champagne or wine. Simmer until the mixture has reduced a little. Dice half the remaining butter and whisk it into the sauce until smooth. Season to taste, then pour the sauce into a blender and process until velvety smooth.

4 Return the sauce to the pan, bring it to just below boiling point, then drop in the oysters. Poach for 1 minute, to warm but barely cook. Keep warm, but do not let the sauce boil.

5 Season the turbot fillets. Heat the remaining butter in a large frying pan, then cook the fillets over medium heat for about 2–3 minutes on each side, until cooked through and golden.

6 Cut each turbot fillet into three pieces and arrange on individual warmed plates. Pile the vegetable julienne on top, place three oysters around the turbot fillets on each plate and pour the sauce around the edge.

Halibut with Leek Energy 364kcal/1520kJ; Protein 39.1g; Carbohydrate 2.7g, of which sugars 2.1g; Fat 21.9g, of which saturates 10.8g; Cholesterol 101mg; Calcium 75mg; Fibre 1.9g; Sodium 221mg.
Fillets of Turbot Energy 752kcal/3125kJ; Protein 66.7g; Carbohydrate 9.2g, of which sugars 8g; Fat 44.1g, of which saturates 23.9g; Cholesterol 106mg; Calcium 252mg; Fibre 1.4g; Sodium 370mg.

Smoked Haddock Bake with a Cheese Crumb

Haddock is available throughout winter and is a very popular and versatile fish. It takes to smoking very well and this is a way of enjoying the fish, even when it isn't in season. Serve this comforting dish as a filling appetizer, or accompany it with crusty bread and a leafy winter salad as a light meal or snack.

Serves 4
350g/12oz smoked haddock
450ml/³⁄₄ pint/scant 2 cups milk
25g/1oz/2 tbsp butter
25g/1oz/4 tbsp plain
   (all-purpose) flour
115g/4oz mature (sharp)
   Cheddar cheese, grated
60ml/4 tbsp fresh breadcrumbs
salt and ground black pepper
crusty bread and a leafy salad,
   to serve

1 Remove and discard all skin and bones from the haddock and cut the fish into strips.

2 Put the milk, butter and flour into a pan and season with salt and black pepper. Over medium heat and whisking constantly, bring to the boil and bubble gently for 2–3 minutes until thick and smooth.

3 Add the haddock and half the cheese to the hot sauce and bring it just back to the boil to melt the cheese.

4 Divide the mixture between individual flameproof dishes or ramekins. Toss together the remaining cheese and the breadcrumbs and sprinkle the mixture over the top of each filled dish.

5 Put the dishes under a hot grill (broiler) until bubbling and golden. Serve immediately with crusty bread.

Cook's Tip
The flavour and colour of this dish is best when made with pale, undyed smoked haddock rather than the bright yellow artificially dyed variety.

Smoked Haddock with Mustard Cabbage

This seasonal dish is very simple and quick to make and yet tastes absolutely delicious. Serve with baked potatoes for a main meal.

Serves 4
1 Savoy or pointu cabbage
675g/1¹⁄₂lb undyed smoked
   haddock fillet
300ml/¹⁄₂ pint/1¹⁄₄ cups milk
¹⁄₂ onion, sliced into rings
2 bay leaves
¹⁄₂ lemon, sliced
4 white peppercorns
4 ripe tomatoes
50g/2oz/¹⁄₄ cup butter
30ml/2 tbsp wholegrain mustard
juice of 1 lemon
salt and ground black pepper
30ml/2 tbsp chopped fresh
   parsley, to garnish

1 Cut the cabbage in half, remove the central core and thick ribs, then shred the cabbage. Cook in a pan of lightly salted, boiling water, or steam over boiling water for about 10 minutes, until just tender. Leave in the pan or steamer until required.

2 Meanwhile, put the haddock in a large shallow pan with the milk, onion and bay leaves. Add the lemon slices and peppercorns. Bring to simmering point, cover and poach until the fish flakes easily when tested with the tip of a sharp knife. Depending on the thickness of the fish, this takes 8–10 minutes. Remove the pan from the heat. Preheat the grill (broiler).

3 Cut the tomatoes in half horizontally, season them with salt and pepper and grill (broil) until lightly browned. Drain the cabbage, refresh under cold water and drain again.

4 Melt the butter in a shallow pan or wok, add the shredded cabbage and toss over the heat for 2 minutes. Mix in the mustard and season to taste, then tip the cabbage into a warmed serving dish.

5 Drain the haddock. Skin and cut the fish into four pieces. Place on top of the cabbage with some onion rings and grilled (broiled) tomato halves. Pour on the lemon juice, then sprinkle with chopped parsley and serve.

Haddock Bake Energy 363kcal/1525kJ; Protein 30.1g; Carbohydrate 21.8g, of which sugars 5.8g; Fat 17.4g, of which saturates 10.8g; Cholesterol 79mg; Calcium 396mg; Fibre 0.5g; Sodium 1073mg.
Smoked Haddock Energy 319kcal/1340kJ; Protein 36.1g; Carbohydrate 14.2g, of which sugars 13.7g; Fat 13.1g, of which saturates 7.3g; Cholesterol 90mg; Calcium 146mg; Fibre 4.2g; Sodium 1512mg.

Haddock with Spicy Puy Lentils

Grey-green Puy lentils have a delicate taste and texture and hold their shape during cooking, which makes them particularly good for slow cooker dishes. Haddock is a highly welcome addition to the winter kitchen.

Serves 4

175g/6oz/³/₄ cup Puy lentils
600ml/1 pint/2½ cups near-
   boiling vegetable stock

30ml/2 tbsp olive oil
1 onion, finely chopped
2 celery sticks, finely chopped
1 red chilli, halved, seeded
   and finely chopped
2.5ml/½ tsp ground cumin
four thick 150g/5oz pieces of
   haddock fillet or steak
10ml/2 tsp lemon juice
25g/1oz/2 tbsp butter, softened
5ml/1 tsp finely grated lemon rind
salt and ground black pepper
lemon wedges, to garnish

1 Put the lentils in a sieve (strainer) and rinse under cold running water. Drain well, then tip into the ceramic cooking pot. Pour over the hot vegetable stock, cover with the lid and switch the slow cooker on to high.

2 Heat the oil in a frying pan, add the onion and cook gently for 8 minutes. Stir in the celery, chilli and cumin, and cook for a further 2 minutes, or until soft but not coloured. Add the mixture to the lentils, stir, re-cover and cook for about 2½ hours.

3 Meanwhile, rinse the haddock pieces and pat dry on kitchen paper. Sprinkle them with the lemon juice. In a clean bowl, beat together the butter, lemon rind, salt and ground black pepper.

4 Put the haddock on top of the lentils, then dot the lemon butter over the top. Cover and cook for 45 minutes–1 hour, or until the fish flakes easily, the lentils are tender and most of the stock has been absorbed. Serve immediately, garnished with the lemon wedges.

> **Cook's Tip**
> *Any firm white fish can be cooked in this way. Both cod and swordfish give particularly good results.*

Kedgeree

A popular Victorian breakfast dish, kedgeree has its origins in kitchiri, an Indian dish of rice and lentils. It can be flavoured with curry powder, but this recipe is mild.

Serves 4

500g/1¼lb smoked haddock
115g/4oz/generous ½ cup
   basmati rice

50g/2oz/4 tbsp butter, diced, plus
   extra for greasing
30ml/2 tbsp lemon juice
150ml/¼ pint/⅔ cup single
   (light) cream or sour cream
pinch of freshly grated nutmeg
pinch of cayenne pepper
2 hard-boiled eggs, peeled and cut
   into wedges
30ml/2 tbsp chopped
   fresh parsley
salt and ground black pepper

1 Put the haddock in a shallow pan, pour in just enough water to cover and heat to simmering point. Poach the fish for about 10 minutes, until the flesh flakes easily when tested with the tip of a sharp knife. Lift the fish out of the liquid, then remove any skin and bones and flake the flesh. Reserve the cooking liquid,

2 Pour the cooking liquid into a measuring jug (cup) and make up the volume with water to 250ml/8fl oz/1 cup.

3 Pour the measured liquid into a pan and bring it to the boil. Add the rice, stir, then lower the heat, cover and simmer for about 10 minutes, until the rice is tender and the liquid has been absorbed. Meanwhile, preheat the oven to 180°C/350°F/ Gas 4 and butter a baking dish.

4 When the rice is cooked, remove it from the heat and stir in the lemon juice, cream, flaked haddock, grated nutmeg and cayenne pepper. Add the egg wedges to the rice mixture and stir in gently.

5 Transfer the rice mixture into the prepared baking dish. Level the surface and dot with butter. Cover the dish loosely with foil and bake for about 25 minutes.

6 Stir the chopped parsley into the baked kedgeree and add seasoning to taste. Serve immediately.

Haddock with Lentils Energy 366kcal/1538kJ; Protein 38.9g; Carbohydrate 25.2g, of which sugars 3.2g; Fat 12.8g, of which saturates 4.3g; Cholesterol 82mg; Calcium 64mg; Fibre 4.7g; Sodium 353mg.
Kedgeree Energy 320kcal/1336kJ; Protein 15.6g; Carbohydrate 46.6g, of which sugars 0g; Fat 7.6g, of which saturates 3.3g; Cholesterol 149mg; Calcium 39mg; Fibre 0g; Sodium 357mg.

Sea Bass with Orange Chilli Salsa

The chilli citrus salsa has a freshness which provides the perfect contrast to the wonderful flavour of fresh sea bass.

Serves 4
4 sea bass fillets
salt and ground black pepper

fresh coriander (cilantro),
    to garnish

For the salsa
2 fresh green chillies
2 oranges or pink grapefruit
1 small onion

1 Make the salsa. Roast the chillies in a dry griddle pan until the skins are blistered, being careful not to let the flesh burn. Put them in a strong plastic bag and tie the top to keep the steam in. Set aside for 20 minutes.

2 Slice the top and bottom off each orange or grapefruit then cut off all the peel and pith. Cut between the membranes and put each segment in a bowl.

3 Remove the chillies from the bag and peel off the skins. Cut off the stalks, then slit the chillies and scrape out the seeds. Chop the flesh finely. Cut the onion in half and slice it thinly. Add the onion and chillies to the orange pieces and mix lightly. Season and chill.

4 Season the sea bass fillets. Line a steamer with baking parchment, allowing extra to hang over the sides to help lift out the fish after cooking. Place the empty steamer over a pan of water and bring to the boil.

5 Place the fish in a single layer in the steamer. Cover and steam for 8 minutes, or until just cooked. Garnish with coriander and serve with the salsa and some seasonal vegetables.

> **Cook's Tip**
> If the fish has not been scaled, do this by running the back of a small filleting knife against the grain of the scales.

Sea Bass in a Salt Crust

Baking fish in a crust of sea salt keeps in the flavours, enhancing the natural taste of the fish. It is a popular way of cooking fish on the Greek islands, where large outside ovens are used to prevent the inside of buildings becoming too hot. Any firm fish can be cooked with a salt crust, but it is well suited to the seasonal sea bass.

Serves 4
1 sea bass, about 1kg/2¼lb, cleaned and scaled
1 sprig fresh fennel
1 sprig fresh rosemary
1 sprig fresh thyme
2kg/4½lb coarse sea salt
mixed peppercorns
seaweed or samphire, blanched, to garnish
salt and ground black pepper
lemon slices, to serve

1 Preheat the oven to 240°C/475°F/Gas 9. Spread half the salt on a shallow baking tray (ideally oval or rectangular).

2 Wash out the sea bass and dry any excess moisture with kitchen paper. Open the fish and lightly season the insides with salt and freshly ground black pepper, then fill the cavity of the fish with all the fresh herbs. Do not worry if the fish does not close properly as the herbs will become much more compact as soon as they have been heated through and cooked.

3 Lay the sea bass on the salt. Cover the fish with a 1cm/½in layer of salt, pressing it down firmly. Moisten the salt lightly by spraying with water from an atomizer. Bake the fish in the hot oven for 30–40 minutes, or until the salt crust is just beginning to colour.

4 Garnish the dish with seaweed or samphire and use a sharp knife to break open the salt crust at the table. Serve with lemon slices.

> **Cook's Tip**
> Make sure that you leave enough time for the oven to heat up properly, as a cooler oven will not be able to set the salt crust.

Sea Bass in a Salt Crust Energy 83kcal/351kJ; Protein 16.1g; Carbohydrate 0g, of which sugars 0g; Fat 2.1g, of which saturates 0.3g; Cholesterol 67mg; Calcium 109mg; Fibre 0g; Sodium 2021mg.
Sea Bass with Orange Energy 181kcal/763kJ; Protein 30.2g; Carbohydrate 6.6g, of which sugars 6.3g; Fat 3.9g, of which saturates 0.6g; Cholesterol 120mg; Calcium 232mg; Fibre 1.3g; Sodium 108mg.

Sea Bass with Leeks

Seasonal sea bass tastes sensational when given this simple treatment.

Serves 4

1 sea bass, about 1.4–1.5kg/
    3–3½ lb, scaled and cleaned
8 spring onions (scallions)
60ml/4 tbsp teriyaki marinade
30ml/2 tbsp cornflour
    (cornstarch)
juice of 1 lemon
30ml/2 tbsp rice wine vinegar
5ml/1 tsp ground ginger
60ml/4 tbsp groundnut
    (peanut) oil
2 leeks, shredded
2.5cm/1in piece fresh root ginger,
    peeled and grated
105ml/7 tbsp fish stock
30ml/2 tbsp dry sherry
5ml/1 tsp caster (superfine) sugar
salt and ground black pepper
cooked rice, to serve

1 Make several diagonal slashes on either side of the sea bass, then season the fish inside and out with salt and ground black pepper. Trim the spring onions, cut them in half lengthways, then slice them diagonally into 2cm/¾ in lengths. Put half of the spring onions in the cavity of the fish and reserve the rest.

2 In a shallow dish, mix together the teriyaki marinade, the cornflour, lemon juice, rice wine vinegar and ground ginger until it makes a smooth, runny paste. Turn the fish in the marinade to coat it thoroughly, working it into the slashes, then leave it to marinate for 20–30 minutes, turning it several times.

3 Heat a wok or frying pan that is large enough to hold the sea bass comfortably. Add the oil, then the leeks and grated ginger. Fry gently for about 5 minutes, until the leeks are tender. Remove the leeks and ginger and drain on kitchen paper.

4 Lift the sea bass out of the marinade and lower it into the hot oil. Fry over medium heat for 2–3 minutes on each side. Stir the stock, sherry and sugar into the marinade. Season with salt and pepper.

5 Pour the marinade mixture over the fish in the wok or pan. Return the leeks, ginger and reserved spring onions to the pan. Cover and simmer for about 15 minutes, until the fish is cooked. Serve immediately, with cooked rice.

Wrapped Sea Bass

This spicy dish is effortless but must be started in advance as the rice needs to be cold before it is used in the little parcels. Once the fish are wrapped, all you have to do is keep them chilled, ready to pop on to the barbecue – if the weather isn't too wintry.

400ml/14fl oz/1⅔ cups
    boiling water
45ml/3 tbsp extra virgin olive oil
1 small onion, chopped
1 fresh mild chilli, seeded and
    finely chopped
8 sea bass fillets, about 75g/3oz
    each, with skin
16 large fresh vine leaves
salt and ground black pepper

Serves 4

90g/3½oz/½ cup Chinese
    black rice

1 Place the rice in a pan. Add the boiling water and simmer for about 5 minutes. Add salt to taste and simmer for a further 10 minutes, or until tender. Drain and transfer to a bowl.

2 Meanwhile, heat half the oil in a frying pan. Fry the onion for 5 minutes until soft. Add the chilli. Stir into the rice mixture, adjust the seasoning and cool. Cover and chill until needed.

3 Season the sea bass fillets. Wash the vine leaves in water, then pat dry with kitchen paper. Lay each leaf in the centre of a double layer of foil. Top with a sea bass fillet.

4 Divide the rice mixture among the fillets, spooning it towards one end. Fold the fillet over the rice, trickle over the remaining oil, lay the second vine leaf on top and bring the foil up around the fish and scrunch together to seal. Chill for up to 3 hours, or until needed.

5 Prepare the barbecue. When the coals are hot, or with a light coating of ash, place the parcels on the edge of a grill rack. Cook for 5 minutes, turning them around 90 degrees halfway through. Open up the top of the foil a little and cook for about 2 minutes more. Gently remove from the foil and transfer the vine parcels to individual plates and serve.

Sea Bass Energy 300kcal/1253kJ; Protein 31.1g; Carbohydrate 7.5g, of which sugars 6.7g; Fat 15.4g, of which saturates 2g; Cholesterol 120mg; Calcium 229mg; Fibre 2.6g; Sodium 271mg.
Wrapped Sea Bass Energy 160kcal/669kJ; Protein 16.8g; Carbohydrate 8.7g, of which sugars 1.1g; Fat 6.4g, of which saturates 1g; Cholesterol 65mg; Calcium 120mg; Fibre 0.4g; Sodium 57mg.

Fillets of Brill in Red Wine Sauce

Forget the old maxim that red wine and fish do not go well together. The robust sauce adds colour and richness to this excellent fish dish, which is ideal for a winter dinner party.

Serves 4
4 fillets of brill, each about
    175g/6oz each, skinned

150g/5oz/10 tbsp chilled butter,
    plus extra for greasing
115g/4oz shallots, thinly sliced
200ml/7fl oz/scant 1 cup robust
    red wine
200ml/7fl oz/scant 1 cup
    fish stock
salt and ground white pepper
fresh chervil or flat leaf parsley
    leaves, to garnish

1 Preheat the oven to 180°C/350°F/Gas 4. Season the fish on both sides with a little salt and plenty of pepper. Generously butter a flameproof dish, which is large enough to take all the brill fillets in a single layer without overlapping.

2 Spread the shallots over the base and lay the fish fillets on top. Pour in the red wine and fish stock, cover the dish and bring the liquid to just below boiling point.

3 Transfer the dish to the preheated oven and bake for about 6–8 minutes, or until the brill is just cooked. It should flake readily if tested with the tip of a sharp knife.

4 Using a metal spatula, carefully lift the fish and shallots on to a serving dish, cover with foil and keep hot.

5 Transfer the dish to the hob and bring the cooking liquid to the boil over high heat. Cook until it has reduced by half.

6 Lower the heat and whisk in the chilled butter or margarine, one piece at a time, to make a smooth, shiny sauce. Season the sauce with salt and ground white pepper, remove from the heat and cover to keep hot.

7 Divide the shallots among four warmed plates and lay the brill fillets on top. Pour the sauce over and around the fish and garnish with the chervil or flat leaf parsley.

Grilled Hake with Lemon and Chilli

Nothing could be simpler than perfectly grilled seasonal fish with a dusting of chilli and lemon rind. This is an ideal meal for those occasions when something light is called for.

Serves 4
4 hake fillets, each 150g/5oz
30ml/2 tbsp olive oil
finely grated rind and juice
    of 1 lemon
15ml/1 tbsp crushed chilli flakes
salt and ground black pepper

1 Preheat the grill (broiler) to high. Brush the hake fillets with the olive oil and place them skin side up on a baking sheet.

2 Grill (broil) the fish for 4–5 minutes, until the skin is crispy, then carefully turn the fillets over in the pan, using a metal spatula or two spoons.

3 Sprinkle the fillets with the lemon rind and chilli flakes and season with salt and ground black pepper.

4 Grill the fillets for a further 2–3 minutes, or until the hake is cooked through. (Test using the point of a sharp knife; the flesh should flake.)

5 Transfer the fillets of hake to individual plates and squeeze over the lemon juice just before serving.

Cook's Tip
A pastry brush is the ideal implement for coating fish with oil, but keep one specifically for the purpose, unless you want your apple pie to taste slightly fishy. Draw a fish on the handle with a marker pen to distinguish it from your pastry brush.

Variation
Any firm white fish can be cooked in this simple, low-fat way. Try haddock, halibut or brill – all of which are in season over the winter. If you haven't got any chilli flakes, use chilli oil.

Fillets of Brill Energy 511kcal/2123kJ; Protein 35.7g; Carbohydrate 1.3g, of which sugars 1.3g; Fat 36.7g, of which saturates 19.5g; Cholesterol 156mg; Calcium 97mg; Fibre 0.4g; Sodium 454mg.
Grilled Hake Energy 188kcal/786kJ; Protein 27g; Carbohydrate 0.1g, of which sugars 0.1g; Fat 8.8g, of which saturates 1.2g; Cholesterol 35mg; Calcium 22mg; Fibre 0g; Sodium 150mg.

Hake with Turnip Tops and Onions

Hake is highly prized in many regions of Europe and is served in numerous different ways. Here, sautéed potatoes and leafy turnip tops are paired with this delicate fish for a truly stunning seasonal result. Serve with spinach or broccoli for a supper.

Serves 4
105ml/7 tbsp olive oil
2 small onions, chopped
2 garlic cloves, chopped
5ml/1 tsp sweet paprika
1 bay leaf
15ml/1 tbsp white wine vinegar
150ml/¼ pint/⅔ cup fish stock
  or water
4 hake steaks, about
  225g/8oz each
200g/7oz turnip tops (the green
  part of the turnip)
8 potatoes, boiled without peeling
4 hard-boiled eggs, halved
salt

1 Preheat the oven to 180°C/350°F/Gas 4. Heat 30ml/2 tbsp of the olive oil in a flameproof casserole. Add the onions, garlic, paprika and bay leaf and cook over a low heat, stirring occasionally, for 5 minutes, until the onions have softened.

2 Add the vinegar and the stock or water, then place the hake in the casserole and season with salt. Cover and cook in the oven for 15 minutes.

3 Meanwhile, steam the turnip tops or cook in a little boiling water for 3–5 minutes, then drain if necessary.

4 Press the cooked turnip tops through a sieve (strainer) into a bowl, mix with 15ml/1 tbsp of the remaining olive oil and keep warm.

5 Peel the potatoes and cut into quarters. Heat the remaining olive oil in a sauté pan or frying pan, add the potatoes and cook, turning occasionally, over medium-low heat for around 7–8 minutes until light golden brown.

6 Using a slotted spatula, transfer the fish to a large serving plate. Add the potatoes, turnip tops and eggs and spoon over the onion sauce. Serve immediately.

Monkfish in Beer

For a long time, fishermen believed that this fish brought bad luck and any that were caught were thrown back into the sea. Fortunately, the sweet taste and dense flesh has since earned it a place on the national menu, especially in the winter season. Here it is combined with leeks and wheat beer.

Serves 4
4 medium fillets of monkfish
50g/2oz/¼ cup unsalted
  (sweet) butter
2 leeks, white parts only,
  finely chopped
25ml/1½ tbsp plain
  (all-purpose) flour
5ml/1 tsp mustard (optional)
300ml/½ pint/1¼ cups Belgian
  Abbey beer or dry white wine
1–2 tbsp capers, rinsed
  and dried
salt and ground black pepper
15ml/1 tbsp chopped fresh
  chives, chervil or parsley,
  to garnish
cooked potatoes or rye bread, and
  lemon wedges, to serve

1 Preheat the oven to 180°C/350°F/Gas 4. Rinse the fish fillets and pat them dry. Season both sides with salt and pepper, and set aside.

2 Melt the butter in a frying pan over medium heat. Add the leeks and sauté for 3 minutes. Add the flour and stir for 2 minutes until it has been absorbed.

3 Stir in the mustard, if using, and continue to stir while gradually adding the beer or wine to the pan.

4 When the sauce thickens, after about 5 minutes, season it with salt and black pepper, then scrape it into a baking dish. Level the surface.

5 Arrange the fish fillets on the sauce, and sprinkle over the capers. Cover the dish with foil and bake for about 30 minutes, or until the fish flakes when tested with the tip of a sharp knife.

6 Garnish with the herbs and serve with the potatoes or rye bread, offering the lemon wedges separately for squeezing.

Hake Energy 614kcal/2571kJ; Protein 51g; Carbohydrate 36.2g, of which sugars 5.7g; Fat 30.7g, of which saturates 5.2g; Cholesterol 242mg; Calcium 102mg; Fibre 3.4g; Sodium 326mg.
Monkfish in Beer Energy 268kcal/1125kJ; Protein 33.3g; Carbohydrate 2.6g, of which sugars 2g; Fat 11.6g, of which saturates 6.8g; Cholesterol 55mg; Calcium 65mg; Fibre 2.3g; Sodium 123mg.

Monkfish with Clams and Coriander

This dish features two delicious riches from the sea – monkfish and clams. They are available throughout the season. This tasty main course manages to brighten up a cold winter's night. Serve with lots of crusty white bread to mop up the delectable juices.

Serves 4

200g/7oz live clams
600g/1lb 6oz monkfish fillet
1 bunch of coriander
   (cilantro), chopped
2 garlic cloves, chopped
105ml/7 tbsp fish stock
50ml/2fl oz/¼ cup olive oil
white bread, to serve

1 Scrub the clams under cold running water. Discard any clams with broken shells or that do not shut when sharply tapped with a knife.

2 Place the cleaned clams into a large, heavy pan that has a tight-fitting lid.

3 Add the monkfish, coriander and garlic to the pan. Pour in the stock and olive oil and stir gently to combine. Cover the pan and cook over medium heat for 15 minutes.

4 Remove and discard any clams that have not opened. Serve immediately with slices of white bread.

Cook's Tip
If you prefer, you can cook this dish in a preheated oven set to 180°C/350°F/Gas 4. Place all the ingredients in a flameproof casserole, cover and bake in the oven for about 20–30 minutes until all the seafood is cooked and tender.

Variation
You can also add a chopped onion, a seeded and diced red (bell) pepper and even some sliced pork sausage or chorizo to this dish.

Monkfish with Potatoes and Garlic

This simple baked dish can be made with other seasonal fish. Sauce tartare or a thick vinaigrette flavoured with chopped gherkins and hard-boiled egg are tasty accompaniments.

Serves 4

1kg/2¼lb waxy potatoes, cut
   into chunks
50g/2oz/¼ cup butter
2 onions, thickly sliced
4 garlic cloves

few fresh thyme sprigs
2–3 fresh bay leaves
450ml/¾ pint/scant 2 cups
   vegetable or fish stock,
   plus 45ml/3 tbsp
900g/2lb monkfish tail in
   one piece, skin and
   membrane removed
30–45ml/2–3 tbsp white wine
50g/2oz/1 cup fresh
   white breadcrumbs
15g/½ oz fresh parsley, chopped
15ml/1 tbsp olive oil
salt and ground black pepper

1 Preheat the oven to 190°C/375°F/Gas 5. Put the chunks of potato in an ovenproof dish. Melt half the butter in a large frying pan and cook the onions gently for 5–6 minutes. Add the onions to the potatoes and mix.

2 Slice 2–3 of the garlic cloves and add to the potatoes with the thyme and bay leaves, and season with salt and pepper. Pour in the main batch of stock over the potatoes and bake, stirring once or twice, for 50–60 minutes, until just tender.

3 Nestle the monkfish into the potatoes and season with salt and pepper. Bake for 10–15 minutes. Mix the 45ml/3 tbsp stock with the wine and use to baste the monkfish during cooking.

4 Finely chop the remaining garlic. Melt the remaining butter and toss it with the breadcrumbs, chopped garlic, most of the chopped parsley and seasoning. Spoon over the monkfish, pressing it down gently with the back of a spoon.

5 Drizzle the oil over the crumb-covered fish, return to the oven and bake for a further 10–15 minutes, until the breadcrumbs are crisp and all the liquid has been absorbed. Sprinkle the remaining fresh parsley on to the potatoes and serve immediately.

Monkfish with Clams Energy 193kcal/809kJ; Protein 27g; Carbohydrate 0.7g, of which sugars 0.3g; Fat 9.2g, of which saturates 1.4g; Cholesterol 34mg; Calcium 51mg; Fibre 0.6g; Sodium 297mg.
Monkfish with Potatoes Energy 529kcal/2230kJ; Protein 45.8g; Carbohydrate 54g, of which sugars 6.5g; Fat 15g, of which saturates 7.4g; Cholesterol 63mg; Calcium 67mg; Fibre 3.5g; Sodium 245mg.

Chicken with Potato Dumplings

Slowly poaching chicken pieces in a creamy sauce, topped with light herb and potato dumplings, makes a delicate yet warming meal for a winter's day.

Serves 6

1 onion, chopped
300ml/½ pint/1¼ cups
   vegetable stock
120ml/4fl oz/½ cup white wine
4 large chicken breast fillets
300ml/½ pint/1¼ cups single
   (light) cream
15ml/1 tbsp chopped
   fresh tarragon
salt and ground black pepper

For the dumplings

225g/8oz maincrop potatoes,
   boiled and mashed
175g/6oz/1¼ cups suet
   (US chilled, grated shortening)
115g/4oz/1 cup self-raising
   (self-rising) flour
50ml/2fl oz/¼ cup water
30ml/2 tbsp chopped mixed
   fresh herbs
salt and ground black pepper

1 Place the onion, stock and wine in a deep-sided frying pan. Add the chicken and simmer, covered, for 20 minutes.

2 Remove the chicken from the stock, cut it into chunks and set aside. Strain the stock and discard the onion. Return the stock to the pan and boil until reduced by one-third. Stir in the single cream and tarragon and simmer until just thickened. Stir in the chicken and season with salt and ground black pepper.

3 Spoon the mixture into a 900ml/1½ pint/3¾ cup ovenproof dish. Preheat the oven to 190°C/375°F/Gas 5.

4 Mix together the dumpling ingredients to make a soft dough. Divide into six and shape into balls with floured hands.

5 Place the dumplings on top of the chicken mixture and bake uncovered for 30 minutes until cooked. Serve immediately.

> **Cook's Tip**
> Make sure that you do not reduce the sauce too much before cooking in the oven as the dumplings absorb quite a lot of liquid.

Chicken with Winter Vegetables

A slow-baked winter casserole of wonderfully tender chicken, seasonal root vegetables and green lentils, finished with crème fraîche, wholegrain mustard and tarragon.

Serves 4

350g/12oz onions
350g/12oz leeks
225g/8oz carrots
450g/1lb swede (rutabaga)
30ml/2 tbsp oil
4 chicken portions, about
   900g/2lb total weight
115g/4oz/½ cup green lentils
475ml/16fl oz/2 cups
   chicken stock
300ml/½ pint/1¼ cups
   apple juice
10ml/2 tsp cornflour (cornstarch)
45ml/3 tbsp crème fraîche
10ml/2 tsp wholegrain mustard
30ml/2 tbsp chopped
   fresh tarragon
salt and ground black pepper
a few fresh tarragon sprigs,
   to garnish

1 Preheat the oven to 190°C/375°F/Gas 5. Roughly chop the onions, leeks, carrots and swede into even pieces.

2 Heat the oil in a large, flameproof casserole. Season the chicken portions with salt and pepper, and fry them until golden. Drain on kitchen paper.

3 Add the onions to the casserole and cook for 5 minutes, stirring, until they begin to soften and colour. Add the leeks, carrots, swede and lentils, and cook, stirring, over medium heat for about 2 minutes.

4 Return the chicken portions to the casserole. Pour in the stock and apple juice, and season with salt and pepper. Bring to the boil and cover with a tight-fitting lid. Cook in the oven for 50 minutes to 1 hour or until the chicken portions are tender.

5 Place the casserole over medium heat. Blend the cornflour with 30ml/2 tbsp water and add to the casserole with the crème fraîche, mustard and tarragon. Adjust the seasoning. Simmer gently for about 2 minutes, stirring. Serve immediately, garnished with tarragon sprigs.

Chicken with Dumplings Energy 552kcal/2300kJ; Protein 28.2g; Carbohydrate 26.5g, of which sugars 2.6g; Fat 37.4g, of which saturates 21g; Cholesterol 121mg; Calcium 83mg; Fibre 1.3g; Sodium 80mg.
Chicken Energy 505kcal/2132kJ; Protein 65.2g; Carbohydrate 43.8g, of which sugars 24.7g; Fat 8.9g, of which saturates 3.9g; Cholesterol 170mg; Calcium 181mg; Fibre 9.7g; Sodium 182mg.

Braised Quail with Winter Vegetables

Roasting and braising are the two classic techniques for cooking quail. Here, they are cooked and served in a red wine sauce, then elegantly displayed on crisp croûtes.

Serves 4
4 quail, cleaned
175g/6oz small carrots, scrubbed
175g/6oz baby turnips
60ml/4 tbsp olive oil

4 shallots, halved
450ml/¾ pint/scant 2 cups
 red wine
30ml/2 tbsp Spanish brandy
salt and ground black pepper
fresh flat leaf parsley, to garnish

For the croûtes
4 slices stale bread,
 crusts removed
60ml/4 tbsp olive oil

1 Preheat the oven to 220°C/425°F/Gas 7. Season the quail with salt and ground black pepper. Using a sharp knife, cut the carrots and baby turnips into chunks. (If the carrots are very small, you can leave them whole if you prefer.)

2 Heat half the oil in a flameproof casserole and add the quail. Fry until evenly browned all over. Remove from the casserole and set aside.

3 Add more olive oil to the casserole with all the vegetables and shallots. Cook until just colouring. Return the quail to the casserole, breast sides down, and pour in the red wine. Cover and cook in the oven for 30 minutes, or until the quail are tender.

4 Meanwhile, make the croûtes. Using a 10cm/4in plain cutter stamp out rounds from the bread. Heat the oil in a frying pan and cook the bread over a high heat until golden on both sides. Drain on kitchen paper and keep warm.

5 Place the croûtes on warm plates and set a quail on top of each. Arrange the vegetables around the quail, and keep hot.

6 Boil the cooking juices hard until reduced to a syrupy consistency. Add the brandy and warm through, then season to taste. Drizzle the sauce over the quail and garnish with parsley, then serve immediately.

Braised Chicken with Mashed Swede

This traditional way of cooking chicken maintains maximum flavour and produces delicious juices in the dish. It is served with a mixture of mashed swede and potato, which absorb the butter to give a delectable creamy purée.

Serves 4
75g/3oz/6 tbsp butter
15ml/1 tbsp oil

1 small bunch fresh parsley
1.6kg/3½lb chicken
salt and ground black pepper

For the mashed swede
450g/1lb swede (rutabaga), cut
 into cubes
675g/1½lb potatoes, cut
 into cubes
about 115g/4oz/½ cup butter
pinch of ground allspice

1 Put half of the butter, parsley, salt and pepper inside the chicken. Heat the oil and the rest of the butter in a flameproof casserole. Add the chicken and brown on all sides. Season the outside of the chicken with salt and pepper.

2 Lower the heat, cover the pan and simmer gently for about 1 hour. Test that the chicken is cooked by inserting the point of a sharp knife into the thickest part of the thigh near the body – the juices that run out should be clear.

3 Prepare the mashed swede. Put the swede in a large pan, cover with water and season with salt. Bring to the boil, lower the heat and simmer for 15 minutes.

4 Add the potatoes to the pan of swede and simmer for 15 minutes. Drain, reserving a little water and return the vegetables to the pan. Mash well, then add the butter and allspice. Season the mashed vegetables with salt and ground black pepper.

5 When cooked, transfer the chicken to a warmed serving dish. Add a little water to the pan to make a simple gravy, stirring to deglaze the pan and scraping up any sediment from the bottom. Serve the chicken immediately with the gravy and mashed swede.

Braised Chicken Energy 821kcal/3410kJ; Protein 43.5g; Carbohydrate 33g, of which sugars 7.9g; Fat 58g, of which saturates 24.9g; Cholesterol 269mg; Calcium 91mg; Fibre 3.8g; Sodium 372mg.
Braised Quail Energy 591kcal/2456kJ; Protein 24.4g; Carbohydrate 14.3g, of which sugars 6.7g; Fat 38.8g, of which saturates 7.6g; Cholesterol 116mg; Calcium 68mg; Fibre 2.5g; Sodium 184mg.

Braised Guinea Fowl with Cabbage

The slightly gamey flavour of guinea fowl is complemented by the sweet cabbage. This slow-cooker dish is the perfect winter warmer.

Serves 4
15ml/1 tbsp unsalted butter
½ red cabbage, about 450g/1lb
1.3kg/3lb oven-ready guinea fowl, jointed
15ml/1 tbsp sunflower oil
3 shallots, very finely chopped
15ml/1 tbsp plain
  (all-purpose) flour
120ml/4fl oz/½ cup chicken stock
150ml/¼ pint/⅔ cup apple juice
15ml/1 tbsp soft light brown sugar
15ml/1 tbsp red wine vinegar
4 juniper berries, lightly crushed
salt and ground black pepper

1 Use half the butter to grease the ceramic cooking pot. Cut the cabbage into wedges, removing any tough outer leaves and the central core. Shred the cabbage finely, then place in the ceramic cooking pot, packing it down tightly.

2 Rinse the guinea fowl portions and pat dry with kitchen paper. Heat the remaining butter and the oil in a pan and brown the guinea fowl on all sides. Lift from the pan, leaving the fat behind, and place on top of the red cabbage.

3 Add the shallots to the frying pan and cook gently for 5 minutes. Sprinkle with the flour, cook for a few seconds, then gradually stir in the stock followed by the apple juice. Bring to the boil, stirring constantly, until thickened. Remove from the heat, stir in the sugar, vinegar and juniper berries, and season.

4 Pour the sauce over the guinea fowl, cover and cook on high for 4 hours, or until the meat and cabbage are tender. Check the seasoning and serve.

Variations
• Other mild-tasting poultry or game such as chicken or pheasant can be used in place of the guinea fowl, if preferred.
• Add to the fruity flavour of the cabbage by adding 15ml/1 tbsp sultanas (golden raisins) to the pot before cooking.

Roast Pheasant

Today, pheasant has a wide appeal and dishes like this one often feature on gastronomic menus, especially during the early winter season. Wild pheasants are the best option, but farmed birds, which have a less gamey flavour, can be used instead.

Serves 4
15ml/1 tbsp vegetable oil, plus extra for greasing
2 young pheasants, cleaned and pan ready
115g/4oz/½ cup butter
200g/7oz bacon slices
8 Belgian endives (chicory), cores and any tough outer leaves removed
pinch of sugar
salt and ground black pepper
celeriac or parsnip purée, to serve

1 Preheat the oven to 180°C/350°F/Gas 4. Grease a roasting pan lightly with oil. Season the pheasants generously inside and out. Put 2.5ml/½ tsp butter in the cavity of each bird.

2 Heat 60ml/4 tbsp of the remaining butter with the oil in a heavy frying pan which is large enough to hold both pheasants. Add the birds, placing them on their sides. Fry over medium heat for about 10 minutes, turning the pheasants until they are golden brown on all sides.

3 Lift out the birds and set the pan aside. When the birds are cool enough to handle, wrap them in the bacon slices, tying them on with kitchen string. Put the pheasants in the greased roasting pan, cover with foil or a lid, and roast in the oven for 45 minutes.

4 Meanwhile, return the frying pan to the heat, reheat the fat, then add the endives in a single layer. Pour in enough water to come halfway up the endives. Dot with 5ml/1 tsp butter and season with salt and pepper. Bring to the boil, reduce the heat, cover and simmer for 20 minutes.

5 Using tongs, turn the endives over, replace the lid and simmer for 15–20 minutes more, until tender all the way through.

6 When the pheasants are done remove them from the roasting pan and put them on a chopping board. Slit the string, remove the bacon and set it aside, then cover the birds with foil and leave to rest for 10 minutes.

7 Lift the endives out of the frying pan and put them on a plate. Pour their cooking liquid into the roasting pan. Place over medium-high heat and boil, stirring frequently, for 8 minutes. Meanwhile, return the endives to the frying pan, sprinkle with the sugar and cook until caramelized on both sides.

8 Add the remaining butter to the reduced sauce in the roasting pan and stir over the heat for 4 minutes or until it thickens. The reserved bacon can be chopped or crumbled and added to the sauce, if you like.

9 Carve the birds and arrange on a heated platter. Arrange the endives around the meat and spoon the sauce over. Serve with the celeriac or parsnip purée.

Braised Guinea Fowl Energy 456kcal/1907kJ; Protein 44.5g; Carbohydrate 20g, of which sugars 15g; Fat 22.5g, of which saturates 6.7g; Cholesterol 225mg; Calcium 96mg; Fibre 3.1g; Sodium 15mg.
Pheasant Energy 896kcal/3738kJ; Protein 90.4g; Carbohydrate 1.9g, of which sugars 1.9g; Fat 58.7g, of which saturates 26.5g; Cholesterol 88mg; Calcium 160mg; Fibre 0.9g; Sodium 1211mg.

Pheasant with Mushrooms, Chestnuts and Bacon

Braising is ideal for pheasants available at the end of the season, when they are no longer tender enough to roast but full of flavour. Here they are cooked with seasonal mushrooms and chestnuts.

Serves 4
2 mature pheasants
50g/2oz/4 tbsp butter
75ml/5 tbsp brandy
50g/2oz unsmoked rindless bacon
12 baby (pearl) onions, peeled
1 celery stick, chopped
45ml/3 tbsp plain
 (all-purpose) flour
550ml/18fl oz/2½ cups
 chicken stock
175g/6oz peeled, cooked chestnuts
350g/12oz/4 cups mixed wild
 mushrooms, trimmed and sliced
15ml/1 tbsp lemon juice
salt and ground black pepper
baby turnips, to serve

1 Preheat the oven to 160°C/325°F/Gas 3. Season the pheasants with salt and pepper. Melt half the butter in a large flameproof casserole and brown on all sides over medium heat. Transfer them to a shallow roasting dish.

2 Pour off the excess fat from the casserole and return it to the heat. Add the brandy, stir to loosen the sediment, then pour over the pheasants.

3 Wipe out the casserole and melt the remaining butter. Cut the bacon into strips and brown in the butter with the onions and celery for 5 minutes. Sprinkle the flour into the casserole and cook, stirring, for 1 minute.

4 Gradually add the chicken stock, stirring until smooth. Add the chestnuts, mushrooms, the pheasants and their juices and bring back to a gentle simmer. Cover the dish, put into the hot oven and cook for 1½ hours or until the pheasants are tender.

5 Bring the sauce back to the boil, add the lemon juice and season to taste. Transfer the cooked pheasants and vegetables to a warmed serving plate. Pour over some of the sauce and serve the rest on the side. Serve with baby turnips.

Roast Partridges with Sage, Thyme and Garlic

It is important that you select young birds for this simple recipe so get them early in the winter season. Basting the meat regularly during the cooking time prevents the flesh from drying out and adds a lovely buttery flavour, and the herbs and garlic add a subtle yet distinctive note.

Serves 4
4 small partridges, cleaned
 and gutted
8 slices pork fat or streaky
 (fatty) bacon
50g/2oz/¼ cup butter, softened,
 plus 5ml/3 tbsp melted butter,
 for basting
10 fresh sage leaves,
 roughly chopped
1 bunch fresh thyme,
 leaves chopped
10 garlic cloves, roughly chopped
salt and ground black pepper
cranberry preserve,
 to serve (optional)

1 Preheat the oven to 190°C/375°F/Gas 5. Season the partridges well inside and out with salt and pepper, then place in a large roasting pan.

2 Lay the slices of pork fat or streaky bacon over the top of the birds. In a bowl, mix together the softened butter, herbs and garlic, and use the mixture to stuff the cavities of the birds.

3 Place in the preheated oven and roast for about 1½ hours, or until the birds are cooked through, basting often with the melted butter.

4 Remove from the oven, cover with foil and allow to rest for 15 minutes before serving. Accompany them with a little cranberry preserve, if you like.

Cook's Tip
To test if they are cooked, pierce the thickest part of the thigh; the juices should run clear.

Pheasant Energy 883kcal/3699kJ; Protein 86.8g; Carbohydrate 32.3g, of which sugars 6.9g; Fat 41.6g, of which saturates 15.8g; Cholesterol 35mg; Calcium 205mg; Fibre 2.9g; Sodium 920mg.
Roast Partridges Energy 866kcal/3619kJ; Protein 118g; Carbohydrate 0.1g, of which sugars 0.1g; Fat 43.6g, of which saturates 16.1g; Cholesterol 59mg; Calcium 145mg; Fibre 0g; Sodium 1006mg.

Braised Partridge with Cabbage

For this seasonal dish, partridges are layered with Savoy cabbage and cooked in stock and beer.

Serves 4

2 mature partridges, cleaned and
   ready to cook
115g/4oz/½ cup butter
1 large Savoy cabbage, sliced
200g/7oz rindless smoked streaky
   (fatty) bacon
4 small pork sausages
4 small smoked sausages
pinch of freshly grated nutmeg
250ml/8fl oz/1 cup chicken stock
750ml/1¼ pints/3 cups dark
   Abbey beer or more hot
   chicken stock
2 bay leaves
4 juniper berries
salt and ground black pepper
mashed potatoes, to serve

1 Cut each partridge in half down the centre. Season with salt and pepper. Melt the butter in a large heavy frying pan. Add the partridge halves and brown them on both sides. Cover the pan with foil or a lid and cook over low heat for 30 minutes.

2 Meanwhile, bring a large pan of water to the boil. Stir in 15ml/1 tbsp salt. Add the cabbage and blanch it for 3 minutes, then drain and pat dry with kitchen paper.

3 Put the browned birds on a plate. Set aside. Reheat the fat in the pan and add the bacon and sausages. Fry for 6–8 minutes, until the bacon is crisp and the sausages are cooked.

4 Preheat the oven to 160°C/325°F/Gas 3. Grease a large baking dish (the partridges should be in a single layer). Spread half the cabbage on the base and season with salt, pepper and nutmeg. Place the partridges on top and arrange the bacon and sausages in between. Cover with the remaining cabbage and season again.

5 Pour over the hot chicken stock and beer (or both quantities of stock). Add the bay leaves and juniper berries, cover the dish and bake in the oven for 1 hour.

6 Adjust the seasoning. Mound the cabbage on a heated platter and arrange the partridges on top, with the bacon and sausages around the side. Serve with the potatoes.

Stuffed Roast Turkey

In this simple recipe, the popular winter turkey is stuffed with a rich herb stuffing and served with seasonal cranberry jelly.

Serves 6

1 turkey, about 4.5–5.5kg/10–12lb,
   washed and patted dry with
   kitchen paper
25g/1oz/2 tbsp butter, melted
salt and ground black pepper
cranberry jelly, to serve

For the stuffing
200g/7oz/3½ cups fresh
   white breadcrumbs
175ml/6fl oz/¾ cup milk
25g/1oz/2 tbsp butter
1 egg, separated
1 calf's liver, about 600g/1lb 6oz,
   finely chopped
2 onions, finely chopped
90ml/6 tbsp chopped fresh dill
10ml/2 tsp clear honey
salt and ground black pepper

1 Make the stuffing. Soak the breadcrumbs in milk until swollen. Melt the butter in a frying pan and mix 5ml/1 tsp with the egg. Heat the remaining butter and fry the liver and onions for 5 minutes, until the onions are golden brown. Set aside to cool.

2 Preheat the oven to 180°C/350°F/Gas 4. Add the cooled liver mixture to the soaked breadcrumbs then add the butter and egg yolk mixture, with the dill, honey and seasoning. Whisk the egg white to soft peaks, then fold into the mixture, stirring gently to combine thoroughly.

3 Season the turkey inside and out. Stuff the cavity with the stuffing mixture, then weigh to calculate the cooking time. Allow 20 minutes per 500g/1¼lb, plus an additional 20 minutes. Tuck the legs inside the cavity and tie the end shut with string. Brush over the outside with butter and transfer to a roasting pan. Place in the oven and roast for the calculated time.

4 Baste the turkey regularly, and cover with foil for the final 30 minutes if the skin gets too brown. To test it is cooked, pierce the thick part of the thigh with a knife; the juices should run clear.

5 Remove the turkey from the oven, cover with foil and leave to rest for about 15 minutes. Carve into thin slices, then spoon over the juices and serve with the stuffing and cranberry jelly.

Braised Partridge Energy 1016kcal/4227kJ; Protein 79.7g; Carbohydrate 15.2g, of which sugars 10g; Fat 66.2g, of which saturates 29g; Cholesterol 139mg; Calcium 219mg; Fibre 2.9g; Sodium 1633mg.
Stuffed Turkey Energy 740kcal/3126kJ; Protein 112.3g; Carbohydrate 35.9g, of which sugars 7.3g; Fat 13.5g, of which saturates 6.6g; Cholesterol 507mg; Calcium 122mg; Fibre 1.7g; Sodium 517mg.

Turkey Patties

Minced turkey makes deliciously light patties, which are ideal for winter meals. The recipe is a flavourful variation on a classic burger and they can also be made using minced lamb, pork or beef.

1 small red onion, finely chopped
grated rind and juice of 1 lime
small handful of fresh
   thyme leaves
15–30ml/1–2 tbsp olive oil
salt and ground black pepper

Serves 6
675g/1½lb minced
  (ground) turkey

1 Mix together the turkey, onion, lime rind and juice, thyme and seasoning. Cover and chill for up to 4 hours to allow the flavours to mingle.

2 Divide the turkey mixture into six equal portions. Shape into round patties with lightly floured hands.

3 Preheat a griddle pan. Brush the patties with oil, then place them on the pan and cook on one side for 10–12 minutes. Turn the patties over with a metal spatula, brush with more oil and cook for a further 10–12 minutes on the second side, or until cooked through. Serve immediately.

> **Cook's Tip**
> Serve the patties in split and toasted buns or pieces of crusty bread, with chutney, salad leaves and chunky fries.

> **Variations**
> • Minced (ground) chicken or minced pork could be used instead of turkey in these burgers.
> • You could also try chopped oregano, parsley or basil in place of the thyme, and lemon rind instead of lime.

Turkey Croquettes

A crisp patty of smoked turkey mixed with mashed potato and spring onions and rolled in breadcrumbs.

115g/4oz/2 cups fresh
  white breadcrumbs
vegetable oil, for deep fat frying
salt and ground black pepper

Serves 4
450g/1lb potatoes, diced
3 eggs
30ml/2 tbsp milk
175g/6oz smoked turkey rashers
  (strips), finely chopped
2 spring onions (scallions),
  finely sliced

For the sauce
15ml/1 tbsp olive oil
1 onion, finely chopped
400g/14oz can tomatoes, drained
30ml/2 tbsp tomato
  purée (paste)
15ml/1 tbsp chopped
  fresh parsley

1 Boil the potatoes for 20 minutes or until tender. Drain and return the pan to low heat to evaporate the excess water.

2 Mash the potatoes with two eggs and the milk. Season well with salt and black pepper. Stir in the turkey and spring onions. Chill for 1 hour.

3 Meanwhile, to make the sauce, heat the oil in a frying pan and fry the onion for 5 minutes until soft. Add the tomatoes and purée, stir and simmer for 10 minutes. Stir in the parsley, season with salt and pepper and keep warm.

4 Remove the potato mixture from the refrigerator and divide into eight pieces. Shape each piece into a sausage shape and dip in the remaining beaten egg and then the breadcrumbs.

5 Heat the oil in a pan or deep-fat fryer to 175°C/330°F and deep fry the croquettes for 5 minutes, or until golden and crisp. Serve with the sauce.

> **Cook's Tip**
> Test the oil temperature by dropping a cube of bread into it. If it sinks, rises and sizzles in 10 seconds the oil is ready to use.

Turkey Croquettes Energy 404kcal/1698kJ; Protein 19.4g; Carbohydrate 47g, of which sugars 7.7g; Fat 16.7g, of which saturates 2.4g; Cholesterol 73mg; Calcium 93mg; Fibre 3.3g; Sodium 315mg.
Turkey Patties Energy 141kcal/596kJ; Protein 24.8g; Carbohydrate 0.8g, of which sugars 0.60g; Fat 4.4g, of which saturates 1.1g; Cholesterol 69mg; Calcium 15mg; Fibre 0.2g; Sodium 62mg.

Sausages with Onions and Apples

Venison's winter season is eagerly awaited all year and this full-flavoured casserole is slow-cooked comfort food at its best. Serve with a heap of mashed potatoes and a glass or two of full-bodied red wine to warm you up on a cold winter's night.

Serves 4
45ml/3 tbsp sunflower oil
450g/1lb venison sausages

2 onions, sliced
15ml/1 tbsp plain
   (all-purpose) flour
400ml/14fl oz/1⅔ cups dry
   (hard) cider
350g/12oz celeriac, cut into
   large chunks
15ml/1 tbsp Worcestershire sauce
15ml/1 tbsp chopped fresh sage
2 small tart cooking apples, cored
   and sliced
salt and ground black pepper

1 Preheat the oven to 180°C/350°F/Gas 4. Heat the oil in a heavy frying pan, add the sausages and fry until evenly browned all over, for about 5–7 minutes. Transfer the browned sausages to a earthenware casserole dish.

2 Drain off any excess oil from the frying pan, leaving about 15ml/1 tbsp. Add the onions and cook for a few minutes, stirring frequently, until softened and golden.

3 Stir in the flour, then gradually add the cider and bring to the boil, stirring. Add the celeriac and cook for 2 minutes. Stir in the Worcestershire sauce and sage. Season well with salt and ground black pepper.

4 Pour the cider and celeriac mixture over the sausages in the casserole dish, then cover and cook in the oven for 30 minutes. Add the apples and cook for 10–15 minutes, or until the apples are just tender. Serve immediately.

> **Variation**
> *Try good-quality pork and herb or duck sausages in this recipe instead of the venison sausages, if you like.*

Marmalade-glazed Goose

Succulent roast goose is the classic centrepiece for a traditional Christmas lunch. Red cabbage cooked with leeks and braised fennel are seasonal accompaniments.

Serves 8
4.5kg/10lb oven-ready goose
1 cooking apple, peeled, cored
   and cut into eighths
1 large onion, cut into eighths
bunch of fresh sage, plus extra
   sprigs to garnish
30ml/2 tbsp ginger
   marmalade, melted
salt and ground black pepper

For the stuffing
25g/1oz/2 tbsp butter
1 onion, finely chopped
15ml/1 tbsp ginger marmalade
450g/1lb/2 cups ready-to-eat
   prunes, chopped
45ml/3 tbsp Madeira
225g/8oz/4 cups fresh
   white breadcrumbs
30ml/2 tbsp chopped fresh sage

For the gravy
1 onion, chopped
15ml/1 tbsp plain
   (all-purpose) flour
150ml/¼ pint/⅔ cup Madeira
600ml/1 pint/2½ cups
   chicken stock

1 Preheat the oven to 200°C/400°F/Gas 6. Prick the skin of the goose all over with a fork and season the bird generously, both inside and out. Mix the apple, onion and sage leaves and spoon the mixture into the rump end of the goose.

2 To make the stuffing, melt the butter in a large pan and cook the onion for 5 minutes, or until softened. Remove the pan from the heat and stir in the marmalade, prunes, Madeira, breadcrumbs and chopped sage.

3 Stuff the neck end of the goose with some of the stuffing, and chill the remaining stuffing. Sew up the bird or secure it with skewers to prevent the stuffing from escaping. Place the goose in a large roasting pan. Butter a piece of foil and use to cover the goose loosely, then place in the oven for 2 hours.

4 Baste the goose frequently during cooking and remove excess fat from the pan as necessary, using a small ladle or serving spoon. (Strain, cool and chill the fat in a covered container: it is excellent for roasting potatoes.)

5 Remove the foil from the goose and brush the melted ginger marmalade over the goose, then roast for 30–40 minutes more, or until cooked through. To check if the goose is cooked, pierce the thick part of the thigh with a metal skewer; the juices will run clear when the bird is cooked. Remove from the oven and cover with foil, then leave to rest for 15 minutes before carving.

6 While the goose is cooking, shape the remaining stuffing into walnut-size balls and place them in an ovenproof dish. Spoon 30ml/2 tbsp of the goose fat over the stuffing balls and bake for about 15 minutes before the goose is cooked.

7 To make the gravy, pour off all but 15ml/1 tbsp of fat from the roasting pan, leaving the meat juices behind. Add the onion and cook for 3–5 minutes. Sprinkle in the flour and then stir in the Madeira and stock. Bring to the boil, stirring constantly, then simmer for 3 minutes, or until thickened. Strain the gravy and serve it with the goose and stuffing. Garnish with sage leaves.

Braised Sausages Energy 538kcal/2240kJ; Protein 43.5g; Carbohydrate 7g, of which sugars 2.8g; Fat 28.2g, of which saturates 8.9g; Cholesterol 170mg; Calcium 50mg; Fibre 1.1g; Sodium 610mg.
Marmalade Goose Energy 823kcal/3443kJ; Protein 57.6g; Carbohydrate 47.1g, of which sugars 23.8g; Fat 43.3g, of which saturates 14g; Cholesterol 177mg; Calcium 106mg; Fibre 4.5g; Sodium 395mg.

Potato and Sausage Casserole

This slow-cooker version of the traditional and popular dish means that it is easy to prepare, and you can simply leave it alone to simmer gently to perfection.

Serves 4
15ml/1 tbsp vegetable oil
8 large pork sausages

4 bacon rashers (strips), cut into
  2.5cm/1in pieces
1 large onion, chopped
2 garlic cloves, crushed
4 large baking potatoes,
  thinly sliced
1.5ml/¼ tsp fresh sage
300ml/½ pint/1¼ cups hot
  vegetable stock
salt and ground black pepper

1 Heat the oil in a frying pan. Gently fry the sausages for about 5 minutes, turning frequently until they are golden but not cooked through. Remove from the frying pan and set aside. Pour away all but about 10ml/2 tsp of fat from the pan.

2 Add the bacon to the pan and fry for 2 minutes. Add the onion and fry for about 8 minutes, stirring frequently until beginning to soften and turn golden. Add the garlic and fry for a further 1 minute, then turn off the heat.

3 Arrange half the potato slices in the base of the ceramic cooking pot. Spoon the bacon and onion mixture on top. Season well with salt and ground black pepper, and sprinkle with the fresh sage. Cover with the remaining potato slices.

4 Pour the stock over the potatoes and top with the sausages. Cover with the lid and cook on high for 3–4 hours, or until the potatoes are tender and the sausages cooked through. Serve hot.

> **Cook's Tips**
> • *For a traditional accompaniment, serve this delicious, hearty casserole with braised green cabbage.*
> • *Choose good-quality sausages because it will make all the difference to the final result. Many artisan butchers sell quality sausages, and it is well worth keeping an eye out for them if you have a butcher nearby.*

Beef Tagine with Sweet Potatoes

This warming dish of tender beef and succulent sweet potatoes is eaten during the winter in Morocco, where it can get surprisingly cold.

Serves 4
675–900g/1½–2lb braising or
  stewing beef
30ml/2 tbsp sunflower oil
a good pinch of ground turmeric
1 large onion, chopped

1 red or green chilli, seeded
  and chopped
7.5ml/1½ tsp paprika
a good pinch of cayenne pepper
2.5ml/½ tsp ground cumin
450g/1lb sweet potatoes
15ml/1 tbsp chopped
  fresh parsley
15ml/1 tbsp chopped fresh
  coriander (cilantro)
15g/½ oz/1 tbsp butter
salt and ground black pepper

1 Cube the beef. Heat the oil in a flameproof casserole and fry the meat, with the turmeric and seasoning, for 3–4 minutes until evenly brown, stirring frequently.

2 Cover the pan with a tight-fitting lid and cook for 15 minutes over a fairly gentle heat, without lifting the lid. Preheat the oven to 180°C/350°F/Gas 4.

3 Add the onion, chilli, paprika, cayenne pepper and cumin to the casserole, with just enough water to cover the meat. Cover tightly and cook in the oven for 1–1½ hours until the meat is very tender, checking occasionally and adding a little extra water to keep the stew moist.

4 Meanwhile, peel the sweet potatoes and slice them straight into a bowl of salted water. Transfer to a pan, bring to the boil and simmer for 3 minutes until just tender. Drain.

5 Stir the herbs into the meat. Arrange the potato slices over the top of the meat and dot with the butter. Cover and bake for 10 minutes more.

6 Increase the oven temperature to 200°C/400°F/Gas 6 or heat the grill (broiler). Remove the lid of the casserole and cook in the oven or under the grill for a further 5–10 minutes until the potatoes are golden.

Potato Casserole Energy 717kcal/2984kJ; Protein 20.5g; Carbohydrate 49.9g, of which sugars 6.1g; Fat 49.8g, of which saturates 18.1g; Cholesterol 78.1mg; Calcium 73mg; Fibre 4g; Sodium 1322mg.
Beef Tagine Energy 301kcal/1254kJ; Protein 21.9g; Carbohydrate 12g, of which sugars 3.2g; Fat 18.7g, of which saturates 4.6g; Cholesterol 61mg; Calcium 18mg; Fibre 1.4g; Sodium 67mg.

Baked Beef with a Potato Crust

This recipe makes the best of braising beef by marinating it in red wine and topping it with a cheesy grated potato crust that bakes to a golden, crunchy consistency.

Serves 4

675g/1½lb stewing beef, diced
300ml/½ pint/1¼ cups red wine
3 juniper berries, crushed
slice of orange peel
30ml/2 tbsp olive oil
2 onions, cut into chunks
2 carrots, cut into chunks

1 garlic clove, crushed
225g/8oz/3 cups button (white) mushrooms
150ml/¼ pint/⅔ cup beef stock
30ml/2 tbsp cornflour (cornstarch)
salt and ground black pepper

For the crust

450g/1lb potatoes, grated
15ml/1 tbsp olive oil
30ml/2 tbsp creamed horseradish
50g/2oz/½ cup mature (sharp) Cheddar cheese, grated
salt and ground black pepper

1 Place the diced beef in a large non-metallic bowl. Add the red wine, juniper berries, and orange peel and season with black pepper. Mix the ingredients together until thoroughly combined and then cover and leave to marinate for at least 4 hours or overnight if possible.

2 Preheat the oven to 160°C/325°F/Gas 3. Drain the beef, making sure to reserve the marinade. Heat the oil in a large flameproof casserole dish and fry the meat in small batches for around 5 minutes until sealed on all sides.

3 Add the onions, carrots and garlic and cook for 5 minutes. Stir in the mushrooms, red wine marinade and beef stock. Simmer. Mix the cornflour with water to make a smooth paste. Stir into the pan. Season, cover and cook for 1½ hours.

4 Make the crust 30 minutes before the end of the cooking time for the beef. Start by blanching the potatoes in boiling water for 5 minutes. Drain and then squeeze out the extra liquid.

5 Stir in the remaining ingredients and then sprinkle over the beef. Increase the oven to 200°C/400°F/Gas 6 and bake for a further 30 minutes so that the top is crisp and browned.

Braised Rabbit

Rabbit is another of the winter game meats. It is delicious slowly braised in this rich sauce, made with stock and cider or stout. Serve with potatoes boiled in their skins and a lightly cooked green vegetable.

Serves 4–6

1 rabbit, prepared and jointed by the butcher
30ml/2 tbsp seasoned flour
30ml/2 tbsp olive oil or vegetable oil

25g/1oz/2 tbsp butter
115g/4oz streaky (fatty) bacon
1 onion, roughly chopped
2 or 3 carrots, sliced
1 or 2 celery sticks, trimmed and sliced
300ml/½ pint/1¼ cups hot chicken stock
300ml/½ pint/1¼ cups dry (hard) cider or stout
a small bunch of parsley leaves, chopped
salt and ground black pepper
leeks, to serve

1 Soak the joints in cold salted water for at least 2 hours, then pat them dry with kitchen paper and toss them in seasoned flour. Preheat the oven to 200°C/400°F/Gas 6.

2 Heat the oil and butter together in a large flameproof casserole. Shake off and reserve any excess flour from the rabbit joints. Cook the meat until evenly browned on all sides. Lift out and set aside.

3 Add the bacon to the casserole and cook for 3–4 minutes, then remove and set aside with the rabbit pieces. Add the vegetables to the casserole and cook gently, stirring occasionally, until just colouring, then sprinkle over any remaining seasoned flour to absorb the fats in the casserole. Stir over low heat for 1 minute to cook the flour. Add the stock and cider or stout, stirring, to make a smooth sauce.

4 Return the rabbit and bacon to the casserole, and add half of the chopped parsley and a light seasoning of salt and black pepper. Mix gently together, then cover with a tight-fitting lid and put into the preheated oven. Cook for 15–20 minutes, then reduce the oven temperature to 150°C/300°F/Gas 2 for about 1½ hours, or until the rabbit is tender. Add the remaining parsley and serve immediately with leeks.

Slow-baked Beef Energy 641kcal/2678kJ; Protein 45.9g; Carbohydrate 36.6g, of which sugars 10.8g; Fat 29.6g, of which saturates 10.6g; Cholesterol 111mg; Calcium 152mg; Fibre 4.2g; Sodium 306mg.
Braised Rabbit Energy 368kcal/1535kJ; Protein 32.9g; Carbohydrate 10.5g, of which sugars 5.8g; Fat 19.7g, of which saturates 8g; Cholesterol 133mg; Calcium 88mg; Fibre 1.4g; Sodium 567mg.

Hare Pot Pies

This winter pie filling is simmered in the slow cooker until tender before being topped with pastry and baked in the oven.

Serves 4
45ml/3 tbsp olive oil
1 leek, sliced
225g/8oz parsnips, sliced
225g/8oz carrots, sliced
1 fennel bulb, sliced
675g/1½lb boneless hare, diced
30ml/2 tbsp plain (all-purpose) flour
60ml/4 tbsp Madeira
300ml/½ pint/1¼ cups game
 or chicken stock
45ml/3 tbsp chopped fresh parsley
450g/1lb puff pastry, thawed
 if frozen
beaten egg yolk, to glaze

1 Heat 30ml/2 tbsp of the oil in a pan. Add the leek, parsnips, carrots and fennel and cook for 10 minutes until soft. With a slotted spoon, transfer the vegetables to a ceramic cooking pot. Cover and switch on the slow cooker to high or auto.

2 Heat the remaining oil in the pan and fry the hare in batches until well browned. When all the meat is browned, return it to the pan. Add the flour and cook, stirring, for a few seconds, then gradually add the Madeira and stock and bring to the boil.

3 Transfer the hare mixture to the ceramic cooking pot and cook for 1 hour. Switch the slow cooker to low or leave on auto and cook for 5–6 hours, until the meat and vegetables are tender. Stir in the chopped parsley, then set aside to cool.

4 To make the pies, preheat the oven to 220°C/425°F/Gas 7. Spoon the filling into four small pie dishes. Cut the pastry into quarters and roll out to make the lids, making them larger than the dishes. Trim any excess pastry and use to line the dish rims.

5 Dampen the pastry rims with cold water and cover with the lids. Pinch the edges together to seal. Brush with beaten egg yolk and make a small hole in the top of each one.

6 Stand the pies on a baking tray and bake for 25 minutes, or until the pastry is golden. If necessary, cover the pies with foil to prevent them becoming too brown. Serve immediately.

Venison Pie

This is a variation on beef cottage pie using rich, slowly simmered minced venison with a seasonal root vegetable topping. The resulting dish will warm up diners on a cold night.

Serves 6
30ml/2 tbsp olive oil
2 leeks, trimmed and chopped
1kg/2¼lb minced (ground) venison
30ml/2 tbsp chopped fresh parsley
300ml/½ pint/1¼ cups
 game consommé
salt and ground black pepper

For the topping
1.5kg/3¼lb mixed root
 vegetables, such as sweet
 potatoes, parsnips and swede
 (rutabaga), coarsely chopped
15ml/1 tbsp horseradish sauce
25g/1oz/2 tbsp butter

1 Heat the oil in a heavy frying pan. Add the leeks and cook, stirring occasionally, for about 8 minutes, or until softened and beginning to brown.

2 Add the minced venison to the pan and cook for about 10 minutes, stirring frequently, or until the meat is well browned. Stir in the chopped parsley, game consommé and seasoning, then bring to the boil. Cover the pan, reduce the heat and simmer for about 20 minutes, stirring occasionally.

3 Meanwhile, preheat the oven to 200°C/400°F/Gas 6 and prepare the topping. Cook the vegetables in boiling, salted water to cover for 15–20 minutes. Drain well and mash the vegetables together with the horseradish sauce and butter, and season with salt and pepper.

4 Spoon the venison mixture into an ovenproof dish and top with the mashed vegetables. Bake for 20 minutes, or until piping hot and beginning to brown. Serve immediately.

Variation
This pie can be made with other minced (ground) meats, such as beef, lamb or pork. If leeks aren't available, then use a large onion and chop coarsely.

Hare Pot Pies Energy 906kcal/3784kJ; Protein 45g; Carbohydrate 60.4g, of which sugars 10g; Fat 53.7g, of which saturates 15.9g; Cholesterol 107mg; Calcium 180mg; Fibre 7.6g; Sodium 553mg.
Venison Pie Energy 307kcal/1291kJ; Protein 39.8g; Carbohydrate 13.2g, of which sugars 12.5g; Fat 12g, of which saturates 4.1g; Cholesterol 93mg; Calcium 154mg; Fibre 5.8g; Sodium 176mg.

Filo Pastry, Ice Cream and Mincemeat Parcels

Looking rather like crispy fried pancakes, these golden parcels reveal hot chunky mincemeat and melting vanilla ice cream when cut open. They can be assembled days in advance, ready for easy, last-minute frying.

Makes 12
1 firm pear
225g/8oz/1 cup mincemeat

finely grated rind of 1 lemon
12 sheets of filo pastry,
 thawed if frozen
a little beaten egg
250ml/8 fl oz/1 cup vanilla
 ice cream
oil, for deep-frying
caster (superfine) sugar
 for dusting

1 Peel, core and chop the pear. Put it in a small bowl and then stir in the mincemeat and lemon rind.

2 Lay one filo sheet on the work surface and cut it into two 20cm/8in squares. Brush one square lightly with beaten egg, then cover with the second square.

3 Lay 10ml/2 tsp mincemeat on the filo, placing it 2.5cm/1in away from one edge and spreading it slightly to cover a 7.5cm/3in area. Lay 10ml/2 tsp of the ice cream over the mincemeat. Brush around the edges of the filo with beaten egg.

4 Fold over the two opposite sides of the pastry to cover the filling. Roll up the strip, starting from the filled end. Transfer to a baking sheet and freeze. Make 11 more rolls in the same way.

5 When you are ready to serve, pour oil into a heavy pan to a depth of 7.5cm/3in. Heat it to 185°C/365°F or until a cube of bread added to the oil browns in 30 seconds.

6 Fry several parcels at a time for 1–2 minutes until pale golden, turning them over during cooking. Drain on kitchen paper while frying the remainder. Dust with caster sugar and serve immediately.

Walnut and Vanilla Ice Cream Palmiers

These walnut pastries can be served freshly baked, but for convenience, make them ahead and reheat them in a moderate oven for 5 minutes. They are perfect for a festive winter meal.

beaten egg, to glaze
45ml/3 tbsp caster
 (superfine) sugar
about 200ml/7fl oz/scant 1 cup
 vanilla ice cream

Makes 6
75g/3oz/³/₄ cup walnut pieces
350g/12oz puff pastry,
 thawed if frozen

1 Preheat the oven to 200°C/400°F/Gas 6. Lightly grease a large baking sheet with butter. Chop the walnuts finely. On a lightly floured surface roll the pastry to a thin rectangle 30 × 20cm/12 × 8in.

2 Trim the edges of the pastry, then brush with the egg. Sprinkle over all but 45ml/3 tbsp of the walnuts and 30ml/ 2 tbsp of the sugar. Run the rolling pin over the walnuts to press them into the pastry.

3 Roll up the pastry from one short side to the centre, then roll up the other side until the two rolls meet. Brush the points where the rolls meet with a little beaten egg. Using a sharp knife, cut the pastry into slices 1cm/½in thick.

4 Lay the slices of pastry on the work surface and flatten them evenly with a rolling pin. Transfer to the baking sheet. Brush with more of the beaten egg and sprinkle with the reserved walnuts and sugar.

5 Bake in the preheated oven for about 15 minutes until pale golden and crisp all over. Serve the palmiers while still warm, in pairs with a scoop or two of vanilla ice cream sandwiched between the pastry layers.

Filo Parcels Energy 183kcal/764kJ; Protein 1.6g; Carbohydrate 23.3g, of which sugars 16.8g; Fat 9.9g, of which saturates 1.9g; Cholesterol 2mg; Calcium 35mg; Fibre 0.8g; Sodium 17mg.
Walnut Palmiers Energy 398kcal/1661kJ; Protein 6.4g; Carbohydrate 38g, of which sugars 16.3g; Fat 25.7g, of which saturates 2.8g; Cholesterol 10mg; Calcium 93mg; Fibre 0.4g; Sodium 205mg.

Passion Fruit Creams

These delicately perfumed creams are light with a fresh flavour from the seasonal passion fruit. Ripe passion fruit should look purple and wrinkled – choose fruit that are heavy for their size. When halved, the fragrant, sweet juicy flesh with small edible black seeds are revealed. These creams can be decorated with mint or geranium leaves and served with cream.

Serves 5–6
600ml/1 pint/2½ cups double
    (heavy) cream, or a mixture
    of single (light) and double
    (heavy) cream
6 passion fruits
30–45ml/2–3 tbsp vanilla sugar
5 eggs

1 Preheat the oven to 180°C/350°F/Gas 4. Line the bases of six 120ml/4fl oz/½ cup ramekins with rounds of baking parchment and place them in a roasting pan.

2 Heat the double cream or mix of single and double creams in a small pan to just below boiling point, then remove the pan from the heat.

3 Strain the flesh of four passion fruits through a sieve (strainer), reserving a little for the garnish, and beat together with the vanilla sugar and eggs until well combined. Whisk in the hot cream and then ladle the mixture into the ramekins.

4 Half fill the roasting pan with boiling water. Bake the creams in the preheated oven for 25–30 minutes, or until set, then leave to cool before chilling in the refrigerator for at least 2 hours until set.

5 When ready to serve the desserts, run a knife around the insides of the ramekins, then invert them on to individual serving plates, tapping the bases firmly to release the contents. Carefully peel off the baking parchment and chill in the refrigerator until ready to serve. Spoon on a little passion fruit flesh just before serving.

Chocolate and Chestnut Pots

The chestnut purée adds substance and texture to these mousses. Crisp, delicate biscuits, such as langues-de-chat, provide a good foil to the richness.

Serves 6
250g/9oz plain
    (semisweet) chocolate
60ml/4 tbsp Madeira
25g/1oz/2 tbsp butter, diced
2 eggs, separated
225g/8oz/scant 1 cup
    unsweetened chestnut purée
crème fraîche or whipped double
    (heavy) cream, to decorate

1 Make a few chocolate curls for decoration by rubbing a grater along the length of the bar of chocolate.

2 Break the rest of the chocolate into squares and melt it in a pan with the Madeira over a gentle heat. Remove from the heat and add the butter, a few pieces at a time, stirring until melted and smooth.

3 Beat the egg yolks quickly into the mixture, then beat in the chestnut purée, mixing until smooth.

4 Whisk the egg whites in a clean, grease-free bowl until stiff. Stir about 15ml/1 tbsp of the whites into the chestnut mixture to lighten it, then fold in the rest smoothly and evenly.

5 Spoon the mixture into six small ramekin dishes and chill in the refrigerator until set.

6 Remove from the refrigerator 30 minutes before serving to allow the flavours to 'ripen'. Serve topped with a spoonful of crème fraîche or cream and decorated with chocolate curls.

Cook's Tips
• If Madeira is not available, use brandy or rum instead.
• These chocolate pots can be frozen successfully for up to 2 months, making them ideal for a prepare-ahead dessert.

Chocolate Pots Energy 348kcal/1455kJ; Protein 5g; Carbohydrate 41.4g, of which sugars 29.9g; Fat 18g, of which saturates 9.9g; Cholesterol 75mg; Calcium 42mg; Fibre 2.6g; Sodium 56mg.
Passion Creams Energy 585kcal/2414kJ; Protein 7.2g; Carbohydrate 8.5g, of which sugars 8.5g; Fat 58.4g, of which saturates 34.7g; Cholesterol 296mg; Calcium 77mg; Fibre 0.5g; Sodium 84mg.

Chocolate Pavlova with Passion Fruit Cream

This winter meringue dish has a delicious chewy centre that is hard to resist.

Serves 6
4 egg whites
200g/7oz/1 cup caster
  (superfine) sugar
20ml/4 tsp cornflour (cornstarch)
45g/1¾oz/3 tbsp unsweetened
  cocoa powder
5ml/1 tsp vinegar
chocolate leaves, to decorate

For the filling
150g/5oz plain (semisweet)
  chocolate, chopped into
  small pieces
250ml/8fl oz/1 cup double
  (heavy) cream
150g/5oz/⅔ cup Greek
  (US strained plain) yogurt
2.5ml/½ tsp vanilla extract
4 passion fruit

1 Preheat oven to 140°C/275°F/Gas 1. Cut a piece of baking parchment to fit a baking sheet. Draw on a 23cm/9in circle.

2 Whisk the egg whites in a clean, grease-free bowl until stiff. Gradually whisk in the sugar and continue to whisk until the mixture is stiff again. Whisk in the cornflour, cocoa and vinegar.

3 Place the baking parchment upside down on the baking sheet. Spread the mixture over the circle; make a slight dip in the centre. Bake for 1½–2 hours.

4 Make the filling. Melt the chocolate in a heatproof bowl over barely simmering water, then remove from the heat and cool slightly. In a separate bowl, whip the cream with the yogurt and vanilla extract until thick. Fold 60ml/4 tbsp into the chocolate, then set both mixtures aside.

5 Halve all the passion fruit and scoop out the pulp with a spoon. Stir half into the plain cream mixture. Carefully transfer the meringue shell to a serving plate. Fill with the passion fruit cream, then spoon over the chocolate mixture and the remaining passion fruit pulp. Decorate with chocolate leaves. Serve immediately.

Winter Cheesecake with a Pomegranate Glaze

This cake is the ideal recipe for winter pomegranates.

Serves 8
225g/8oz oat biscuits (crackers)
75g/3oz/6 tbsp unsalted
  butter, melted

For the filling
45ml/3 tbsp orange juice
15ml/1 tbsp powdered gelatine
250g/9oz/generous 1 cup
  mascarpone cheese
200g/7oz/scant 1 cup full-fat
  soft cheese

75g/3oz/⅔ cup icing
  (confectioners') sugar, sifted
200ml/7fl oz/scant 1 cup
  coconut cream
2 egg whites

For the topping
2 pomegranates, peeled and
  seeds separated
grated rind and juice of 1 orange
30ml/2 tbsp caster
  (superfine) sugar
15ml/1 tbsp arrowroot, mixed to a
  paste with 30ml/2 tbsp Kirsch
red food colouring (optional)

1 Grease a 23cm/9in springform cake tin (pan). Crumb the biscuits in a food processor or blender. Add the butter and process briefly. Spoon into the tin, press in well, then chill.

2 Make the filling. Pour the orange juice into a heatproof bowl, sprinkle the gelatine on top and set aside for 5 minutes. Place the bowl in a pan of hot water; stir until the gelatine dissolves.

3 Beat together both cheeses and the icing sugar, then beat in the coconut cream. Whisk the egg whites in a grease-free bowl to soft peaks. Stir the melted gelatine into the coconut mixture and fold in the egg whites. Pour over the base and chill until set.

4 Make the topping. Place the pomegranate seeds in a pan and add the orange rind and juice and sugar. Bring to the boil, then lower the heat, cover and simmer for 5 minutes. Add the arrowroot paste and heat, stirring, until thickened. Stir in a few drops of food colouring, if using. Leave to cool.

5 Pour the glaze over the top of the set cheesecake, then chill. Remove from the tin and cut into slices to serve.

Chocolate Pavlova Energy 541kcal/2260kJ; Protein 7.3g; Carbohydrate 56.4g, of which sugars 52.3g; Fat 33.6g, of which saturates 20.4g; Cholesterol 59mg; Calcium 96mg; Fibre 1.9g; Sodium 146mg.
Winter Cheesecake Energy 407kcal/1702kJ; Protein 8.2g; Carbohydrate 37.3g, of which sugars 26.1g; Fat 26.1g, of which saturates 15.2g; Cholesterol 56mg; Calcium 57mg; Fibre 1.1g; Sodium 336mg.

Chocolate Mandarin Trifle

Rich chocolate custard is combined with seasonal mandarin oranges to make a trifle that is utterly delectable and impossible to resist.

Serves 6–8
4 trifle sponges
14 amaretti
60ml/4 tbsp Amaretto di Saronno
   or sweet sherry
8 mandarin oranges

For the custard
200g/7oz plain (semisweet)
   chocolate, broken into squares

25g/1oz/2 tbsp cornflour
   (cornstarch) or custard powder
25g/1oz/2 tbsp caster
   (superfine) sugar
2 egg yolks
200ml/7fl oz/scant 1 cup milk
250g/9oz/generous 1 cup
   mascarpone

For the topping
250g/9oz/generous 1 cup
   mascarpone or fromage frais
chocolate shapes
mandarin slices

1 Break up the trifle sponges and place them in a large glass serving dish. Crumble the amaretti over and then sprinkle with Amaretto or sweet sherry.

2 Squeeze the juice from two of the mandarins and sprinkle into the dish. Segment the rest and put in the dish.

3 Make the custard. Melt the chocolate in a heatproof bowl over hot water. In a separate bowl, mix the cornflour or custard powder, sugar and egg yolks to a smooth paste.

4 Heat the milk in a pan until almost boiling, then pour in a steady stream on to the egg mixture, stirring constantly. Return to the pan and simmer until the custard is thick and smooth.

5 Stir in the mascarpone until melted, then add the melted chocolate; mix well. Spread over the trifle, cool, then chill to set.

6 To finish, spread the mascarpone or fromage frais over the custard, then decorate with chocolate shapes and the remaining mandarin slices just before serving.

Pineapple Custard

These pineapple crème caramels are the perfect winter dinner party dessert. They are very easy to make, especially if you buy prepared fresh pineapple from the supermarket.

Serves 6
350g/12oz peeled fresh
   pineapple, chopped

150g/5oz/²⁄₃ cup caster
   (superfine) sugar
4 eggs, lightly beaten

For the caramel
60ml/4 tbsp granulated
   (white) sugar
juice of 1 lime

1 Put the pineapple in a blender or food processor and process until smooth. Scrape the purée into a pan and add the sugar. Cook for 5 minutes or until reduced by one-third. The mixture should be thick but not jam-like, so add a little water if it is too thick. Transfer to a bowl and leave to cool.

2 Meanwhile make the caramel. Place the granulated sugar in a heavy pan over medium heat. As the sugar caramelizes around the edges, shake the pan to mix the sugar, but do not stir.

3 Remove the pan from the heat as soon as all the sugar has dissolved and the caramel has become golden brown. Immediately stir in the lime juice, taking care not to burn yourself. The hot caramel will spit when the lime juice is added, but this will stop. Divide the caramel among six ramekins and turn them so that they are coated evenly.

4 Preheat the oven to 180°C/350°F/Gas 4. Stir the eggs into the cool pineapple mixture. Divide the mixture equally among the ramekins. Place the moulds in a roasting pan and pour in warm water to come halfway up their sides. Cover with foil and bake for 45 minutes, until set. Allow to cool.

5 Just before serving, unmould the custards directly on to dessert plates. Loosen the edges of the custards with a knife, invert a dessert plate on top of each mould and quickly turn both over. Serve immediately.

Chocolate Trifle Energy 569kcal/2394kJ; Protein 12.5g; Carbohydrate 80.3g, of which sugars 61.3g; Fat 23.1g, of which saturates 12.8g; Cholesterol 135mg; Calcium 162mg; Fibre 2.9g; Sodium 115mg.
Pineapple Custard Energy 211kcal/895kJ; Protein 4.6g; Carbohydrate 42.5g, of which sugars 42.5g; Fat 3.8g, of which saturates 1g; Cholesterol 127mg; Calcium 48mg; Fibre 0.7g; Sodium 50mg.

Iced Christmas Torte

This makes an exciting alternative to traditional Christmas pudding – but don't feel that you have to limit it to the festive season.

Serves 8–10
75g/3oz/¾ cup dried cranberries
75g/3oz/scant ½ cup
  pitted prunes
50g/2oz/⅓ cup sultanas
  (golden raisins)
175ml/6fl oz/¾ cup port
2 pieces preserved stem ginger,
  finely chopped
25g/1oz/2 tbsp unsalted butter
45ml/3 tbsp light muscovado
  (brown) sugar
90g/3½oz/scant 2 cups fresh
  white breadcrumbs
600ml/1 pint/2½ cups
  double (heavy) cream
30ml/2 tbsp icing
  (confectioners') sugar
5ml/1 tsp ground allspice
75g/3oz/¾ cup brazil nuts,
  finely chopped
sugared bay leaves and fresh
  cherries, to decorate

1 Put the cranberries, prunes and sultanas in a food processor or blender and process briefly. Transfer them to a bowl and add the port and ginger. Leave to absorb the port for 2 hours.

2 Melt the butter in a frying pan. Add the sugar and heat gently until the sugar has dissolved. Add the breadcrumbs, stir lightly, then fry over a low heat for about 5 minutes, until lightly coloured and turning crisp. Leave to cool.

3 Turn the breadcrumbs into a food processor or blender and process to finer crumbs. Sprinkle a third into an 18cm/7in loose-based springform tin (pan) and freeze.

4 Whip the cream with the icing sugar and spice until the mixture is thick but not yet standing in peaks. Fold in the brazil nuts with the dried fruit mixture and any port remaining.

5 Spread a third of the mixture over the breadcrumb base in the tin, taking care not to dislodge the crumbs. Sprinkle with another layer of the breadcrumbs. Repeat the layering, finishing with a layer of the cream mixture. Freeze the torte overnight. Serve immediately decorated with sugared bay leaves and fresh cherries.

Dried Fruit Compote

This dessert uses a mix of frozen fruit and dried fruits. It doesn't take long to prepare, but must be made ahead of time, to allow the dried fruit to plump up and flavours to blend. It is also good for breakfast.

Serves 4
115g/4oz/½ cup ready-to-eat
  dried apricots, halved
115g/4oz/½ cup ready-to-eat
  dried peaches, halved
750ml/1¼ pints/3 cups water
1 pear
1 apple
1 orange
115g/4oz/1 cup frozen
  mixed raspberries and
  blackberries, thawed
1 cinnamon stick
50g/2oz/¼ cup caster
  (superfine) sugar
15ml/1 tbsp clear honey
30ml/2 tbsp lemon juice

1 Place the dried apricots and peaches in a large pan and pour in 600ml/1 pint/2½ cups of the water.

2 Peel and core the pear and apple, then dice. Remove the peel and pith from the orange and cut into wedges. Add all the cut fruit to the pan with the raspberries and blackberries.

3 Pour in the remaining water. Add the cinnamon stick, stir in the sugar and honey, and heat gently, stirring until the sugar and honey have dissolved. Bring to the boil. Cover and simmer for 10 minutes, then remove the pan from the heat.

4 Stir in the lemon or lime juice. Leave to cool completely, then transfer the fruit and syrup to a bowl, cover with clear film (plastic wrap) and chill for 1–2 hours before serving.

> **Variation**
> Depending on the season and what is available, you can swap the fruits around, using dried apples and pears and fresh apricots and peaches instead of the combination suggested in the recipe. Seasonal cranberries are a delicious alternative to the raspberries and blackberries.

Iced Christmas Torte Energy 504kcal/2098kJ; Protein 6.3g; Carbohydrate 38.4g, of which sugars 21g; Fat 36.4g, of which saturates 17.8g; Cholesterol 61mg; Calcium 92mg; Fibre 2.3g; Sodium 209mg.
Dried Fruit Salad Energy 190kcal/811kJ; Protein 3.3g; Carbohydrate 46g, of which sugars 46g; Fat 0.5g, of which saturates 0g; Cholesterol 0mg; Calcium 75mg; Fibre 6g; Sodium 13mg.

Christmas Rice Pudding with Prunes and Brandy

This festive rice pudding can be topped with some substantial winter fruit, such as prunes. The scope for adding ingredients that are associated with winter and Christmas, such as almonds or spices, is endless.

Serves 4
90g/3½oz/½ cup short grain rice
1.2 litres/2 pints/5 cups milk
pinch of salt
15ml/1 tbsp ground cinnamon

200ml/7fl oz/scant 1 cup double (heavy) cream
50g/2oz/¼ cup caster (superfine) sugar
25g/1oz/¼ cup toasted flaked (sliced) almonds

To serve
100g/3¾oz/scant ½ cup prunes
50ml/2fl oz/¼ cup brandy

1 Put the rice and milk in a pan and bring to the boil. Add the salt, lower the heat, cover and simmer gently for about 1 hour, until the rice has absorbed most of the milk and is almost tender. Stir frequently to prevent the rice from sticking and burning on the bottom of the pan.

2 Add the cinnamon, cream, sugar and almonds to the rice and cook for a further 10 minutes, until the rice is tender.

3 Meanwhile, put the prunes and brandy in a pan and heat gently for 5–6 minutes until the prunes are heated through and have absorbed some of the brandy. Serve the rice in individual serving bowls and spoon the prunes on top.

> **Cook's Tip**
> A blanched almond is traditionally pressed into the rice pudding, in a similar way to the sixpence that is hidden inside a Christmas pudding. It is meant to bring good luck to whoever finds the almond.

Chocolate and Orange Scotch Pancakes

These fabulous mini pancakes in a rich orange liqueur sauce are perfect for a winter treat.

Serves 4
115g/4oz/1 cup self-raising (self-rising) flour
30ml/2 tbsp unsweetened cocoa powder
2 eggs
50g/2oz plain (semisweet) chocolate, broken into squares
200ml/7fl oz/scant 1 cup milk

finely grated rind of 1 orange
30ml/2 tbsp orange juice
butter or oil, for frying
60ml/4 tbsp chocolate curls, to decorate

For the sauce
2 large oranges
25g/1oz/2 tbsp unsalted butter
40g/1½oz/3 tbsp light muscovado (brown) sugar
250ml/8fl oz/1 cup crème fraîche
30ml/2 tbsp orange liqueur

1 Sift the flour and cocoa into a bowl and make a well in the centre. Add the eggs and beat well, gradually incorporating the surrounding dry ingredients to make a smooth batter.

2 Mix the chocolate and milk in a heavy pan. Heat gently until the chocolate has melted, then beat into the batter until smooth and bubbly. Stir in the grated orange rind and juice.

3 Heat a large frying pan or griddle. Grease with a little butter or oil. Drop large spoonfuls of batter into the pan and cook over medium heat until lightly browned underneath and bubbling on top; flip them over to cook the other side. Slide on to a plate and keep hot, then make more in the same way.

4 Make the sauce. Grate the rind of one orange into a bowl and set aside. Peel both oranges, discarding the peel and pith, then slice thinly. Gently heat the butter and sugar, stirring until the sugar dissolves. Stir in the crème fraîche and heat gently.

5 Add the pancakes and orange slices to the sauce, heat gently for 1–2 minutes, then spoon on the liqueur. Sprinkle with the reserved orange rind. Sprinkle over chocolate curls and serve.

Rice Pudding Energy 617kcal/2577kJ; Protein 14.7g; Carbohydrate 54.9g, of which sugars 36.8g; Fat 35.7g, of which saturates 20.2g; Cholesterol 86mg; Calcium 419mg; Fibre 1.9g; Sodium 145mg.
Chocolate Pancakes Energy 752kcal/3131kJ; Protein 12.1g; Carbohydrate 58.1g, of which sugars 35.5g; Fat 53.2g, of which saturates 27g; Cholesterol 185mg; Calcium 282mg; Fibre 3.9g; Sodium 304mg.

Chocolate Orange Marquise

Here is a cake for people who are passionate about chocolate. The rich, dense flavour is accentuated by fresh seasonal orange to make it a truly delectable winter treat.

Serves 6–8
200g/7oz/1 cup caster (superfine) sugar
60ml/4 tbsp freshly squeezed orange juice
350g/12oz dark (bittersweet) chocolate, broken into squares
225g/8oz/1 cup unsalted butter, diced, plus extra for greasing
5 eggs
finely grated rind of 1 orange
45g/1¾oz/3 tbsp plain (all-purpose) flour
icing (confectioners') sugar and finely pared strips of orange rind, to decorate

1 Preheat the oven to 180°C/350°F/Gas 4. Grease a 23cm/9in shallow cake tin (pan) with a depth of 6cm/2½in. Line the base of the tin with baking parchment.

2 Place 90g/3½oz/½ cup of the sugar in a pan. Add the orange juice and stir over a low heat until dissolved.

3 Remove from the heat and stir in the chocolate until melted, then add the butter, piece by piece, until melted.

4 Whisk the eggs with the remaining sugar in a large bowl, until the mixture is pale and very thick. Add the orange rind, then lightly fold the chocolate mixture into the egg mixture. Sift the flour over the top and fold in.

5 Pour the mixture into the prepared tin. Place in a roasting pan, then pour hot water into the roasting pan to reach about halfway up the sides of the cake tin.

6 Bake for 1 hour, or until the cake is firm to the touch. Remove the tin from the roasting pan and cool for 20 minutes. Turn out the cake on to a baking sheet, place a serving plate upside down on top, then carefully turn the plate and baking sheet over together. Dust with a little icing sugar, decorate with strips of orange rind and serve slightly warm or chilled.

Cranberry and Chocolate Squares

These delicious little morsels are packed with winter flavour thanks to the inclusion of cranberries, which are at their peak in the early winter months.

Makes 12
150g/5oz/1¼ cups self-raising (self-rising) flour, plus extra for dusting
115g/4oz/½ cup unsalted butter
60ml/4 tbsp unsweetened cocoa powder
215g/7½oz/1¼ cups light muscovado (brown) sugar
2 eggs, beaten
115g/4oz/1⅓ cups fresh or thawed frozen cranberries
75ml/5 tbsp coarsely grated plain (semisweet) chocolate, for sprinkling

For the topping
150ml/¼ pint/⅔ cup sour cream
75g/3oz/6 tbsp caster (superfine) sugar
30ml/2 tbsp self-raising (self-rising) flour
50g/2oz/4 tbsp soft margarine
1 egg, beaten
2.5ml/½ tsp vanilla extract

1 Preheat oven to 180°C/350°F/Gas 4. Grease a 27 × 18cm/ 10½ × 7in cake tin (pan) and dust lightly with flour. Combine the butter, cocoa powder and sugar in a pan and stir over low heat until melted and smooth.

2 Remove the melted mixture from the heat and stir in the flour and eggs, beating until thoroughly mixed.

3 Stir in the cranberries, then spread the mixture in the tin. Make the topping by mixing all the ingredients in a bowl. Beat until smooth, then spread over the base.

4 Sprinkle with the chocolate and bake for 40–45 minutes, or until risen and firm. Cool in the tin for 10 minutes, then cut into 12 squares. Remove from the tin and cool on a wire rack.

Cook's Tip
Make these treats in early winter with fresh cranberries as the season for these berries tails off after the Christmas period.

Chocolate Marquise Energy 553kcal/2309kJ; Protein 3.1g; Carbohydrate 59.1g, of which sugars 54.4g; Fat 35.5g, of which saturates 22g; Cholesterol 63mg; Calcium 41mg; Fibre 1.3g; Sodium 176mg.
Cranberry Squares Energy 343kcal/1439kJ; Protein 4.8g; Carbohydrate 42.9g, of which sugars 30.8g; Fat 18.2g, of which saturates 8.7g; Cholesterol 76mg; Calcium 63mg; Fibre 1.4g; Sodium 164mg.

Chocolate and Fruit Puddings

Drenched in a thick chocolate syrup and packed with winter fruit, this slow-cooker pudding is pure indulgence.

Serves 4

1 apple, peeled and cored, diced
25g/1oz/¼ cup cranberries, thawed if frozen
175g/6oz/¾ cup soft dark brown sugar
115g/4oz/½ cup soft margarine
2 eggs, lightly beaten
50g/2oz/½ cup self-raising (self-rising) flour, sifted
45ml/3 tbsp unsweetened cocoa powder

For the syrup

115g/4oz plain (semisweet) chocolate, chopped
30ml/2 tbsp clear honey
15g/½oz/1 tbsp unsalted butter
2.5ml/½ tsp vanilla extract

1 Pour 2.5cm/1in of hot water into the cooking pot and switch the slow cooker to high. Grease four individual heatproof bowls with oil, then line with baking parchment.

2 Place the diced apple in a bowl, and add the cranberries and 15ml/1 tbsp of the sugar. Mix well, then divide among the four bowls, gently patting it down into the base of each one.

3 Place the remaining sugar in a clean mixing bowl and add the margarine, eggs, flour and cocoa. Beat together until smooth. Spoon into the bowls and cover each with a double thickness of greased foil. Place the bowls in the cooking pot and pour in hot water to come two-thirds of the way up the sides of the bowls.

4 Cover with the lid and cook on high for 1½–2 hours, or until the puddings are well-risen and firm. Carefully remove from the slow cooker and leave to stand for 10 minutes.

5 Meanwhile, make the chocolate syrup. Put the chocolate, honey, butter and vanilla extract in a heatproof bowl and place in the hot water in the slow cooker. Leave for 10 minutes, until the butter has melted, then stir until smooth.

6 Run a knife around the edge of the puddings to loosen, then turn over on to plates. Serve immediately, with the syrup.

Christmas Pudding

This rich, slowly steamed pudding is a must for any Christmas feast. Serve with a traditional hot white sauce, flavoured with whiskey, brandy or rum, or simply offer a jug of cream liqueur, to be poured over the pudding as a sauce.

Makes 2 puddings, each serving 6–8

275g/10oz/5 cups fresh breadcrumbs
225g/8oz/1 cup light muscovado (brown) sugar
225g/8oz/1 cup currants
275g/10oz/2 cups raisins
225g/8oz/1⅓ cups sultanas (golden raisins)
50g/2oz/⅓ cup chopped (candied) peel
115g/4oz/½ cup glacé (candied) cherries
225g/8oz shredded suet (US chilled, grated shortening), or vegetarian equivalent
2.5ml/½ tsp salt
10–20ml/2–4 tsp mixed (apple pie) spice
1 carrot, coarsely grated
1 apple, peeled, cored and finely chopped
grated rind and juice of 1 small orange
2 large (US extra large) eggs, lightly whisked
450ml/¾ pint/scant 2 cups stout
white sauce, to serve

1 Mix the breadcrumbs, sugar, dried fruit and peel in a bowl. Shred and add the suet, salt, mixed spice, carrot, apple and orange rind. Mix until well combined. Stir in the orange juice, eggs and stout. Leave the mixture overnight, giving it a stir occasionally, if convenient.

2 Well grease and line two 1.2 litre/2 pint/5 cup heatproof bowls with baking parchment. Stir the mixture and turn into the bowls. Cover with buttered circles of baking parchment, then tie pudding cloths over the top, or tightly cover them with several layers of baking parchment and foil, tied under the rim.

3 Steam for about 6–7 hours. Ensure the puddings do not go off the boil, and top up with more water as needed.

4 When cool, re-cover the puddings with paper or foil and store in a cool, dry place for at least a month. When required, steam for another 2–3 hours. Serve hot, with a traditional white sauce.

Choc Puddings Energy 739kcal/3094kJ; Protein 9.1g; Carbohydrate 88.3g, of which sugars 77.2g; Fat 41.3g, of which saturates 14.4g; Cholesterol 124mg; Calcium 103mg; Fibre 3.1g; Sodium 438mg.
Christmas Pud Energy 7171kcal/30,432kJ; Protein 38.8g; Carbohydrate 1596.3g, of which sugars 1479.8g; Fat 112.9g, of which saturates 58g; Cholesterol 321mg; Calcium 1071mg; Fibre 13.8g; Sodium 1965mg.

Vanilla Snow

While a good-quality vanilla essence is perfectly acceptable for flavouring drinks, a far more aromatic taste will be achieved using a vanilla pod. This simple smoothie is deliciously scented, creamy and thick, and well worth the extravagance of using a whole vanilla pod. Its lovely, snowy whiteness is delightfully speckled with tiny black vanilla seeds.

Makes 3 glasses
1 vanilla pod (bean)
25g/1oz/2 tbsp caster
    (superfine) sugar
3 eating apples
300g/11oz/1⅓ cups natural
    (plain) yogurt

1 Using the tip of a sharp knife, split open the vanilla pod lengthways. Put it in a small pan with the sugar and 75ml/5 tbsp water. Heat until the sugar dissolves, then boil for 1 minute. Remove from the heat and leave to steep for 10 minutes.

2 Cut the apples into large chunks and push through the juicer, then pour the juice into a large bowl or jug (pitcher).

3 Lift the vanilla pod out of the pan and scrape the tiny black seeds back into the syrup. Pour into the apple juice.

4 Add the yogurt to the bowl or jug and whisk well by hand or with an electric mixer until the smoothie is thick and frothy. Pour into glasses and serve.

Cook's Tip
Like most smoothies, this one should ideally be served well chilled. Either use apples and yogurt straight from the refrigerator, or you can chill the smoothies briefly before serving. to make a thick, icy version, you could try making the smoothies with frozen yogurt.

Passionata

The combination of ripe passion fruit with sweet caramel is gorgeous in this dreamy milkshake. For convenience, you can easily make the caramel syrup and combine it with the fresh passion fruit juice in advance, so it's all ready for blending with the milk. For the best results, make sure you use really ripe, crinkly passion fruit.

Makes 4 glasses
90g/3½oz/1/2 cup caster
    (superfine) sugar
juice of 2 large oranges
juice of 1 lemon
6 ripe passion fruit, plus
    extra for garnish
550ml/18fl oz/2½ cups
    full cream
(whole) milk
ice cubes

1 Put the sugar in a small, heavy pan with 200ml/7fl oz/scant 1 cup water. Heat gently, stirring with a wooden spoon until the sugar has dissolved.

2 Bring the mixture to the boil and cook, without stirring, for about 5 minutes until the syrup has turned to a deep golden caramel. Watch closely towards the end of the cooking time because caramel can burn very quickly. If this happens, let the caramel cool, then throw it away and start again.

3 When the caramel has turned deep golden, immediately lower the base of the pan into cold water to prevent it from cooking any further.

4 Carefully add the orange and lemon juice, standing back slightly as the mixture will splutter. Return the pan to the heat and cook gently, stirring continuously, to make a smooth syrup. Transfer the syrup to a small heatproof bowl and set aside until it has cooled completely.

5 Cut the passion fruit in half and, using a spoon, scoop out the seeds into a blender or food processor. Add the caramel and milk to the blender and mix until the mixture is smooth and frothy. Pour over ice and serve immediately with a passion fruit garnish.

Vanilla Snow Energy 124kcal/527kJ; Protein 5.4g; Carbohydrate 25.1g, of which sugars 25.1g; Fat 1.1g, of which saturates 0 .5g; Cholesterol 1mg; Calcium 198mg; Fibre 1.6g; Sodium 86mg.
Passionata Energy 197kcal/828kJ; Protein 5.4g; Carbohydrate 33.2g, of which sugars 33.2g; Fat 5.5g, of which saturates 3.5g; Cholesterol 19mg; Calcium 179mg; Fibre 0.8g; Sodium 67mg.

Foaming Citrus Eggnog

For most of us, eggnog is inextricably associated with the festive season. This version, however, pepped up with orange rind and juice for a lighter, fresher taste, has a much wider appeal. Whether you sip it as a late-night soother, serve it as a wintry dessert or enjoy it as a cosy tipple on a wet afternoon, it's sure to bring a warm, rosy glow to your cheeks.

Makes 2 glasses
2 small oranges
150ml/¼ pint/⅔ cup single
   (light) cream
plenty of freshly grated nutmeg
2.5ml/½ tsp ground cinnamon
2.5ml/½ tsp cornflour (cornstarch)
2 eggs, separated
30ml/2 tbsp light muscovado
   (brown) sugar
45ml/3 tbsp brandy
extra nutmeg, for
   sprinkling (optional)

1 Finely grate the rind from the oranges, then squeeze out the juice and pour it into a jug (pitcher).

2 Put the rind in a small heavy pan with the cream, nutmeg, cinnamon and cornflour. Heat gently over a low heat, stirring frequently until bubbling.

3 Whisk the egg yolks with the sugar, using a handheld whisk.

4 Stir the hot citrus cream mixture into the egg yolks, then return to the pan. Pour in the orange juice and brandy and heat very gently, stirring until slightly thickened.

5 Whisk the egg whites in a large, clean bowl until foamy and light.

6 Strain the cream mixture through a sieve into the whisked whites. Stir gently and pour into heatproof punch cups, handled glasses or mugs. Sprinkle over a little extra nutmeg before serving, if you like.

> **Cook's Tip**
> Note that this recipe contains almost raw egg.

Pomegranate Plus

Pomegranates have an exotic and distinctive flavour that is quite delicious. A reddish skin is usually a sign that the seeds inside will be vibrant and sweet. Pomegranate juice makes a delicious base for this treat of a juice, which is mildly spiced with a hint of ginger.

Serves 2
2 pomegranates
4 fresh figs
15g/½oz fresh root
   ginger, peeled
10ml/2 tsp lime juice
ice cubes and lime wedges,
   to serve

1 Halve the pomegranates. Working over a bowl to catch the juices, pull away the skin to remove the seeds.

2 Quarter the figs and roughly chop the ginger. Push the figs and ginger through a juicer. Push the pomegranate seeds through, reserving a few for decoration. Stir in the lime juice. Pour over ice cubes and lime wedges, then serve.

Ruby Dreamer

Fresh figs are at their best in winter when ruby oranges are also in season.

15ml/1 tbsp dark muscovado
   (molasses) sugar
30–45ml/2–3 tbsp lemon juice
crushed ice

Makes 2 glasses
6 large ripe figs
4 ruby oranges

1 Cut off the hard, woody tips from the stalks of the figs, then use a sharp knife to cut each fruit in half.

2 Squeeze the oranges and pour the juice into a blender or food processor. Add the figs and sugar. Process well until the mixture is smooth and fairly thick.

3 Add the lemon juice and blend. Pour over the ice and serve.

Pomegranate Plus Energy 224kcal/951kJ; Protein 3.4g; Carbohydrate 52.3g, of which sugars 52.3g; Fat 1.6g, of which saturates 0g; Cholesterol 0mg; Calcium 233mg; Fibre 6.9g; Sodium 58mg.
Ruby Dreamer Energy 417kcal/1776kJ; Protein 7.2g; Carbohydrate 97.8g, of which sugars 97.8g; Fat 2.5g, of which saturates 0g; Cholesterol 0mg; Calcium 443mg; Fibre 13.8g; Sodium 96mg.
Citrus Eggnog Energy 375kcal/1566kJ; Protein 9.1g; Carbohydrate 29.6g, of which sugars 29.6g; Fat 19.9g, of which saturates 10.7g; Cholesterol 232mg Calcium 112mg; Fibre 0.1g; Sodium 98mg.

Index

aioli, fried new potatoes with 19
almond
 and apricot stuffed chicken 110
 avocado, orange and almond salad 29
 biscuits, quince mousse with 188
 and pear tart 187
apple
 bacon with 149
 baked stuffed 185
 Charlottes 185
 chocolate and fruit puddings 249
 Christmas chutney 199
 and cider relish 141
 and cider sorbet 183
 and gingerbread sundaes 183
 mini toffee apples 184
 old-fashioned apple cake 184
 and potato rösti, pork escalopes with 178
 roast duck with prunes and 177
 roast pork, apples and glazed potatoes 179
 sweet sharp shock 193
asparagus
 asparagus, bacon and leaf salad 32
 and cheese flan 36
 and chicken tartlets 23
 Dutch 51
 and egg terrine 17
 garganelli with spring vegetables 37
 grilled spring onions, Parma ham and 27
 with lemon sauce 35
 and pea soup 9
 risotto with 35
 with salmon 46
 salmon rolls with butter sauce and 45
 scrambled eggs with 36
 spring, with egg 34
 stir-fried noodles in shellfish sauce 43
aubergine
 aubergine, lemon and caper salad 89
 conchiglie with roasted vegetables 96
 crispy seven-spice 77
 dip, creamy 75
 and garlic custards, roasted, with red
  pepper dressing 93
 grilled vegetable pizza 96
 grilled vegetable terrine 80
 mackerel in lemon samfaina 105
 moussaka 115
 parcels, grilled 92
 roast chicken with summer vegetables and
  potatoes 113
 roasted ratatouille moussaka 99
 roasted vegetable quesadillas with melted
  mozzarella 97
 rolls 92
 soup with mozzarella and gremolata 70
 and spinach pie 39
 stewed, with tomatoes and red wine 93
 summer vegetable kebabs with harissa and
  yogurt dip 98
avocado
 avocado, onion and spinach salad 25
 avocado, orange and almond salad 29
 chilled avocado soup with cumin 8
 eggs mimosa 16
 green devil 66
 guacamole 14
 hot avocado halves 17
 prawn, egg and avocado mousse 21
 with salmon salad 30
 tortilla wrap with tabbouleh 18

bacon
 with apples 149
 asparagus, bacon and leaf salad 32
 cream of duck soup 139

Galacian broth 13
 and leek soup 9
 mackerel with nutty bacon stuffing 104
 pâté with mushrooms and 149
 peas and carrots with 37
 scallops with fennel, mascarpone and 170
 stir-fried spring greens 34
banana
 and chocolate chip pudding 251
 milkshake 67
 roast, with Greek yogurt 250
 and rum waffles 251
beef
 baked, with a potato crust 240
 with chanterelle in cream sauce 181
 golden beef and potato puffs 207
 meatballs in tomato and wine sauce 116
 polpettes with mozzarella and tomato 116
 spiced beef roll 56
 spicy beefburgers 117
 steak ciabatta with hummus 117
 steak and mushroom pudding with a
  herby suet crust 181
 stuffed cabbage leaves 180
 and sweet potato salad 213
 tagine with peas and saffron 56
 tagine with sweet potatoes 239
black pudding 50
blueberry
 purple haze 131
 relish 139
 and vanilla crumble 122
bombe, spicy pumpkin and orange 182
brill fillets in red wine sauce 229
broad beans
 broad bean salad 27
 broad beans with sausages 50
 baked chicken with broad beans 50
Brussels sprouts with bacon and caraway
 seeds 214
butternut squash
 and blue cheese risotto soup 138
 cinnamon squash 192
 and maple pie 191
 roasted garlic and butternut squash soup
  with tomato salsa 138
 roasted shallot and butternut squash
  salad 154

cabbage
 braised guinea fowl with 234
 braised partridge with 236
 braised red 216
 colcannon 215
 crispy winter 216
 curried red cabbage slaw 208
 hunter's stew 180
 sauerkraut pie 217
 spiced greens 215
 stuffed cabbage leaves 180
 winter coleslaw 209
 winter salad with coconut and lime
  dressing 211
calabrese, florets polonaise 34
calf's liver and hare terrine 206
caramelized apricots with pain perdu 125
caramelized shallot and garlic tarte tatin 20
cauliflower
 florets polonaise 34

soup, curried 194
 stir-fried, with garlic crumbs 214
celeriac, spicy root vegetable gratin 165
cheese
 and asparagus flan 36
 aubergine rolls 92
 aubergine and spinach pie 39
 baked leek and potato gratin 220
 baked tomatoes with mint 95
 and broccoli mina 160
 butternut squash and blue cheese risotto
  soup 138
 cheese-stuffed pears 144
 cheesy creamy leeks 219
 chicken flautas 111
 chicory salad with Roquefort 209
 courgette fritters with chilli jam 79
 courgette with green chillies and 90
 courgette roulade 91
 creamy aubergine soup with mozzarella
  and gremolata 70
 garlic with goat's cheese pâté 146
 grilled aubergine parcels 92
 grilled goat's cheese toasts with
  beetroot 20
 grilled halloumi and bean salad 28
 grilled vegetable pizza 96
 Gruyère and potato soufflés 202
 halloumi and grape salad 151
 Idaho potato slices 203
 Jerusalem artichoke au gratin 219
 kefalotyri cubes spiked with bay leaves 76
 leek and onion tartlets 201
 leek soufflé 201
 moussaka 115
 mushroom soup with croûtes 137
 onions stuffed with goat's cheese 165
 pear and Roquefort soup 136
 pears with Cashel Blue cream and
  walnuts 150
 pies with raisins and nuts 142
 polpettes with mozzarella and
  tomato 116
 roast pepper terrine 80
 roasted mixed pepper and Parmesan
  risotto 98
 roasted ratatouille moussaka 99
 roasted vegetable quesadillas with melted
  mozzarella 97
 rocket and tomato pizza 95
 Roquefort and walnut salad 151
 scallops with fennel, mascarpone and
  bacon 170
 smoked haddock bake with a cheese
  crumb 225
 spiced couscous with halloumi and
  courgette ribbons 159
 strawberry and ricotta semi-freddo 121
 stuffed baby squash 156
 sweet romanos stuffed with two cheeses
  and cherry peppers 97
 tart 63
 tomato and black olive tart 94
 tomato and mozzarella salad 85
 warm halloumi and fennel salad 152
 wild mushroom and fontina tarts 163
 yellow courgette wraps with spinach and
  mozzarella 90
cheesecakes
 raspberry and white chocolate 124
 spring cheesecake with cinnamon 64
 winter, with pomegranate glaze 244
cherry
 clafoutis 61
 ice cream with hot black cherry sauce 62
 noodle pudding with cherries and nuts 62
 strudel 61
chicken
 apricot and almond stuffed 110
 and asparagus tartlets 23
 baked, with broad beans 50

bitki 148
 braised, with mashed swede 233
 and broccoli salad 31
 chicken wings with blood oranges 207
 coq au vin 175
 escalopes with vegetables 49
 fajitas 111
 fillets with Serrano ham 110
 flautas 111
 grilled skewered 109
 and lentil broth 12
 lettuce parcels 83
 marinated chicken salad with spring
  onions 33
 and mushroom donburi 174
 with peas 49
 and pork in peanut sauce 175
 with potato dumplings 232
 with prawns 112
 rice con pollo 112
 roast, with summer vegetables and
  potatoes 113
 roasted, with grapes and fresh root
  ginger 174
 satay, pandanus-flavoured, with hot cashew
  nut sambal 108
 soup 196
 tandoori drumsticks with kachumbar 109
 with tomatoes, cinnamon and honey 113
 with winter vegetables 232
chickpea
 and parsnip stew 221
 rissoles 143
chicory 16
 salad with Roquefort 209
chilled pepper soup 68
chilli
 chilli crabs 22
 chilli curls 66
 gazpacho juice 130
 green, courgette with cheese and 90
 grilled hake with lemon and 229
 husk-grilled corn on the cob 156
 jam, courgette fritters with 79
 lemon, chilli and garlic relish 140
 onion and red chilli relish 198
 peppery egg, watercress and chilli salad 88
 pineapple with ginger and 208
 and raspberry dip, butterfly prawn
  skewers with 81
 red onion and tomato relish 114
 roasted vegetable quesadillas with melted
  mozzarella 97
 salsa, classic tomato 74
 salsa verde 15
 salsa, yogurt soup with 73
 sea bass with orange chilli salsa 227
 spaghetti with broccoli and red chilli 161
chocolate
 and chestnut pots 243
 chocolate chip and banana pudding 251
 chocolate redcurrant torte 123
 and cranberry squares 248
 devilish chocolate roulade 63
 and fruit puddings 249
 mandarin trifle 245
 orange marquise 248
 and orange Scotch pancakes 247
 pavlova with passion fruit cream 244
 pears in chocolate fudge blankets 187
 raspberry and white chocolate
  cheesecake 124
chouriço 50
Christmas chutney 199
Christmas pudding 249
Christmas rice pudding with prunes and
 brandy 247
chutney, Christmas 199
ciabatta, steak, with hummus 117
cider
 and apple relish 141

and apple water ice 183
Christmas chutney 199
and cream broth, mussels in a 166
clafoutis, cherry 61
clams
    monkfish with coriander and 231
    and mussels in banana leaves 167
    seafood spaghetti parcels 168
    with tomato sauce 168
clapshot 218
cobbler, peach 126
coconut
    halibut with peppers and 105
    and lime dressing, winter cabbage salad
      with 211
    paste, roasted sweet potatoes, onions and
      beetroot in 223
    and pumpkin soup 135
cod
    baked, with beer and lemon 107
    three-fish terrine 205
colcannon 215
coleslaw, winter 209
compote, dried fruit 246
conchiglie with roasted vegetables 96
confit of slow-cooked onions and prunes 142
coq au vin 175
coriander
    monkfish with clams and 231
    relish, crab soup with 11
corn on the cob, husk-grilled 156
courgette
    with cheese and green chillies 90
    chunky courgette and tomato soup 71
    conchiglie with roasted vegetables 96
    farfalle with prawns and 100
    fritters with chilli jam 79
    grilled vegetable pizza 96
    grilled vegetable terrine 80
    and halloumi ribbons, spiced couscous
      with 159
    mackerel in lemon samfaina 105
    pan-fried ham and Mediterranean
      vegetables with eggs 114
    roasted ratatouille moussaka 99
    roulade 91
    summer vegetable kebabs with harissa
      and yogurt dip 98
    tempura 77
    and tofu with tomato sauce 91
    and tomato timbales 79
    yellow courgette wraps with spinach and
      mozzarella 90
couscous, spiced, with halloumi and courgette
    ribbons 159
crab
    bake 43
    chilli crab 22
    dim sum with chives, steamed 22
    egg and avocado mousse 21
    soft-shell, with chilli and salt 42
    soufflés, hot 41
    soup with coriander relish 11
    spring crab cakes 41
    stuffed spider crab 42
cranberry
    baked stuffed apples 185
    chocolate and fruit puddings 249

and chocolate squares 248
    iced Christmas torte 246
cream of vegetable soup 11
crispy seven-spice aubergines 77
croquettes, turkey 236
crostini 75, 137
croûtons 87, 194
crumble
    blueberry and vanilla 122
    rhubarb and raspberry 59
cucumber
    dip 143
    gazpacho 68
    gazpacho juice 130
    light and fragrant tiger prawns with dill
      and 100
    and prawn soup, chilled 72
    and tomato salad with yogurt dressing 84
cumin, chilled avocado soup with 8
curried
    cauliflower soup 194
    parsnip soup 133
    pumpkin and leek soup 135
    red cabbage slaw 208
    salmon chowder 12
curry, sweet pumpkin and peanut 158
custards
    pineapple 245
    roasted garlic and aubergine, with red
      pepper dressing 93

date
    cheese-stuffed pears 144
    date, orange and carrot salad 29
    sweet dream 192
devilish chocolate roulade 63
dill
    farfalle with salmon and 46
    light and fragrant tiger prawns with
      cucumber and 100
    rice with green peas, mint and 39
    sauce, salted salmon with potatoes in 45
dim sum, steamed crab, with chives 22
dips
    cajun 202
    chilli and raspberry 81
    creamy aubergine 75
    cucumber 143
    harissa and yogurt 98
donburi, chicken and mushroom 174
dried fruit compote 246
duck
    with plum sauce 176
    roast, with prunes and apples 177
    roasted duckling on honeyed potatoes 48
    salad with poached eggs 155
    sausages with plum sauce 176
    and sesame stir-fry 48
dumplings 196
    potato, chicken with 232
    venison medallions with 57
    white fish 44
Dutch asparagus 51

eel, fried, with creamy potatoes 101
egg
    and asparagus terrine 17
    broccoli and cheese mina 160
    Caesar salad 87
    duck salad with poached eggs 155
    Dutch asparagus 51
    florets polonaise 34
    kedgeree 226
    mimosa eggs 16
    pan-fried ham and Mediterranean
      vegetables with eggs 114
    pea and mint omelette 38
    peppery egg, watercress and chilli salad 88
    pineapple custard 245
    potato salad with egg and lemon 25
    prawn, egg and avocado mousse 21

    roasted garlic and aubergine custards with
      red pepper dressing 93
    salad Niçoise 88
    scrambled, with asparagus 36
    spring asparagus with 34
    tapenade and quail's eggs 78
    timbales, tomato and courgette 79
    warm dressed salad with eggs 87
elderberry wine, farm pigeon with 177

fajitas, chicken 111
farfalle
    with courgettes and prawns 100
    with salmon and dill 46
farm pigeon with elderberry wine 177
fennel
    grilled fennel salad 152
    and halloumi salad, warm 152
    and leek salad 29
    roast chicken with summer vegetables and
      potatoes 113
    scallops with mascarpone, bacon and 170
fig
    figs and pears in honey with cardamom
      189
    honey baked figs with hazelnut ice cream
      189
    Roquefort and walnut salad 151
    sweet dream 192
    and walnut torte 190
filo cigars stuffed with creamy prawns 81
fish
    and chermoula mini pies 83
    dumplings 44
    see also individual types of fish
fishcakes
    pilchard and leek potato cakes 21
    salmon 44
    salmon, sesame and ginger 23
    spring crab cakes 41
flan, cheese and asparagus 36
flautas, chicken 111
florets polonaise 34
fragrant mushrooms in lettuce leaves 153
frisée 32
fritters, leek 200
fusilli with wild mushrooms 162

Galacian broth 13
gâteau, soft fruit and meringue 60
gazpacho 68
gazpacho juice 130
Génoise cake 118
ginger
    halibut with leek and 224
    kachumbar 109
    kan shao green beans 99
    and kiwi sorbet 58
    kiwi and stem ginger spritzer 67
    papaya baked with 190
    papaya, lime and ginger salad 150
    pear and gingerbread sundaes 183
    pineapple with chilli and 208
    rhubarb and ginger wine torte 58
    roasted chicken with grapes and fresh
      root ginger 174
    salmon, sesame and ginger fishcakes 23
    steamed scallops with 171
    teriyaki salmon fillets with ginger strips 47

globe artichoke
    braised artichokes with fresh peas 160
    salad 26
gnocchi
    potato 222
    pumpkin, with chanterelle parsley
      cream 159
golden beef and potato puffs 207
goose, marmalade-glazed 238
gooseberry and clotted cream ice cream 121
granita, watermelon 119
grape
    and halloumi salad 151
    red defender 130
    roasted chicken with fresh root ginger
      and 174
grapefruit, pink and perky 193
gravlax 45
green beans
    and grilled halloumi salad 28
    kan shao 99
    salad Niçoise 88
    soup Niçoise with seared tuna 71
    summer, in a light batter 76
green devil 66
gremolata, creamy aubergine soup with
    mozzarella and 70
griddled tomatoes on soda bread 78
grouse, roast, with rowanberry and wine
    sauce 178
Gruyère and potato soufflés 202
guacamole 14
guinea fowl, braised, with cabbage 234

haddock
    kedgeree 226
    smoked haddock bake with a cheese
      crumb 225
    smoked haddock chowder 196
    smoked haddock with mustard
      cabbage 225
    with spicy Puy lentils 226
    three-fish terrine 205
hake
    grilled, with lemon and chilli 229
    with turnip tops and onions 230
halibut
    with leek and ginger 224
    with peppers and coconut 105
halloumi
    and bean salad, grilled 28
    and courgette ribbons, spiced couscous
      with 159
    and fennel salad, warm 152
    and grape salad 151
ham
    Dutch asparagus 51
    Galacian broth 13
    grilled spring onions, asparagus and Parma
      ham 27
    pan-fried, and Mediterranean vegetables
      with eggs 114
    sauerkraut pie 217
    Serrano, chicken fillets with 110
    and veal pie 55
    warm salad of Bayonne ham 32
harissa 148
    and yogurt dip, summer vegetable kebabs
      with 98
hay-wrapped leg of lamb 54
hazelnut
    ice cream, honey baked figs with 189
    winter coleslaw 209
herb-crusted rack of lamb with Puy lentils 53
herring in oatmeal 103
hollandaise sauce 17, 46
honey
    baked figs with hazelnut ice cream 189
    chicken with tomatoes, cinnamon and 113
    figs and pears in honey with
      cardamom 189

honey-seared melon with lavender and
  raspberries 128
summer parcels with apricots and honey
  glaze 125
horse mackerel, stuffed 104
horseradish
  dressing, roasted beetroot with 211
  squash soup with 133
hummus, steak ciabatta with 117
hunter's stew 180
husk-grilled corn on the cob 156

ice cream
  apricot and amaretti 120
  blackberry 191
  filo, ice cream and mincemeat parcels 242
  gooseberry and clotted cream 121
  hazelnut, honey baked figs with 189
  with hot black cherry sauce 62
  peach and cardamom 120
  pear and gingerbread sundaes 183
  rhubarb and ginger 59
  simple raspberry 129
  simple strawberry 129
  spicy pumpkin and orange bombe 182
  walnut and vanilla ice cream palmiers 242
iced Christmas torte 246
Idaho potato slices 203

Jerusalem artichoke
  au gratin 219
  with garlic 218
  roasted 219
julienne 12

kachumbar 109
kale
  chorizo and potato soup 197
  colcannon 52
  with mustard dressing 215
  spiced greens 215
kan shao green beans 99
kebabs
  lamb, with mint chutney 51
  summer vegetable, with harissa and
    yogurt dip 98
kefalotyri cubes spiked with bay leaves 76
kidney beans
  mushroom and bean pâté 145
  winter farmhouse soup 195
kirsch 61
kiwi
  and ginger sorbet 58
  and stem ginger spritzer 67
kugel, noodle, flavoured with apple and
  cinnamon 186

lamb
  burgers with red onion and tomato
    relish 114
  casserole with broad beans 52
  hay-wrapped leg of 54
  herb-crusted rack of, with Puy lentils 53
  kebabs with mint chutney 51
  moussaka 115
  with oregano and basil 52
  roast leg of, with rosemary and garlic 53
  sweet and sour 52
  with tomatoes and peppers 115
lavender
  honey-seared melon with raspberries
    and 128
  and strawberry sorbet 118
leek
  and apple relish 14
  barley risotto with roasted squash 157
  cheesy creamy leeks 219
  chicken with winter vegetables 232
  and fennel salad 29
  fritters 200
  halibut with ginger and 224

and onion tartlets 201
and pilchard potato cakes 21
and potato gratin, baked 220
and pumpkin soup, curried 135
sea bass with 228
soufflé 201
vichyssoise 73
lemon
  aubergine, lemon and caper salad 89
  baked cod with beer and 107
  butter, plaice fillets with sorrel and 106
  cinnamon squash 192
  grilled hake with chilli and 229
  lemon, chilli and garlic relish 140
  and papaya relish 140
  potato salad with egg and 25
  preserved lemons 27
  samfaina, mackerel in 105
  sauce, asparagus with 35
lentils
  chicken and lentil broth 12
  chicken with winter vegetables 232
  Puy, herb-crusted rack of lamb with 53
  spiced red lentil soup 10
  spicy Puy, haddock with 226
lettuce
  Caesar salad 87
  fragrant mushrooms in lettuce leaves 153
  parcels 83
  and peas, braised 38
  salad Niçoise 88
  steamed lettuce-wrapped sole 40
  warm dressed salad with eggs 87
light and fragrant tiger prawns with cucumber
  and dill 100
lime
  and coconut dressing, winter cabbage
    salad with 211
  papaya, lime and ginger salad 150
  quinoa salad with citrus dressing 86
  seared swordfish with citrus dressing 173
  syrup and sorbet, grilled mango cheeks
    with 128
lobster thermidor 172

macaroni, winter farmhouse soup 195
mackerel
  in lemon samfaina 105
  with nutty bacon stuffing 104
  with rhubarb sauce 103
mandarin trifle, chocolate 245
mangetout, scrambled eggs with 36
mango
  grilled mango cheeks with lime syrup and
    sorbet 128
  with sticky rice 127
  wontons with raspberry sauce 127
matzo meal 200
meatballs
  beef, in tomato and wine sauce 116
  polpettes with mozzarella and tomato
    116
melon
  frozen 119
  honey-seared, with lavender and
    raspberries 128
  mixed melon and orange salsa 74
  watermelon granita 119
merguez sausages with iced oysters 205
meringue
  cake with raspberries 129
  chocolate pavlova with passion fruit
    cream 244
  pie, rhubarb 65
  and soft fruit gateau 60
mina, broccoli and cheese 160
mincemeat, filo pastry and ice cream
  parcels 242
mini toffee apples 184
mint
  baked tomatoes with 95

beetroot with fresh 208
chutney, lamb kebabs with 51
and pea omelette 38
rice with green peas, dill and 39
monkfish
  in beer 230
  with clams and coriander 231
  with potatoes and garlic 231
  seafood and spring onion skewers 40
moussaka 115
  roasted ratatouille 99
mousse
  prawn, egg and avocado 21
  quince, with almond biscuits 188
mozzarella
  creamy aubergine soup with gremolata
    and 70
  grilled aubergine parcels 92
  grilled vegetable pizza 96
  roasted vegetable quesadillas with
    melted 97
  rocket and tomato pizza 95
  sweet romanos stuffed with two cheeses
    and cherry peppers 97
  and tomato salad 85
  yellow courgette wraps with spinach and
    90
muesli layer, raspberry 60
mushroom
  and bean pâté 145
  beef with chanterelle in cream sauce 181
  braised tofu with 162
  caviar 144
  chicken bitki 148
  and chicken donburi 174
  deep-fried layered shiitake and scallop 147
  fragrant, in lettuce leaves 153
  fusilli with wild mushrooms 162
  garlic chive rice with mushrooms 164
  garlic mushrooms 145
  with hot garlic sauce 163
  hunter's stew 180
  lettuce parcels 83
  marinated button mushrooms with
    sherry 153
  mixed mushroom soup 134
  pâté with bacon and 149
  pheasant with chestnuts, bacon and 235
  pumpkin gnocchi with chanterelle parsley
    cream 159
  soup with croûtes 137
  and steak pudding with a herby suet
    crust 181
  stroganoff 164
  wild mushroom and fontina tarts 163
mussels
  in a cider and cream broth 166
  and clams in banana leaves 167
  marinated 146
  mussel risotto 167
  seafood spaghetti parcels 168
  shelled, with garlic and herbs 147
  soup with pumpkin 139
  steamed, with onions and celery 166
mustard
  cabbage, smoked haddock with
    mustard 225
  dip, potato skewers with 18
  dressing, kale with 215

noodles
  cold somen 69
  lettuce parcels 83
  noodle kugel flavoured with apple and
    cinnamon 186
  noodle pudding with cherries and nuts 62
  stir-fried, in shellfish sauce 43

oatmeal, herring in 103
old-fashioned apple cake 184
olives
  black olive ciabatta toasts 70
  black and orange salad with a spicy
    dressing 210
  cheese-stuffed pears 144
  potato salad with capers and 210
  soup Niçoise with seared tuna 71
  summer salad with capers and 84
  tapenade and quail's eggs 78
  tomato and black olive tart 94
omelette, pea and mint 38
oysters
  fillets of turbot with 224
  merguez sausages with iced 205
  oysters Rockefeller on the half shell 204

pakoras, spiced onion 143
palmiers, walnut and vanilla ice cream 242
pancakes
  with hot black cherry sauce 62
  lacy potato 19
  Scotch, chocolate and orange 247
pandanus-flavoured chicken satay with hot
  cashew nut sambal 108
papaya
  baked with ginger 190
  and lemon relish 140
  papaya, lime and ginger salad 150
Parmesan and roasted mixed pepper
  risotto 98
parsley
  pumpkin gnocchi with chanterelle parsley
    cream 159
  pumpkin salad with red onion and 154
  and rocket salad 24
parsnip
  and apple soup 132
  and carrot purée 221
  and chickpea stew 221
  creamy potato and potato bake 222
  curried parsnip soup 133
  and sweet potato soup 134
partridge
  braised, with cabbage 236
  roast, with sage, thyme and garlic 235
passion fruit
  chocolate pavlova with passion fruit
    cream 244
  creams 243
pasta
  conchiglie with roasted vegetables 96
  farfalle with courgettes and prawns 100
  farfalle with salmon and dill 46
  fusilli with wild mushrooms 162
  garganelli with spring vegetables 37
  penne with tomatoes and basil 99
  seafood spaghetti parcels 168
  spaghetti with broccoli and red chilli 161
  tagliatelle with scallops 169
  winter farmhouse soup 195
pastry
  aubergine and spinach pie 39
  butternut squash and maple pie 191
  cheese and asparagus flan 36
  cheese pies with raisins and nuts 142
  cheese tart 63
  fig and walnut torte 190
  filo cigars stuffed with creamy prawns 81
  filo, ice cream and mincemeat parcels 242
  golden beef and potato puffs 207
  hare pot pies 241

leek and onion tartlets 201
one-crust rhubarb pie 65
onion tart 94
pear and almond tart 187
rhubarb meringue pie 65
sauerkraut pie 217
tartlets with seafood and chicken
  fillings 23
tomato and black olive tart 94
veal and ham pie 55
wild berry tart 124
wild mushroom and fontina tarts 163
pâté
  with bacon and mushrooms 149
  garlic with goat's cheese 146
  hare 206
  mushroom and bean 145
patties
  beetroot 200
  turkey 236
pavlova, chocolate, with passion fruit
  cream 244
peach
  and cardamom ice cream 120
  cobbler 126
  dried fruit compote 246
  melba, sparkling 131
  and tomato jus with prawns 69
peanut
  and potato soup 195
  and pumpkin curry, sweet 158
  sauce, chicken and pork in 175
pear
  and almond tart 187
  apple and leek relish 14
  with Cashel Blue cream and walnuts 150
  cheese-stuffed 144
  in chocolate fudge blankets 187
  figs and pears in honey with cardamom
    189
  and gingerbread sundaes 183
  pink and perky 193
  poached, in red wine 186
  and Roquefort soup 136
  and sauternes sorbet 182
  and watercress salad 25
peas
  braised lettuce and 38
  and carrots with bacon 37
  with chicken 49
  fresh, braised artichokes with 160
  garganelli with spring vegetables 37
  pea and asparagus soup 9
  pea and mint omelette 38
  rice with green peas, mint and dill 39
  spiced scallops and sugar snaps 171
  summer pea and chive soup 72
  tagine of beef with saffron and 56
pecan nut
  baked stuffed apples 185
  and maple croissant pudding 250
penne with tomatoes and basil 99
peppers
  chargrilled pepper salad 86
  chilled pepper soup 68
  conchiglie with roasted vegetables 96
  gazpacho 68
  gazpacho juice 130
  grilled vegetable pizza 96
  grilled vegetable terrine 80
  halibut with coconut and 105
  lamb with tomatoes and 115
  mackerel in lemon samfaina 105
  red onion and tomato relish 114
  roast chicken with summer vegetables
    and potatoes 113
  roast pepper terrine 80
  roasted garlic and aubergine custards with
    red pepper dressing 93
  roasted mixed pepper and Parmesan
    risotto 98

roasted pepper salad
roasted ratatouille moussaka 99
roasted vegetable quesadillas with melted
  mozzarella 97
sour cream cooler 75
summer vegetable kebabs with harissa
  and yogurt dip 98
sweet romanos stuffed with two cheeses
  and cherry peppers 97
tomato salad with marinated peppers and
  oregano 85
peppery egg, watercress and chilli salad 88
pesto
  spicy, salmon with 47
pheasant
  with mushrooms, chestnuts and bacon 235
  roast 234
pies
  aubergine and spinach 39
  broccoli and cheese mina 160
  butternut squash and maple 191
  cheese, with raisins and nuts 142
  fish and chermoula mini 83
  hare pot 241
  one-crust rhubarb 65
  rhubarb meringue 65
  sauerkraut 217
  veal and ham 55
  venison 241
pigeon with elderberry wine 177
pilchard and leek potato cakes 21
pimento 85
pine nuts
  cheese pies with raisins and nuts 142
  mackerel with nutty bacon stuffing 104
pineapple
  custard 245
  with ginger and chilli 208
  relish, piquant 199
  and rum cream, grilled 250
pink and perky 193
piquant pineapple relish 199
pizzas
  grilled vegetable 96
  rocket and tomato 95
plaice
  fillets with sorrel and lemon butter 106
  fried, with tomato and basil sauce 106
plum sauce
  duck sausages with 176
  duck with 176
polpettes with mozzarella and tomato 116
pomegranate glaze, winter cheesecake
  with 244
pork
  and chicken in peanut sauce 175
  escalopes with apple and potato rösti 178
  roast, with apples and glazed potatoes 179
potato
  and apple rösti, pork escalopes with 178
  baked beef with a potato crust 240
  and beef puffs, golden 207
  beetroot, apple and potato salad 212
  and beetroot salad 155
  cakes, pilchard and leek 21
  clapshot 218
  dumplings, chicken with 232
  Dutch asparagus 51
  fried eel with creamy potatoes 101

fried new potatoes with aioli 19
glazed, roast pork with apples and 179
gnocchi 222
grated potato casserole 223
grilled halloumi and bean salad 28
and Gruyère soufflés 202
Idaho potato slices 203
kale, chorizo and potato soup 197
and leek gratin, baked 220
monkfish with garlic and 231
and onion cakes with beetroot relish 204
pancakes, lacy 19
and parsnip bake, creamy 222
and peanut soup 195
potato skins with cajun dip 202
and radish salad 24
roast chicken with summer vegetables
  and 113
roasted duckling on honeyed potatoes 48
salad with capers and black olives 210
salted salmon with potatoes in dill sauce 45
and sausage casserole 239
skewers with mustard dip 18
spicy root vegetable gratin 165
Swiss soufflé potatoes 203
vichyssoise 73
prawns
  butterfly prawn skewers with chilli and
    raspberry dip 81
  chicken with 112
  creamy, filo cigars stuffed with 81
  farfalle with courgettes and 100
  fish and chermoula mini pies 83
  light and fragrant tiger prawns with
    cucumber and dill 100
  prawn and cucumber soup, chilled 72
  prawn, egg and avocado mousse 21
  prawn salad 31
  prawn tartlets 23
  salt and pepper 82
  scallops and tiger prawns 170
  seafood salad with fragrant herbs 31
  seafood spaghetti parcels 168
  seafood and spring onion skewers 40
  tomato and peach jus with 69
purple haze 131

quail, braised, with winter vegetables 233
quesadillas, roasted vegetable with melted
  mozzarella 97
quince
  mousse with almond biscuits 188
  soufflés, hot 188
quinoa salad with citrus dressing 86

rabbit, braised 240
radish and potato salad 24
raspberry
  and chilli dip, butterfly prawn skewers
    with 81
  honey-seared melon with lavender
    and 128
  meringue cake with raspberries 129
  muesli layer 60
  and rhubarb crumble 59
  sauce, mango wontons with 127
  simple raspberry ice cream 129
  sparkling peach melba 131
  sponge cake with fruit and
    cream 118
  and white chocolate cheesecake 124
red alert 66
red cabbage
  braised 216
  slaw, curried 208
red defender 130
redcurrant
  chocolate redcurrant torte 123
  soft fruit and meringue gateau 60
relish
  apple and cider 141

apple and leek 14
beetroot 198, 204
blueberry 139
lemon, chilli and garlic 140
onion and red chilli 198
papaya and lemon 140
piquant pineapple 199
red onion and tomato 114
toffee onion 141
rhubarb
  and ginger ice cream 59
  and ginger trifles 64
  and ginger wine torte 58
  mackerel with rhubarb sauce 103
  meringue pie 65
  pie, one-crust 65
  and raspberry crumble 59
rice
  aubergine rolls 92
  aubergine and spinach pie 39
  butternut squash and blue cheese risotto
    soup 138
  chicken and mushroom donburi 174
  Christmas rice pudding with prunes and
    brandy 247
  con pollo 112
  garlic chive rice with mushrooms 164
  with green peas, mint and dill 39
  kedgeree 226
  mangoes with sticky rice 127
  and spinach soup 132
  stuffed baby squash 156
  stuffed cabbage leaves 180
ricotta
  aubergine rolls 92
  cheese-stuffed pears 144
  roasted ratatouille moussaka 99
  and strawberry semi-freddo 121
  sweet romanos stuffed with two cheeses
    and cherry peppers 97
risotto
  with asparagus 35
  barley, with roasted squash 157
  butternut squash and blue cheese risotto
    soup 138
  mussel 167
  roasted mixed pepper and Parmesan 98
  scallop 169
rissoles, chickpea 143
rocket
  and parsley salad 24
  and tomato pizza 95
Roquefort
  chicory salad with 209
  and pear soup 136
  and walnut salad 151
rosemary, roast leg of lamb with garlic and 53
rösti, apple and potato, pork escalopes with 178
roulades
  courgette 91
  devilish chocolate 63
rum
  and banana waffles 251
  and pineapple cream, grilled 250
rye bread with sour cream 16

saffron, tagine of beef with peas and 56
salads
  asparagus, bacon and leaf 32
  aubergine, lemon and caper 89
  avocado, onion and spinach 25
  avocado, orange and almond 29
  baked sweet potato 212
  beef and sweet potato 213
  beetroot, apple and potato 212
  beetroot and potato 155
  beetroot and red onion 28
  black and orange, with a spicy dressing 210
  broad bean 27
  Caesar 87
  chargrilled pepper 86

chicken and broccoli 31
chicory, with Roquefort 209
cucumber and tomato, with yogurt
    dressing 84
date, orange and carrot 29
duck, with poached eggs 155
fragrant mushrooms in lettuce leaves 153
globe artichoke 26
grilled fennel 152
grilled halloumi and bean 28
halloumi and grape 151
kachumbar 109
leek and fennel 29
marinated chicken salad with spring
    onions 33
Niçoise 88
papaya, lime and ginger 150
parsley and rocket 24
peppery egg, watercress and chilli 88
potato, with capers and black olives 210
potato, with egg and lemon 25
potato and radish 24
prawn 31
pumpkin, with red onion and parsley 154
quinoa, with citrus dressing 86
roasted pepper 89
roasted shallot and butternut squash 154
Roquefort and walnut 151
salmon with avocado 30
seafood, with fragrant herbs 31
seared mixed onion 213
spinach and roast garlic 26
summer, with capers and olives 84
tomato, with marinated peppers and
    oregano 85
tomato and mozzarella 85
warm chorizo salad with baby spinach 33
warm dressed salad with eggs 87
warm halloumi and fennel 152
warm salad of Bayonne ham 32
watercress and pear 25
winter cabbage, with coconut and lime
    dressing 211
winter coleslaw 209
salmon
    with asparagus 46
    with avocado salad 30
    curried salmon chowder 12
    farfalle with dill and 46
    fish cakes 44
    rolls with asparagus and butter sauce 45
    salted, with potatoes in dill sauce 45
    sesame and ginger fishcakes 23
    with spicy pesto 47
    tartare 30
    teriyaki fillets with ginger strips 47
    three-fish terrine 205
    yogurt soup with chilli salsa 73
salsa verde 15
salt and pepper prawns 82
salted and grilled sardines 101
salted salmon with potatoes in dill sauce 45
samfaina, lemon, mackerel in 105
sardines
    cutlets 102
    salted and grilled 101
    in summer marinade 102
sauces
    hollandaise 17, 46
    lemon 35
    plum 176
    sambal 108
    samfaina 105
    tartare 40
sauerkraut
    hunter's stew 180
    pie 217
sausages
    broad beans with 50
    caramelized onion and sausage tarte
        tatin 179

chorizo, kale and potato soup 197
duck, with plum sauce 176
hunter's stew 180
kale, chorizo and potato soup 197
merguez, with iced oysters 205
with onions and apples 238
potato and sausage casserole 239
warm chorizo salad with baby spinach 33
sauternes and pear sorbet 182
scad, stuffed 104
scallops
    deep-fried layered shiitake and 147
    with fennel, mascarpone and bacon 170
    scallop risotto 169
    seafood salad with fragrant herbs 31
    seafood and spring onion skewers 40
    steamed, with ginger 171
    and sugar snaps, spiced 171
    tagliatelle with 169
    and tiger prawns 170
Scotch pancakes, chocolate and orange 247
sea bass
    with leeks 228
    with orange chilli salsa 227
    in a salt crust 227
    wrapped 228
sea trout, marinated 107
seafood spaghetti parcels 168
seafood and spring onion skewers 40
semi-freddo, strawberry and ricotta 121
shrimps, grey, tomatoes stuffed with 82
smoked haddock chowder 196
sole, steamed lettuce-wrapped 40
sorrel, plaice fillets with lemon butter and 106
soufflé potatoes, Swiss 203
soufflés
    Gruyère and potato 202
    hot crab 41
    hot quince 188
    leek 201
soups
    asparagus and pea 9
    butternut squash and blue cheese
        risotto 138
    carrot and orange 10
    chicken 196
    chicken and lentil broth 12
    chilled avocado, with cumin 8
    chilled cucumber and prawn 72
    chilled pepper soup 68
    chunky courgette and tomato 71
    classic gazpacho 68
    crab, with coriander relish 11
    cream of duck 139
    cream of tomato, with black olive ciabatta
        toasts 70
    cream of vegetable 11
    creamy aubergine, with mozzarella and
        gremolata 70
    curried cauliflower 194
    curried parsnip 133
    curried pumpkin and leek 135
    curried salmon chowder 12
    Galacian broth 13
    hare 197
    kale, chorizo and potato 197
    leek 9
    mixed mushroom 134
    mushroom, with croûtes 137
    mussel, with pumpkin 139
    parsnip and apple 132
    peanut and potato 195
    pear and Roquefort 136
    pumpkin and coconut 135
    roasted garlic and butternut squash, with
        tomato salsa 138
    roast vegetable medley 194
    simple cream of onion 136
    smoked haddock chowder 196
    soup Niçoise with seared tuna 71
    spiced red lentil 10

spicy roasted pumpkin 137
spinach and rice 132
squash, with horseradish 133
summer pea and chive 72
sweet potato and parsnip 134
sweet-and-sour vegetable borscht 13
tomato and peach jus with prawns 69
vichyssoise 73
watercress 8
winter farmhouse 195
yogurt soup with chilli salsa 73
sour cream
    cooler 75
    rye bread with 16
spaghetti
    with broccoli and red chilli 161
    seafood spaghetti parcels 168
spiced beef roll 56
spiced greens 215
spiced onion pakoras 143
spiced red lentil soup 10
spiced scallops and sugar snaps 171
spicy beefburgers 117
spicy pumpkin and orange bombe 182
spicy roasted pumpkin soup 137
spinach
    and aubergine pie 39
    avocado, onion and spinach salad 25
    oysters Rockefeller on the half shell 204
    red alert 66
    and rice soup 132
    and roast garlic salad 26
    three-fish terrine 205
    warm chorizo salad with baby 33
    yellow courgette wraps with mozzarella
        and 90
sponge cake with fruit and cream 118
spring greens, stir-fried 34
squash
    butternut squash and blue cheese risotto
        soup 138
    butternut squash and maple
        pie 191
    stuffed baby squash 156
    winter, in tomato sauce 157
squid
    pan-fried baby squid with spices 148
    stuffed with garlic pork 173
    vegetable-stuffed 172
strawberry
    and champagne water ice 183
    cream shortbreads 122
    devilish chocolate roulade 63
    and lavender sorbet 118
    red defender 130
    and ricotta cheese semi-freddo 121
    simple strawberry ice cream 129
    simply strawberry 67
    snow 126
    soft fruit and meringue gateau 60
    sponge cake with fruit and
        cream 118
summer parcels with apricots and honey
    glaze 125
summer pudding 123
summer vegetable kebabs with harissa and
    yogurt dip 98
sundaes, pear and gingerbread 183
sweet dream 192

sweet romanos stuffed with two cheeses and
    cherry peppers 97
sweet sharp shock 193
sweet and sour lamb 52
sweet-and-sour vegetable borscht 13
Swiss soufflé potatoes 203
swordfish, seared, with citrus dressing 173

tagliatelle with scallops 169
tandoori drumsticks with kachumbar 109
tapenade and quail's eggs 78
tartare, salmon 30
tartare sauce 40
tarte tatin
    caramelized onion and sausage 179
    caramelized shallot and garlic 20
tartlets with seafood and chicken fillings 23
tempura
    courgette 77
    summer green beans in batter 76
teriyaki salmon fillets with ginger strips 47
terrines
    asparagus and egg 17
    grilled vegetable 80
    hare and calf's liver 206
    roast pepper 80
    three-fish 205
tomato
    baked tomatoes with mint 95
    and black olive tart 94
    chicken with cinnamon, honey and 113
    chilled pepper soup 68
    chunky courgette and tomato soup 71
    clams with tomato sauce 168
    conchiglie with roasted
        vegetables 96
    and courgette timbales 79
    cream of tomato soup with black olive
        ciabatta toasts 70
    fried plaice with tomato and basil
        sauce 106
    griddled tomatoes on soda bread 78
    mackerel in lemon samfaina 105
    polpettes with mozzarella and 116
    roasted ratatouille moussaka 99
    salsa, classic 74
    salsa, roasted garlic and butternut squash
        soup with 138
    sauce, courgettes and tofu
        with 91
    sour cream cooler 75
    summer vegetable kebabs with harissa
        and yogurt dip 98
    tomatoes stuffed with grey
        shrimps 82
tortilla wrap with tabbouleh 18
tuna
    salad Niçoise 88
    seared, soup Niçoise with 71
    yogurt soup with chilli salsa 73
turbot
    fillets of, with oysters 224
    three-fish terrine 205
turkey
    croquettes 236
    patties 236
    stuffed roast 236

veal
    braised, with prunes 55
    casserole with broad beans 54
    and ham pie 55
venison
    medallions with dumplings 57
    pie 241
    stew 57

yogurt
    simply strawberry 67
    soup with chilli salsa 73
    sweet dream 192